Language and Bilingual Cognition

Language and Bilingual Cognition

Edited by Vivian Cook and Benedetta Bassetti

Ψ Psychology Press
Taylor & Francis Group

NEW YORK AND HOVE

Published in 2011
by Psychology Press
270 Madison Avenue
New York, NY 10016
www.psypress.com

Published in Great Britain
by Psychology Press
27 Church Road
Hove, East Sussex BN3 2FA

*Psychology Press is an imprint of the Taylor & Francis Group,
an Informa business*

Copyright © 2011 by Taylor & Francis

Typeset in Times by
RefineCatch Limited, Bungay, Suffolk
Printed in the USA by
Sheridan Books, Inc. on acid-free paper
Cover design by Aubergine Creative Design

10 9 8 7 6 5 4 3 2 1

Library of Congress Cataloging in Publication Data
A catalog record for this book is available from the Library of Congress.

ISBN: 978-1-84872-924-7

Contents

Preface and acknowledgments

It has been a great delight working on this book because of the interest that our contributors have provided. We are privileged to have had the chance to publish such stimulating contributions to the new and exploding field of language and bilingual cognition research, and would like to thank the contributors for their willingness to take part in this long and complicated project. Benedetta Bassetti would like to thank her parents for their continuous support while she was working on this volume. Vivian Cook would like to remember Karen Woo, whom he knew for more than twenty years, one of the finest contemporary dancers of her generation, who retrained as a doctor and gave her life while treating the people of Nuristan.

As always the book would never have been finished without the constant assistance of (on one author's loudspeakers) Sonny Rollins, Humphrey Lyttelton, and Branford Marsalis, and (on the other's) Heinrich Ignaz Franz Biber, Jacques Duphly, and Jean-Philippe Rameau—fortunately seldom playing simultaneously in the same office.

Contributors

Jeanette Altarriba, The University at Albany, SUNY, Department of Latin American, Caribbean, and US Latino Studies, 1400 Washington Avenue, SS-250, Albany, New York 12222, USA. E-mail: Ja087@cnsunix.albany.edu

Panos Athanasopoulos, School of Linguistics and English Language, Bangor University, Bangor, Gwynedd LL57 2DG, UK. E-mail: panos@bangor.ac.uk

Benedetta Bassetti, Department of Educational Studies, University of York, Heslington, York YO10 5DD, UK. E-mail: benedetta@benedetta-bassetti.org

Mary Besemeres, School of Language Studies, The Australian National University, Canberra ACT 0200, Australia. E-mail: Mary.Besemeres@anu.edu.au

Keith Brooke, Department of Literature, Film, and Theatre Studies, University of Essex, Colchester CO4 3SQ, UK. E-mail: keith@keithbrooke.co.uk

Hsin Chin Chen, Department of Psychology, National Chung Cheng University, 168 University Rd, Ming-Hsiung Chai-Yi, Taiwan. E-mail: psyhcc@ccu.edu.tw

Jenn-Yeu Chen, Institute of Cognitive Science, National Cheng Kung University of Tainan, No.1, University Road, Tainan City 701, Taiwan. E-mail: psyjyc@mail.ncku.edu.tw

Vivian Cook, King George VI Building, School of ECLS, University of Newcastle, Queen Victoria Road, Newcastle upon Tyne NE1 7RU, UK. E-mail: Vivian.Cook@newcastle.ac.uk

Kenny R. Coventry, School of Psychology & Sports Science, Northumbria University, Northumberland Building, City Campus, Newcastle upon Tyne NE1 8ST, UK. E-mail: kenny.coventry@northumbria.ac.uk

Debbie S. Cunningham, Department of Modern Languages, Ohio University, Athens, OH 45701, USA. E-mail: debc@neo.tamu.edu

Natalia Czechowska, Collegium Novum, Department of English Language Acquisition, School of English, Adam Mickiewicz University, Poznań, Poland. E-mail: nczechowska@ifa.amu.edu.pl

Susan Ervin-Tripp, 3315 Tolman Hall, University of California, Berkeley, CA 94720–1670, USA. E-mail: ervintripp@berkeley.edu

Vyvyan Evans, Department of Linguistics & English Language, Bangor University, Gwynedd LL57 2DG, UK. E-mail: vyv@vyvevans.net

Anna Ewert, Collegium Novum, Department of English Language Acquisition, School of English, Adam Mickiewicz University, Poznań, Poland. E-mail: eanna@ifa.amu.edu.pl

Chiyoko Kobayashi Frank, Department of Psychology, Cornell University, 211 Uris Hall Cornell University Ithaca, NY 14853, USA. E-mail: chiyokok@hotmail.com

Virginia G. Mueller Gathercole, School of Psychology, University of Bangor, Adeilad Brigantia, Penrallt Road, Gwynned LL57 2AS, UK. E-mail: v.c.gathercole@ bangor.ac.uk

David W. Green, Department of Psychology, University College London, Gower Street, London WC1E 6BT, UK. E-mail: d.w.green@ucl.ac.uk

Pedro Guijarro-Fuentes, Plymouth Business School, CKY320, Cookworthy Building, Drake Circus, Plymouth, Devon PL4 8AA, UK. E-mail: pedro.guijarro-fuentes@plymouth.ac.uk

Henriette Hendriks, Research Centre for English and Applied Linguistics, 9 West Road, University of Cambridge CB3 9DP, UK. E-mail: hpjmh2@cam.ac.uk

Maya Hickmann, Laboratoire Structures Formelles du Langage, CNRS & Université Paris 8, Paris, France. E-mail: maya.hickmann@sfl.cnrs.fr

Erland Hjelmquist, Department of Psychology, Göteborgs Universitet, Haraldsgatan 1, Box 100, 405 30 Göteborg, Sweden. E-mail: erland.hjelmquist@psy.gu.se

Juliane House, Institut für Allgemeine und Angewandte Sprachwissenschaft, Von-Melle-Park 6, II. Stock, D-20146 Hamburg, Germany. E-mail: jhouse@fastmail.fm

Hugh Knickerbocker, University at Albany, State University of New York, 1400 Washington Avenue, SS-250, Albany, New York 12222, USA. E-mail: hughknickerbocker@gmail.com

John A. Lucy, Department of Comparative Human Development, University of Chicago, 5730 S. Woodlawn Avenue, Chicago, IL 60637, USA. E-mail: jalucy1@gmail.com

David Luna, Baruch College/CUNY, Zicklin School of Business, One Bernard Baruch Way, New York, NY 10010, USA. E-mail: David_Luna@baruch.cuny.edu

Giuliana Salvato, Dept of Languages, Literatures and Cultures, University of Windsor, 6th Floor Lambton Tower, Windsor, Ontario N9B 3P4, Canada. E-mail: gsalvato@uwindsor.ca

Peter Sercombe, School of ECLS, King George VI Building, University of Newcastle, Queen Victoria Road, Newcastle upon Tyne NE1 7RU, UK. E-mail: peter.sercombe@ncl.ac.uk

Michael Siegal, Department of Psychology, University of Sheffield, Western Bank, Sheffield S10 2TP, UK. E-mail: M.Siegal@Sheffield. ac.uk

Jui-Ju Su, Department of Psychology, National Chung Cheng University, 168 University Rd, Ming-Hsiung Chai-Yi, Taiwan. E-mail: sujuiju@ gmail.com

Luca Surian, Department of Cognitive Sciences and Education, University of Trento, Corso Bettini n. 31, 38068 Rovereto, Italy. E-mail: luca.surian@unitn.it

Chris Swoyer, Department of Philosophy, University of Oklahoma, 627 Dale Hall Tower, 455 West Lindsey Street, Norman, OK 73019–2006, USA. E-mail: cswoyer@ou.edu

Barbara Tversky, Jordan Hall, Building 420, Department of Psychology, Stanford University, Stanford, CA 94305–2130, USA. E-mail: bt@psych.stanford.edu

Jyotsna Vaid, Department of Psychology, Texas A&M University, College Station, TX 77843–4235, USA. E-mail: jxv@psyc.tamu.edu

Berenice Valdés, Departamento de Psicología Básica, Facultad de Psicología, Universidad Complutense de Madrid (UCM), Madrid, Spain. E-mail: bvaldes@pdi.ucm.es

Anna Wierzbicka, Department of Linguistics, Australian National University, Baldessin Precinct Building (110), Ellery Crescent, ANU, Canberra ACT 0200, Australia. E-mail: Anna.Wierzbicka@anu.edu.au

Tony Young, School of ECLS, F7 King George VI Building, University of Newcastle, Queen Victoria Road, Newcastle upon Tyne NE1 7RU, UK. E-mail: tony.young@ncl.ac.uk

Part A

Language and cognition

The overall structure of this volume is first to establish a firm foundation of current work on the relationship between cognition and language, laid down by leading authorities from relevant fields in Chapters 2–6. Second, it extends this work to the relationship of thinking and language in people who know more than one language in Chapters 7–21. Third it suggests applications and implications for other areas such as language teaching in Chapters 22–25. It ends with an epilogue.

Part A 'Language and Cognition' presents linguistic relativity from the perspectives of different areas of linguistics, psychology, and other language-related disciplines. It starts by introducing the concept of research into language and cognition (Cook). It then presents authoritative views of the research area from the perspective of philosophy (Swoyer), anthropology (Lucy), cognitive linguistics (Evans), developmental psychology (Gathercole), and cognitive psychology (Tversky).

1 Relating language and cognition: The speaker of one language

Vivian Cook

A central question for philosophers, psychologists and linguists for many years has been how what we think relates to what we say. This introduction sketches some possible relationships between cognition and language as a prologue to the rest of the book. It is intended as an impressionistic snapshot from an applied linguist to involve readers with some of the issues and potentialities of this exciting area of research. Bilingualism is the subject of a separate overview in Chapter 7.

One logical possibility is that the way people think influences the language they use. Another possibility is that language influences how people think. Or it may be impossible to separate the two: Thinking and language are essentially the same thing. Or indeed language and thinking may be linked simply through convenience; neither language nor thinking crucially affects the other.

Alongside these synchronic relationships between cognition and language at a particular moment of time go diachronic and developmental issues about how the relationship works over longer periods of time: How did these connections come into being in societies and how do they emerge in the minds of individual children? Issues also arise concerning people who know two systems: Does an English second language (L2) user of Japanese in Tokyo think in a Japanese way, maintain their English way of thinking, or think in a new way born out of the two?

QUESTIONS OF COGNITION AND LANGUAGE

The possible relationships between cognition and language can be expressed in many ways. Gumperz and Levinson (1996, p. 25) spell out one approach as follows. Given that (1) differences occur in linguistic categories across languages, and (2) linguistic categories determine aspects of individuals' cognition, then (3) aspects of individuals' cognition differ across linguistic communities according to the language they speak.

Lucy (1997) puts it as a logical choice between

- structure-centered approaches that see what linguistic differences imply for cognition;
- domain-centered approaches that see how 'experienced reality' may be represented differently across languages;
- behavior-centered approaches that see how different behaviors are linked to language differences.

We will discuss the relationship as a set of four interrelated questions—the extension to people who know more than one language is made in Chapter 7.

Question 1. Do people think differently?

One question is whether there are differences between the cognition of groups or individuals—Do English people think differently from Japanese people in general? Does a particular English person think differently from a particular Japanese person? The question is deliberately couched in general terms that could apply to any group of people. Research into the relationship between language and cognition has usually restricted itself to groups that differ in culture, language or age rather than gender, disability, handedness, literacy or other areas where differences might also occur.

Let us take five disparate examples of apparent differences in cognition between groups out of the many that could be used.

Visual perception

The Müller-Lyer illusion, familiar from introductions to psychology, asks which of two lines seems longer. 'Westerners' see:

>———< as longer than: ←——→

although they are actually the same length. People from 'non-Western' cultures, such as Zulus and Bushmen in southern Africa and Hanunóo in the Philippines, see them as the same length (Segall, Campbell, & Herskovitz, 1966). Even an apparently straightforward matter of optical illusion varies between groups of people.

Taste and smell

Malaysians are able to make finer distinctions than English speakers between solutions differing in saltiness (O'Mahony & Muhiudeen, 1977); Germans and Japanese people differ over perceived pleasantness and intensity of odors (Ayabe-Kanamura et al., 1998). People's perception of taste and smell differs across groups, even if such sensations are hard to verbalize in any language.

Spatial orientation

Guugu-Yimidhirr people in north-east Australia do not orient themselves by their own bodies (front/back, left/right) but by points of the compass (north/south, east/west) (Levinson, 1996). Spatial reference is relative to the body of the speaker for some groups, absolute for others, or indeed based on other types of reference: for speakers of Pirahã by orientation to the nearest river (Everett, 2008) and for the inhabitants of Santiago de Chile by closeness to the Andes—'up town' is towards the Andes, 'down town' is away.

Objects and substances

When classifying simple objects, the Japanese are influenced by the idea of their material rather than their shape; Americans are the reverse (Imai & Gentner, 1997). Asked to choose whether a plastic pyramid or a piece of cork is most like a cork pyramid, Japanese prefer the piece of cork, English speakers the plastic pyramid. Similar preferences for material versus shape have been found in Yucatec versus English (Lucy, 1992) and for shape and color in Navaho versus English (Carroll & Casagrande, 1958).

Color

Speakers of Berinmo in Papua New Guinea and speakers of English perceive different boundaries between the two pairs of colors *nol/wor* and *blue/green* respectively (Davidoff, Davies, & Roberson, 1999); Davies (1998) found that speakers of Setswana were more likely to group 'green' and 'blue' together than speakers of English and Russian.

The examples here so far have followed the logic expressed by Lucy (1997, p. 295): 'Without the relation to thought more generally (i.e. beyond that necessary for the act of speaking itself), it [linguistic relativity] is merely linguistic diversity.' The goal is, then, to see how language impinges on *non*-language areas of cognition: 'Does thinking for speaking a particular language have an effect on how people think when not thinking for speaking that language?' (Boroditsky, Schmidt, & Phillips, 2003, p. 62). As Cardini (2009) points out, this requires research techniques which involve language as little as possible; it also has the problem of trying to establish language-neutral aspects of cognition unaffected by the language and culture of the researcher (Lucy, Chapter 3 this volume; Wierzbicka, Chapter 8 this volume).

Some language and cognition researchers, however, now work with Slobin's (1996) concept of 'language for thinking'—'a special form of thought that is mobilized for communication' (p. 76); they concentrate on whether people differ when they communicate ideas rather than in the ideas themselves. The question is whether people differ when they turn particular concepts they want to say into words, rather than whether they think differently when actual communication is not involved. This may be compatible with a view in which human thinking is universal; particular languages draw out or enable particular ways of expressing our common mental concepts. Of course, like observations of electrons, the difference between language for thinking and non-language cognition is filtered through the mind of the observer, which inevitably relies on the medium of language to function.

While it is always possible to attack the design and methodology of individual research paradigms, for example Li and Gleitman (2002)'s criticism of Levinson's approach, nevertheless the sheer bulk and range of the studies constitute a body of evidence that some aspects of cognition do vary between groups of human beings, unavailable at the time when the relationship between language and cognition became a focus of discussion in the early twentieth century: At least some aspects of human cognition are not universal.

Question 2. Do differences in cognition go with different features of language?

A preliminary issue is whether language and cognition are indeed distinct at some level. Writers like Jackendoff (1992) would claim they were one and the same and deny that they can be meaningfully separated. To those who deny any difference, this question is pointless: If people indeed think differently, this is necessarily reflected in their language: 'language does not affect cognition; it is one form that cognition can take' (Tomasello, 2003, p. 56). At the opposite extreme, Chomskyan theory has always maintained the modularity of language as a distinct faculty of the mind. In the current Minimalist Program (e.g., Chomsky, 1995), an interface keeps the computational system of language distinct from the conceptual-intentional system (Chomsky, 1995).

Question 2 correlates differences in cognition with differences in language. Language is, however, not the only factor that could be correlated with cognition. The differences in susceptibility to the Müller-Lyer illusion were ascribed by Segall et al. (1966) to the square lines of 'carpentered' buildings versus the flowing contours of 'uncarpentered' ones, that is to say, features of the environment. However, recent work in shape representation finds common perception of shapes among US students and members of an isolated tribe, the Himba (Biederman, Yue, & Davidoff, 2009). The taste and smell differences of O'Mahony and Muhiudeen (1977) and Ayabe-Kanamura et al. (1998) may be due to cooking styles, i.e. an aspect of culture, or indeed of early habituation (Rozin & Schiller, 1980)—hot curries in childhood apparently raise your tolerance for chilli for life. Thus, environment or non-language cultural factors can also be correlated with cognition differences.

So what is the evidence for direct links between cognition and language itself? Let us look at a handful of research-based studies.

Grammatical gender and perception of objects

Grammatical gender is a formal property of many languages in which different elements in the sentence such as adjectives and verbs 'agree' with nouns by having a consistent set of properties (Corbett, 1991), i.e. it should not be confused with the everyday meaning of gender as 'sex'. Languages have an arbitrary number of genders in this sense, Polish for example having five. In languages with 'natural' gender such as English, feminine pronouns like *she* go with nouns referring to females like *woman*, masculine *he* with nouns referring to males like *man*, and neuter *it* with nouns referring to inanimates like *rock*. In languages with 'arbitrary' gender such as French, nouns are assigned to genders regardless of whether they are male, female or neuter, although there are often semantic or phonological patterns to such assignment, French feminine nouns, for instance, having more syllables (Matthews, 2009); often gender agreement in arbitrary gender languages goes beyond pronouns to include adjectives, verb inflections, articles and prepositions. In Italian a toothbrush is masculine *spazzolino*, while a key is feminine *chiave*; in German a ball is masculine *Ball*, while a girl is notoriously neuter *Mädchen*. So do people who speak languages with natural gender systems ascribe gender to objects differently from people who speak arbitrary gender languages? Sera, Forbes, Burch, and Rodriquez (2002) found that children over the age of 8 who spoke French and Spanish, both arbitrary gender languages, associated female voices with objects referred to by nouns with feminine gender in their language, differing from children who spoke English and from those who spoke German, another arbitrary gender language. Thus the semantic difference between arbitrary and natural gender seems to go with how gender is assigned to objects in the world.

Direction of writing and representation of time

The direction in which a script is read or written is crucial to reading and writing, varying inter alia between right-to-left, as in Arabic, Hebrew, and Urdu, and left-to-right, as in English, Cyrillic, and Devanagari. Children who speak Hebrew or Arabic represent temporal concepts visually from right to left, for instance ranging pictures of daily meals in a right-to-left sequence, whereas English-speaking children order them from left to right (Tversky, Kugelmass, & Winter, 1991). Writing directionality differs from most spoken language in that it is explicitly taught to children, although it does also occur in the environment, for example the left-to-right sequence of English before-and-after advertisements for weight loss, home improvement and the like. An aspect of the language system is linked with the way that children organize temporal concepts, discussed further in Tversky (Chapter 6 this volume). The same applies to perception of geometrical shapes: Japanese children trained in a predominantly visual writing system remember shapes better than English children with a mostly phonologically based script (Mann, 1986). Other aspects of literacy have also been linked to cognition: Goody (2000) sees literacy itself as introducing a profound change in human memory systems; Luria (1976) showed that literate people reason in a more abstract way.

Verb expression and motion

Languages vary in how they describe change of location: Spanish speakers typically use verbs that specify the path of a motion event and describe the manner of motion separately, as in *entra caminando* 'he enters walking'; the verb *entra* shows the path 'from outside to inside' and *caminando* shows the manner 'walking', rather than, say, running or cycling. English speakers specify the manner with path using a particle *he walked in*—verb-framed versus satellite languages (Talmy, 1985). Native English speakers and Spanish speakers living in the US indeed judge the similarity of pictures of motion events depending on the 'salience of the path dimension in the linguistic descriptions' (Gennari, Sloman, Malt, & Fitch, 2002). Von Stutterheim, Bastin, Carroll, Flecken, and Schmiedtová (in press) show that people's eyes explore images of motion differently according to the motion structure used in their language. Czechowska and Ewert (Chapter 13 this volume) extend such differences to pairs of languages even within the same overall group. So a preferred way of describing motion may be linked to an aspect of cognition.

Countable/uncountable (count/mass) nouns and classification

In English, nouns such as *flour* are called uncountable, i.e. they have a zero article *flour* rather than an indefinite article *a flour* and seldom occur in the plural *flours*; countable nouns like *bottle* on the other hand can have an indefinite article *a bottle* and occur in the plural *bottles*. Uncountables can, if necessary, be counted through a phrase *a bag of flour*. Japanese nouns are uncountable in that there are no articles in Japanese; they are 'counted' through a range of classifiers that vary according to the type of object referred to, *issatsu no hon*, literally 'one-classifier book', and *ippai no mizu* 'one-classifier water'. The material/shape distinction in cognition mentioned above is related to this count/mass difference by Imai and Gentner (1997): The reason why American children categorize objects more by shape, Japanese children more by material, may be their respective languages. The way in which people classify nouns therefore connects with how they classify objects in the world.

Overall, question 2 receives a positive answer: Some aspects of cognition seem to go with particular aspects of language in a measurable way. The question differs from the structure-based approach in Lucy (1997; Chapter 3 this volume) only by relating established differences in cognition to language rather than by relating descriptions of language differences to cognition; the attempt to relate aspects of language and aspects of cognition is the same in both cases.

THE LANGUAGE IN LANGUAGE AND COGNITION

Before continuing, we need to comment briefly on the other partner in the two-way relationship—language—which is often taken for granted (Cook, 2010). The meanings of the English word *language* are not necessarily found in other languages: The distinction in French between *langue*, *langage*, and *parole* (de Saussure, 1916/1976), for instance, has always been a bugbear for English-speaking linguists. Given that the language of academic discussion for most research in language and cognition is English, researchers may indeed be constrained by the English interpretation of *language*.

At its most general, language and cognition research concerns language as a property of human beings: The semantic primes of Wierzbicka (1996) such as 'part', 'kind' (the relationship between things) or 'big', 'small' (the size of things) make good candidates for a central inalienable core of human language and human cognition; Lucy (1997, p. 292) describes a semiotic level at which 'speaking any natural language at all may influence thinking'—people think differently from apes because they have language. At a more specific level, the research concerns internalized language in people's minds—how individuals know properties of nouns such as mass/count—which is by no means isomorphic with the institutionalized 'standard' language of grammar books and dictionaries; the fact that the grammar books state particular syntactic rules for English does not mean that Geordies do not say *Thank yous* when addressing two people, and individuals like a former UK Foreign Secretary do not say *people like you and I*. Research into language and cognition, if it is not clear about the meaning of *language* involved, tends to fall back by default on traditional school grammar and common sense rather than the scientific study of language practiced in the twenty-first century. The three alternative approaches proposed by Lucy (1997), which Lucy (Chapter 3 this volume) cuts down to two by eliminating behavior-centered, essentially come down to different interpretations of what language is.

Vyvyan Evans (Chapter 4 this volume) describes the Cognitive Commitment to provide 'a characterization of language that accords with what is known about the mind and brain from other disciplines'

(p. 71). But there is also the Linguistic Commitment to employ views of language consonant with theories and descriptions from the language-related disciplines. To meet this, terms like *grammatical gender* and *mass/count* need a clear basis in contemporary theories and descriptions of language.

The Language Commitment also eventually involves investigating a broader range of aspects of language than the semantics of syntactic forms such as grammatical gender and the referential meaning of limited sets of words; as Sapir (1921/n.d., p. 181) pointed out, 'the linguistic student should never make the mistake of identifying a language with a dictionary'. There are for instance a host of cross-linguistic syntactic differences crying out to be tested against cognition, such as the differences between configurational languages with phrase structure and non-configurational languages without (Hale, 1983); the preposition/postposition divide between languages such as English and Japanese; the variable order of subject (S), verb (V) and object (O) in the world's languages (SOV, SVO, VSO, VOS, OVS/OSV) (Tomlin, 1986); and whether subjects are compulsory in the sentence (Whorf, 1941b/1956, p. 243), alias the pro-drop or null-subject parameter (Chomsky, 1981): All of these might well have as interesting links to cognition as the semantic aspects of grammatical form.

Question 3. Does a correlation of cognition with language imply a causation, either from cognition to language or from language to cognition?

Assuming that some aspects of cognition do indeed correlate with aspects of language (question 2), question 3 examines whether one causes the other and the direction of the causality. Whether language creates differences in cognition or reflects pre-existing cognitive differences is the central and most bitterly controversial problem of research into language and cognition.

This question raises the historical ghosts of linguistic relativity in linguistics and philosophy, illustrated in the quotations in the box. To von Humboldt (1836/1999), cognition imposes general laws on language but in turn language gives form to cognition (although Humboldt is mostly concerned with language as the possession of a nation, i.e. a group, not of an individual). Boas (1920/1940) sees culture as confined by specific features of language, more or less as an aside to his general ideas on culture. Bally regards language as a straitjacket on cognition: '*définer un type de langue, c'est définer la manière dont elle déforme la realité*' (defining a kind of language means defining the ways in which it distorts reality) (Forel, 2008, p. 123). Sapir (1921/n.d.) on the other hand calls language a 'garment for thought': It is not separate from thought, it is its highest form—in some ways an antecedent of cognitive linguistics; different languages predispose

Historic quotations

von Humboldt (1836/1999):
. . . the requirements that *thinking* imposes on language, from which the *general laws* of language arise . . . language is the formative organ of *thought*. (p. 54)

Boas (1920/1940):
The categories of language compel us to see the world arranged in certain definite conceptual groups which, on account of our lack of knowledge of linguistic processes, are taken as objective categories and which, therefore, impose themselves upon the form of our thoughts. (p. 289)

Sapir:
From the point of view of language, thought may be defined as the highest latent or potential content of speech . . . (1921/n.d., p. 14)

What if language is not so much a garment as a prepared road or groove? (1921/n.d., p. 15)

. . . nor can I believe that language and culture are in any true sense causally related. Culture may be defined as what a society does and thinks. Language is a particular how of thought. (1921/n.d., p. 216)

. . . we see and hear and otherwise experience very largely as we do because the language habits of our community predispose certain choices of interpretation. (1929, p. 210)

Whorf
Concepts of 'time' and 'matter' are not given in substantially the same form by experience to all men but depend upon the nature of the language or languages through the use of which they have been developed. . . . probably the apprehension of space is given in substantially the same form by experience irrespective of language. (1941a/1956, p. 158)

. . . the 'linguistic relativity principle', which means, in informal terms, that users of markedly different grammars are pointed by their grammars towards different types of observations and different evaluations of externally similar acts of observation, and hence are not equivalent as observers but must arrive at somewhat different views of the world. (1940/1956, p. 221) people to particular ways of thinking (although his views on language and thought amount to a few asides in a general account of language). Whorf (1940/1956) develops the idea of languages constraining cognition more extensively through 'the linguistic relativity principle' that a person's way of seeing the world is relative to the language they speak.

Out of the writings of Sapir and Whorf others drew the Whorf-Sapir hypothesis that language affects cognition: How you speak structures how you think. An infuriating aspect of the discussion of the linguistic relativity issue is the tendency for people to debate not the actual issues involved, but their interpretation of the writings of Whorf and Sapir in terms of such slogans as 'determinism' and 'weak and strong' versions of relativity (see Casasanto, 2008; Lucy, Chapter 3 this volume), rather like the exegesis of a sacred text.

The slender evidence provided for these claims in the writings of these pioneers has mostly been disputed or ridiculed—for example Whorf's claim that Inuit languages have seven words for snow—leaving them as the precursors of later work rather than as a foundation for enquiry. Sometimes, as Lenneberg (1953) points out, Whorf's evidence depends on translation from another language into English—what would this mean if it were English?—rather than any independent proof of different cognition; Wierzbicka (Chapter 8 this volume) discusses the dangers in treating English as a universal metalanguage for discussing cognition. One distinction between these early approaches and later ones is that the early evidence comes from observation of language in use rather than from the psychology-style experiments used from the 1950s onwards (Lucy, 1996); Ervin-Tripp (Chapter 9 this volume) provides a fascinating account of the seminal work in this area.

A crucial though seldom-made distinction, touched on implicitly by Whorf (1941a/1956) in his concept of 'habitual thought', is that between short-term causation in which the specific language used affects access during processing, and long-term causation in which the specific language learnt affects the long-lasting cognition of the user, essentially on-line performance versus perma-store competence. One dimension to this is the relationship between language and cognition in the development of the individual; another is the relationship between Whorf's habitual thought in the adult and what Lucy (1997, p. 307) calls 'linear real-time processing of thinking'. That is to say, whether the cognitive development of a human child over many years depends on language is a different question from whether the mature cognitive apparatus of the adult depends on language during mental processing. The links between language and cognition might be the sand carried by the stream or the sand deposited on the lake bottom (as Weinreich famously said about language transfer, 1953, p. 11)—a diachronic process that occurs throughout development or a synchronic process happening at the moment of speaking. Sera et al. (2002, p. 396) show how 'grammatical gender can lead speakers of a language to think about inanimate objects in terms of properties they associate with males and females', varying between natural gender languages such as English and arbitrary gender languages such as French. A linguistic system here correlates with a cognitive difference—a short-term processing link. Indeed Stapel and Semin (2007) point out that such staples of psychology research as semantic priming, discussed by Knickerbocker and Altarriba (Chapter 20 this volume), rely on short-term effects of language on cognition. Siegal, Kobayashi Frank, Surian, and Hjelmquist (Chapter 19 this volume) see Theory of Mind awareness in children as arising from certain types of conversational interaction, such as hearing other people talking about their interpretations of people's actions—long-term development. De Villiers (2000) indeed points to the syntactic underpinning of cognition necessary for the child to understand the instructions in Theory of Mind tasks.

The results of temporal sequence research seem unequivocal: Children taught to read from right to left think differently from children taught left-to-right direction, a long-term effect (Tversky et al., 1991). Apart from minor environmental influences, the cause can only be the language difference. Still researchers vary in their views of the relationship between language and child development. Tversky et al. (1991) take it more as a process of selecting from a set of concepts available to children: 'The similarity of systems invented repeatedly by different children and by different cultures can be taken as evidence for some compelling cognitive correspondences between people's conceptions of the world and their external representations of them' (pp. 551–552). In their classification study, Imai and Gentner (1997, p. 169) claim that 'children universally make a distinction between individuals and non-individuals in word learning but that the nature of the categories and the boundary between them is influenced by language'. Barner, Inagaki, and Li (2009, p. 329) also suggest that 'speakers of Mandarin, English, and Japanese draw on a universal set of lexical meanings, and that mass-count syntax allows speakers of English to select among these meanings'. This approach does not commit researchers to a straightforward causal relationship between language and cognition so much as a view that cognition is universal and a particular language in some way constrains the elements available—very similar to the Chomskyan view of cognition as a set of innate universal concepts 'essentially available prior to experience' (Chomsky, 1991, p. 29). The conclusion of the motion studies in Gennari et al. (2002) is similar: The language effect occurred only when language was relevant during initial encoding: 'Linguistic descriptions directed attention to certain aspects of the events later used to make a non-linguistic judgement' (p. 77). In other words, language did not so much impinge on the concept of motion itself as on the ways people accessed the concept through language—thinking for language.

Translating correlation into causation is notoriously hard, often resting more on unassailable arguments and accumulation of evidence than on the straightforward outcome of experiments. Correlation may be caused by some underlying factor not tested for. When the link between lung cancer and smoking depended on correlation alone, at one time it was argued that the underlying cause of cancer might be genetic or personality differences which correlated with a propensity to smoke rather than smoking itself. So, in the case of language and cognition, it could be culture, environment, or still other factors. To settle the language/cognition relationship developmentally would require bringing children up in two groups with particular languages in the identical physical environment, rather like a mammoth twin study, clearly an ethically forbidden experiment—except for King Psammetichus who, according to Herodotus (ca 430 BC) isolated children with a silent shepherd for two years to see which language emerged spontaneously (Thomas, 2006), and for the fictional treatment in *The Embedding* (Watson, 1973) in which children become superhuman by learning to handle multiply-embedded constructions.

To sum up, these studies do not make a conclusive case for language being the cause of some aspects of cognition. Mostly they are concerned with the synchronic processing of language and cognition rather than with the diachronic development of language and cognition. Overall they seem to support a so-called 'weak' version of linguistic relativity in which language facilitates cognition, rather than a 'strong' version in which language determines cognition—if in fact the strong relativity position has actually ever been held by someone rather than acting as a straw man to be denigrated (Swoyer, Chapter 2, and others in this volume debate the weak and strong versions of linguistic relativity at greater length).

The alternative possibility that cognition drives language development has received less attention. Yet in developmental terms, Sapir (1921/n.d., p. 16) claimed 'The point of view that we have developed does not by any means preclude the possibility of the growth of speech being in a high degree dependent on the development of thought.' In Piagetan research the assumption was that cognitive development triggered language acquisition, explored for instance by Sinclair-de-Zwart (1967) and Bruner (1983). The influential review by Cromer (1974) concluded that, while language development does not always relate to cognition, when there *is* a relationship, language depends on cognitive development. Gathercole (Chapter 5 this volume, p. 109) similarly believes 'extensive pursuit over the last decades of meticulous work exploring the relationship between language and cognitive development has indicated that language and cognition interact in development'. Bowerman (1996, p. 170) nonetheless feels that 'spatial thought—undeniably one of our most basic cognitive capacities—bears the imprint of language'.

Presumably all theories that deny that language is a specific module in the mind, whether emergentism or behaviorism, will see a common underlying source for all cognitive processes. The view from cognitive linguistics (V. Evans, Chapter 4 this volume, p. 69) is that 'the concepts we have access to, and the nature of the "reality" we think and talk about, are grounded in the multimodal representations that emerge from our embodied experience'. Language and cognition are then an interrelated inseparable system, and causation is irrelevant, or at any rate partial.

Question 4. Can cognition be changed by appropriate language control or teaching for individuals, children or societies?

If questions 1–3 are answered affirmatively, there still remains the question for an applied linguist of whether deliberately changing people's language actually alters their cognition. This section extends the discussion outside the narrow academic discussion of cognition and language to the powerful if vague influences on human life which often feature in popular discussions. The intention is to remind us that the academic study of language and cognition has, or should have, consequences for everyday problems and issues facing individuals and governments.

One relevant attempt to cause cognitive change through language correlated language level with Piagetan stage and then taught children the language of the next stage, with little effect (Sinclair-de-Zwart, 1967). Ervin-Tripp (Chapter 9 this volume) describes Carroll's discovery that Navaho children sort objects by form because of their language, American children acquire it from playing with blocks in pre-schools. One education approach in the UK is known as 'teaching thinking'—'an umbrella term used to describe a range of interventions, which have been classified into three groups: context independent, . . . subject-based programmes, . . . and subject infusion' (Leat & Lin, 2003, p. 385). Worthwhile as these approaches may be on other educational grounds, in so far as they involve changing thinking by language intervention, we still do not know that language change promotes changes in cognition, even if educationalists often take this for granted (and this could arguably be said to be the heart of all education). The 1970s saw organized intervention to redress disadvantaged groups in society such as *Sesame Street* and *Talk Reform* (Gahagan & Gahagan, 1970), with language being a key ingredient; the overall benefits of *Sesame Street* for its child viewers have been well documented (Fisch & Truglio, 2001). In as much as attempts to teach learning-disabled children to use Makaton or children with reading difficulties to handle letter shapes go beyond their language briefs, these too rely on the idea of changing cognition through language intervention. As indeed do claims for the educational and social advantages of learning another language, as we shall see in Chapter 7. In reverse, the practice of Steiner schools is not to teach reading until the child's milk-teeth have dropped out (Steiner, 1968/1997), making language development clearly depend on physical maturation.

COGNITION AND LANGUAGE IN MODERN LIFE

Despite the reluctance of researchers over the years to commit themselves to the view that language determines cognition, in everyday life this is precisely what popular movements have assumed, particularly the attempts to improve the workings of society and the minds of individuals by changing their language. One form this takes is control of language through 'anti-ism', whether anti-sexism deploring the effects of male-dominated language such as the use of *chairman*, anti-racism concerned with the effects of race-tinged language such as the use of *Paki* or *gyppo*, or anti-classism concerned with the effects of 'elaborated' middle-class language on working-class children's education (Bernstein, 1971), such as the working-class preference for exophoric pronouns relating language to the immediate environment rather than anaphoric pronouns referring to aspects of discourse. The items of language discussed change from decade to decade; yesterday's ban on *girl* for 'mature women' is superseded by today's use of *girl* for 'vital female youth', as in *Spice Girls*. Academic research is not immune to these pressures. However much they disagree with linguistic relativity, researchers are careful to submit papers with non-specific gender *he/she* or *they* for people in general and with *participant* rather than *subject* (Stapel & Semin, 2007); the publishers' instructions to contributors to this book say 'Avoid the use of "he" (when he or she is meant) wherever possible, either through the use of "they" or by repeating the noun' (Psychology Press, no date).

The worthy belief that changing the language improves the world is often put down by being labeled political correctness—the *Guardian* once called it 'petty bourgeois linguistic anti-racism': We can lessen the discrimination against particular groups by censoring the language we use about them. It is certainly best, for example, not to use the word *schizophrenic* to mean when people 'seem to have very different purposes or opinions' (COBUILD, 1995), exemplified in the 'rather schizophrenic way in which the Whorfian question has been viewed' (Gentner & Goldin-Meadow, 2003, p. 3). Such use 'does an injustice to the enormity of the public health problems and profound suffering associated with this most puzzling disorder of the human mind' (Gottesman, 1991) and is in fact banned in some, if not all, newspaper style sheets. The proscriptions on vocabulary do affect language usage: The numbers of the pronoun *she* in *Time Magazine* almost doubled between 1960 and the present, while the numbers of *he* went down; indeed the usage of several contributors to this volume is evidence of changes in gender choice in pronoun use. Whether this affects people's cognition and attitudes is another matter; Khosroshahi (1989) found that adopting non-sex-marked generic pronouns affected women's drawing of generic objects but not men's; avoiding the split-personality meaning of *schizophrenic* may improve politeness, but have little effect on attitudes to mental illness.

Language, then, can be blamed for the general ills of humankind. For example the theories of Western scientists may be constrained by the notions of Noun and Verb (Whorf, 1941b/1956), say imposing a dichotomy between light as a noun-like particle or as a verb-like wave; as with much subsequent discussion in linguistic relativity research, this treats Noun and Verb as a semantic rather than a syntactic category. Halliday (1990/2001) sees growthism as built-in to the use of scientific language through elaborate nominal groups such as *interpretations of experiments on syntactic processing in cotton-top tamarin* and through the use of uncountable nouns for natural resources—*water* suggests inexhaustibility, *a water* suggests finiteness. The field of ecolinguistics has indeed developed the concept of language interfacing with society for good or for ill (Fill & Muhlhausler, 2001). Recent years have shown many examples of the entrenched belief that saying the words will in itself change people's thinking, whether political slogans like 'Education, education, education' or mission statements such as 'Regionally rooted, nationally influential, and globally respected' (Cook, 2009).

One intriguing possibility is the effect of computer languages and computer programs on our cognition. Iverson (1980) talked of the positive advantages of using the computer language APL (which he invented); 'Programming languages, because they were designed for the purpose of directing computers, offer important advantages as tools of thought' p. 445 The computer language Prolog has been taught to children for similar reasons (Colbourn & Light, 1987). On the negative side, Tufte (2003) attributes poor thinking, and indeed the crash of the space shuttle, to the ubiquitous use of Powerpoint. Eco (1994), writing on PC users versus Mac users, speculates 'One may wonder whether, as time goes by, the use of one system rather than another leads to profound inner changes'.

The aircrash with the biggest loss of life to date may have been caused by a confusion in the specialized international English of air traffic control (Tajima, 2004). A Dutch pilot of a Boeing 747 departing from Tenerife announced *We are now at take-off*, meaning 'we are now actually taking off'; the Spanish air traffic controller understood 'we are now waiting at the take-off position', with tragic consequences. Reforming particular specialized areas of language to remove ambiguities or unclarities for safety reasons alone seems a useful enterprise; airlines rely on passengers understanding the emergency command *brace brace*, an untypical use of a low-frequency verb and a puzzle to non-native speakers of English. Indeed one of Whorf's original motivations for pursuing linguistic relativity was the kind of language problems he encountered as a fire inspector (Whorf, 1941a/1956); for example a little-used electric fire on a wall was seen as 'a place to put coats'; when someone turned on what they thought was 'the light switch', the building caught fire. Hence one practical interest is how the short-term processing of language impacts on cognition: How we encode the environment at the moment of speaking affects our behavior.

Many proposals have gone further than the banning of particular words or meanings. The most notorious was the general semantics movement based on Korzybski (1933), which attempted to make language more logical by abandoning Aristotelian either/or choices, fictionalized in the Van Vogt (1948) classic *The World of Null-A* (A for Aristotelian). Reforming language removes undesirable thoughts. At the positive end of the scale comes Halliday's consciousness-raising of the environmental implications of linguistic behavior for society and the world (Halliday, 1990/ 2001). At the negative end comes the thought control of Newspeak specially designed by Big Brother in *Nineteen Eighty Four* 'not only to provide a medium of expression for the world-view and mental habits proper to the devotees of Ingsoc [English Socialism] but to make all other forms of thought impossible' (Orwell, 1949). The proposals for various kinds of simplified language such as Basic English (Ogden, 1937) often have overtones of language control of thought.

So, as well as continuing to fascinate and infuriate researchers, the language/cognition interface is also involved in many aspects of everyday life, including government policies. It would seem well to establish its strengths and limitations on as firm a basis as possible to inform people how feasible such implementations are likely to be.

The crucial element missing from the discussion so far is individuals or groups who use two or more languages. In terms of the numbers of human beings alive today, this is a colossal oversight common to most of the research in this area. There may well be more people who use two or more languages in their everyday lives than there are monolinguals in the world. In addition the advantage of second language users for research into language and cognition is that these can be desynchronized, unlike first language development and use: 'It would be highly useful if we could, so to speak, disengage the two processes of language and cognitive development and look at people whose level of thinking is out of step with their level of language' (Cook, 1981, p. 255). For these reasons the role of second language users is at the center of this book, starting with the background to language and cognition in Chapter 7 and becoming the focus of Chapters 8 to 21.

REFERENCES

Ayabe-Kanamura, S., Schicker, I., Laska, M., Hudson, R., Distel, H., & Kobayakawa, T. (1998). Differences in perception of everyday odours: A Japanese–German cross-cultural study. *Chemical Senses, 23,* 31–38.

Barner, D., Inagaki, S., & Li, P. (2009). Language, thought, and real nouns. *Cognition, 111,* 329–344.

Bernstein, B. (1971). *Class, codes and control: Volume 1.* London: Routledge & Kegan Paul.

Biederman, I., Yue, X., & Davidoff, J. (2009). Representation of shape in individuals from a culture with minimal exposure to regular simple artefacts. *Psychological Science, 20*(12), 1437–1442.

Boas, F. (1920/1940). The methods of ethnology. *American Anthropologist, 22,* 311–322. [Reprinted in F. Boas (1940). *Race, language and culture* (pp. 281–289). New York: Free Press.]

Boroditsky, L., Schmidt, L. A., & Phillips, W. (2003). Sex, syntax, and semantics. In D. Gentner & S. Goldin Meadow (Eds.), *Language in mind: Advances in the study of language and thought* (pp. 61–80). Cambridge, MA: MIT Press.

Bowerman, M. (1996). The origins of children's spatial semantic categories: Cognitive versus linguistic determinism. In J. J. Gumperz & S. C. Levinson (Eds.), *Rethinking linguistic relativity* (pp. 145–176). Cambridge, UK: Cambridge University Press.

Bruner, J. (1983). *Child's talk*. Oxford, UK: Oxford University Press.

Cardini, F-E. (2009). Evidence against Whorfian effects in motion conceptualization. *Journal of Pragmatics, 42*(5), 1442–1459.

Carroll, J. B., & Casagrande, J. B. (1958). The function of language classifications in behavior. In E. Maccoby, T. M. Newcomb, & E. L. Hartley (Eds.), *Readings in social psychology* (pp. 18–31). New York: Holt Rinehart & Winston.

Casasanto, D. (2008). Who's afraid of the big bad Whorf? Crosslinguistic differences in temporal language and thought. *Language Learning, 58,* 63–79.

Chomsky, N. (1981). *Lectures on government and binding*. Dordrecht: Foris.

Chomsky, N. (1991). Linguistics and cognitive science: Problems and mysteries. In A. Kasher (Ed.), *The Chomskyan turn* (pp. 26–53). Oxford, UK: Blackwell.

Chomsky, N. (1995). *The minimalist program*. Cambridge, MA: MIT Press.

COBUILD. (1995). *Collins COBUILD dictionary*. Glasgow, UK: Collins.

Colbourn, C. J., & Light, P. H. (1987). Social interaction and learning using Micro-PROLOG. *Journal of Computer Assisted Learning, 3*(3), 130–140.

Cook, V. J. (1981). Some uses for second language learning research. *Annals of the New York Academy of Sciences, 379,* 251–258.

Cook, V. J. (2009). *It's all in a word*. London: Profile.

Cook, V. J. (2010). Prolegomena to second language learning. In P. Seedhouse, S. Walsh, & C. Jenks (Eds.), *Conceptualizing language learning*. London: Palgrave Macmillan.

Corbett, G. G. (1991). *Gender*. Cambridge, UK: Cambridge University Press.

Cromer, R. F. (1974). The development of language and cognition: The cognition hypothesis. In B. Foss (Ed.), *New perspectives in child development* (pp. 184–252). Harmondsworth, UK: Penguin.

Davidoff, J., Davies, I., & Roberson, D. (1999). Color categories in a stone-age tribe. *Nature, 398,* 203–204.

Davies, I. R. L. (1998). A study of color grouping in three languages: A test of linguistic relativity hypothesis. *British Journal of Psychology, 89*(3), 433–452.

de Saussure, F. (1916/1976). *Cours de Linguistique Générale*. [Edited by C. Bally & A. Sechehaye (1916). Critical edition by T. de Maurio.] Paris: Payothèque, Payot.

De Villiers, J. (2000). Language and Theory of Mind: What are the developmental relationships? In S. Baron-Cohen, H. Tager-Flusberg, & D. Cohen (Eds.), *Understanding other minds: Perspectives from autism* (pp. 83–123). Oxford, UK: Oxford University Press.

Eco, U. (1994). La bustina di Minerva [column]. *Espresso*, September 30th.

Everett, D. L. (2008). *Don't sleep: There are snakes*. London: Profile.

Fill, A., & Muhlhausler, P. (Eds.). (2001). *The ecolinguistics reader*. London: Continuum.

Fisch, S. M., & Truglio, R. T. (Eds.). (2001). *G is for growing: Thirty years of research on children and Sesame Street*. Mahwah, NJ: Lawrence Erlbaum Associates Inc.

Forel, C. (2008). *La linguistique sociale de Charles Bally*. Genève: Librarie Droz.

Gahagan, D. M., & Gahagan, G. A. (1970). *Talk reform*. London: Routledge.

Gennari, S. P., Sloman, S. A., Malt, B. C., & Fitch W. T. (2002). Motion events in language and cognition. *Cognition, 83*, 49–79.

Gentner, D., & Goldin-Meadow, S. (2003). Whither Whorf. In D. Gentner & S. Goldin-Meadow (Eds.), *Language in mind: Advances in the study of language and thought* (pp. 1–15). Cambridge, MA: MIT Press.

Goody, J. (2000). *The power of the written tradition*. Washington, DC: Smithsonian Institute.

Gottesman, I. (1991). *Schizophrenia genesis*. Oxford/New York: W. H. Freeman.

Gumperz, J. J., & Levinson, S. C. (Eds.). (1996). *Rethinking linguistic relativity*. Cambridge, UK: Cambridge University Press.

Hale, K. (1983). Warlipiri and the grammar of non-configurational languages. *Natural Language and Linguistic Theory, 1*, 5–47.

Halliday, M. A. K. (1990/2001). New ways of meaning: The challenge to applied linguistics. In A. Fill & P. Muhlhausler (Eds.), *The ecolinguistics reader* (pp. 175–202). London: Continuum.

Imai, M., & Gentner, D. (1997). A cross-linguistic study of early word meaning: Universal ontology and linguistic influence. *Cognition, 62*, 169–200.

Iverson, K. E. (1980). Notation as a tool of thought. *Communications of the ACM, 23*(8), 444–465.

Jackendoff, R. (1992). *Languages of the mind*. Cambridge, MA: MIT Press.

Khosroshahi, F. (1989). Penguins don't care but women do: A social identity analysis of a Whorfian problem. *Language in Society, 18*, 505–525.

Korzybski, A. (1933). *Science and sanity: An introduction to non-Aristotelian systems and general semantics*. New York: Institute of General Semantics.

Leat, D., & Lin, M. (2003). Developing a pedagogy of metacognition and transfer: Some signposts for the generation and use of knowledge and the creation of research partnerships. *British Educational Research Journal, 29*(3), 383–415.

Lenneberg, E. H. (1953). Cognition in ethnolinguistics. *Language, 29*(4), 463–471.

Levinson, S. (1996). Relativity in spatial conception and description. In J. J. Gumperz & S. C. Levinson (Eds.), *Rethinking linguistic relativity* (pp. 177–202). Cambridge, UK: Cambridge University Press.

Li, P., & Gleitman, L. (2002). Turning the tables: Language and spatial reasoning. *Cognition, 83*, 265–294.

Lucy, J. A. (1992). *Grammatical categories and cognition: A case study of the linguistic relativity hypothesis*. Cambridge, UK: Cambridge University Press.

Lucy, J. A. (1996). The scope of linguistic relativity. In J. J. Gumperz & S. C. Levinson (Eds.), *Rethinking linguistic relativity* (pp. 37–69). Cambridge, UK: Cambridge University Press.

Lucy, J. A. (1997). Linguistic relativity. *Annual Review of Anthropology, 26*, 291–392.

Luria, A. R. (1976). *Cognitive development: Its cultural and social foundations.* Cambridge, MA: Harvard University Press.

Mann, V. A. (1986). Temporary memory for linguistic and non-linguistic material in relation to the acquisition of Japanese kanji and kana. In H. S. R. Kao & R. Hoosain (Eds.), *Linguistics, psychology, and the Chinese language* (pp. 55–167). Hong Kong: University of Hong Kong Press.

Matthews, C. (2009). On the nature of phonological cues in the acquisition of French gender categories: Evidence from instance-based learning models. *Lingua, 120*(4), 879–900.

Ogden, C. K. (1937). *Basic English: A general introduction with rules and grammar.* London: Paul, Trench Trubner & Co.

O'Mahony, M., & Muhiudeen, H. (1977). A preliminary study of alternative taste languages using qualitative description of sodium chloride solutions: Malay versus English. *British Journal of Psychology, 68,* 275–278.

Orwell, G. (1949). *Nineteen eighty four.* London: Secker & Warburg.

Psychology Press. (no date). *Instructions for contributing authors.* Hove, UK: Psychology Press.

Rozin, P., & Schiller, D. (1980). The nature and acquisition of a preference for chili pepper by humans. *Motivation and Emotion, 4,* 77–101.

Sapir, E. (1921/n.d.). *Language: An introduction to the study of speech.* [Reprinted no date.] New York: Harcourt Brace & Co.

Sapir, E. (1929). The status of linguistics as a science. *Language, 5,* 207–214.

Segall, M. H., Campbell, D. T., & Herskovits, M. J. (1966). *The influence of culture on visual perception.* New York: Bobbs-Merrill.

Sera, M. D., Forbes, J., Burch, M. C., & Rodriquez, W. (2002). When language affects cognition and when it does not: An analysis of grammatical gender and classification. *Journal of Experimental Psychology: General, 131,* 377–397.

Sinclair-de-Zwart, H. (1967). *Acquisition du langage and développement de la pensée.* Paris: Dunod.

Slobin, D. I. (1996). From 'thought and language' to 'language for thinking'. In J. J. Gumperz & S. C. Levinson (Eds.), *Rethinking linguistic relativity* (pp. 70–96). Cambridge, UK: Cambridge University Press.

Stapel, D. A., & Semin, G. R. (2007). The magic spell of language: Linguistic categories and their perceptual consequences. *Journal of Personality and Social Psychology, 93*(1), 23–33.

Steiner, R. (1968/1997). *The roots of education.* [Reprinted by Hudson.] New York: Anthroposophic Press.

Tajima, A. (2004). Fatal miscommunication: English in aviation safety. *World Englishes, 23*(3), 451–470.

Talmy, L. (1985). Lexicalization patterns: Semantic structure in lexical forms. In T. Shopen (Ed.), *Language typology and lexical description: Vol. 3. Grammatical categories and the lexicon* (pp. 36–149). Cambridge, UK: Cambridge University Press.

Tomasello, M. (2003). *Constructing a language.* Cambridge, MA: Harvard University Press.

Tomlin, R. S. (1986). *Basic word order: Functional principles.* London: Croom Helm.

Thomas, M. (2006). The evergreen story of Psammetichus' inquiry. *Historiographia Linguistica, 34,* 37–62.

Tufte, E. (2003). *The cognitive style of Powerpoint*. Cheshire, CT: Graphics Press.

Tversky, B., Kugelmass, S., & Winter, A. (1991). Cross-cultural and developmental trends in graphic productions. *Cognitive Psychology, 23,* 515–557.

Van Vogt, A. E. (1948). *The world of null-A*. New York: Simon & Schuster.

von Humboldt, W. (1836/1999). *On language* (Translated by P. Heath.) Cambridge, UK: Cambridge University Press.

von Stutterheim, C., Bastin, D., Carroll, M., Flecken, M., & Schmiedtová, B. (in press). How grammaticized concepts shape event conceptualization in the early phases of language production: Insights from linguistic analysis, eye tracking data and memory performance. *Linguistics*.

Watson, I. (1973). *The embedding*. London: Victor Gollancz.

Weinreich, U. (1953). *Languages in contact*. The Hague: Mouton.

Whorf, B. L. (1940/1956). Science and linguistics. *Technology Review, 42*(8), 229–231, 247–248. [Reprinted in J. B. Carroll (Ed.). (1956). *Language, thought, and reality: Selected writings of Benjamin Lee Whorf* (pp. 207–219). Cambridge, MA: MIT Press.]

Whorf, B. L. (1941a/1956). The relation of habitual thought and behavior to language. [Reprinted in J. B. Carroll (Ed.). (1956). *Language, thought, and reality: Selected writings of Benjamin Lee Whorf* (pp. 134–159). Cambridge, MA: MIT Press.]

Whorf, B. L. (1941b/1956). Languages and logic. [Reprinted in J. B. Carroll (Ed.). (1956). *Language, thought, and reality: Selected writings of Benjamin Lee Whorf* (pp. 233–245). Cambridge, MA: MIT Press.]

Wierzbicka, A. (1996). *Semantics: Primes and universals*. Oxford, UK: Oxford University Press.

2 How does language affect thought?

Chris Swoyer

There has been a long, often passionate, debate over the ways in which language affects thought. The claim that a person's language influences how they experience or think about the world is known as the *linguistic relativity hypothesis* or *linguistic relativism*. Such influences are causal, and because many different aspects of language could in principle influence many different aspects of thought, the linguistic relativity hypothesis is really a family of claims about these potential influences.

My aim here is to sketch a context for thinking about linguistic relativity. I begin with a very short history of linguistic relativity doctrines (which I shall denominate collectively as the *linguistic relativity hypothesis*), stressing the influence of the ambient intellectual climate on its formulations and fortunes. I then note several quite distinct versions of the doctrine, examine problems that arise in testing them, and discuss avenues for future work.

There are many snares in the neighborhood. Many participants in the debates over linguistic relativity oversimplify the views of their opponents. The problem is exacerbated because relativistic theses often come in two forms: a bold and arresting version, which is proclaimed, and a weaker, less vulnerable version, which is defended—with the first having a tendency to morph into the second when under attack. Moreover, although relativistic lines of thought often lead to quite implausible conclusions, there is something seductive about them and, even when the arguments are weak, they have captivated a wide range of thinkers from a wide range of traditions.

Discussions of relativism are also frequently marred by all-or-none thinking: Either virtually everything is relative or virtually nothing is. But usually the question is whether there is a space for an interesting and plausible version of relativism between claims that are banal (the Babylonians did not have a counterpart of the word *telephone* so they did not think about telephones) and those that are dramatic but almost certainly false (those who speak different languages see the world in totally different ways). And it could turn out that some versions of the thesis are true while others are false.

Although I will not defend specific empirical claims about the hypotheses here, the discussion will suggest several morals. First, even if all humans are biologically endowed with a rich set of linguistic and cognitive universals, there may still be room for interesting ways in which differences in language could lead to differences in thought. Second, as of now, many versions of the relativity hypothesis (and many natural languages) have not been tested at all. In the relatively few cases where they have, the methodology is not always impeccable nor the results univocal. The results thus far are limited, qualified, and piecemeal. Finally, tests of interesting versions of the hypothesis are *very difficult* to perform. What is needed now is less polemics and more detailed empirical work involving as many different methods as possible.

LINGUISTIC RELATIVITY

What counts as a substantive difference?

People could agree that two languages differ in some way or that two groups engage in rather different forms of reasoning, yet disagree as to whether the difference is big enough to matter. Take concepts, for example. Some concepts are much more *central* to our thought than others. For instance, our concepts of 'causation', 'physical object', 'person', 'space', and 'color' are more central to our thought than our concepts of 'avocado', 'pickup truck', and 'toothpick'. More interesting versions of relativity involve larger differences like the former rather than the latter. Such debates pit those who see a glass as half full against those who see the same glass as half empty. Whether a difference is large enough to be of interest depends heavily on how large the difference has been thought to be by previous thinkers. Against the background of Whorf's extreme claims of linguistic relativity, many recently discovered differences seem rather trivial. Given the recent fashion for innate capacities and cognitive universals, the same differences appear more substantive.

A preliminary statement of the linguistic relativity hypothesis

There are around four to five thousand languages in use today, each quite different from many of the others. Differences are especially pronounced between languages of different families, e.g., Indo-European languages like English and German and Latin, on the one hand, and non-Indo-European languages like Hopi and Japanese and Swahili, on the other.

Many thinkers have urged that large differences in language lead to large differences in experience or thought. They may even hold that each language embodies a worldview, with quite different languages embodying quite different views, so that speakers of different languages think about the world in quite different ways or even, in a common and pungent—if hazy—metaphor, may live in 'different worlds'.

Such suggestions have an intuitive appeal for many readers, but questions about the impact of language on thought are *empirical questions* that can only be answered by *empirical investigation*. Despite considerable progress in the last quarter-century, the enthusiasm of partisans on both sides of the debate often far outstripped the available evidence.

A (slightly) more careful statement of the hypotheses

Interesting versions of the linguistic relativity hypothesis embody two claims:

I   *Linguistic diversity*: Languages can differ in substantial ways from one another.
II   *Linguistic influence on thought*: Features of a person's language influence how they think, and they influence it in systematic ways.

The thesis of linguistic diversity can be construed uncontroversially. Even if all human languages share numerous abstract linguistic universals, there are often large differences in their syntactic structures and their lexicons, as anyone who has learned a second language can attest. The second claim is more controversial, but because linguistic forces could shape thought in various ways and to varying degree, this thesis comes in more and less plausible forms.

As a first approximation, we can think of language as the independent variable and cognition as the dependent variable. We must replace these general notions with much more fine-grained features of language and thought, however, to obtain testable versions of the general hypothesis. We should try to answer three questions:

1   *Which aspects* of language influence *which aspects* of thought in a systematic way?
2   What *form* does this influence take?
3   How *strong* is the influence?

For example, certain features of a language's syntax (e.g., whether there is a distinction between intransitive verbs and adjectives) or its lexicon (e.g., what color words or spatial vocabulary it contains) might be hypothesized to influence perception, classification, or memory (e.g., in recall tests) in clearly specifiable ways.

LINGUISTIC INFLUENCE ON THOUGHT: A VERY BRIEF HISTORY

Background

Current thought about linguistic relativity has its roots in debates that began in late-eighteenth- and nineteenth-century Germany, particularly in the work of Johann Georg Hamann (1730–88), Johann Wilhelm von Humboldt (1767–1835), and especially Gottfried Herder (1744–1803). That work was part of the Romantic reaction to various Enlightenment ideas.

We can view the debates as staking out positions along a continuum between two poles, betwixt two ideal types. At one end of the spectrum we find the views of Leibniz, Hume, Voltaire, Condillac and other Enlightenment figures who believed in the *constancy of human nature* or, more to the point here, the *constancy of the basic mechanisms and concepts of human thought*. True, they allowed that there might be interesting differences between various languages (like English and Hebrew). But these differences were seen as a patina over shared basic concepts and modes of thought, and with intellectual care and ingenuity they could be peeled off to reveal the cognitive uniformities underneath.

Many later thinkers, particularly anthropologists, took a more empirical route to a similar destination, often taking a cue from the German anthropologist Adolf Bastian's (1826–1905) postulate of *the psychic unity of mankind*. And far more sophisticated variations on these ideas have been popular in recent decades among proponents of substantive linguistic and cognitive universals (linguistic and cognitive features that are the biological endowment of *all* normal human beings).

At the other end of the spectrum we have various versions of the linguistic relativity hypothesis. From this perspective there *are* striking differences among some (not necessarily all) languages, and at least some of these differences lead to non-trivial differences in how their users perceive and think about the world. Many of the early champions of this view, including the Romantics, were exceptionally erudite, with a command of an array of divers languages. Later champions of linguistic relativity based their claims on more direct empirical contact with the users of different languages rather than just the texts they left behind.

Few thinkers occupy either extreme of the spectrum, but many are much closer to one end than the other. Roughly speaking, the relativists dominated the Western intellectual climate in the first half of the twentieth century and their opponents dominated the second half.

The big names

It will be easier to see why the linguistic relativity hypothesis captivated so many thinkers if we briefly consider the more arresting claims of Edward

Sapir (1884–1936) and Benjamin Lee Whorf (1897–1941). Sapir was an American anthropological linguist who, like many American anthropologists of his day, was a student of the Dean of American anthropologists, Franz Boas. Whorf, a businessman and amateur linguist, was a student of Sapir. Unlike many earlier champions of linguistic relativity, Sapir and Whorf based their claims on first-hand encounters with the languages and cultures they described, and this gave their accounts a vividness earlier discussion typically lacked. A few quotations will convey the flavor.

Sapir

In 1929 Sapir averred:

> Human beings do not live in the objective world alone, nor alone in the world of social activity as ordinarily understood, but are very much at the mercy of the particular language which has become the medium of expression for their society. It is quite an illusion to imagine that one adjusts to reality essentially without the use of language and that language is merely an incidental means of solving specific problems of communication or reflection.
>
> (Sapir, 1929, p. 209)

Our language affects how we perceive things:

> Even comparatively simple acts of perception are very much more at the mercy of the social patterns called words than we might suppose. . . . We see and hear and otherwise experience very largely as we do because the language habits of our community predispose certain choices of interpretation.
>
> (Sapir, 1929, p. 210)

But the differences do not end with perception:

> The fact of the matter is that the 'real world' is to a large extent unconsciously built up on the language habits of the group. No two languages are ever sufficiently similar to be considered as representing the same social reality. The worlds in which different societies live are distinct worlds, not merely the same worlds with different labels attached.
>
> (Sapir, 1929, p. 209)

Whorf

The linguistic relativity hypothesis gained its widest audience, and notoriety, through the work of Whorf, whose collected writings became something of a relativistic manifesto. Even by the rather lax standards of early discussions of the hypothesis, Whorf is unclear and inconsistent, sliding back and forth between very brash claims and more guarded ones. Debate continues about his considered views, but there is little doubt that his bolder claims were what captivated many readers.

When languages are similar, Whorf tells us, they are not likely to issue in dramatic cognitive differences. But languages that differ markedly from English and other Western European languages (which Whorf calls, collectively, 'Standard Average European') often *do* lead their speakers to think in very different ways, even to the point of having very different worldviews.

> We are thus introduced to a *new principle of relativity*, which holds that all observers are not led by the same physical evidence to the same picture of the universe, unless their linguistic backgrounds are similar, or can in some way be calibrated. . . . The *relativity of all conceptual systems*, ours included, and their dependence upon language stand revealed.
>
> (Whorf, 1956, p. 214f, italics added)

> We dissect nature along lines laid down by our native languages. The categories and types that we isolate from the world of phenomena we do not find there because they stare every observer in the face; on the contrary, the world is presented in a kaleidoscopic flux of impressions which has to be organized by our minds—and this means largely by the linguistic systems in our minds. [. . .] no individual is free to describe nature with absolute impartiality but is constrained to certain modes of interpretation even while he thinks himself most free.
>
> (Whorf, 1956, pp. 213–214)

And:

> . . . users of markedly different grammars are pointed by their grammars toward different types of observations and different evaluations of externally similar acts of observation, and hence are not equivalent as observers but must arrive at somewhat different views of the world.
>
> (Whorf, 1956, p. 221)

In yet a third essay 'facts are unlike to speakers whose language background provides for unlike formulation of them' (Whorf, 1956, p. 235). Indeed,

> [Western] Science . . . has not yet freed itself from the illusory necessities of common logic which are only at bottom necessities of

grammatical pattern in Western Aryan grammar; necessities for substances which are only necessities for substantives in certain sentence positions . . .

(Whorf, 1956, pp. 269–270)

Both Whorf's and Sapir's discussions brim with metaphors of coercion: Our thought is 'at the mercy' of our language, it is 'constrained' by it; no one is free to describe the world in a neutral way; we are 'compelled' to read certain features into the world. Here the influence of language on thought is almost preternaturally strong.

Linguistic relativism was defended by numerous other thinkers from many backgrounds. Here is a vivid encapsulation from the philosopher Ernst Cassirer (1874–1945):

. . . the distinctions which here are taken for granted, the analysis of reality in terms of things and processes, permanent and transitory aspects, objects and actions, do not precede language as a substratum of given fact, but that language itself is what initiates such articulations, and develops them in its own sphere.

(Cassirer, 1923/55, p. 12)

Because the linguistic relativity hypothesis came to prominence through the work of Sapir and Whorf, it is often called the 'Sapir-Whorf hypothesis' or simply the 'Whorf hypothesis' in deference to them. I will stick with the label 'linguistic relativity', however, for although it is not perfect, it makes it easier to separate the hypothesis from the details of Sapir's and Whorf's views. The basic ideas can even be generalized, as the work of Nelson Goodman (1978) suggests, to the claim that symbol systems— including computer languages, conventions for diagrams, even styles of painting—influence perception and thought, but I will focus on natural languages here.

Linguistic relativity hypotheses were popular among many American anthropologists during the first half of the twentieth century, and some anthropologists (who seem less affected by nativist trends than other social scientists) still endorse it. The hypothesis also received succor from behaviorism, the dominant approach in psychology (and to a lesser extent other social sciences) during this period. Many behaviorists found the hypotheses congenial, because they thought that many aspects of human behavior and thought were learned ('conditioned') rather than innate, so that people with quite different learning histories might well end up with quite different modes of thought. However, with the emphasis on behavior, inner episodes of thought were often held to be beyond the reach of science, or even beyond the pale, so behaviorists could easily slide into the view that nothing remains for language to influence, and the relativity hypothesis becomes a non-issue.

The demise of linguistic relativity

A half-century after Whorf, the linguistic relativity hypothesis had degenerated into the poster child for shoddy empirical work coupled with speculative excess. What happened?

Cognitive science

Cognitive science happened. As a result of several mutually reinforcing trends beginning in the mid-1950s, behaviorism began to wither and was eventually replaced by cognitive psychology and, more recently, cognitive science (an interdisciplinary approach to the study of cognition). One stimulus for this was the development of the computer and the information sciences, and (despite their differences) most cognitive scientists came to view the human mind as an information encoding and processing system and mental operations as functionally specifiable computational mechanisms which process information.

This picture is compatible with various versions of linguistic relativity, for example with the view that language and concepts are acquired by very general learning mechanisms through which we might acquire quite different languages or styles of thought. The rise of the cognitive sciences restored the study of inner mental processes (like perception, attention, memory, decision making) to respectability. It also killed behaviorism with its anti-nativist tendencies, and it required a fairly rich picture of our biological cognitive endowment, which at least allowed for a rich set of innate linguistic and cognitive universals.

Chomsky and nativism

A second major cause of the passing of the linguistic relativity hypothesis was the work of the linguist Noam Chomsky who has argued for over half a century that human beings could only learn natural languages if they had a good deal of innate linguistic equipment to guide their way (e.g., Chomsky, 2000). Chomsky characterized this equipment in different ways over the years, but the abiding theme is that unless infants entered the world with such a biological inheritance, they could never progress beyond the sparse set of utterances they hear to the rich linguistic ability they achieve.

After all, in just a few years all normal children acquire the language that is spoken by those around them. They pick up a highly complex and virtually unbounded ability to distinguish sentences from non-sentences, and to understand and utter a virtually unlimited number of sentences they have never encountered before on the basis of the utterances they hear and the feedback (rarely in the form of corrections) they receive. The problem is that children's data are very unsystematic and sparse compared to the systematic and nearly unbounded linguistic competence they achieve in just a few years.

Hence, the argument continues, the child needs help to progress from this impoverished input to the rich output (viewed as the acquisition of acquisition of a grammar with recursive rules for a complex natural language). This help can only be provided by something innate that constrains and guides the child in their construction of the grammar. Furthermore, because any child can learn any human language, the innate endowment must put constraints on which of the countless logically possible languages are humanly possible (otherwise the data would be compatible with too many possible languages for children to single one out). In recent years this line of thought is sometimes reinforced by considerations drawn from formal learning theory (e.g., Matthews & Demopoulos, 1989).

If the features of human languages are limited by such innate language acquisition mechanisms, there is less scope for the large differences among languages that the more extreme linguistic relativists have imagined. Furthermore, if there are innate cognitive universals, as many have also urged (e.g., Brown, 1991; cf. Chiang & Wynn, 2000; Spelke & Newport, 1998; Xu & Carey, 1996), the scope narrows even further. But it is now increasingly recognized that even quite rich linguistic and cognitive universals could leave room for interesting linguistic and cognitive variations within the space of humanly possible languages and modes of thought. The question is whether or not they do.

Cognitive modules

Inspired in part by Chomsky's claims on behalf of an innate language acquisition 'module' in the brain, many cognitive psychologists went on to argue that the human mind is composed of a number of distinct modules for processing various types of information. Although the classic account of a module (Fodor, 1983) is now generally thought to be too strong, many cognitive scientists still believe that the human mind is composed of relatively independent modules, perhaps many of them. Candidates include modules for acquiring the syntax of one's native language, for recognizing human faces, and even for detecting cheaters.

If such cognitive modules exist, some of the empirical issues about linguistic relativity will translate into issues concerning the ways in which various modules can influence one another. Moreover, champions of modules tend to see many of our cognitive capacities as innate, which tends to run counter to the relativity hypothesis. However, many claims about specific cognitive modules are very difficult to test, and some are based on little more than the Just-So Stories of evolutionary psychologists. The issues here are empirical and the jury is still out. Still, even many of those skeptical of modules in general admit that there is a pretty good case for the existence of one or more language modules, and so some version of linguistic nativism certainly seems far more plausible than it did 60 years ago.

Finally, as we will see shortly, the demise of linguistic relativity hypotheses also resulted partly from a few empirical results that were, until recently, often taken to show that the facts on the ground simply did not support them.

TESTING THE HYPOTHESIS

Preliminaries

There are two general strategies for assailing the linguistic relativity hypothesis. First, one might argue that natural languages are not nearly as different from one another as is often supposed. To be sure, there are many surface differences, many features that make a second language difficult to learn, but at a more abstract level these are just surface variations on an underlying core of similarity (involving different settings of the same several dozen Chomskyian parameters, for example). If this is true, many versions of the relativity thesis are nipped in the bud. Perhaps large differences in languages *would* have led to large differences in thought, but because there are not large differences among human languages, such possibilities do not arise. Here the question of what counts as a difference large enough to be interesting—the half-empty–half-full problem—surfaces yet again.

The second general strategy for attacking the linguistic relativity hypothesis is to argue that although natural languages *do* sometimes (maybe often) differ in substantive ways, these differences do *not* lead to substantive differences in cognition. Either languages are a crust over human thought that can, with luck, be pried off with careful experimentation to reveal species-wide cognitive universals underneath, or else, *if* there are large cognitive differences among human groups, they are due to something other than language (e.g., non-linguistic aspects of culture).

Example: Color language and color cognition

The more extreme versions of the relativity hypothesis have little support (e.g., Malotki, 1983), but this leaves room for more modest versions. The first step in assessing relativity hypotheses is to take clearer and much more manageable versions of the hypothesis into the lab or out into the field to test. For example, instead of the grand claim that the lexicon of one's native language influences all aspects of thought, one might test the claim that the vocabulary of one's language influences how one will perceive, classify, or remember plants or animals or types of snow.

As it happened, much of the most punctilious investigation of the relativity hypothesis in the 1950s and 1960s involved color language and color cognition. At the outset this was an area where linguistic relativity seemed plausible. On the one hand, there is nothing in the physics of light (e.g., in facts about surface spectral reflectances) that suggests drawing boundaries between colors at one place rather than another; in this sense, our segmentations of the spectrum are arbitrary. On the other hand, it was well known that different languages had color terms which sliced the color spectrum in different spots. So, since nothing in the physics of color could determine how humans thought about color, it was natural to conclude that a person's color cognition follows the grooves laid down by their color language.

Color was also an auspicious object of study because investigators could use Munsell color chips (a widely used, standardized set of chips of different colors) or similar stimulus materials with participants all over the globe. This assured that whatever differences they found in their cognitive (dependent) variables really did involve the same independent variable, *color* (as anchored in the chips), rather than some more nebulous construct.

Brent Berlin and Paul Kay (Berlin & Kay, 1969; cf. Kay & McDaniel, 1978) did the most significant work on color. It did much to raise the quality of empirical work on the linguistic relativity hypothesis. And together with much subsequent work it suggested to many that the more robust versions of the linguistic relativity hypothesis were false when it comes to color. Indeed, this and related work (much of it involving ethnobiological and kinship terms) led many to conclude that language did not influence thought in any interesting way.

We now know that colors may be a rather special case, however, for although there is nothing in the physics of color that suggests particular segmentations of the spectrum, the opponent-process theory of color vision, now well confirmed, tells us that there are neurophysiological facts about human beings which influence many of the ways we perceive colors. We do not know of any comparable innate mechanisms that would channel thought about causation or space or social traits into similarly deep, cross-cultural grooves. There may well be similarities in the ways human beings think about such things, but we cannot conclude this from the research done on color.

Most versions of the hypothesis have never been tested

At least until recently, a close look would have shown that the case of each side of the debate was shaky. Often the only consideration cited in favor of linguistic relativity hypotheses was to point to a difference between two languages and assert that it adds up to a difference in modes of thought. But this simply assumes what needs to be shown, namely that such linguistic differences *give rise to* cognitive differences. On the other hand, refutations of the hypothesis often target implausibly extreme versions or proceed as if refutations in one domain (e.g., color language and color cognition) show that it is false in others like spatial language and cognition (whereas in fact it remains open whether, say, differences in spatial vocabulary influence navigation or the interpretation of directions).

Extreme versions of the linguistic relativity hypothesis are dead, and good riddance. But several things have recently breathed new life into more circumspect versions.

First, at least some of the empirical work thought to undermine linguistic relativity has been criticized on methodological grounds.

Second, we have seen great progress over the last quarter-century on both the methodological and the theoretical sides in the study of language and cognition.

Third, highly regarded empirical work (often employing these new tools) suggests that some aspects of language *do* influence some aspects of thought (one notable example is the work of Melissa Bowerman and her collaborators; e.g., Majid, Bowerman, Kita, Haun, & Levinson, 2004). There is even some literature suggesting that more sweeping negative conclusions about color cognition were premature (e.g., Davies & Corbett, 1997; Winawer et al., 2007).

Finally, as we will now see, it has become increasingly clear that many aspects of language and thought have not been tested for relativity at all.

Why the hypothesis is so difficult to test

Deciding to reopen the case for the linguistic relativity hypothesis is one thing. Adequately testing it is another. There are several reasons why it is very difficult to pin down the influence of specific aspects of a language (or language use) on specific aspects of thought.

Pinning down the independent and dependent variables

First, despite the efforts of able theorists and experimenters, there is still little consensus about many features of *our own* language and thought, which of course makes it difficult to get clear about those of quite alien cultures. To be sure, we have learned a great deal in the last half-century about the phonology and syntax of a large number of languages. But in the latter case we have almost been too successful, for we now have numerous approaches to the syntactic theory, along with seemingly endless disputes among their adherents.

When we turn to other aspects of language, the situation is far worse. For example, it seems reasonable to suppose that *if* a language does affect the way its users think, the meanings of its words and phrases are a strong candidate for having such an impact. But the fragmentary nature of current syntactic theories is nothing compared to the chaos surrounding current theories of linguistic meaning (semantic theories). There are numerous, hotly contested accounts of what meaning *is* and few signs of movement toward agreement about even the most fundamental issues. Nor is there any theoretical consensus about the nature and mechanisms of language *use*. Indeed, there is even debate over what a language *is, what one learns* when learning one, and *what sort of thing would even count as a solution* to these problems.

Things are little better when we turn to cognitive (dependent) variables. Although there has been impressive progress in many areas one would expect to bear on the linguistic relativity debate, much remains up for grabs. For example, there are large and irreconcilable differences about the nature and mechanisms of human judgment and decision making (e.g., Swoyer, 2002) or inductive inference (e.g., Feeney & Heit, 2007)

Or consider concepts. Concepts are relevant here, because at least in the case of linguistically encoded concepts (roughly those with 'names'), differences in the lexicon could plausibly be supposed to lead to differences in concepts. But there is much dispute about what concepts even are; indeed, there is probably less accord now than there was 20 years ago. The only thing most theorists can agree on is that none of the theories now on display offers a satisfactory account of all concepts, and in some cases it's not clear they can account for any (e.g., Margolis & Laurence, 1999). This is especially relevant to the relativity hypothesis because concepts do more than classify. Classification is rarely an end in itself, and concepts underlie all of our higher mental processes, including inference, prediction, planning, learning, and explanation. So, if a difference between two languages leads to a difference in the concepts their users deploy, this difference would ramify throughout their modes of thought.

Even if we assume that we are clear enough about the nature of concepts to investigate specific examples, we are not all that clear about many of these. 'Causation', for example, is one of our most central concepts (and one that concerned Whorf). But despite classic psychological work by Piaget and Michotte and much 'conceptual analysis' by philosophers, careful empirical study of casual learning and causal reasoning is only now getting under way, and there is still uncertainty about just what our concept (or concept*s*) of causation amounts to (e.g., Penn & Povinelli, 2007). Hence, it will be difficult to compare our causal cognition (if it is unified enough to be profitably compared with anything else) with that of a quite different culture. In short, we have at best a tentative handle on many of the central linguistic and cognitive variables that seem likely to be relevant to linguistic relativity hypotheses.

Interactions, aggregation, and confounding

Testing relativity hypotheses is also difficult because most things that happen, and certainly many things involving language and cognition, are the effects of multifarious causal influences that interact with each other in delicate and non-linear ways. Even if we had good models (which we do not) for how certain linguistic variables affect cognitive variables if nothing else interfered, in the real world something always does. When matters are this complex, it is extremely difficult to avoid confounding variables.

In the physical sciences it is sometimes possible to create conditions that shield disturbing influences so that we can ascertain the source, magnitude, and direction of a force whose influence is swamped outside the lab. Once we have learned this, we know that the force will add together with other forces, in conformity with the rules of vector addition for physical forces, and that an object acted on by this sum of forces will behave (by accelerating in accordance with Newton's second law) in just the way that it would if this resultant force vector were the only force acting on it. We typically cannot determine all the forces in the real world, of course, and when it comes to predicting where a leaf blowing in the wind will land, the natural scientists' forecasting powers are not that far ahead of the cognitive scientists. Still, in vector addition we have a simple theoretical picture about how physical forces interact.

Unfortunately, we have nothing remotely comparable in the case of cognitive mechanisms. When several linguistic or other cognitive mechanisms operate at the same time they might reinforce each other, cancel each other out, exhibit some sort of interference effect, or interact in a way that depends on 22 of the other psychological processes then taking place. Hence, even if we can learn about the behavior of specific mechanisms in the lab, this does not tell us how those mechanisms would behave over a range of circumstances in the outside world. Here we encounter a virulent example of the familiar trade-off between studying a realistic situation (in the field) and control (in the lab), a trade-off between internal validity (control) and external validity (realism and generalizability).

When the topic is linguistic relativity, we need to do much of our work in the field, where we have even less grip on what causes what. There has been impressive progress in recent years on isolating causes in such conditions (Pearl, 2009, is state of the art), but in practice the problems remain daunting. If we do discover a difference in the color perception of two groups, is it due to language or to some other variable(s) that is entangled with the language users' culture, physiological traits (e.g., eye pigmentation), or the like? Put another way, a language is a vital part of a culture, and many aspects of a person's culture are likely to covary with aspects of their language in ways that are difficult to tease apart. It is always possible that a generalization will become so hedged in by qualifications that it evaporates into a mist of ever-higher-order interactions as experimenters probe an ever-wider range of cases (C causes E, unless B is present, though if we have C, B, and D we do get E, unless . . .).

In light of such difficulties, it is scarcely surprising that some empirical results bearing on linguistic relativity seem to conflict with others, or that there are even claims about wholesale failures to replicate earlier results (e.g., January & Kako, 2007). None of this means that testing the relativity hypothesis is impossible, but it does suggest that a series of related tests will often be needed to establish a firm conclusion. On the positive side, we now have much better tools and methods for studying language and cognition (from developmental psychology through psychology of aging), and a much better understanding of the issues involved than people did even a couple of decades ago. We do not always know what accounts are right, but we now know that many earlier accounts were wrong, and we know about various phenomena that any adequate account would need to explain. So we seem to be on the right track.

RELEVANT VARIABLES

The pendulum swung from relativistic views during the first half of the twentieth century to anti-relativistic views during the second half. Now it is drifting back to a let's-go-look-and-see middle. It may help fix ideas if we conclude with a brief look at a few more specific variables that currently appear relevant in testing hypotheses about linguistic relativity.

Linguistic (independent) variables

Various aspects of language could easily affect cognition.

Grammar

Languages can differ in their grammar or syntax. Many earlier discussions of the linguistic relativity hypothesis focused on grammar and lexicon as independent variables. For instance, many of Whorf's contentions, e.g., his claims about the way Hopi thought about time, were based on (what he took to be) large-scale differences between Hopi and Standard Average European that included grammatical and lexical differences (e.g., Whorf, 1956, p. 158).

To take a simpler example, typical word order may vary between languages. In English the common order is subject, verb, object. In Japanese it is subject, object, verb. In Welsh it is verb, subject, object. And of course there are many subtler grammatical differences between languages. It should be noted that grammar does not mean the prescriptive grammar we learned in grammar school but the syntactic structure of a language. In this sense, a grammar comprises a set of rules (or some equivalent device) that can generate all and only the sentences of a given language. Actual tests will have to be more specific still (this is also true for the variables mentioned below), focusing on specific, manageable aspects of grammar. For instance, languages can differ in whether they make a distinction between intransitive verbs and adjectives. Does this affect any aspects of their users' mental lives?

Lexicon

Different languages have different lexicons (vocabularies, roughly), and the lexicons of different languages may classify things in different ways. For example, the color lexicons of some pairs of languages segment the color spectrum at different locations.

Semantics

Different languages might have different semantic features (over and above differences in lexical semantics).

Pragmatics

It is increasingly clear that context plays a vital role in the use and understanding of language (as well as in cognition; e.g., Philip & Aydede, 2008; Swoyer, 2002). So it is possible that differences in the way speakers of different languages *use* their languages in concrete settings affect their mental life.

Metaphor

Different languages employ different metaphors or employ them in different ways.

Cognitive (dependent) variables

Thought

Language might influence many different aspects of thought. Most empirical work has focused, appropriately enough, on those aspects of cognition that are easiest to assess without relying on language. This is important because we otherwise risk finding influences of one aspect of language on some related aspect *of language*, rather than on some aspect of thought. Commonly studied cognitive variables include perceptual discrimination, availability in memory, and classification. But we also need to ask whether features of one's native language influence one's judgment and decision making, problem solving, inductive inference, or various aspects of social cognition, e.g., classifying people in terms of various traits, or explaining behavior more by citing traits or situations.

Differences in language might also affect more general styles of thought (cf. e.g., Nisbett, Peng, Choi, & Norenzayan, 2008). Again, several recent theorists have proposed dual-process accounts of cognition. Different writers develop this distinction in different ways, but the basic idea is that human beings have two quite different cognitive subsystems (or two types of subsystems). There is an 'explicit' subsystem that is largely conscious, symbolic, verbal, rule-governed, serial, flexible, and capable of reflection. But there is also an 'implicit' subsystem that is largely non-conscious, associative, impulsive, affective, and that reacts automatically to stimuli (e.g., Chaiken & Trope, 1999; Sloman, 1996). Aspects of language might well influence one system more than the other, or influence the two systems in different ways.

We already know that cultural differences (which are entangled with language) can affect social cognition (e.g., Norenzayan, Choi, & Nisbett, 2002). As we employ more tools and techniques and approaches, we may also encounter some quite unexpected things. For example, it now appears that the effects of linguistic relativity are stronger in the right visual field than in the left (Gilbert, Regier, Kay, & Ivry, 2007), something no one would have even considered several decades ago.

Example of influence

By way of example, certain features of syntax or of the lexicon might exert a causal influence on certain aspects of visual perception (e.g., on which colors we can discriminate), classification (e.g., on how we sort things by color), or long-term memory (e.g., on which differences among colors we remember most accurately) in clearly specifiable ways. If there is such an influence we would also like to know what mechanisms mediate it, but until we have a better idea whether such difference exist, we are not well positioned to answer deeper questions like this.

Table 2.1 presents a set of choices as in a Chinese menu illustrating a few (of the many) families of variables that are plausibly hypothesized to be relevant to linguistic relativity theses. Here, one or more variables in

Table 2.1 Some linguistic and cognitive variables

Aspects of language (*Families of independent variables*)	Aspects of thought (*Families of dependent variables*)
Grammar (syntax)	Perception
Lexicon	Attention
Meaning (semantics)	Concepts
Use (pragmatics)	Memory
Metaphor	Decision making
	Inductive inference
	Explanation
	Social cognition
	Systems (processes) of thought

the left-hand column (in the proper context) might be thought to influence one or more variables in the right-hand column. Of course, even these variables are too general for a direct test, and in actual empirical work we would consider quite restricted examples of them. For example, one would not test memory in general but, say, some quite specific recall task after priming.

There are many combinations of variables that could matter, and when we observe that they might only be active under certain conditions (e.g., it might require priming to elicit a certain memory effect), there seem to be hundreds of things to test. The point is not to emphasize such numbers but to indicate how many aspects of the linguistic relativity hypothesis there are, and how implausible glib and general claims about them are likely to be.

CONCLUSION: WHERE ARE WE NOW?

In addition to careful studies of more variables and more languages, we need to employ as many different methods and approaches as possible. The skills of the experimental psychologist, the field linguist, and the scholar of ancient languages all are relevant. Cross-cultural psychology (e.g., Berry, Poortinga, & Pandey, 1996) and cognitive anthropology (e.g., D'Andrade, 1995) will play an ever more prominent role, as will neuropsychology (with its array of methods of brain imaging and, one expects, more powerful tools on the horizon) and biological psychology. Among the approaches here, those that focus on bilinguals will surely be very important. If quite different methods converge on similar conclusions, we will know that we have found something worth knowing.

Given our strong nativist Zeitgeist, it is important to stress that substantive linguistic and cognitive universals are entirely compatible with substantive linguistic and cognitive differences between languages and cultures (and subcultures and other groups). Universals mean that the variations will be played out within a restricted space, but that space may well allow dramatic and unexpected differences. Conversely, finding interesting linguistic or cognitive differences between two groups would not rule out the existence of interesting linguistic or cognitive universals.

I have not tried to provide a comprehensive overview of the issues surrounding the linguistic relativity hypotheses or to cite much of the field's voluminous literature. My aim has been to provide orientation and to motivate the conclusions that questions about the impact of a variable on cognition are empirical, and that they are questions about *what causes what* and *how it does so*. Such questions can only be answered once we specify *which aspects* of an independent variable influence *which aspects* of thought, and what form that influence takes. Such hypotheses can vary greatly in specificity, strength, and scope. And because small samples make for weak inductions, a comparison of more than a handful of linguistic communities is needed to draw any firm conclusions. Furthermore, testing a specific version of the hypothesis requires a combination of skills, including those of a good ethnographer, linguist, and experimental psychologist. Progress will be slow, often painful, sometimes hard to discern. But that's the thing about science.

REFERENCES

Berlin, B., & Kay, P. (1969). *Basic color terms: Their universality and evolution.* Berkeley, CA: University of California Press.

Berry, J. W., Poortinga, Y. H., & Pandey J. (1996). *Handbook of cross-cultural psychology: Volume 1, Theory and method* (2nd ed.). Needham Heights, MA: Allyn & Bacon.

Brown, D. E. (1991). *Human universals.* New York: McGraw-Hill.

Cassirer, E. (1923/1955). *Philosophie der symbolischen Formen, Berlin: Bruno Cassirer, Volume 1* [(R. Manheim, Trans.) *The philosophy of symbolic forms, Volume 1: Language.* New Haven, CT: Yale University Press].

Chaiken, S., & Trope, Y. (1999). *Dual-process theories in social psychology.* New York: Guilford Press.

Chiang, W., & Wynn, K. (2000). Infants' tracking of objects and collections. *Cognition, 77,* 169–195.

Chomsky, N. (2000). *New horizons in the study of language and mind.* Cambridge, UK: Cambridge University Press.

D'Andrade, R. G. (1995). *The development of cognitive anthropology.* Cambridge, UK: Cambridge University Press.

Davies, I. R. L., & Corbett, G. C. (1997). A cross-cultural study of color-grouping: Evidence for weak linguistic relativity. *British Journal of Psychology, 88,* 493–517.

Feeney, A., & Heit, E. (2007). *Inductive reasoning: Experimental, developmental, and computational approaches.* Cambridge, UK: Cambridge University Press.

Fodor, J. A. (1983). *The modularity of mind.* Cambridge, MA: MIT Press.

Gilbert, B., Regier, T., Kay, C. A., & Ivry, R. B. (2007). Support for lateralization of the Whorf effect beyond the realm of color discrimination. *Brain and Language, 105,* 91–98.

Goodman, N. (1978). *Ways of worldmaking.* Indianapolis, IN: Hackett.

January, D., & Kako, E. (2007). Re-evaluating evidence for linguistic relativity: Reply to Boroditsky (2001). *Cognition, 104,* 417–426.

Kay, P., & McDaniel, C. K. (1978). The linguistic significance of meanings of basic color terms. *Language, 54,* 610–646.

Majid, A., Bowerman, M., Kita, S., Haun, D. B. M., & Levinson, S. C. (2004). Can language restructure cognition? The case for space. *Trends in Cognitive Sciences, 8,* 108–114.

Malotki, E. (1983). *Hopi time: A linguistic analysis of the temporal concepts in the Hopi language.* Berlin: Mouton.

Margolis, E., & Laurence, S. (1999). Concepts and cognitive science. In E. Margolis & S. Laurence (Eds.), *Concepts: Core readings* (pp. 3–81). Cambridge, MA: MIT Press.

Matthews, R. J., & Demopoulos, W. (1989). *Learnability and linguistic theory*. New York: Springer.

Nisbett, R. E., Peng, K., Choi, I., & Norenzayan, A. (2008). Culture and systems of thought: Holistic versus analytic cognition. In J. E. Adler & L. J. Rips (Eds.), *Reasoning: Studies of human inference and its foundations* (pp. 956–985). New York: Cambridge University Press.

Norenzayan, A., Choi, I., & Nisbett, R. E. (2002). Cultural similarities and differences in social inference: Evidence from behavioral predictions and lay theories of behavior. *Social Psychology Bulletin, 28,* 109–120.

Pearl, J. (2009). *Causality: Models, reasoning and inference* (2nd ed.). Cambridge, UK: Cambridge University Press.

Penn, D. C., & Povinelli, D. J. (2007). Causal cognition in human and non-human animals: A comparative, critical review. *Annual Review of Psychology, 58,* 97–118.

Philip, P., & Aydede, M. (2008). *The Cambridge handbook of situated cognition*. Cambridge, UK: Cambridge University Press.

Sapir, E. (1929). The status of linguistics as science. *Language, 5,* 207–214.

Sloman, S. A. (1996). The empirical case for two systems of reasoning. *Psychological Bulletin, 119,* 3–22.

Spelke, E. S., & Newport, E. (1998). Nativism, empiricism, and the development of knowledge. In R. Lerner (Ed.), *Handbook of child psychology, Vol. 1: Theoretical models of human development* (5th ed.). New York: Wiley.

Swoyer, F. C. (2002). Judgment and decision making: Extrapolations and applications. In R. Gowda & J. Fox (Eds.), *Judgments, decisions, and public policy* (pp. 9–45). Cambridge, UK: Cambridge University Press.

Whorf, B. L. (1956). *Language, thought and reality* (Ed. J. B. Carroll). Cambridge, MA: MIT Press.

Winawer, J., Witthoft, N., Frank, M., Wu, L., Wade, A., & Boroditsky, L. (2007). Russian blues reveal effects of language on color discrimination. *Proceedings of the National Academy of Sciences USA, 104,* 7780–7785.

Xu, F., & Carey, S. (1996). Infants' metaphysics: The case of numerical identity. *Cognitive Psychology, 30,* 111–153.

3 Language and cognition: The view from anthropology

John Lucy

In 1888, ethnologist Daniel Brinton wrote an essay entitled 'The Language of Paleolithic Man' which aimed to gain insight into the historical emergence of language through the study of existing Native American languages, conceived of as being closer to the primitive precursors of modern language. In discussing these languages, he noted that

> the phonetic elements . . . are, in many American languages, singularly vague and fluctuating. If in English we were to pronounce the three words, *loll*, *nor*, *roll*, indifferently as one or the other, you see what violence we should do to the theory of our alphabet. Yet analogous examples are constant in many American languages. Their consonants are 'alternating,' in large groups, their vowels 'permutable.'
>
> (Brinton, 1888, p. 217)

The following year Franz Boas, the founding father of American anthropology, produced a rejoinder, his classic paper 'On Alternating Sounds'. He reviewed psychological evidence showing that people often recognize or mis-hear speech sounds because they utilize categories familiar from past experience to guide perception. He then showed that even well-trained observers show the influence of their native language when they describe an unknown language and try to transcribe its sounds. He concluded:

> For this reason I maintain that there is no such phenomenon as synthetic or alternating sounds, and that their occurrence is in no way a sign of primitiveness of the speech in which they are said to occur; that alternating sounds are in reality alternating apperceptions [by the observer] of one and the same sound.
>
> (Boas, 1889, pp. 51–52)

The problem, Boas argued, lay not with the Native American languages, but rather with Brinton's misunderstanding of them, grounded in his own language experience as framed by certain hierarchical value judgments.

In this exchange we see in microcosm the chief lineaments of the emerging anthropological orientation towards language: Recognition of the behavioral importance of linguistic differences, rejection of hierarchical rankings of languages, and identification of the conceptual and methodological ethnocentrism underlying such hierarchical judgments. The anthropological approach to language and cognition begins from this distinctive orientation towards language diversity. Even when methods and findings produced within this tradition appear to be quite similar to those in other fields, they are in fact shaped throughout by this distinctive orientation. This essay aims to clarify that guiding orientation and then to articulate and exemplify through representative works how it yields a distinctive set of methodological problems, solutions, and empirical efforts.

LANGUAGE DIVERSITY

The diversity of human languages has long given rise to speculation about its sources and consequences. Why do languages render the same reality so differently and what are the consequences of language differences for human thought? These two questions are in fact intimately related: How we understand *language diversity*, the ways languages differ in their renderings of reality, greatly affects our approach to understanding *linguistic relativity*, the effects of linguistic diversity on thought. To understand the distinctiveness of the anthropological approach, we need to review how this diversity has been treated historically, then look at the distinctive stance of anthropology toward diversity, and finally show how that stance challenges and reshapes traditional views.

Historical approaches to language diversity

The interpretation of language diversity in terms of evaluative hierarchies has a long history. It emerges clearly in the two approaches that have dominated Western understandings of language diversity over the past several hundred years (see Aarsleff, 1982).

First, there are those who have adopted the Leibnitzian view that there is a natural (or absolute) connection between language and the world. Confronted by the empirical diversity of languages, those holding this view have two ways of explaining how it arose. For some, existing languages all represent various sorts of decline; that is, what we see is an accumulation of human corruption upon some earlier pristine form of language, the language of Adam or the ancient Hebrews being the classic reference points, but any idealized historical reference point may be invoked. The route to grasping this uncorrupted form lies through the historical reconstruction of the original language. One can hear echoes of this view in any language ideology about the supposed slovenliness of contemporary modern speech as contrasted with earlier, even ancient forms or even in the common complaints by parents about the sloppy speech of their children. Alternatively, within this approach, one can imagine that the pristine form still lies secure within each language and that all we have to do is peel back the superficial encrustation concealing it and we will find the original natural logic of language revealed. One hears echoes of this view in all those ideologies about underlying competence, deep structures, universal primitives, and the like; ideologies typically held by those who purport to have discovered the key to uncovering these common treasures lying beneath apparent diversity. Ultimately, however, in their search for a common universal language, such views dismiss the theoretical and practical importance of variation among languages.

Second, there are those who have adopted the Lockean view that languages by their nature bear an artificial (or conventional) relation to reality. Hence the diversity among languages is an intrinsic and unavoidable feature of languages. Some celebrate this diversity as of local historical significance: Languages contain in their form living traces of history and are to be treasured as repositories of the genius of a people. Although such views embrace diversity as a good thing, they are often coupled with a more or less explicit evaluation of one or another language (or language type) as superior—along with the culture and thought of the people who created it. (One thinks especially of Humboldt in this regard; see Aarsleff, 1988.) Alternatively, some take a more neutral view of this diversity, but recognize that the lack of a uniform natural relationship presents obstacles to clear communication, especially in philosophy and science. However, the very conventional nature of language, its intrinsic flexibility, allows us to build up specialized vocabularies and professional jargons as needed to convey our views accurately. Our inheritance from Adam, then, is not a particular language but the liberty to create language. So instead of seeing diversity as a sign of decline and corruption as in the first approach, languages here are seen both as the repository of the historical genius of a people and at the same time holding the potential for the progress and perfection of language and discourse. Here we find both the impetus to prize diversity and to transcend it, typically by making it more transparent through the development of precise technical terms and other language refinements. (One variant of this approach seeks to substitute formal mathematical models for language. However, the knowledge embodied in these formalisms can only be set free by recourse to the language of some discursive community, whereupon all the usual problems return.)

Despite the differences between these two dominant approaches to understanding language diversity, they share the common underlying assumptions that there is a single unitary reality and an ideal relation of language to it, however elusive. In one case, that ideal relation has been lost and has to be recovered or uncovered. In the other, the ideal remains a goal to be attained, at least by some peoples or in some activities. But either way, the common assumption of an ideal relation between language and reality is tacitly embraced.

The anthropological approach to language diversity

The anthropological approach to language diversity is deeply informed by the culture concept, especially as developed by the American school led by Franz Boas (1966). Historically, there has been much less interest in language within the various European anthropological traditions. For example, early attention to language in British anthropology by Malinowski and others did not lead to an ongoing concern with language. Likewise, in French anthropology the influence of structural linguistics as a methodological model for social analysis, especially in the work of Levi-Strauss, was not accompanied by a concern for everyday language.

The Boasian school argued for the importance of cultures, that is, bodies of historically developed traditions, in explaining how humans differ from other species, in explaining differences among human groups, and in explaining differences within groups (Sapir, 1993). Cultural explanations provided an important alternative to various nineteenth-century theories that explained human differences in terms of innate racial capacities. Likewise, the anthropological approach to language (seen here as part of culture) also rejects explanations in terms of racial differences. Instead, the capacity for language distinguishes humans from other species, all normal humans are capable of learning a natural language, and differences among languages spring from history not race. This much of the anthropological perspective has been broadly accepted in the human sciences.

The anthropological approach also characteristically rejects hierarchical views that cast some cultures and languages as more primitive or advanced than others (Boas, 1966), a view that reproduces nineteenth-century racial hierarchies as cultural hierarchies. Instead, each culture is regarded as worthy of respect as a valid way of life. Similarly, the understanding of language also rejects hierarchical views that see one language as intrinsically superior or inferior to another. From a historical point of view the rejection of hierarchical evaluations of languages was quite revolutionary. And despite its egalitarian impulse, which many today would embrace in principle, it has been a very difficult position to implement and sustain in practice. The difficulty in escaping hierarchical views stems in large part from the unwitting tendency to take one's own language as a guide in understanding and evaluating other languages. So the anthropologists' critical stance toward ethnocentric evaluations of other cultures includes a similar stance against unwitting lingua-centrism, that is, the interpretation and evaluation of other languages in terms that are ultimately rooted in one's own language.

During the 1930s these anthropological assumptions about language diversity were extended to concerns about the relation of language and thought, particularly in the work of Edward Sapir (1921) and Benjamin Whorf (1941/1956) (see Lucy, 1985, 1992b for reviews). Whorf in particular sought to apply the principle that all languages were equally valid instruments of communication while simultaneously accepting the diversity of how they represented reality. This led him to question the existence of a single ideal relation of language to reality and in precisely this sense to question also our conceptualization of a unitary reality, since its qualities would vary as a function of the language used to describe it. If there is no ideal relation of language to reality, hence a fundamental uncertainty about the character of that reality, then the whole problem of the relation of language to experience changes. Claims for universality in the relation of language to reality cannot now simply be presumed but require empirical proof. And no language, whether ancient or modern, received or constructed, can be judged inferior or superior, corrupted or perfected in light of its match with reality. Crucially, we lack a language-neutral standard against which to form such judgments; that is, no single language can provide, through its system of categories, a reliable guide to reality for the purposes of research. Whorf also argued that the language we speak influences the way we habitually see reality outside of language. So in his view it is also not trivial to circumvent language by direct appeals to our understanding of reality. In short, he questioned the fundamental assumptions that had long guided research and speculation on language diversity and its relation, thought.

Whorf's challenge disturbed many people and led to unusually strong negative reactions against such research. Their reactions against this 'linguistic relativism' have their root in the recognition, explicitly or implicitly, that his view challenges the researcher's own claims to have an unmediated grasp of reality. By way of rebuttal, such researchers typically caricature his position in one of three ways: as saying that languages bear *no* relation to reality, as saying that we cannot think *at all* without language, or as saying that each language so completely *determines* our thought that we can never establish whether he is right. None of these misrepresentations can sustain close scrutiny (see Lucy, 1992b), but collectively they have provided a comforting rationale that there is no need to engage in further research on his proposals. So virtually no empirical research on the relation of language diversity and thought has emerged from these critics of Whorf's ideas.

However, others have taken up the conceptual and empirical challenge of developing ways of investigating the relation of language and thought without privileging the vision of reality in our own language from the outset. Some have been favorable to the view that language influences thought, while others have been opposed to such a conclusion, but all have recognized in one way or another that something new was now required, namely, a more neutral method for characterizing the differences among languages in regards to how they represent reality.

LANGUAGE DIVERSITY AND THOUGHT

Two strategies of research

Since the appearance of Whorf's formulation of the language and thought problem, two primary strategies of empirical research have emerged aiming to solve the problem of how to provide a neutral metalanguage (or frame of reference) for comparing languages (see full review in Lucy, 1997a). Each approach has characteristic advantages and drawbacks, but each takes seriously the problem of how to provide an operationally unbiased characterization of language, reality, and cognition.

The domain-centered strategy

One strategy, which I call *domain-centered*, selects a domain of experience (such as color or time or space) and seeks to describe it on language-independent grounds, in order first to ask how individual languages treat the domain and subsequently how speakers then treat that domain during cognitive activity. The domain-centered strategy seeks to solve the comparison problem by asking how different languages partition the same domain of reality. Although the strategy offers a number of advantages for comparative purposes, it tends to suffer from two weaknesses. First, the representation of the domain is typically drawn from one linguistic and cultural tradition. As such it begs the question being asked, namely, whether such representations, or even the domain itself, are universally recognized. Acknowledging this problem, some seek to anchor the description in well-established scientific concepts to help assure neutrality and objectivity. This can be illuminating, but more often one ends up with a description of reality in terms of parameters drawn from natural or biological science and not from parameters semantically or structurally relevant to actual linguistic systems; this in turn can lead to a dramatic misrepresentation of the languages at issue. Further, by adopting one vision of reality, even a scientifically refined one, as the standard for comparison, one still necessarily favors the original language and culture from which it arose. This leads, not surprisingly, to any number of demonstrations of difference in which a hierarchy quietly (re)emerges: In effect such efforts simply show how well languages do or do not represent the semantic values of the language system framing the comparison. The method used for creating a neutral system based on reality thus often undermines the very possibility of fair comparison.

Perhaps the best-known example of work using this strategy is the long tradition of research on color terms. This line of research was begun in the 1950s by psycholinguists Brown and Lenneberg (1954) as a way of addressing the Whorfian methodological challenge. From the late 1960s until the present, work on color terms has been continued by anthropologists Berlin and Kay and their colleagues (e.g., Berlin & Kay, 1969; Kay, Brent, Maffi, & Merryfield, 1997; Kay & McDaniel, 1978) who interpret their findings as evidence against Whorf's claims. In this research one represents reality though a selection of color chips designed to sample a color space and then asks speakers of different languages how they partition this space. The difficulties are legion: The proper definition and sampling of a color space is far from obvious; some languages don't even have color terms and they certainly are not central to the semantic structure of many languages; and languages that do have relevant terms may deploy them quite differently, such that they are often misanalyzed by those unfamiliar with the language or simply disqualified for inclusion in the study. But the most important difficulty is that any color systems encountered are ultimately arrayed or scaled along an 'evolutionary' cline of how finely they represent this color space; that is, how closely they approach our own system of dedicated color terms. Here we see the re-emergence of the old hierarchical portrayal of languages in terms of how well they match the underlying natural relation of language to reality, where the 'natural' in this case corresponds to the system in our own language (Lucy, 1997b). Ironically, even under these constraints, all reliable evidence still indicates that variations in color language predict cognitive performance more accurately than do the purportedly underlying natural relations (Davidoff, Davies, & Roberson, 1999; Roberson & Hanley, 2010).

The structure-centered strategy

A second strategy, which I call *structure-centered*, selects some grammatical structure (such as number or gender or aspect marking), asks how it differs across languages, and how reality might appear differently from the vantage of each relevant system. Structure-centered strategies build squarely on a long tradition of comparative work in linguistics, seeking to characterize individual languages by the types of categories they employ and then to compare these structures of meaning. But the strategy is difficult to implement: Comparing categories across languages requires extensive linguistic work in terms of both local description and typological framing, can be derailed by blindness to categories very different from one's own, and may not easily yield referential entailments suitable for an independent assessment of cognition. Nonetheless, this strategy holds the most potential for closely respecting the linguistic differences and thus holds the greatest promise for identifying structural differences and directing the search for cognitive influences in appropriate directions.

The classic example of a structure-centered strategy is Whorf's own comparison of number marking patterns in English and Hopi (Whorf, 1941/1956; see also Lucy, 1992b). Whorf argued that English speakers measure and count cyclic experiences such as the passage of a day or a year in the same way as ordinary objects with a form and a substance. This leads ultimately by analogy to the projection of these cycles as forms (or containers) for a homogeneous substance 'time'. By contrast, the Hopi language differentiates these cycles as a distinct type of recurrent event and its speakers are not therefore led to the same view of time as English speakers. From these linguistic observations Whorf was led to identify patterns in habitual behavior that he felt bore the impress of this difference in outlook toward time. There are difficulties in Whorf's work to be sure, notably the anecdotal quality of the characterization of effects on thought or cognition. But his approach does illustrate the structure-centered strategy of beginning comparison with an analysis of language structure and then building a characterization of reality through the categories provided by the languages themselves. And, crucially, this approach does not entail any hierarchical evaluation of the languages with respect to a pre-given reality or other metric.

In sum, these two dominant strategies seek to address the new concerns about presuming a unique, optimal language-to-reality mapping. One attempts to describe reality (in the guise of a selected referential domain) independently of languages, and then asks how that reality is partitioned by languages. The other seeks to describe languages (typically in the form of particular structural categories) independently of prior assumptions about reality, and then asks how reality would look from the perspective of each system. The first tends to suffer from implicit bias and semantic irrelevancy in characterizing the domain, the second from descriptive complexity and difficulty in cognitive comparison. And it is fair to say that both strategies were at first much more concerned with characterizing language differences than with mounting systematic efforts to assess the effects of those language differences on cognition.

Two contemporary innovations

The period since 1980 has been marked by two dominant trends that crosscut the two traditions described above. First, there has been an increased effort to ground language comparisons in systematic language description and typology. Second, there has been an effort to provide direct assessment of whether individual cognition can be influenced by language. Although these innovations first arose within the structure-centered tradition in the work of Lucy (1992a), they have been most widely applied and influential within the domain-centered tradition associated with Levinson (2003) and his colleagues at the Max Planck Institute for Psycholinguistics, Nijmegen.

Innovations in domain-centered research

The most successful recent effort at domain-centered research has been undertaken in the domain of space (Levinson, 2003; Majid, Bowerman,

Kita, Haun, & Levinson, 2004; Pederson et al., 1998). Spatial conceptualization has been widely regarded as invariant within philosophical, psychological, and linguistic circles and yet these researchers have been able to show that there is considerable cross-linguistic variability in its encoding. They have accomplished this by undertaking many careful cross-linguistic comparisons of referential practice with respect to a wide range of spatial phenomena using a variety of innovative techniques in order to compare 'the meaning patterns that consistently emerge from domain-directed interactive discourse . . .' (Pederson et al., 1998, p. 565). Indeed, it is fair to say that one of the most important contributions of this research effort has been to create a new kind of linguistic typology, a typology of referential practice, that inventories and characterizes systematically all the ways a given domain can be referred to by each language and then builds a series of typological generalizations from a comparison of these systems (for examples, see esp. Levinson & Wilkinson, 2006).

One example can serve to illustrate the approach. This group has been particularly concerned to develop a typology of the spatial frames of reference that speakers can use to locate objects in space. The full typology (Levinson, 2003, Ch. 2), which is based on many languages, identifies three basic frames of reference in language: Intrinsic, in which objects are located with respect to other objects; Absolute, in which objects are located with respect to an environmentally anchored coordinate system; and Relative, in which objects are located with respect to a viewer. (Critics such as Li & Gleitman, 2002, often truncate this typology; see discussion in Levinson, Kita, Haun, & Rasch, 2002.) For example, many European languages favor the use of Relative frames linked to a viewer (e.g., 'the man is to the left of the tree') whereas other languages such as Guugu Yimithirr (Australian) and Tzeltal (Mayan) favor Absolute systems anchored in 'absolute' cardinal direction terms or topographic features respectively (e.g., 'the man is to the east/uphill of the tree'). These frames can be formally distinguished from one another by their transitivity relations and invariance under rotation, each of which can be anchored in displaced origos (or deictic reference points), and more than one system can be used in combination, creating hybrid systems.

Using field experiments, these researchers have been able to show that speakers differ in their approach to a variety of cognitive tasks (i.e., memory, inference, etc.) as a function of the frame of spatial reference they would routinely employ in describing the spatial configurations involved in a task. So in the example given above, speakers using a Relative system in a task will maintain the left–right orientation of an array of items even as they turn their body around to recreate the array in another location across a room, whereas speakers using an Absolute system will maintain the east–west orientation of the array under a similar rotation. These experimental results have proven robust across a wide range of languages from all over the world. And the experimental results are supplemented by an array of naturalistic evidence. For example, speakers who routinely use Absolute means of spatial description typically orient their co-speech gestures absolutely and are more accurate in dead-reckoning tasks that require indicating the exact locations of landmarks not in sight. In short, it appears that speakers of languages that represent space in different ways verbally also routinely think about space in different ways in nonverbal tasks. The results strikingly refute the common view that spatial cognition is uniform across human populations and suggest that language resources play an important role in shaping it.

This research has attempted to gain the advantages of precise, extensive comparison characteristic of a domain-centered approach while simultaneously avoiding its chief pitfalls by explicitly incorporating extensive linguistic description and typology into the project from the outset. And it rigorously avoids entering into an evaluation of which type of semantic system is superior or more natural, seeing each as having characteristic costs and benefits. In these respects this effort escapes the usual weakness of domain-centered approaches. But it does so only by allowing serious slippage with regard to the original concern with linguistic structure: A single 'language' may use more than one semantic approach to spatial description, and languages considered the 'same' in their referential usage may in fact be using radically different structural means. In the end then, the linguistic analysis and typology are not concerned so much with the meaning conveyed by particular linguistic structures (i.e., systems of 'sense') but rather with the patterns of linguistic usage (i.e., systems of 'reference'); and a single language can be used to implement more than one referential strategy depending on local context (e.g., using absolute frames in rural setting and relative ones in urban settings; Pederson, 1993).

Innovations in structure-centered research

The most extensive recent effort to extend and improve a structure-centered approach is my own comparative study of the relation between grammatical number marking and cognition among speakers of American English and Yucatec Maya (Lucy, 1992a). The study develops a comparative linguistic analysis of the two languages within a broad typological framework, which allows a neutral characterization of their differences, draws from these differences specific inferences about how reality is being construed, and then provides systematic assessments to text whether reality is being thought about differently.

This study begins with a grammatical contrast of English and Yucatec number-marking patterns. The two languages differ in the way they signal plural for nouns. English speakers obligatorily signal plural for some nouns (e.g., *chair/chairs*) but not for others (e.g., *mud*, but not *muds*). By contrast, Yucatec speakers are never obliged to signal plural for any noun, although they often do apply an optional plural to those referring to animate referents. The two languages also contrast in the way they enumerate nouns. English speakers directly modify some nouns with a numeral (e.g., *one candle, two candles*), but for others they must provide an extra form indicating the unit to be counted (e.g., *one clump of dirt, two clumps of dirt*). By contrast, Yucatec requires that *all* constructions with numerals be supplemented by such an extra form called a 'unitizer' (or 'numeral classifier') that indicates a unit (e.g., *'un ts'iit kib'*, 'one long-thin candle', *ká'a ts'iit kib'*, 'two long-thin candle'). Crucially, these patterns of plural marking and numeral modification are in complementary distribution: Plurals are obligatory only for nouns for which unitizers are not required and unitizers are obligatory only for nouns for which plurals are not required. This complementary distribution suggests that the two patterns form part of a single number-marking structure within the language.

The interaction of these two aspects of number marking forms part of a regular typological pattern across languages (Lucy, 1992a, pp. 61–71). First, broadly speaking, languages with obligatory plurals tend not to require unitizers and languages with obligatory unitizers tend not to require plurals. Second, for languages that have both forms, the obligatory uses tend to appear in complementary distribution. Although the specific boundary point between obligatory plurals and obligatory unitizers can vary, it does so in a systematic way governed by a hierarchy of noun phrase types based on semantic features. This cross-language typological patterning makes it possible to characterize any given language within a much broader, neutral framework that does not require taking either language as the baseline for characterizing the other.

Within this framework, the contrasting formal patterns of English and Yucatec can be interpreted substantively as follows. English treats some of its nouns as indicating a quantificational unit (or form) in their lexical meaning, others as not indicating a quantificational unit. Yucatec essentially treats all nouns as if they were semantically unspecified as to quantificational unit, almost as if they all referred to unformed substances. So, for example, the semantic sense of the Yucatec word *kib'* glossed as 'candle' in the example just cited actually refers to the substance and is better translated into English as 'wax' (i.e., 'one long-thin wax'). In ordinary speech, when occurring alone without a numeral modifier, the form *kib'* can routinely *refer* to objects that we would call candles, but the *semantic* value of the word does not contain any element signaling form or function—it can be used equally well for anything made of wax. Given the quantificational neutrality of the noun it becomes clear why one must specify a unit when counting, since expressions such as 'one wax' do not make quantificational sense. In short, whereas English is neutral about unit only for some nouns, Yucatec is neutral about this aspect of meaning for all of its nouns.

To assess whether traces of these contrasting verbal patterns appear in speakers' cognitive activities more generally, we need first to draw out the implications of these grammatical patterns for the general interpretation of experience. If we consider the denotational meaning of nouns referring to discrete concrete referents—that is, *stable objects* that maintain their physical appearance over time—then certain regularities appear from which cognitive implications can be drawn.

The quantificational unit presupposed by English nouns referring to objects of this type is frequently the *shape* of the object. Hence use of these English lexical items routinely draws attention to the shape of a referent as the basis for incorporating it under some lexical label and assigning it a number value. Here, to draw on our example above, is a contemporary definition of *candle* from *Webster's Seventh New Collegiate Dictionary* (1965, p. 121): '1: a long slender cylindrical mass of tallow or wax containing a loosely twisted linen or cotton wick that is burned to give light. 2: something resembling a candle in shape or use . . .'. Although the shape and structure now predominate in the definition, historically the light-giving function apparently predominated—compare the related *(in)candescent* and Latin *candere* 'shine, glow, gleam (white), etc.'. The material can be any suitable fuel such as tallow, wax, or, nowadays, paraffin—it is not criterial to the use of the word.

By contrast, Yucatec nouns referring to objects of this type, lacking such a specification of quantificational unit, do not draw attention to shape and, in fact, fairly routinely draw attention to the *material* composition of the referent as the basis for incorporating it under some lexical label. If these linguistic patterns translate into a general cognitive sensitivity to these properties of referents of the discrete type, then we can draw the following prediction: Yucatec speakers should attend relatively more to the material composition of stable objects (and less to their shape), whereas English speakers should attend relatively less to the material composition of stable objects (and more to their shape). And for objects that are not stable, which we can call *malleable* objects, the two groups should attend equally to material.

These cognitive implications have been tested with speakers from both languages (Lucy, 1992a; Lucy & Gaskins, 2001, 2003). One example will serve to illustrate the approach. Speakers in each language group were shown 15 triads of familiar objects. Each triad consisted of an original *pivot* object and two *alternate* objects, one of the same shape as the pivot and one of the same material as the pivot. So, for instance, speakers were shown a plastic comb with a handle as the pivot and asked whether it was more like a wooden comb with a handle or more like a plastic comb without a handle. The expectation was that English speakers would match the pivot to the other comb with a handle, whereas the Yucatec speakers would match it with the other comb made of plastic. Speakers were shown a large number of such triads, which, across the stimulus set, controlled for size, color, function, wholeness, malleability, and familiarity. The predicted classification preference was strongly confirmed, with adult English speakers choosing the material alternate only 23% of the time and adult Yucatec speakers favoring it 61% of the time. Clearly the groups classify these objects differently and in line with the expectations based on the underlying lexico-grammatical structures of the two languages. Further, when presented with malleable stimuli, where the languages agree on the material focus, there were no differences between the two groups. And, when presented with other sorts of tasks involving memory and reasoning, the same effects appear. In short, the patterns observed in language structure predict cognitive responses. That language plays the shaping role here is suggested by the appearance of similar effects in societies otherwise widely divergent in other aspects of culture including religion, mode of subsistence, education, modernity, etc. (Lucy, 2004).

This research remedies some of the traditional difficulties of structure-centered approaches by framing the linguistic analysis typologically so as to enhance comparison and by supplementing ethnographic observation with a rigorous assessment of individual thought. This then makes possible the realization of the benefits of the structure-centered approach: Placing the languages at issue on an equal footing, exploring semantically significant lexical and grammatical patterns, and developing connections to related semantic patterns in the languages.

Distinctive contributions of the anthropological approach

The domain- and structure-centered approaches differ fundamentally, the former focusing on referential use and the later on semantic structure. In this they reflect the fundamentally dual nature of language itself in which reference and sense are distinguishable, irreducible, and yet constantly interacting. In this respect, the gap between the two approaches may be narrowed but never ultimately closed. However, when we examine the trajectory of contemporary research here, we see that the two approaches have converged in some other ways that are significant and distinctive. They share the recognition that there must be a neutral framework of comparison, that the surest route to such a framework is through cross-linguistic typology built on close linguistic descriptions of the sense or reference systems of many languages, and that the cognitive entailments of observed language differences need to be tested in controlled ways to assess their impact on how actual speakers engage with the world. In respect to these three issues, both approaches contrast with most other research on linguistic relativity: Research that adopts a metalanguage that is little more than a formalization of the categories of the investigator's own language, research that pays no attention to the language as a structured system or to observable patterns of typological variation in such systems, research that speculates about effects on cognition but which never actually investigates them (e.g., most research in the color tradition exhibits all of these properties). From this vantage point, this anthropological approach to exploring the effects of language diversity on thought represents the most theoretically coherent and empirically powerful approach currently available. And the resulting empirical research strongly suggests a distinctive role for language in shaping cognition.

LANGUAGE DIVERSITY AND INTELLECTUAL DEVELOPMENT

The first tenet of the anthropological approach to language is that normal children are capable of learning any culture and any natural language. This implies that normal children everywhere begin with similar intellectual and verbal capacities and that differences emerge as part of the process of enculturation. Indeed, the capacities enabling cultural diversity must lie at the heart of what distinguishes humans from other species (see Lucy, 1996, and Haun, 2007, for discussions). Hence understanding the relation of language diversity and thought requires attention to the mechanisms that allow stable differences to emerge from common, shared capacities. Anthropologists have focused on the evolutionary emergence, or *phylogenesis*, of these shared capacities and, to a lesser extent, on their developmental unfolding, or *ontogenesis*, in childhood. The discussion here will be confined to those studies that engage directly with the domain- and structure-centered approaches.

Phylogenesis: Continuities and discontinuities

A recent line of research has used the domain-centered approach to explore the development of language-related cognitive differences in non-human primates and children (Haun, 2007; Haun, Rapold, Call, Janzen, & Levinson, 2006). The broad aim is to identify the continuities and discontinuities between humans and their closest animal relatives in the spatial domain. The research has two specific strategies. The first concerns the general effects of language and contrasts the spatial preferences of the great apes with those of human infants. The second concerns the specific effects of language and contrasts the spatial preferences of children who speak different languages. Two examples can serve to illustrate the approach.

One study compared great apes with human children regarding strategies in spatial memory (Haun, 2007). The task involves hiding a reward under one of three distinct objects in a row. Then the row is occluded and either the reward is moved to a new position under the same object or it is left in the same position under a different object. When the participants are allowed to see the array again, the question is whether they will look for reward in the original position or under the original covering object.

Both great apes and 1-year-old children prefer the original position. This suggests a degree of continuity across primates in their innate preferences. However, by 3 years of age human children switch to preferring feature strategies; that is, looking under the same covering object. This shift suggests to Haun (2007) that increasing language proficiency and enculturation lead to a change or 'masking' of the innate cognitive strategy preference. The shift seems clear enough. But to claim that early strategies are *masked* by later strategies suggests the former are real and the latter merely obscure them. From a developmental point of view, however, several other possibilities exist: The later strategy may replace, complement, or consummate the earlier strategy. Indeed, other studies show that some cross-species continuities, such as preferring the use of environmental cues for processing spatial relations, extend to even later ages.

A second study (Haun, 2007) compared Dutch and Namibian elementary school children at about age 8 regarding their preferred frames of spatial orientation (Haun et al., 2006). The two cultures differ in the way they prefer to express spatial relations verbally: The Dutch prefer speaking using a relative (left–right type) frame of reference and the Namibians prefer speaking using an absolute frame (east–west type) of reference. In a nonverbal task the children were shown a row of animal figures and then asked to reconstruct that row in another location where they had been rotated 90 degrees and placed with respect to a local landmark (so that use of distinct frames of reference can be distinguished). The results showed that the Dutch children preferred to reconstruct the array using a relative frame of orientation, whereas the Namibian children preferred an absolute frame of orientation. A separate task that increased the difficulty of the array and prompted children to use their dispreferred strategy revealed that they made many more errors, showing that it was difficult for them to switch from their habitual preferences. This study suggests, then, that the adult language patterns predict the children's cognition by as early as age 8, a pattern that then continues into adulthood. Related studies suggest that the use of this relative frame of orientation may be more difficult for young children to implement (Haun, 2007).

Together these studies show that there is continuity in certain spatial relational preferences using position and environmental cues within the primates, but that there is also discontinuity, in that humans are able to use other features in spatial relational tasks by age 3 and they exhibit diversity by age 8 in the spatial frames of reference that they use in cognitive tasks, frames that are in line with the patterns of language usage in their community. This suggests that humans have new representational capacities that enable departure from innate preferences and hence diversity within the species as well. And it suggests that language use is a key driver and shaper of this diversity.

One further development in this tradition bears mention. The domain-centered approach focuses on the full range of linguistic resources that can be used to convey specific referential information. This in turn leads quite naturally to looking at the full range of communicative resources outside of the linguistic code proper which can also play a role in conveying such information. Thus within this tradition there has long been interest in pointing gestures and other forms of nonverbal communication. From this expansion beyond the spoken language modality, it is but a small step to more recent work that considers the entire multimodal communicative interaction as the proper unit of analysis. And it is within interaction or, more precisely, the set of capacities necessary to mount interaction, that the evolutionary roots of human sociality are located (Enfield & Levinson, 2006). In this way of thinking, language plays a secondary role, extending the power of interactional strategies that are, ultimately, independent of it and grounded in individual cognitive skills (e.g., Theory of Mind), interpersonal skills (e.g., turn taking), and bodies of shared information (e.g., cultural traditions). Although this work on interaction has produced some excellent new comparative work on both the commonalities and differences in interactional engagement across cultures, it leaves behind a concern for the specific role of language in shaping cognition and has yet to engage the question of how general interaction strategies influence cognition.

Ontogenesis: The growth of mind in middle childhood

A recent line of research has used the structure-centered approach to explore the development of language-related cognitive differences in child-hood (Lucy & Gaskins, 2001, 2003). This research program effectively joins a Whorfian question about the impact of language differences on thought with a Vygotskian one about the impact of language on the development of conceptual thought in middle childhood (Lucy, 2010). The research has two aims. First, developmental research can provide a new way to address the question of which comes first, the language pattern or the cognitive pattern. Although many factors suggest that the language categories must be the leading force here (see Lucy, 1992a), direct developmental evidence can provide an important confirmation of the order of emergence. Second, once we have an adult contrast, we can use it to help us diagnose when and how language and thought interact in development. This provides us insight into the timing and mechanism of the developmental process.

Pilot work indicated that the distinctive cognitive patterns were appearing at around age 8. Accordingly, we then administered the full set of the triads described earlier to samples of American English and Yucatec Maya children at ages 7 and 9. Looking first at stable objects, we obtained the results shown in Figure 3.1. As you can see, English-speaking and Yucatec-speaking 7-year-olds showed an identical early bias toward shape —choosing material alternates only 12% of the time. But by age 9 the adult pattern was visible: English-speaking children continued to favor shape,

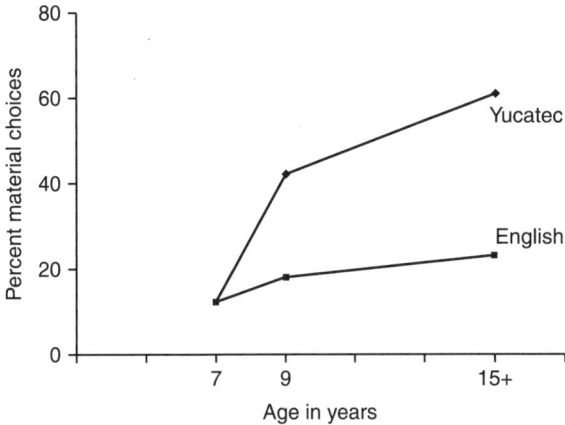

Figure 3.1 Developmental pattern for English and Yucatec classification preferences with stable objects: Material versus shape. *Source:* Reprinted
from Lucy (2004, p. 13).

choosing material alternates only 18% of the time, whereas Yucatec-
speaking children were now choosing material alternates 42% of the time.
Finally, on the far right are the adult results reported earlier. Thus, the
same kind of language-group difference found among adult speakers is
also found in children by age 9—and this result is statistically reliable.

Turning next to the results for malleable objects, where we expect the two
groups to look alike, we find that English-speaking and Yucatec-speaking
7-year-olds both showed a substantial number of material choices, as
shown in Figure 3.2. English-speaking children choose the material alternate 42% of the time and Yucatec-speaking children choose the material
alternate 46% of the time. At age 9 there is essentially no change: English
children choose material alternates 43% of the time and Yucatec children
choose them 50% of the time. And again, the adult responses appear on
the right. Overall, the similarity of response found among adult speakers
for referents of this type also appears in children. However, now viewed
in contrast to the developmental data, we can see that the adult results
appear more strongly differentiated in a manner reminiscent of the stable
object results—which perhaps suggests some general transfer of effect
from the stable object category to these malleable object stimuli.

We can bring both of these results together to display the interaction
of referent type and language type across age, as shown in Figure 3.3. This
composite chart shows that 7-year-olds show clear sensitivity to referent
type independently of language group membership. They show a relative
preference for material as a basis of classification with malleable objects
and relative preference for shape as a basis of classification with stable
objects. Both bases of classification respond to stimulus properties and are

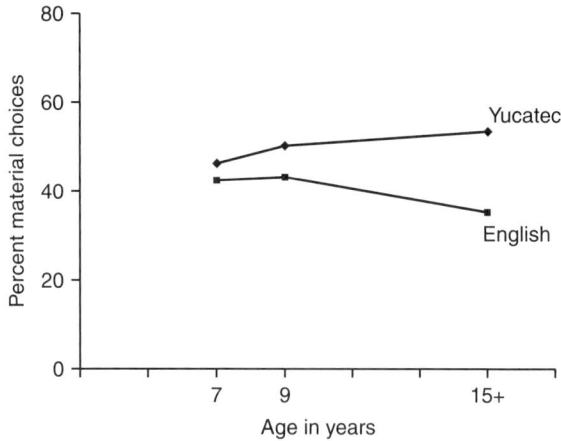

Figure 3.2 Developmental pattern for English and Yucatec classification preferences with malleable objects: Material versus shape. *Source:* Reprinted
from Lucy (2004, p. 15).

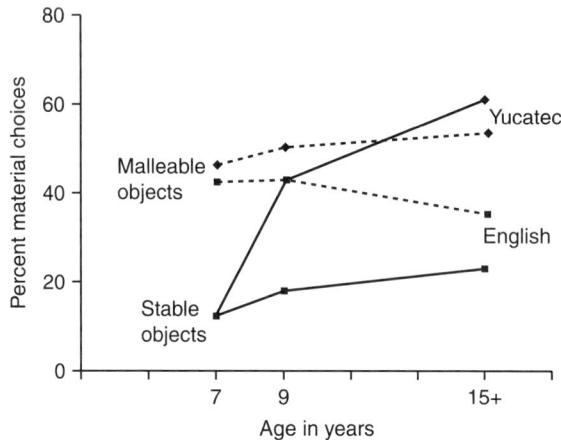

Figure 3.3 Developmental pattern for English and Yucatec classification preferences with both stable and malleable objects: Material versus shape.
Source: Reprinted from Lucy (2004, p. 17).

fully available to and used by both groups. Apparently, referent type but
not language type is the dominant factor in these nonverbal cognitive
tasks at this age. Simply having a linguistic form in the language is not
enough in itself to shape cognition. By contrast, 9-year-olds show differential sensitivity to referent type along adult lines: Their classification
preferences differ where the languages differ and correspond where the
languages correspond. This suggests that language categories increase in

their importance for cognition between ages 7 and 9; that is, that category patterns in the linguistic structure become important in a new way. Adult responses continue to show these language-specific patterns but also show a trend towards consolidation into a dominant pattern for each group. The Yucatec responses converge towards material choices and the English responses towards shape choices. The split-marking pattern in English obviously militates against the complete erasure of the distinctions among referent types in that language, hence the overall trend necessarily remains subordinate to the main effect of cognition aligning with the specific linguistic treatment of a referent type. Research on other unitizer languages such as Japanese produces results similar to those found in Yucatec (see discussion in Lucy & Gaskins, 2003). We can summarize the overall pattern of these results by saying that *young children begin by grouping different referent types in the same way and then shift during middle childhood to grouping the same referent types in quite different ways as a function of the structure of their language.*

Note that most of the central elements of the grammar, including number marking, have been in place for many years for these children. Just as English-speaking children have substantial command of plurals by age 7, so too do Yucatec-speaking children have substantial command of numeral classifiers by this age. Seven-year-old Yucatec-speaking children reliably use classifiers when counting, draw appropriate semantic distinctions among them in comprehension tasks, and will judge a number construction lacking them as faulty. However, they do still fall short of having the full adult range of classifiers in comprehension and production. Insofar as the cognitive results derive from basic structural characteristics of the language rather than mastery of the full range of lexemes, there is no reason the effects should not appear at age 7 rather than several years later. Something new must be happening during this middle childhood period.

These results are bolstered by other studies. These effects of language on thought are not merely mediated through lexical categories: The associated inflectional pattern of plural marking has other direct effects on cognition (see Lucy, 1992a, Ch. 3). Likewise, effects are not limited to simple classification tasks: Similar patterns appear in complex classification tasks (Lucy & Gaskins, 2001), in memory tasks (Lucy & Gaskins, 2003), and in everyday behavior (Lucy, 2004). And these structural effects emerge during middle childhood, in accordance with Vygotsky's (1934/ 1987) views. Taken together, these findings suggest that the specific structure of the language one speaks takes on new significance for cognition during this age period.

Understanding how language and thought come to relate in this new way will require taking a closer look at language development during this period. This is not a period of child language that has been heavily studied, but the available research shows that children develop many new verbal skills during this period and most of these changes suggest that the structural element of language comes into new significance as the child engages in more demanding discursive tasks. In terms of language structure, children continue their lexical development, adding new forms and reorganizing old ones so as to converge on the meanings held by adults (Ameel, Malt, & Stoorms 2008). In terms of grammatical structure, they master constructions such as passives (Chomsky, 1969) and the anaphoric use of demonstratives (Karmiloff-Smith, 1979) that enhance discourse cohesion. They also rework existing structural resources to create more coherent narratives through the sophisticated handling of temporal ordering and reported speech (Berman & Slobin, 1994; Hickmann, 1993, 2003). All of these structural developments involve taking existing structural alignments of form and meaning and either overriding or manipulating them in the service of various discursive ends. In terms of language function, children during this period also begin to use language for new forms of verbal humor and insult, as well as specialized stances such as sarcasm and flirting (e.g., Hoyle & Adger, 1998; Romaine, 1984). These skills all involve deploying one line of referential meaning while a second, sometimes diametrically opposed, meaning is also evoked in order to express a stance the speaker is taking towards the material. In formal terms, the child has learned to exploit the reflexive poetic potential of language such that one level of the message effectively 'comments' on another and a new message emerges from the conjuncture. At the same time, new metalinguistic skills emerge as children become able to explain the meanings of words more effectively, setting one construction into equation with another, and as their self-corrections grow beyond a concern with referential accuracy to a concern with communicative appropriateness and rhetorical effect. In particular, the ability to recognize and appeal to a listener's presuppositions and then to manipulate their expectations and reactions suggests a growing enmeshment of language with the surrounding socially shared reality.

Collectively, these new skills reflect a growing sensitivity to and mastery of the full structural implications of language forms. This includes the realization that these implications are recognized and used by others, and therefore that they can be relied on achieving a variety of effects in communicative interaction. For the child to draw on the full latent power of the shared structural means in the language and erect new functions upon it, the structure must itself be thoroughly mastered (Karmiloff-Smith, 1979). The child's new capabilities seem to be of three general types. First, there is deeper, more flexible mastery of the fundamentals of the meaning structure, mastery sufficient to permit the use of a single form for multiple meanings and to signal a given meaning through multiple forms. This flexibility permits greater referential precision and allows users to coordinate several messages in a single utterance, whether as speakers or hearers. Second, there is a deeper, subtler mastery of the fundamentals of the discursive space. These new discursive capacities necessarily involve shaping a message for the participants in a particular speech event. This implies an ability to understand the likely response a given utterance will elicit from a listener in a given situation and what, in turn, their interlocutors' own responses entail for them. In formal terms, what is emerging is the ability to co-construct and sustain a shared reality, a common ground for the purposes of conversation. Third, both of these shifts depend on re-analyzing the deictic forms that anchor linguistic structures in ongoing discourse: person, tense, modality, and evidentials (Jakobson, 1957/1971). Hereafter, such deictic forms not only have reference to the default, taken-for-granted, immediate speech situation that dominates in young children's speech, they also have reference to the broader shared social and interactive context, including language structures themselves, which adult speech both presupposes and helps create.

Interestingly, precisely during this period of enhanced structural mastery and associated verbal competence, children also begin to lose some of their former flexibility in language learning. Children learning a second language later in life will typically exhibit this loss of flexibility in the form of an accent; that is, a structurally driven interference with the new language. And the structures at issue here arise not only in the realm of sound but also in the realm of meaning. That is, children will develop a *semantic accent* and systematically apply the structural meanings of one or another prior language when interpreting a new language (Lucy, 2006). In bilingualism research, the terms *transfer* or *cross-linguistic influence* are more commonly used to discuss the effects of one set of language categories on another (e.g., Jarvis & Pavlenko, 2008). The term *accent* is preferred here because it carries the connotations that such effects are normal, unconscious, durable, and value laden. It also puts more emphasis on the role of an early language on the reception of a language learned later. It is as if the child, in order to implement more sophisticated forms of discourse, is forced in some way to crystallize the existing language system in a way that interferes with later language learning. In other words, new verbal powers seem to be purchased at the expense of structural openness. And henceforth, each new language is 'heard' through the structural paradigms of the first-learned language(s).

The results of the case study reported here indicate that something similar happens with cognition during this period. For it is precisely during this period of emerging verbal skill, resting on virtuoso structural mastery and commitment to local discursive realities, that linguistic relativity effects appear. We not only see new languages through the lens of our own language in the form of a semantic accent, it seems we also come to see and think about other aspects of reality itself through categories of our language. Even as the use of language structures helps liberate us from living and thinking only in the immediate reality, 'enriching' our vision, its structures and their shared entailments are also becoming 'habitual' constraints on our vision of reality.

This suggests that that engagement with the inner structural logic of a language and the particular discursive world it enables provides the leverage needed to transcend the immediate moment so as to re-envision reality, to re-think it, and ultimately to re-make it—precisely the practices that distinguish humans from other species. From this vantage point, linguistic relativity effects are not some unfortunate side-effect of language development, but are rather its intended achievement as we recruit the inner face of our particular language structure to the shared task of re-imagining the reality around us. It is crucial to see that the structural patterns in language that support this development *are* the telos of language development, the end towards which it develops. And this telos is latently there from the beginning both as a presupposition of the developmental process and as its central achievement. The structure of language allows us to reach beyond the immediate speaking moment to construe a historically specific reality, a reality which represents the stable and enduring legacy of each language to its speakers.

CONCLUSION

The distinctive anthropological approach to the study of language and thought derives from the view that no language has an intrinsically superior representation of reality such that it can be taken as the standard for evaluating others. This leads directly to efforts to find ways to compare languages in a more neutral way, in particular by reference to how languages partition domains characterized independently of language or by reference to how structural contrasts between languages implicate different realities. Later refinements of these approaches have converged on the use of referential and semantic typologies to characterize language differences and the use of systematic experimental comparisons to characterize nonverbal consequences of the language differences. Recent work explores the evolutionary and ontogenetic origins of the capacity for diversity and of the specific mechanisms in development associated with the emergence of linguistic relativity effects. These effects seem to be associated with a fundamental trade-off whereby a deeper commitment to the structures of one's language goes hand in hand with the emergence of more sophisticated verbal and intellectual capabilities.

The anthropological approach makes clear that research on the impact of language diversity is inherently difficult because the bias of our own language pervades the research process. First, our understanding of the meaning structure of another language can be impeded by the categories of our own language, what I have called here our semantic accent. Like any other accent, semantic accents are normal, systematic, resistant to change, and value laden. Second, our understanding of the nature of reality can be shaped by the categories of our own language, what is usually called linguistic relativity. Our categories not only bias how we habitually see the world, they also seem to us uniquely suited to capturing that reality. Third, both of these effects, semantic accent and linguistic relativity, converge to create interpretive problems when we try to understand how another people are seeing reality. Insofar as we interpret their *language* through our categories and then interpret *reality* through our categories, it becomes almost impossible to recognize difference, let alone relativity. If, on the one hand, we observe that their language categories match ours and match our reality, we conclude that languages are not really so different after all, and there is no relativity. If, on the other hand, we observe that their language categories do not match our language or our reality, we may conclude not that there is relativity, but that their language is simply deficient by comparison with ours. It is difficult to recognize the third possibility, that their language is different than ours and represents reality equally well. It is unlikely that this difficulty can be overcome by good intentions in the form of an egalitarian mindset—these biases are too deeply ingrained and useful in other contexts. Rather, from the point of view of research, they can be overcome only through embracing a theoretically informed methodology that forces us to follow the logic of another language on its own terms, to frame the comparison in neutral terms, and then to assess directly the contrasting views of reality held by ourselves and by others. And the execution of this theoretical methodology, in turn, requires sustained practical engagement with other languages.

ACKNOWLEDGMENTS

Portions of this paper were written while the author was an Andrew W. Mellon Fellow at the Center for Advanced Study in the Behavioral Sciences, Stanford, CA, USA. I thank the volume editors for their useful comments and good-humored patience.

REFERENCES

Aarsleff, H. (1982). *From Locke to Saussure: Essays on the study of language and intellectual history*. Minneapolis MN: University of Minneapolis Press.

Aarsleff, H. (1988). Introduction. In W. von Humboldt (Trans. P. Heath), *On language: The diversity of human language-structure and its influence on the mental development of mankind* (pp. vii–lxv). Cambridge, UK: Cambridge University Press.

Ameel, E., Malt, B., & Storms, G. (2008). Object naming and later lexical development: From baby bottle to beer bottle. *Journal of Memory and Language, 58,* 262–285.

Berlin, B., & Kay, P. (1969). *Basic color terms: Their universality and evolution.* Berkeley, CA: University of California Press.

Berman, R., & Slobin, D. (1994). *Relating events in narrative: A crosslinguistic developmental study.* Hillsdale, NJ: Lawrence Erlbaum Associates Inc.

Boas, F. (1889). On alternating sounds. *American Anthropologist, 2*(1), 47–54.

Boas, F. (Ed.). (1966). *Race, language, and culture.* New York: The Free Press.

Brinton, D. (1888). The language of Palaeolithic man. *Proceedings of the American Philosophical Society, 25*(128), 212–225.

Brown, R., & Lenneberg, E. (1954). A study in language and cognition. *Journal of Abnormal and Social Psychology, 49,* 454–462.

Chomsky, C. (1969). *The acquisition of syntax in children from 5 to 10.* Cambridge, MA: MIT Press.

Davidoff, J., Davies, I., & Roberson, D. (1999). Colour categories of a stone-age tribe. *Nature, 398,* 203–204.

Enfield, N., & Levinson, S. (Eds.). (2006). *Roots of human sociality: Culture, cognition, and interaction.* Oxford, UK: Berg.

Haun, D. (2007). *Cognitive cladistics and the relativity of spatial cognition.* PhD thesis, Radboud Universiteit Nijmegen.

Haun, D., Rapold, C., Call, J., Janzen, G., & Levinson, S. C. (2006). Cognitive cladistics and cultural override in Hominid spatial cognition. *Proceedings of the National Academy of Sciences, 103,* 17568–17573.

Hickmann, M. (1993). The boundaries of reported speech in narrative discourse: Some developmental aspects. In J. Lucy (Ed.), *Reflexive language: Reported speech and metapragmatics* (pp. 63–90). Cambridge, UK: Cambridge University Press.

Hickmann, M. (2003). *Children's discourse: Person, space, and time across languages.* Cambridge, UK: Cambridge University Press.

Hoyle, S., & C. Adger (Eds.). (1998). *Kids talk: Strategic language use in later childhood.* Oxford, UK: Oxford University Press.

Jakobson, R. (1957/1971). Shifters, verbal categories, and the Russian verb. In *Selected writings, Volume 2: Word and language* (pp. 130–147). The Hague: Mouton.

Jarvis, S., & Pavlenko, A. (2008). *Crosslinguistic influence in language and cognition.* New York: Routledge.

Karmiloff-Smith, A. (1979). *A functional approach to child language: A study of determiners and reference.* Cambridge, UK: Cambridge University Press.

Kay, P., Brent, B., Maffi, L., & Merrifield, W. (1997). Color naming across languages. In C. Hardin & L. Maffi (Eds.), *Color categories in thought and language* (pp. 20–56). Cambridge, UK: Cambridge University Press.

Kay, P., & McDaniel, C. (1978) The linguistic significance of the meanings of basic color terms. *Language, 54*(3), 610–646.

Levinson, S. (2003). *Space in language and cognition: Explorations in cognitive diversity.* Cambridge, UK: Cambridge University Press.

Levinson, S., Kita, S., Haun, D., & Rasch, B. (2002). Returning the tables: Language affects spatial reasoning. *Cognition, 84*(3), 155–88.

Levinson, S., & Wilkinson, D. (Eds.). (2006). *Grammars of space: Explorations in cognitive diversity.* Cambridge, UK: Cambridge University Press.

Li, P., & Gleitman, P. (2002). Turning the tables: Language and spatial reasoning. *Cognition, 83,* 265–294.

Lucy, J. (1985). Whorf's view of the linguistic mediation of thought. In E. Mertz & R. Parmentier (Eds.), *Semiotic mediation: Sociocultural and psychological perspectives* (pp. 73–97). Orlando, FL: Academic Press.

Lucy, J. (1992a). *Grammatical categories and cognition: A case study of the linguistic relativity hypothesis.* Cambridge, UK: Cambridge University Press.

Lucy, J. (1992b). *Language diversity and thought: A reformulation of the linguistic relativity hypothesis.* Cambridge, UK: Cambridge University Press.

Lucy, J. (1996). The scope of linguistic relativity: An analysis and review of empirical research. In J. Gumperz & S. Levinson (Eds.), *Rethinking linguistic relativity* (pp. 37–69). Cambridge, UK: Cambridge University Press.

Lucy, J. (1997a). Linguistic relativity. *Annual Review of Anthropology, 26,* 291–312.

Lucy, J. (1997b). The linguistics of 'color'. In C. Hardin & L. Maffi (Eds.), *Color categories in thought and language* (pp. 320–346). Cambridge, UK: Cambridge University Press.

Lucy, J. (2004). Language, culture, and mind in comparative perspective. In M. Achard & S. Kemmer (Eds.), *Language, culture, and mind* (pp. 1–21). Stanford, CA: Center for the Study of Language and Information Publications.

Lucy, J. (2006). *Linguistic relativity and the problem of semantic accent.* Plenary address, 2nd Language, Culture, and Mind Conference. Paris, July 17–20.

Lucy, J. (2010). Language structure, lexical meaning, and cognition: Whorf and Vygotsky revisited. In B. Malt & P. Wolff (Eds.), *Words and the mind: How words capture human experience* (pp. 268–288). Oxford, UK: Oxford University Press.

Lucy, J., & Gaskins, S. (2001). Grammatical categories and the development of classification preferences: A comparative approach. In S. Levinson & M. Bowerman (Eds.), *Language acquisition and conceptual development* (pp. 257–283). Cambridge, UK: Cambridge University Press.

Lucy, J., & Gaskins, S. (2003). Interaction of language type and referent type in the development of nonverbal classification preferences. In D. Gentner & S. Goldin-Meadow (Eds.), *Language in mind: Advances in the study of language and thought* (pp. 465–492). Cambridge, MA: MIT Press.

Majid, A., Bowerman, M., Kita, S., Haun, D., & Levinson, S. (2004). Can language restructure cognition? The case for space. *Trends in Cognitive Sciences, 8*(3), 108–114.

Pederson, E. (1993). Geographic and manipulable space in two Tamil linguistic systems. In A. U. Frank & I. Campari (Eds.), *Spatial information theory* (pp. 294–311). Berlin: Springer-Verlag.

Pederson, E., Danziger, E., Levinson, S., Kita, S., Senft, G., & Wilkins, D. (1998). Semantic typology and spatial conceptualization. *Language, 74,* 557–589.

Roberson, D., & Hanley, J. R. (2010). Relatively speaking: An account of the relationship between language and thought in the color domain. In B. Malt & P. Wolff (Eds.), *Words and the mind: How words capture human experience* (pp. 183–198). Oxford, UK: Oxford University Press.

Romaine, S. (1984). *The language of children and adolescents: The acquisition of communicative competence.* New York: Blackwell.

Sapir, E. (1921). *Language: An introduction to the study of speech.* New York: Harcourt Brace & Co.

Sapir, E. (1993). *The psychology of culture: A course of lectures* (Reconstructed and edited by J. T. Irvine). Berlin: Mouton de Gruyter.

Vygotsky, L. (1934/1987). Thinking and speech. In R. W. Rieber & A. S. Carton (Eds.), *The collected works of L.S. Vygotsky. Vol. I: Problems of general psychology* (trans. N. Minnick) (pp. 39–285). New York: Plenum.

Webster's seventh new collegiate dictionary (1965). Springfield, MA: G. & C. Merriam.

Whorf, B. (1941/1956). The relation of habitual thought and behavior to language. In J. B. Carroll (Ed.), *Language, thought, and reality: Selected writings of Benjamin Lee Whorf* (pp. 134–159). Cambridge, MA: MIT Press.

4 Language and cognition: The view from cognitive linguistics

Vyvyan Evans

Cognitive linguistics is a modern school of linguistic thought and practice, concerned with investigating the relationship between human language, the mind, and socio-physical experience. For comprehensive and detailed overviews of cognitive linguistics see Evans and Green (2006), which is suitable for the neophyte, or the more voluminous Geeraerts and Cuyckens (2007). For collections of fundamental readings see Evans, Bergen, and Zinken (2007) and Geerearts (2006). For a glossary covering many of the technical terms of cognitive linguistics see Evans (2007).

Cognitive linguistics has its origins in scholarship which emerged in the 1970s, conducted by a small number of researchers. These include Charles Fillmore (e.g., 1975), George Lakoff (e.g., 1977; Lakoff & Thompson, 1975), Ronald Langacker (e.g., 1978) and Leonard Talmy (e.g., 1975, 1978). This research arose out of dissatisfaction with formal approaches, then dominant in the disciplines of linguistics and philosophy. While its origins were, in part, philosophical in nature, as is evident in the landmark 1980 publication, *Metaphors We Live By*, by Lakoff and Johnson, cognitive linguistics has always been strongly influenced by theories and findings from the other cognitive sciences as they emerged during the 1960s and 1970s, particularly cognitive psychology, and more recently by the brain sciences, especially the interdisciplinary perspective known as cognitive neuroscience. In recent years, cognitive linguistic theories have become sufficiently sophisticated and detailed to begin making predictions that are testable using a broad range of converging methods from the cognitive and brain sciences. González-Márquez, Mittelberg, Coulson, and Spivey (2006), for instance, provide a review of some of the methodologies currently deployed in cognitive linguistics.

Perhaps what is most distinctive about cognitive linguistics is that it is not a single articulated theoretical perspective or methodological toolkit. Nor is it subject to the *ex cathedra* pronouncements of a single theoretical authority. Rather, cognitive linguistics constitutes an enterprise characterized by a number of core commitments and guiding assumptions. It constitutes a loose confederation of theoretical perspectives united by these shared commitments and guiding assumptions. The worldview that emerges has resonated with increasingly large numbers of researchers such that the rise and take-up of cognitive linguistics, particularly since the 1990s when it began to become increasingly institutionalized with the development of the International Cognitive Linguistics Association (ICLA), has been rapid and inexorable. At the time of publication, cognitive linguistics is arguably the most rapidly growing school of thought and practice within linguistics. It exerts an increasing influence on many subdisciplines of language science, as well as a number of cognate disciplines in the cognitive, brain, and social sciences, as well as the humanities.

Cognitive linguists have typically adopted a number of distinct (although complementary) foci. Some have been exercised by the study of language structure and organization. This constitutes a subbranch of cognitive linguistics sometimes referred to as 'cognitive approaches to grammar'. Notable exemplars include Croft (2002), Goldberg (1995, 2006), Lakoff (1987, case study 3), Langacker (e.g., 1987, 1991a, 1991b, 1999, 2008), and Talmy (e.g., 2000). Others have employed language as a means of studying aspects of conceptual organization and structure. The study of aspects of the mind, such as knowledge representation and meaning construction, employing language as a lens for doing so, is sometimes referred to as *cognitive semantics* Exemplars include Fauconnier (1985/1994, 1997), Fauconnier and Turner (2002), and Lakoff and Johnson (1980, 1999). A further subbranch relates to the study of word meanings, sometimes referred to as *cognitive lexical semantics*. Notable exemplars include Evans (2004), Geeraerts (1997) and Tyler and Evans (2003). Some scholars have attempted to integrate the study of all three areas. A recent example is Evans (2009).

The main purpose of this chapter is to survey the theoretical position and main findings of cognitive linguistics as it bears on the relationship between language and cognition. The chapter is organized as follows. In the next section I provide an overview of the two primary commitments of cognitive linguistics, its axiomatic base. Then I consider the five theses of cognitive linguistics: its postulates. It is subscription to these that gives a particular theoretical architecture or approach its distinctive cognitive linguistic character. The next section considers the distinctive cognitive linguistic worldview that emerges, and the subsequent section considers some of the models of language that have emerged within cognitive linguistics. I also consider the way in which these models reflect the underlying commitments and theses of the cognitive linguistics enterprise. Then I examine the way in which cognitive linguistics theories have additionally been employed to investigate aspects of conceptual structure and organization. The next section reviews cognitive linguistic theories of how language interfaces with non-linguistic aspects of mental representation in order to model linguistically mediated meaning construction. The chapter concludes by briefly considering what cognitive linguistics might offer the researcher in bilingual cognition.

THE TWO PRIMARY COMMITMENTS OF COGNITIVE LINGUISTICS

Cognitive linguistics is distinct from other movements in linguistics, both formalist and functionalist, in two respects. First, it takes seriously the cognitive underpinnings of language, the so-called cognitive commitment (Lakoff, 1990). Cognitive linguists attempt to describe and model language in the light of convergent evidence from other cognitive and brain sciences. Second, cognitive linguists subscribe to a generalization commitment: a commitment to describing the nature and principles that constitute linguistic knowledge as an outcome of general cognitive abilities (see Lakoff, 1990)—rather than viewing language as constituting, for instance, a wholly distinct encapsulated module of mind. In this section I briefly elaborate on these two commitments which lie at the heart of the cognitive linguistics enterprise.

The cognitive commitment

The hallmark of cognitive linguistics is the cognitive commitment (Lakoff, 1990). This represents a commitment to providing a characterization of language that accords with what is known about the mind and brain from other disciplines. It is this commitment that makes cognitive linguistics cognitive, and thus an approach which is fundamentally interdisciplinary in nature.

The cognitive commitment represents the view that principles of linguistic structure should reflect what is known about human cognition from the other cognitive and brain sciences, particularly psychology, artificial intelligence, cognitive neuroscience, and philosophy. In other words, the cognitive commitment asserts that the models of language and linguistic organization proposed should reflect what is known about the human mind, rather than purely aesthetic dictates such as the use of particular kinds of formalisms or economy of representation (Croft, 1998).

The cognitive commitment has a number of concrete ramifications. First, linguistic theories cannot include structures or processes that violate what is known about human cognition. For example, if sequential derivation of syntactic structures violates time constraints provided by actual human language processing, then it must be jettisoned. Second, models that employ established cognitive properties to explain language phenomena are more parsimonious than those that are built from a priori simplicity metrics (such as Chomskyan elegance). For instance, given the amount of progress cognitive scientists have made in the study of categorization, a theory that employs the same mechanisms that are implicated in categorization in other cognitive domains in order to model linguistic structure is simpler than one that hypothesizes a separate system. Finally, the cognitive linguistic researcher is charged with establishing convergent evidence for the cognitive reality of components of any model proposed—whether or not this research is conducted by the cognitive linguist (Gibbs, 2006).

The generalization commitment

The generalization commitment (Lakoff, 1990) represents a dedication to characterizing general principles that apply to all aspects of human language. This goal reflects the standard commitment in science to seek the broadest generalizations possible. In contrast, some approaches to the study of language often separate what is sometimes termed the 'language faculty' into distinct areas such as phonology (sound), semantics (word and sentence meaning), pragmatics (meaning in discourse context), morphology (word structure), syntax (sentence structure), and so on. As a consequence, there is often little basis for generalization across these aspects of language, or for study of their interrelations.

Generative linguistics, for instance, attempts to model language by positing explicit algorithmic procedures operating on theoretical primitives in order to generate all the possible grammatical sentences of a given language. This approach has attempted precise formulations by adopting formalisms originally inspired by artificial intelligence, mathematics, and logic, as represented in the work of Noam Chomsky (e.g., 1965, 1981, 1995). In somewhat related fashion, formalisms deriving from these disciplines inform, even more explicitly, the tradition known as formal semantics, inspired by philosopher of language Richard Montague (1970, 1973; see Cann, 1993 for a review).

Within the generative grammar tradition it is often assumed that areas such as phonology, semantics, and syntax concern significantly different kinds of structuring principles operating over different kinds of primitives. For instance, the syntax concerns a particular kind of knowledge that is hypothesized to be specialized for arranging words into well-formed sentences, whereas a phonology subsystem is specialized for arranging sounds into patterns (e.g., CV structure) permitted by the rules of a given language, and by human language in general. This modular view of mind reinforces the idea that modern linguistics is justified in separating the study of language into distinct subdisciplines, not only on grounds of practicality, but also because the types of knowledge that make up language are wholly distinct and, in terms of their primitives and organizational principles, incommensurable.

While cognitive linguists acknowledge that it may often be useful to treat areas such as syntax, semantics, and phonology as being notionally distinct, cognitive linguists do not start with the assumption that the 'subsystems' of language are organized in significantly divergent ways. Hence, the generalization commitment represents a commitment to openly investigating how the various aspects of linguistic knowledge emerge from a common set of human cognitive abilities upon which they draw, rather than assuming that they are produced in an encapsulated module of the mind, consisting of distinct knowledge types, or subsystems.

The generalization commitment has concrete consequences for studies of language. First, cognitive linguistic studies focus on what is common among aspects of language, seeking to re-use successful methods and explanations across these aspects. For instance, just as word meaning displays prototype effects—there are better and worse examples of referents of given words, related in particular ways (see Lakoff, 1987)—so various studies have applied the same principles to the organization of morphology (e.g., Taylor, 2003), syntax (e.g., Goldberg, 1995, 2006), and phonology (e.g., Jaeger & Ohala, 1984). Generalizing successful accounts over distinct domains of language isn't just good scientific practice, this is also the way biology works; reusing existing structures for new purposes, both on evolutionary and developmental timescales.

THE FIVE THESES OF COGNITIVE LINGUISTICS

In addition to the two primary commitments of cognitive linguistics, the enterprise also features a number of guiding assumptions: its postulates or theses. There are at least five distinctive theses that make up the cognitive linguistics perspective. These are:

1   the thesis of embodied cognition,
2   the thesis of encyclopedic semantics,
3   the symbolic thesis,
4   the thesis that meaning is conceptualization, and
5   the usage-based thesis.

Together with the two primary commitments, these theses give rise to a distinctive worldview, which I elaborate on below.

The thesis of embodied cognition

The thesis consists of two related parts. The first part holds that the nature of reality is not objectively given, but is a function of our species-specific and individual embodiment—this is the subthesis of 'embodied experience' (see Lakoff, 1987; Lakoff & Johnson, 1980, 1999; Tyler & Evans, 2003). Second, our mental representation of reality is grounded in our embodied mental states: mental states captured from our embodied experience—this is the subthesis of 'grounded cognition' (see Barsalou, 2008; Evans, 2009; Gallese & Lakoff, 2005).

The subthesis of embodied experience maintains that due to the nature of our bodies, including our neuro-anatomical architecture, we have a species-specific view of the world. In other words, our construal of 'reality' is mediated, in large measure, by the nature of our embodiment. One example of the way in which embodiment affects the nature of experience is in the realm of color. While the human visual system has three kinds of photoreceptors (i.e., color channels), other organisms often have a different number (Varela, Thompson, & Rosch, 1991). For instance, the visual system of squirrels, rabbits, and possibly cats, makes use of two color channels, while other organisms, including goldfish and pigeons, have four color channels. Having a different range of color channels affects our experience of color in terms of the range of colors accessible to us along the color spectrum. Some organisms can see in the infrared range, such as rattlesnakes which hunt prey at night and can visually detect the heat given off by other organisms. Humans are unable to see in this range. The nature of our visual apparatus—one aspect of our embodiment—determines the nature and range of our visual experience.

A further consequence of the subthesis of embodied experience is that as individual embodiment within a species varies, so too will embodied experience across individual members of the same species. There is now empirical support for the position that humans have distinctive embodied experience due to individual variables such as handedness. That is, whether one is left- or right-handed influences the way in which one experiences reality (Casasanto, 2009).

The fact that our experience is embodied—that is, structured in part by the nature of the bodies we have and by our neurological organization—has consequences for cognition: the subthesis of grounded cognition. In other words, the concepts we have access to, and the nature of the 'reality' we think and talk about, are grounded in the multimodal representations that emerge from our embodied experience. More precisely, concepts constitute re-activations of brain states that are recorded during embodied experience. Such re-activations are technically referred to as 'simulations'. (I give an example below, relating to the word *red*, which illustrates this notion.) These simulations are grounded in multimodal brain states which arise from our action and interaction with our socio-physical environment. Such experiences include sensory-motor and proprioceptive experience, as well as states that arise from our subjective experience of our internal (bodily) environment, including our visceral sense, as well as experiences relating to mental evaluations and states and other subjective experiences, including emotions and affect more generally, and experiences relating to temporal experience. From the grounded cognition perspective, the human mind bears the imprint of embodied experience. The embodied experience and grounded cognition perspectives together make up the thesis of embodied cognition.

The thesis of encyclopedic semantics

The thesis of encyclopedic semantics is also made up of two parts. First, it holds that semantic representations in the linguistic system, what is often referred to as *semantic structure*, relate to—or interface with—representations in the conceptual system. The precise details as to the nature of the relationship can, and indeed do, vary however, across specific cognitive linguistic theories. For instance, Langacker (e.g., 1987) equates semantic structure with conceptual structure, whereas Evans (2009) maintains that semantic structure and conceptual structure constitute two distinct representational formats, with semantic structure facilitating access to (some aspects of) conceptual structure. It is worth noting that the 'representational' view associated with the thesis of encyclopedic semantics is directly at odds with the 'denotational' perspective, what cognitive linguists sometimes refer to as 'objectivist semantics', as exemplified by some formal (i.e., truth-conditional) approaches to semantics.

The second part of the thesis relates to the view that conceptual structure, to which semantic structure relates, constitutes a vast network of structured knowledge, a semantic potential (Evans, 2009) which is hence encyclopedia-like in nature and in scope.

By way of illustration, consider the lexical item *red*. The precise meaning arising from any given instance of use of the lexical item *red* is a function of the range of perceptual hues associated with our encyclopedic set of mental representations for red, as constrained by the utterance context in which red is embedded. For instance, consider the following examples:

(1) The school teacher scrawled in red ink all over the pupil's exercise book.
(2) The red squirrel is almost extinct in the British Isles.

In each of these examples, a distinct re-activation of perceptual experience, a simulation, is prompted for. In the example in (1) the perceptual simulation relates to a vivid red, while in (2) the utterance prompts for a brown/dun hue of red. In other words, the meaning of the lexical item *red* arises from an interaction between linguistic and conceptual representations, such that the most relevant conceptual knowledge is activated upon each instance of use. Examples such as those in (1) and (2) suggest that word meaning does not arise by unpacking a purely linguistic representation. Rather, it involves access to a potentially vast body of encyclopedic knowledge. A simulation, then, is a re-activation of part of this non-linguistic encyclopedic knowledge.

A consequence of this is that each individual instance of word use potentially leads to a distinct interpretation. For instance, *fast* means something quite different in *fast car*, *fast driver*, and *fast lane of the motorway*. This follows as any instance of use constitutes a distinct usage event that may activate a different part of the encyclopedic knowledge potential to which a lexical item facilitates access.

The symbolic thesis

The symbolic thesis holds that the fundamental unit of grammar is a form–meaning pairing, or symbolic unit. The symbolic unit is variously termed a 'symbolic assembly' in Langacker's cognitive grammar, or a 'construction' in construction grammar approaches (e.g., Goldberg's cognitive construction grammar, 1995, 2006). Symbolic units run the full gamut from the fully lexical to the wholly schematic. For instance, examples of symbolic units include morphemes (for example, *dis-* as in *distasteful*), whole words (for example, *cat*, *run*, *tomorrow*), idiomatic expressions such as *He kicked the bucket*, and sentence-level constructions such as the ditransitive (or double object) construction, as exemplified by the expression: *John baked Sally a cake* (see Goldberg, 1995). Some examples of symbolic units are given in Table 4.1.

More precisely, the symbolic thesis holds that the mental grammar consists of a form, a semantic unit, and symbolic correspondence that relates the two. This is captured in Figure 4.1. In other words, the symbolic thesis holds that our mental grammar comprises units which consist of pairings of form and meaning.

One consequence of the symbolic thesis is that units that do not consist of pairings of form and meaning, such as the abstract rules posited in the generative tradition, are excluded from a language user's mental grammar. Langacker (1987) for instance, posits a *content requirement*, a principle that asserts that units of grammar must involve actual content: units of semantic structure and phonological form (even if phonologically schematic) that are linked by a symbolic correspondence.

Table 4.1 Examples of symbolic units

Type of symbolic unit	Traditional name	Example
Complex and (mostly) schematic	Syntax	NP *be*-TENSE VERB- *en by* NP/[ACTION FROM PERSPECTIVE OF PATIENT]
Complex and (mostly) specific	Idiom	*pull*-TENSE NP's *leg*/[TO TEASE AS A JOKE]
Complex but bound	Morphology	NOUN-*s*/[MORE THAN ONE OF SOMETHING], VERB-TENSE/[TIME REFERENCE WITH RESPECT TO CODING TIME]
Atomic and schematic	Word classes	NOUN/[THING], VERB/[TEMPORALLY GROUNDED RELATION]
Atomic and specific	Lexical items	*The*/[THE], *jumper*/[JUMPER]

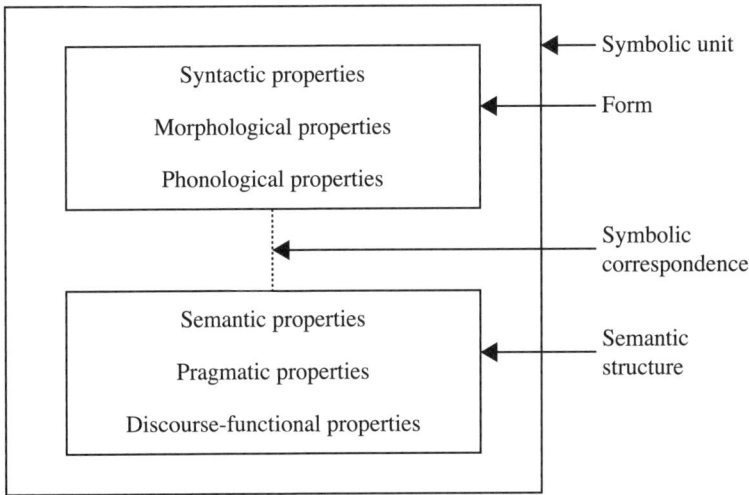

Figure 4.1 A symbolic unit.

The adoption of the symbolic thesis has a number of important consequences for a model of grammar. Because the basic unit is the symbolic unit, meaning achieves central status in cognitive linguistic approaches to grammar. This follows as the basic grammatical unit is a symbolic unit: form cannot be studied independently of meaning.

The second consequence is that as there is not a principled distinction between the study of semantics and syntax—the study of grammar is the study of the full range of units that make up a language, from the lexical to the grammatical. Cognitive linguists posit a 'lexicon–grammar continuum' (Croft, 2002; Langacker, 1987) to capture this perspective. While the grammar of a language is made of symbolic units, symbolic units exhibit qualitative differences in terms of their schematicity. At one extreme are symbolic units which are highly specified in terms of their lexical form, and in terms of the richness of their semantic content. Such symbolic units, such as words, lie at the 'lexical' end of the lexicon–grammar continuum. At the other end lie highly schematic symbolic units, schematic both in terms of phonological and semantic content. An example of a symbolic unit of this kind is the sentence-level ditransitive construction studied by Goldberg (e.g., 1995) and discussed in more detail below. Lexically unfilled sentence-level syntactic templates such as the ditransitive construction are held to have a schematic form and schematic meaning conventionally associated with them as exemplified in (3):

(3) a. Form: SUBJ VERB NP1 NP2
     b. Meaning: X CAUSES Y TO RECEIVE Z

Symbolic units of this sort lie at the 'grammatical' end-point of the lexicon–grammar continuum. While fully 'lexical' and 'grammatical' symbolic units differ in qualitative terms, they are the same in principle, being symbolic in nature, in the sense described. Moreover, examples such as these are extreme exemplars. A range of symbolic units exist in all languages which occupy various points along the continuum that are less extreme.

A third consequence is that symbolic units can be related to one another, both in terms of similarity of form and semantic relatedness. One manifestation of such relationships is in terms of relative schematicity or specificity, such that one symbolic unit can be a more (or less) specific instantiation of another. Cognitive linguists model the relationships between symbolic units in terms of a network, arranged hierarchically relating to levels of schematicity. This is an issue I return to below when I discuss the usage-based thesis.

Finally, constituency structure—and hence the combinatorial nature of language—is a function of symbolic units becoming integrated or fused in order to create larger grammatical units, with different theorists proposing slightly different mechanisms for how this arises. For instance, Langacker (e.g., 1987) holds that constituency structure emerges from what he terms 'conceptually dependent (or relational) predications', such as verbs, encoding a schematic slot, termed an 'elaboration site'. The elaboration site is filled by 'conceptually autonomous (or nominal) predications', such as nouns. In contrast, Goldberg (e.g., 1995), in her theory of cognitive construction grammar, argues that integration is due to a fusion process that takes place between verb-level slots, what she terms 'participant roles', and sentence-level 'argument roles', discussed further below (see Evans, 2009, for further discussion of these issues).

The thesis that meaning is conceptualization

Language understanding involves the interaction between semantic structure and conceptual structure, as mediated by various linguistic and conceptual mechanisms and processes. In other words, linguistically mediated meaning construction doesn't simply involve compositionality, in the Fregean sense, whereby words encode meanings which are integrated in monotonic fashion such that the meaning of the whole arises from the sum of the parts (see Evans, 2006, 2009 for critical discussion of this notion of compositionality). Cognitive linguists subscribe to the position that linguistically mediated meaning involves conceptualization—which is to say, higher-order cognitive processing some, or much, of which is non-linguistic in nature. In other words, the thesis that meaning is conceptualization holds that the way in which symbolic units are combined during language understanding gives rise to a unit of meaning which is non-linguistic in nature—the notion of a simulation introduced above—and relies, in part, on non-linguistic processes of integration.

There are two notable approaches to meaning construction that have been developed within cognitive linguistics. The first is concerned with the sorts of mechanisms central to meaning construction that are fundamentally non-linguistic in nature. Meaning construction processes of this kind have been referred to as 'backstage cognition' (Fauconnier, 1985/ 1994, 1997). There are two distinct, but closely related, theories of backstage cognition: mental spaces theory, developed in two monographs by Gilles Fauconnier (1985/1994, 1997), and conceptual blending theory, developed by Gilles Fauconnier and Mark Turner (2002), both of which are explicated later in the chapter. Mental spaces theory is concerned with the nature and creation of 'mental spaces', small packets of conceptual structure built as we think and talk. Conceptual blending theory is concerned with the integrative mechanisms and networks that operate over collections of mental spaces in order to produce emergent aspects of meaning—meaning that is in some sense novel.

A more recent approach is LCCM theory (Evans, 2006, 2009), named after the two central constructs in the theory: the 'lexical concept' and the 'cognitive model'. LCCM theory is concerned with the role of linguistic cues and linguistic processes in meaning construction (lexical concepts), and the way in which these lexical concepts facilitate access to non-linguistic knowledge (cognitive models) in the process of language understanding. Accordingly, as the emphasis is on the nature and the role of linguistic prompts in meaning construction, LCCM theory represents an attempt to provide a 'front-stage approach' to the cognitive mechanisms, and specifically the role of language, in meaning construction. LCCM theory is discussed in slightly more detail below.

The usage-based thesis

The final thesis to be discussed is the usage-based thesis. This holds that the mental grammar of the language user is formed by the abstraction of symbolic units from situated instances of language use: utterances— specific usage events involving symbolic units for purposes of signaling local and contextually relevant communicative intentions. An important consequence of adopting the usage-based thesis is that there is no principled distinction between knowledge of language, and use of language (competence and performance, in generative grammar terms), since knowledge emerges from use. From this perspective, knowledge of language *is* knowledge of how language is used.

The symbolic units that come to be stored in the mind of the language user emerge through processes of 'abstraction' and 'schematization' (Langacker, 2000), based on 'pattern recognition' and 'intention reading' abilities (Tomasello, 1999, 2003). Symbolic units thus constitute what might be thought of as 'mental routines' (Langacker, 1987), consisting, as we have seen, of conventional pairings of form and meaning.

One of the consequences of the usage-based thesis is that symbolic units exhibit degrees of 'entrenchment'—the degree to which a symbolic unit is established as a cognitive routine in the mind of the language user. If the language system is a function of language use, then it follows that the relative frequency with which particular words or other kinds of symbolic units are encountered by the speaker will affect the nature of the grammar. That is, symbolic units that are more frequently encountered become more entrenched. Accordingly, the most entrenched symbolic units tend to shape the language system in terms of patterns of use, at the expense of less-frequent and thus less-well-entrenched words or constructions. Hence, the mental grammar, while deriving from language use, also influences language use.

A further consequence of the usage-based thesis is that by virtue of the mental grammar reflecting symbolic units that exist in language use, and employing cognitive abilities such as abstraction in order to extract them from usage, the language system exhibits redundancy. That is, redundancy is to be expected in the mental grammar.

As noted earlier, symbolic units are modeled in terms of a network. Redundancy between symbolic units is captured in terms of a hierarchical arrangement of 'schema–instance' relations holding between more schematic and more specific symbolic units. By way of illustration, Figure 4.2 captures the schema–instance relationships that hold between the more abstract [P [NP]] symbolic unit and the more specific instances of this abstract schema, such as [*to me*]. The usage-based thesis predicts that as [P [NP]] is a feature of many (more specific) instances of use, it becomes entrenched in long-term memory along with its more specific instantiations. Moreover, the schema ([P [NP]]) and its instances (e.g., [*to me*]), are stored in related fashion, as illustrated in Figure 4.2.

THE COGNITIVE LINGUISTICS WORLDVIEW

The primary commitments and theses of cognitive linguistics give rise to a specific and distinctive worldview, which has a number of dimensions. Collectively, these give rise to a distinctive cognitive linguistic perspective on (i) the nature of language, (ii) its interaction with non-linguistic aspects

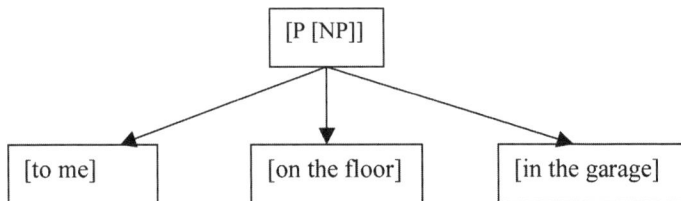

Figure 4.2 Schema–instance relationships.

of cognition, and (iii) the nature of the human mind. In this section I identify five dimensions of the cognitive linguistics worldview and briefly elaborate on these:

- Language reflects the embodied nature of conceptual organization.
- Language is a lens for studying conceptual organization.
- Language provides a mechanism for construal.
- Language can influence aspects of non-linguistic cognition.
- Humans have a common conceptualizing capacity.

Language reflects conceptual organization

Following the thesis of embodied cognition, cognitive linguists view language as reflecting the embodied nature of conceptual structure and organization. Hence, cognitive linguists study language by taking seriously the way language manifests embodied conceptual structure.

An outstanding example of this is the study of 'conceptual metaphor' (e.g., Lakoff & Johnson, 1980, 1999; Lakoff & Turner, 1989). For instance, we use language relating to more abstract domains such as time, in terms of space, as exemplified by the example in (4), or states in terms of locations exemplified in (5), precisely because at the level of conceptual structure time is systematically structured in terms of conceptual structure recruited from the domain of space, and states are structured in terms of locations in space. I consider the issue of conceptual metaphor in more detail later on.

(4) Christmas is *approaching*.
(5) She is *in* love.

Language is a lens on the mind

Second, language serves as a lens for studying aspects of the mind. It does so precisely because it reflects organizational principles of embodied cognition. For instance, by studying metaphorical patterns in language, the cognitive linguist is able to discern patterns in the nature and organization of conceptual structure. Conceptual metaphors, qua cross-domain mappings—mappings that relate distinct conceptual domains—are evidenced by virtue of examining distinctive and productive patterns in language in order to uncover their existence.

Of course, in keeping with the cognitive commitment, linguistic evidence for conceptual structure must be supplemented with *converging evidence* from the other cognitive sciences. Evidence supporting some of the main claims made by conceptual metaphor theory, for instance with respect to time-as-space metaphors, has emerged on the basis of gestural studies (Núñez & Sweetser, 2006), and behavioral experiments (e.g., Boroditsky, 2000; Casasanto & Boroditsky, 2008; Gentner, Imai, & Boroditsky, 2002).

Language provides a mechanism for construal

Third, as language is constituted of a language-specific inventory of symbolic units, following the symbolic thesis, any given language provides a means of viewing the same state, situation, or event from the range of perspectives that are conventionally available to the language user, given the language-specific symbolic resources available. In other words, a language provides the language user with resources for viewing the same scene in multiple, and hence alternative, ways. This constitutes a mechanism for 'construal'. Construal is a technical term for the facility whereby the same situation can be linguistically encoded in multiple ways. For example, someone who is not easily parted from his or her money could be either described as *stingy* or as *thrifty*. In keeping with the thesis of encyclopedic semantics, each of these words is understood with respect to a different background frame or cognitive model, which provides a distinct set of evaluations. While *stingy* represents a negative assessment against an evaluative frame of giving and sharing, *thrifty* relates to a frame of careful management of resources (husbandry), against which it represents a positive assessment. Hence, lexical choice provides a different way of framing ostensibly the same situation, giving rise to a different construal.

Indeed, any given language, by virtue of containing a language-specific set of symbolic units, thereby provides a ready-made language-specific repertoire for construing human experience and the world in, necessarily, different ways. One reason for this is because different languages often encode culture-specific ideas and hence perspectives. For instance, the Korean word *nunchi*, which might be translated as 'eye-measure' in English, provides a conventionalized means of encoding the idea that a host evaluates whether a guest requires further food or drink in order to avoid the guest being embarrassed by having to request it.

Of course, languages provide conventional means of alternate construals even when two similar ideas are both conveyed in two different languages. For instance, both English and French—related genetically and by area—have conventional means of expressing the notion of containment: the preposition *in* for English and *dans* for French. Yet the scene depicted by Figure 4.3, involving a woman walking in the rain, is conventionally construed, in English, as exhibiting a 'containment' relationship as evidenced by (6), but in French as exhibiting an 'under' relationship, as encoded by the French preposition *sous*, evidenced in (7).

(6)   The woman is walking in the rain.
(7)   *La femme marche sous la pluie.*
      The woman walks under the rain.
      'The woman is walking in the rain'

What is remarkable about these examples is how they illustrate the way in

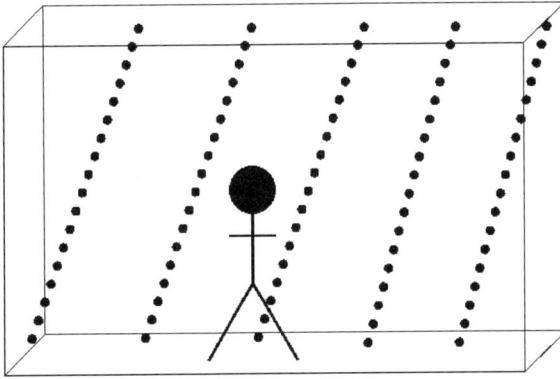

Figure 4.3 The woman walks in the rain.

which two relatively closely related languages conventionally construe a similar, everyday experience in what amounts to quite different ways.

Language influences non-linguistic cognition

The discussion of the English and French utterances in (6) and (7) also helps illustrate the fourth dimension of the cognitive linguistics world-view. As language provides a means of construing reality in alternate ways, and moreover remains connected to conceptual representation, it has a transformative function: It can influence aspects of non-linguistic cognition. That is, language doesn't merely reflect conceptual representation; it can influence and affect it. For instance, as French and English each have conventionalized alternative ways of encoding a particular spatial scene, this leads to what Slobin (e.g., 2003) has labeled differences in 'thinking for speaking': Users of any given language must pay attention to particular aspects of their experienced reality, at the expense of others, in order to package their thoughts for purposes of linguistic communication.

Cognitive linguists hold that this language-specific 'packaging' has profound consequences on non-linguistic cognition. That is, language influences how we categorize aspects of our socio-physical environment, and how we think about reality, independently of language. For example, in experimental work, Lera Boroditsky (2001; Boroditsky, Schmidt, & Phillips, 2003) has found that different ways of construing both time and gender in language influence performance of non-linguistic activities. This view is of course part of a resurgence in work by linguists of various theoretical stripes who are increasingly vocal in advocating a neo-Whorfian perspective on the relationship between language and non-linguistic cognition. Notable exemplars include the work of Stephen Levinson (e.g., 2003) on space, and Athanasopolous (e.g., Thierry, Athanasopoulos, Wiggett, Dering, & Kuipers, 2009) on color perception.

A simple illustration of the way in which language can influence thought comes from an experiment described by Gentner and Gentner (1982), in which they trained different English-speaking participants in 'analogical models' of electricity. An analogical model relies on a relatively well-known scenario or system for understanding a less-well-known system, where the parts and relations of the well-known system stand in a similar relation to those in the less-well-known system, here electricity. Through analogy, participants can reason about electricity using the well-known model.

In the experiment, one group was taught that electricity can be represented as a teeming crowd of people, while another group was taught that electricity can be represented as water flowing through a pipe, as in a hydraulic system. The mappings between these two analogical models and an electrical circuit are summarized in Tables 4.2 and 4.3.

Importantly, each analogical model correctly predicted different aspects of the behavior of an electrical circuit, but was no help with other aspects. For example, a circuit with batteries connected serially will produce more current than a circuit with batteries in parallel. This is predicted by the analogy based on the hydraulic system, where serial pumps one after the

Table 4.2 Hydraulic system model

Hydraulic system	Electric circuit
Pipe	Wire
Pump	Battery
Narrow pipe	Resistor
Water pressure	Voltage
Narrowness of pipe	Resistance
Flow rate of water	Current

Based on Gentner and Gentner 1982, p. 110.

Table 4.3 Moving crowd model

Moving crowd	Electric circuit
Course/passageway	Wire
Crowd	Battery
People	Resistor
Pushing of people	Voltage
Gates	Resistance
Passage rate of people	Current

Based on Gentner and Gentner, 1982, p. 120.

other will produce a greater flow rate of water. In the moving crowd model, where the battery corresponds simply to the crowd, it is difficult to think of a meaningful contrast between a serial and a parallel connection.

Serial resistors in an electrical circuit reduce current, while parallel resistors increase it. The moving crowd model is better at predicting this aspect of the behavior of electricity, where resistance is modeled in terms of gates. Parallel gates allow more people through, while serial gates allow fewer people through.

Gentner and Gentner (1982) hypothesized that if participants used different analogical models to reason about the circuit, then each group should produce dramatically divergent results, which is exactly what they found. Participants who were trained in the hydraulic system model were better at correctly predicting the effect of serial versus parallel batteries on current, while those who were familiar with the moving crowd model were better at predicting the effect of serial versus parallel resistors on current.

This study reveals that different 'choices' of language for representing concepts can indeed affect non-linguistic thought, such as reasoning and problem solving.

A common human conceptualizing capacity

Of course, one of the charges that has been leveled at those who subscribe to a (neo)Whorfian perspective is that this entails that language determines how the world is viewed and categorized. If this view were correct, language would effectively provide a straitjacket, resulting in wholly distinct ways of conceptualization across languages and language users, which would be insurmountable.

However, the cognitive linguistics worldview treats language as but one of the mechanisms whereby humans construct their perceptual, cognitive, and socio-cultural reality. Cognitively modern humans have a common conceptualizing capacity: we share with our conspecifics a similar range of cognitive mechanisms and processes that provide us with multiple ways of construing reality. Language is but one modality, and hence but one way in which we interact with and learn about our environment, our socio-cultural reality, others around us, and ourselves. Cognitive linguists fully recognize that there are myriad ways in which humans experience their environment, including sense-perceptory experience, proprioception, and subjective experiences including affect, the visceral sense, and diverse cognitive evaluations and states. All of these experiences provide a rich basis for a multiplicity of mental representations, providing often complementary and even competing 'views' of reality. From the perspective of cognitive linguistics, semantic structure encoded by language can influence our conceptualizations, and other outputs of cognitive function, such as categorization, for instance. However, language does not determine them.

MODELING LANGUAGE: LANGUAGE AS REFLECTING COGNITION

In this section I examine the way language has been modeled by cognitive linguists in order to exemplify the various commitments, theses, and world-view of cognitive linguistics. I focus on three distinct but related proposals:

- The lexical and grammatical systems approach (Leonard Talmy)
- Cognitive grammar (Ronald Langacker)
- Cognitive construction grammar (Adele Goldberg)

In particular, I show that, in slightly different ways, each of these three approaches reveals how linguistic structure and organization reflects and interacts with aspects of cognition.

The interplay between language and conceptual structure

In this section I consider the nature of the conceptual structure which gets encoded in language. I do so by considering the lexical and grammatical systems approach of Talmy (e.g., 2000). Talmy suggests that language serves to encode and externalize an experiential complex, which he refers to as the 'cognitive representation' (CR). The CR might relate to an objectively verifiable state, concerning some aspect of the world, as in the expression in (8), or it might relate to a cognitive or affective state, such as the expression of unrequited love in (9):

(8)   It is raining in London.
(9)   John is desperate for Susan's love but she hasn't even noticed him.

Talmy holds that language expresses the CR of the language user by means of two distinct subsystems: language is made up of two systems, each of which brings equally important but very different dimensions to the scene that they jointly prompt for. These systems are the 'conceptual structuring (or "grammatical") system' and the 'conceptual content (or "lexical") system'. While the grammatical or conceptual structuring system, as its name suggests, provides the structure, skeleton, or 'scaffolding' for a given scene, the lexical or content system provides the majority of rich substantive detail. It follows from this view that the meaning associated with the grammatical system is highly schematic in nature, while the meaning associated with the lexical system is rich and highly detailed. This distinction is captured in Figure 4.4.

The bifurcation in content externalized by language relates, Talmy contends, to a well-known distinction in the phonological forms that make up the symbolic units of a given language. Open-class forms encode rich aspects of conceptual content, while closed-class forms encode the more

```
┌─────────────────────────────────────┐
│     COGNITIVE REPRESENTATION         │
└─────────────────────────────────────┘
```

┌─────────────────────────────┐   ┌─────────────────────────────┐
│ CONCEPTUAL STRUCTURING   │   │   CONCEPTUAL CONTEXT   │
│   SYSTEM   │   │   SYSTEM   │
│   'GRAMMAR'   │   │   'LEXIS'   │
│   delineates structural   │   │ provides rich contentful detail │
│ properties of a given scene │   │   of a particular scene   │
└─────────────────────────────┘   └─────────────────────────────┘

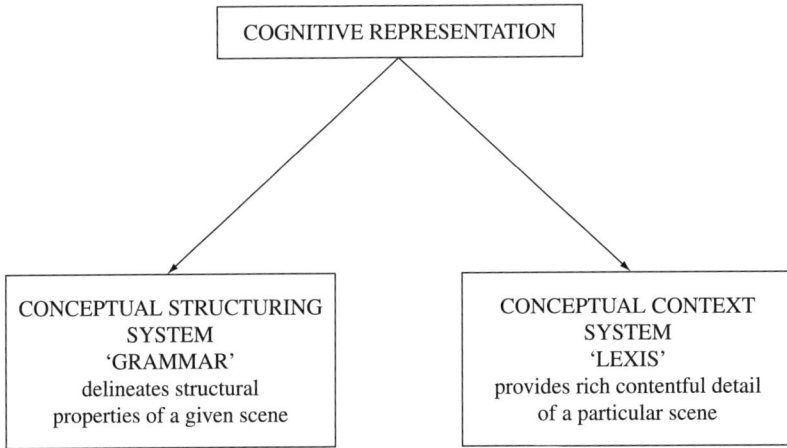

Figure 4.4 The bifurcation in content encoded by the grammatical and lexical systems.

schematic or structural aspects of conceptual content. In other words, closed-class forms relate to the schematic meanings encoded by the grammatical system while open-class forms encode the rich meanings associated with the lexical system. To illustrate, consider (10), in which closed-class forms are highlighted in bold while the open-class forms appear in italics:

(10)   **A** *waiter serv***ed the** *customer***s.**

The lexical system, encoded by open-class forms, relates to things, people, places, events, properties of things, and so on. The grammatical system, encoded by closed-class forms, relates to content having to do with topological aspects of space, time, and number, whether a piece of information is old or new, and whether the speaker is providing information or requesting information, and so on.

In addition to closed-class forms that have an overt phonetic realization —those marked in bold face in (10)—closed-class forms can also be phonetically abstract. A central claim made by Talmy, in keeping with the symbolic thesis, is that even abstract closed-class forms encode (schematic) content. Examples of such forms include lexical classes: e.g., noun, verb; lexical subclasses: e.g., count noun, mass noun; grammatical relations: e.g., subject, object; declarative versus integrative forms, active voice versus passive voice, and clause-level symbolic units such as the ditransitive construction, and so forth.

Tables 4.4 and 4.5 present a Talmy-style analysis for the example in (10) in order to illustrate the distinction in terms of schematic versus rich content encoded by closed-class versus open-class forms.

While the contribution of both the lexical and grammatical systems is

Table 4.4 Schematic content encoded by closed-class forms

Closed-class vehicles	Schematic semantic content
a	Introduces a referent which the hearer is held to be unable to readily identify (from context or preceding discourse)
a	Designates a unitary instantiation of the referent
the	Introduces a referent which the hearer is held to be able to readily identify (from context or preceding discourse)
-s	Designates multiple instantiations of a referent
-er	Designates performer of a particular action or activity
Lexical class: verb (for *serve*)	Designates entity as an event (as one possibility)
Lexical class: noun (for *waiter/customer*)	Designates entity as an object (as one possibility)
Grammatical relation: subject (for *waiter*)	Designates entity as being the primary or focal entity in a designated relationship
Grammatical relation: object (for *customers*)	Designates entity as less important or secondary entity in a designated relationship
Active voice (through verb form)	Designates point of view being situated at the agent
Declarative word order	Speaker knows the situation to be true and asserts it to the hearer

Table 4.5 Rich content encoded by open-class forms

Open-class vehicles	Rich semantic content
Waiter	Person with a particular function, and sometimes appearance, who works in a particular setting
Serve	Particular mode of activity involving two or more people and, typically, an entity with which one of the participants is provided by the other
Customer	Person who is provided with a particular object or service (of various sorts) in exchange for, typically, money

essential to encoding the CR, in his research Talmy primarily focuses on the nature of the conceptual content that gets encoded by the grammatical system. He does this for at least two reasons. First, as the content encoded by the grammatical system is structural and hence schematic in nature, it provides a set of schematic semantic content which is potentially finite in nature. In terms of practicality then, the content associated with the grammatical system can, in principle, be fully described. As the lexical system relates to rich content, it is less clear that the range of meanings encoded are finite. Hence, they are not susceptible to a complete description. On grounds of practicality then, it makes sense to target the schematic content associated with the grammatical system.

Second, as the schematic content encoded by closed-class forms is finite, it provides an inventory of meanings upon which all languages are likely to draw. Indeed, even for prepositions, which have a large number of distinct senses associated with them, we cannot create new meanings as effortlessly as new meanings can be created for open-class forms such as nouns. There are constraints that apply to the range of meanings that are and can be associated with closed-class forms such as prepositions (see Tyler & Evans, 2001). This is due to the nature and quality of the meaning encoded by closed-class forms (see Evans, 2009). As such, the study of the nature of the schematic meanings encoded by the grammatical system is likely to reveal details as to which aspects of conceptual content are foundational in terms of facilitating a structuring function cross-linguistically.

Talmy proposes that the grammatical system is arranged in terms of a limited number of large-scale 'schematic systems' (Talmy, 2000). These provide the basic organization of the CR, upon which the rich content encoded by open-class elements can be organized and supported. Various schematic systems collaborate to structure a scene that is expressed via language. Each schematic system contributes different structural aspects of the scene, resulting in the overall delineation of the scene's skeletal framework. In his work, Talmy has primarily elucidated four schematic systems, although he acknowledges there are likely to be others. These are given in Figure 4.5.

Schematic systems can be further divided into 'schematic categories'. By way of illustration, I elucidate one schematic category from one schematic system: The configurational system. This schematic system structures the temporal and spatial properties associated with an experiential complex, such as the division of a given scene into parts and participants. Consider the schematic category which Talmy identifies as 'degree of extension'. 'Degree of extension' relates to the degree to which matter (space) or action (time) is extended. The schematic category 'degree of extension' has three values: a point, a bounded extent, or an unbounded extent.

To make this clear, consider the examples in (11) to (13). These employ closed-class elements in order to specify the degree of extension involved.

(11) Point $at + NP_{\text{point-of-time}}$
     The train passed through at [noon]
(12) Bounded extent $in + NP_{\text{extent-of-time}}$
     She went through the training circuit in [five minutes flat]

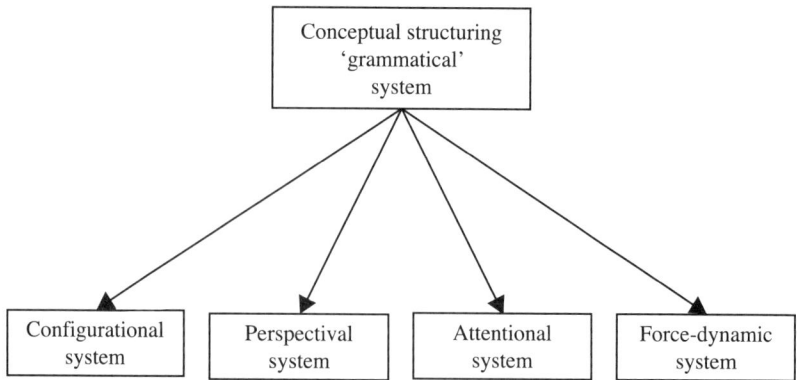

Figure 4.5 The schematic systems identified by Talmy (2000).

(13)   Unbounded extent   '*keep -ing*' + '*-er and -er*'
       The plane kept going higher and higher

As these examples illustrate, some closed-class elements encode a particular degree of extension. For instance, in (11) the preposition *at*, together with an NP that encodes a temporal point, encodes a point-like degree of extension. The NP does not achieve this meaning by itself: If we substitute a different preposition for instance, a construction containing the same NP *noon* can encode a bounded extent (e.g., *The train arrives between noon and 1 pm*). The punctual nature of the temporal experience in example (11) forms part of the grammatical system, and is conveyed in this example by closed-class forms. The nature of the punctual event—that is, the passage of a train through a station rather than, say, the flight of a flock of birds overhead—relates to content drawn from the lexical system, e.g., the selection of the form *train* versus *birds*.

In the example in (12), the preposition *in*, together with an NP that encodes a bounded extent encodes a bounded degree of extension. In (13) the closed-class elements *keep -ing + -er and -er* encode an unbounded degree of extension. This closed-class construction provides a grammatical 'skeleton' specialized for encoding a particular value within the schematic category 'degree of extension'. The lexical system can add dramatically different content meaning to this frame (e.g., *keep singing louder and louder*; *keep swimming faster and faster*; *keep getting weaker and weaker*), but the schematic meaning contributed by the structuring system remains constant —in all these examples, time has an unbounded degree of extension.

The interplay between language and cognitive mechanisms

In this section I briefly consider the way in which cognitive linguistics views language structure and organization as an outcome of generalized conceptual mechanisms. In so doing, I draw on the seminal work of Langacker (1987, 1991a, 1991b, 1999, 2008), as exemplified in his theory of cognitive grammar.

In his work, Langacker has developed a model of language which treats linguistic structure and organization as reflecting general cognitive organizational principles. In particular, mechanisms relating to cognitive aspects of attention are claimed to underpin the organization of linguistic structure. Langacker defines attention as being 'intrinsically associated with the intensity or energy level of cognitive processes, which translates experientially into greater prominence or salience' (1987, p. 115). I briefly consider two theoretical constructs posited in cognitive grammar which are held to be central to attention in general and which also show up in linguistic organization. These are the notions of 'profile–base organization' and 'trajector–landmark organization'.

Profile–base organization

Profile–base organization has to do with the semantic pole of a symbolic unit. It assumes that word meaning, for instance, involves focusing attentional resources on one aspect of a particular structure, such that a particular facet is highlighted or profiled. For instance, consider the symbolic unit *hypotenuse*, employed by Langacker to make this idea clear. This lexical item designates a substructure—the longest side in a right-angled triangle—but does so with respect to a larger structure—the right-angled triangle, as illustrated in Figure 4.6.

In Figure 4.6 the longest side, labeled A, is the subpart of the larger structure designated, and thus constitutes the profile. The entire triangle, involving sides A-B-C constitutes the base, the entity with respect to which the profile receives special prominence. Profile–base organization is thus a feature of linguistic semantics, but it reflects a deeper cognitive impulse, namely the selection of a particular substructure for attentional prominence against some larger structure.

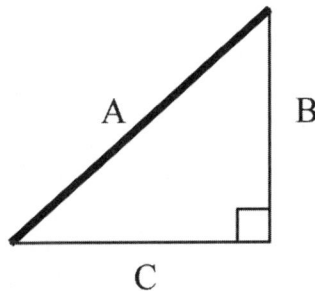

Figure 4.6 Profile–base organization for *hypotenuse*.

Trajector–landmark organization

The second theoretical construct, trajector–landmark organization, is motivated by a related attentional phenomenon concerning the relative prominence assigned to entities involved in a relationship of some sort. For instance, in events involving energy transfer, what Langacker refers to as an 'action chain' (e.g., *John started the ball rolling*) one participant typically transfers energy to another entity, thereby affecting it. As such, the affecting participant is more salient.

Langacker maintains that the assignment of relative prominence to entities at the perceptual and cognitive levels is also a fundamental design feature of language. Indeed, he claims that it shows up at the level of the word, phrase, and clause, and is therefore fundamental for constituency, and hence the ability of symbolic units to be combined with one another in order to form larger units. To illustrate this idea, consider the distinction between the following two utterances:

> (14)   John ate all the pizza.
> (15)   All the pizza was eaten by John.

These utterances relate to an action chain in which some activity, namely eating, is performed by John on the pizza so that there is no pizza left. Yet each utterance assigns differential relative prominence to the participants in this action chain, namely *John* and *pizza*. In English, and in language in general, the first participant slot in an utterance, commonly referred to as the subject position, is reserved for participants that are most prominent. The participant in a profiled relationship that receives greatest prominence, what Langacker terms *focal prominence*, is referred to as the *trajector* (TR). The participant that receives lesser prominence, referred to as secondary prominence, is termed the *landmark* (LM). The distinction, then, in the utterances above is that in (14) *John* corresponds to the TR and *pizza* to the LM, while in (15) *pizza* corresponds to the TR and *John* to the LM. This distinction is captured by Figure 4.7. The distinction between TR and LM approximates the more traditional distinction between subject and object. The advantage is that it provides a conceptual basis for the distinction.

The diagrams in Figure 4.7 reveal the following. While the transfer of energy is still the same across the two utterances, as indicated by the direction of the arrows, the participants are assigned differential prominence across the two utterances. Put another way, the active and passive constructions, as exemplified by the two utterances, in fact encode a distinction in terms of the focal prominence associated with the two participants involved in the relationship being conveyed. This distinction, which is central to the way language encodes the relationship between agents and patients, in fact reflects a more general cognitive mechanism:

TR   LM

JOHN   PIZZA
John ate all the pizza

LM   TR

JOHN   PIZZA
All the pizza was eaten by John

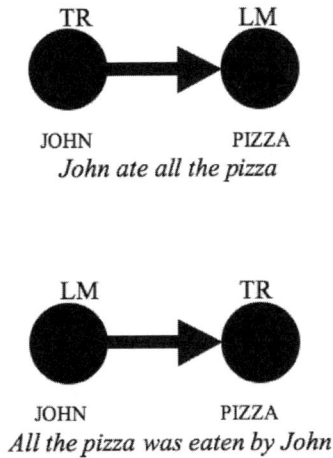

Figure 4.7 The distinction between TR–LM alignment across agent–patient reversal.

distinguishing between the relative prominence paid and assigned to participants in an action chain.

The interplay between language and embodied experience

In this section I consider the way in which cognitive linguistics views language organization as reflecting embodied experience, in the sense defined above. I do so by considering the theory of cognitive construction grammar developed in the work of Adele Goldberg (e.g., 1995, 2006).

In her work, Goldberg has studied sentence-level symbolic units, what she refers to as constructions. In keeping with the symbolic thesis, Goldberg claims that sentences are themselves motivated by sentence-level symbolic units, consisting of a schematic meaning and a schematic form. For instance, consider the following example:

(16)   John gave Mary the flowers.

Goldberg argues that a sentence such as (16) is motivated by the ditransitive construction. This is essentially a symbolic unit that has the schematic meaning: X CAUSES Y TO RECEIVE Z, and the form: Subj Verb NP1 NP2. As with many other symbolic units associated with the grammatical system (in the sense of Talmy), the ditransitive construction is phonetically implicit. That is, its form consists of a syntactic template which is not lexically filled, but which stipulates the nature and range of the lexical constituents that can be fused with it (see Goldberg, 1995, for discussion and evidence for positing sentence-level constructions; see also Goldberg, 2006, and Evans, 2009).

A crucial question for Goldberg concerns what motivates the semantics and the form of such sentence-level constructions. That is, what motivates such constructions to emerge in the first place? In keeping with the thesis of embodied cognition, she posits what she terms the 'scene encoding hypothesis'. According to this hypothesis, sentence-level constructions emerge from humanly relevant scenes that are highly recurrent and salient in nature. For instance, on many occasions each day we experience acts of transfer. Such acts involve three participants: The agent who effects the transfer, the recipient of the act of the transfer, and the entity trans-ferred. In addition, such acts involve a means of transfer. Goldberg holds that the sentence-level construction is motivated by the human need to communicate about this highly salient scene. Indeed, the semantics and the form associated with this construction are uniquely tailored to encoding such humanly relevant scenes. In this way, grammatical organization, Goldberg suggests, reflects fundamental aspects of human embodied experience.

The construction grammar perspective has also been applied cross-linguistically in the work of William Croft (e.g., 2002). Indeed, based on a wide range of typologically diverse languages, Croft argues that con-struction grammar provides the most appropriate means of modeling languages from a typological perspective.

MODELING CONCEPTUAL STRUCTURE: LANGUAGE AS LENS

The human conceptual system is not open to direct investigation. Never-theless, cognitive linguists maintain that the properties of language allow us to reconstruct the properties of the conceptual system, and to build a model of that system. The logic of this claim is as follows. As language structure and organization, as revealed in the previous section, reflect various known aspects of cognitive structure, by studying language, which is observable, we thereby gain insight into the nature of the con-ceptual system. The subbranch of cognitive linguistics concerned with employing language as a lens, in order to study otherwise hidden aspects of conceptual structure, is often referred to as cognitive semantics.

One of the earliest, and perhaps best-known, cognitive semantic theor-ies is conceptual metaphor theory, developed by Lakoff and Johnson (1980, 1999). The central insight of this approach is that figurative patterns in language reflect underlying, highly stable associations, known as *map-pings*, which hold between domains in the conceptual system. Sets of mappings holding between two distinct conceptual domains are referred to as conceptual metaphors, which is what gives the theory its name. For instance, one particularly common way in which we talk and think about a love relationship is in terms of journeys. To illustrate, consider the following everyday expressions, drawn from Lakoff and Johnson (1980), which we might use to describe aspects of a love relationship:

(17)   a. Look *how far* we've *come.*
       b. We're at *a crossroads.*
       c. We'll just have to *go our separate ways.*
       d. We can't *turn back* now.
       e. I don't think this relationship is *going anywhere.*
       f. This relationship is *a dead-end street.*
       g. Our marriage is *on the rocks.*
       h. This relationship *is foundering.*

According to Lakoff and Johnson, utterances such as these are motivated by an entrenched pattern in our conceptual system: A conceptual metaphor. The conceptual metaphor can be stated as LOVE IS A JOURNEY. This conceptual metaphor is made up of a fixed set of established mappings which structure concepts that are located in the more abstract domain of LOVE, in terms of concepts belonging to the more concrete domain of JOURNEY. For instance, in the domain of LOVE we have concepts for lovers, the love relationship, events that take place in the love relationship, difficulties that take place in the relationship, progress we make in resolving these difficulties, and in developing the relationship, choices about what to do in the relationship, such as moving in together, whether to split up, and so on, and the shared and separate goals we might have for ourselves in the relationship, and for the relationship itself. Similarly, we represent a range of concepts relating to the domain of JOURNEYS. These include concepts for the travelers, the vehicle used for the journey, plane, train, or automobile, the distance covered, obstacles encountered, such as traffic jams, that lead to delays and hence impediments to the progress of the journey, our decisions about the direction and the route to be taken, and our knowledge about destinations.

The conceptual metaphor, LOVE IS A JOURNEY, provides a means of systematically mapping these knowledge slots from the domain of JOURNEY onto corresponding slots in the domain of LOVE. This means that slots in the LOVE domain are structured *in terms of* knowledge from the domain of JOURNEY. For instance, the lovers in the domain of LOVE are structured in terms of travelers such that we understand lovers in terms of travelers. Similarly, the love relationship itself is structured in terms of the vehicle used on the journey. For this reason we can talk about marriage *foundering, being on the rocks,* or *stuck in a rut* and understand expressions such as these as relating, not literally to a journey, but rather to two people in a long-term love relationship that is troubled in some way. In other words, we must have knowledge of the sort specified by the conceptual metaphor stored in our heads if we are to be able to understand these English expressions: to understand lovers in terms of travelers, and the relationship in terms of the vehicles, and so on. The linguistic expressions provide compelling evidence for the conceptual metaphors. The mappings implicated by the linguistic evidence are given in Table 4.6.

In essence, the claim at the heart of conceptual metaphor theory is that the mappings, which lie at the level of conceptual structure, are revealed by evidence from language, as exemplified by the sentences in (17) for instance. Language can thus be employed as a key methodological tool for revealing conceptual patterns that underlie language use.

MEANING CONSTRUCTION: THE INTERACTION BETWEEN LANGUAGE AND COGNITION

In this section I consider the way in which cognitive linguistics has modeled the contribution of language to meaning construction. The essential insight is that language provides relatively impoverished prompts for the construction of meaning. These linguistic prompts interface with non-linguistic conceptual mechanisms specialized for the construction of meaning, and with non-linguistic knowledge representation. In other words, cognitive linguists take the view that meaning construction involves an interaction between language on the one hand, and cognitive mechanisms and representations on the other.

In the remainder of this section I explore two distinct, albeit related, cognitive semantic approaches to meaning construction. The first approach relates to what I earlier referred to as the backstage cognition perspective, associated with the scholarship of Gilles Fauconnier, and Mark Turner. Fauconnier (1985/1994, 1997), and Fauconnier and Turner (2002) have shown that much of the complexity and some of the most interesting aspects of meaning construction involving language occur

Table 4.6 Mappings for LOVE IS A JOURNEY

Source domain: *JOURNEY*	*Mappings*	Target domain: *LOVE*
TRAVELERS	→	LOVERS
VEHICLE	→	LOVE RELATIONSHIP
JOURNEY	→	EVENTS IN THE RELATIONSHIP
DISTANCE COVERED	→	PROGRESS MADE
OBSTACLES ENCOUNTERED	→	DIFFICULTIES EXPERIENCED
DECISIONS ABOUT DIRECTION	→	CHOICES ABOUT WHAT TO DO
DESTINATION OF THE JOURNEY	→	GOALS OF THE RELATIONSHIP

behind the scenes. That is, meaning construction predominantly involves a battery of conceptual mechanisms that serve to integrate hugely complex assemblies of knowledge. Accordingly, language provides relatively impoverished prompts which are hence but the tip of the iceberg.

A related, and more recent approach, developed by V. Evans (e.g., 2006, 2009) takes what I have referred to as the front-stage cognition perspective. While this approach also assumes that language provides relatively impoverished prompts for backstage processes of meaning construction, Evans maintains that there is nevertheless significant complexity associated with these linguistic prompts. Evans proceeds by studying the nature of this complexity and the way in which linguistic prompts interface with 'backstage' aspects of knowledge representation inhering in the conceptual system.

Mental spaces and conceptual integration

The backstage cognition perspective involves two distinct, although closely related, theoretical proposals. The first, mental spaces theory, was developed in two book-length treatments by Gilles Fauconnier (1985/1994, 1997). The second, which builds on mental spaces theory is termed conceptual integration theory, and develops the mechanisms referred to as 'blending'. This latter theory, and the mechanism of blending, are developed in a (2002) book-length treatment by the architects of the theory: Gilles Fauconnier and Mark Turner.

The backstage cognition perspective holds that, when we think and talk, humans assemble what are referred to as mental spaces, briefly introduced earlier. These are 'packets' of conceptual material, assembled 'on the fly' for local purposes of language understanding and conceptual processing. Moreover, material from these mental spaces qua conceptual packets, can be selectively projected in order to form a hybrid mental space drawn from a number of so-called input mental spaces. This hybrid mental space is referred to as a 'blended space', also known as a 'blend'.

In order to briefly illustrate the process of mental space formation and blending consider the following joke:

(18)   Q. What do you get if you cross a kangaroo with an elephant?
       A. Holes all over Australia!

The backstage cognition perspective holds that in order to understand and hence 'get' the joke, we have to perform conceptual integration across mental spaces and thus construct a blend. While we have complex bodies of knowledge available to us concerning elephants and kangaroos, including their size, means of locomotion, and their geographical region of abode, all of which gets diffusely activated by the question, the punch-line prompts us to selectively project only specific aspects of our knowledge relating to elephants and kangaroos, in order to build a blended space. In the blend we integrate information relating to the abode and manner of locomotion associated with kangaroos, with the size of elephants. The hybrid organism we come up with, that exists only in the blend, which is to say 'in' our heads, has the size of an elephant, lives in Australia, and gets about by hopping. Such an organism would surely leave holes all over Australia. The joke is possible (and possibly funny) only because the operation of blending is a fundamental aspect of how we think. Moreover, blending is revealed by language use; linguistically mediated meaning construction relies upon it.

In essence, then, the backstage cognition perspective is concerned with the mechanisms of mental space construction and blending, processes that are primarily conceptual in nature.

LCCM theory

The front-stage cognition perspective developed in Evans (2006, 2009) is embodied in the theory of lexical concepts and cognitive models (LCCM theory). LCCM theory was developed in order to account for variation in word meanings across contexts of use, although it has been applied to a wider range of linguistic semantic phenomena including metaphor and metonymy.

The main premise of the theory is that there is a distinction in the nature of the semantic representations that populate the linguistic and conceptual systems. The semantic representational format of the linguistic system is modeled in terms of the theoretical construct of the lexical concept, while the semantic representational format of the conceptual system is modeled in terms of the construct of the cognitive model—notions that give LCCM theory its name. A cognitive model is a composite multimodal knowledge structure grounded in the range of experience types processed by the brain, including sensory-motor experience, proprioception, and subjective experience. In contrast, a lexical concept—the semantic pole of a symbolic unit—consists of a bundle of different types of schematic knowledge encoded in a format that can be directly represented in the time-pressured auditory–manual medium that is manifested by the world's spoken and signed natural languages.

In LCCM theory, although linguistic representations are schematic in nature they nevertheless exhibit significant complexity. For instance, lexical concepts encode what are referred to as 'parameters': digitized dimensions abstracted from across rich perceptual experience. Building on insights developed by Talmy (e.g., 2000), Evans claims that one aspect of the schematic nature of content encoded by lexical concepts is that they provide topological rather than Euclidean reference. That is, linguistic content encodes schematic aspects of sensory-motor, proprioceptive, and subjective experience, while conceptual content, to which open-class lexical concepts facilitate access, relates to precise, metric distinctions.

To illustrate consider the closed-class lexical concepts associated with the demonstrative forms *this* and *that*. These lexical concepts encode a distinction between an entity construed as proximal to the speaker, glossed as [THIS], versus an entity construed as distal, glossed as [THAT]. Consider (19):

(19)   Sit on this chair not that one!

In this utterance, the chair that the addressee is being asked to sit on is the one closer to the speaker: 'this chair' as opposed to 'that one'. Nevertheless, the distinction between [THIS] versus [THAT] does not rely on precise metric details such as the exact distance from the speaker, in terms of meters, centimeters, and millimeters. After all, it is immaterial how far the chairs are from the speaker (within reason), as long as one is closer to the speaker than the other. In other words, closed-class lexical concepts are 'magnitude neutral', where magnitude has to do with metric properties relating to distance. This is what it means to say that closed-class lexical concepts provide topological reference. In contrast, the open-class lexical concepts facilitate access to conceptual content, and hence can be employed to express metric details of distance giving rise to Euclidean reference, as illustrated by (20):

(20)   Sit on the chair 2.54 meters away from me!

The expression '2.54 meters' involves open-class lexical concepts rather than closed-class lexical concepts, and serves to evoke the chair precisely.

One of the distinctive aspects of LCCM theory is that it proposes specific mechanisms that facilitate the interaction of linguistic and conceptual representations belonging to two distinct representational systems in service of meaning construction. While I do not present an overview of the compositional mechanisms involved here (for that see Evans, 2009), I present below an informal illustration of the way in which lexical concepts interface with cognitive models in providing an utterance-level simulation.

Consider the following four utterances:

(21)   a. France is a country of outstanding natural beauty.
       b. France is one of the leading nations in the European Union.
       c. France beat New Zealand in the 2007 Rugby World Cup.
       d. France voted against the EU constitution in the 2005 referendum.

In each of these examples the semantic contribution associated with the form *France* is slightly distinct. That is, the semantic contribution provided by *France* varies across these distinct utterances. The key insight of LCCM theory is that the reason for this variation is due to differential activation of non-linguistic knowledge structures, the cognitive models, to which the lexical concept associated with *France* affords access. The linguistic and non-linguistic processes that give rise to this differential activation, which relate, in part, to the differences in the four linguistic contexts in which *France* is embedded, are highly complex. LCCM theory represents a pro- grammatic attempt to identify the sorts of mechanisms involved in this activation process.

The meaning associated with *France* in each of these examples concerns France as a geographical landmass in (21a), France as a political entity, a nation state, in (21b), the 15 players who make up the French Rugby team in (21c), and in (21d) that proportion of the French electorate who voted *non* when presented, in a 2005 referendum, with the proposal to endorse a constitution for the European Union.

In order to provide these distinct interpretations, LCCM posits that the lexical concept glossed as [FRANCE], facilitates access to a wide range of cognitive models, its 'cognitive model profile'. This, in informal terms, provides a semantic potential, part of which can be activated by a given linguistic (or extra-linguistic context). In each of the examples in (21), the different reading for France arises precisely because a different aspect of the cognitive model profile accessed via the lexical concept [FRANCE] is activated. Put another way, the lexical concept [FRANCE] provides an 'access site' for a cognitive model profile that, at the very least, includes the cognitive models indicated in Figure 4.8.

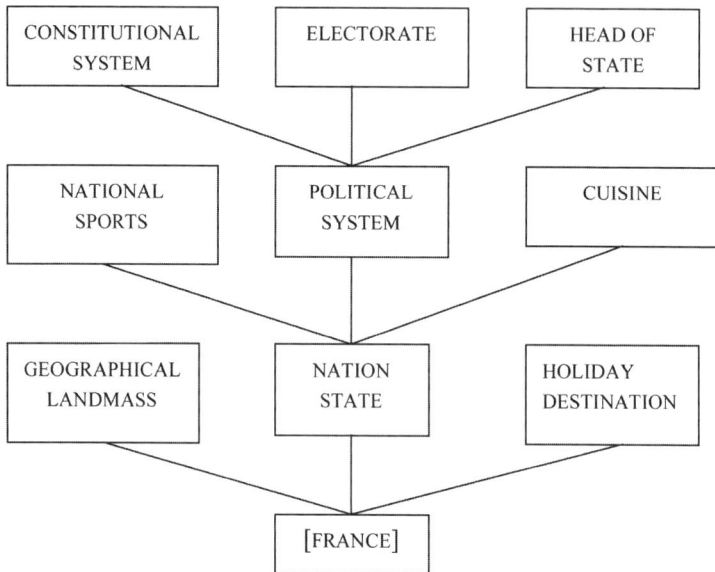

Figure 4.8 Partial cognitive model profile for [FRANCE].

Figure 4.8 captures the sort of knowledge that language users must have access to when speaking and thinking about France. In Figure 4.8 the lexical concept [FRANCE] provides access to a potentially large number of cognitive models. As each cognitive model consists of a complex and structured body of knowledge which provides access to other sorts of knowledge, LCCM theory distinguishes between cognitive models which are directly accessed via the lexical concept—'primary cognitive models'—and those cognitive models which form substructures of those that are directly accessed—'secondary cognitive models'. These secondary cognitive models are indirectly accessed via the lexical concept.

The lexical concept [FRANCE] affords access to a number of primary cognitive models. These include: GEOGRAPHICAL LANDMASS, NATION STATE, and HOLIDAY DESTINATION. Each of these cognitive models provides access to further cognitive models. In Figure 4.8 a flavor of this is given by virtue of the various secondary cognitive models which are accessed via the NATION STATE cognitive model. These include NATIONAL SPORTS, POLITICAL SYSTEM, and CUISINE. For instance we may know that, in France, the French engage in national sports of particular types, such as football, rugby, athletics, and so on, rather than others: the French don't typically engage in American football, ice hockey, cricket, and so on. We may also know that as a sporting nation they take part in international sports competitions of various kinds, including the FIFA football world cup, the Six Nations rugby competition, the rugby world cup, the Olympics, and so on. That is, we may have access to a large body of knowledge concerning the sorts of sports French people engage in. We may also have some knowledge of the funding structures and social and economic conditions and constraints that apply to these sports in France, France's international standing with respect to these particular sports, and further knowledge about the sports themselves including the rules that govern their practice, and so on. This knowledge is derived from a large number of sources including direct experience and through cultural transmission.

With respect to the secondary cognitive model of POLITICAL SYSTEM, Figure 4.8 illustrates a sample of further secondary cognitive models which are accessed via this cognitive model. In other words, each secondary cognitive model has further (secondary) cognitive models to which it provides access. For instance, (FRENCH) ELECTORATE is a cognitive model accessed via the cognitive model (FRENCH) POLITICAL SYSTEM. In turn the cognitive model (FRENCH) POLITICAL SYSTEM is accessed via the cognitive model NATION STATE. Accordingly, NATION STATE is a primary cognitive model while ELECTORATE and POLITICAL SYSTEM are secondary cognitive models.

In view of all this, LCCM theory accounts for differential interpretations associated with *France* in (21) as follows. In (21a) the interpretation associated with the form *France*, which relates to a particular geographical region, derives from activation of the GEOGRAPHICAL LANDMASS cognitive model. That is, individual language users have knowledge relating to the physical aspects of France, including its terrain and its geographical location. In this example, the utterance context serves to activate this part of the cognitive model profile accessed by the lexical concept [FRANCE]. In the second example, the utterance context serves to activate a different part of the cognitive model profile to which the lexical concept [FRANCE] affords access. In this example, the reading for *France* relates to the cognitive model of France as a political entity. This is due to activation of the NATION STATE cognitive model. In example (21c) the use of *France* relates to the group of 15 French individuals who play as a team and thereby represent the French nation on the rugby field. Hence, it is the NATIONAL SPORTS cognitive model which is activated. In the example in (21d) the form *France* relates not to a geographical landmass, nor a political entity, a nation state, nor to a group of 15 rugby players who happen to be representing the entire population of France. Rather, it relates to that portion of the French electorate that voted against ratification of the EU constitution in a referendum held in 2005. Accordingly, what is activated here is the ELECTORATE cognitive model.

In essence, LCCM theory treats semantic variation in word meaning as a function of interaction between linguistic and conceptual content. The distinctive semantic contribution of a particular word in any given context of use results from the differential activation of the encyclopedic multimodal knowledge structures to which words facilitate access.

CONCLUSION: IMPLICATIONS FOR RESEARCH ON BILINGUAL COGNITION

Research conducted by scholars investigating bilingualism has, among other things, been concerned with modeling how the bilingual mind stores and processes distinct linguistic systems and the way in which the distinct linguistic systems interface with conceptual structure. For instance, one issue concerns whether bilingual cognition deploys a single unified set of conceptual representations, or whether two distinct linguistic systems require distinct sets of conceptual structures. A related issue concerns distinctions that may (or may not) arise in the mind of the bilingual versus the monolingual speaker. That is, does representing more than one linguistic system in the mind have consequences for other aspects of cognitive function and processing?

While cognitive linguistics has not directly explored such issues, the cognitive linguistics enterprise proffers researchers on bilingual cognition fresh perspectives and, perhaps importantly, a rich set of cognitively realistic analytical frameworks with which to better address some of the key issues in bilingual cognition research. In particular, cognitive linguistics provides the bilingual researcher with theories of language structure, conceptual structure, and the relationship between the two that take seriously psychological plausibility, and hence are more cognitively realistic than many previous models of language structure and processing. Moreover, cognitive linguistics specifies and clarifies the relationship between language and conceptual structure in terms of the relative contribution of each. Accordingly, it sheds light on how language and non-linguistic cognition interface, in terms of both meaning construction and linguistically mediated communication. As such, cognitive linguistics provides a rich and diverse set of findings, theoretical frameworks, and methodologies which can potentially serve the bilingual researcher in investigating a number of the key empirical concerns that are central to a better understanding of bilingual cognition.

There are at least three specific areas of research in bilingual cognition for which recent research in cognitive linguistics is likely to have implications. These are the following:

1   the nature of linguistic representation in the bilingual mind,
2   the nature of conceptual structure in the bilingual mind, and
3   the influence of different linguistic codes on cognitive structure and function in the bilingual mind

In terms of the first issue, bilingualism researchers are 'generally agreed now that the languages of the bilingual child are represented [in the mind] in underlyingly different ways' (Genesee, 2001, p. 158). They develop as autonomous systems. The recent models of linguistic organization that emerge from cognitive linguistics developed by scholars such as Langacker, Goldberg, and others reveal why this must be so. A language consists of a vast inventory of constructions, language-specific form–meaning pairings. Moreover, infants do not come with an inbuilt prespecification for language in the Chomskyan sense. Rather, language acquisition is a dynamic usage-based process, which is constructed in an item-based way. To be sure, humans have impressive schematization and abstraction skills, and this facilitates the development of rules, of a grammar. But the rules of grammar emerge from use rather than being prewired in the first place (Langacker, 2008; Tomasello, 2003, 2008). This constructional usage-based view provides a fresh perspective for scrutinizing the findings arising from research on language organization and development in the bilingual mind. Moreover, as the acquisition of constructions is usage based, this may go some way to shedding light on the well-known finding that bilingual children are adept at using expressions from both their L1 and L2 in language-specific ways and contexts, and, moreover, address their carer in the appropriate language from early in infancy (see Baker, 2006, for review).

In terms of the second issue, the nature of conceptual structure in the bilingual mind, it has often been observed that bilinguals are adept at 'translating' ideas between languages. An influential account relates to the work of Cummins (e.g., 1981) who advocates a common underlying proficiency model for the bilingual L1 and L2. Recent work on the nature of conceptual structure in cognitive linguistics and the way it interfaces with linguistic representation provides a fresh perspective on this particular issue. Some aspects of knowledge representation are likely to be universal (or at least nearly universal), such as primary metaphors (Grady, 1997; Lakoff & Johnson, 1999), while others are likely to be culture specific. The nature and organization of the meaning construction processes that draw upon conceptual structure, such as the mechanisms of conceptual integration (Fauconnier & Turner, 2002) are likely to be universal. In contrast, the way in which specific languages interface with conceptual structure is likely to be language specific (Evans, 2009). Hence, some aspects of conceptual structure and conceptualization in the bilingual mind may underpin both L1 and L2 while other aspects may be specific to the requirements of each language. In any case, this is an area of investigation which is likely to be enriched by an awareness of ideas from cognitive linguistics.

Finally, the worldview provided by cognitive linguistics bears on the issue of the nature of the influence exerted by language on non-linguistic cognition. This is an issue that is particularly relevant for research in bilingual cognition as, if language does indeed influence non-linguistic aspects of conceptual structure and function, then it remains to be established what the influence is in the case of the bilingual mind where there are two languages at play. Cognitive linguists contend both that language provides a mechanism for construal, and that language can influence aspects of non-linguistic cognition. The various findings provided by cognitive linguists will insightfully inform ongoing and future research in bilingual cognition.

REFERENCES

Baker, C. (2006). *Foundations of bilingual education and bilingualism*. Bristol, UK: Multilingual Matters.

Barsalou, L. (2008). Grounded cognition. *Annual Review of Psychology, 59,* 617–645.

Boroditsky, L. (2000). Metaphoric structuring: Understanding time through spatial metaphors. *Cognition, 75*(1), 1–28.

Boroditsky, L. (2001). Does language shape thought? English and Mandarin speakers' conceptions of time. *Cognitive Psychology, 43*(1), 1–22.

Boroditsky, L., Schmidt, L., & Phillips, W. (2003). Sex, syntax, and semantics. In D. Gentner & S. Goldin-Meadow (Eds.), *Language in mind: Advances in the study of language and cognition* (pp. 61–79). Cambridge, MA: MIT Press.

Cann, R. (1993). *Formal semantics*. Cambridge, UK: Cambridge University Press.

Casasanto, D. (2009). Embodiment of abstract concepts: Good and bad in right- and left-handers. *Journal of Experimental Psychology: General, 138*(3), 351–367.

Casasanto, D., & Boroditsky, L. (2008). Time in the mind: Using space to think about time. *Cognition, 106,* 579–593.

Chomsky, N. (1965). *Aspects of the theory of syntax*. Cambridge, MA: MIT Press.

Chomsky, N. (1981). *Lectures on government and binding*. Dordrecht: Foris.

Chomsky, N. (1995). *The minimalist program*. Cambridge, MA: MIT Press.

Croft, W. (1998). Mental representations. *Cognitive Linguistics, 9*(2), 151–174.

Croft, W. (2002). *Radical construction grammar: Syntactic theory in typological perspective*. Oxford, UK: Oxford University Press.

Cummins, J. (1981). The role of primary language development in promoting educational success for language minority students. In California State Department of Education (Ed.), *Schooling and language minority students: A theoretical framework* (pp. 3–49). Los Angeles: Evaluation, Dissemination and Assessment Center California State University.

Evans, V. (2004). *The structure of time. Language, meaning and temporal cognition*. Amsterdam: John Benjamins.

Evans, V. (2006). Lexical concepts, cognitive models and meaning-construction. *Cognitive Linguistics, 17*(4), 491–534.

Evans, V. (2007). *A glossary of cognitive linguistics*. Edinburgh, UK: Edinburgh University Press.

Evans, V. (2009). *How words mean*. Oxford, UK: Oxford University Press.

Evans, V., Bergen, B. K., & Zinken, J. (2007). *The cognitive linguistics reader*. London: Equinox.

Evans, V., & Green, M. (2006). *Cognitive linguistics: An introduction*. Edinburgh, UK: Edinburgh University Press.

Fauconnier, G. (1985/1994). *Mental spaces*. Cambridge, UK: Cambridge University Press.

Fauconnier, G. (1997). *Mappings in thought and language*. Cambridge, UK: Cambridge University Press.

Fauconnier, G., & Turner, M. (2002). *The way we think: Conceptual blending and the mind's hidden complexities*. New York: Basic Books.

Fillmore, C. (1975). An alternative to checklist theories of meaning. *Proceedings of the First Annual Meeting of the Berkeley Linguistics Society, 1,* 123–131.

Gallese, V., & Lakoff, G. 2005. The brain's concepts: The role of the sensory-motor system in reason and language. *Cognitive Neuropsychology, 22,* 455–479.

Geeraerts, D. (1997). *Diachronic prototype semantics*. Oxford, UK: Oxford University Press.

Geeraerts, D. (2006). *Cognitive linguistics: Basic readings*. Berlin: Mouton de Gruyter.

Geeraerts, D., & Cuyckens, H. (2007). *The Oxford handbook of cognitive linguistics*. Oxford, UK: Oxford University Press.

Genesee, F. (2001). Bilingual first language acquisition: Exploring the limits of the language faculty. *Annual Review of Applied Linguistics, 21,* 153–168

Gentner, D., & Gentner, D. R. (1982). Flowing waters or teeming crowds: Mental models of electricity. In D. Gentner & A. Stevens (Eds.), *Mental models* (pp. 99–129). Hillsdale, NJ: Lawrence Erlbaum Associates Inc.

Gentner, D., Imai, M., & Boroditsky, L. (2002). As time goes by: Evidence for two systems in processing space time metaphors. *Language and Cognitive Processes, 17*(5), 537–565.

Gibbs, R. W. (2006). Why cognitive linguists should care more about empirical evidence. In M. González-Márquez, I. Mittelberg, S. Coulson, & M. J. Spivey (Eds.), *Empirical methods in cognitive linguistics* (pp. 2–18). Amsterdam: John Benjamins.

Goldberg, A. (1995). *Constructions: A construction grammar approach to argument structure*. Chicago: Chicago University Press.

Goldberg, A. (2006). *Constructions at work: The nature of generalization in language*. Oxford, UK: Oxford University Press.

González-Márquez, M., Mittelberg, I., Coulson, S., & Spivey, M. J. (Eds.). (2006). *Empirical methods in cognitive linguistics*. Amsterdam: John Benjamins.

Grady, J. (1997). *Foundations of meaning*. Unpublished doctoral thesis, Linguistics Department, University of California, Berkeley.

Jaeger, J., & Ohala, J. (1984). On the structure of phonetic categories. *Proceedings of the 10th Annual Meeting of the Berkeley Linguistics Society* (pp. 15–26). Berkeley, CA: Berkeley Linguistics Society.

Lakoff, G. (1977). Linguistic gestalts. *Papers from the 13th Regional Meeting of the Chicago Linguistics Society, 13,* 236–287.

Lakoff, G. (1987). *Women, fire and dangerous things: What categories reveal about the mind*. Chicago: University of Chicago Press.

Lakoff, G. (1990). The invariance hypothesis: Is abstract reason based on image-schemas? *Cognitive Linguistics, 1*(1), 39–74.

Lakoff, G., & Johnson, M. (1980). *Metaphors we live by*. Chicago: University of Chicago Press.

Lakoff, G., & Johnson, M. (1999). *Philosophy in the flesh: The embodied mind and its challenge for western thought*. New York: Basic Books.

Lakoff, G., & Thompson, H. (1975). Introduction to cognitive grammar. *Proceedings of the 1st Annual Meeting of the Berkeley Linguistics Society* (pp. 295–313). Berkeley, CA: Berkeley Linguistics Society.

Lakoff, G., & Turner, M. (1989). *More than cool reason: A field guide to poetic metaphor*. Chicago, IL: University of Chicago Press.

Langacker, R. (1978). The form and meaning of the English auxiliary. *Language, 54,* 853–882.

Langacker, R. (1987). *Foundations of cognitive grammar, Volume I*. Stanford, CA: Stanford University Press.

Langacker, R. (1991a). *Foundations of cognitive grammar, Volume II*. Stanford, CA: Stanford University Press.

Langacker, R. (1991b). *Concept, image, symbol: The cognitive basis of grammar* (2nd ed.) Berlin: Mouton de Gruyter.

Langacker, R. (1999). *Grammar and conceptualization*. Berlin: Mouton de Gruyter.

Langacker, R. (2000). A dynamic usage-based model. In M. Barlow & S. Kemmer (Eds.), *Usage-based models of language*. Stanford, CA: CSLI Publications.

Langacker, R. (2008). *Cognitive grammar: A basic introduction*. Oxford, UK: Oxford University Press.

Levinson, S. (2003). *Space in language and cognition*. Cambridge, UK: Cambridge University Press.

Montague, R. (1970). Universal grammar. *Theoria, 36,* 373–398.

Montague, R. (1973). The proper treatment of quantification in ordinary English.

In K. Hintikka, E. Moravcsik, & P. Suppes (Eds.), *Approaches to natural language* (pp. 221–242). Dordrecht: Reidel.

Núñez, R., & Sweetser, E. (2006). With the future behind them: Convergent evidence from Aymara language and gesture in the crosslinguistic comparison of spatial construals of time. *Cognitive Science, 30*(3), 401–450.

Slobin, D. I. (2003). Language and thought online: Cognitive consequences of linguistic relativity. In D. Gentner & S. Goldin-Meadow (Eds.), *Language in mind: Advances in the investigation of language and thought* (pp. 157–191). Cambridge, MA: MIT Press.

Talmy, L. (1975). Semantics and syntax of motion. In J. P. Kimball (Ed.), *Syntax and semantics 4* (pp. 181–238). New York: Academic Press.

Talmy, L. (1978). Figure and ground in complex sentences. In J. Greenberg, C. Ferguson, & J. Moravcsik (Eds.), *Universals of human language, Volume 4* (pp. 221–242). Stanford, CA: Stanford University Press.

Talmy, L. (2000). *Toward a cognitive semantics*. Cambridge, MA: MIT Press.

Taylor, J. (2003). *Linguistic categorization* (3rd ed.). Oxford, UK: Oxford University Press.

Thierry, G., Athanasopoulos, P., Wiggett, A., Dering, B., & Kuipers, J-R. (2009). Unconscious effects of language-specific terminology on preattentive color perception. *Proceedings of the National Academy of Sciences of the USA, 106* (11), 4567–4570.

Tomasello, M. (1999). *The cultural origins of human cognition*. Cambridge, MA: Harvard University Press.

Tomasello, M. (2003). *Constructing a language*. Cambridge, MA: Harvard University Press.

Tomasello, M. (2008). *Origins of human communication*. Cambridge, MA: MIT Press.

Tyler, A., & Evans, V. (2001). Reconsidering prepositional polysemy networks. *Language, 77*(4), 724–765.

Tyler, A., & Evans, V. (2003). *The semantics of English prepositions: Spatial scenes, embodied meaning and cognition*. Cambridge, UK: Cambridge University Press.

Varela, F., Thompson, E., & Rosch, E. (1991). *The embodied mind*. Cambridge, MA: MIT Press.

5   Interactive influences of language and cognition

Virginia C. Mueller Gathercole

Let us open this chapter with something of a thought experiment. Take a moment and think of everything you can about time. How do you conceive of time? My guess is that you think of time as something of a progression of units through the day and night, which move eventually through days and weeks and months and years. Those units are probably thought of as having stable duration (an 'hour' or a 'minute' or a 'second', or even an unspecified 'moment'), with there being 60 minutes in an hour, 24 hours in a day, and so forth. The unit of time is constant. Every hour is like every other hour in length. We measure activities in terms of the number of hours they will take, or portions of hours. A 'long' movie might take over 3 hours. A short phone call might take only a quarter of an hour. The daylight in the summer has more hours in it than the daylight in winter and, hence, corresponds to 'long' days; conversely, the night time in summer has fewer hours than the night time in winter and, hence, corresponds to 'short' nights; and so forth.

Now imagine that instead of the units of time having constant duration, so that the number of hours of daylight varies from one season to another, time were divided up instead in such a way that the number of units in the daylight portion of a day were constant. That is, what if the 'length' of an hour varied, so that there were, for example, 12 of them in whatever daylight period there was. In the summer these daytime hours would last long; in the winter the daytime hours would last for a shorter period. If clock time were organized in this way, there might be 12 'hours' to a daylight period, 6 for the morning, 6 for the afternoon, and the 'hour' could be faster or slower, depending on the speed with which the sun passes through the sky from dawn to dusk.

While such a scenario might at first seem odd or difficult to conceptualize, it is in fact how we conceive of musical 'timing' in Western music. There might be four beats to a measure, one quarter note to a beat, two eighth notes to a beat, four sixteenth notes to a beat, etc., and the 'beat' can be speeded up or slowed down, according to the conductor's or musician's preference when performing. The number of beats in a measure remains constant, the duration of each beat varies. If this schema for musical 'time' were applied to clock 'time', we would have precisely the type of flexible 'hours' mentioned above.

It may be hard for us in the twenty-first century to imagine thinking of clock 'time' like musical 'time', but this thought experiment actually has its basis in historical fact (Boorstin, 1983). The evolution of the constant hour took centuries. Time was initially divided into two parts, sunlight and dark. The sunlight portion went through several variants over the ages in how it was divided, including centuries of 'elastic units' dividing up only the daylight period. This included, for example, the sixth-century Benedictine division of daylight time into seven canonical hours: First light/dawn ('Matins' or 'Lauds'), sunrise ('Hora Prima'), mid-morning ('Hora Teria'), noon ('Hora Sexta' or 'Meridies'), mid-afternoon ('Hora Nona'), sunset ('Vespers'), and nightfall ('Compline') (Boorstin, 1983). Clock makers eventually developed water and mechanical clocks that could allow for and measure units of time that varied in length from season to season, in line with the conceptualization of time in terms of flexible time units. The division of a period into these flexible units of time in turn was eventually extended for use not only for sunlight periods but also for dark periods of the day. The evolution of the concept of an invariant hour, the standardization of clock time and the division of the day finally into 24 equally spaced hours did not occur until around AD 1330 (Boorstin, 1983).

The received conventions on how to express and conceptualize one element of reality—in this case, time—can pervade and frame our thinking about that reality. It is extremely hard in the modern age to conceive of time in any way other than as a sequence of equally spaced, constant units of measurement; it takes a genius like Einstein to break out of such a conceptual frame. If we were like the monks of the middle ages, on the other hand, our received conventions would, instead, lead us to think about time as elastic and only relevant to the daylight period. It took humans countless centuries to move away from this mode of conceiving time.

Is language like the water and mechanical clocks that led to the reconceptualization of the passage of time? These new devices allowed for a way of thinking about time that differed from what sundials allowed— they led to the conceptualization and division of the flow of time in a way that could expand time beyond daylight to night time and in a way in which the units of time could be thought of as constant. While all human beings must on some level experience and have a sense of the passing of time (with the movement of the sun, changes in human bodies with age, etc.), the new devices for the conventionalization of clock time provided a 'packaging' of time in a way that affected the conceptualization of time.

Is it the case that, just as different types of clocks invented over the centuries packaged time differently and influenced the conceptualization of time, languages also package our experiences in ways that are radically different? And, if so, how do concepts and the linguistic means for express-ing concepts emerge in children's development of both cognition and lan-guage? This is the question to which we now turn.

INTRODUCTION

Over the last half century much research on first language acquisition has focused on the important question of the relationship between language and cognition. The interest in this question arose from two directions, one from a general resurgence in interest in the Sapir-Whorf hypothesis (Sapir, 1924/1949; Whorf, 1940/1956) on the influence of language on cognition, the other from a serious search for the major determinants of developments in children's acquisition of language. The former high-lighted the question of whether language serves simply to map onto the world and the things in it or, instead, helps us to 'construct models' of the world (Grace, 1987), so that differences across languages might lead to differences in 'thinking for speaking' (Slobin, 1996a). If language does help humans to construct models of the world, then how far down would one find evidence of such influence of language on thinking?

The second concern, the search for determinants of development in language, arose out of the growing awareness of the complexity of language and the inordinate task the child must face in order to acquire it (e.g., Chomsky, 1972; Pinker, 1995). Perhaps children start with some universal starting space or starting point for language development. That starting space might consist of some innate knowledge of universal grammar, the Chomskyan position, or it might consist of infant cognitive knowledge present either in the pre-linguistic period or early on in the child's grow-ing knowledge of the world. The pursuit of insights into what controls children's language development—what determines first steps into lan-guage, how universal are those first steps into language, and what deter-mines the order and timing of the development of particular linguistic constructs—provided a major impetus behind exploration into the rela-tionship between language and cognition in development. An obvious candidate for at least one factor that might be controlling linguistic devel-opment could be the child's developing cognitive understanding of the concepts underlying the linguistic forms being learned. There are countless parallel developments in the realms of linguistic and cognitive advances in children, and many related developments appear to occur at approxi-mately the same time in development. Is it possible that developments in cognition are preconditions for developments in language? If language development occurs as a process of the child finding the means available in the language s/he is learning to express the concepts s/he is gaining, then linguistic development would be easy to explain, language-acquisitional processes should be similar across languages, and the acquisition of particular linguistic structures would be dependent on the concomitant or prior development of the underlying conceptual underpinnings.

Researchers have speculated on potential links between cognition and language on the basis of commonalities of timing of development and content or realm of knowledge, and such potential links are found more or less across the linguistic spectrum in acquisition. The first steps in language may begin with some of the most basic elements of any grammar, including word classes (nouns, verbs), thematic roles (agents, patients), grammatical roles (subjects, objects of verbs), and grammatical modulations such as tense and number marking. The child's development of these linguistic elements might be related intimately with the emergence of the child's concepts of objects and object permanence (Baillargeon, 1987; Gentner & Boroditsky, 2009; Piaget, 1952; Spelke, 1990; Spelke, Breinlinger, Macomber, & Jacobson, 1992), with early infant cognition (Huntley-Fenner, Carey, & Solimando, 2002; Xu & Carey, 1996), and with universal aspects of cognizing the world and objects, relations, actions, states, and events in it.

The link between language and cognition in development may extend to more complex linguistic encoding and more complex conceptual understanding, such as the expression and understanding of number and scalarity, perspective taking, and inferencing. Linguistic elements that encode these, such as scalar predicates and quantification and quantifier scope, the choice of definite and indefinite referential forms, the framing of topics and focus in conversational interaction, and the expression of presuppositional and assertional components, may well be contingent on the development of corresponding cognitive abilities, such as seriation (or the ability to rank items according to relative size, volume, or number), decentration (or the ability to see things from perspectives other than one's own), and hypothetical thinking (being able to think about non-present phenomena, beyond the here and now). If linguistic development is built on cognition, two things will follow. First, children's initial steps into language will be associated with cognitive primitives, or with infant or early-developing cognitive concepts. Second, children's first linguistic steps will be universal, since children's entry into the linguistic system will be based on the universal cognitive abilities of infants, with concepts onto which language will be mapped. The evidence accruing over the last few decades fails to support either of these predictions, at least in a strong version of the cognition-first position, whereby language merely maps directly onto cognition.

IS LANGUAGE BUILT UP BY MAPPING ONTO COGNITIVE CONCEPTS?

First, research has shown a wealth of areas in which language does not necessarily build on attested cognitive knowledge. In the 1970s, for example, the search was on for evidence showing that first steps into language, such as the emergence of first words or the emergence of two-word speech, built on Piagetian (e.g., Piaget, 1952) notions such as object permanence and tool use (Bloom, 1970, 1973; Bloom & Lahey, 1978). The concurrence in timing of these cognitive and linguistic developments made them prime candidates for testing the cognition-first position. Yet on close examination of children's development of the linguistic and cognitive abilities, Bates and her colleagues (Bates, 1979; Bates, Camaioni, & Volterra, 1975) found that there was no direct link between children's language abilities and the comparable Piagetian cognitive abilities, with individual children showing different patterns for the relative timing of the emergence of potentially related cognitive and linguistic abilities. Bates concluded that, rather than developments in either domain being a prerequisite for developments in the other, the evidence supported a position in which cognitive developments and linguistic developments 'share common structures because the associated tasks require the invention of independent but structurally similar solutions' (Bates, 1979, p. 136); she argued for 'homology through shared underlying "software" ' (p. 138). Examples of underlying shared software might include resources involving memory and attention.

More recent work has drawn on studies showing that infants have sophisticated cognitive abilities even in the first year of life. Infants show pre-linguistic knowledge of the stability and coherence or spatiotemporal continuance of objects (Baillargeon, 1987; Spelke, 1990; Spelke et al., 1992); discrimination of numbers of individuals (one vs two, two vs three) (Antell & Keating, 1983; Bijeljac-Babic, Bertoncini, & Mehler, 1991; Carey, 2001; Starkey & Cooper, 1980; Starkey, Spelke, & Gelman, 1983; Strauss & Curtis, 1981; Van Loosbroek & Smitsman, 1990; Wynn, 1996); discrimination of object-like entities from continuous substances (Huntley-Fenner et al., 2002; Xu & Carey, 1996); and understanding of dynamic events and of the potential for reversibility of movements across time and space (McCune, 2006).

Again, children's linguistic abilities often seem to develop separately from these cognitive abilities. Take, for example, the acquisition of nouns. Children's first usage of nouns does not seem to build on notions of stable, coherent objects. In Dromi's (1987, 1993, 1999, 2009) study of her daughter's earliest uses of words, for example, she found a high incidence of 'unclassified' usage, involving shifting reference (e.g., use of the Hebrew word *sus* 'horse' for bouncing movements, for riding, and for horses) and frequent occurrence of associative rather than referential use (e.g., *dod* 'uncle' used whenever the child heard noises coming from outside). This is not what one would expect if nouns and word meanings are mapped directly onto pre-developed conceptualizations of objects and actions. Similarly, the acquisition of number relies heavily on linguistic achievements well beyond infant cognitive knowledge (Carey, 2004); the acquisition of the mass-count linguistic distinction occurs independently of knowledge of objects and substances (Gathercole, 1985a, 1986; Gordon, 1982, 1988); and dynamic events get encoded in language-specific ways in the earliest utterances of children across languages (McCune, 2006) (see discussion in Gathercole, in press).

A related set of proposals that could be interpreted as falling into the cognition-first view is work positing innate mappings between certain concepts or attentional preferences and linguistic forms. Pinker's (1984, 1987, 1989) semantic bootstrapping, for example, proposed that there is specific in-born knowledge concerning which types of concepts or meanings get mapped onto (which aspects of) language. According to the theory, children's innate linguistic endowment provides specific guidelines concerning what types of concepts map onto what types of linguistic elements: e.g., concepts for objects, actions, agents are linked universally with specific linguistic categories or grammatical functions like noun, verb, subject, respectively. The prediction is that this linkage will provide the entry into the linguistic system to be learned (even though the child's linguistic system cannot remain at this level if it is to accommodate non-prototypical members into the linguistic categories). If the semantic bootstrapping hypothesis is correct, the earliest acquired linguistic forms should be ones that conform to these innate linkages: Nouns should be words for objects, verbs words for actions, subjects words for expressing agents, and so forth. Alternatively, the categories of nouns, verbs, and subjects will be constructed around such prototypical instances.

A similar type of proposal came from a very different theoretical position, in Slobin's (1973, 1985) work on operating principles, or principles used by children to break into the linguistic code of the particular language being learned. Among those principles, for example, Slobin proposed that cross-linguistically children rely on 'prototypical scenes/events' to build up language. One of the most salient types of events was what he termed the 'manipulative activity scene'—corresponding to Lakoff and Johnson's (1980) 'prototypical direct object manipulation'—in which an intentional, active agent performs some action that directly affects some patient, or receiver of the action. Slobin argued that children take advantage of such prototypical scenes to map grammatical elements onto concepts. Thus, the child's first use of linguistic means for marking direct objects (with accusative markers, word order, and the like) will occur in relation to patients involved in such prototypical object manipulation; and the child's first marking of subjects of sentences will be in relation to active agents performing acts on patients. Thus, for example, the prediction is that a child who is learning Japanese as a first language will associate the subject marker *ga* and the object marker *o* with such agents and patients before using them with less-prototypical subjects and objects.

The evidence for both types of proposals failed to support the predictions. For example, Bowerman (1990) and Uziel-Karl (2006, 2007;

Uziel-Karl & Budwig, 2007) demonstrated that children do not rely on the innate linkages proposed to establish argument structure in their language. In fact, their data point to considerable verb-by-verb learning and influence of the input (Uziel-Karl, 2006, 2007), as well as the slow emergence of more abstract grammars relatively late in development (Morris, Cottrell, & Elman, 2000). In relation to manipulative activity scenes, Bowerman (1989) examined data on the acquisition of nominative–accusative languages versus the acquisition of ergative–absolutive languages. The two types of language both differentiate the marking of subjects and objects in transitive sentences, but they differ in whether the subjects of intransitive sentences are aligned with subjects or objects of transitives (does one say, for example, *He sleeps* or ***Him sleeps***?). In nominative–accusative languages, subjects of intransitive sentences are treated like subjects of transitive sentences (e.g., with both marked for nominative case); in ergative–absolutive languages, in contrast, subjects of intransitive sentences are treated like objects of transitive sentences. Intransitive sentences, critically, tend not to express events or states that fall into Slobin's prototypical manipulative activity scene type. Bowerman argued, then, that subjects of intransitive verbs should be more difficult than subjects or objects of transitive sentences: Children may be able to apply Slobin's operating principle to the arguments of transitive verbs, but they will have to figure out independently whether the subjects of intransitives in their language act like subjects of transitives (*he sleeps*) or like objects of transitives (***him sleeps***). This is not what is found, however. Children learning both types of language make their intransitive subjects conform with the structure of the language they are learning from the very start (Bowerman, 1989). With regard to the question of whether linguistic forms are built by mapping language onto already developed cognitive concepts, then, the weight of the evidence fails to support this. Instead, language can develop as its own system, independent from what the child may be learning cognitively.

ARE THE EARLIEST STEPS INTO LANGUAGE UNIVERSAL?

Let us turn to the question of the possible universality of linguistic developments. According to a cognition-first position, children's first steps into language should be uniform: What children appear to be trying to say across languages, and the way in which children attempt to put their non-linguistic knowledge into language, should be very similar, if not identical. As was the case with the cognition-first predictions, the bulk of the evidence shows that, at least for many aspects of language, this is not the case.

Differences in children's first steps into language across languages are increasingly apparent. On close examination of children's earliest entry into several aspects of language, researchers have repeatedly found that from the earliest stages, even by age 2 or 2½, children's expression is influenced by the structure of the language they are learning. This has been documented for the expression of spatial relations (Bowerman, 1996a, 1996b; Bowerman & Choi, 2001; Choi, 1997; Choi & Bowerman, 1991), for the expression of motion (Berman & Slobin, 1994; Choi & Bowerman, 1991; Slobin, 1996b, 1997), for the interpretation of new nominal forms as referring to whole objects versus substances (Gathercole & Min, 1997; Imai & Gentner, 1997) or to individuals versus collections (Gathercole, Thomas, & Evans, 2000), for the expression of aspect and tense (Li, 2009; Weist, 2009), and for the initial level of abstraction versus specificity of terms (de León, 2001, 2009; Narasimhan & Brown, 2009). The data reveal little support, then, for a position positing universal first steps in language based on universality of infant cognition. Children learning different languages must be guided from the beginning, at least in part, by the language they are learning.

THE INTERACTION OF LANGUAGE AND COGNITION

So the acquisition of language is not built directly onto a cognitive base, nor are first steps into the structure of language guided directly by such a base. This means one of two things: Either cognitive development and linguistic development are totally independent or cognitive development and linguistic development interact with each other, without one being totally dependent on the other.

To examine the extent to which cognition and language are independent or interact, one can start, at least, with an exploration of the relative timing of the two. First, if the two are totally independent, one could expect that, even if linguistic developments differ across languages or cultures or individual children, cognitive development should be fairly uniform and unaffected by linguistic differences. Second, within individual children the timing of development of apparently related cognitive and linguistic items should be no different from the timing of development of apparently unrelated items.

There is some evidence that cognitive abilities can, indeed, be affected by the language being learned. Gopnik and Choi (1990) provided one of the earliest elegant demonstrations that what children were learning in language may provide a guide for children's cognitive development and may affect the order in which cognitive skills emerge. These researchers examined English-, French-, and Korean-learning 17-month-old children's developing use of language concerning disappearance, success and failure, and naming, and compared this with their cognitive knowledge of object permanence, means–ends relations (e.g., using a tool to obtain a toy), and categorization. The languages differ crucially in the prevalence of verbs in the input; Korean places verbs in sentence-final position, and nominal arguments are not obligatory. The question was whether this higher occurrence of verbs in Korean would correlate with greater capacities for concepts associated with verb-type meanings, including success–failure and means–ends. The results indicated that Korean children used more verbs than the other two groups of children, and the Korean children all developed means–ends knowledge before object permanence. The English-speaking children, in contrast, developed categorization earlier than the Korean children, which seemed to be linked with the predominance of nouns over verbs in the English input. For all groups, the cognitive abilities were closely linked in time with the development of the related linguistic abilities.

At the same time, linguistic differences do not always seem to lead to cognitive differences. Weist, Lyytinen, Wysocka, and Atanassova (1997) examined cognitive and linguistic developments in Polish- and Finnish-speaking children. They reasoned that the morphological structure of Polish might favor the development of temporal concepts, and the structure of Finnish might facilitate spatial knowledge. On cognitive tasks they found support for their hypothesis regarding Finnish, but not for Polish. (In a later study, Weist, Atanassova, Wysocka, & Pawlak, 1999, failed to find a cognitive difference across groups for either spatial or temporal concepts.)

With regard to the relative timing of linguistic and cognitive developments, the evidence is mixed. In some cases, developments for related items appear closely tied in time. In Gopnik and Choi's (1990) study, for example, there was a striking link in timing in the development of related linguistic and cognitive developments (within 10 to 14 days of each other), while unrelated cognitive and linguistic developments were more spread apart (28 to 69 days). In Choi's later work on children's early development of spatial terms and concepts, she focuses on differences in Korean and English encoding of spatial relations: Whereas English encodes containment within (*put X in Y*) and surface support (*put X on Y*), Korean highlights tightness or looseness of fit (*kkita* 'put X into/onto a tight fit relation with Y' and *nehta* 'put X into/onto a loose fit relation with Y'). Choi again reports a link in time between the acquisition of the linguistic forms for expressing spatial relations and changes in infants' attentional behavior in relation to space. The language appears to heighten attention to the linguistically relevant distinctions and reduce attention to those not relevant. Thus, for example, before English-speaking children learn the preposition *in* or show a high level of vocabulary, they show attention, like Korean-learning babies, to tight- versus loose-fit situations (McDonough, Choi, & Mandler, 2003), but later, when they've learned more language, this attention diminishes in English-speaking babies (Choi, 2006). Weist and colleagues (Weist, 2008, 2009; Weist et al., 1997, 1999) similarly found a high correlation in children's linguistic and cognitive abilities related to time and space.

At the same time, such a close relationship in the timing of related linguistic and conceptual advances does not appear necessary; advancement in one can occur independently of the other. For example, at least for some structures, children appear to be able to gain some level of productivity with linguistic forms before they gain a full cognitive appreciation of their semantic import. Shirai and Miyata (2006), for example, examined the early acquisition of the past tense marker *-ta* in four Japanese-speaking children's speech and found that the children had productive use of *-ta* before they gained a full appreciation of its temporal meaning. Gathercole (2009b) examined children's usage of a variety of scalar expressions like *too X, catch up with, as X as*, and found extensive use of these before children gain an appreciation of their scalar import (see below).

These studies together point to interactive influences between language and cognition. They indicate that initial steps to language development and cognitive development can be taken independently, with language-specific linguistic structure influencing the nature of what is learned early. At the same time, the cognitive preparedness of the child seems to set a framework and some outer limits on meanings the child may be able to entertain as associated with the linguistic constructs being learned. In turn, the language being learned can bring a child's attention to certain aspects of the world or relations in it, and this can foster related cognitive advances. As the child gains knowledge in both realms, these begin to be brought together more and more into a complex network of associations; these, in turn, may affect attentional patterns in the cognitive realm and restructuring of the whole system (Bowerman, 1982a, 1982b; Carey, 2004; Gathercole, 2006; Karmiloff-Smith, 1992; Li, 2009).

TWO EXTENDED EXAMPLES

Two recent sets of studies from our own work can demonstrate how such a developmental progression can affect acquisition in monolinguals and bilinguals. The first example is taken from my own analyses of children's acquisition of scalar predicates in English (Gathercole, 2009b), the second from our current work on linguistic categorization in bilinguals (Gathercole, 2009a; Gathercole et al., 2009; Gathercole & Moawad, 2010; Stadthagen-González, Pérez Tattam, Yavas, & Campusano, 2009).

English monolinguals and the acquisition of scalar predicates

Gathercole (2009b) traces the flowering of the use of a wide range of scalar predicates in the speech of two English-speaking children, from the earliest uses before age 2 through complex uses by age 6. The structures examined include simple, equative, comparative, and superlative forms of adjectives and quantifiers (e.g., simple: *big, much, many*; equative: *as big (as)*, *as much as*; comparative: *bigger (than)*, *more beautiful (than)*, *more (than)*, *less (than)*; superlative: *the biggest*, *the most beautiful*, *the most*, *the least*), modifications of adjectives and quantifiers with relevant adverbs and determiners (e.g., *so big*, *very big*, *too big*, *big enough*, *so much*, *so many*, *too much*, *that many*, etc.), and multiply-modified forms (e.g., *so much bigger*, *that much too big*, *way too much*, *so very many*, *that many*, *too many*, etc.). These structures are relevant here because they are used to express complex concepts related to intensification, comparison, contrast, location along a scale, relative location along a scale, and so forth.

The data reveal a progression that is in line with the model described here—initial developments in the linguistic realm demonstrating piecemeal uptake of linguistic forms offered by the language-specific properties of the language being learned, English; the influence of cognitive preparedness on what types of meanings the child is equipped to associate with the linguistic structures being learned; and a complex process of the interweaving of emerging linguistic and cognitive knowledge over the trajectory of their development.

The two children studied, Rachel and Sadie, both began the acquisition of the linguistic forms by picking up piecemeal, disconnected linguistic elements from the input being learned. For example, both children started with bare forms of adjectives (As) and quantifiers (Qs), such as *heavy*, *stinky*, *more*, *first*. These were associated quite soon in each case with certain types of modifiers—e.g., *so A*, *all A*, *very A* in Sadie's case, and *A-er*, *A-est*, and reduplication (*big big X*) in Rachel's case. Both children soon picked up the co-occurrence of *more* with *no* and *any* (*no more*, *any more*); and Rachel's earliest uses of *many* were all associated with age: e.g., *This is the many I'm gonna be. I'm gonna be three in a minute* (2;11.6) (Gathercole, 2009b, p. 375). Both children's earliest uses of *much* were always accompanied by a determiner, usually restricted to *too* or *that*, and were never associated with adjectives.

Each of these linguistic forms had a life of its own as it expanded gradually to become less and less restricted. The children drew out generalization by generalization and gradually extended the use of forms beyond these earliest restricted uses. For example, Sadie began by expanding the forms *so*, *all*, and *very* + *A* to incorporate other modifiers, such as *freezing* and *heck-out: freezing tired*, *heck-out dirty water*; both children extended their use of *no more* and *any more* to other modifiers, e.g., *a little bit more*, *a lot more*, *some more*, even *yes more*: 'I want **yes more baguette**. I want **yes more cheese!**' (Sadie 2;3.7) (Gathercole, 2009b, Table 11.2D, p. 357). (Following Gathercole, 2009b, underlining in child utterances indicates stress, bold type indicates the structure of relevance.) These in turn got extended in Sadie's speech to incorporate other quantifier forms in the place where *more* occurred: *a little bit some, one . . 2 . . . 3 . . . 4 . . 5 bit*.

Beyond these developments, later modifications of quantifiers were rooted in the *too/that* + *much* forms and the *no*, *any*, *a lot*, *some* + *more* forms. The former expanded, first, with the use of new determiners, previously associated with adjectives only, with *much*: e.g., *very much, so much*; the latter with the entry of quantifier modifiers, previously only occurring before *more*, before adjectives (and beyond to verbs): *a-little-bit-loose diaper, a lot salty pretzels, somewhat better, a lot similar, a lot so love you, and even later, any spicy, some good*. These got expanded even further in Sadie's speech to the incorporation of numbers in the modifier position: '20 fun!', '150 tired', '199 tired', '20 hundred and 750 lucky', as in the following:

> It was so much fun. It was **20 fun**! 1, 2, 3, 4, 5, 6, 7, 8, 9, 10, 11, 12, 13, 14, 15, 16, 17, 18, 19, 20. It takes a long time to get to 20. 3;4.8
> That doesn't make **any sense**. Not **one single** {sent/cent}. 3;8.24
> Is everybody as tired as I am? I'm **150 tired** . . . I'm **199 tired**. 3;9.22
> You're very lucky. You're **20 hundred and 750 lucky**. 3;9.24
> (Gathercole, 2009b, Table 11.8, p. 371)

In Rachel's speech the expansion took a somewhat different route: The modifiers she used in her X + A forms got extended to use with *A-er*: *much + A-er, how + A-er, even + A-er, so + A-er, very + A-er*, and eventually *more + A-er*. This last was then expanded further to *even more + A-er* and *much more + A-er*.

These linguistic developments were taking place alongside concurrent cognitive developments. At the earliest stages, Sadie's and Rachel's (as well as other children's) expressions focused on fairly non-complex notions of likeness, extreme ends, and intensification. These notions provide a fairly good match with some linguistic forms, such as, respectively, *as* (for *like*—cf. *its fleece was white as snow*); the superlative; and *so, very*, and reduplication. They are a less-good match for others, such as the comparative, the full meaning of *as . . . as, too X*. These latter forms all require an understanding of scalarity and relative position on a scale for proper use. So, if a child uses these latter forms early on, prior to the understanding of scalarity, they will very likely use the forms—in most instances—to express one of the less-complex notions, such as to express the simple presence of a property or for intensification, as in Rachel's *My shoes are **littler than** my feet* (3;1.28) in a context in which she was insisting that her shoes did in fact fit her feet (Gathercole, 2009b: Table 11.11A, p. 379). (Note, however, that the forms do not seem to 'mean' those less-complex meanings, if one takes into consideration the complete range of usage, see Gathercole, 1983, 1985b.)

On the face of it, this might be taken as evidence in favor of a cognition-first approach for acquisition: The meanings children attached to complex linguistic forms were associated with their developing cognitive abilities. However, there are two elements of the acquisition of these forms that argue in favor of an interactionist view. First, a cognition-first approach cannot adequately explain the full usage of these forms in children's earliest speech. *Some* uses of the comparative, for example, appear appropriate. I have argued (Gathercole, 1983, 2009b) that the full range of usage can be better explained in terms of acquisition of the linguistic forms in context. The child learns a given form with an associated, appropriate context, and from this draws out patterns of usage. That early context acts as a kind of prototypical usage that provides a kind of grounding of the usage and from which the child discovers the application of the form. The child's understanding of that prototypical usage may be limited to some extent by the conceptual underpinnings s/he can entertain. This is not the same as saying that the linguistic form has been *mapped onto* those concepts.

But a second factor that argues in favor of an interactionist view is this: It appears that the process of acquiring the complete linguistic system plays an important role in the development of the subtle semantics that ultimately should be associated with the forms in question. Thus, for example, in the case of the equative and the comparative, it is the acquisition of the forms themselves that may push the child to develop complex semantic underpinnings. In particular, the acquisition of the obligatory association of the degree marker *as* with the standard marker *as* (*as quiet as a mouse*) and of the degree marker *-er* with the standard marker *than* may be key to the child's discovery of the fact that both of these require for their proper understanding that two elements are being compared along some scale. It is striking that children's adherence to use of *than* with *-er* (rather than their more immature use of, for example, *from* or *like* as standard markers) coincides with their consistently correct use of *A-er* for comparative meaning (Gathercole, 2009b).

Similarly, children's movement into *scalar* understanding of the predicates *too X, A-er, A enough*, among others, seems to be connected intimately with their incorporation of number into the linguistic structures expressing these, as in Sadie's *20 fun, 150 tired*, and Rachel's *sweating three times, tired two times*:

> [R comparing amount she's sweating and amount she's tired:]
> I'm sweating *three times*, and I'm tired *two times*.
> [i.e., sweating at a value of 3 and tired at a value of 2.] 4;11.25
> (Gathercole, 2009b, Table 11.15H, p. 397)

It is possible that, to some extent, the child's growing understanding of number and scales helps to push his or her acquisition of language, but it is likely also that to some extent, the child's developing linguistic system pushes him or her to gain a better and more sophisticated appreciation of scalarity.

The acquisition of this whole range of structures and their organization into a system provides a rich field in which to explore these questions, and further research will help to establish even better what the exact relationship is between language and cognition in their developing trajectory.

Bilinguals and categorization

An intriguing question that arises as an outgrowth of the above research has to do with the interaction of language and cognition in children learning two or more systems. When the linguistic systems being learned package semantics and meaning differently, what effect might this have on the cognitive knowledge of such children and on the ways in which language and cognition interact?

There are several hypotheses one might entertain. One is that, if language can affect the timing of cognitive advances, then we might expect children who speak two languages to perhaps attain certain cognitive insights before their monolingual counterparts. This could be especially true in cases in which one language emphasizes one aspect (e.g., tightness versus looseness of fit) while the other language emphasizes another (containment versus surface support). With two languages providing distinct ways of 'thinking for speaking' (Slobin, 1996a), we might predict that children learning those languages will gain facility in both ways of conceptualizing the world or the relevant aspects of the world. We know that bilingual children gain metalinguistic awareness before their monolingual peers (Bialystok, 1993), indicating an earlier appreciation of the fact that language is arbitrary. And there is evidence that even monolingual infants are able to quickly learn a system different from their own: Casasola, Wilbourn, and Yang (2006) taught English-speaking toddlers a novel word to express placing objects into a tight-fit relation, and these children were able to learn the Korean tight-fit relation after hearing the novel word only 32 times, 8 times each in relation to four different sets of toys. Casasola et al. (2006) highlight that these toddlers did this even though the tight-fit relation cross-cut their existing spatial categories for *in* and *on*. The children were thus able to take on an alternative way of grouping actions on the basis of fairly limited exposure: 'language appears to motivate young children to recognize as equivalent those actions that they previously were unable to group into a single category, supporting the notion that language can facilitate the acquisition of a particular concept' (Casasola et al., 2006, pp. 199–200). If monolingual children can, on the basis of very limited exposure, adjust their attention and take on new ways of categorizing according to new linguistic information in the input, how much more easily should bilingual children be able to adjust attention and take on alternative ways of categorizing on the basis of extensive daily exposure?

In other cases we might predict that bilingual children's conceptualizations might show some convergence of the ways in which their two languages package the world. Recent work has examined the extent to which bilinguals' categorization in their two languages corresponds to that of monolinguals, and this work is beginning to confirm this prediction. (See discussion in Chapter 7.) Some of this work has focused on L2 learners' uptake of the L2 system (Jiang, 2002, 2004; Malt & Sloman, 2003), some has shown influence of the L2 on the L1 conceptualization (Pavlenko, 2003; Wolff & Ventura, 2009), and some has reported bidirectional influence in L2 learners (Brown & Gullberg, 2008). Some work has examined categorization in simultaneous bilinguals and has reported some convergence across systems. For example, Ameel and colleagues (Ameel, Malt, Storms, & Van Assche, 2009; Ameel, Storms, Malt, & Sloman, 2005) have recently found that simultaneous Dutch–French bilinguals showed some convergence of categories of bottles and dishes across their two languages, so that their semantic groupings were distinct in both languages from what was observed for monolinguals. Bilinguals showed both less-complex categories and semantic convergence for both the centers and the boundaries of the cross-language categories.

An interesting aspect of this work is that the amount and loci of convergence appear to be a function of the interaction of the semantic content and the relationship of referents in the cognitive space. Our own work is beginning to show that those categories that encode members from closely linked cognitive spaces are more likely to undergo cross-linguistic influence than those that encode members from more distantly linked cognitive spaces. We are particularly focusing on words for which one language makes a distinction that the other does not, or for which one word in one of the languages has a wider range of application than those in the other language. Some simple examples are: the word *hill* in English corresponds to two in Welsh, *bryn* (a mini-mountain) and *(g)allt* (an incline); Spanish *dedo* corresponds to two words in English, *finger* and *toe*; Arabic *yistad* corresponds to two words in English, *hunt* (V) and *fish* (V).

In some cases, the meaning of the word in the wider language (i.e., with the word with broader application) can be defined in terms of necessary and sufficient conditions (e.g., *dedo* in Spanish can be defined as 'an appendage, one of five, extending from a human limb'), or can be classified as a 'classical' category (Lakoff, 1987); sometimes it cannot. Sometimes, instead, it can be seen to have 'radial' structure, wherein a core use has conventionally been extended in a number of directions, but the combined uses of the word cannot be defined in terms of necessary and sufficient conditions. An example would be the category *sister*. At its core, this word applies to biological female siblings. But it also applies (on the basis of a metaphorical or metonymic extension from the core meaning), equally legitimately, e.g., to nuns, to good female friends, and (in British English) to nurses.

We have been examining bilinguals' processing of such categories in several contexts—Arabic–English bilinguals in Saudi Arabia, Welsh–English bilinguals in Wales, and Spanish–English bilinguals in Miami (Gathercole, 2009a; Gathercole et al., 2009; Gathercole & Moawad, 2010;

Stadthagen-González et al., 2009). We have reasoned that, if children are developing linguistically relevant categories alongside their cognitive development, then we should find more interaction between a bilingual's two languages when the members of a category are close in the conceptual space than when the members are more distant in the conceptual space. In other words, classical categories, whose members share criterial characteristics and are thus close in conceptual space, should be more subject to convergence in bilinguals' two languages than radial categories, whose members do not share criterial characteristics and are thus more distant in the conceptual space. This is precisely what we have been finding in our work. And the interaction appears more likely to occur in early bilinguals, those who either learnt both languages from birth or began the second language before age 6, than in late bilinguals. The best interpretation of this appears to relate to the interaction of the cognitive and semantic structures during language development in bilingual children.

Although these studies are just beginning to explore these issues regarding semantic interaction, this line of research promises to provide considerable new insight into the relation between language and cognition, using especially rich information that can be gleaned from the systems established in bilinguals.

CONCLUSION

In conclusion, extensive pursuit over the last decades of meticulous work exploring the relationship between language and cognitive development has indicated that language and cognition interact in development. The two undergo some amount of independent progress in children's emerging systems, but they together form a complex network through which they are interconnected and interwoven. Language, like clocks, provides some packaging of conceptual material. It helps to provide lines that divide categories (Hampton, 2007), and it affects what speakers pay attention to, as shown by work to date.

Future work in the area of both first and bilingual language development will continue to provide further insights into the precise relationship between language and cognition. Such cross-linguistic work and work examining cognition and language in both monolinguals and bilinguals promises to provide stimulating new insights in the future.

ACKNOWLEDGMENTS

This work was supported in part by ESRC & WAG/HEFCW grant RES-535-30-0061, ESRC Centre for Research on Bilingualism in Theory and Practice, whose support is gratefully acknowledged. I am also grateful for discussions on these issues and comments on earlier drafts from Lisa Bedore, Enlli Thomas, Rocío Pérez Tattam, and Hans Stadthagen-González.

REFERENCES

Ameel, E., Malt, B. C., Storms, G., & Van Assche, F. (2009). Semantic convergence in the bilingual lexicon. *Journal of Memory and Language, 60*(2), 270–290.

Ameel, E., Storms, G., Malt, B., & Sloman, S. (2005). How bilinguals solve the naming problem. *Journal of Memory and Language, 53,* 60–80.

Antell, S., & Keating, D. (1983). Perception of numerical invariance in neonates. *Child Development, 54,* 695–701.

Baillargeon, R. (1987). Object permanence in 3.5- and 4.5-month-old infants. *Developmental Psychology, 23,* 655–664.

Bates, E. (1979). The emergence of symbols: Ontogeny and phylogeny. In W. A. Collins (Ed.), *Children's language and communication: The Minnesota symposia on child psychology, Vol. 12* (pp. 121–155). Hillsdale, NJ: Lawrence Erlbaum Associates Inc.

Bates, E., Camaioni, L., & Volterra, V. (1975). The acquisition of performatives prior to speech. *Merrill-Palmer Quarterly, 21*(3), 205–226.

Berman, R. A., & Slobin, D. I. (1994). *Relating events in narrative: A crosslinguistic developmental study.* Hillsdale, NJ: Lawrence Erlbaum Associates Inc.

Bialystok, E. (1993). Metalinguistic awareness: The development of children's representations of language. In C. Pratt & A. Garton (Eds.), *Systems of representation in children: Development and use* (pp. 211–233). London: Wiley.

Bijeljac-Babic, R., Bertoncini, J., & Mehler, J. (1991). How do four-day-old infants categorize multi-syllabic utterances? *Developmental Psychology, 29,* 711–721.

Bloom, L. (1970). *Language development: Form and function in emerging grammars.* Cambridge, MA: MIT Press.

Bloom, L. (1973). *One word at a time.* The Hague: Mouton.

Bloom, L., & Lahey, M. (1978). *Language development and language disorders.* New York: John Wiley & Sons.

Boorstin, D. J. (1983). *The discoverers.* New York: Random House.

Bowerman, M. (1982a). Reorganizational processes in lexical and syntactic development. In E. Wanner & L. Gleitman (Eds.), *Language acquisition: The state of the art* (pp. 319–346). Cambridge, UK: Cambridge University Press.

Bowerman, M. (1982b). Starting to talk worse: Clues to language acquisition from children's late speech errors. In S. Strauss & R. Stavy (Eds.), *U-shaped behavioral growth* (pp. 101–146). New York: Academic Press.

Bowerman, M. (1989). Learning a semantic system: What role do cognitive predispositions play? In R. L. Schiefelbusch & M. L. Rice (Eds.), *The teachability of language.* Baltimore: Paul H. Brooks Publishing Co.

Bowerman, M. (1990). Mapping thematic roles onto syntactic functions: Are children helped by innate linking rules? *Linguistics, 28,* 1253–1289.

Bowerman, M. (1996a). Learning how to structure space for language: A cross-linguistic perspective. In P. Bloom, M. A. Peterson, L. Nadel, & M. F. Garrett (Eds.), *Language and space* (pp. 385–436). Cambridge, MA: MIT Press.

Bowerman, M. (1996b). The origins of children's spatial semantic categories: Cognitive versus linguistic determinants. In J. J. Gumperz & S. C. Levinson (Eds.), *Rethinking linguistic relativity* (pp. 145–176). Cambridge, UK: Cambridge University Press.

Bowerman, M., & Choi, S. (2001). Shaping meanings for language: Universal and language-specific in the acquisition of spatial semantic categories. In M. Bowerman & S. C. Levinson (Eds.), *Language acquisition and conceptual development* (pp. 475–511). Cambridge, UK: Cambridge University Press.

Brown, A., & Gullberg, M. (2008). Bidirectional crosslinguistic influence in L1–L2 encoding of manner in speech and gesture. *Studies in Second Language Acquisition, 30,* 225–251.

Carey, S. (2001). Bridging the gap between cognition and developmental neuroscience: The example of number representation. In C. A. Nelson & M. Luciana (Eds.), *Handbook of developmental cognitive neuroscience* (pp. 415–431). Cambridge, MA: MIT Press.

Carey, S. (2004). Bootstrapping and the origin of concepts. *Daedalus, Winter,* 59–68.

Casasola, M., Wilbourn, M. P., & Yang, S. (2006). Can English-learning toddlers acquire and generalize a novel spatial word? *First Language, 26*(2), 187–205.

Choi, S. (1997). Language-specific input and early semantic development: Evidence from children learning Korean. In D. I. Slobin (Ed.), *The crosslinguistic study of language acquisition, Vol. 5: Expanding the contexts* (pp. 111–133). Mahwah, NJ: Lawrence Erlbaum Associates Inc.

Choi, S. (2006). Influence of language-specific input on spatial cognition: Categories of containment. *First Language, 77,* 207–232.

Choi, S., & Bowerman, M. (1991). Learning to express motion events in English and Korean: The influence of language-specific lexicalization patterns. *Cognition, 41,* 83–121.

Chomsky, N. (1972). *Language and mind.* New York: Harcourt Brace Jovanovich.

de León, L. (2001). Finding the richest path: Language and cognition in the acquisition of verticality in Tzotzil (Mayan). In M. Bowerman & S. C. Levinson (Eds.), *Language acquisition and conceptual development* (pp. 544–565). Cambridge, UK: Cambridge University Press.

de León, L. (2009). Mayan semantics in early lexical development: The case of the Tzotzil verbs for 'eating' and 'falling down'. In V. C. M. Gathercole (Ed.), *Routes to language: Studies in honor of Melissa Bowerman* (pp. 69–94). New York: Psychology Press.

Dromi, E. (1987). *Early lexical development.* London: Cambridge University Press.

Dromi, E. (1993). The mysteries of early lexical development. In E. Dromi (Ed.), *Language and cognition: A developmental perspective* (pp. 32–60). Norwood, NJ: Ablex Publishing Corporation.

Dromi, E. (1999). Early lexical development. In M. Barrett (Ed.), *The development of language* (pp. 99–131). Hove, UK: Psychology Press.

Dromi, E. (2009). Old data—new eyes: Theories of word meaning acquisition. In V. C. Mueller Gathercole (Ed.), *Routes to language: Studies in honor of Melissa Bowerman* (pp. 39–59). New York: Psychology Press.

Gathercole, V. C. (1983). Haphazard examples, prototype theory, and the acquisition of comparatives. *First Language, 4,* 169–196.

Gathercole, V. C. (1985a). 'He has too much hard questions': The acquisition of the linguistic mass-count distinction in *much* and *many*. *Journal of Child Language, 12,* 395–415.

Gathercole, V. C. (1985b). More and more and more about *more*. *Journal of Experimental Child Psychology, 40,* 73–104.

Gathercole, V. C. (1986). Evaluating competing linguistic theories with child language data: The case of the mass–count distinction. *Linguistics and Philosophy, 9,* 151–190.

Gathercole, V. C. M. (2006). Introduction to special issue: Language-specific influences on acquisition and cognition. *First Language, 26*(1), 5–17.

Gathercole, V. C. M. (2009a). *All categories are not created equal: Semantic interaction effects in bilinguals.* Paper presented at the Symposium on Bilingual Development: The Acquisition of Form and Meaning, XIV European Conference on Developmental Psychology, 18–22 August, Vilnius, Lithuania.

Gathercole, V. C. M. (2009b). 'It was so much fun. It was 20 fun!' Cognitive and linguistic invitations to the development of scalar predicates. In V. C. M. Gathercole (Ed.), *Routes to language: Studies in honor of Melissa Bowerman* (pp. 319–443). New York: Psychology Press.

Gathercole, V. C. M. (in press). Relation of language and cognition in development. In M. Vihman & V. C. Gathercole (Eds.), *Language development: Issues, models, empirical evidence.* Oxford, UK: Blackwell.

Gathercole, V. C. M., & Min, H. (1997). Word meaning biases or language-specific effects? Evidence from English, Spanish, and Korean. *First Language, 17,* 31–56.

Gathercole, V. C. M., & Moawad, R. A. (2010). Semantic interaction in early and late bilinguals: All words are not created equally. *Bilingualism: Language and Cognition, 13*(4), 1–22.

Gathercole, V. C. M., Moawad, R. A., Stadthagen-González, H., Thomas, E. M., Pérez Tattam, R., Yavas, F., et al. (2009). *The semantics–cognition interface in bilingual systems: Not all words are created equally.* Paper presented at the Conference on Mind–Context Divide: Language Acquisition & Interfaces of Cognitive-Linguistic Modules, Iowa City, Iowa, April 30–May 2.

Gathercole, V. C. M., Thomas, E. M., & Evans, D. (2000). What's in a noun? Welsh-, English-, and Spanish-speaking children see it differently. *First Language, 20,* 55–90.

Gentner, D., & Boroditsky, L. (2009). Early acquisition of nouns and verbs: Evidence from Navajo. In V. C. M. Gathercole (Ed.), *Routes to language: Studies in honor of Melissa Bowerman* (pp. 5–36). New York: Psychology Press.

Gopnik, A., & Choi, S. (1990). Do linguistic differences lead to cognitive differences? A cross-linguistic study of semantic and cognitive development. *First Language, 10,* 199–215.

Gordon, P. (1982). *The acquisition of syntactic categories: The case of the count/mass distinction* (Ph.D. dissertation). Cambridge, MA: MIT.

Gordon, P. (1988). Count/mass category acquisition: Distributional distinctions in children's speech. *Journal of Child Language, 15,* 109–128.

Grace, G. W. (1987). *The linguistic construction of reality.* London: Croom Helm.

Hampton, J. A. (2007). Typicality, graded membership, and vagueness. *Cognitive Science: A Multidisciplinary Journal, 31*(3), 355–384.

Huntley-Fenner, G., Carey, S., & Solimando, A. (2002). Objects are individuals but stuff doesn't count: Perceived rigidity and cohesiveness influence infants' representations of small groups of discrete entities. *Cognition, 85,* 203–221.

Imai, M., & Gentner, D. (1997). A crosslinguistic study of early word meaning: Universal ontology and linguistic influence. *Cognition, 62,* 169–200.

Jiang, N. (2002). Form–meaning mapping in vocabulary acquisition in a second language. *Studies in Second Language Acquisition, 24,* 617–638.

Jiang, N. (2004). Semantic transfer and its implications for vocabulary teaching in a second language. *Modern Language Journal, 88,* 416–432.

Karmiloff-Smith, A. (1992). *Beyond modularity*. Cambridge, MA: MIT Press.

Lakoff, G. (1987). *Women, fire, and dangerous things*. Chicago, IL: The University of Chicago Press.

Lakoff, G., & Johnson, M. (1980). *Metaphors we live by*. Chicago, IL: University of Chicago Press.

Li, P. (2009). Meaning in acquisition: Semantic structure, lexical organization, and crosslinguistic variation. In V. C. M. Gathercole (Ed.), *Routes to language: Studies in honor of Melissa Bowerman* (pp. 257–283). New York: Psychology Press.

Malt, B. C., & Sloman, S. A. (2003). Linguistic diversity and object naming by non-native speakers of English. *Bilingualism: Language and Cognition, 6,* 47–67.

McCune, L. (2006). Dynamic event words: From common cognition to varied linguistic expression. *First Language, 26*(2), 233–255.

McDonough, L., Choi, S., & Mandler, J. (2003). Understanding spatial relations: Flexible infants, lexical adults. *Cognitive Psychology, 46,* 229–59.

Morris, W. C., Cottrell, G. W., & Elman, J. L. (2000) A connectionist simulation of the empirical acquisition of grammatical relations. In S. Wermter & R. Sun (Eds.), *Hybrid neural symbolic integration* (pp. 175–193). Dordrecht: Springer Verlag.

Narasimhan, B., & Brown, P. (2009). Getting the INSIDE story: Learning to express containment in Tzeltal and Hindi. In V. C. M. Gathercole (Ed.), *Routes to language: Studies in honor of Melissa Bowerman* (pp. 97–132). New York: Psychology Press.

Pavlenko, A. (2003). Eyewitness memory in late bilinguals: Evidence for discursive relativity. *International Journal of Bilingualism, 7*(3) 257–281.

Piaget, J. (1952). *The origin of intelligence in children*. New York: Norton.

Pinker, S. (1984). *Language learnability and language development*. Cambridge, MA: Harvard University Press.

Pinker, S. (1987). The bootstrapping problem in language acquisition. In B. MacWhinney (Ed.), *Mechanisms of language acquisition*. Hillsdale, NJ: Lawrence Erlbaum Associates Inc.

Pinker, S. (1989). *Learnability and cognition: The acquisition of argument structure*. Cambridge, MA: MIT Press.

Pinker, S. (1995). *The language instinct: How the mind creates language*. New York: Harper Perennial.

Sapir, E. (1924/1949). The grammarian and his language. *American Mercury, 1,* 149–155. [Reprinted in D. G. Mandelbaum (Ed.). (1949). *Selected writings of Edward Sapir in language, culture, and personality* (pp. 150–159). Berkeley: University of California Press, & London: Cambridge University Press.]

Shirai, Y., & Miyata, S. (2006). Does past tense marking indicate the acquisition of the concept of temporal displacement in children's cognitive development? *First Language, 26*(1), 45–66.

Slobin, D. I. (1973). Cognitive prerequisites for the development of grammar. In C. A. Ferguson & D. I. Slobin (Eds.), *Studies of child language development* (pp. 175–208). New York: Holt, Rinehart & Winston.

Slobin, D. I. (1985). Crosslinguistic evidence for the language-making capacity. In D. I. Slobin (Ed.), *The crosslinguistic study of language acquisition, Vol. 2* (pp. 1158–1249). Hillsdale, NJ: Lawrence Erlbaum Associates, Inc.

Slobin, D. I. (1996a). From 'thought and language' to 'thinking for speaking'. In J. J. Gumperz & S. C. Levinson (Eds.), *Rethinking linguistic relativity* (pp. 70–96). Cambridge, UK: Cambridge University Press.

Slobin, D. I. (1996b). Two ways to travel: Verbs of motion in English and Spanish. In M. Shibatani & S. A. Thompson (Eds.), *Grammatical constructions: Their form and meaning* (pp. 195–217). Oxford, UK: Oxford University Press.

Slobin, D. I. (1997). Mind, code, and text. In J. Bybee, J. Haiman, & S. A. Thompson (Eds.), *Essays on language function and language type: Dedicated to T. Givón* (pp. 437–467). Amsterdam: John Benjamins.

Spelke, E. S. (1990). Principles of object perception. *Cognitive Science, 14,* 29–56.

Spelke, E. S., Breinlinger, J., Macomber, J., & Jacobson, K. (1992). Origins of knowledge. *Psychological Review, 99,* 605–632.

Stadthagen-González, H., Pérez Tattam, R., Yavas, F., & Campusano, G. (2009). *Language dominance and interaction of L_A and L_B in Spanish–English adults in Miami.* Paper presented at the Colloquium on The Semantics–Cognition Interface in Bilinguals: Interaction Effects, Direction of Influence, Age of Acquisition, and Language Dominance, International Symposium on Bilingualism 7, Utrecht, July 8–11, 2009.

Starkey, P., & Cooper, R. (1980). Perception of numbers by human infants. *Science, 210,* 1033–1035.

Starkey, P., Spelke, E. S., & Gelman, R. (1983). Detection of intermodal numerical correspondences by human infants. *Science, 222,* 179–181.

Strauss, M., & Curtis, L. (1981). Infant perception of numerosity. *Child Development, 52,* 1146–1152.

Uziel-Karl, S. (2006). Acquisition of verb argument structure from a developmental perspective: Evidence from child Hebrew. In N. Gagarina & I. Gülzow (Eds.), *The acquisition of verbs and their grammar: The effect of particular languages. Studies in theoretical psycholinguistics* (pp. 15–44). Dordrecht: Springer.

Uziel-Karl, S. (2007). *Nativist vs. input based accounts of VAS acquisition: The case of Hebrew.* Paper presented in Workshop on Argument Structure and Syntactic Relations, University of the Basque Country, Vitoria-Gasteiz, Spain, May 23–25.

Uziel-Karl, S., & Budwig, N. (2007). The acquisition of non-agent subjects in child Hebrew: The role of input. In I. Gülzow & N. Gagarina (Eds.), *Frequency effects in language acquisition* (pp. 117–144). Berlin: Mouton de Gruyter.

Van Loosbroek, E., & Smitsman, A. (1990). Visual perception of numerosity in infancy. *Developmental Psychology, 26,* 916–922.

Weist, R. M. (2008). One-to-one mapping of temporal and spatial relations. In J. Guo, E. Lieven, S. Ervin-Tripp, N. Budwig, S. Özçalişkan, & K. Nakamura (Eds.), *Crosslinguistic approaches to the psychology of language: Research in the tradition of Dan Isaac Slobin* (pp. 69–80). Hillsdale, NJ: Lawrence Erlbaum Associates Inc.

Weist, R. M. (2009). Children think and talk about time and space. In P. Łobacz, P. Nowak, & W. Zabrocki (Eds.), *Language, science, and culture* (pp. 349–378). Poznań: Wydawnictwo Naukowe UAM.

Weist, R. M., Atanassova, M., Wysocka, H., & Pawlak, A. (1999). Spatial and temporal systems in child language and thought: A cross-linguistic study. *First Language, 19,* 267–312.

Weist, R. M., Lyytinen, P., Wysocka, J., & Atanassova M. (1997). The interaction of language and thought in children's language acquisition: A crosslinguistic study. *Journal of Child Language, 24,* 81–121.

Whorf, B. L. (1940/1956). Science and linguistics. *Technological Review, 42,* 229–231, 247–248. [Reprinted in J. B. Carroll (Ed.). (1956). *Language, thought, and reality* (pp. 207–219). Cambridge, MA: MIT Press.]

Wolff, P., & Ventura, T. (2009). When Russians learn English: How the semantics of causation may change. *Bilingualism: Language and Cognition, 12*(2), 153–176.

Wynn, K. (1996). Infants' individuation and enumeration of physical actions. *Psychological Science, 7,* 164–169.

Xu, F., & Carey. S. (1996). Infants' metaphysics: The case of numerical identity. *Cognitive Psychology, 30,* 111–153.

6   Tools for thinking

Barbara Tversky

For some reason the idea that the language one speaks affects the way one thinks, the Whorf or Sapir-Whorf hypothesis (e.g., Sapir, 1921; Whorf, 1956), is repugnant to some and stirring to others. Perhaps because of the passion it arouses, it produces clever experiments. Take speakers of Guugu Yimithirr, a language that uses only the cardinal directions to locate things in space, and drive them around every which way, and ask them to point home. They do so remarkably accurately. Take speakers of Dutch, a language that uses egocentric relations as well as cardinal directions to locate things in space and do the same—they point randomly (e.g., Levinson, 1996, 2003). Ask native German speakers to describe objects like a *bridge* in English. Some use terms like *elegant, fragile*, or *slender*. Ask the same of native Spanish speakers. Some use terms like *strong, sturdy*, or *towering* (Boroditsky, Schmidt, & Phillips, 2003). Why? In German, the word for *bridge* is feminine, whereas in Spanish it is masculine. Ask people who speak languages that refer to objects like boxes as units of substance, similar to 'pieces of cardboard', whether a plastic box or a piece of cardboard goes better with a cardboard box. They tend to group by stuff; they pick the piece of cardboard as often as the plastic box. In contrast, speakers of languages like English that individuate objects tend to group by kind; they pick the plastic box (e.g., Imai & Gentner, 1997; Lucy, 1992; Lucy & Gaskins, 2001, 2003). Effects of language have been shown for time (e.g., Boroditsky, 2001) as well as space, for color and shape as well as for substance/object (e.g., Roberson, Davidoff, & Shapiro, 2002; Roberson, Davies, & Davidoff, 2000). As for the effects of language on spatial cognition, the effects of language on perception of color, objects, and substance have been challenged. Sometimes the challenge is specific, that alternative explanations seem more plausible for the case at hand (e.g., Li, Dunham, & Carey, 2008), but sometimes the challenge is general, to the very idea that the language one speaks can affect the way one thinks (e.g., Li & Gleitman, 2002; but see Levinson, Kita, Haun, & Rasch, 2002).

Perhaps a broader perspective is needed. What kinds of things do affect thought? And how do they affect thought? Let's start close to controversy, with effects of language within a language. There are simply more things and features of things, and relations among things and relations among their features, and actions of things and relations among their actions and their features in the world, than there are words. Words select among that multitude of features, acting as pointers or filters. Word associations to names of objects are more stereotyped and focused than word associations to pictures of objects, presumably because they are less affected by the visual properties inevitably apparent in pictures of objects or objects themselves (Deno, Johnson, & Jenkins, 1968; Otto, 1962; Wicker, 1970; Winn, 1976).

Language can do more than select features. Language can favor some kinds of features over other kinds of features. Significantly, using language can focus attention on features such as function not readily available in perception; that is, from momentary views of static objects. For example, when people compared two pictures of bodies with a part highlighted to verify whether the same part was highlighted in both, reaction times were fastest for parts that were perceptually salient; specifically, high in contour distinctiveness. However, when people compared a name of a body part to a picture of a body with a part highlighted, reaction times were fastest for parts that were functionally significant, as rated independently (Morrison & Tversky, 2005). Functional significance is not readily apparent from seeing bodies; it depends on knowing what different body parts do, even ones hidden inside the body, and how what they do affects one's life. Words for things arouse abstract features of the things more than the things themselves. A related phenomenon occurs when people provide the words themselves, by giving play-by-play descriptions for ongoing actions, simple everyday activities such as making beds and doing dishes. Those who described the activities as they watched them organized them more hierarchically than those who simply watched (Zacks, Tversky, & Iyer, 2001). The descriptions give clues to why describing had the effect of organizing perception. The descriptions were primarily of completed goals and subgoals, completed actions on objects, such as *putting on the bottom sheet* or *rinsing the plate*. The act of describing ongoing action (a longer discussion) focused attention on completion of actions. Since action completions are hierarchically organized—*smoothing the sheet* is the last part of *putting on the sheet*, which is in turn a middle part of *making a bed*— describing in language served to increase hierarchical organization of the perception of ongoing action.

Because language can select certain features at the expense of others, it can also be detrimental. It may focus on the wrong features for the task. Faces, notoriously difficult to describe, provide an example. Describing faces while viewing them can make them more difficult to recognize later (Schooler, 1997). Describing appears to focus attention on features that are easy to describe. Those features, such as eye color or hair texture, do not seem to be useful in discriminating old faces from new ones. At the same time, describing takes attention away from features of faces such as configurations of features that are hard to describe but central to recognition.

Language can go beyond selecting certain features of things and ignoring others. Language can signal that something belongs to a category. Being in a category has consequences for relations to other things within the category as well as for relations of things in the category to things in other categories. This is apparent in performance of children in matching tasks. Children are shown a picture of a target object and asked to select which of two pictures of other objects goes better with, or is another example of, or is the same as, the target object. When children are shown a picture of a bee, for example, and asked to find what 'goes better' with the bee, an ant or a flower, they pick the flower. They pick the flower even when asked to 'find me the same kind of thing as this'. However, when they are shown the picture of the bee and asked to find another *sud*, they are more likely to pick the ant, and less likely to pick the thematically related object, the flower (Markman & Hutchinson, 1984). Using a name, a word, a label, even if a nonsense word, is what matters. Languages typically use names or labels to refer to categories of things that share features, such as 'tiny, wiry creatures with heads and legs that fly or crawl', which we call *insects*, but languages typically don't use names to refer to themes that relate different objects, such as 'bees extract nectar from flowers'. The label seems to signal to the child that the bee belongs to a category and to focus on the features shared by the category rather than on interactions of the bee with other things. Language can call attention to relations between categories as well as to category membership. Providing preschoolers with words for spatial relations, such as *top*, *middle*, or *bottom* helps them solve a spatial analogy problem in which they are asked to place a card in the same relative position as a previous one (Lowenstein & Gentner, 2005).

Note that many of the effects of language on thought are not effects of words per se. The attribution of feminine features to bridges by German speakers and masculine features to bridges by Spanish speakers described earlier is an effect of grammatical gender, not of specific words (Boroditsky et al., 2003). Simply the way words are arbitrarily ordered affects thought. When a person is described with a list of varied personality attributes, some positive, some negative, the first descriptor carries the greatest weight in later ratings of likability (Anderson & Hubert, 1963). The weight people give to the descriptors in estimating likability declines with the serial order of the descriptor.

Many of these effects of language within a language go beyond 'thinking for speaking', the analysis Slobin (1996) proposed for Whorfian effects. Language used by others affects the thought of listeners as well as speakers. As noted, children are more likely to group taxonomically instead of thematically when they hear a pseudo category label (Markman & Hutchinson, 1984), and adults are more likely to attend to functional features of body parts when they are named than when they are presented visually (Morrison & Tversky, 2005). The case that turned insurance investigator Whorf into a linguist is yet another example (Whorf, 1956). He investigated fires that were caused by people who were careless with matches around oil barrels because the barrels had been described as 'empty'.

Equally important, language appears to have longer-term off-line effects, encouraging people to attend to certain things, aspects, distinctions, and relations in the world and instilling associations to things, aspects, distinctions, and relations not directly given in perception. The ability to maintain orientation in space by speakers of a language that locates things in space using an absolute (cardinal directions) system is one example (Levinson, 2003). Another example comes from research within a language. A longitudinal study of language and cognitive development found that toddlers who heard and used more spatial language later performed a variety of spatial tasks better, specifically mental rotation, block designs, and spatial analogies (Levine, Huttenlocher, Gunderson, Rowe, & Pruden, 2009). If language biases thought within a language, then it is likely to do so across languages as well. Many of the mechanisms are similar, for example focusing attention on some aspects of things and not others.

Language is not unitary; it has many communicative strands, delicately interwoven. Yet other aspects of language affect thinking. Gesture is one of them. One's own gestures aid thought; sitting on the hands interferes with finding words (e.g., Krauss, Chen, & Gottesman, 2000). Others' gestures aid thought: Teachers' gestures help students learn math (e.g., Singer & Goldin-Meadow, 2005; Valenzano, Alibali, & Klatzky, 2003). Language can be written as well as spoken. The direction of reading and writing seems to be a chance and arbitrary convention, in that many languages are written left to right and many others are written right to left. Nevertheless, writing direction has dramatic effects on thought. Time is thought to go from left to right by speakers of languages that are written and read from left to right, and to go from right to left by speakers of languages written from right to left (e.g., Santiago, Román, Ouellet, Rodríguez, & Pérez-Azor, 2010; Tversky, Kugelmass, & Winter, 1991). A person depicted on the left is perceived as more agentive than one on the right for left–right languages but the opposite for right–left languages (Chatterjee, 2001). Action from left to right is perceived as stronger than right to left action by readers of left-to-right languages, but the reverse is true for readers of right-to-left languages (Maass, Pagani, & Berta, 2007). Aesthetic judgments (Chokron & De Agostini, 2000) and interpretation of facial expressions (Vaid & Singh, 1989) correspond to writing direction. Even more purely perceptual processing like apparent motion (Morikawa & McBeath, 1982) and perceptual exploration (Nachshon, 1985) are affected by reading order.

Language is a cognitive tool, one of many designed to expand the mind and foster the communication and coordination on which human society rests (e.g., Norman, 1993; Tversky, 2001). Like other cognitive tools—our bodies, pencil and paper, calculators, abaci, maps, graphs, design sketches, even the environment around us—language can help (or hinder) thought. Language encodes, encapsulates, emphasizes, summarizes, organizes, and transforms certain meanings and relations and not others. Language can serve communication, it can direct our own thoughts and actions, it can direct the thoughts and actions of others. Frequently, what language encodes and emphasizes is useful, but on occasion what it ignores might have been useful as well, true of any tuned and adaptive filtering or processing mechanism. Focusing, filtering, reducing, and transforming information has benefits and costs, depending on the task.

Thought is multifaceted, as are the interrelations of thought and the cognitive tools that serve it. Counting and arithmetic provide examples of the rich interactions between tools and thought. People who speak languages that have count-words solve certain problems better than people who speak languages that lack count-words (e.g., Frank, Everett, Fedorenko, & Gibson, 2008; Gordon, 2004). Some numerical competence—for example, estimating which of two quantities is larger—is possible without the training in counting that number words enable. People speaking languages without count-words can use one-to-one correspondence to compare two quantities when the quantities are spatially aligned in parallel. However, training in counting with number words augments this capacity, so that determining one-to-one correspondence for spatially disparate displays is easy for those speaking languages with count-words, but those speaking languages without count-words make errors. Note, however, the important role that actions, pointing and moving, have in learning to count and in determining one-to-one correspondences. Later, counting with the eyes can often substitute for counting with the fingers. Count-words allow inspecting and summing each display separately and using the final number as a memory aid for the entire array to compare arrays. Even the length of the words used to count makes a difference. Working memory capacity depends on number of syllables, so it is greater for shorter words with fewer syllables than for words with many syllables. As a consequence, speakers of languages whose count-words have fewer syllables, like Chinese, have longer number memory spans than speakers of languages whose count-words have many syllables, like Welsh (Baddeley & Hitch, 1974; Chen & Stevenson, 1988). Doing multiplication is easier with Arabic numerals than with Roman numerals (Zhang & Norman, 1995); try 36 times 9 versus XXXVI times IX. Doing multiplication with paper and pencil is easier than doing it in the mind. Training in arithmetic using an abacus alters the way children do mental arithmetic and the ways they think about numbers (Stigler, 1983). Both words for counting and devices for arithmetic are cognitive tools, and each tool, language and device, affects thought.

Many external cognitive tools affect thought in many different ways. Using an abacus is one example. Even the simple tool of pencil and paper affects thought. In many cases, marks on paper, diagrams or sketches, aid thinking, from to-do lists to computing square roots to designing buildings (e.g., Goldschmidt, 1994; Schon, 1983; Suwa & Tversky, 1997). However, just as for language, sketches and diagrams can bias thinking, not always for the best. Students checking diagrams of information systems, connections among computers, servers, clients, and the like, tend to scan them in reading order, from left to right. When many components need to be checked, students often neglect checking the later ones, leading to systematic errors (Corter, Rho, Zahner, Nickerson, & Tversky, 2009; Nickerson, Corter, Tversky, Zahner, & Rho, 2008). People tend to interpret lines on paper as connections, even as physical routes (Tversky, 2001), so that many students interpret lines in diagrams of components of information systems as routes through the system, and think that information must pass through all the intervening components to get from the leftmost to the rightmost component, an inference that can be erroneous (Corter et al., 2009; Nickerson et al., 2008).

The general claim should be clear by now. Language is one of many cognitive tools for thinking, a toolbox that also includes gestures, diagrams, training in a multitude of skills, like counting and arithmetic, and more. Each of these can affect thinking in diverse ways, but not necessarily. Cognitive tools, and specifically language, don't always affect thought. For example, languages differ widely in the dominant ordering of subjects, verbs, and objects. However, when asked to explain how to perform a variety of actions on objects using only gestures, speakers of languages with many different syntactic orders nevertheless ordered their gestures identically, subject–object–verb (Goldin-Meadow, So, Ozyurek, & Mylander, 2008).

If thought can be affected by so many different cognitive tools, why wouldn't the language one speaks be among those cognitive tools, given the multiplicity of ways that language is used and the multiplicity of ways that different languages cut up the world, spatially, temporally, causally, emotionally, and more? The evidence presented here, a small fraction of that available, illustrates only few of those multiple ways. If so, why does the very idea that the language one speaks affects how one thinks arouse so much resistance? Of course, challenging ideas is the usual business of science: proposing alternative hypotheses and finding evidence supporting them. However, some seem to fear that the Whorf hypothesis implies the frightening thought that speakers of different languages are doomed to never understand one another. To which one could point out that speakers of the same language, even within the same family, sometimes appear to have the same trouble. Underlying some of the passion in this debate seems to be differing worldviews: Are different peoples fundamentally the same or are the differences among different peoples substantial and significant? These different worldviews, universalist or particularist, are not unique to language and thought.

There remains an important issue on which there are no data. How large are the effects of language on thinking? How do they compare to the other influences on thought, home, education, religion, culture, gender, genes? How extensive are the effects of language on behavior? Do speakers of *stuff* languages find it easier to recycle than speakers of *kind* languages? Do speakers of languages without a future tense have more problems with future planning? Would a German architect be more likely to design a delicate frilly bridge and a Spanish designer more likely to design a massive, sturdy one? Either way, the forecast is for more insightful research.

REFERENCES

Anderson, N. H., & Hubert, S. (1963). Effects of concomitant verbal recall on order effects in personality impression formation. *Journal of Verbal Learning & Verbal Behavior, 2,* 379–391.

Baddeley, A. D., & Hitch, G. J. (1974). Working memory. In G. A. Bower (Ed.), *Recent advances in learning and motivation, Volume 8* (pp. 47–89). New York: Academic Press.

Boroditsky, L. (2001). Does language shape thought? Mandarin and English speakers' conceptions of time. *Cognitive Psychology, 43,* 1–22.

Boroditsky, L., Schmidt, L., & Phillips, W. (2003). Sex, syntax, and semantics. In D. Gentner & S. Goldin-Meadow (Eds.), *Language in mind: Advances in the study of language and thought* (pp. 61–78). Cambridge, MA: MIT Press.

Chatterjee, A. (2001). Language and space: Some interactions. *Trends in Cognitive Science, 5,* 55–61.

Chen, C., & Stevenson, H. W. (1988). Cross-linguistic differences in digit span of preschool children. *Journal of Experimental Child Psychology, 46,* 150–158.

Chokron, S., & De Agostini, M. (2000). Reading habits influence aesthetic preference. *Cognitive Brain Research, 10,* 45–49.

Corter, J. E., Rho, Y-J, Zahner, D., Nickerson, J. V., & Tversky, B. (2009). Bugs and biases: Diagnosing misconceptions in the understanding of diagrams. In N. A. Taatgen & H. van Rijn (Eds.), *Proceedings of the 31st Annual Conference of the Cognitive Science Society* (pp. 756–761). Austin, TX: Cognitive Science Society.

Deno, S. L., Johnson, P., & Jenkins, J. R. (1968). Associative similarity of words and pictures. *AV Communication Review, 16,* 280–286.

Frank, M. C., Everett, D. L, Fedorenko, E., & Gibson, E. (2008). Number as a cognitive technology: Evidence from Pirahã language. *Cognition, 108,* 810–824.

Goldin-Meadow, S., So, W-C., Ozyurek, A., & Mylander, C. (2008). The natural order of events: How speakers of different languages represent events nonverbally. *Proceedings of the National Academy of Sciences, 105,* 9163–9168.

Goldschmidt, G. (1994). On visual design thinking: The vis kids of architecture. *Design Studies, 15,* 158–174.

Gordon, P. (2004). Numerical cognition without words. Evidence from Amazonia. *Science, 306,* 496–499.

Imai, M., & Gentner, D. (1997). A crosslinguistic study of early word meaning: Universal ontology and linguistic influence. *Cognition, 62,* 169–200.

Krauss, R. M., Chen, Y., & Gottesman, R. F. (2000). Lexical gestures and lexical access: A process model. In D. McNeill (Ed.), *Language and gesture* (pp. 261–283). New York: Cambridge University Press.

Levine, S. C., Huttenlocher, J., Gunderson, E. A., Rowe, M. L., & Pruden, S. (2009). *Preschoolers' number and spatial knowledge: Relation to early parent–child interactions.* Paper presented at the Society for Research in Child Development Biennial Meeting, Denver, Colorado, April 2–4.

Levinson, S. C. (1996). Frames of reference and Molyneux's question: Cross-linguistic evidence. In P. Bloom, M. A. Peterson, L. Nadel, & M. Garrett (Eds.), *Space and language* (pp. 109–169). Cambridge, MA: MIT Press.

Levinson, S. C. (2003). *Space in language and cognition: Explorations in cognitive diversity.* Cambridge, UK: Cambridge University Press.

Levinson, S. C., Kita, S., Haun, D. B. M., & Rasch, B. H. (2002). Returning the tables: Language affects spatial reasoning. *Cognition, 84,* 155–188.

Li, P., Dunham, Y., & Carey, S. (2008). Of substance: The nature of language effects on entity construal. *Cognitive Psychology, 58,* 487–524.

Li, P., & Gleitman, L. (2002). Turning the tables: Spatial language and spatial cognition. *Cognition, 83,* 265–294.

Lowenstein, J., & Gentner, D. (2005). Relational language and the development of relational mapping. *Cognitive Psychology, 50,* 315–353.

Lucy, J. (1992). *Grammatical categories and cognition: A case study of the linguistic relativity hypothesis.* Cambridge, UK: Cambridge University Press.

Lucy, J., & Gaskins, S. (2001). Grammatical categories and the development of classification preferences: A comparative approach. In M. Bowerman & S. Levinson (Eds.), *Language acquisition and conceptual development* (pp. 257–283). Cambridge, UK: Cambridge University Press.

Lucy, J. A., & Gaskins, S. (2003). Interaction of language type and referent type in the development of nonverbal classification preferences. In D. Gentner & S. Goldin-Meadow (Eds.), *Language in mind: Advances in the issues of language and thought* (pp. 465–492). Cambridge, MA: MIT Press.

Maass, A., Pagani, D., & Berta, E. (2007). How beautiful is the goal and how violent is the fistfight? Spatial bias in the interpretation of human behavior. *Social Cognition, 25,* 833–852.

Markman, E. M., & Hutchinson, J. E. (1984). Children's sensitivity to constraints on word meaning: Taxonomic vs. thematic relations. *Cognitive Psychology, 16,* 1–27.

Morikawa, K., & McBeath, M. (1992). Lateral motion bias associated with reading direction. *Vision Research, 32,* 1137–1141.

Morrison, J. B., & Tversky, B. (2005). Bodies and their parts. *Memory and Cognition, 33,* 696–709.

Nachson, I. (1985). Directional preferences in perception of visual stimuli. *International Journal of Neuroscience, 25,* 161–174.

Nickerson, J. V., Corter, J. E., Tversky, B., Zahner, D., & Rho, Y-J. (2008). The spatial nature of thought: Understanding information systems design through diagrams. In R. Boland, M. Limayem, & B. Pentland (Eds.), *Proceedings of the 29th International Conference on Information Systems.* Paris: Association for Information Systems.

Norman, D. A. (1993). *Things that make us smart*. Reading, MA: Addison-Wesley.

Otto, W. (1962). The differential effects of verbal and pictorial representations of stimuli upon responses. *Journal of Verbal Learning and Verbal Behavior, 1*, 192–196.

Roberson, D., Davidoff, J., & Shapiro, L. (2002). Squaring the circle: The cultural relativity of good shape. *Journal of Cognition and Culture, 2*, 29–53.

Roberson, D., Davies, I., & Davidoff, J. (2000). Color categories are not universal: Replications and new evidence from a Stone-Age culture. *Journal of Experimental Psychology: General, 129*, 369–398.

Santiago, J., Román, A., Ouellet, M., Rodríguez, N., & Pérez-Azor, P. (2010). In hindsight, life flows from left to right. *Psychological Research, 74*(1), 59–70. doi 10.1007/s00426-008-0220-0

Sapir, E. (1921). *Language*. New York: Harcourt, Brace, & World.

Schon, D. A. (1983). *The reflective practitioner*. New York: Harper Collins.

Schooler, J. (1997). The verbal overshadowing effect: Why descriptions impair face recognition. *Memory and Cognition, 25*, 129–139.

Singer, M. A., & Goldin-Meadow, S. (2005). Students learn when their teachers' gesture and speech differ. *Psychological Science, 16*, 85–89.

Slobin, D. (1996). From 'thought and language' to 'thinking for speaking.' In J. J. Gumperz & S. C. Levinson (Eds.), *Rethinking linguistic relativity* (pp. 70–96). Cambridge, UK: Cambridge University Press.

Stigler, J. (1983). 'Mental abacus': The effect of abacus training on Chinese children's mental calculation. *Cognitive Psychology, 16*, 145–176.

Suwa, M., & Tversky, B. (1997). What architects and students perceive in their sketches: A protocol analysis. *Design Studies, 18*, 385–403.

Tversky, B. (2001). Spatial schemas in depictions. In M. Gattis (Ed.), *Spatial schemas and abstract thought* (pp. 79–111). Cambridge, MA: MIT Press.

Tversky, B., Kugelmass, S., & Winter, A. (1991). Cross-cultural and developmental trends in graphic productions. *Cognitive Psychology, 23*, 515–557.

Vaid, J., & Singh, M. (1989). Asymmetries in the perception of facial effects: Is there an influence of reading habits? *Neuropsychologia, 27*, 1277–1286.

Valenzano, L. Alibali, M. W., & Klatzky, R. (2003). Teachers' gestures facilitate students' learning: A lesson in symmetry. *Contemporary Educational Psychology, 28*, 187–204.

Whorf, B. L. (1956). The relation of habitual thought and behavior to language. In J. B. Carroll (Ed.), *Language, thought, and reality: Selected writings of Benjamin Lee Whorf* (pp. 134–159). Cambridge, MA: MIT Press.

Wicker, F. (1970). Continuous restricted associations to pictorial and verbal items. *AV Communication Review, 18*, 431–439.

Winn, W. (1976). The structure of multiple free associations to words, black-and-white pictures and color pictures. *AV Communication Review, 24*, 273–293.

Zacks, J., Tversky, B., & Iyer, G. (2001). Perceiving, remembering, and communicating structure in events. *Journal of Experimental Psychology: General, 136*, 29–58.

Zhang, J. J., & Norman, D. A. (1995). A representational analysis of numeration systems. *Cognition, 57*, 271–295.

Part B

Bilingual cognition

The intention of Part B is to present the new research area of bilingual cognition, arising out of the general views seen in Part A but now taking on an independent life of its own. Part B starts with an introduction giving the background to current research (Bassetti & Cook). It then presents three papers by distinguished researchers looking at semantic differences between languages and their relationship to thinking in bilinguals (Wierzbicka), at the pioneering days of research into linguistic relativity and bilingualism (Ervin-Tripp), and at the bilingual mind and brain (Green). It goes on to look at specific examples of current research into the minds of those who know two languages, covering a variety of areas: color (Athanasopoulos), spatial location (Coventry, Guijarro-Fuentes, & Valdés), motion (Czechowska & Ewert; Hendriks & Hickmann), time perception (Chen & Su), concepts of animals (Bassetti), gesture (Salvato), causation (Cunningham, Vaid, & Chen), Theory of Mind (Siegal, Kobayashi Frank, Surian, & Hjelmquist), and emotions (Knickerbocker & Altarriba; Besemeres). Part B, then, demonstrates the broad range of topics and methodologies used in current bilingual cognition research.

7 Relating language and cognition: The second language user

Benedetta Bassetti and Vivian Cook

If differences in linguistic representation lead to differences in cognition among speakers of different languages, what happens to people who know more than one language? Knowing two languages that instantiate two different ways of looking at the world may lead bilinguals to look at the world differently from monolinguals, and may help them see beyond what the first language represents.

Bilingualism has two possible cognitive outcomes. One is that the very knowledge and use of two languages affects cognition, regardless of the languages involved—the macro level. An example of this may be increased metalinguistic awareness (Bialystok, 2001) or delayed onset of Alzheimer's (Bialystok, Craik, Klein, & Viswanathan, 2004). Another outcome is that the learning of two languages affects cognition because of the characteristics of the languages involved, and how the languages code a given aspect of the world. We may refer to this as the micro level. For instance, suppose a monolingual user of Russian linguistically encodes two different shades of blue where a monolingual user of English has one: In this case a bilingual who speaks both English and Russian may distinguish two colors that monolingual English speakers consider to be one. An English–Dutch bilingual, however, would not differ from an English monolingual, because these two languages do not have different classifications of blue. While this volume is mostly directed at the micro outcome, the macro outcome (or interactions between the micro and the macro levels) is also widely studied (e.g., see Green, Chapter 9, this volume).

WHAT IS A BILINGUAL?

A starting point is to consider what bilingualism actually *is*. Intuitively, it is the knowledge of more than one language, as opposed to mono-lingualism, but a scientific definition seems hard to pin down. A variety of definitions have been proposed, surveyed usefully in Hoffman (1991). Most definitions cluster into two groups. One consists of a maximal assumption where being bilingual means speaking two languages with equal fluency in every situation, as in Bloomfield's (1933) 'native-like control of two languages' (p. 56). This probably corresponds best to the everyday concept of bilingualism, namely that a bilingual has a high level of proficiency in both languages. The other definition takes the minimal view that bilingualism refers to any real-life use of more than one language at whatever level; Haugen (1953, p. 7) for instance claims that bilingualism starts at 'the point where a speaker can first produce complete meaningful utterances in the other language'. These definitions then oppose 'complete' knowledge of two (or more) languages against 'any' ability to use the second language at all; they differ in how much of the second language (L2) they consider it takes to be bilingual. Concealed in the maximal/minimal question is a second issue of 'knowledge' of another language versus 'ability to use' another language. Weinreich, for example, defines bilingualism as 'the practice of alternately using two languages' (Weinreich, 1953, p. 1); that is, a straightforward use definition.

Both types of definition have a fatal flaw, as pointed out by Romaine (1989, p. 282): 'it is clear that a reasonable account of bilingualism cannot be based on a theory which assumes monolingual competence as its frame of reference'. The maximal definition assumes that the target for a bilingual is the linguistic competence of a monolingual native speaker in both languages; the use definition assumes that a bilingual uses language in the same way as a monolingual native speaker in both languages. But people who know more than one language have different knowledge of both their first and second languages from monolingual native speakers of either (Cook, 2003), and they have uses for language that no monolingual has, such as code-switching and translation: In short a bilingual is *not* two monolinguals in one person (Grosjean, 1998); 'For the vast majority of bilinguals, "bilingual competence" is not measurable in terms of monolingual standards' (Hoffman, 1991, p. 23).

In support of the minimal definition, it seems that even a smattering of knowledge of another language is enough to change from a monolingual's way of thinking. For instance, it took just a few months of English for a group of Hebrew-speaking schoolchildren to change their concept of time flow (see below). It took 1 hour of Italian a week for 1 year for a group of English kindergarten children to develop a different concept of 'word' (Yelland, Pollard, & Mercuri, 1993). Experimental studies also found effects of very short (e.g., as little as 15 minutes) second language learning of an artificial language on performance on non-language cognitive tasks (e.g., Boroditsky, 2001). In other words it would be wrong to assume that any cognitive consequences of bilingualism only appear in maximal bilinguals who have acquired and used the language for many years; effects may manifest themselves at a comparatively low level of knowledge and use of the second language after a matter of hours.

The use definition needs to acknowledge the so-called language 'skills'—listening, speaking, reading, and writing; the Language Passport (Council of Europe, 2000) of the Council of Europe for instance asks people to rate themselves on six levels of second language ability under the headings Understanding, Speaking, and Writing. Bilingualism may thus vary according to the skill involved. One of the present authors would come out very differently on these scales, being able to follow academic committee meetings in French with no problems but being unable to speak at them except in English; the other author can read entire novels in French but cannot buy a box of chocolates in Brussels. There is a difference between productive and receptive knowledge of a second language; a bilingual may comprehend one of their languages at a different level of proficiency from which they produce it. Someone who is a fluent listener or reader of a language but cannot speak it is indeed a bilingual, just as a monk with a vow of silence is still a native speaker of his first language. A particularly interesting case in point is the bimodal bilingualism of the Deaf (Grosjean, 2008): A Deaf signer may be a native user of say British Sign Language and an L2 user of written English, with no use of spoken English. Furthermore, conceptual changes can be instigated not only by knowledge of spoken language, but also by knowledge of written language—someone who cannot speak two languages but can read two languages is not identical to a monoliterate person.

Another, related, crucial distinction is between academic knowledge or study of a language and the ability to actually use it (also captured by the distinction between natural and instructed bilingualism). For the purposes of bilingual cognition research, someone who learnt Latin in school and understood the intricacies of its tense and aspect system hardly qualifies as a monolingual any more, although this person may never have spoken a full sentence of Latin. The impact of a second language on thinking needs to be extended to different types of L2 knowledge, ranging from the scholar who writes entire grammars of languages they cannot speak to the English-speaking child who has been taught the French subjunctive at school.

It might be impossible ever to provide a satisfactory definition of bilingualism. More importantly for the present volume, it might be undesirable. Different groups of people need different definitions, depending on their purposes. For instance, for educators a use-based definition is more useful, e.g., a bilingual child is one 'who regularly needs to understand or use more than one language (e.g., at home and at school)' (Frederickson & Cline, 2002, p. 246). For the purposes of bilingual cognition research, a bilingual is someone who knows more than one language, regardless of ability to produce the languages, and regardless of whether the languages are spoken, written or signed. While language production can be evidence of knowledge, there is no evidence that it is needed for the process of acquiring new concepts. Nor is it is necessary to know the spoken language, as new ideas can be acquired by reading.

Furthermore, in this volume, the term *bilingual* includes *multilingual*, *trilingual*, and so on, except where the specific issue of cognition in bilinguals versus multilinguals is discussed below. To avoid prejudging all these issues, some researchers now use the more neutral term *L2 users* rather than *bilinguals* (Cook, 1994), not committing themselves to a multiple-monolingual definition of bilingualism, and the term will be used in this chapter to talk about someone who knows more than one language, whether spoken, written, or signed, regardless of the number of languages known, the level of proficiency, how they were learnt, and whether knowledge is productive or receptive.

BILINGUALISM IN THE EARLY DAYS OF LINGUISTIC RELATIVITY

Historically, scientific research into the relationship of language and thought took its inspiration from the principle of 'linguistic relativity' proposed by Benjamin Lee Whorf (Whorf, 1940/1956) and Edward Sapir, as mentioned in most contributions to this volume. From its very beginnings, the concept of linguistic relativity was associated with people who knew more than one language, coming out of the strong US nineteenth- and early twentieth-century tradition of anthropological linguistics, as described in Lucy's contribution to this volume (Chapter 3). Edward Sapir (who was Whorf's mentor) was a German Jew who had ended up in the USA and so was a user of more than one language— bilingual in the maximal sense. Whorf himself probably developed his ideas about linguistic relativity as a consequence of studying American Indian languages.

The idea that learning another language changes your worldview was not, of course, new. A century before Whorf, von Humboldt had said:

> To learn a foreign language should therefore be to acquire a new standpoint in the world-view hitherto possessed, in fact to a certain extent this is so, since every language contains the whole conceptual fabric and mode of presentation of a portion of mankind.
>
> (von Humboldt, 1836/1988, p. 60).

Still, he pessimistically went on to add:

> But because we always carry over, more or less, our own world-view, and even our own language-view, this outcome is not purely and completely experienced.

Sapir and Whorf were more enthusiastic about bilingualism. Sapir wrote:

> Perhaps the best way to get behind our thought processes and to eliminate from them all the accidents or irrelevances due to their

linguistic garb is to plunge into a study of exotic modes of expression. At any rate, I know of no better way to kill spurious 'entities'.

(Sapir, 1924/1985, p. 157)

Whorf also believed that learning other languages could free people from the bias of their language and clarify thinking. To him the stranglehold that language has on thinking could be overcome by becoming aware of it through knowledge of other languages; as Lee puts it, Whorf 'believed that awareness achieved by studying the way different languages embody different analyses of experience has the capacity, at least potentially, to free conceptual activity, including reasoning, from monolingual constraints' (Lee, 1996, p. 239). Whorf repeatedly makes the point that a more object-ive understanding of reality comes from learning how other languages represent reality, styled 'multilingual awareness':

> Western culture has made, through language, a provisional analysis of reality and, without correctives, holds resolutely to that analysis as final. The only corrective lies in all those other tongues which by aeons of independent evolution have arrived at different, but equally logical, provisional analyses.
>
> (Whorf, 1941/1956, p. 244)

But he seems to think that this insight is to be achieved through formal study, not naturalistic acquisition. In his 1940 article 'Science and lin-guistics', Whorf wrote: 'The person most nearly free [to describe nature with absolute impartiality] would be a linguist familiar with very many widely different linguistic systems' (Whorf, 1940/1956, p. 214).

Indeed, Whorf appeared to believe that the linguist with an academic knowledge of languages was better equipped to understand how language invisibly affects thinking than the polyglot who can communicate in more than one language:

> These background phenomena [the phenomena of language that are outside the consciousness and control of its speakers] are the province of the grammarian—or of the linguist, to give him his more modern name as a scientist. . . . a person who can quickly attain agreement about subject matter with different people speaking a number of dif-ferent languages . . . is better termed a polyglot or a multilingual.
>
> (Whorf, 1940/1956, p. 211)

Not that Whorf was always consistent. On the one hand, he believes him-self capable of understanding the worldview of Hopi speakers as pre-sented in their language, unfettered by his native English. On the other hand, he seems to treat his Hopi informants as monolingual Hopi speakers rather than Hopis who spoke English—his main informant was living in

New York after all—assuming that they think in uniquely Hopi ways, without appreciating that their knowledge of English may have affected what they are presenting to him. So, for instance, he writes (1937/1956, pp. 103–104) that the 'bilingual English-speaking Hopi informant' has two or more fundamental meaning categories in his own language corresponding to just one category in English (inceptive, or 'begin doing', and projective, or 'do with a forward movement').

At any rate, in spite of these caveats, from the early days of linguistic relativity bilingualism was seen as the solution to the problem of language's effects on thought that had just been discovered. Yet research on bilingual cognition was still far off.

THE DEVELOPMENT OF RESEARCH ON LINGUISTIC RELATIVITY AND BILINGUAL COGNITION

Indeed the possibility that bilingualism affects cognition did not become a research topic for another 60 years after Whorf, although early linguistic relativity research that included bilinguals had shown from the very early days that bilinguals differed from monolinguals. During the 1950s and the 1960s, when linguistic relativity research focused on color perception, a handful of studies indeed looked at bilinguals. Brown and Lenneberg (1954) and Lenneberg and Roberts (1956) showed that when a language does not have separate lexical labels for two colors (e.g., Zuni has one word for 'yellow' and 'orange'), its speakers do not remember these colors as well as speakers of a language with two lexical labels (e.g., English). Ervin (1961) found that learning L2 English changes Navaho speakers' color naming and color prototypes, and that these are affected by language dominance (whether English-dominant or Navaho-dominant). Similar findings were published a few years later (Caskey-Sirmons & Hickerson, 1977). In short, these pioneer studies showed that bilinguals do not share the same color categories as monolinguals.

By the 1970s, linguistic relativity had fallen out of favor with researchers, partly because evidence of the universality of color perception was generally accepted (see Berlin & Kay, 1969), but also due to a change in the zeitgeist, as linguists inspired by Chomsky concentrated increasingly on language universals and psychologists had other preoccupations (see Ervin-Tripp, Chapter 9 this volume). Research into linguistic relativity itself became rare and was sometimes vilified. As a consequence, research on bilingual cognition too faded away (with very rare exceptions, such as the study of person cognition in Hoffman, Lau, & Johnson, 1986).

Yet it was also during this time that a fairly strong claim about the effects of bilingual cognition was advanced, in Bloom's study of counterfactual reasoning in Chinese speakers that included Chinese users of L2 English (Bloom, 1981). The English language distinguishes between a counterfactual conditional (a conditional that describes the consequences of events that did not happen, as in *If John had seen Mary, he would have known that she was pregnant*—i.e., John did not see Mary) and a factual conditional (*If John saw Mary, he knew she was pregnant*—i.e., we don't know whether John saw Mary). The Chinese language does not distinguish between these two types of conditionals either lexically or grammatically, and so gives no information as to whether an event happened or not. Bloom created a counterfactual story about what would have happened if a philosopher named Bier had known Chinese, and asked Chinese speakers to answer questions about the story. Chinese monolingual speakers mostly did not interpret the story counterfactually, but those who knew L2 English did so more often. Although the research only used bilinguals as a test-bed for research on monolinguals, it provided clear evidence of effects of bilingualism on cognition. It was also the first study of bilinguals to look at 'grammaticalized concepts', i.e., concepts encoded in morphology and syntax, rather than 'lexicalized concepts', i.e., concepts encoded in words, such as colors—a distinction that has become highly relevant to current research.

Bloom's research happened to be published at a time when linguistic relativity was seen as theoretically and methodologically suspect. Such research was even seen as something to be avoided on ethical grounds, as is evident from the following comment on Bloom's work:

> [A] cross-cultural study of a possible difference in basic cognitive ability that happened to get favorable results for linguistic relativity inevitably leads to the implied degradation of one of the compared cultures. Given the indecisive nature of cross-cultural research, it does not seem to be advisable to conduct cross-cultural studies of linguistic relativity, the most reliable accomplishment of which may be the creation of hostility among different cultures in this already complicated world.
>
> (Takano, 1989, p. 161)

Ironically, it was precisely his finding that Chinese–English bilinguals out-performed monolinguals that might have saved Bloom from taunts of racism. If learning a second language makes this type of reasoning easier, this makes it a *language* problem, not one of race or culture. Many researchers criticized Bloom's work on methodological grounds and failed to obtain the same results (with modified materials—for example Au, 1983, 1984; Cheng, 1985; Liu, 1985). One could say that Bloom's book was dismissed partly because it came out at the wrong time. Only recently have researchers dared to re-open the topic of Chinese counterfactuals (Yeh & Gentner, 2005, on monolinguals; Bassetti, 2008, on bilinguals).

There was then a hiatus in research into bilingual cognition, barring the occasional paper or thesis (e.g., Kiyak, 1982). The late 1990s saw the appearance of calls for research specifically on bilingual cognition

(Cook, 2002; Green, 1998; Pavlenko, 1999); the term 'conceptual transfer' made its appearance (e.g., Jarvis, 1998); and theses and conference papers started emerging (Chalikia & Vaid, 1999; Han, 1998). In the 2000s came the first workshop devoted to the topic at the European Second Language Association conference (2002), which included presentations by the present authors with colleagues (Bassetti et al., 2002) and by others (Athanasopoulos, 2002). In 2005 two overviews were published (Odlin, 2005; Pavlenko, 2005), and the field has been steadily growing since.

One reason for the increased interest was the rehabilitation of linguistic relativity in the 1990s, documented in most of the chapters in this volume and in such landmark works as Gumperz and Levinson (1996), Niemeier and Dirven (2000), Hunt and Agnoli (1991), and Lucy (1992a, 1992b, 1997). New theories and methodologies were used to investigate language influences on non-language behavior through cross-linguistic comparison. Some researchers defined themselves as neo-Whorfians, in order to distance themselves from criticisms previously leveled at the Sapir-Whorf hypothesis, particularly from the 'linguistic determinism' attributed to linguistic relativity research by its opponents. Research looked not only at lexicalized concepts, but also at grammaticalized concepts, probably closer to Whorf's original idea than the codability wave of research like Brown and Lenneberg (1954).

The second reason for the rebirth of bilingual cognition research was the rehabilitation of bilingualism itself which, following much research sparked by the landmark study of bilinguals' IQ by Peal and Lambert in 1962, was no longer seen as a deficit, but as an advantage. Research on bilingualism became respectable; in the past decade or so there has been a veritable explosion of conferences, journals, and research focusing on the psychology of bilingualism. Bilingualism research has also started to merge with its sister discipline, second language acquisition research, which had come out of an applied linguistics tradition rather than from psychology.

The crucial difference from earlier days is, however, that now researchers are investigating bilingual cognition for its own sake, rather than as a spin-off to confirm or disconfirm findings from monolinguals. Nowadays there are then two sources of evidence on bilingual cognition. There are studies that are designed on purpose to test the effects of bilingualism on cognition; and there are studies that are interested in cross-linguistic comparisons, where bilinguals are included for one reason or another, such as Romney, Moore, and Rusch (1997) for emotion; Hoffman et al. (1986) for person cognition; and Jameson and Alvarado (2003) for color. However important the findings from these latter studies, they had not been specifically designed to investigate bilingualism, and their results are not explained beyond how they do or do not confirm monolinguals' behavior or provide convergent evidence. In fact, there may even be much more bilingual cognition research than we think, as many cross-linguistic studies that purportedly compared speakers of different languages in fact studied bilinguals, although the participants' knowledge of other languages is ignored and not reported, as if this were immaterial, including the famous Berlin and Kay study of colors (1969).

This new wave of bilingualism-oriented research encompasses not only color but also time, space, motion, emotion, etc., as described below; the present volume includes bilingual cognition research on spatial location (Coventry, Guijarro-Fuentes, & Valdes, Chapter 12), temporal representations (Chen & Su, Chapter 15), motion (Czechowska & Ewert, Chapter 13; Hendriks & Hickmann, Chapter 14), color (Athanasopoulos, Chapter 11), Theory of Mind (Siegal, Kobayashi Frank, Surian, & Hjelmquist, Chapter 19), causality (Cunningham, Vaid, & Chen, Chapter 18), concepts of animals (Bassetti, Chapter 16), and emotions (Knickerbocker & Altarriba, Chapter 20; Besemeres, Chapter 21)—as wide a range as cross-linguistic research, and rapidly growing. Furthermore, researchers in various disciplines are nowadays looking at the consequences of bilingual cognition for practical applications, such as marketing to bilinguals and legal trials of bilinguals, as discussed in Part C of this volume.

CAN LEARNING ANOTHER LANGUAGE CHANGE THE WAY PEOPLE THINK?

Not only linguistic relativity researchers, but also laypeople (including policymakers) seem to think that knowledge of more than one language has positive effects on thinking. The question then is—how and why does this happen? This section mostly concentrates on sequential bilinguals, i.e., those who learnt an additional language once they had already established one (or more) language system(s) and related conceptual system(s), although the same issues apply to simultaneous bilinguals.

The layperson's view of language learning as an eye-opener

Among non-specialists there is a widespread view that learning new linguistic representations of the world changes the way people think about it. There has long been a popular view that learning another language 'opens one's mind', or 'widens one's horizons'. Traditionally this was considered an effect of learning Latin and Greek. Both authors of this chapter spent 7 years or more learning Latin and one spent 5 years learning Ancient Greek, with the main aim of learning to think better, or 'brain training' as it was often called. This view has still not been abandoned. The current Mayor of London Boris Johnson proclaimed recently 'Latin and Greek are great intellectual disciplines, forcing young minds to think in a logical and analytical way.' (Mulholland, 2010). In a recent discussion on Italian Facebook about the teaching of Latin and Classical Greek in schools, many Italians wrote that these languages *insegnano a ragionare* ('teach reasoning'), *servono alla logica* ('are useful for logic'), and that studying them *apre la mente* ('opens the mind'; Facebook, 2010). It is not clear whether the perceived miracle of increased thinking capability is due to the classical languages themselves or to the intellectually demanding grammar-translation method traditionally employed to teach them.

A category of laypersons with more clout than Facebook users are policymakers. The European Union is strongly pushing its citizens, especially schoolchildren, to learn other European languages, for a variety of social, economic, and political reasons. At the same time, EU officials seem convinced that knowing two languages improves thinking. The Director General for Education and Culture of the European Commission states that '[t]here is a clear link between multilingualism and creativity because knowledge of languages gives access to other ways of thinking and to other cultures, reinforcing our creative capacities'. The European Union Commission for Multilingualism insists that 'The ability to communicate in several languages . . . enhances creativity, breaks cultural stereotypes, encourages thinking "outside the box", and can help develop innovative products and services' (European Commission on Multilingualism, 2010).

The layperson's view is partly supported by scientific evidence. Bilingual children do better than monolinguals in some tests of both verbal and non-verbal intelligence and in some other linguistic and non-linguistic tasks, and there is currently a widespread view among psychologists that bilinguals outperform monolinguals in tasks that require cognitive control, i.e., the ability to concentrate on some stimuli while ignoring others (Green, Chapter 10 this volume). Knowing or learning another language may indeed have a positive effect on cognition. Whether it 'opens up the mind' or 'broadens horizons' is much more difficult to say, although some chapters in this volume indeed report conceptual changes in this direction (e.g., Chapters 11, 15, and 16, among others). The following section discusses whether knowing more than one language can affect cognition.

Does learning an additional language result in conceptual changes?

The first possibility is that learning another language does not have any conceptual effects. New linguistic items—whether lexical labels or grammatical rules—are learnt, and communication with users of another language is achieved, without any conceptual change. It is possible to learn to communicate in another language without changing one's concepts. If the bilinguals differ from monolinguals, it is then only in how they think about reality in order to encode it for speech, aka 'thinking-for-speaking' (Slobin, 1996), not in how they think.

The other possibility is that L2 learning affects non-linguistic cognition. We saw in Part A of this volume that first language acquisition can lead to the emergence of new concepts, and to changes in existing ones. What about a second language? Research shows that very young children who are taught a new label develop a new concept that does not exist in their linguistic community. Casasola, Bhagwat, and Burke (2006) taught English-speaking 18-month-old infants a made-up word (*toke*) that represents tight fit, as in Korean *kkita*, showing them videos of actions that end with two objects being in contact. This label represents the new concept of 'close contact' which is not represented in English and cuts across the distinctions drawn by English speakers, as it is used regardless of whether the objects are 'in' or 'on' each other. After seeing just a few events, children could when requested put two objects *toke*, showing that they had acquired the concept of 'toke', or being in tight contact.

Can adults also learn new concepts labeled in a second language word? Some experimental evidence comes from research that used artificial language learning tasks. Although in the researchers' intentions artificial language learning studies should shed light on first language acquisition, participants are adults with fully developed language and conceptual systems, unlike children who are at the same time learning language and learning about the world, possibly being guided by language in their conceptualization of the world. Artificial language learning studies, then, shed light on the effects of second language learning. Results show that adults can learn new concepts through exposure to another language. These concepts are learnt quickly, affect performance on non-language cognitive tasks, and can be learnt from both new words and new grammatical (morphological and syntactical) rules, as well as other language elements such as metaphors. In one study (Boroditsky, Schmidt, & Phillips, 2003), English adults learnt a micro artificial language that divides nouns into two classes, one for nouns for male humans and some objects, the other for nouns for female humans and other objects. Later, participants rated the objects as more similar to male or female humans, and described some objects with more masculine adjectives and other objects with more feminine adjectives, depending on whether their nouns were 'oosative' or 'soupative', a behavior normally observed in native speakers of languages that have such noun classes (see Cook, Chapter 1, this volume).

How much L2 learning is needed to have conceptual change? English speakers behave like Greek speakers on a time estimation task after learning Greek-style time metaphors for just half an hour (Casasanto, 2008). It appears that very short exposures indeed are needed to develop new concepts, at least in these studies. This is not the experience of second language learners, who typically undergo a long process with uncertain outcomes. In first language acquisition as well it takes much longer to acquire such linguistic and conceptual categories—even taking into account the maturational differences between adults and children, it seems unlikely that a more cognitively mature child could acquire noun classes such as 'oosative' and 'soupative' (i.e., grammatical gender) in half an hour. So how is one to explain the cognitive consequences of artificial language learning? Perhaps these tasks provide participants a key to understand how to perform an arguably meaningless task—since it makes no sense to rate the similarity of objects and humans, participants rely on the newly learnt categories of oosative and soupative. Alternatively, these are short-lived effects—participants' performance could be affected by the temporary accessibility of a concept, due to recency or novelty. So these experiments show that new concepts can be learnt from learning a new language, that these concepts affect performance on non-language cognitive tasks, and that they are acquired through exposure to a language without exposure to culture (which is a confounding variable in many bilingualism studies). But do these conceptual changes happen outside the psycholinguistic laboratory, and do they last in the long term?

In real-life second language learning there is some evidence that when a second language concept is first introduced it has immediate effects on cognitive tasks, which then become weaker in time. For instance, as seen in Chapter 1, Hebrew-speaking children represent temporal sequences as going from right to left, in line with the directionality of their writing system, for instance putting a picture of breakfast to the right of a picture of lunch (Tversky, Kugelmass, & Winter, 1991), and naming sets of objects starting from the right and moving towards the left (Kugelmass & Lieblich, 1979). Shortly after they learn to read English, Hebrew children show a change of directionality in their representations of temporal sequences, using both right-to-left and left-to-right directions (Kugelmass & Lieblich, 1979; Tversky et al., 1991); these effects then become weaker as time goes by (Tversky et al., 1991), but they do not disappear. A bilingual does not revert to the conceptual system of a monolingual.

Why does an additional language affect cognition? Codability and habitual thought

Why does another language affect cognition? One issue is the 'codability' of concepts. Some concepts are 'lexicalized' (expressed in an item of vocabulary) or 'grammaticalized' (expressed in a item of syntax or morphology) in one language but not in another. This does not mean that people cannot talk about those concepts in all languages, but in one language the concept label is immediately available as a single lexical item. For instance, in the Alaskan language Dena'ina there are verbs for how trees grow on the mountains, e.g., 'growing on the upper mountain slope', 'growing up the mountain in strips', 'growing up the mountainsides', and 'growing through the pass' (Lord, 1996). Learning Dena'ina as a second language means learning what aspects of tree growth are expressed in that language.

Languages can segment a continuum into different categories, for instance labeling different categories within the color spectrum or degrees of saltiness; speakers of two languages might therefore have to categorize the same experiences (such as two shades of a color or two savoury tastes) as being the same in one language or belonging to two different categories in the other. For instance, since Italian has a label for 'light blue' (*azzurro*) and English does not, English learners of Italian are exposed to a new concept through a new word. Languages can also create categories that are purely linguistic, for instance a category that includes fire, dangerous things, and women (Lakoff, 1987). Speakers of two languages must learn which animate and inanimate entities belong to the same category in their languages—categories that cannot be influenced by reality or perception, as is the case with number or color. For instance, English learners of Italian have to learn that 'skirt', 'hen', and 'gun' belong to the same category. The lexical and grammatical categories of a second language correspond to conceptual categories, which L2 learners can acquire.

However, the presence of a label in a language might not be enough if the lexical or grammatical item is not used. Some concepts are often represented in a language, and speaking in that language requires one to use them. Languages can require speakers to encode different aspects of reality, for instance singular and plural, witnessed and unwitnessed events, completed and uncompleted actions, so that speakers of different languages have to notice, remember, and specify how many entities there are, whether actions are completed or not, whether events were personally witnessed or not, or other aspects of the world around them. In this way, the 'habitual thought' of bilinguals differs from that of monolinguals. But, instead of being just thinking-for-speaking, this ultimately affects how bilinguals also think when they are not producing language.

The related issues of 'codability' and 'habitual thought' can affect nonlinguistic cognition. The following section reviews some areas where bilinguals have been shown to 'think' differently from monolinguals as a consequence of knowing two specific languages.

LANGUAGE AND BILINGUAL COGNITION: SOME AREAS OF INVESTIGATION

Research on cognition in bilinguals largely, but not always, follows crosslinguistic research in its topics and emphases. Historically, the first area to be investigated was color, because linguistic relativity researchers working with monolinguals also tested bilinguals. An areas that is currently attracting much attention is the conceptualization of motion events, as we see in this volume, largely due to the popularity of the theories of Talmy and Slobin. Bilingual emotion has also been much researched, in this case perhaps more than among cross-linguistic researchers.

Here is a far from complete list of some aspects of bilingual cognition that have been investigated, giving first the aspect of language involved and then the aspect of cognition to which it relates. This section includes findings both from studies created to investigate bilingual cognition and from cross-linguistic studies that included bilinguals. It attempts to provide a quick sketch of a few areas of investigation, in the hope of providing food for thought, with no pretence of completeness. Also it mostly limits itself to non-language behavior; while there are many differences in the way time, space, etc. are expressed linguistically by bilinguals and monolinguals, and especially L2 learners compared with native speakers, this is not necessarily evidence of conceptual differences, but might be straightforward linguistic differences, or thinking-for-speaking. Italian speakers of English might correctly use the English words *on* and *upon* (both translated as *sopra* in Italian), but this does not mean that they differ from an Italian monolingual in spatial cognition. The fact that a person describes the same action as *run inside* when speaking English and *entrare di corsa* ('go-in running') when speaking Italian does not mean that they conceptualize motion differently when speaking different languages. So conceptual change can only be revealed by analysing L2 users' performance in both linguistic and non-linguistic tasks. Some aspects of linguistic behavior can provide windows on conceptual effects of bilingualism (e.g., code switching and translation can show that a new concept has been acquired from LX that does not exist in LY, verbal descriptions of events can show which aspects of the event are noticed at least in order to describe the event, etc). On the other hand, looking only at language production and comprehension cannot provide evidence of conceptual effects of bilingualism in the absence of evidence of non-linguistic performance.

Sensory perception and categorization

Compared with color, other aspects of sensory perception in bilinguals have received less attention. Still, there is research on senses other than vision, such as the perception and categorization of (non-linguistic) sound, and concepts of taste.

Color terms and color perception and categorization

The traditional area for linguistic relativity research has been color, as described above and in Ervin-Tripp and Athanasopoulos (Chapters 9 and 11 this volume). Early cross-linguistic researchers found that bilinguals' color categories differed from those of monolingual speakers of their L1 in shifting towards the categories of their second language (which in this research meant exclusively English) and were between the L1 and L2 categories. For instance there was a shift in the description of focal yellow (more or less, the best example of 'yellow') in Navaho–English bilinguals (Ervin, 1961). Other shifts were found in color concepts in speakers of various first languages who knew L2 English, leading for example to changes in the concept of 'green' in Korean–English bilinguals

(Caskey-Sirmons & Hickerson, 1977). More recent cross-linguistic research that included bilinguals confirmed that their color categories are in between those of monolingual speakers of their two languages. For instance, color-naming behavior in Vietnamese–English bilinguals falls in between the naming behaviors of Vietnamese and English monolinguals. Vietnamese does not have a label for 'orange'; monolingual Vietnamese name 'orange' as 'dark yellow' or 'red'; bilinguals tested in L1 Vietnamese, however, use a new color name to name this color category which they learnt from L2 English (Jameson & Alvarado, 2002, 2003). Several results confirm that bilinguals perform in between monolingual speakers of their two languages in linguistic and non-linguistic tasks. For instance, Russian–English bilinguals consider dark and light blue as more similar than do Russian monolinguals (Andrews, 1994), as do Greek–English bilinguals with higher English proficiency compared with bilinguals with lower proficiency (Athanasopoulos, 2009, and Chapter 11 this volume).

Linguistic tone, pitch patterns in languages, and musical tone perception

The concentration on color by researchers does not mean that other aspects of sensorial perception and classification than vision are unaffected by bilingualism. With regard to hearing, language seems to link to pitch perception. Some studies related language and pitch perception by looking at the perception of the *tritone paradox*, a pattern of two musical tones separated by a half-octave (tritone) interval created so that their pitch class is clear but their octave placement is not (e.g., one note is clearly a C, but it could be in the middle octave or in the octaves above or below)—this is perceived as ascending or descending depending on the pitch range of the hearer's first language. A late 1990s study found differences in the perception of tritones between English–Spanish bilinguals and English monolinguals, attributed to differences between the pitch patterns of the two languages (Chalikia & Vaid, 1999; see also Chalikia, Norberg, & Paterakis, 2000, on Greek–English bilinguals).

Researchers have also looked at the ability to perceive and produce musical tones in bilinguals who speak a 'tone language' (in a tone language—such as Chinese and some dialects of Norwegian—the same syllable has different meaning according to its pitch contour, e.g., in Chinese /ba/ pronounced with level tone means 'eight', but with descending tone it means 'dad'). In another tritone perception study, Deutsch (2004) linked differences between Vietnamese–English bilinguals and English monolinguals to Vietnamese, a tone language; knowledge of English did not seem to affect performance, as English- and Vietnamese-dominant bilinguals both differed from English monolinguals but not from each other, which Deutsch attributed to a critical period. Mang (2006) also showed that Cantonese-speaking children are more in tune when they sing an English language song than English-speaking children. The cause may be that Cantonese is tone-based; speakers of tone languages might have absolute pitch more often than speakers of other languages (Deutsch, Henthorn, & Dolson, 2004). While it appears that the factor affecting bilinguals' musical tone perception is their first language rather than their bilingualism, Chalikia and Vaid (1999) claimed that bilinguals differed from monolinguals regardless of which of the two languages was their chronological L1, i.e., a later-learnt L2 could also affect pitch perception.

Taste terms and taste concepts

Taste concepts have also been investigated. As there are primary colors, so there are basic tastes, but while in western languages these are 'sweet', 'salty', 'bitter', and 'sour', the Chinese and Japanese languages also label another taste concept called *umami* in Japanese (and more recently also in English). This combines attributes of savoriness and meaty taste, as found for instance in soy sauce, parmesan cheese, and Marmite. Cross-linguistic studies found differences in the perception of umami (O'Mahony & Ishii, 1986). One study showed that English speakers can learn the Japanese concept of umami (then unknown to Americans) by exposure to linguistic definition and actual (Japanese) food samples, and that learning this new lexical item affects their food categorization (Ishii & O'Mahony, 1989).

Time, space, and motion events

Perhaps the most widely studied areas in bilingual cognition are motion events, as the chapters in this volume demonstrate, for example in relation to verbs and adjuncts (Czechowska & Ewert, Chapter 13; Hendriks & Hickmann, Chapter 14). In this volume, Coventry, Guijarro-Fuentes, and Valdés (Chapter 12) look at spatial prepositions and concepts of location in space in English–Spanish bilinguals and find that 'sensitivity to functional relations occurs earlier than sensitivity to fine-grained geometric relations' (p. 280). Temporal representations have also been studied, in relation to time metaphors and to verb morphology (in this volume, see Chen & Su, Chapter 15).

Verbs and conceptualization of motion events

Since Talmy (1985, 2005) conceptualized motion events as consisting of figure, ground, path, and motion, much research has looked at learners' conceptualization of motion events. In satellite-framed languages such as English and Polish, typically verbs express manner of motion, and path is expressed in a satellite such as a preposition (e.g., *run inside*); verb-framed languages such as French and (mostly) Italian express path in verbs and manner in satellites (e.g., *entrare di corsa*; *entrare* = 'go in'; *di corsa* =

'running'). Descriptions of motion events in L2 learners are affected by their first language (Jarvis & Odlin, 2000), and even when their speech production is close to native speakers their gestures reveal thinking patterns typical of their L1 (Kellerman & van Hoof, 2003). On the other hand, the L2 also affects the conceptualization of motion events: Japanese–English bilinguals encode manner in L1 Japanese speech more often than Japanese monolinguals, although this is limited to linguistic output, as their gestures do not represent manner more than monolinguals (Brown & Gullberg, 2008); L1 descriptions of motion events are affected by L2 in choice of manner and path verbs in both early (before age 5) and late (after age 12) sequential bilinguals (Hohenstein, Eisenberg, & Naigles, 2006; but see Pavlenko, 2010). In this volume, Czechowska and Ewert (Chapter 13) look at differences between the degree of satellite-framedness in English and Polish, showing 'conceptual shift towards the L2 in the least-proficient bilinguals and restructuring of the conceptual domain in the two most proficient groups' (p. 302). Covering the same area, Hendriks and Hickmann (Chapter 14, this volume) found that 'English learners of French have clear difficulties expressing the same level of density (P+M) [path and manner] in their second language as they would in their source language' (p. 331), and in order to convey the information they deem necessary they 'flout some of the target language rules' (p. 334).

Results are varied, and much more research has appeared than can be reviewed here (e.g., Brown & Gullberg, 2010, in press; Cadierno, 2008; Cadierno & Robinson, 2009; Navarro & Nicoladis, 2005; Slobin, 2003; etc. For reviews, see Czechowska and Ewert, Chapter 13, and Hendriks and Hickmann, Chapter 14, this volume). In general much research has found effects of both languages in conceptualization and expression of motion in L2 learners and users.

Other differences between bilinguals' and monolinguals' conceptualizations of motion events are related to knowledge of one language that has a perfectivity marker (perfective/imperfective morphology marking whether an action is completed or not, e.g., *he is eating an apple*) and one that does not (*he has eaten an apple*); again knowing two languages affects the conceptualization of motion events, for instance the amount of attention paid to endpoints (e.g., the monastery in *walking towards a monastery*; see among others Bylund, 2009; Flecken, in press; Schmiedtová, Carroll, & von Stutterheim, 2007).

Verb inflections, metaphors, and temporal representations

Researchers also examined the relationship between tense and aspect and representations of events. In as-yet unpublished conference presentations, Boroditsky and colleagues have reported that bilinguals notice differences between completed and uncompleted actions more often than monolingual speakers of their L1 if verbs convey this information in their second language but not in their first language. For instance, Indonesian–English bilinguals are more affected by the tense of action (whether completed, undergoing, or going to happen) than Indonesian monolinguals in rating the similarity of pictures of actions and in remembering which picture they had seen before (Boroditsky, Ham, & Ramscar, 2002; see also similar findings from Russian–English bilinguals in Boroditsky and Trusova 2003); the Indonesian bilinguals also perform differently depending on the language of the instructions (Boroditsky et al., 2002). Chen and Su (Chapter 15, this volume) investigated temporal awareness and found 'Chinese–English bilinguals with a high level of English proficiency perceive the future and the past phases of an action event, as encoded in a picture, more readily than bilinguals with a low level of proficiency' (p. 354).

Research has also looked at the relationship between time metaphors and the representation of the directionality of time. One study (Boroditsky, 2001) correlated Chinese–English bilinguals' age of onset of acquisition (reported age when they started learning English) with their preference for thinking about time vertically, attributed to the debatable idea that English uses horizontal spatial metaphors, Chinese vertical ones (as in *shang ge yue*, lit. 'above-month', 'last month'). Earlier bilinguals consequently represent time directionality as horizontal more than later bilinguals; with increased exposure to English, L2 users move towards English speakers, whose true/false responses to statements such as 'March comes earlier than April' were faster after a horizontal prime (e.g., a picture of two worms one to the left of the other), whereas Chinese speakers' answers were faster after a vertical prime (e.g., a picture of two balls one above the other). Nevertheless, a subsequent study found no differences between bilinguals and monolinguals (Tse & Altarriba, 2008); and two studies failed to replicate Boroditsky's monolingual results with Chinese speakers (Chen, 2007; January & Kako, 2006).

Finally, some research linked the directionality of writing (left to right, right to left, or top to bottom) with mental representations of time. Children who learn an L2 with different writing directionality change their representations of time directionality: While English children put a picture of lunch on the left of a picture of dinner and Arab children do the opposite, Arab children learning English do both; bilinguals also name sets of objects starting both from the left and the right (Kugelmass & Lieblich, 1979; Tversky et al., 1991. Writing directionality also affects the directionality of face scanning, Vaid, 1995; and of the illusory rotation of objects, Morikawa & McBeath, 1992; Vaid, 2010).

Concepts and categorization of entities

Bilingualism can affect concepts and categorization of entities such as artifacts, animals, natural kinds, and abstract entities, e.g., 'clock', 'tiger', 'moon', and 'freedom'.

Object nouns and object categorization

Different languages assign objects to different categories. L2 users of English differ from English monolinguals in object naming and object typicality judgments, due to the linguistic categorization in their first languages, for instance considering a 'dish' what English speakers consider a 'bowl' (Malt & Sloman, 2003). There are also effects of language knowledge and exposure: The less-experienced learners (in terms of length of stay, length of study, and proficiency self-rating) differed more from L2 native speakers in naming and typicality ratings of housewares (e.g., concepts of 'chair' and 'stool'; Graham & Belnap, 1986; Jarvis, 2000). Vice versa, L2 nouns also affect bilinguals' naming and typicality ratings of 'bottles' and 'dishes' in their two languages, showing convergence of L1 and L2 (Ameel, Malt, Storms, & Van Assche, 2009; Ameel, Storms, Malt, & Sloman, 2005; Pavlenko & Malt, in press). It appears that categorization of objects is affected by bilingualism, as reflected in naming tasks.

Grammatical number and the classification of objects and substances

In English objects are generally referred to with count nouns that can be plural and can be preceded by a numeral (e.g., *two books*), while substances are referred to with mass nouns that do not take plurals and can be preceded by a classifier (e.g., *two glasses of water* but not **two waters*); in Japanese both objects and substances are referred to in the same way (with either bare noun or numeral-classifier-noun, e.g., *futatsu no hon*, 'two-classifier book', and *nihai no mizu*, 'two-classifier water'). In one study (Cook, Bassetti, Kasai, Sasaki, & Takahashi, 2006), Japanese–English bilinguals with longer stays in an English-speaking country differed in their classification of entities that were borderline between objects and substances from bilinguals with shorter stays, attributable ultimately to the differences between English and Japanese article systems. Other studies have also found a preference for shape-based classification in Japanese high-proficiency users of L2 English compared with those with lower proficiency (Athanasopoulos, 2007; Athanasopoulos & Kasai, 2008). Effects of bilingualism were also found on the similarity rating of pictures that contained the same number of objects or the same amount of substances (Athanasopoulos, 2006): English monolinguals rate pictures with the same number of objects as more similar than pictures with the same amount of substances, whereas Japanese–English bilinguals pay equal attention to similarity in the number of objects and in the amount of substances if they are less proficient in English, and behave more like English monolinguals if they are more proficient.

Finally, Kuo and Sera (2009) looked at the effects of classifiers on the categorization of objects. Participants matched pictured objects (mostly complex objects, i.e., having a complex shape and a function) with objects that had either the same function, or the same shape and the same classifier (e.g., a broom could be matched with either a vacuum cleaner, i.e., same function, or a garden fork, i.e., same shape and classifier). Overall participants classified mostly by function, which is a universal preference in the classification of complex objects. Yet Chinese–English bilinguals relied on shape-classifier for classification more often than English monolinguals, but they were more similar to English monolinguals than Chinese speakers who were not living in an English speaking country. The bilinguals again performed in-between.

Grammatical gender and concepts, and classification of entities

In some languages all nouns belong to agreement classes called 'genders'. In many Indo-European languages the genders are masculine, feminine, and in some cases neuter. While some of these nouns refer to biologically male or female referents (e.g., 'uncle'), most do not (e.g., 'tiger' is masculine in German *der Tiger* and feminine in Italian *la tigre*). Cross-linguistic research found that speakers of such languages think of referents as being more or less masculine or feminine depending on their grammatical gender, so that German speakers consider an apple more masculine than Spanish speakers (Boroditsky et al., 2003).

English is a natural gender language in which gender goes with biological sex, as reflected in choice of pronouns. When native speakers of a grammatical gender language learn a natural gender language, their L1 grammatical gender assignment still affects their performance in various tasks, such as describing entities with adjectives—German speakers describe bridges in English as 'elegant' and Spanish speakers describe them as 'robust', in line with the grammatical gender of the noun 'bridge' in the two languages. These bilinguals also learn English names for objects more easily when the name is consistent with the grammatical gender of the noun in their L1 (e.g., *Patrick* versus *Patricia* for an apple). Studies with learning of micro artificial languages also show that when English speakers learn an artificial language where one category of nouns is used for male humans and some objects, and the other is used for female humans and other objects, performance in object–human similarity judgment tasks is affected by the object's gender in the artificial language (Boroditsky et al., 2003).

On the other hand, when bilinguals know two grammatical gender languages, the effects of grammatical gender are reduced or disappear. Phillips and Boroditsky (2003) found that when bilinguals with German and Spanish rated the similarity of various objects to male or female humans, the effects of each language's grammatical gender correlated with the bilingual's fluency in that language. In Bassetti (2007), Italian native-speaking children chose a male or female voice for a series of objects as they would be talking in a cartoon. Italian children chose female voices for objects that were grammatically feminine in Italian, but Italian–German bilingual children were not affected by grammatical gender. Bassetti (Chapter 16, this volume) found that Italian–German bilinguals perform in between Italian and German monolinguals in rating animals on a semantic differential task that measures masculinity–femininity when these animals are grammatically masculine in one of their languages and feminine in the other. From these studies, it appears that knowledge of two languages that assign opposite gender to the same entity reduces the effects of grammatical gender, at least for those entities. On the other hand, there is some evidence that learning a second language with grammatical gender can introduce a grammatical gender bias in native speakers of a language with natural gender. English-speaking child learners of Spanish choose male or female voices for objects depending on the objects' grammatical gender in L2 Spanish, and this effect correlates with L2 proficiency (Kurinski & Sera, in press).

Reasoning

Some effects of bilingualism have been found in reasoning, for instance in mathematical reasoning, counterfactual reasoning, and causal reasoning. Bilingual children also generally develop Theory of Mind earlier than monolinguals (see Siegal et al., Chapter 19, this volume), although this seems a generic macro effect of bilingualism rather than a consequence of knowing two specific languages.

Mathematical terminology, mathematical concepts, and mathematical reasoning

Research on mathematical reasoning has found differences in mathematical cognition tasks between bilinguals and monolinguals due to their language combinations. Some Chinese mathematical terms are more transparent than their English equivalents, e.g., the English *diagonal* in Chinese is *dui jiao xian*, 'line-opposed-to-angle', and *equilateral triangle* is *deng bian san jiao xing*, 'equal-side three-corner-figure'. English–Chinese bilingual high-school students understand such mathematical concepts better than English monolinguals, as shown in tasks such as identifying the picture of an equilateral triangle; their performance correlates with proficiency in Chinese (Han & Ginsburg, 2001).

Conditionals and counterfactual reasoning

The controversies about counterfactual reasoning were discussed earlier. From the bilingualism perspective, Bloom (1981) demonstrated that Chinese speakers who know English reason more like English speakers than Chinese monolinguals on tasks involving comprehension of a complex counterfactual story. A recent study reported in a conference presentation (Bassetti, 2008) confirms and extends Bloom's findings, showing that preference for counterfactual interpretations of stories in Chinese–English bilinguals correlates with levels of academic English proficiency, and is more frequent when the same stories are presented in English than in Chinese.

The expression of causality and causal reasoning

Causal reasoning has also been investigated with reference to bilinguals. For instance, due to differences in causal expressions in English and Russian, causal events are described differently by Russian–English and English–Russian bilinguals and monolingual speakers of their L1, as bilinguals tend towards speakers of their L2 when describing videos of actions in L1 Russian (Wolff & Ventura, 2009). Cunningham, Vaid, and Chen (Chapter 18, this volume) found that when describing accidental occurrences Spanish–English bilinguals are more likely to use constructions that de-emphasize agency in Spanish than in English; however, non-agentive constructions are more prevalent in English among bilinguals as compared to English monolinguals, suggesting a carryover influence of Spanish.

Linguistic categories

Bilingualism can also affect concepts of linguistic categories. Bilingual children are known to develop some concepts of language earlier than monolinguals. For instance bilingual preschoolers have greater awareness of syllable onsets and rimes, basically the ability to separate the initial consonant or consonant cluster from the rest of the syllable (Bruck & Genesee, 1995), because exposure to more than one language makes language more transparent and open to analysis (Bialystok, 2001). They also develop earlier than monolingual peers the ability to distinguish between a word and its referent, for instance understanding that *train* is a short word but a long thing and *caterpillar* is a long word but a comparatively short creature (Bialystok, 2001; Yelland et al., 1993). While this widely studied phenomenon is a macro effect of bilingualism, there are also micro effects of knowledge of two specific languages. Some researchers argue that bilinguals who speak a language with a 'simpler' phonology (generally measured broadly in terms of syllable complexity, or number of different vowels, etc.) might develop some aspects of phonological awareness in a language with more 'complex' phonology faster than monolingual speakers of the latter language. For instance, 5-year-old children with a reportedly more phonologically complex first language (English) and a less phonologically complex second language (Greek) outperform English monolingual children in tasks measuring awareness of phonemes; on the other hand, when the second language is more phonologically complex than the first, L2 learning does not affect awareness, i.e., Greek children who learn English do not perform better than Greek monolinguals (Loizou & Stuart, 2003). English children attending an English–Italian bilingual school outperform English monolinguals in selecting the one English word in a set that has a different initial phoneme, and in repeating words without the first syllable (Campbell & Sais, 1995); Spanish–English bilingual children outperform English monolinguals in segmenting words into phonemes (Bialystok, Majumder, & Martin, 2003). The way a bilingual's two languages cut up the sound space used for language production, then, affects the child's ability to identify and manipulate linguistic sounds.

Concepts of language that develop simultaneously with exposure to written language, such as the concept of phoneme or word, develop faster in biliterates than in monoliterate children when the biliterates know a written language that has more regular correspondences between units of writing and units of language. For instance, the concept of Chinese word in English–Chinese adults differs from the Chinese monolinguals' concept, probably because words are separated by word spaces in written English words but not in Chinese (Bassetti, 2005).

Emotion and person cognition

Research on emotion in bilinguals has received much attention; for reviews, see Knickerbocker and Altarriba (Chapter 20, this volume), Pavlenko (2006, 2008) and Dewaele (2010).

Emotion terms and emotion concepts

One area is the relationship between emotion terms in the bilinguals' two languages and their concepts of emotions. Some emotion terms only exist in one of the bilinguals' two languages, and cannot be translated (e.g., Wierzbicka, Chapter 8, this volume, discusses the untranslatability of the English concept of 'frustration' into Russian, and of the Russian concept of '*dosada*' into English). In an early cross-linguistic study that included bilinguals (Romney et al., 1997), participants judged the similarity of 15 emotion terms, resulting in a model that shows the semantic structure of emotion terms (e.g., 'anger' and 'hate' are close, but far from 'happy'). In spite of the similarities across monolingual and bilingual groups, the Japanese–English bilinguals' models differed from Japanese monolinguals when tested in Japanese, and when tested in English were in between the two monolingual groups. Greek–English bilinguals cannot translate English *frustration* into Greek, and Greek *stenahoria* ('discomfort/sadness/suffocation') into English; they use code-switching to talk about these emotions in the language that does not have a term for them, showing the acquisition of the relevant emotion concept (Panayiotou, 2004). Researchers have also looked at purportedly universal emotions using facial expressions. In one study researchers had planned to use photographs of seven 'universal' emotions, but had to drop two ('contempt' and 'disgust') because they could not find a term for these emotions in Hindi. When Hindi–English bilinguals were shown photographs of facial expressions of the remaining five emotions, they named three more consistently in English than in Hindi ('anger', 'fear', and 'sadness') (Matsumoto & Assar, 1992). In Spanish–English bilinguals too some emotion labels are more accessible in English than in their first language (Matsumoto, Anguas-Wong, & Martinez, 2008).

Emotional language and emotional responses

Various studies revealed different levels of emotional responses to emotional words and expressions in the bilingual's two languages. On the one hand, L1 emotional words may be more emotional than L2 ones: For example, sequential bilinguals respond more to reprimands (e.g., 'don't do that') and taboo words in their first language than in the second language (e.g., Sutton, Altarriba, Gianico, & Basnight-Brown, 2007) and remember L1 emotion terms and emotional words more than L2 ones in recall tasks (Annoshian & Hertel, 1994). On the other hand, other studies found that the level of emotional response depends on proficiency rather than age of acquisition (Harris, 2004); swearwords and taboo words are perceived as more emotional in the language with higher proficiency and frequency of use, and even 'I love you' has different emotional weights in the bilingual's languages (Dewaele, 2004, 2008a, 2008b). In this volume (Chapter 20) Knickerbocker and Altarriba describe how 'bilingual individuals process and experience emotional words differently in English and in Spanish' (p. 467); Besemeres (Chapter 21) also shows the difficulty of adjusting concepts of friendship when moving from one language to another.

Personality descriptors and person cognition

Bilingualism might also affect people's reasoning about personality and human relationships, for instance due to the effects of different personality descriptors in the two languages on person cognition. English and Chinese have different personality descriptors, or terms that describe a set of characteristics, such as *artistic* in English, which includes characteristics such as unconventionality, and has no equivalent in Chinese, and Chinese *shi gu*, which includes world experience and family orientation. When evaluating the personality traits of fictional characters, Chinese–English bilinguals were affected by stereotypes associated with different terms in their two languages, and also performed differently in different languages, for instance attributing unconventionality to characters who were described as *artistic* in English, but not to the same characters described in Chinese (Hoffman et al., 1986).

SOME SUGGESTIONS FOR FUTURE RESEARCH ON BILINGUAL COGNITION

The review above, albeit highly selective, provides a taste of the rapid growth and variety of research in bilingual cognition, still just scratching the surface. This section makes some suggestions for future research.

More replications of cross-linguistic studies of monolinguals

The most straightforward approach to bilingual cognition research uses evidence of cross-linguistic differences among speakers of different languages as a basis for looking at bilinguals who know both languages involved. Bilingual cognition researchers find themselves in an easier position than researchers working on cross-linguistic comparisons, who must start from observed cognitive differences among speakers of different languages, or from linguistic differences among pairs of languages (see Cook, Chapter 1, this volume). Bilingual cognition researchers can choose one of the already known cross-linguistic differences to check out with bilinguals.

Future research could then continue to follow this path of extending cross-linguistic discoveries to bilingualism. For instance, Chinese children develop Theory of Mind earlier than English-speaking children because their language has different verbs for false beliefs (i.e., *xiang/dang*, 'to believe' and *yi wei*, 'to believe incorrectly'; for examples from other languages, see Siegal et al., Chapter 19, this volume). These linguistic effects could then be investigated in bilingual children. There are many differences among speakers of different languages that have not been investigated in bilinguals, from perception of saltiness in bilinguals with say Korean and English (for cross-linguistic differences, see O'Mahony & Muhiudeen, 1977), to concepts of kinship and family relations (see Anggoro & Gentner, 2003), to concepts of teen numbers in bilingual children with English and Chinese (English has individual nouns for teen numbers—*eleven, twelve*—whereas Chinese nouns are formed by rule, with decade noun followed by unit noun—11 = *shi yi*, 'ten-one', 22 = *er shi er*, 'two-ten-two'; Chinese children learn the number system faster than English children, Miller, Major, Shu, & Zhang, 2000). These and endless other cross-linguistic differences can provide a starting point for bilingualism researchers.

The Linguistic Commitment

Research on bilingual cognition needs to provide an adequate description of the linguistic phenomena under analysis, both in general and in reference to the specific languages involved, called the Linguistic Commitment in the introduction to Part A of this volume (Cook, Chapter 1). The bridge between language and cognition has to have a firm foundation on both banks. This is particularly important in ensuring that effects are truly linked to language rather than to other factors. A scientific description of the language phenomena supposedly related to cognitive differences is fundamental to any claims of co-occurrence of linguistic and cognitive phenomena in bilinguals.

Descriptions of the aspects of language involved should meet some basic requirements. For a start, descriptions should be consonant with contemporary linguistic views of language (or clearly state how they disagree from current approaches), rather than coming out of a general common-sense view of language, or the Latin-based school tradition of grammar. This does not mean that linguistic descriptions necessarily have to be completely up to date—linguistic theories are notoriously prone to change. Linguistics also comes in all shapes and sizes and flavors. But any statement about language implies a theory, whether it is the phonological theory of the term 'phoneme' or the semantic theory of satellite and verb-framed languages; adequate research into bilingual cognition requires an explicitly stated language theory or description.

Research has mostly concentrated on small-scale aspects of language. Older lexically based research looked at limited areas of the lexicon, such as whether there is a word for 'green' or not, or what is meant by the words 'chair' and 'stool'. Much recent research continues to concentrate on small areas of the lexicon, such as color terms, or whether verbs convey information on manner or path of motion, a minute fragment of English grammar probably unknown to most teachers of English and indeed most grammarians. Some researchers have turned to more complex linguistic phenomena in morphology and syntax (as Whorf originally suggested), for instance grammatical gender or tense markers. Still, there are many less-obvious aspects of linguistic systems. For instance, research on causal reasoning in bilinguals has looked at differences between languages that obligatorily convey agentives but has not looked, say, at pro-drop and non-pro-drop languages (languages where the subject can or cannot be omitted, e.g., English *he sings* vs Italian *canta* 'sings' or Chinese *chang ge*, 'sing'; for a cross-linguistic study, see Jisa, Reilly, Verhoeven, Baruch, & Rosado, 2002). Such areas of research could emerge from contemporary linguistic theories, e.g., semantic or syntactic theories, rather than common-sense semantics or ad hoc syntax. While this shift towards contemporary linguistic theories should probably originate in cross-linguistic studies and then be extended to bilingual cognition studies, it is equally vital for bilingual cognition studies, and researchers in this area could take the lead.

The Linguistic Commitment also implies the duty of observational adequacy—do people really say *a tree* and *water* rather than *tree* or *a water*, or is the countable/uncountable distinction something merely handed down in the grammar-book tradition? Actual linguistic descriptions need to be provided for the relevant aspects of both languages involved. Descriptions should be linked to real-world language use, not based on prescriptive grammar books. In bilingual cognition research it does not matter what an idealized highly schooled speaker would say or write, but what actual people say or write. It is important to avoid confusing idealized with real-life language production, standard with non-standard varieties of language, written with spoken varieties, and so on. This is particularly relevant whenever cognitive effects are attributed to habitual thought: A prescriptive description might be beside the point, as speakers might never have come across that aspect of language outside grammar books, which typically say whether something exists in a language at all, not how common it is. Among other factors, it might be necessary to say how frequent a certain phenomenon is in all the languages involved—easy enough these days with the availability of large corpora. For instance, classifiers affect object categorization more in Chinese than in Japanese speakers because classifiers are more frequently used in Chinese (Imai & Saalbach, 2010). Yet frequency of use is scarcely ever reported in bilingual cognition (and indeed linguistic relativity) studies. If language X affects language Y it might simply be that the phenomenon occurs more often in language X than in language Y.

Language pairs and the position of English

The English language is all-pervasive in bilingual cognition research. Since researchers are largely (native or non-native) English speakers and, more often than not, based in English-speaking countries, most research involves bilinguals or second language learners who have English either as their first or second language, because English language learners are widely available everywhere, and native English-speaking learners of other languages are available in the English-speaking countries where most researchers are based. Studies of bilinguals or L2 learners with no English in their language combination are rare (e.g., Spanish–Swedish bilinguals in Bylund, 2009; Italian–German bilinguals in Bassetti, Chapter 16, this volume; Quechua–Spanish bilinguals in Sánchez, 2004).

This bias towards English means that there is little research on linguistic phenomena that do not exist in English. Research mostly looks at how something that exists in English but not in language X is acquired by language X-speaking learners of English, or its consequences for language X–English and/or English–language X bilinguals; or less frequently at how a phenomenon that exists in language X but not in English is acquired by English-speaking learners of language X and used by bilinguals. Potentially interesting language combinations have not been studied even where there are cross-linguistic differences among monolingual speakers: For instance, Thai children learn the concept of 'speed' faster than Japanese children, whose language has no separate spoken forms for 'early' and 'fast' (Mori, Koyima, & Tadang, 1976). Also, there has been considerable research (reported above) on tense and aspect and conceptualization of time in bilinguals who are native speakers of languages with no inflectional morphology like Chinese, and whose second language English does, to some extent. On the other hand, there has been no research on evidentiality in bilinguals. Languages with evidentiality mark morphologically whether there is evidence for what is being reported, and what type of evidence it is; for example in Turkish there is a difference between direct and indirect experience as in *geldi*, '[he] came' (I saw it) vs *gelmis*, '[he] came' (apparently, reportedly; Slobin & Aksu, 1982). Tosun, Vaid, and Geraci (2010) found differences in memory of events between Turkish and English speakers, due to the presence of evidentials in Turkish but not in English. While evidentiality may not be marked in English morphology, it is marked in those of a substantial number of the languages of the world (see Aikhenvald, 2004), and so is worth investigating in bilinguals. While Tosun et al. report planning a bilingual replication of their study, it is rarer to find research about language phenomena that exist in other languages but not in English, compared with phenomena that exist in English but not in other languages. More in general, it is hard to find bilingual cognition research where English is not involved.

One urgent issue is then to look into bilinguals with different language combinations in which English does not take part. At present, bilingual cognition research mostly shows that learning English widens the mind and opens new horizons. It would be stimulating to read more research where English speakers have their minds opened by learning another language. This might counteract any linguistic imperialistic beliefs that learning English is good for users of other languages, while the opposite effect is never tested. Instead of reading that Navaho speakers discover 'orange' from learning English, why can't we read how English speakers discover that there are two types of 'blue' from learning Italian or Greek? English may be convenient because of the ready availability of L1 and L2 English users; from the point of view of bilingual cognition research, it is only one of the 7000-odd languages in the world.

MULTI-COMPETENCE, BILINGUAL CONCEPTS, AND THE OUTCOMES OF BILINGUALISM

In general, this volume makes the point that knowing more than one language gives access to more than one description of the world, and therefore bilinguals should have a clearer mental representation at least for those aspects of the world that are described differently in their two languages. This positive effect of bilingualism should then be seen on a concept-by-concept case, applying to some concepts but not all—a contrastive analysis of differences between two languages and two groups of speakers does not necessarily predict what will happen in bilinguals. For example, Jameson and Alvarado (2003) found that their sample of Vietnamese–English bilinguals were closer to English monolinguals in the categorization of 'orange', and closer to Vietnamese monolinguals in the categorization of 'blue' and 'green'. For reasons to be discovered, some L2 lexical items affect concepts more than others. Of course there is also the possibility that, once bilinguals realize that language affects their cognition, they can develop a greater sensitivity than monolinguals to the potential impact of language on cognition, therefore leading to a general cognitive effect of bilingualism that goes beyond the specific effects on specific aspects of reality.

This section introduces the theory of multi-competence, proposes a categorization of bilingual concepts and of bilinguals, discusses whether bilingualism's effects on cognition are always positive, and highlights some variables that modulate bilingualism effects.

Multi-competence and bilingual cognition

The assumption behind most linguistic relativity research, and indeed much research in linguistics and in second language acquisition, is that the human mind normally knows one language; another language is an optional added extra. Hence people who know two languages are treated as exceptions and studied in spin-off applied disciplines rather than as part of the mainstream in psychology and linguistics. However, people who use two languages are perhaps in the majority among human beings today; the potential of all human beings is that they can learn and use more than one language if exposed to it (Cook, 2009). For 20 years the idea has been spreading that L2 users should be studied in their own right (Grosjean, 1998), called by some 'multi-competence' (Cook, 2008). An engrained idea in most language research is that monolingual native speakers are the ideal and that L2 users should be measured against them, whether in terms of language proficiency or in terms of cognition: If the L2 user does it differently from the native speaker, they are wrong; if they approximate the native speaker they are improving. A typical view is 'Very few L2 learners appear to be fully successful in the way that native speakers are' (Towell & Hawkins, 1994, p. 14). From the multi-competence perspective, using a native speaker standard for measuring L2 users is like describing apples in terms of pears; it may yield some insights—there are cone-shaped apples called Worcester Pearmains—but it distorts the picture considerably and it never yields the distinctive qualities of apples that make them different from pears. L2 users have to be treated sui generis; any comparison with monolingual native speakers is a methodological device for understanding them, not a way of cataloging their alleged deficiencies.

Language and cognition in L2 users

Looked at from the multi-competence perspective, four relationships for language and cognition are possible, illustrated here with the example of 'lunch' in English–Italian L2 users. When the present authors googled images of *lunch*, the first page of results contained only photographs of sandwiches with bags of crisps (indeed, Google helpfully suggested the related search term *sandwich*). The authors then googled images of *pranzo* (Italian for 'lunch'), and the first page showed meals with pasta and a main course, or pasta dishes; not a single photograph of sandwiches showed up. The concept labeled by the English word *lunch*, then, seems to refer to sandwiches and crisps, whereas the Italian word *pranzo* refers to a pasta dish and a main course such as fish or meat, as seen in Figure 7.1.

Lunch   Pranzo

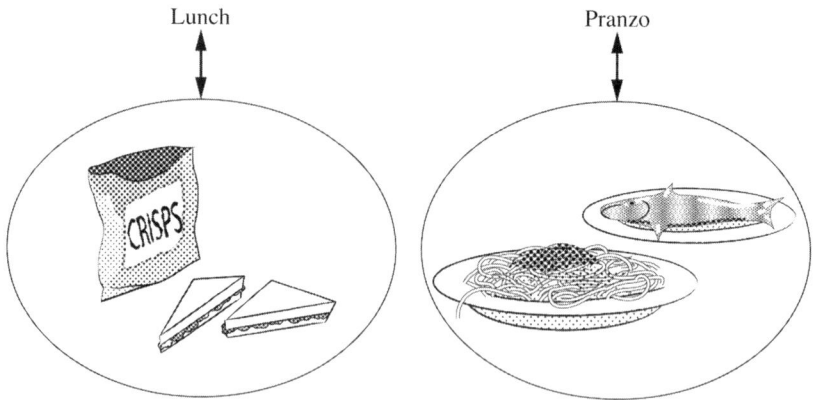

Figure 7.1 The concept of 'lunch' in Italian monolinguals and English monolinguals.

So what does an English–Italian L2 user have for lunch? Here are four possible scenarios, illustrated briefly and tentatively from the literature and sketched in Figures 7.2–7.5.

(1) *The one-concept scenario.* In this case the L2 user has a single concept 'lunch', with two labels attached—Italian *pranzo* and English *lunch*. The concept can be a language X concept (sandwich and crisps) or a language Y concept (pasta and fish), depending on various factors. No matter whether talking about *lunch* or *pranzo*, some English–Italian L2 users will be thinking about sandwiches and crisps, others about pasta and a main course (see Figure 7.2). Presumably an English beginner in Italian will be thinking of sandwiches and crisps, while an advanced learner might be thinking of pasta and fish/meat.

A more well-known example is colors. The Italian language distinguishes two colors: *blu* and *azzurro*, the former referring to darker shades of blue and the latter to lighter shades, such as 'sky blue'. The English *blue* covers all colors called *blu* and *azzurro* in Italian. The Italian *blu* therefore labels a range of darker blues compared to English *blue* (since lighter shades are *azzurro*), while the English *blue* labels a wider range of color shades and its focus (best example) is lighter than the focus for Italian *blue* (for Greek and English, see Athanasopoulos, Chapter 11, this volume). So in the one-concept scenario the L2 user has two labels, Italian *blu* and English *blue*, but these are used for the same color, which will be a lighter blue (for instance, for an English beginner learner of Italian) or a darker blue (for instance, for an advanced learner).

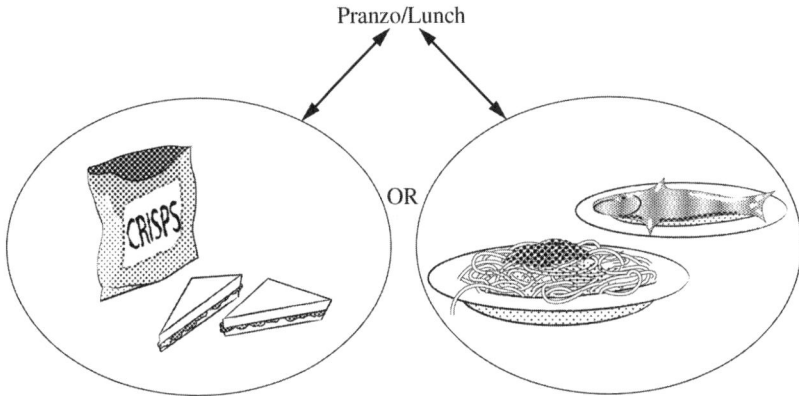

Figure 7.2 The concept of lunch in English–Italian bilinguals: The one-concept scenario.

Evidence from less-proficient bilinguals and L2 learners supports the view that they use L1 concepts with both L1 and L2 labels—the one-concept scenario. Various researchers found that L2 learners were relying on L1 concepts regardless of the language they were speaking (for instance, see Malt & Sloman, 2003, for object categorization; Jarvis & Odlin, 2000, and Kellerman & van Hoof, 2003, for motion events). This is more common among less-proficient L2 users (e.g., Graham & Belnap, 1986; Jarvis, 2000).

(2) *The double-concepts scenario.* The L2 user has two separate concepts, and thinks differently when speaking different languages. When speaking in English, *lunch* suggests sandwiches and crisps; speaking in Italian, *pranzo* suggests pasta and meat/fish (see Figure 7.3). In terms of colors, this means that, speaking in English, an L2 user says *blue* and

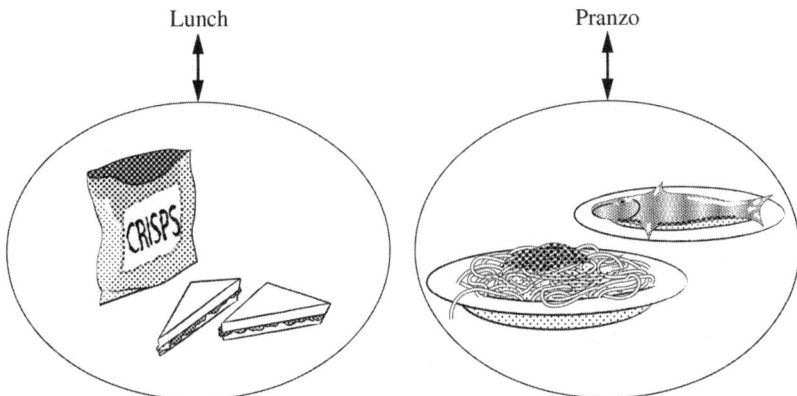

Figure 7.3 The concept of lunch in English–Italian bilinguals: The double-concept scenario.

thinks of a lighter blue, but speaking Italian says *blu* and thinks of a darker blue.

The double-concepts scenario is supported by evidence that L2 users 'think' differently when speaking different languages (for instance, see Hoffman et al., 1986, for person cognition; Sutton et al., 2007, for emotional language; Boroditsky et al., 2002, for temporal representations).

(3) *The one-integrated-concept scenario.* The L2 user combines the L1 and L2 concepts into a single concept in between those of the two languages, and so thinks differently from monolingual speakers of either language. For instance, an Italian–English L2 user might think of a dish of pasta accompanied by a packet of crisps (see Figure 7.4). In colors the L2 user has a single concept of 'blue', whose focus is darker than *blue* and lighter than *blu*.

Lunch/Pranzo

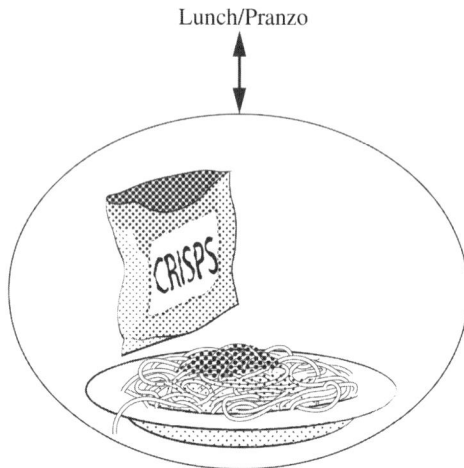

Figure 7.4 The concept of lunch in English–Italian bilinguals: The one-merged-concept scenario.

Much evidence seems to support the one-integrated-concept scenario—so that L2 users think differently from monolingual speakers of both their first and second language. Most designs have compared monolingual speakers of language X and monolingual speakers of language Y with L2 users who know both X and Y to see whether they have concepts in between. Most of the chapters in this volume provide evidence for this scenario, e.g., Bassetti (Chapter 16) for concepts of animals, Chen and Su (Chapter 15) for temporal representations, Czechowska and Ewert (Chapter 13) for motion conceptualization, etc. (outside this volume, this was also found in object naming and typicality rating by Ameel et al., 2009, in motion conceptualization by Brown & Gullberg, 2008, etc.)

(4) *The original-concept scenario.* The L2 user creates concepts that differ from those of either language. The L2 user might reject a lunch made of

sandwiches and crisps, thinking, like all Italians, that these are awful, and might reject a lunch made of pasta and fish, thinking, like English people, that this is too heavy—and might develop a new concept of 'lunch', maybe pasta with a cup of tea (see Figure 7.5). Indeed, in real-life experience the Italian co-author of this chapter embarrasses her parents by insisting on tea after her lunch in Italian restaurants. In the case of *blue* versus *blu*, the L2 user might have a concept of 'blue', which is neither (1) *blue* or *blu*, nor (2) in between *blue* and *blu*, but is (3) a different shade of blue.

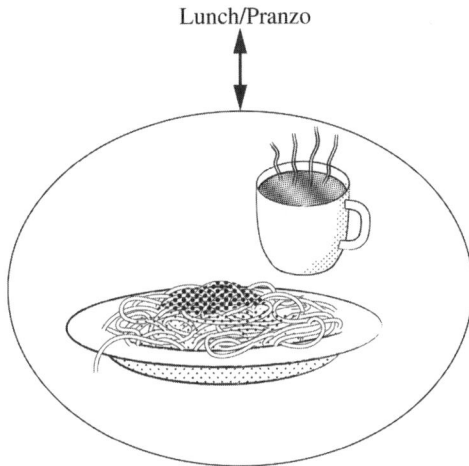

Figure 7.5 The concept of lunch in English–Italian bilinguals: The original-concept scenario.

The original-concept scenario relates to research such as Athanasopoulos (Chapter 11, this volume) that Greek–English L2 users have a concept of '*ghalazio*' ('light blue') that is lighter than Greek monolinguals. This cannot be predicted by the one-integrated-concept scenario (which only predicts that their concept of '*ble*' will approximate the concept of L2 English 'blue'). It is a new color category that L2 users have created for themselves that does not lie in between the concepts in their two languages but is something of its own. Czechowska and Ewert (Chapter 13, this volume) also found that highly proficient L2 users notice aspects of motion differently from native speakers of both L1 and L2, in ways that are not predictable from their language combination.

The four scenarios described above apply to concepts rather than people, so that the same bilingual individual can have concepts belonging to different types. An English–Italian L2 user might have a different concept of 'lunch' compared with a monolingual, having compounded *pranzo* with *lunch*, but might share the concept of 'blue' with an English monolingual, having not changed it as a consequence of learning the words *blu* and *azzurro*. Indeed, even within the same field such as colors, L2 users can have single concepts for some colors and integrated concepts for others, for instance having a new concept with a new name for 'orange' (coded in L2 but not in L1 Vietnamese), but without any effects from the L2 on their 'blue' and 'green' (Jameson & Alvarado, 2003).

Nevertheless it is possible to categorize individual L2 users in terms of the scenario they use most. Bilinguals who have mostly single concepts from one of their languages might be considered type 1 bilinguals (dominant in one language); those who mostly have double concepts (one for each language) might be type 2 bilinguals; those with integrated concepts might be type 3 bilinguals; and those with original concepts might be type 4 bilinguals.

This classification resembles the three familiar types of bilinguals proposed by Weinreich (1953): subordinate, coordinate, and compound. The main differences are that subordinate bilingualism is here conceived of more as cross-linguistic influence which also includes effects of L2 on L1 (Cook, 2003); and that L2 users can have concepts that are new creations—in the present conception, L2 users are active and creative learners and users of their languages.

Are bilingualism-induced conceptual changes always positive?

Mostly in the review above we have seen that bilinguals know concepts that are unknown to monolingual speakers of one of their languages, e.g., the concept of 'orange' in Vietnamese–English bilinguals, or that bilinguals' concepts differ from those of monolinguals as a consequence of knowing more than one way of representing the world, e.g., Italian–German bilinguals think that storks are less feminine than Italian monolinguals. But can L2 learning and bilingualism have negative effects? Knowing L2 English, a language with a smaller motion lexicon than L1 Russian, does not lead to an impoverished perception of motion in Russian speakers (as pointed out by Czechowska and Ewert in Chapter 13 of this volume, with reference to Pavlenko, 2010); on the other hand, Russian–English bilinguals show attrition of the distinction between dark and light blue (Andrews, 1994). Some cognitive consequences of bilingualism could be considered negative. Kurinski and Sera (in press) found that learning Spanish leads English-speaking children to consider objects as more masculine or feminine, in line with their grammatical gender—presumably learning Spanish introduced a language bias that was not present in English children. Bassetti (2008) also argued that learning English negatively affects the understanding of counterfactual stories in Chinese speakers.

Bilingualism is currently mostly portrayed as a positive thing. It increases metalinguistic awareness, improves literacy, increases selective attention (Bialystok, 2005), it even delays cognitive aging (Bialystok et al., 2004). Of course, this rosy picture is not the whole story; for instance bilingualism can slow down children's vocabulary development in the first language (for overviews of negative effects, see Ardila & Ramos, 2007;

Bialystok, 2009). The results reported above show that bilingualism can also introduce language-induced biases that were not there in the first place, and so cloud bilinguals' representations of reality.

What factors modulate the effects of bilingualism on cognition?

We have seen, then, that there may be variation in the effects of learning a second language both on concepts and on L2 users. What causes this variation? Ideally one would look at the comprehensive list of variables that affect bilinguals' performance in Grosjean (1998). Here are a few factors that seem particularly relevant to bilingual cognition research.

Age of onset of acquisition of the two languages

The age at which sequential bilinguals begin to acquire their two languages has been shown to be important, for instance by Bylund (2009) with motion events conceptualization, Harris (2004) with emotional expressions, and Boroditsky (2001) with temporal representations. And of course age is doubly important when the people studied are still children in process of maturation; research testing effects of grammatical gender on concepts below the age of 8 found no effects (see Sera et al., 2002, for cross-linguistic research, and Kurinski & Sera, in press, for bilingual research).

Length and type of stay in the two linguistic environments

Researchers have found effects of length of stay in an L2-speaking country on object categorization (Cook et al., 2006) and color categorization (Athanasopoulos, 2009), although such exposure is not a necessary condition as L2 effects on bilingual cognition have been found in bilinguals who have never lived in an L2-speaking country (Bassetti, 2007; Chen & Su, Chapter 15, this volume). The purposes of the stay are also crucial, whether as expat birds of passage, permanent immigrants, indigenous speakers of minority languages, schoolchildren, etc. (see Ervin-Tripp, Chapter 9, this volume, on Japanese war brides).

Proficiency and use of both languages

Effects of language proficiency have been found, among others, on emotion (Sutton et al., 2007) and numerical cognition (Han & Ginsburg, 2001); Chen and Su (Chapter 15, this volume) found effects on temporal representations. Problems arise of how to assess proficiency, whether using vocabulary tests (Cook et al., 2006), self-rating (Bassetti, 2007), placement tests (Coventry et al., Chapter 12, this volume) or other means, and how to assess knowledge of the specific language phenomenon under analysis.

Other languages known

The other languages known to an L2 user as well as the two under analysis could also affect results, not only because of the macro effects of knowing more than two languages but also because of the particular interrelationships involved. In studies of grammatical gender for instance (see Bassetti, Chapter 16, this volume), it is particularly important to be aware of the gender system of all the languages the person knows. This is crucial nowadays, as some English is almost always lurking in the background of any L2 user regardless of which two languages are ostensibly being compared.

THE RELATIONSHIP OF LANGUAGE TO BILINGUAL COGNITION: OVERALL QUESTIONS

Let us sum up the general issues involved in bilingual cognition research by rephrasing the four questions raised in the introduction to this volume about the relationship of language to cognition in terms of bilingualism research (Cook, Chapter 1, this volume).

The first question was whether different groups of people think differently. Recasting this in terms of bilingualism means asking whether there are differences in thinking between groups of people who do and do not speak more than one language. To test this question one would want to compare bi- or multilingual communities with monolingual ones. This has, so far, not been done in linguistic relativity studies, except accidentally. The assumption among language researchers has been that communities share only a single language; as Mackey wrote: 'An individual's use of two languages supposes the existence of two different language communities; it does not suppose the existence of a bilingual community' (Mackey, 1962, p. 51). The Common European Framework of Reference (CEFR) developed by the Council of Europe insisted on the goal of plurilingualism rather than the creation of a pan-European multilingual community (Council of Europe, 2001). Brutt-Griffler (2002) has indeed proposed 'the multi-competence of the community'. However, rather than starting with the assumption that communities have a single language, it may be better to consider how languages relate to each other within a community.

The second question in the introduction was 'do differences in cognition go with different features of language?' As much of the research in this volume attests, the major research paradigm for looking at language and bilinguals has been the comparison of the thinking of individuals who know only a single language with that of individuals who know more than one language, with one of the languages involved being typically English for practical reasons. The aim is to show that the experience of knowing more than one language affects the L2 users' thinking both in the language-tied perspective of thinking for speaking, where the question is whether thought is structured in order to produce language, and in the language-free linguistic relativity perspective, in which thinking involves non-language concepts. In our own early research with three colleagues reported above (Bassetti et al., 2002; Cook et al., 2006), the aim was to take an area where speakers of language X had been shown experimentally to think differently from speakers of language Y (in this case, the categorization of objects and substances) and then to see how this worked in people who knew both language X and Y. Japanese L2 users of English had indeed moved to some extent towards the classificatory preferences of English people. The studies reviewed in this chapter and those reported in Part B of this volume tend to show that people who know two or more languages have slightly different cognition from monolinguals in areas such as colors, space, time, objects, and so on, not necessarily having concepts in between the LX and LY, but sometimes concepts that are different from either. The conclusion is that L2 users indeed think differently from monolinguals in most areas tested.

The third question in the introduction was 'does a correlation of cognition with language imply a causation'; does acquiring the syntax of, say, classifiers in Chinese actually affect Chinese speakers' categorization of objects (Imai & Saalbach, 2010)? The debate over causation has been long and bitter, but bilingualism research can help address this important issue. In L1 development many other things are happening at the same time as language development, cognitively, emotionally, socially, and physically; any of these might be the underlying source of cognitive differences between language groups, with language being a side-effect. Language-external factors can reinforce language-based representations. For instance, someone walking in the street and looking at public art or flags in different countries will see different things that reflect the local language: Statues representing freedom are women in Italy (reflecting the grammatical gender of 'freedom' in Italian) but men in the Czech Republic; the rainbow in the (American) gay pride flag has only one blue stripe while the rainbow in the (originally Italian) peace flag has one dark blue stripe and one light blue stripe (reflecting the fact that dark and light blue are named in two different ways *blu* and *azzurro* in Italian but are both called *blue* and therefore perceived as a single color category in English). Material culture constantly reinforces differences that are due to language, making it difficult to disentangle what is due to language and what to culture.

However, this is precisely where bilingualism can provide a sharper focus. Many L2 users live in exactly the same environment as their monolingual peers; the only difference is the additional language. A Japanese child learning English in Tokyo is still in Tokyo, not magically transported to London. So, if there is an effect of learning English on the child's thinking, this can only be due to language; for instance, Bassetti (2007) found differences between Italian- and Italian–German-speaking children living in the same

Italian town. Bilingualism, then, provides a clearer answer to the causation question than is possible through studying monolingualism, by separating language out from other developmental factors: 'L2 research can be used as a kind of touchstone to test ideas in developmental psychology' (Cook, 1981, p. 256). A powerful argument for studying bilingual cognition is that it permits one to isolate the effects of language from those of the environment. If L2 users think differently from monolinguals who live in the same environment, then language is the likely cause of the cognitive difference— or at least there are far fewer alternatives to consider. A consequence of this approach is having to treat the L2 user as a whole with a single mind that combines the two languages into one system. Much research has shown how the L2 user is unable to totally isolate the two languages but has both accessible at some level of activation whichever is being used, whether in syntax, vocabulary, or phonology (Cook, 2003). It is not, then, that we can treat the L2 user as a monolingual when they are processing one language or the other, efficient in their L1, less efficient in their L2, but that they are L2 users at all times. So it cannot be assumed that the L2 user has a monolingual's knowledge of the syntax of their first language (or indeed their second) nor that they think in an L1-related way or an L2-related way. Their difference from monolinguals is the constantly changing balance between the two languages in their minds. On this view, bilingual cognition research takes a much more central role in linguistic relativity research; it is not a fringe activity but something at its very heart. One consequence is the need for linguistic relativity research to exert more control over the choice of participants. It is vital to control the other languages that participants know. L2 users are not suitable participants for monolingual studies of linguistic relativity, *pace* Whorf. If true monolinguals cannot be found, researchers need to be aware of the possibility that their results are due to the other languages their participants know. It may be possible to find monolinguals in some remote enclave of the Amazon rainforest or the New Guinea Highlands, but in most places people are 'contaminated' by other languages whether in multilingual communities or in classrooms. It is still an empirical issue how much of a second language needs to be learnt to affect cognition, and this may vary in all sorts of ways. Until this is settled, it cannot be assumed that L2 users think in the same ways as monolingual native speakers.

The above question, whether language affects thinking, leads naturally to the fourth question in the introduction: 'Can cognition be changed by language control or teaching?' Many L2 users acquire their language 'naturally', that is to say, by being immersed in a situation where they learn another language to deal with other groups within their own country or their new country of immigration; restaurant staff in London acquire Spanish as a lingua franca (Block, 2006), their counterparts in Toronto learn Italian (Norton, 2000); Arabic-speaking prisoners in Israeli jails learn Hebrew; English children in Swiss sanatoria pick up the languages of the other patients. Thus, unlike the relatively homogeneous context of monolingual L1 acquisition of L1, L2 learning and bilingual first language acquisition occur in a variety of circumstances (Cook, 2010). However, very many L2 users are actually *taught* the second language to a greater or lesser extent; their language and learning environment is under tight control from a teacher. Cook (Chapter 22, this volume) discusses what bilingual cognition research means for L2 teachers, arguing that 'the objective of language teaching can be precisely the enhancements to cognitive processing that knowing another language brings' (p. 514). Language teaching is in essence a vast uncontrolled experiment in language and cognition where the variables of language and situation are systematically manipulated by teachers. This does involve some disadvantages; in the case of people who are formally taught a second language, it is a question of whether the methodological advantages of exemption from other factors outweigh the sometimes imponderable variables induced by the teaching method involved, which can range from the physical actions of the Total Physical Response Method to the ratiocination of Focus on Form instruction and to the conversational interaction of communicative language teaching (Cook, 2008). The question about effects of language on bilingual cognition is intertwined with the question of whether language learnt by the 'studial process' (Palmer, 1926) is the same as language knowledge 'naturally' acquired from use.

Apart from the four main questions discussed above, there are many questions that spring from the area of bilingual cognition that have barely started to be considered in their own right, although the research in this volume hints at possible answers:

- Does conceptual change relate to a critical or sensitive period for language acquisition, or is conceptual change possible with language learning at any age?
- How much contact with another language leads to conceptual change? Does a small amount of contact have any effects?
- Is multilingualism 'better' than bilingualism? In other words, are there more cognitive changes the more languages are known? As Whorf put it, does an objective view of reality come from knowing 'very many . . . linguistic systems' (1940/1956, p. 214)?
- Do some language combinations lead to more conceptual change than others? For instance, so far as cognitive changes are concerned, is learning Korean for a speaker of English better than learning German (examples of the 'widely different linguistic systems' suggested by Whorf, 1940/1956, p. 214)?
- Does formal language study lead to more conceptual change than 'natural' language acquisition, or vice versa?
- Do effects of language on bilingual cognition cross the modalities of speech, writing, and signing? This is suggested for instance by the effects of written language on non-linguistic cognition reviewed in Cook and Bassetti (2005), and by research on sign language and

bilingualism by Emmorey and her colleagues (e.g., Emmorey & McCullough, 2009).
- Is 'passive' use of a language, say by reading, as change-inducing as active use in speaking?
- What roles does culture rather than language play in bilingual cognition change?

The study of bilingual cognition, then, can benefit the whole enterprise of research into the relationship between language and cognition, as well as being of interest to researchers (and indeed practitioners) working with bilinguals. But it also has practical consequences for everyday human life in these days when a large proportion of people in the world knows more than one language, even if it is just a smattering of school English. Whorf was preoccupied with the effects of language on behavior, for instance how language could avoid accidents in the workplace. It is likely that having different concepts might affect real-life behavior of bilinguals, for instance affecting a marital relationship if an English–Italian bilingual spouse has a different concept of 'love' from their English monolingual spouse. Part C of this book raises such practical issues, ranging from language teaching (Cook, Chapter 22) to translation (House, Chapter 23), intercultural communication (Sercombe & Young, Chapter 24), and marketing (Luna, Chapter 25).

ACKNOWLEDGMENTS

We are grateful to Professor Jyotsna Vaid for her comments on a previous version of this chapter, and to Stefano Ferrari for preparing the illustrations.

REFERENCES

Aikhenvald, A. Y. (2004). *Evidentiality*. Oxford, UK: Oxford University Press.
Ameel, E., Malt, B., Storms, G., & Van Assche, F. (2009). Semantic convergence in the bilingual lexicon. *Journal of Memory and Language, 60,* 270–290.
Ameel, E., Storms, G., Malt, B., & Sloman, S. A. (2005). How bilinguals solve the naming problem. *Journal of Memory and Language, 53,* 60–80.
Andrews, D. R. (1994). The Russian color categories *sinij* and *goluboj*: An experimental analysis of their interpretation in the standard and emigré languages. *Journal of Slavic Linguistics, 2,* 9–28.
Anggoro, F., & Gentner, D. (2003). Sex and seniority: The effects of linguistic categories on conceptual judgments and memory. In R. Alterman & D. Kirsh (Eds.), *Proceedings of the twenty-fifth annual meeting of the Cognitive Science Society.* Mahwah, NJ: Lawrence Erlbaum Associates Inc.
Annoshian, L., & Hertel, P. (1994). Emotionality in free recall: Language specificity in bilingual memory. *Cognition and Emotion, 8*(6), 503–514.

Ardila, A., & Ramos, E. (2007). Bilingualism and cognition: The good, the bad and the ugly of bilingualism. In A. Ardila & E. Ramos (Eds.), *Speech and language disorders in bilinguals* (pp. 213–234). New York, NY: Nova Science Publishers.

Athanasopoulos, P. (2002). *Colour perception of blue in Greek bilinguals and monolinguals*. Paper presented at the 12th Conference of the European Second Language Association, Basel, Switzerland, 18–21 September.

Athanasopoulos, P. (2006). Effects of the grammatical representation of number on cognition in bilinguals. *Bilingualism: Language and Cognition, 9,* 89–96.

Athanasopoulos, P. (2007). Interaction between grammatical categories and cognition in bilinguals: The role of proficiency, cultural immersion, and language of instruction. *Language and Cognitive Processes, 22,* 689–699.

Athanasopoulos, P. (2009). Cognitive representation of colour in bilinguals: The case of Greek blues. *Bilingualism: Language and Cognition, 12*(1), 83–95.

Athanasopoulos, P., & Kasai, C. (2008). Language and thought in bilinguals: The case of grammatical number and nonverbal classification preferences. *Applied Psycholinguistics, 29*(1), 105–123.

Au, T. K-F. (1983). Chinese and English counterfactuals: The Sapir-Whorf hypothesis revisited. *Cognition, 15,* 155–187.

Au, T. K-F. (1984). Counterfactuals: In reply to Alfred Bloom. *Cognition, 17*(3), 289–302.

Bassetti, B. (2005). Effects of writing systems on second language awareness: Word awareness in English learners of Chinese as a foreign language. In V. J. Cook & B. Bassetti (Eds.), *Second language writing systems* (pp. 335–356). Clevedon, UK: Multilingual Matters.

Bassetti, B. (2007). Bilingualism and thought: Grammatical gender and concepts of objects in Italian–German bilingual children. *International Journal of Bilingualism, 11*(3), 251–273.

Bassetti, B. (2008). *Counterfactual reasoning in Chinese–English bilinguals*. Paper presented at the International Conference on Language, Communication and Cognition, Brighton, UK, 4–7 August.

Bassetti, B., Cook, V. J., Kasai, C., Sasaki, M., Takahashi, J. A., & Tokumaru, Y. (2002). *Perception of shape and material in Japanese users of English*. Paper presented at the 12th Conference of the European Second Language Association, Basel, 18–21 September.

Berlin, B., & Kay, P. (1969). *Basic color terms: Their universality and evolution.* Berkeley, CA: University of California Press.

Bialystok, E. (2001). *Bilingualism in development: Language, literacy, and cognition.* Cambridge, UK: Cambridge University Press.

Bialystok, E. (2005). Consequences of bilingualism for cognitive development. In B. Kroll & A. M. B. de Groot (Eds.), *Handbook of bilingualism: Psycholinguistics perspectives* (pp. 417–432). Oxford, UK: Oxford University Press.

Bialystok, E. (2009). Bilingualism: The good, the bad, and the indifferent. *Bilingualism: Language and Cognition, 12*(1), 3–11.

Bialystok, E., Craik, F. I., Klein, R., & Viswanathan, M. (2004). Bilingualism, aging, and cognitive control: Evidence from the Simon task. *Psychology and Aging, 19*(2), 290–303.

Bialystok, E., Majumder, S., & Martin, M. M. (2003). Developing phonological awareness: Is there a bilingual advantage? *Applied Psycholinguistics, 24,* 27–44.

Block, D. (2006). *Multilingual identities in a global city: London stories*. London: Palgrave.

Bloom, A. (1981). *The linguistic shaping of thought: A study in the impact of language on thinking in China and the West*. Mahwah, NJ: Lawrence Erlbaum Associates Inc.

Bloomfield, L. (1933). *Language*. New York: Henry Holt.

Boroditsky, L. (2001). Does language shape thought? English and Mandarin speakers' conceptions of time. *Cognitive Psychology, 43*(2), 1–22.

Boroditsky, L., Ham, W., & Ramscar, M. (2002). What is universal in event perception? Comparing English and Indonesian speakers. In W. D. Gray & C. D. Schunn (Eds.), *Proceedings of the twenty-fourth annual conference of the Cognitive Science Society* (pp. 136–141). Mahwah, NJ: Lawrence Erlbaum Associates Inc.

Boroditsky, L., Schmidt, L. A., & Phillips, W. (2003). Sex, syntax and semantics. In D. Gentner & S. Goldin-Meadow (Eds.), *Language in mind: Advances in the study of language and thought* (pp. 61–78). Cambridge, MA: MIT Press.

Boroditsky, L., & Trusova, E. (2003). Cross-linguistic differences in the representation of events: Verb aspect and completion in English and Russian. In R. Alterman & D. Kirsh (Eds.), *Proceedings of the twenty-fifth annual conference of the Cognitive Science Society* (pp. 13–19). Mahwah, NJ: Lawrence Erlbaum Associates Inc.

Brown, A., & Gullberg, M. (2008). Bidirectional crosslinguistic influence in L1–L2 encoding of manner in speech and gesture: A study of Japanese speakers of English. *Studies in Second Language Acquisition, 30*(2), 225–251.

Brown, A., & Gullberg, M. (2010). Changes in encoding of path of motion after acquisition of a second language. *Cognitive Linguistics, 21*(2), 263–286.

Brown, A., & Gullberg, M. (in press). Bidirectional crosslinguistic influence in event conceptualization? Expressions of path among Japanese learners of English. *Bilingualism: Language and Cognition*.

Brown, R., & Lenneberg, E. (1954). A study in language and cognition. *Journal of Abnormal and Social Psychology, 49,* 454–462.

Bruck, M., & Genesee, F. (1995). Phonological awareness in young second language learners. *Journal of Child Language, 22,* 307–324.

Brutt-Griffler, J. (2002). *World English: A study of its development*. Clevedon, UK: Multilingual Matters.

Bylund, E. (2009). Effects of age of L2 acquisition on L1 event conceptualization patterns. *Bilingualism: Language and Cognition, 12*(3), 305–322.

Cadierno, T. (2008). Learning to talk about motion in a foreign language. In P. Robinson & N. C. Ellis (Eds.), *Handbook of cognitive linguistics and second language acquisition* (pp. 239–275). London: Routledge.

Cadierno, T., & Robinson, P. (2009). Language typology, task complexity and the development of L2 lexicalization patterns for describing motion events. *Annual Review of Cognitive Linguistics, 7,* 245–276.

Campbell, R., & Sais, E. (1995). Accelerated metalinguistic (phonological) awareness in bilingual children. *British Journal of Developmental Psychology, 13,* 61–68.

Casasanto, D. (2008). Who's afraid of the big bad Whorf? Crosslinguistic differences in temporal language and thought. *Language Learning, 58*(1), 63–69.

Casasola, M., Bhagwat, J., & Burke, A. S. (2006). Learning to form a spatial category of tight-fit relations: How experience with a label can give a boost. *Developmental Psychology, 45*(3), 711–723.

Caskey-Sirmons, L. A., & Hickerson, N. P. (1977). Semantic shift and bilingualism: Variation in the color terms of five languages. *Anthropological Linguistics, 19,* 358–367.

Chalikia, M. H., Norberg, A. M., & Paterakis, L. (2000). Greek bilingual listeners perceive the tritone stimuli differently from speakers of English. *Journal of the Acoustical Society of America, 108*(5), 25–72.

Chalikia, M. H., & Vaid, J. (1999). *Do bilinguals perceive the tritone paradox as monolinguals do?* Poster presentation, Acoustical Society of America annual meeting, Columbus, OH.

Chen, J-Y. (2007). Do Chinese and English speakers think about time differently? Failure of replicating Boroditsky (2001). *Cognition, 104,* 427–436.

Cheng, W-j. (1985). Pictures of ghosts: A critique of Alfred Bloom's *The Linguistic Shaping of Thought. American Anthropologist, 87*(4), 917–922.

Cook, V. J. (1981). Some uses for second-language-learning research. *Annals of the New York Academy of Sciences, 279,* 251–258.

Cook, V. J. (1991). The poverty-of-the-stimulus argument and multi-competence. *Second Language Research, 7*(2), 103–117.

Cook, V. J. (1994). The metaphor of access to universal grammar. In N. Ellis (Ed.), *Implicit learning and language* (pp. 477–502). New York: Academic Press.

Cook, V. J. (2002). Background to the L2 user. In V. J. Cook (Ed.), *Portraits of the L2 user* (pp. 21–28). Clevedon, UK: Multilingual Matters.

Cook, V. J. (Ed.). (2003). *The effects of the second language on the first.* Clevedon, UK: Multilingual Matters.

Cook, V. J. (2008). *Second language learning and language teaching* (4th ed.). London: Hodder Education.

Cook, V. J. (2009). Multilingual Universal Grammar as the norm. In I. Leung (Ed.), *Third language acquisition and universal grammar* (pp. 55–70). Bristol: Multilingual Matters.

Cook, V. J. (2010). Prolegomena to second language learning. In P. Seedhouse, S. Walsh, & C. Jenks (Eds.), *Conceptualising language learning.* London: Palgrave Macmillan.

Cook, V. J., & Bassetti, B. (2005). Introduction to researching *Second Language Writing Systems.* In V. J. Cook & B. Bassetti (Eds.), *Second language writing systems* (pp. 1–67). Clevedon, UK: Multilingual Matters.

Cook, V. J., Bassetti, B., Kasai, C., Sasaki, M., & Takahashi, J. A. (2006). Do bilinguals have different concepts? The case of shape and material in Japanese L2 users of English. *International Journal of Bilingualism, 10*(2), 137–152.

Council of Europe. (2000). *Europass Language Passport.* Available from: http://www.coe.int/T/DG4/Portfolio/documents/Pass_2spr.pdf (accessed March 1, 2010).

Council of Europe. (2001). *Common European framework of reference for languages.* Cambridge, UK: Cambridge University Press. [Available from: http://www.coe.int/t/dg4/linguistic/CADRE_EN.asp (accessed January 15, 2009).]

Deutsch, D. (2004). Speech patterns heard early in life influence later perception of the tritone paradox. *Music Perception, 21*(3), 357–372.

Deutsch, D., Henthorn, T., & Dolson, M. (2004). Absolute pitch, speech, and tone language: Some experiments and a proposed framework. *Music Perception, 21*(3), 339–356.

Dewaele, J-M. (2004). The emotional force of swearwords and taboo words in the speech of multilinguals. *Journal of Multilingual and Multicultural Development, 25,* 204–222.

Dewaele, J-M. (2008a). Dynamic emotion concepts of L2 learners and L2 users: A second language acquisition perspective. *Bilingualism: Language and Cognition, 11*(2), 173–175.

Dewaele, J-M. (2008b). The emotional weight of 'I love you' in multilinguals' languages. *Journal of Pragmatics, 40,* 1753–1780.

Dewaele, J-M. (2010). *Emotions in multiple languages.* London: Palgrave Macmillan.

Emmorey, K., & McCullough, S. (2009). The bimodal bilingual brain: Effects of sign language experience. *Brain and Language, 109*(2–3), 124–132.

Ervin, S. M. (1961). Semantic shift in bilingualism. *American Journal of Psychology, 74,* 233–241.

European Commission on Multilingualism. (2010). *Language teaching: Creativity and language.* Available from: http://ec.europa.eu/education/languages/language-teaching/doc34_en.htm (accessed 5 April 2010).

Facebook. (2010). *Topic: I miei figli NON faranno mai il liceo classico* [*My children will NEVER go to classical high school*]. Available from: http://www.facebook.com/topic.php?uid=24770815378&topic=5160 (accessed April 5, 2010).

Flecken, M. (in press). Event conceptualization by early bilinguals: Insights from linguistic and eye tracking data. *Bilingualism: Language and Cognition.* Advance online publication. Retrieved July 29, 2010. doi 10.1017/5136672810000180

Frederickson, N., & Cline, T. (2002). *Special educational needs, inclusion and diversity: A textbook.* Buckingham, UK: Open University Press.

Graham, R. C., & Belnap, K. R. (1986). The acquisition of lexical boundaries in English by native speakers of Spanish. *International Review of Applied Linguistics, 24*(4), 275–286.

Green, D. W. (1998). Bilingualism and thought. *Psychologica Belgica, 38,* 253–278.

Grosjean, F. (1998). Studying bilinguals: Methodological and conceptual issues. *Bilingualism: Language and Cognition, 1,* 131–149.

Grosjean, F. (2008), The bilingualism and biculturalism of the Deaf. In F. Grosjean (Ed.), *Studying bilinguals* (pp. 221–240). Oxford, UK: Oxford University Press.

Gumperz, J. J., & Levinson, S. C. (Eds.). (1996). *Rethinking linguistic relativity.* Cambridge, UK: Cambridge University Press.

Han, A. Y. (1998). *Chinese and English mathematics language: The relation between linguistic clarity and mathematics performance.* PhD thesis, Columbia University, OH.

Han, A. Y., & Ginsburg, H. P. (2001). Chinese and English mathematics language: The relation between linguistic clarity and mathematics performance. *Mathematical Thinking and Learning, 3,* 201–220.

Harris, C. L. (2004). Bilingual speakers in the lab: Psychophysiological measures of emotional reactivity. *Journal of Multilingual and Multicultural Development, 25,* 223–247.

Haugen, E. (1953). *The Norwegian language in America.* Philadelphia, PA: University of Pennsylvania Press.

Hoffman, C. (1991). *An introduction to bilingualism.* London: Longman.

Hoffman, C., Lau, I. Y-M., & Johnson, D. R. (1986). The linguistic relativity of person cognition: An English–Chinese comparison. *Journal of Personality and Social Psychology, 51*(6), 1097–1107.

Hohenstein, J., Eisenberg, A., & Naigles, L. (2006). Is he floating across or crossing afloat? Cross-influence of L1 and L2 in Spanish–English bilingual adults. *Bilingualism: Language and Cognition, 9,* 249–261.

Hunt, E., & Agnoli, F. (1991). The Whorfian hypothesis: A cognitive psychology perspective. *Psychology Review, 98*(3), 377–389.

Imai, M., & Saalbach, H. (2010). Categories in mind and categories in language: Do classifier categories influence conceptual structure? In B. Malt & P. Wolff (Eds.), *Words and the mind: How words capture human experience*. Oxford, UK: Oxford University Press.

Ishii, R., & O'Mahony, M. (1989). Group taste concept measurement: Verbal and physical definition of the umami taste concept for Japanese and Americans. *Journal of Sensory Studies, 4*(4), 215–227.

Jameson, K. A., & Alvarado, N. (2002). The use of modifying terms in the naming and categorization of color appearances in Vietnamese and English. *Journal of Cognition and Culture, 2,* 53–80.

Jameson, K. A., & Alvarado, N. (2003). Differences in color naming and color salience in Vietnamese and English. *COLOR Research and Application, 28,* 113–138.

January, D., & Kako, E. (2006). Re-evaluating evidence for linguistic relativity: Reply to Boroditsky (2001). *Cognition, 104,* 417–426.

Jarvis, S. (1998). *Conceptual transfer in the interlanguage lexicon*. Bloomington, IN: Indiana University Linguistics Club Publications.

Jarvis, S. (2000). Methodological rigor in the study of transfer: Identifying L1 influence in the interlanguage lexicon. *Language Learning, 50,* 245–309.

Jarvis, S., & Odlin, T. (2000). Morphological type, spatial reference, and language transfer. *Studies in Second Language Acquisition, 22,* 535–557.

Jisa, H., Reilly, J., Verhoeven, L., Baruch, E., & Rosado, E. (2002). Passive voice constructions in written texts: A cross-linguistic developmental study. *Written Language and Literacy, 5,* 163–181.

Kellerman, E., & van Hoof, A-M. (2003). Manual accents. *International Review of Applied Linguistics, 41,* 251–269.

Kiyak, H. A. (1982). Interlingual interference in naming colour words. *Journal of Cross-Cultural Psychology, 13,* 125–135.

Kugelmass, S., & Lieblich, A. (1979). The impact of learning to read on directionality in perception: A further cross-cultural analysis. *Human Development, 22,* 406–415.

Kuo, J. Y-C., & Sera, M. D. (2009). Classifier effects on human categorization: The role of shape classifiers in Mandarin Chinese. *Journal of East Asian Linguistics, 18,* 1–19.

Kurinski, E., & Sera, M. (in press). Does learning Spanish grammatical gender change English-speaking adults' categorization of inanimate objects? *Bilingualism: Language and Cognition*.

Lakoff, G. (1987). *Women, fire, and dangerous things: What categories reveal about the mind*. Chicago, IL: University of Chicago Press.

Lee, P. (1996). *The Whorf theory complex: A critical reconstruction*. Amsterdam: John Benjamins.

Lenneberg, E. H., & Roberts, J. M. (1956). The language of experience: A study in methodology. Supplement to *International Journal of American Linguistics, 22,* 2.

Liu, L. G. (1985). Reasoning counterfactually in Chinese: Are there any obstacles? *Cognition, 21*(3), 239–270.

Loizou, M., & Stuart, M. (2003). Phonological awareness in monolingual and bilingual English and Greek five-year-olds. *Journal of Research in Reading, 26*(1), 3–18.

Lord, N. (1996). Native tongues: The languages that once mapped the American landscape have almost vanished. *Sierra, 8*(16), 46–69.

Lucy, J. (1992a). *Grammatical categories and cognition: A case study of the linguistic relativity hypothesis*. Cambridge, UK: Cambridge University Press.

Lucy, J. (1992b). *Language diversity and thought: A reformulation of the linguistic relativity hypothesis*. Cambridge, UK: Cambridge University Press.

Lucy, J. (1997). Linguistic relativity. *Annual Review of Anthropology, 26,* 291–312.

Mackey, W. F. (1962). The description of bilingualism. *Canadian Journal of Linguistics, 7,* 51–85.

Malt, B., & Sloman, S. A. (2003). Linguistic diversity and object naming by non-native speakers of English. *Bilingualism: Language and Cognition, 6*(1), 47–67.

Mang, E. (2006). The effects of age, gender and language on children's singing competency. *British Journal of Music Education, 23*(2), 161–174.

Matsumoto, D., Anguas-Wong, A. M., & Martinez, E. (2008). Priming effects of language on emotion judgments in Spanish–English bilinguals. *Journal of Cross-Cultural Psychology, 39,* 335–342.

Matsumoto, D., & Assar, M. (1992). The effects of language on judgments of universal facial expressions of emotion. *Journal of Nonverbal Behavior, 16*(2), 85–99.

Miller, K., Major, S. M., Shu, H., & Zhang, H. (2000). Ordinal knowledge: Number names and number concepts in Chinese and English. *Canadian Journal of Experimental Psychology, 54,* 129–139.

Mori, I., Koyima, M., & Tadang, K. (1976). The effect of language on a child's perception of speed. *Science Education, 60*(4), 531–534.

Morikawa, K., & McBeath, M. (1992). Lateral motion bias associated with reading direction. *Vision Research, 32*(6), 1137–1141.

Mulholland, H. (2010). Boris Johnson lobbies Tories to add Latin to state-school curriculum. (Wednesday 17 March 2010.) Retrieved September 13, 2010, from http://www.guardian.co.uk/politics/2010/mar/17/boris-johnson-lobbies-tories-latin-curriculum

Navarro, S., & Nicoladis, E. (2005). Describing motion events in adult L2 Spanish narratives. In D. Eddington (Ed.), *Selected proceedings of the 6th conference on the acquisition of Spanish and Portuguese as first and second languages* (pp. 102–107). Somerville, MA: Cascadilla Proceedings.

Niemeier, S., & Dirven, R. (Eds.). (2000). *Evidence for linguistic relativity*. Amsterdam: John Benjamins.

Norton, B. (2000). *Identity in language learning*. London: Longman.

Odlin, T. (2005). Crosslinguistic influence and conceptual transfer: What are the concepts? *Annual Review of Applied Linguistics, 25,* 3–25.

O'Mahony, M., & Ishii, R. (1986). A comparison of English and Japanese taste languages. *British Journal of Psychology, 77,* 161–174.

O'Mahony, M., & Muhiudeen, H. (1977). A preliminary study of alternative taste languages using qualitative description of sodium chloride solutions: Malay versus English. *British Journal of Psychology, 68,* 275–278.

Palmer, H. E. (1926), *The principles of language study*. London: Harrap.

Panayiotou, A. (2004). Bilingual emotions: The untranslatable self. *Estudios de Sociolingüística, 5*(1), 1–19.

Pavlenko, A. (1999). New approaches to concepts in bilingual memory. *Bilingualism: Language and Cognition, 2*(3), 209–230.

Pavlenko, A. (2005). Bilingualism and thought. In A. M. B. de Groot & J. F. Kroll (Eds.), *Handbook of bilingualism: Psycholinguistics perspectives*. Oxford, UK: Oxford University Press.

Pavlenko, A. (2006). *Emotions and multilingualism*. Cambridge, UK: Cambridge University Press.

Pavlenko, A. (2008). Emotion and emotion-laden words in the bilingual lexicon. *Bilingualism: Language and Cognition, 11*(2), 147–164.

Pavlenko, A. (2010). Verbs of motion in L1 Russian of Russian–English bilinguals. *Bilingualism: Language and Cognition, 13*(1), 49–62.

Pavlenko, A., & Malt, B. (in press). Kitchen Russian: Cross-linguistic differences and first-language object naming by Russian–English bilinguals. *Bilingualism: Language and Cognition*. Advance online publication. Retrieved July 13, 2010. doi 10.1017/5136672891000026X

Peal, E., & Lambert, W. E. (1962). The relation of bilingualism to intelligence. *Psychological Monographs, 76*(27), 1–23.

Phillips, W., & Boroditsky, L. (2003). Can quirks of grammar affect the way you think? Grammatical gender and object concepts. In R. Alterman & D. Kirsh (Eds.), *Proceedings of the twenty-fifth annual meeting of the Cognitive Science Society*. Mahwah, NJ: Lawrence Erlbaum Associates Inc.

Romaine, S. (1989). *Bilingualism*. Oxford, UK: Blackwell.

Romney, K. A., Moore, C. C., & Rusch, C. D. (1997). Cultural universals: Measuring the semantic structure of emotion terms in English and Japanese. *Proceedings of the National Academy of Sciences, 94*, 1–5.

Sánchez, L. (2004). Functional convergence in the tense, evidentiality and aspectual systems of Quechua–Spanish bilinguals. *Bilingualism: Language and Cognition, 7*, 147–162.

Sapir, E. (1924/1985). The grammarian and his language. [Originally in *American Mercury, 1*, 149–155.] In D. G. Mandelbaum (Ed.), *Selected writings in language, culture, and personality* (pp. 150–159). Berkeley, CA: University of California Press.

Schmiedtová, B., Carroll, M., & von Stutterheim, C. (2007). *Implications of language-specific L1 patterns in event construal of advanced second language learners*. Paper presented at the annual conference of the American Association for Applied Linguistics, Costa Mesa, CA, 24 April.

Sera, M., Elieff, C., Forbes, J., Burch, M. C., Rodríguez, W., & Dubois, D. P. (2002). When language affects cognition and when it does not: An analysis of grammatical gender and classification. *Journal of Experimental Psychology: General, 131*(3), 377–397.

Slobin, D. I. (1996). From 'thought and language' to 'thinking for speaking'. In J. Gumperz & S. Levinson (Eds.), *Rethinking linguistic relativity* (pp. 70–96). Cambridge, UK: Cambridge University Press.

Slobin, D. I. (2003). Language and thought online: Cognitive consequences of linguistic relativity. In D. Gentner & S. Goldin-Meadow (Eds.), *Language in mind: Advances in the study of language and thought* (pp. 157–191). Cambridge, MA: MIT Press.

Slobin, D. I., & Aksu, A. A. (1982). Tense, aspect and modality in the use of the Turkish evidential. In P. J. Hopper (Ed.), *Tense–aspect: Between semantics and pragmatics*. Amsterdam: John Benjamins.

Sutton, T. M., Altarriba, J., Gianico, J. L., & Basnight-Brown, D. M. (2007). The automatic access of emotion: Emotional Stroop effects in Spanish–English bilingual speakers. *Cognition and Emotion, 21,* 1077–1090.

Takano, Y. (1989). Methodological problems in cross-cultural studies of linguistic relativity. *Cognition, 31*(2), 141–162.

Talmy, L. (1985). Lexicalization patterns: Semantic structure in lexical forms. In T. Shopen (Ed.), *Language typology and lexical description: Vol 3. Grammatical categories and the lexicon* (pp. 36–149). Cambridge: Cambridge University Press.

Talmy, L. (2005). The fundamental system of spatial schemas in language. In B. Hampe (Ed.), *From perception to meaning: Image schemas in cognitive linguistics.* Berlin/New York: Mouton de Gruyter.

Tosun, S., Vaid, J., & Geraci, L. (2010). *Mary (reportedly) missed her flight. Evidentials, memory and source knowledge: A comparison of Turkish and English.* Poster presented in the Department of Psychology, Texas A&M University, Texas.

Towell, R., & Hawkins, R. (1994). *Approaches to second language acquisition.* Clevedon, UK: Multilingual Matters.

Tse, C-S., & Altarriba, J. (2008). Evidence against linguistic relativity in Chinese and English: A case study of spatial and temporal metaphors. *Journal of Cognition and Culture, 8*(3–4), 335–357.

Tversky, B., Kugelmass, S., & Winter, A. (1991). Cross-cultural and developmental trends in graphic productions. *Cognitive Psychology, 23*(4), 515–557.

Vaid, J. (1995). Script directionality affects nonlinguistic performance: Evidence from Hindi and Urdu. In I. Taylor & D. R. Olson (Eds.), *Scripts and literacy: Reading and learning to read alphabets, syllabaries and characters* (pp. 295–310). Dordrecht: Kluwer.

Vaid, J. (2010). Asymmetries in representational drawing: Alternatives to a laterality account. In A. Maas & T. Schubert (Eds.), *Spatial dimensions of social thought.* The Hague: Mouton de Gruyter.

von Humboldt, W. (1936/1988). *On language: The diversity of human language-structure and its influence on the mental development of mankind* [trans. by P. Heath]. Cambridge, UK: Cambridge University Press.

Weinreich, U. (1953). *Languages in contact.* The Hague: Mouton.

Whorf, B. L. (1937/1956). Discussion of Hopi linguistics. Letter reprinted in J. B. Carroll (Ed.), *Language, thought and reality: Selected writings of Benjamin Lee Whorf* (pp. 102–111). Cambridge, MA: MIT Press.

Whorf, B. L. (1940/1956). Science and linguistics. In J. B. Carroll (Ed.), *Language, thought and reality: Selected writings of Benjamin Lee Whorf* (pp. 207–219). Cambridge, MA: MIT Press.

Whorf, B. L. (1941/1956). Languages and logic. In J. B. Carroll (Ed.), *Language, thought and reality: Selected writings of Benjamin Lee Whorf* (pp. 233–245). Cambridge, MA: MIT Press.

Wolff, P., & Ventura, T. (2009). When Russians learn English: How the meaning of causal verbs may change. *Bilingualism: Language and Cognition, 12*(2), 153–176.

Yeh, D., & Gentner, D. (2005). Reasoning counterfactually in Chinese: Picking up the pieces. *Proceedings of the twenty-seventh annual meeting of the Cognitive Science Society,* 2410–2415.

Yelland, G. W., Pollard, J., & Mercuri, A. (1993). The metalinguistic benefits of limited contact with a second language. *Applied Psycholinguistics, 14*(4), 423–444.

8 Bilingualism and cognition: The perspective from semantics

Anna Wierzbicka

WHAT IS 'BILINGUALISM' AND WHAT IS 'COGNITION'?

A perspective from semantics is one that pays attention to the meaning of words, and this includes the words in the title of this chapter. What do we mean, then, by *bilingualism* and what do we mean by *cognition*? In this article I will focus predominantly on the second of these questions, but I do want to make one point in relation to the first: there is a difference between 'bilingualism' in the sense of 'being able to speak' two languages and 'bilingualism' in the sense of 'living with' two languages. As I will discuss more fully in the conclusion, it is bilingualism in this second sense which is now increasingly recognized as a vital source of insight into human cognition in general.

The word *cognition*, not an everyday word in English, is used differently by different writers. The *Collins Cobuild English Language Dictionary* (1991) defines it as follows: '*cognition* is a mental process of knowing, learning and understanding things; a formal or technical word. For example, we have little evidence about how the brain functions in cognition.' The word *knowing* is well chosen here. To explain to a child, or a non-native speaker, what 'cognition' is meant to be about, one would need to say, as a first approximation, that it is about ways of thinking and ways of knowing.

The phrase 'mental process' is more problematic and less explanatory. Presumably, the intention behind it is to hint that cognition refers not only to 'conscious' thinking and knowing but also to some things that happen in a person's 'mind' that this person may not be aware of, and that happen not because this person wants them to happen. The example referring to the brain underscores this point: the word *cognition* intends to build a bridge between, on the one hand, thinking-and-knowing (and perhaps even feeling) and on the other, the brain and neurophysiology; and sometimes, *cognition* is bleached of any thinking-and-knowing and reduced, by and large, to what happens in the brain.

In this chapter I will assume that the question concerns ways of thinking-and-knowing, and ways of speaking. I do not mean only fully conscious thinking-and-knowing but also, for example, the categorization of what is seen and felt, which speakers, especially monolingual ones, are likely to take for granted and never make the subject of conscious attention.

Of course questions about processes occurring in the brain are also important, but any discussion of the relations between thinking-and-knowing and the brain requires a prior consideration of thinking-and-knowing as such.

Does the same apply to the relation between thinking-and-knowing and speaking? Here the answer must be no: We cannot discuss cognition (in the sense of thinking-and-knowing) without using language. The key question is: In what language can we discuss it if we want to arrive at an unbiased and culture-independent account?

For many scholars who don't have the experience of living with two languages and cultures this question simply doesn't arise: Even if they know two (or more) languages in an academic way, their thinking may be so conditioned by the only language in which they are living their life that this language is invisible to them, so that they take the categories embedded in it for granted. In today's English-dominated world, cognitive science, psychology, and even linguistics often proceed in just such a fashion: Many Anglophone scholars assume that English words—for example, *cognition, mind, colour, emotion, appraisal, consciousness, behaviour, information, communication, society, privacy*—are culture-independent scientific tools which allow them to discuss subjects such as 'human cognition' in an unbiased and objective way.

This is where bilingualism—not just in the sense of competence in two languages but in the sense of lived bilingual experience—comes in, as a source of insight and understanding which may not be accessible to purely monolingual English-based science. To people who have such experience it will be clear that many words that English speakers take for granted are in fact language- and culture-specific and have no equivalents in other languages. *Cognition* is one such word (semi-technical, to be sure, but widely used in academic English). For example, there is no equivalent to *cognition* in my native Polish. The closest Polish counterpart of this word is *poznanie* (close to the German *Erkentniss*)—a word which (like *Erkentniss*) refers to the acquisition of knowledge and does not include in its meaning any reference to thinking. (The adjective *kognitywny* is used in academic language as a calque from English.)

Psychologists, like other scholars, often insist that their discipline cannot rely on ordinary language and that it requires a technical language of its own. In practice, however, the technical language of psychology and cognitive science depends to a very considerable extent on English, and various current theories of human cognition (and emotion) are simply not translatable into other languages, because of their dependence on English (cf. e.g., Wierzbicka, in press).

We should recall Francis Bacon's (1620, p. 68) warning about 'the idols imposed by words on the understanding' (quoted in Mandler & Kesson, 1959, pp. 9–10). There are two kinds of such words, according to Bacon: Those which imply the existence of something that doesn't in fact exist, for example *Fortune*, and those which are widely used but which have no stable and clearly defined meaning. The word 'cognition' may well be an example of this second category.

To avoid the pitfalls that Bacon was warning about we need to anchor our discussion in words which are reliable; that is, words which are self-explanatory and whose meanings are not restricted to English but can be found in any human language. Decades of painstaking cross-linguistic investigations have established that the words KNOW, THINK, SAY, HOW (WAY) and PEOPLE (along with 60 or so others) are such words (see the next section). The work on human cognition, both theoretical and applied, can draw on these findings.

To illustrate, here is how a psychiatrist tries to explain 'hope', on the occasion of Easter 2009: 'hope means being able to think about the future hypothetically in a way that generates possibilities' (quoted in Zwartz, 2009). This explanation, which uses complex and obscure words, may sound scientific and authoritative, but it is hard to understand and impossible to translate into most languages of the world. On the other hand, if we use simple and universal human concepts we can explain 'hope' in a way which is both intelligible to all speakers of English and readily translatable into any other language, along the following lines: When someone has hope, this someone often thinks like this: 'I want good things to happen, I know that these things can happen, this is good'; and when this someone thinks like this, this someone feels something good. In addition to being easier to understand, such simpler formulae are also easier to verify intuitively. In this particular case, intuitive verification allows us to identify some important gaps in the psychiatrist's explanation of 'hope', such as the absence of references to 'good', 'want', and 'feel', which are, arguably, essential to the concept of 'hope'. (The phrase *I hope* can be used with reference to thoughts alone, without a 'feel' component. However, the noun *hope* is often used as an opposite of *fear*, and one can speak of 'a feeling of hope'.)

As the psychiatrist's Easter message of 'hope' illustrates, cognitive psychology often seeks not only to understand human beings (of any ethnic and cultural background) but also to help people (including immigrants in English-speaking countries such as the US, UK, or Australia) by encouraging them to adopt certain patterns of thought. But such desirable patterns of thought cannot be communicated effectively if they are formulated in a language which is difficult to understand and impossible to translate into the native language of the addressee. The use of simple and universal human concepts can help us to understand other people's ways of thinking and knowing more faithfully and to communicate about them more effectively. It is on these concepts, then, that I intend to rely in my discussion of the relation between 'bilingualism' and 'cognition'.

NSM ENGLISH: A MINI-ENGLISH FOR THE STUDY OF LANGUAGE AND COGNITION

'NSM' is a 'natural semantic metalanguage' based on natural language and representing the intersection of all natural languages, and 'NSM English' is an English-based version of this metalanguage. Every NSM is a tightly constrained yet flexible mini-language of simple indefinable meanings ('universal semantic primes'), along with their inherent universal grammar. To define the meaning of a word or an expression in NSM (NSM English or any other version of NSM) means to explain, or 'explicate' it through simple and universal human concepts that do not require further explanation themselves and that can be found as words (or word-like elements) in all languages. Cross-linguistic evidence shows that KNOW and THINK are among their numbers (for discussion, see Goddard & Wierzbicka, 2002).

The most distinctive feature of the NSM approach is that it takes seriously the idea advanced by seventeenth-century European philosophers like Descartes, Arnauld, and above all Leibniz, that only a small repertoire of self-explanatory simple concepts (the 'alphabet of human thoughts') can provide the bedrock of all human understanding.

The NSM approach to semantics has adopted this idea, and its practitioners have engaged, over more than three decades, in theoretical and empirical investigations, seeking to identify, by trial and error, a set of self-explanatory semantic primes which could free semantic analysis from pseudo-explanations involved in paraphrasing complex and obscure expressions in terms of other equally complex and obscure expressions (see e.g., Goddard, 1998; Wierzbicka, 1972, 1996). To this end, NSM researchers have undertaken wide-ranging experimentation over many semantic domains across many diverse languages, and have identified matching minimal sets of lexically embodied simple meanings in terms of which all complex meanings and ideas can be intelligibly explained and compared.

The natural semantic metalanguage (NSM), built through extensive cross-linguistic investigations, is described in great detail in many publications, especially in Goddard and Wierzbicka (2002), which also contains six studies demonstrating that the posited semantic primes and their basic syntactic frames exist in a set of typologically and genetically diverse languages. A sizable bibliography is available on the NSM homepage (http://www.une.edu.au/bcss/linguistics/nsm). The full NSM lexicon of universal semantic primes is set out, in summary form, in Table 8.1, using English exponents (capitals represent semantic primitives). (For equivalent tables in many other languages see Goddard, 2008; Goddard & Wierzbicka, 2002; Peeters, 2006.)

Empirical investigations carried out within the NSM framework suggest that similar tables can be drawn up for any language and, moreover, that

Table 8.1 Semantic primes (in capitals), grouped into categories

I, YOU, SOMEONE, SOMETHING/THING, PEOPLE, BODY	Substantives
KIND, PART	Relational substantives
THIS, THE SAME, OTHER/ELSE	Determiners
ONE, TWO, SOME, ALL, MUCH/MANY	Quantifiers
GOOD, BAD	Evaluators
BIG, SMALL	Descriptors
THINK, KNOW, WANT, FEEL, SEE, HEAR	Mental predicates
SAY, WORDS, TRUE	Speech
DO, HAPPEN, MOVE, TOUCH	Action, events, movement, contact
BE (SOMEWHERE), THERE IS, HAVE, BE (SOMEONE/SOMETHING)	Location, existence, possession, specification
LIVE, DIE	Life and death
WHEN/TIME, NOW, BEFORE, AFTER, A LONG TIME, A SHORT TIME, FOR SOME TIME, MOMENT	Time
WHERE/PLACE, HERE, ABOVE, BELOW, FAR, NEAR, SIDE, INSIDE	Space
NOT, MAYBE, CAN, BECAUSE, IF	Logical concepts
VERY, MORE	Intensifier, augmentor
LIKE	Similarity

the semantic primes listed share a set of combinatory properties. This means that every natural language has as its semantic core a language-like structure, with a mini-lexicon and a mini-grammar. Each such mini-language is in fact a surface realization of one and the same underlying system (cf. Lehrman, 2006). This universal mini-language can be used effectively as a natural semantic metalanguage for exploring and comparing the ways of thinking and categorizing experience reflected in different languages of the world, and in different historical states of the same language.

In addition to semantic primes ('atoms of meaning'), many NSM explications also rely (in a limited way) on 'semantic molecules', built out of primes, especially in the area of concrete vocabulary. In particular, body part concepts often function as 'semantic molecules' in the meaning of verbs of physical activity, such as *walk* ('legs', 'feet'), *lick* ('tongue'), *bite* ('teeth'), and *eat* and *drink* ('mouth') (Wierzbicka, 2007a, 2009b). As we will see below ('In what colors did Nabokov see the world?'), color words rely, to a considerable extent, on environmental and bodily molecules such as 'sky', 'sun', 'day', and 'blood', as well as on the molecule 'color'. (The concept of 'color', which is far from universal, constitutes an important semantic molecule in languages like English. It is based on the universal concept of 'seeing'. Roughly speaking, it stands for something that people can know about some things when they see those things (and only in this way. For discussion, see Wierzbicka, 2007b, 2008).

Semantic molecules, marked in explications (i.e., NSM-style definitions) with the symbol [M], function as units in the meaning of more complex concepts. From a cognitive point of view, they effect a kind of chunking that makes it easier to manipulate and process complex semantic information. Like semantic primes, semantic molecules must be lexical meanings in the language concerned. For example, it wouldn't do to postulate for Russian a semantic molecule which could be expressed as a word in English but not in Russian itself. All molecules can be explicated in terms of universal semantic primes.

LANGUAGE DIVERSITY AND LANGUAGE UNIVERSALS

The NSM theory of language and cognition is based on the assumption that semantic diversity and semantic universals are two sides of the same coin: NSM primes allow us to show that complex language-specific meanings are in fact language-specific configurations of universal human concepts.

Generally, linguists assume that all languages share certain features, and these features are often referred to as 'language universals'. Throughout the Chomskyan era, however, the emphasis was on purely structure-based syntactic universals rather than on semantic universals, and this focus on abstract syntactic universals has continued into the post-Chomskyan era, despite the fact that many contemporary linguists have renounced the 'syntactocentrism' of generative grammar (Jackendoff, 2002, p. 107).

It is no doubt a healthy sign that various unquestioned assumptions of Chomskyan linguistics are being more and more widely rejected as myths (see e.g., N. Evans & Levinson, 2009), including the putative syntactic universal of 'recursion' (allegedly 'the only uniquely human component of the faculty of language', Hauser, Chomsky, & Fitch 2002, p. 1569. The term 'recursion' is commonly used with reference to rules that apply to their own output, creating loops which can go on indefinitely, see e.g., Cook & Newson, 2007, p. 79). But such well-justified challenges to 'universal grammar' as conceived by Chomsky and his followers can sometimes lead to a wholesale rejection of the very idea of language universals, including those universals that Chomskyan linguistics had no interest in but which are central to the study of human cognition and bilingualism, that is, semantic universals.

Cross-linguistic evidence strongly suggests that alongside huge diversity there is also a shared, universal core of human thinking and knowing. This shared core includes, in effect, what Leibniz called 'the alphabet of human thoughts', i.e., a small set of universal semantic primes, and an even smaller set of foundational building blocks of human knowledge, i.e., a very limited number of universal semantic molecules. The first set is given in Table 8.1. The second one includes, on current indications, molecules like 'sky', 'ground', 'sun', 'day', 'night', 'water', 'fire', 'hands', 'blood', 'men', 'women', and 'children' (cf. Goddard, 2010).

Of course human knowledge builds on semantic primes as well as on semantic molecules, and human thinking, too, operates with both primes and molecules. Jointly, these two universal sets of building blocks constitute a basis of human cognition, which can be accessed through the lexical core of English, or any other language.

A good example of over-reaction to Chomskyan claims about 'universal grammar' is a recent paper entitled 'The myth of language universals: Language diversity and its importance for cognitive science' (N. Evans & Levinson, 2009), which denies the existence of any universals (including semantic ones), and thus throws the baby out with the bath water.

If the authors' main purpose was to attract attention to their theme at any cost, then it is likely that this purpose will be achieved. But the costs are high. They include, first, an arbitrary dismissal of very substantial evidence supporting the existence of shared human concepts expressed by simple words in all languages (e.g., Goddard, 2008; Goddard & Wierzbicka, 2002; Peeters, 2006); second, disregard for bilingual experience of conceptual continuities as well as differences (cf. e.g., Besemeres, 2002; Besemeres & Wierzbicka, 2007; Pavlenko, 2006); and third, the inability to account for the possibility of translation and intercultural understanding.

To start with the third of these points, it is not clear how speakers of one language could ever understand anything that speakers of another language want to communicate if the two groups had no shared concepts. At the simplest level, for example, how could a simple English sentence like *this is good* be translated into other languages if these other languages didn't have words matching in meaning *this* and *good*? Universal human experience indicates that cross-cultural understanding is fraught with danger and that translatability has its limits, but not that *nothing* can ever be translated or understood.

The experience of bilingual people is crucial in this regard and it suggests that while *some* things cannot be faithfully translated into other languages or fully understood by those who don't speak a given language, other things can be translated and understood perfectly well. No bilingual (or trilingual) person was more conscious of the limits of such transferability of thoughts than the Russian poet Marina Tsvetaeva, whose testimony was '*inye mysli na inom jazyke ne mysljatsja*', 'some thoughts can only be thought in some languages but not in others' (1972, p. 151). The word *inye* 'some' is crucial here. To understand bilingual experience, we need to accept that some thoughts, and concepts, are perceived as untransferable, and that they differ in this respect from some others.

Finally, there is a great deal of empirical evidence showing that while most words in most languages carry meanings which are not universal, there are several dozen words with matching and universal meanings, and also that in addition to a set of universal words (or, strictly speaking, word meanings) there is a set of universal semantic structures. For example, it is not only words like *this*, *good*, and *bad* which have their exact semantic equivalents in all languages, but also sentences like *this is good* and *this is bad*. Similarly, it is not only words like *something*, *happen*, and *now* whose meanings match across language boundaries, but also sentences like *something good is happening now*. This explains why intercultural communication, while difficult, is in principle possible: A basic set of tools for it is hardwired.

As for *bilingual* cognition, it is important that the ways of thinking, knowing, and feeling of Russian–English bilinguals, for example, can be described through a metalanguage with two versions, English and Russian. To try to explain the 'cognition and emotion' of Russian–English bilinguals in an analytical language that is tied to English and cannot be translated into Russian is likely to be counterproductive; it is also unnecessary.

In his recent paper entitled 'Grammar and psychosocial cognition: What linguistic diversity can tell us about social cognition', Nicholas Evans (2009) quotes, with approval, the philosopher John Searle (1999, p. 2070): 'Epistemic objectivity of method does not preclude ontological subjectivity of subject matter. Thus there is no objection in principle to having an epistemically objective science of an ontologically subjective domain, such as human consciousness.' To anyone interested in bilingualism and cognition this must be a welcome statement. The key question, however, is this: In what language can an objective science of human cognition in general, and bilingual cognition in particular, be formulated?

Along with many other Anglophone philosophers and psychologists, Searle appears to assume that it can be done in English (see Wierzbicka, 2000b). But English, like any other language, brings with it concepts and categories of a particular culture. As a result, the purportedly objective science of human cognition formulated in English is bound to bring with it a culture-specific (Anglo) bias (Wierzbicka, 1993, 2006a, 2010). The same applies to psychology, psycholinguistics, and linguistics.

N. Evans (2009, handout p. 1) writes:

> Though psychologists have begun to investigate social cognition in detail (. . .), most of their work has concentrated on speakers of English or closely-related languages. Yet different languages and cultures promote and sensitize attention and representations of quite different aspects of social reality, so this risks giving a distorted and impoverished picture of what human social cognition is capable of. Linguistic investigation offers us a glimpse into rather different social universes.

The goal of investigating many different languages is of course important. One must wonder, however, how such investigations can lead to insights into different social and psychological universes if they are to be conducted through cognitive categories tied to *one* such universe (English). If we use culture-specific English categories as a yardstick it is not clear how we can ever discover what the anthropologist Clifford Geertz famously called 'the native's point of view' (Geertz, 1971).

In my view, it is also an illusion to think that we can obtain a valid picture of human cognition by multiplying psycholinguistic experiments involving speakers of different languages, as N. Evans puts it, 'Nijmegen-style'.

The phrase 'Nijmegen-style', which I have used myself in my critique of this approach (Wierzbicka, 2007a, 2009a), refers to the work of the Cognitive Anthropology Group of the Max Planck Institute at Nijmegen. The hallmark of this approach is the use of standardized externalist elicitation techniques (including video clips) to study the cognition of many different human groups around the globe. In these studies, indigenous consultants are presented with various external stimuli, such as Munsell color chips and other kinds of physical objects or pictorial representations of objects, and given some tasks involving them. The consultants' verbal responses are then recorded and analyzed. The language in which the analysis is conducted is, of course, English, with the effect that the consultants' responses end up re-coded in English, usually in terms which would be untranslatable into the original language.

As I have argued in my critique of this approach, such techniques cannot bring to light 'the native's point of view' because the outcomes of the experimentation depend largely on the conceptual framework underlying both the experiments and the conclusions drawn from them. Since psycholinguistic experiments of this kind re-code the cognitive categories of the native consultants into those of the experimenters (Goddard, 2007), they often tell us how the experimenters think but not how the respondents do, i.e., they tell us more about the cognition of the researchers than about that of their participants.

I agree with N. Evans (2009) that to study human cognition we need to investigate what he calls 'internal representations'. But here the crucial question is that of the metalanguage. If we end up portraying the 'internal representations' of speakers of different languages through the linguistic categories specific to English, we will inevitably 'anglicize' them.

To compare 'internal representations' linked with different languages (including the two languages of a bilingual), we need a common measure. If English is to be the lingua franca of cognitive science (which given the current global realities it seemingly has to be for the foreseeable future) then this lingua franca needs to be based on a mini-English, i.e., a subset of English with matching subsets in other languages. NSM research has identified such a subset of English. This subset (with matching counterparts in all other languages) consists of lexical and grammatical universals.

In particular, if putative 'internal representations' of bilingual persons are formulated in English (macro-English), they cannot be discussed with the people whose cognition they are supposed to represent. If, on the other hand, they are formulated in a mini-English with a matching mini-version of the bilingual person's other language (that is, in NSM English) then they can be discussed with bilingual consultants and revised in accordance with their linguistic intuitions.

For example, NSM explications of Russian emotion terms such as *dosada* or Russian color terms such as *goluboj* and *sinij* (see the next two sections) can be discussed with Russian–English bilinguals. Consultations of this kind always lead to revisions and improvements. Such a process of testing, validation, and adjustment would not be possible if one were simply modeling 'internal representations' of the Russian terms through English (macro-English).

EMOTIONS AND COGNITIVE SCENARIOS: 'FRUSTRATION' AND *DOSADA*

More often than not, emotion terms are language-specific in meaning and reflect culturally salient expectations, attitudes, and values. Testimonies of bilingual speakers and lexical borrowing occurring in their speech highlight both the lack of correspondence between emotion concepts encoded in different languages and the significance of such differences in bilingual lives. In this section I will seek to illustrate this with bilingual testimonies concerning the English emotion term *frustration*, followed by a semantic analysis of its meaning.

As discussed in detail elsewhere (see Besemeres & Wierzbicka, 2009; Wierzbicka, 1999), *frustration* is a unique English concept, spreading now, through borrowings from English, in other languages, especially in the technical language of psychology. Testimonies of Russian–English bilinguals highlight the absence from colloquial Russian of any words corresponding to the English *frustration*. In her article 'Emotion and emotion-laden words in the bilingual lexicon', the psycholinguist Aneta Pavlenko (a Russian–English bilingual herself) illustrates this point with the following example (for other bilingual testimonies and further discussion, see Besemeres & Wierzbicka, 2009):

> . . . in her Russian-language memoir, a well-known Russian actress, Elena Koreneva, who had lived for a while in the United States with her American husband, revealed that she came to rely on the Anglo concept of 'frustration' in her thinking and behavior. In her defense, she argued that '*frustration*—"čuvstvo neudovletvorenija, smešannoe

s dosadoj, kotoroe voznikaet posle bol'šix ožidanij" [frustration—a feeling of dissatisfaction mixed with vexation/annoyance that appears after great expectations] ([Koreneva, 2003,] p. 383) is impossible to translate into Russian with one word . . .

(Pavlenko, 2008, p. 151).

Pavlenko comments that, to acquire concepts like 'frustration', Russian learners of English 'have to (. . .) learn what events and phenomena commonly elicit such emotions, in what contexts and how these emotions are commonly displayed, and what consequences they might lead to'. For my part, I would prefer to say that, to acquire the concept of 'frustration', Russian learners of English have to learn (at some level of consciousness) the cognitive scenario encoded in this English word. Using NSM, we can pin down this scenario in the following explication:

she felt frustration
a. she felt something bad at that time, like someone can feel when this someone thinks like this:
b. 'I want to do something
c. I thought like this before: 'I can do it after a short time'
d. I can't think like this any more
e. I think like this now: 'maybe I can't do it, this is bad'

This scenario is different from those encoded in any of the Russian words offered as counterparts to *frustration* in either dictionaries or ad hoc comments by bilingual speakers. In particular, it is different from the scenario of the Russian word *dosada*, which was used in Koreneva's autobiographical account and which from an English point of view looks like a blend of *anger, dissatisfaction, irritation*, and *vexation*. The *Oxford Russian–English Dictionary* (1980) glosses it as 'vexation, disappointment, spite', but none of these glosses fits the whole range of *dosada*'s use. Two examples from Ožegov's (1972) Russian dictionary:

Tanja uexala s neopredelennym čuvstvom dosady. Ona ne obidelas' na Semena Semenoviča, no ej ne ponravilos' čto-to v ego tone. (Kazakevič) 'Tanya left with a vague feeling of irritation (*dosada*). She didn't get offended by what Semen Semenovič had said, but there was something in his tone that she didn't like.'

Po prirode stydlivaja i robkaja, ona dosadovala na svoju zastenčivost' i s dosady nasil'stvenno staralas' byt' razvjaznoj i smeloj. (Turgenev) 'By nature diffident and shy, she was so irritated ("*dosada*", Verb) by her own timidity that for precisely that reason (out of *dosada*) she tried desperately hard to seem to be bold and disdainfully at ease.'

A cognitive scenario compatible with the whole range of use of *dosada* can be formulated as in the following explication (which I will adduce here in two versions, English and Russian):

she felt 'dosada'
a.   she felt something bad at that time, like someone can feel when this someone feels something because this someone thinks like this:
b.   'something bad happened to me a short time before
c.   I don't want things like this to happen to me
d.   I want to do something because of this
e.   maybe I can't do anything
f.   this is bad'

ona čuvstvovala dosadu
a.   ona čuvstvovala čto-to ploxoe, kak kto-to možet čuvstvovat' kogda ėtot kto-to čuvstvuet čto-to potomu čto on dumaet tak:
b.   'čto-to ploxoe slučilos' so mnoj nedavno
c.   ja ne xoču, čtoby takie vešči so mnoj slučalis'
d.   potomu ja xoču čto-to sdelat'
e.   možet byt' ja ne mogu ničego sdelat'
f.   ėto ploxo'

What is missing from *dosada* (in comparison with *frustration*) is the initial 'I can do it' assumption—followed by the subsequent realization that 'maybe I can't do it, after all'. It is the perception that one is not in control of the situation as one has expected to be that is often reflected in the comments of immigrants to English-speaking countries.

The cognitive scenario spelled out in the explication of *frustration* reflects an expectation that a sustained, goal-related activity will bring about a desired outcome. This expectation is not met ('frustrated', in the older sense of the word) and the 'doer' (agent) 'feels something bad'. The whole attitude to life reflected in this scenario is based on the assumption that when people want something to happen and act energetically and persistently to make it happen, this thing is likely to happen. This assumption is culture-specific.

Finally, it is worth noting that in books written in English by Russian 'language migrants' (Besemeres, 2002) one can often come across the word *frustration* used in a non-English way—clearly a conceptual transfer from the immigrant's first language in which there is no such concept.

For example, in Nabokov's *Lolita* the pedophile Humbert 'moans with frustration' (1955, p. 234) thinking that he could have immortalized Lolita playing tennis by taking photos of her at the time. Frustration? Not regret? The Russian version of *Lolita* gives us a clue to why *frustration* may have seemed to Nabokov a more fitting word here than *regret*, because in

Russian he uses the word *obida*. This word suggests that the narrator is not merely regretting his failure to record Lolita's movements but as it were mentally kicking himself for it; this failure pains him and makes him angry with himself. This 'active' mental attitude makes *obida* more appropriate here than *regret*, and since there is no *obida* in English, he reaches for the word *frustration*. But as the explication of *frustration* shows, this word doesn't really fit the context here. The narrator didn't try (and fail) to record Lolita, he simply didn't think of doing it.

Similarly, in her autobiographical book *The Multilingual Self*, the Russian immigrant in America, Natasha Lvovič (1997, p. xv) confesses to having felt, for many years, 'frustrated about [her] differentness' from the people around her. This appears to imply an unsuccessful struggle to blend in, but it is clear from the book that this is not what the author meant. She felt 'bad feelings', but not exactly 'frustration'. Yet *frustration* is the word which she uses, in the absence of one that would fit her experience better; and to someone 'living in English' the word *frustration*, which one hears in English all the time, readily comes to mind.

THE COLOR OF THE SKY IN ENGLISH, POLISH AND RUSSIAN: EVIDENCE FROM BILINGUALS

A key question in any consideration of 'bilingualism and cognition' is that of the bilingual lexicon. There are two sets of words in this lexicon, but are these two different sets of words linked with two different sets of meanings?

No doubt some words in a bilingual person's mental lexicon have, for this person, meanings restricted to one of their two languages, whereas some other words have for them meanings shared by both. The degree to which the meanings stored in the mind of a bilingual person can be sorted out into two sets varies of course from one bilingual person to another and depends on many different factors. It is not my purpose to survey these factors here. Rather, I want to address the following question: Are there any identifiable kinds of concepts which tend to resist 'bifurcation' in the bilingual mind?

From my reading of the relevant literature, and also from my personal experience as a Polish–English bilingual and the mother of two English–Polish bilinguals, there emerges the following generalization: Two kinds of concepts which resist such 'bifurcation' are those which are deeply rooted in perception and those which are linked with a given lingua-culture's cultural key words.

For example, I think that in my own mental lexicon the concept linked with the Polish color word *niebieski* (from *niebo* 'sky') has never been replaced with the English concept 'blue'. Furthermore, while I know *about* the range of the English *blue* (much wider than that of *niebieski*) I don't think I ever use this word to refer to shades which fall outside the range of the Polish *niebieski*. After 35 years living in Australia, it still seems strange to me that, for example, jeans, which in Polish would never be described as *niebieskie* (plural), should be referred to in English as 'blue jeans'.

My two daughters, who were raised in Australia and for whom English is the dominant language, had the opposite problem. While their Polish is excellent, for many years they have tended to extend their use of the Polish word *niebieski* beyond its normal Polish range and to give it the range of the English *blue*.

I will return to the problem of color concepts in bilingual cognition later. Here let me simply restate the point which I made in various earlier publications (see e.g., Wierzbicka, 1996, 2005) that the difference in the range of use of *niebieski* and *blue* follows from different concepts, and that these different concepts are anchored in different conceptual prototypes: the daytime sky (*niebo*) in the case of *niebieski* and the combination of the sky and the sea in the case of *blue*. Using NSM and building on the semantic molecules 'sky', 'sun', 'day', and 'sea', we can represent these different concepts, 'blue' and 'niebieski', as follows:

X is blue
a.   when people think about the color [M] of X, they can think like this:
b.   'the color [M] of the sky [M] can be like this at many times
c.   it can be like this during the day when people can see the sun [M]
d.   it can be like this at many other times
e.   the color [M] of the sea [M] can be like this at many times'

X is niebieski
a.   when people think about the color [M] of X, they can think like this:
b.   'the color [M] of the sky [M] can be like this at many times during the day [M]
c.   it can be like this when people can see the sun [M]
d.   it can be like this when people can't see the sun [M]'

The evidence supporting the claim that the two words, *niebieski* and *blue*, are indeed associated with the prototypes indicated above has been discussed elsewhere (see e.g., Wierzbicka, 1996, 2005). But the main argument in favor of the proposed prototypes is their explanatory power: They account both for the similarities and the differences in the use of these words, both for the overlaps in their use and for their different boundaries.

Both words refer to the sky in their meaning (and *niebieski* is also related to *niebo* 'sky' in its form), but they do so in different ways. The sky-related prototype of *niebieski* includes a wide range of shades, but all these shades are restricted to the daytime appearance of the sky. By contrast, the sky-related prototype of *blue* does not explicitly exclude the night sky, and moreover it is combined in the meaning of the word *blue* with a second prototype, the sea. This explains why the denotational range of *blue* is considerably wider than that of *niebieski*, and why in English, *navy-blue* can be seen as a kind of 'blue', whereas in Polish, *granatowy* (the color of navy uniforms) cannot be seen as a kind of *niebieski*.

These conclusions drawn from my own experiences and reading are corroborated by an experimental study of the use of the Russian words *goluboj* and *sinij* (usually glossed in English, inaccurately, as 'light blue' and 'dark blue') in the speech of Russians living in Russia and of bilingual Russian immigrants in the United States.

According to this study (Andrews, 1994), young adults who had emigrated from the Soviet Union as children or teenagers, or who were born in the US to Russian-speaking families, came to 'treat *sinij* and *goluboj* in much the same way that English-speakers treat "dark blue" and "light blue"—not as two basic terms, but as the dark and bright variations of a single category' (p. 25). Andrews interprets this, convincingly, 'as a result of American acculturation' (p. 26). On the other hand, those immigrants who had left the Soviet Union as adults have maintained their Russian concepts '*goluboj*' and '*sinij*'. Andrews concludes that 'both *sinij* and *goluboj* are bona fide basic color terms in standard Russian (. . .) and (. . .) this interpretation is fixed by adulthood and remains unaffected by subsequent bilingualism' (p. 25).

From my point of view what matters here is, first, that the words *goluboj* and *sinij* are used in standard Russian to encode language-specific concepts, different from, but on a par with, the English concept 'blue'; second, that in the speech of bilingual speakers who emigrated to the United States as adults these concepts are preserved intact; and third, that in the speech of young acculturated bilinguals, they have been replaced with the English concept 'blue'. This is fully consistent with my own experience concerning the Polish word *niebieski*. The concepts encoded in the words *goluboj* and *sinij* as used in standard Russian are explicated below.

X is goluboj
a.   when people think about the color [M] of X, they can think like this:
b.   'it is like the color [M] of the sky [M] at times when people can see the sun [M]
c.   at those times the color [M] of the sky [M] on all sides of the sun [M] can be like this'

X is sinij
a.   when people think about the color of X, they can think like this:
b.   'the color [M] of the sky [M] can be like this during the part of the day [M] when people can't see the sun [M] any more
c.   the color [M] of the sea [M] can be like this'

IN WHAT COLORS DID NABOKOV SEE THE WORLD?

Different languages encourage different ways of looking at the world. Two languages which both have a word for the concept of 'color' and which are both associated with a great deal of 'color talk', can still encourage their speakers to see the world, as it were, in different colors. This applies even to languages which are relatively close, in genealogical as well as geographical and cultural terms; for example, to English and Russian.

But what about a bilingual person, for example, a Russian–English bilingual? Would such a person have, so to speak, double vision and switch from one vision to the other when switching from one language to the other or would they rather see the world, predominantly, in terms of visual categories embedded in one of their two languages? In this section I will examine this question in relation to two versions of the same novel, *Lolita*, which Nabokov first wrote in English and then translated into Russian. Since I cannot undertake here an exhaustive study of this topic, I will focus mainly on one word which occurs again and again in the English *Lolita* and on its many different counterparts in the Russian text. The word is *russet*.

Russet is not a common word in English and its frequent occurrence in the English *Lolita* seems to reflect, above all, the *absence* from English of certain visual descriptors widely used in colloquial Russian. These colloquial Russian descriptors serve Nabokov as habitual interpretive tools when he is looking at the world through his Russian lens—and one suspects that it is the absence of equivalent tools from the English conceptual kit which has led Nabokov to fall back, again and again, on the rather marginal English word *russet*. Let us examine some examples.

The very first time when the pedophile Humbert Humbert has a chance to speak to the 12-year-old girl-child Lolita (and she allows him to lick a speck out of her eye) Lolita's face is described, somewhat oddly, as 'russet'. In the quotes from *Lolita*, 'E' indicates the English original (1955), and 'R', the Russian translation (1967):

> (. . .) she noticed the pucker of my approaching lips. 'Okay,' she said cooperatively, and bending forward her warm upturned russet face (. . .) Humbert pressed his mouth to her fluttering eyelid. She laughed and brushed past me out of the room.
>
> (E. pp. 45–46)

In the Russian version of the novel, Lolita's face (*lico*) is described as '*ryževato-rozovoe*'. *Ryževato* is an untranslatable adverb, carrying the connotations of the familiar-slangy-expressive adjective *ryževatyj*, derived from *ryžij*, which is normally used for what is called in English *red hair*. The suffix *-ovat/-evat* can be compared to the English *-ish* in *reddish*. But since the adjective *ryžij* itself has no equivalent in English, neither does the adjective *ryževatyj* or the adverb *ryževato*.

To appreciate the difference between the everyday Russian word *ryžij* (and its derivatives) and the very rare English word *russet*, it is worth comparing the frequency of these words in corpora. Thus, in the Russian National Corpus, *ryžij* occurs about 60 times per million words, while in the Cobuild Bank of English, *russet* occurs once per million words. This is a spectacular difference. For comparison, we can note that *pink*—which is an everyday English word—occurs in Cobuild 40 times per one million words. This shows that *ryžij* is a much more frequent word in Russian than *pink* is in English. With *russet*, there is simply no comparison.

Rozovyj is glossed in Russian–English dictionaries as *pink*, and vice versa, but the two are not really semantically equivalent. Combined with abstract nouns such as *nadeždy* 'hopes' or *mečtanija* 'dreams', *rozovyj* implies 'good thoughts' and 'good feelings', rather like *rosy* does in English. When it is used in a visual sense, it *can* be purely descriptive, but when it is used with reference to human bodies it normally has positive connotations (reminiscent, as mentioned above, of roses and of the dawn, and again comparable to, though not identical with, those of *rosy*). Clearly, Lolita's '*ryževato-rozovoe lico*' (R. p. 33) evokes an image different from, and far richer than the English 'russet face' (E. p. 76).

The phrase *rozovato ryžij*, used about Lolita in another context, is similarly rich and untranslatable. Obviously, *pinkishly russet* would not work and something like *rosy-ishly russet* is totally inconceivable. (Incidentally, Nabokov's phrase *rosy lips* [E. p. 228] sounds less natural in English than its Russian translation *rozovye guby* [R. p. 207]. The phrase *rosy cheeks* is so common as to be a cliché, but *rosy lips* can be suspected of being a mental translation from Russian.)

When Humbert finds his beloved 'nymphet' again after 3 years of agonizing separation from her, he suddenly notices how much she resembles—has always resembled—Botticelli's '*ryževataja*' Venus. The word *ryževataja* is the feminine form of an expressive derivate of the highly colloquial adjective *ryžij* (fem. *ryžaja*), which was mentioned earlier. The image, and the emotional tone, of the *ryževataja Venera* (R. p. 251) couldn't be more different than that of the 'russet Venus' (E. p. 272). It carries with it all the familiar and jocularly pejorative overtones of the adjective *ryžij*, normally used only about people's hair, and that in a country (Russia) where 'normally' people did not have what in English is called 'red hair'.

The lovesick Humbert never sees Lolita as simply *ryžaja*, he can only so describe other girl-children, whom he might like to ogle but about whom he doesn't really give a damn (*ryžie ot solnca nimfetki*, R. p. 54), and in English as *russet nymphets* (E. p. 68). But in the English version *russet* is used indiscriminately about Lolita and other 'nymphets'.

Another word which plays an important role in the Russian version of the novel is *rusyj* (fem. *rusaja*), glossed by the *Oxford Russian Dictionary* as 'light brown', and by Ožegov's (1972) Russian dictionary as '*svetlo-koričnevyj*', literally also 'light brown (of hair)'. For example, when Humbert unexpectedly sees Lolita (for the second time in his life), he is struck by her 'chestnut head of hair' (E. p. 4), and in Russian, by her '*rusaja šapka volos*', 'a *rusaja* cap of hair' (R. p. 29). On another occasion, Humbert watches Lolita playing tennis, with her 'sunny-brown curls' hanging forward (E. p. 169). In the Russian version of the novel, Lolita's hair is described not as 'sunny-brown' but as 'sunny *rusye*' (plural), *solnečno-rusye volosy* (R. p. 146).

Later still, Humbert suffers agonies of jealousy at seeing Lolita at the edge of a swimming pool, 'dipping and kicking her long-toed feet in the water', while on either side of her there crouches an adolescent drawn to her by her 'russet beauty and the quicksilver in the baby folds of her stomach' (E. p. 169). In Russian, Lolita's beauty (*krasota*) is described in the corresponding passage as '*rusaja*' (*rusaja krasota*), as someone might say in English 'her golden beauty', but hardly 'her russet beauty'.

Elsewhere in the book, the Russian word *rusyj* (fem. *rusaja*) is used to describe Lolita as *blestjašče rusaja* (R. p. 59), 'dazzlingly *rusaja*', to which in the English version corresponds the phrase (E. p. 67) 'the Lolita of the rich brown hair' (*blestjašče* means, literally, 'shiningly', and also 'dazzlingly').

Thus, Lolita's '*rusaja krasota*' in the Russian version suggests shining, dazzling, rich light brown hair (as well perhaps as an overall image of *rusalka* 'mermaid/nymph'). Again, little of this comes across in the English phrase *russet beauty*. If the prosaic word *ryžaja* is used with reference to Lolita at all, it is always combined with some positively charged words, in collocations evoking fairytale charm, and often in combination with *rusaja*, as in the following sentence referring to her: '*ničego net konserva-tivnee rebenka, osoblivo devočki, bud' ona samoj čto ni na est' basnoslovnoj, rusoj, rozovato-ryžej nimfetkoj v zolotoj dymke oktjabrskogo vertograda*' (R. p. 168).

In the English *Lolita* this sentence reads: 'There is nothing more con-servative than a child, especially a girl-child, be she the most auburn and russet, the most mythopoeic nymphet in October's orchard-haze' (E. p. 188). The style and tone of this English sentence could not be more different from the highly emotive and poetic but by no means literary or recherché Russian version. There is nothing in the Russian version that would be comparable to *russet* or *auburn*, as there is nothing comparable to *mythopoeic*. The combination of poetry, enchantment, a fairytale qual-ity, and a smiling down-to-earthness of the Russian sentence is completely absent from its English counterpart. The colors with which the image of

Lolita is endowed here are as different from *auburn* and *russet* as the bookish and erudite word *mythopoeic* is from poetic but not erudite *basnoslovnyj*, roughly, 'fairytale-like'.

And yet one suspects that the visual and phonetic form of *russet*, so reminiscent of that of *rusyj*, did secretly appeal to Nabokov. It is worth mentioning here that Nabokov's first love, the 15-year-old Tamara, had *rusye volosy* (hair), that he described her as a *rusalka* (mermaid), and that when he left Russia for ever he was leaving behind both his *rusaja rusalka* Tamara and Russia—his home country whose very name (*Rus', Rossija*) is phonetically, if not etymologically, akin to *rusyj*.

As we have seen, in the English version of *Lolita*, the word *russet* doesn't always correspond to *rusyj* in the Russian version, it can also correspond to *ryžij* and its derivatives, which Nabokov seemed to be missing in English as much as he was missing *rusyj*. Thus in yet another episode Lolita is described in English as 'rosy and russet' (E. p. 245) and in Russian, as '*takaja rozovaja, s zolotoj ryžinkoj*'. Even if we could assume that *rozovaja* can be equated with *rosy* and that the phrase *takaja rozovaja* could be glossed in English as 'so rosy', we would have to acknowledge that the phrase *s zolotoj ryžinkoj* cannot be rendered in English at all (without a significant loss or distortion of meaning).

Ryžij, as already mentioned, is an adjective which refers to what is described in English as 'red hair' but which is full of its own conceptual and attitudinal overtones. *Ryžinka* is a noun built on the model of *sedinka* 'a patch of gray hair' (thought of not as a kind of hair but as a visual image). The suffix -*k* indicates here an affectionate diminutive. Thus, the phrase *s ryžinkoj* implies something like 'with a dear-little admixture of color reminiscent of the color of the hair of "red-haired" people'. This diminutive noun *ryžinka* (in the instrumental case, and with the preposition *s*, 'with', *s ryžinkoj*) is modified in Nabokov's Russian sentence by the adjective *zolotoj*, meaning 'gold/golden'. The overall image, visual and emotional, is very different from that conveyed by the rather literary English phrase 'rosy and russet'.

I will also note that in Nabokov's visual world, things which in the English *Lolita* are described as 'red' or 'pink', in the Russian version are often 'cherry-like', 'raspberry-like', or 'apricot-like'. For example, the car pursuing Humbert and Lolita is always described in English as 'red', whereas in Russian, it is *višnevyj* ('cherry', adjective). In Russian Lolita has an *abrikosovyj* ('apricot', adjective) tan on arms and legs as well as an *abrikosovaja golaja pojasnica* (R. p. 212) and *obajatel'nye lopatki s abrikos-ovym puškom na nix* (R. p. 212), while in English she has 'adorable apricot-colored limbs' (E. p. 232), 'adorable apricot shoulder blades', and an 'apricot midriff' (E. p. 233). But these English expressions sound like a translation from Nabokov's mental Russian, and in any case, they do not correspond exactly in meaning to their Russian counterparts, which do not need to add anything like *colored* to the name of the fruit.

The phrase *abrikosovyj pušok*, which means, literally, 'apricot-like down' (on Lolita's shoulder blades), highlights the fact that in Russian, the appearance of Lolita's arms, legs, and shoulder blades (and probably mid-riff, too), is compared to the appearance of apricots more globally than the English word *apricot-colored* would imply. It is not just the color, but also the 'downy' skin on the exposed parts of Lolita's body which in Russian brings to mind the appearance (and texture) of apricots.

Another Russian word which Nabokov uses to describe the beauty of Lolita's skin (as perceived by Humbert) is *zolotistyj*, a word which is derived from *zolotoj* 'golden' and which means something like 'beautifully shining and golden'. Thus, when Humbert sees Lolita bending over a window sill, he notes in his diary: *'Vid so spiny. Poloska zolotistoj koži meždu beloj majkoj i belymi trusikami.'* (R. p. 43). In English the passage reads: 'Dorsal view. Glimpse of shiny skin between T-shirt and white gym shorts' (E. p. 56).

My point is that words like *russet*, *auburn*, and *vermeil* are rare and bookish in English and sound like somewhat labored substitutes for interpretive tools which for Russians are second nature. The very fact that *ryžij*, *ryževatyj*, *rusyj*, *rozovyj*, *višnevyj*, and *malinovyj* are high-frequency words in Russian (unlike *russet*, *vermeil*, or *auburn* in English) shows that their role in Russian discourse is different from that of words like *russet*, *vermeil*, or *auburn* in English. They are everyday words, rich in connota-tions, and often suggestive of feelings and attitudes. They belong to what Russian linguists often call 'Russkaja jazykovaja kartina mira' (Apresjan, 2006; Zalizniak, Levontina, & Shmelev, 2005), literally, 'Russian linguistic picture of the world', or 'the picture of the world embedded in the Russian language'. The picture is different from that embedded in the English language, and not just chromatically different. For example, words like *rozovyj* 'pink' and *goluboj* 'the color of the sky on a sunny day' have in some contexts positive connotations, absent from *pink* and *blue*.

Furthermore, Russian has many words which are widely used to describe aspects of visual appearance, including color, which have no equivalents in English. As we have seen, *ryžij* (used of 'red hair'), *sedoj* (used of 'gray hair'), *zolotoj* (translating both *gold* and *golden*) and also *zolotistyj* ('beautifully shining and golden'), *višnevyj* (from *višnja* 'cherries', but close in shade to *maroon*), and *malinovyj* (from *malina* 'raspberries') are among their number.

BILINGUAL VISION AND SELF-TRANSLATION

I asked in the previous section whether a bilingual person could be expected to see the world through two pairs of spectacles or through one. The answer could of course be different for different bilinguals, but in the case of Nabokov the evidence seems to point to a single vision rather than double vision, and also to indicate that his vision was, predominantly, the one reflected in his Russian *Lolita* and suggested to him by the resources of the Russian language. When he was translating *Lolita* from English into Russian, he was moving from English phrases like *rosy and russet Venus* to a phrase like *ryževataja Venera*, but what he saw in his mind's eye while writing the English *Lolita* may well have been a *ryževataja* Venus in the first place.

It is hard not to think that Nabokov's use of the word *russet*, and on a smaller scale of words like *auburn* and *vermeil*, suggests that he was (consciously or unconsciously) looking for words like *ryžij*, *ryževatyj*, *rusyj*, *rozovyj*, *rozovatyj*, *malinovyj*, *višnevyj*, and *zolotistyj*, which were indispensable parts of his mental palette.

In the closing passage of his postscript to the English *Lolita* Nabokov lamented:

> My private tragedy, which cannot, and indeed should not, be anybody's concern, is that I had to abandon my natural idiom, my untrammelled, rich, and infinitely docile Russian tongue for a second-rate brand of English, devoid of any of those apparatuses—the baffling mirror, the black velvet backdrop, the implied associations and traditions—which the native illusionist, frac-tails [sic] flying, can magically use to transcend the heritage in his own way.
>
> (1955, p. 318)

The 'natural idiom' is not only a matter of style but also a matter of vision, of the 'natural' way of seeing the world, made available to us by our native language. Nabokov returned to the question of living between two languages on a number of occasions. When an interviewer asked him, 'Do you feel you have any conspicuous secret flaw as a writer?' he replied:

> The absence of a natural vocabulary. An odd thing to confess, but true. Of the two instruments in my possession, one—my native tongue—I can no longer use, and this not only because I lack a Russian audience but also because the excitement of verbal adventure in the Russian medium has faded away gradually after I turned to English in 1940. My English, this second instrument I have always had, is however a stiffish, artificial thing, which may be all right for describing a sunset or an insect, but which cannot conceal poverty of syntax and paucity of domestic diction when I need the shortest road between warehouse and shop. An old Rolls-Royce is not always preferable to a plain jeep.
>
> (Nabokov, 1973, p. 106)

Arguably, however, the problem goes even deeper than that. Certainly, words like *ryžij*, *ryževatyj*, *rusyj*, *malinovyj*, or *višnevyj* provided for Nabokov a 'natural vocabulary' and a 'domestic diction' which could not be replaced to his satisfaction with words like *russet, vermeil*, or *red*. But perhaps Russian was for Nabokov not only an instrument for speaking but also a lens through which to see the world. Widely recognized as 'a grand master of English prose' (Jin, 2008, p. 48), Nabokov seems to have felt that he had never achieved through English the 'natural' way of relating to the world, including the visual world, which he had in his native Russian.

In her discussion of Nabokov's 'self-translation' Mary Besemeres (2002, p. 108) notes that 'in a letter to his wife, written after he had wrenched himself away from writing in Russian, Nabokov speaks movingly of the vicissitudes of his relationship with English as his new artistic medium' and she quotes, inter alia, the following passage:

> Yesterday (. . .) on my walk I was pleasantly pierced by a lightning bolt of inspiration, I had a passionate desire to write, and write in Russian, and I must not. I don't think that anyone who has not experienced this feeling can really understand its tortuousness, its tragic aspect. The English language in this light is illusion and *ersatz*.

When Besemeres speaks of Nabokov's 'self-translation' she is not referring to his translating his work from English into Russian (as in the case of *Lolita*) but of his 'translating his self' from Russian into English: 'Because Nabokov cannot reach his reading audience through Russian, he is forced constantly to translate himself, a process which, however appealing to the literary chameleon in him, in the case of *Pnin* involves self-parody' (Besemeres, 2002, p. 33).

Pnin, the hero of Nabokov's eponymous novel, is 'a Russian emigrant whose fate has left him dangling in the alien English language' (Besemeres, 2002, p. 85). Besemeres' reading of *Pnin* 'as an allegory of the author's personal and cultural transformation' (2002, p. 85) is very convincing, and her analysis of 'Pninian English' resonates with the experience of many Russian (and Polish) immigrants in English-speaking countries. *Lolita* is of course different from *Pnin* in not involving any elements of conscious self-parody. But 'a muted Russian-speaking voice echoing, or shadowing, the narrator's English' (Besemeres, 2002, p. 93) can be heard in the background of this novel too, especially in the narrator's description of colors.

One lesson worth highlighting here is that the way one perceives the world is deeply influenced by the visual vocabulary acquired, experientially and existentially, through one's native language. To think that native speakers of Russian see both the bright sky and the darkish sea as 'blue', or 'essentially blue', even though they tend to talk about the former as *goluboe* and about the latter as *sinee*, is deeply wrong, because seeing involves interpreting, and the words *goluboe* and *sinee* provide Russian speakers with their natural tools for interpreting the images that hit their retinas and get transmitted to their brains.

Arguably, the whole fallacy that color terms are the tools of 'naming' rather than instruments of interpretation rests on this (Wierzbicka, in press). Of course, it is possible that some people—especially those who have grown up with two languages—may have access to two sets of interpretive tools, and that both these sets feel natural to them. The way bilingual people interpret their visual experience requires much further study. It seems clear, however, that this study cannot get seriously off the ground if the visual experience of bilinguals is to be studied within an interpretive framework derived from English and imposing on this experience an Anglo/English perspective. (The phrase 'Anglo/English perspective' is a condensed way of referring to 'Anglo' culture reflected in English. For an extensive discussion of 'Anglo culture' see my book *English: Meaning and Culture*, Wierzbicka, 2006a).

CONCLUSION: OVERCOMING ANGLOCENTRISM IN THE STUDY OF BILINGUALISM AND COGNITION

N. Evans (2009, handout p. 11) quotes Wittgenstein's words: 'Philosophy must plough over the whole language', and he responds: 'yes, but which language(s)?', pointing out that 'to draw the most insight from the world's linguistic diversity we need an approach equally able to gather data from a wide range of languages and to synthesize it into an overall model'.

I agree that philosophy (as well as psychology and cognitive science) needs to 'plough' over many different languages, not just one. But in which language shall we do our ploughing? And if we do it in English, how will we avoid the danger of imposing cognitive categories embedded in English on all the other languages of the world?

Bilingual experience is a crucial source of insight into human cognition and into the inadequacy of purely English-based 'data gathering' aimed at discovering cognitive categories of speakers of different languages. The relevant data in this area must include self-reports, and these self-reports will normally include indigenous categories. To accurately interpret these categories in English, we need to use not only macro-English (which would reflect English-specific cognitive categories) but also a mini-English which can be transposed, without distortion, into other languages. To quote Goddard's conclusion to his examination of a number of mental state concepts in a number of different languages:

> ... the ethnopsychological constructs of individual languages, when appropriately analysed, are revelatory of widely differing folk models of mental experience. Because they are embodied in the words and phrases of everyday talk and because they represent 'experience-near' concepts, such models find their way into people's self-understandings and into their narrative of life experience. There can be little hope

of understanding the subjective quality of mental experience of people from other languages and cultures unless we can 'crack into' such ethnopsychological constructs and come to appreciate them. At the same time, however, it is equally important to 'crack into' the ethno-psychological categories of the English language (categories such as *mind, emotion*, and *memory*; cf. Amberber, 2007), which are taken for granted in much mainstream cognitive science. Analysis into semantic primes provides a new and powerful technique to achieve these ends.

(Goddard, 2007, p. 29)

The role of bilingual consultants is crucial here, because while they can't be expected to analyze their own thoughts and categories into semantic primes, they can understand explications couched in primes (such as, e.g., those of *dosada*), or in primes and molecules (such as, e.g., those of *goluboj*), test them against their intuitions and propose adjustments. This means that such consultants can be treated as conversational partners capable of understanding the meaning of their own words and sentences, instead of being reduced to silent objects of the investigation carried out in English, by Anglo investigators, and to producers of data to be re-coded by linguists into technical English.

In addition to being the linguists' conversational partners, bilingual persons can contribute a great deal by recording their own self-observation and reflections. In particular, recent language memoirs, starting with Eva Hoffman's (1989) ground-breaking *Lost in Translation*, show that bilingual writers can throw a great deal of light on human cognition as expert witnesses capable of analyzing their own experience. Especially revealing are the observations of 'language migrants' (to use a term introduced by Besemeres, 2002); that is, people who are forced to 'translate themselves into the English language' (Besemeres, 2002, p. 278) and who experience, like the 13-year-old Eva Hoffman, 'the sudden, unwelcome awareness of the relativity of meanings' (Hoffman, 1989, p. 49).

> Hoffman's most striking contribution to the debate over the relationship between the self and language is her insistence that any language implies a cultural universe, whose contours remain invisible as long as they are shared but which become unmistakeable upon collision with another such world, another language.
>
> (Besemeres, 2002, p. 41)

The testimonies of 'language migrants' are so revealing because these authors have experienced that shock of collision. Such testimonies tell us not only about what happens in the heads of people moving from one language to another but also in the heads of people who are settled in one language: Without the experience of collision, people normally take most categories of their native language for granted. Besemeres' book *Translating one's self: Language and selfhood in cross-cultural autobiography* contends that:

> . . . writing by language migrants can challenge the monolingual, monocultural assumptions of contemporary literary theory and philosophy of language alike, which are not concerned, as immigrants must be, with the impact of specific natural languages on actual lives: the most significant way in which language is constitutive of the self.
>
> (Besemeres, 2002, p. 278)

These monolingual and monocultural assumptions also pervade psychology, cognitive science, and much of linguistic theory (Goddard & Wierzbicka, in press).

Nearly a century has passed since Edward Sapir, himself a 'language migrant', formulated his deep insight: 'The fact is that the "real world" is to a large extent unconsciously built up on the language habits of the group' (1929/1949, p. 102). The 'real world' built unconsciously on the language habits of speakers of English includes interpretations of 'human cognition' built, unconsciously, on cognitive categories of the English language. Many theorists of cognition reject the so-called 'Sapir-Whorf hypothesis' in all its versions, claiming that there is no evidence for it (see e.g., Pinker, 1994, 1997). But as the Cuban-American writer Gustavo Pérez Firmat (2003, p. 13) points out, 'what is crucial is that many bilinguals relate to their languages in ways that enact some version of this hypothesis'. This is why 'deep bilinguals', and especially 'language migrants'—not polyglots, but those for whom two languages are 'woven into the fabric of their lives' (Pérez Firmat, 2003, p. 71)—can challenge the monolingual, Anglocentric perspective on language and cognition.

The philosopher van Brakel (2004, p. 21) remarks ironically that the assumption that English is hardwired is pervasive. The good news arising from cross-linguistic semantic investigations is that *part* of English is indeed hardwired—that part which matches the shared core of all other languages; and this good news is compatible both with the well-documented possibility of successful intercultural communication and with bilingual experience. It is on this part of English that a transnational and transcultural science of human cognition can build.

ACKNOWLEDGMENTS

Several explications included in this chapter have been developed jointly with Cliff Goddard. I have also benefited greatly from discussions with Anna Gladkova, and incorporated her suggestions in the revised formulae.

REFERENCES

Amberber, M. (Ed.). (2007). *The language of memory in a crosslinguistic perspective*. Amsterdam/New York: John Benjamins.

Andrews, D. (1994). The Russian color categories *Sinij* and *Goluboj*: An experimental analysis of their interpretation in the standard and emigré languages. *Journal of Slavic Linguistics, 2*(1), 9–28.

Apresjan, Ju. D. (2006). *Jazykovaja Kartina Mira i Sistemnaja Leksikografija*. Moscow: Jazyki Slavjanskix Kul'tur.

Bacon, F. (1620). *Instauratio magna. Novum organum*. London: John Bill.

Besemeres, M. (2002). *Translating one's self: Language and selfhood in cross-cultural autobiography*. Oxford, UK: Peter Lang.

Besemeres, M., & Wierzbicka, A. (Eds.). (2007). *Translating lives: Living with two languages and cultures*. St Lucia, Queensland: University of Queensland Press.

Besemeres, M., & Wierzbicka, A. (2009). The concept of *frustration*: A culture-specific emotion and a cultural key word. In A. Błachnio & A. Przepiorka (Eds.), *Closer to emotions III* (pp. 211–226). Lublin, Poland: Wydawnictwo KUL.

Collins Cobuild English language dictionary (1991). London and Glasgow: Collins.

Cook, V. J., & Newson, M. (2007). *Chomsky's universal grammar: An introduction*. Oxford, UK: Blackwell.

Evans, N. (2009). *Grammar and psychosocial cognition: What linguistic diversity can tell us about social cognition*. Paper presented at the Australian National University, March 25.

Evans, N., & Levinson, S. (2009). The myth of language universals: Language diversity and its importance for cognitive science. *Behavioral and Brain Sciences, 32*(5), 429–492.

Geertz, C. (1971). From the native's point of view: On the nature of anthropological understanding. In K. Basso & H. Selby (Eds.), *Meaning in anthropology*. Albuquerque, NM: University of New Mexico Press.

Goddard, C. (1998). *Semantic analysis: A practical introduction*. Oxford, UK: University Press.

Goddard, C. (2007). A culture-neutral metalanguage for mental state concepts. In A. C. Schalley & D. Khlentzos (Eds.), *Mental states. Volume 2: Language and cognitive structure* (pp. 11–35). Amsterdam: John Benjamins.

Goddard, C. (Ed.) (2008). *Cross-linguistic semantics*. Amsterdam: John Benjamins.

Goddard, C. (2010). Semantic molecules and semantic complexity (with special reference to 'environmental molecules'). *Review of Cognitive Linguistics, 8*(1), 123–155.

Goddard, C., & Wierzbicka, A. (Eds.). (2002). *Meaning and universal grammar: Theory and empirical findings*. Amsterdam: John Benjamins.

Goddard, C., & Wierzbicka, A. (in press). Semantics and cognition. *Wires Cognitive Science* (Wiley online library, July 9, 2010).

Hauser, M. D., Chomsky, N., & Fitch, W. T. (2002). The faculty of language: What is it, who has it, and how does it evolve? *Science, 298*, 1569–1579.

Hoffman, E. (1989). *Lost in translation: A life in a new language*. New York: Dutton.

Jackendoff, R. (2002). *Foundations of language*. New York: Oxford University Press.

Jin, H. (2008). *The writer as migrant*. Chicago: The University of Chicago Press.

Lehrman, A. (2006). Meaning as grammar. *Language Sciences, 28*, 497–507.

Lvovič, N. (1997). *The multilingual self: An inquiry into language learning.* Mahwah, NJ: Lawrence Erlbaum Associates Inc.

Mandler, G., & Kesson, W. (1959). *The language of psychology.* New York: John Wiley.

Nabokov, V. (1955). *Lolita.* New York: G. P. Putnam.

Nabokov, V. (1967). *Lolita.* [Translated from the English into Russian by the author.] New York: Phaedra Publishers.

Nabokov, V. (1973). *Strong opinions.* New York: McGraw-Hill.

Ožegov, S. I. (1972). *Slovar' russkogo jazyka.* (Russian Language Dictionary, 9th ed.). Moscow: Sovetskaja Enciklopedija.

Pavlenko, A. (Ed.). (2006). *Bilingual minds: Emotional experience, expression and representation.* Clevedon, UK: Multilingual Matters.

Pavlenko, A. (2008). Emotion and emotion-laden words in the bilingual lexicon. *Bilingualism: Language and Cognition, 11*(2), 147–164.

Peeters, B. L. (Ed.). (2006). *Semantic primes and universal grammar: Empirical evidence from the Romance languages.* Amsterdam: John Benjamins.

Pérez Firmat, G. (2003). *Tongue ties: Logo-eroticism in Anglo-Hispanic literature.* New York: Palgrave Macmillan.

Pinker, S. (1994). *The language instinct.* New York: William Morrow.

Pinker, S. (1997). *How the mind works.* New York: Norton.

Sapir, E. (1929/1949). The status of linguistics as a science. *Language, 5,* 207–214. [Reprinted in 1949: 160–166.]

Searle, J. R. (1999). The future of philosophy. *Philological Transactions of the Royal Society of London, Series B,* 2069–2080.

Tsvetaeva, M. (1972). *Neizdannye pis'ma.* Paris: YMCA-Press.

van Brakel, J. (2004). The empirical stance and the colour war. *Divinatio, 20,* 7–26

Wierzbicka, A. (1972). *Semantic primitives.* Frankfurt: Athenäum.

Wierzbicka, A. (1993). A conceptual basis for cultural psychology. *Ethos, 21*(2), 205–231.

Wierzbicka, A. (1996). *Semantics: Primes and universals.* Oxford, UK: Oxford University Press.

Wierzbicka, A. (1999). *Emotions across languages and cultures: Diversity and universals.* Cambridge, UK: Cambridge University Press.

Wierzbicka, A. (2005). There are no 'color universals', but there are universals of visual semantics. *Anthropological Linguistics, 47,* 217–244.

Wierzbicka, A. (2006a). *English: Meaning and culture.* New York: Oxford University Press.

Wierzbicka, A. (2006b). 'Experience' in John Searle's account of the mind: Brain, mind, and Anglo culture. *Intercultural Pragmatics, 3,* 241–255.

Wierzbicka, A. (2007a). Bodies and their parts: An NSM approach to semantic typology. *Language Sciences, 29,* 14–65.

Wierzbicka, A. (2007b). Shape and colour in language and thought. In A. C. Schalley & D. Khlentzos (Eds.), *Mental states. Volume 2: Language and cognitive structure* (pp. 37–60). Amsterdam: John Benjamins.

Wierzbicka, A. (2008). Why there are no 'colour universals' in language and thought. *Journal of the Royal Anthropological Institute (N.S.), 14,* 407–425.

Wierzbicka, A. (2009a). Reciprocity: An NSM approach to linguistic typology and social universals. *Studies in Language, 33*(1), 103–175.

Wierzbicka, A. (2009b). All people eat and drink. Does this mean that 'eat' and 'drink' are universal human concepts? In J. Newman (Ed.), *The linguistics of eating and drinking* (pp. 65–89). Amsterdam: John Benjamins.

Wierzbicka, A. (2010). *Experience, evidence and sense: The hidden cultural legacy of English*. New York: Oxford University Press.

Wierzbicka, A. (in press). How much longer can the Berlin and Kay paradigm dominate visual semantics? English, Russian and Warlpiri seen 'from the native's point of view'. In D. Young (Ed.), *Rematerializing colour*. Cambridge, UK: Scholars' Press.

Zalizniak, A., Levontina, I., & Shmelev, A. (2005). *Ključevye idei russkoj jazykovoj kartiny mira*. Moscow: Jazyki Slavjanskoj Kul'tury.

Zwartz, B. (2009). The season of hope. *Sydney Morning Herald* (Easter weekend edition, news report). April 10, 2009.

9 Advances in the study of bilingualism: A personal view

Susan Ervin-Tripp

The editors of this volume asked me to reflect on changes since the 1950s in my thinking about the relationship between bilingualism and cognition. A field then sparse has since blossomed. My 1955 dissertation on bilingual personality change with language was stimulated by the comment of a close college friend, a French bilingual poet, Jacqueline Bourguignon Frank, whose later poetry collection was called *No One Took a Country From Me*, that she felt like a different person in her two languages. More recently Anna Wierzbicka (1985) made the same comment about herself.

Why personality? That seems odd now. While personality theories now are oriented mainly to temperament and to measuring the Big Five personality dimensions, the theories of personality in the 1950s included motivations and attitudes, which are profoundly affected by cultural milieu and by the language of experience. G. H. Mead (1934) suggested that our notions of the self as well as our social norms are internalized from social interaction, as a kind of inner speech. The data I collected, which included word associations, sentence completions, and picture narratives, could also be seen as assessing cognitive differences according to language of report.

Psychological research on bilingualism before 1950 was primarily focused on handicaps, as found in intelligence tests in English, in an era when there was political opposition in the US to immigration. Psychologists paid no attention then to the research of linguists. Linguists had already done detailed descriptions of their bilingual children's language development (e.g., Leopold, 1939–49; Ronjat, 1913), and because of the attention to historical change with contact, there was detailed study of bilingual communities in terms of phonological, semantic, lexical, and grammatical consequences, such as the studies by Haugen (1953) of Norwegian–American English bilingualism and by Weinreich (1953) of Swiss bilingual communities. These studies showed clearly that as immigrants became bilingual, their first languages were changed by contact.

Was anybody thinking then about the relation of bilingualism to cognition? Yes, in the sense of change of lexical meanings with language, and the spread of grammatical-semantic features with bilingualism, but only in this restricted sense. Linguists knew that some meanings didn't appear to exist until one borrowed a word, so clearly there were novel concepts in the languages that gave us *omelet*, *rodeo*, and *kindergarten*. Anybody who worked in translation had dealt with the issue of both referential and emotional meaning differences.

While the Gestalt theorists were able to bring complex visual perception into psychology, and Piaget had studied reasoning in children for decades by careful observation, American studies of complex human behavior and learning in 1950 were derived from experiments, learning, and from the dominant operant conditioning theory of Skinner. Considerations of language appeared only in word associations. Verplanck famously remarked 'To risk a pun, the writer remains ignorant of what a cognition is. So far as he knows, he has never had one, and no one has ever been able to correct him on this, or tell him how to have one or how to recognize it if he did' (1957, p. ii).

Some historians of science attribute the development of modern cognitive research to 1956, the date of the publication of key works by George Miller, Chomsky, and Bruner. For others, the final blow to the dominance of operant conditioning was Chomsky's devastating review of Skinner's 1957 book *Verbal Behavior* in the linguistic journal *Language* in 1959, which was widely reprinted. The Harvard Center for Cognitive Studies was organized by Bruner and Miller in 1960. So cognition made its American appearance.

But the tradition of studies of word association was strong. Osgood tried to extend word association through complex mediating networks. In the early 1950s, prodded by John Carroll, a psychometrician who had edited Whorf's work on language and thought (Whorf, 1956), the leading American interdisciplinary organization, the Social Science Research Council, set up a Committee on Psychology and Language to create a new field of research. The dominant theoretical paradigms at the time were Bloomfieldian descriptive linguistics, associationist psychology, and information theory, which described complex language in terms of sequential probabilities. After a summer workshop with these three components, associated with a Linguistic Society Summer Institute in Bloomington, Indiana, the field called *psycholinguistics* was launched with a monograph (Osgood & Sebeok, 1954).

These theoretical foundations seemed a very unpromising ancestry for developing studies of language and cognition. We did consider bilingualism in the monograph, developing a translation of Weinreich's semantic compound and coordinate bilingualism into Osgood's mediating associations (Ervin & Osgood, 1954). Weinreich's distinction is still in use (e.g., Ameel, Storms, Malt, & Sloman, 2005). Later, when I had both bilingual and monolingual measures to compare, it became clear that there was too much variation within individuals across measures for it to be a useful general classifier of persons in my samples.

One of the first of the committee-sponsored interdisciplinary conferences in 1954 was on bilingualism. I gave a paper on 'Identification and bilingualism' (Ervin-Tripp, 1973) reporting differences in sentence completions and stories about pictures in Japanese and English by bilingual Nisei (second-generation immigrant) students. I found that the same speaker would shift thematic focus with language in a way consistent with cultural differences. At that conference I met Wallace Lambert, who had developed a program of research on bilingualism and a measure of attitudes towards speech varieties at McGill University in Montreal. I later adapted his method for measuring language dominance by relative picture-naming speed to my work with French, Navajo, Italian, and Japanese bilinguals.

The most important of the experiences I had as assistant to the Social Science Research Council committee in 1954–7 was to help create testing materials and a field manual for the Southwest Project in Comparative Psycholinguistics, in which we developed projects in six languages of the American southwest: English, Spanish, Zuni, Navajo, Hopi, and Tewa. John Carroll had conceived of this program as a test for the Whorf hypothesis that language affects cognition. To do such a test, one compared languages. Our topics included the effects of lexical categories on color discrimination and hue memory, the effects of Navajo form classifiers on color/form preferences and on memory, the commonalities and differences in synesthesia (Osgood, 1960) and in semantic differential connotative structure in different languages, and the effects of language dominance on color naming and on associations in bilinguals. Because the primary purpose of the project was testing the Whorf hypothesis, cognitive issues were central.

Spending two summers doing linguistic interviews of Navajo speakers, where there were then many monolinguals, and living near the reservation was a profound experience that persuaded me that one cannot do good psycholinguistic research on bilinguals without sociolinguistic and anthropological/cultural knowledge. The life conditions and life history of monolinguals and bilinguals often differ. In research on immigrants it is also common to find that the culture that provided monolingual 'norms' has changed. So it was naïve to think that the typical bilingual was two monolinguals co-existing in one head.

Carroll and Casagrande (1958) published a prototypic Whorf test study from the project, intended to show the effects of the Navajo form classifiers on child cognition. Previous studies had shown that toddlers sort by color earlier than form. Form classifiers are obligatory on verbs of handling in Navajo; since children talk a lot about handling objects, these are learned early. A blanket laid out flat requires a different verb stem from a rolled-up blanket, for instance. It was not surprising that children who spoke Navajo sorted blocks by form rather than by color earlier than Navajo children who spoke English at home rather than Navajo. But when Carroll got back to Harvard, he tested children in pre-schools, and found that the typical manufactured form blocks and sorting toys in pre-schools can have the same training effect on anglophone children. So we could see that cognition could be changed by either verbal or non-verbal experience, in this case two modes of calling attention to form.

COLOR COGNITION

Among the several studies I did with the Navajo in that project were two specifically directed to bilinguals, on color names and on picture recall. Because of the work of Brown and Lenneberg (1954) on color naming, and because the Navajo color terminology system is quite different from English, we collected data on Munsell color chip naming, and on reaction times in naming from monolinguals and bilinguals. The relative dominance test turned out to be important, because it became clear that minimal knowledge of English led to some remarkable replies. It is unforgettable to hear a purple chip called *green*. Haugen had invented the term *diamorph* to identify lexical matches, including those in which semantic equivalence may be over-extended. Thus a Navajo learner of English who hears what he calls *dootl'izh* called *green* by an English speaker might at first assume that the referential extension is the same. But the Munsell hues called *dootl'izh* by Navajo monolinguals ranged from those called *green* by English monolinguals to those they called *purple*, the center being around turquoise. Color and form have continued to be aspects of perceptual codification that recent, much more sophisticated bilingual studies examine.

Color naming is an easy place to apply the model of implicit verbalizing, or verbal mediation. This is a mediating verbal codification effect, which has been demonstrated for categories of objects as well as for perceptual continua. My interpretation of the difference in naming hues in L1 by the bilinguals was entirely based on relative 'codability' of the hue in the two languages, and the effect of 'implicit verbalization' or mediating codification in the fast-response language for that hue (Ervin, 1961b).

What has happened since through extensive research is that there seems to be evidence of an underlying shift in boundaries in bilinguals (Athanasopoulous, 2009). The best test might be a left-visual-field sorting test of bilinguals in comparison to monolinguals, to see if actual perceptual grouping unaffected by verbalization is changed in bilinguals (Gilbert, Regier, Kay, & Ivry, 2008).

RECALL OF OBJECT PICTURES

The idea was that, if one is asked to remember, one rehearses verbally, so rehearsal is thinking for speaking. In this research we made an assumption that may be false: that everyone uses verbal rehearsal in remembering.

Currently, from observing individual differences in memory, I suspect some people have better visual memory and rely less on verbal storage. But there has been, as far as I know, no work on individual differences in visual/verbal memory, though Vera John-Steiner (1985) showed strong differences in visualization in creative thinking. Of course the issue in research on bilinguals was measuring or controlling which linguistic category system they used for rehearsal, if any.

At the time of the Navajo fieldwork, I did a study with Navajo and also with Italians in Boston that dealt with the notion of a possible contrast between the language of a new experience and the language used in recall (Ervin, 1961a). This study used pictures of objects known to be nameable in both languages, and to influence language choice for storage the pictures to be recalled were named aloud on first presentation. In the Italian bilingual study exposure time during learning was also controlled.

There were two groups of Italian bilinguals. The first-generation group had learned English either in late childhood or in adulthood and spoke Italian more easily than English. The second-generation sample grew up in the US and used both languages interchangeably since childhood. The task was an explicit recall task, with an intervening task (the gender study below) to disrupt rehearsal of the pictured items named during learning. In the Navajo study there were Navajo-dominant bilinguals and English-dominant bilinguals, and the results of the two groups were a mirror image. The model and the results suggest that participants covertly store names in their language of quickest response for the item. When asked to recall in their weaker language, or one in which they have had no latent practice for the item, they are slower. Thus the worst condition was naming pictured objects in the dominant language and recall in the weaker language.

COGNITION AND GENDER MARKING

As a filler task in the Italian memory study, I assessed gender connotations of nonsense words accruing from grammatical marking by final vowels in Italian. Recent studies of gender semantics have used real words, male or female voices, or images; in the primitive days before current video technology we used the stopwatch and nonsense words, showing that there are accrued connotations for gender suffixes in speakers whose childhood language was Italian, on Osgood's universal semantic differential dimensions of value and strength (Ervin, 1962). This finding has been much enriched by the excellent recent research on such gender semantics, which shows it develops in speakers by age 8. Boroditsky, Schmidt, and Phillips (2003), using a delicate measure such as giving a gendered person's name to an object, found that the semantics from first languages with grammatical gender carried over into naming objects in L2 English, which is indifferent to noun genders for inanimate objects. But if a multilingual's languages conflict in gender assignments, these connotative associations are washed out. So Bassetti concludes that 'for monolingual native speakers grammatical gender is not simply grammatical but also conceptual' (2007, p. 269). While in my study the judgments simply used the suffix as the only cue that had meaning, the Boroditsky and the Bassetti effects must have been conceptual for the reference objects.

PERSONALITY

The research on French bilinguals for my 1955 dissertation addressed the hypothesis of personality being temporarily changed by the language in use. The participants were all French speakers who came to the United States as adults, many as war brides, and my method was obtaining narratives in each language about ambiguous photographs (Thematic Apperception Test pictures). This was easy, since I lived in Washington where there were many French speakers and I was fluent in second-language French. Predicting projections of needs and values, I scoured the literature on French culture to identify contrasts and predicted that the English stories would have more themes of physical violence, fewer themes of verbal argument and social withdrawal, and more achievement themes in the women. The last three predictions proved significant. It seemed such narrative differences might arise in bilingual adults from many sources—differences in the perception and recall of their own experience, mass media thematic contrasts, differences in verbally expressed values in the two societies, or role or attitude shifts associated with life in the respective language communities. I had no way to discriminate these explanations. A recent version of this research can be seen in Koven's (2007) study of Portuguese–French bilinguals.

WORD ASSOCIATIONS AND SENTENCE COMPLETIONS

Five years later, when I was teaching in the Speech Department at the University of California, Berkeley, in 1960–62, I was able to get National Science Foundation funding to expand a replication of my dissertation. I found California Japanese bilinguals, hired a Japanese bilingual assistant, collected monolingual data in Japan for comparison rather than relying on hypotheses of culture contrast, and included a control procedure testing whether trying to sound typical affected responses (i.e., culture 'set'). The samples were from two pools. One was of Japanese 'war brides', women who came to the US after World War II as wives of American servicemen, having grown up in Japan. The women had typically been speaking English for 15 years. A subset of the participants were born in the United

States but spent the war years in Japan with their relatives—these are known as Kibei Nisei. They had learned English first as children in bilingual families in the United States. The war brides were like the French bilinguals in that they had been monolinguals as children and experienced a culture shift and a shift of milieu coincidental with becoming bilingual.

A frequent area of research in the 1960s was associations. Word associations were a simple way of getting at differences in bilingual semantics. In the Japanese study we gave a Japanese or American weight to a response in terms of its frequency in the monolingual samples. The Nisei tended to give American-like responses in both languages, whereas the war brides had distinctive responses by language. In both the word associations and in sentence completions the content differences with language were more contrasted for the war brides, whose Japanese had been acquired in a different cultural milieu than their English. The Nisei tended to give responses in both languages that were close to American monolinguals.

Were they just giving culturally stereotyped answers? The set instructions, to give Japanese-typical replies, had the effect of increasing Japanese-ness of associations in Japanese, but the women did not know how to sound more like American monolinguals in their associations intentionally. They were more successful for sentence completions and story completions, where the topics drew on salient culture differences.

NARRATIVES

In both the French study and the Japanese study, the bilinguals told stories twice about ambiguous pictures, with a session in each language. There were significant differences for the French speakers with language, but in the Japanese project when we had monolingual women for comparison (albeit years after the bilinguals left Japan) we found that the actual monolingual stories often didn't fit cultural stereotypes.

Some women gave more American responses in both languages; they turned out to be less conservative and more acculturated in interviews than those who were more Japanese in replies. Those who shifted story content with language typically had close American friends. Studies of bilingual narratives, mostly narratives of personal history, have more recently been richly explored by Koven (2007), Pavlenko (2003), and others. It is clearly a far more complex topic than the study of color vocabulary.

In 1955 I moved from Washington to the Harvard School of Education, doing both teaching about child language and research on child cognition. My milieu there was anthropologists doing cross-cultural studies of child socialization, interacting with Chomsky, Bruner, and Roger Brown. When I moved to Berkeley, I started a longitudinal project on child syntax. Child syntax was a rapidly developing field at that time, and by 1965 I had children of my own to observe. Bilingualism, except for Lambert in

Montreal, was not a thriving field at the time, and I was not myself bilingual, so my research focus shifted.

WHAT HAS REMAINED OF THESE OLD ISSUES?

The current components of psychologists' research on bilingualism are studies of the brain, of cognition, of psycholinguistics, and of linguistics. In the 1950s, what was known of the bilingual brain came only from brain injuries; brain imaging during mental tasks was yet to be.

There has been extraordinary proliferation in the analysis of specific domains of cognition, of colors, of number, of object classes, of grammatical gender, of time metaphors, with subtle methods. The study of bilingual cognition has become rich and detailed. Some testing materials show a difference between bilinguals and monolinguals, and others do not, possibly subtly reflecting whether implicit verbalization played a role in the ostensibly non-verbal tasks.

A recent study of color and object perception found that either using forced left visual field rather than right visual field use, or preoccupying verbal memory could reduce the influence of verbal classifications on perceptual memory, since they presumably require left lateral processing (Gilbert et al., 2008).

There is now much more knowledge of what is conceptual and what is facilitated by language. Spelke and Tsivkin (2001), in an elegant study of memory for trained material by bilinguals, showed that 'a specific natural language contributes to the representation of large, exact numbers but not to the approximate number representations that humans share with other mammals' (p. 45). Thus there is language specificity in training effects for large number precise calculations but not for estimations.

But these are primarily studies at the visual, sorting, and calculating end of the cognitive process, and some of my work with bilinguals has involved more complex issues of personality, values, and social behavior. Hunt and Agnoli (1991) suggested that differences in the pragmatics in a bilingual's two communities could mean that changing language reinforces contrasts in social meanings, values, and social cognition. This proposal brings us to a seemingly independent development in the study of bilingualism, the analysis of interaction, as it controls attention, cognition, and signifiers of allegiance and of interpretive context. Here is a domain far more difficult to study experimentally, but remaining for the future.

REFERENCES

Ameel, E., Storms, G., Malt, B. C., & Sloman, S. A. (2005). How bilinguals solve the naming problem. *Journal of Memory and Language, 53,* 60–80.

Athanasopoulos, P. (2009). Cognitive representation of colour in bilinguals: The case of Greek blues. *Bilingualism: Language and Cognition, 12*(1), 83–95.

Bassetti. B. (2007). Bilingualism and thought: Grammatical gender and concepts of objects in Italian–German bilingual children. *International Journal of Bilingualism, 11,* 251–273.

Boroditsky, L., Schmidt, L., & Phillips, W. (2003). Sex, syntax, and semantics. In D. Gentner & S. Goldin-Meadow (Eds.), *Language in mind: Advances in the study of language and cognition* (pp. 61–79). Cambridge, MA: MIT Press.

Brown, R. W., & Lenneberg, E. H. (1954). A study in language and cognition. *The Journal of Abnormal and Social Psychology, 49,* 454–462.

Carroll, J. B., & Casagrande, J. B. (1958). The function of language classifications in behavior. In E. E. Maccoby, T. M. Newcomb, & E. L. Hartley (Eds.), *Readings in social psychology* (pp. 18–31). New York: Henry Holt.

Chomsky, N. (1959). Review of *Verbal Behavior*, by B. F. Skinner. *Language, 35*(1), 26–57.

Ervin, S. M. (1955). *The verbal behavior of bilinguals: The effect of language of report on the Thematic Apperception Test stories of adult French bilinguals*. PhD thesis, University of Michigan.

Ervin, S. M. (1961a). Learning and recall in bilinguals. *American Journal of Psychology, 74,* 446–451.

Ervin, S. M. (1961b). Semantic shift in bilingualism. *American Journal of Psychology, 74,* 233–241.

Ervin, S. M. (1962). The connotations of gender. *Word, 18,* 249–261.

Ervin, S. M., & Osgood, C. E. (1954). Second language learning and bilingualism. In C. E. Osgood & T. E. Sebeok (Eds.), *Psycholinguistics: A survey of theory and research problems*. Supplement to *International Journal of American Linguistics (Memoir 10), 20*(4), 139–145.

Ervin-Tripp, S. M. (1973). *Language acquisition and communicative choice: Essays by Susan M. Ervin-Tripp* (ed. A. Dil). Stanford, CA: Stanford University Press.

Gilbert, A. L., Regier, T., Kay, P., & Ivry, R. B. (2008). Support for lateralization of the Whorf effect beyond the realm of color discrimination. *Brain and Language, 105,* 91–98.

Haugen, E. (1953). *The Norwegian language in America: A study in bilingual behavior*. Philadelphia: University of Pennsylvania Press.

Hunt, E., & Agnoli, F. (1991). The Whorfian hypothesis: A cognitive psychology perspective. *Psychological Review, 98,* 377–389.

John-Steiner, V. (1985). *Notebooks of the mind: Explorations of thinking*. Albuquerque, NM: University of New Mexico Press.

Koven, M. (2007). *Selves in two languages: Bilinguals' verbal enactments of identity in French and Portuguese*. Amsterdam: John Benjamins.

Leopold, W. (1939–49). *Speech development of a bilingual child: A linguist's record*. Evanston, IL: Northwestern University.

Mead, G. H. (1934). *Mind, self, and society from the standpoint of a social behaviorist* (edited with an introduction by C. W. Morris). Chicago, IL: University of Chicago Press.

Osgood, C. E. (1960). The cross-cultural generality of visual–verbal synesthetic tendencies. *Behavioral Science, 5*(2), 146–169.

Osgood, C. E., & Sebeok, T. A. (Eds.). (1954). *Psycholinguistics: A survey of theory and research problems*. Supplement to *International Journal of American Linguistics (Memoir 10), 20*(4), 139–145.

Pavlenko, A. (2003). Eyewitness memory in late bilinguals: Evidence for discursive relativity. *International Journal of Bilingualism, 7*(3), 257–281.

Ronjat, J. (1913). *Le développement du langage observé chez un enfant bilingue.* Paris: H. Champion.

Skinner, B. F. (1957). *Verbal behavior.* New York: Appleton-Century-Crofts.

Spelke, E. S., & Tsivkin, S. (2001). Language and number: A bilingual training study. *Cognition, 78,* 45–88.

Verplanck, W. S. (1957). A glossary of some terms used in the objective science of behavior. *Psychological Review (Supplement), 64*(6), 1–42.

Weinreich, U. (1953). *Language in contact: Findings and problems.* New York: Linguistic Circle of New York.

Whorf, B. (1956). *Language, thought, and reality* (ed. J. B. Carroll). Cambridge, MA: MIT Press.

Wierzbicka, A. (1997). The double life of a bilingual: A cross-cultural perspective. In M. Bond (Ed.), *Working at the interface of cultures: Eighteen lives in social science* (pp. 113–115). London: Routledge.

10 Bilingual worlds

David W. Green

Languages differ markedly in their grammars, suggesting different design solutions to constraints of a socio-historical and cognitive nature rather than permutations of a fixed universal grammar (Evans & Levinson, 2009). Different languages direct attention to different aspects of events (Slobin, 2004) and help shape our perceptions of fundamental properties of our worlds (Whorf, 1956) such as the sense of ourselves in space (Levinson, Kita, Haun, & Rasch, 2002) and our perceptions of the color of objects (Tan et al., 2008; Thierry, Athanasopoulos, Wiggetta, Deringa, & Kuipers, 2009). It is true that blocking the use of language may eliminate such effects (e.g., Winawer et al., 2007) but in everyday life we experience the world as beings who do use language—we talk to ourselves, we talk to others, and we use language to guide our actions (Vygotsky, 1960).

If we now think of bilingual, let alone multilingual, speakers, there is an explosion of variety. Maybe their first language was an Indo-European language and their second Mandarin; maybe their first language was Straits Salish (Evans & Levinson, 2009) with no noun–verb distinction and they learnt Spanish; maybe they were brought up speaking more than one language with similar or with radically distinct properties. What neural and mental means permit such variety? What personal and inter-personal worlds are created? We are at the beginning of the endeavor to understand such questions. However, there is one area where substantial progress has already been made, and it strongly suggests that use of two or more languages has significant cognitive consequences.

Language is fundamental to practical action because it allows us to coordinate with one another. To make a social arrangement, for example, the parties must discuss and agree the best option. The cognitive demands on them depend on the extent of their shared experience of the world (have they met before?), on the nature of the local environment (is it quiet or noisy?) and, in the case of bilingual speakers, on the languages that can be used. Effective coordination requires that bilingual speakers monitor the language in use, select one language rather than another and inhibit use of the other. For instance, when speaking to a monolingual speaker, a bilingual speaker must avoid switching into the non-shared language and ensure fluency by overcoming interference from non-shared language words or phrases. In contrast, when coordinating arrangements with two monolingual speakers of different languages, a bilingual needs to switch rapidly from one language to another, translating from language A to language B in order to speak to one addressee and translating from language B to language A in order to speak to the other addressee. Language control in these different contexts requires the dynamic regulation of two language systems and specific patterns of coordination.

In one approach to language control, the *inhibitory control model* (Green, 1986, 1998a), inhibitory processes play a central role in suppressing activation in the non-target language where just one language is in play and in modulating language activation when both languages are in play. Critically, dynamic regulation of two languages involves control systems external to the system mapping thought to expression and makes use of systems involved in the control of action in general.

On this supposition, Bialystok (see Bialystok, 2009, for a recent review) proposed that the continued exercise of the systems involved in language control (e.g., monitoring the language in use, selecting one language and inhibiting the other) should lead to enhanced skills in executive (cognitive) control even on non-verbal tasks. The additional cognitive demands imposed on bilingual speakers relative to monolingual speakers may then have profound consequences for the way in which bilinguals engage with the social and physical world over the life span. In contrast to an earlier evaluation (Green, 1998b), data from experimental research now strongly suggest that such demands do exert widespread cognitive effects (Bialystok, 2009). Bilinguals are specific speaker-hearers (Grosjean, 1998, 2001) not only in terms of the lexical concepts they recruit or their procedures for thinking for speaking, but also in terms of the very processes that help coordinate cognition and that lie at the heart of human adaptive behavior.

In this chapter I examine the cognitive demands on bilingual speakers in order to identify key differences from monolingual speakers. I argue that the key factor is the dynamic regulation of two languages and the control processes associated with such regulation. I then consider how these demands may affect the effectiveness or efficiency of the networks involved in cognitive control and so mediate a bilingual advantage in switching between different tasks or in controlling interference. In a final section I argue that it is important to understand the behavioral ecology of bilingual speakers in order to account for individual differences in any cognitive advantage and to examine the associations of genes and executive attention by carrying out genetic studies of speakers in primarily bilingual and primarily monolingual societies.

COGNITIVE DEMANDS ON BILINGUAL SPEAKERS

If language control involves the network used in cognitive control in general and if we assume that cognitive demands affect the effectiveness or efficiency of the network, what cognitive demands challenge the control system in bilingual speakers?

There is good evidence that the goal of using one language does not preclude the activation of lexical alternatives in the other language (e.g., Colomé, 2001; Costa, Santesteban, & Ivanova, 2006; Hermans, Bongaerts, de Bot, & Schreuder, 1999; Lee & Williams, 2001; Sandoval, Gollan, Ferreira, & Salmon, 2010). However there is debate as to whether such alternatives compete for selection. On the supposition that proficiency in another language induces a functionally separable module (Hernandez, Li, & MacWhinney, 2005; Kroll & Stewart, 1994) or subsystem (Paradis, 2001, 2004, 2009), language selection may seem to require no more than the differential activation of one subsystem (Costa et al., 2006; La Heij, 2005; Schwieter & Sunderman, 2008). On this account, once the subsystem is activated, competitive processes will solely reflect competition within it and so will not differ from that experienced by monolingual speakers. How justified is this account?

We can imagine minimal competition between languages when one language is not selected for a long time, but even that state does not imply that competitive effects are identical within the selected language to those experienced by monolingual speakers of that language. It is possible that lexical representations in a later-acquired language, for instance, are more densely represented and elicit stronger competitive effects (Zhao & Li, 2007) that invoke inhibitory control.

In fact, in selecting one language rather than another, bilingual speakers must coordinate potentially competing representations of a gestural, prosodic, syntactic, and lexical nature that differ between languages. It is perhaps this process of continually negotiating a more complex multimodal internal space containing a manifold of competing alternatives or attractor states (see Spivey & Dale, 2006) that distinguishes the subjective worlds of bilingual and monolingual speakers.

The extent to which the growth of an utterance (its epigenesis) reveals evidence of its competitive trajectory in overt behavior depends on the circumstance. It may be apparent when individuals first switch into their other language—they may pause or pronounce a word incorrectly. Certainly, experimental data indicate that deliberate switching between languages incurs a cost (e.g., Gollan & Ferreira, 2009; Meuter & Allport, 1999) and one that is consistent with the suppression of the non-selected language (Philipp & Koch, 2009). Deliberate switching (in contrast to involuntary code switching) between languages may then yield a cognitive benefit because this activity enhances the bilingual's facility in suppressing/reinstating an action goal or the plans that implement it.

Evidence of competitive effects may be masked as speakers continue in the selected language. In fact, even in such conditions, tacit, transitory reactions indicative of contact with lexical representations of the non-target language can be revealed using evoked reaction potential (ERP) methods in the absence of overt behavioral differences (e.g., Thierry & Wu, 2007). In such circumstances regulation may arise at the level of language goals because activation in the non-target language stimulates the alternative language goal, requiring its reactive inhibition and the engagement of systems involved in executive control.

The dynamic regulation of two languages may therefore exercise those systems involved in executive control primarily when speakers deliberately switch between languages and when they deliberately seek to maintain fluency in the selected language.

THE BILINGUAL ADVANTAGE

We focus here on the non-verbal cognitive advantages of bilingualism. There are also advantages in the learning of new languages (Kaushanskaya & Marian, 2009; Van Hell & Mahn, 1997) and small costs in word recognition and in picture naming (see Bialystok, 2009) reflecting perhaps the reduced experience in using each language relative to monolingual speakers (Gollan & Kroll, 2001).

Three questions are key to the current research agenda on the bilingual advantage. First, which aspects of cognitive control are enhanced in bilinguals and how do these vary over the life span? Second, to what extent is it possible to distinguish effects of bilingualism on cognitive control from other factors that modulate executive functioning such as social class and culture? Third, what are the neural bases of language control and the bilingual advantage?

We can distinguish different executive processes (e.g., Bunge, Dudukovic, Thomason, Vaidya, & Gabrieli, 2002; Miyake, Friedman, Emerson, Witzki, & Howerter, 2000) associated with different kinds of tasks (interference suppression, response suppression, and task switching). In some tasks individuals must attend to a target stimulus and suppress interference from a competing cue. In a non-verbal flanker task, for example, the target stimulus is a central arrow pointing either left or right and the competing cues are arrows pointing in the same direction as the central arrow on a congruent trial (i.e., → → → → →) or in the opposite direction on an incongruent trial (i.e., ← ← → ← ←). The need for inhibitory control arises because the task is to press one button if the central arrow points right and another button if it points left. In other tasks individuals must suppress an habitual response to a stimulus (e.g., overriding a right button press to a rightward-pointing arrow when the task demands a response opposite to the direction of the arrow). In other cases individuals must switch between one task and another, as when they are required to respond to the shape of a stimulus or to its color. In this case, on switch trials they must resist performing the prior task (e.g., responding to the shape of the stimulus) and its associated responses and reinstate the alternative task (e.g., responding to the color of the stimulus).

The current consensus is that bilinguals show an advantage in suppressing interference (e.g., Bialystok & Viswanathan, 2009; Costa, Hernández, & Sebastián-Gallés, 2008) and in task switching (Bialystok & Viswanathan, 2009; Prior & MacWhinney, 2010) but not necessarily in response suppression (Martin-Rhee & Bialystok, 2008). These advantages in experimental tasks have correlates that are socially and practically important. Developmentally, one correlate of enhanced inhibitory control is that bilingual children ('crib bilinguals', i.e., those bilingual from birth) are advanced in the performance of Theory of Mind tasks (Kovács, 2009). Across the life span, from young adulthood through middle- and old-age, bilinguals suffer less task interference—an effect that is most marked in the elderly (Bialystok, Craik, Klein, & Viswanathan, 2004). Clinically, perhaps because of adaptive changes in the brain, bilingualism may act as a kind of cognitive reserve and as a protective factor against the onset of Alzheimer's disease (Bialystok, Craik, & Freedman, 2007).

Social class and culture are also important factors that modulate executive functioning (Carlson & Meltzoff, 2008; Hedden, Ketay, Aron, Markus, & Gabrieli, 2008) and so it is important to distinguish a bilingual advantage from such factors. This question can be addressed by comparing bilinguals with diverse language backgrounds with monolingual speakers—a strategy adopted in Martin-Rhee and Bialystok (2008). In this study, bilinguals showed an advantage in tasks requiring interference suppression but no advantage in tasks requiring response suppression. An alternative approach is to contrast bilingual groups in different cultures with monolingual controls (Bialystok & Viswanathan, 2009). In this case, bilinguals showed an advantage in inhibitory control and in switching response sets—an aspect of task switching.

In terms of the neural bases of language control and the bilingual advantage, Abutalebi and Green (2007) argued that language control recruits the same cortical and subcortical structures involved in the control of interference and in task switching in monolingual speakers. Language control, in other words, recruits a network involved in executive control of action and so the data strongly suggest that the bilingual advantage arises either from adaptive changes to that network in bilingual speakers or from their more effective recruitment of the network. Of particular importance are cortical regions that monitor task cues, detect and control interference, and initiate new response mappings along with subcortical regions that help select between competing actions and are active during language switching (e.g., Abutalebi et al., 2007; Crinion et al., 2006; see Abutalebi & Green, 2007, for details).

The precise mechanisms and neural substrate underlying an advantage in inhibitory control remain to be determined. It is likely that different loci are involved (Abutalebi & Green, 2007; Kroll, Bobb, & Wodniecka, 2006). An important distinction is between transient and sustained control processes (Braver, Reynolds, & Donaldson, 2003; Christoffels, Firk, & Schiller, 2007; Wang, Kuhl, Chen, & Dong, 2009). In the non-verbal flanker task, bilinguals are faster on both congruent and incongruent trials (Costa et al., 2008). Conceivably, bilinguals suppress competing cues (whether valid or invalid) and maintain such suppression over a sequence of trials. Differences in inhibitory control may then reflect not only transient control processes (that is, a more rapid response to a task cue and/or more effective response to interference) but also control processes that are sustained over time and that are presumably invoked when individuals continue to speak in one language and avoid speaking in another.

In task-switching studies, activation associated with sustained control can be isolated by contrasting neural response to non-switch trials in a block where individuals are switching from one task to another with neural response to the same trials presented in a block of trials of the same type. Activation associated with transient control can be isolated by contrasting response to switch compared with non-switch trials. Research on monolinguals (Braver et al., 2003) and on bilinguals (Wang et al., 2009) confirms that distinct regions are associated with these two forms of control. Such results pave the way for studies that explicitly contrast monolingual and bilingual speakers performing the same non-verbal task.

At the time of writing, only one published neuroimaging study meets this criterion (Bialystok et al., 2005). It contrasted two early bilingual groups (French–English and Cantonese–English) with a monolingual English group. Participants pressed the right-hand button if there was a red square and the left button if there was a green square. On congruent trials the target square (e.g., a red square) appeared on the same side as the correct response button (i.e., right) whereas it appeared on the opposite side on incongruent trials. Bialystok et al. used magneto-encephalography (MEG) to identify the neural basis of any bilingual advantage. The data indicate a common network with subtle differences in how interference is controlled. For instance, attentional control processes for congruent and incongruent trials appeared similar for the two groups but were stronger for the bilinguals. Neuroimaging studies of bilinguals and monolinguals performing the same task are needed to isolate the different sources of advantage (e.g., to sustained and/or to transient control processes) and to identify the key regions and connections.

Functional demand can induce changes in brain structure (e.g., Crinion et al., 2009; Draganski et al., 2004; Mechelli et al., 2004) and so it is also vital to examine structural differences in the regions mediating control. Changes may arise in cortical or subcortical regions involved in control and/or in the white matter tracts that connect these regions. Conceivably, increased gray matter density in control regions provides an additional resource to resist interference. For instance, it may improve the effectiveness of sustained control or permit more effective transient control.

THE BEHAVIORAL ECOLOGY OF BILINGUALS

Languages are learned and used within particular environments. Constraints on plasticity (Hernandez & Li, 2007; Li & Farkas, 2002; Li & Green, 2007; Li, Zhao, & MacWhinney, 2007) or on the nature of the learning process may affect the involvement of different neural regions, especially those coding for grammar (see for example, Paradis, 2001, 2004, 2009; Ullman, 2001; see also Green, 2003). The precise pattern of usage of different languages (e.g., one language at work, another at home; use of code switching) and the precise skills of the user (e.g., in simultaneous translation) may also affect how language is produced and controlled and underlie individual variability in any bilingual cognitive advantage. For instance, in communities where code switching predominates in conversation, switching between languages may reflect automatic processes (Green, 1998a; Paradis, 2009) and restrict the engagement of executive control mechanisms in language selection. In such a context, any bilingual advantage may be quite restricted in turn.

Evolutionary factors may also be at work, shaping the process of learning multiple languages and favoring traits that facilitate language control. According to Romaine (2004), 70% of the 6000–8000 natural languages are found in 20 of the 200 nation-states on the planet. There are then concentrations of bilingual societies among cultures that are effectively monolingual. This pattern provides the opportunity for large-scale genetic studies that contrast the associations of genes mediating executive attention (Fossella et al., 2002) in different types of bilingual community (e.g., those with and without extensive code switching) and primarily monolingual communities.

Even in the absence of such specific associations, it is worth exploring the extent to which bilingualism, at least within bilingual societies, affects the relative attractiveness of males to females; i.e., is bilingualism a sexual selection fitness indicator? Evolutionary theories already offer the best account of how women's preferences for masculine-sounding voices change over the menstrual cycle (e.g., Jones et al., 2008). Such studies tightly control confounding factors by varying properties of the same voice to sound more or less masculine. Might hearing the voice speak one or two languages of the community affect preference? If so bilingualism may be a sexual selection fitness indicator in such communities, and with increased migration, it may become one even more generally.

CONCLUSION

Research has linked language control in bilinguals to a bilingual advantage in the control of interference and task switching. We do not yet know the full extent of such an advantage nor the relative contribution of different processes (e.g., sustained or transient control processes). Work is needed too to explore the range of competitive representations contacted but not selected in the speech of bilinguals. Is the experiential basis of lexical concepts (Vigliocco, Meteyard, Andrews, & Kousta, 2009) equally available in both languages? How does the mental simulation of sentence meaning (e.g., Glenberg & Kaschak, 2002) differ in the speaker's two languages? What kind of syntactic procedures can handle widely different grammars within one brain? The diversity of bilingual worlds points to the need to understand the behavioral ecology of bilingual/multilingual speakers and to develop neurocomputational accounts that render such variety comprehensible.

REFERENCES

Abutalebi, J., Brambati, S. M., Annoni, J-M., Moro, A., Cappa, S. F., & Perani, D. (2007). The neural cost of the auditory perception of language switches: An event-related functional magnetic resonance imaging study in bilinguals. *Journal of Neuroscience, 27,* 13762–13769.

Abutalebi, J., & Green, D. W. (2007). Bilingual language production: The neuro-cognition of language representation and control. *Journal of Neurolinguistics, 20,* 242–275.

Bialystok, E. (2009). Bilingualism: The good, the bad and the indifferent. *Bilingualism: Language and Cognition, 12,* 3–11.

Bialystok, E., Craik, F. I. M., & Freedman, M. (2007). Bilingualism as a protection against the onset of symptoms of dementia. *Neuropsychologia, 45,* 459–464.

Bialystok, E., Craik, F. I. M., Grady, C., Chau, W., Ishii, R., Gunji, A., et al. (2005). Effects of bilingualism on cognitive control in the Simon task: Evidence from MEG. *NeuroImage, 24,* 40–49.

Bialystok, E., Craik, F. I. M., Klein, R., & Viswanathan, M. (2004). Bilingualism, aging, and cognitive control: Evidence from the Simon task. *Psychology and Aging, 19,* 290–303.

Bialystok, E., & Viswanathan, M. (2009). Components of executive control with advantages for bilingual children in two cultures. *Cognition, 112,* 494–500.

Braver, T. S., Reynolds, J. R., & Donaldson, D. I. (2003). Neural mechanisms of transient and sustained cognitive control during task switching. *Neuron, 39,* 713–726.

Bunge, S. A., Dudukovic, N. M., Thomason, M. E., Vaidya, C. J., & Gabrieli, J. D. E. (2002). Immature frontal lobe contributions to cognitive control in children: Evidence from fMRI. *Neuron, 33,* 301–311.

Carlson, S. M., & Meltzoff, A. N. (2008). Bilingual experience and executive functioning in young children. *Developmental Science, 11,* 282–298.

Christoffels, I. K., Firk, C., & Schiller, N. O. (2007). Bilingual language control: An event-related brain potential study. *Brain Research, 1147,* 192–208.

Colomé, A. (2001). Lexical activation in bilinguals' speech production: Language-specific or language-independent? *Journal of Memory and Language, 45,* 721–736.

Costa, A., Hernández, M., & Sebastián-Gallés, N. (2008). Bilingualism aids conflict resolution: Evidence from the ANT task. *Cognition, 106,* 59–86.

Costa, A., Santesteban, M., & Ivanova, I. (2006). How do highly-proficient bilinguals control their lexicalization process? Inhibitory and language-specific selection mechanisms are both functional. *Journal of Experimental Psychology: Learning, Memory, and Cognition, 32,* 1057–1074.

Crinion, J., Green, D. W., Chung, R., Ali, N., Grogan, A., Price, G., et al. (2009). Neuroanatomical markers of speaking Chinese. *Human Brain Mapping, 30,* 4108–4115.

Crinion, J., Turner, R., Grogan, A., Hanakawa, T., Noppeney, U., Devlin, J. T., et al. (2006). Language control in the bilingual brain. *Science, 312,* 1537–1540.

Draganski, B., Gaser, C., Busch, V., Schuierer, G., Bogdahn, U., & May, A. (2004). Changes in grey matter induced by training. *Nature, 427,* 311–312.

Evans, N., & Levinson, S. C. (2009). The myth of language universals: Language diversity and its importance for cognitive science. *Behavioral and Brain Sciences, 32,* 429–448.

Fossella, J., Sommer, T., Fan, J., Wu, Y., Swanson, J. M., Pfaff, D. W., et al. (2002). Assessing the molecular genetics of attention networks. *BMC Neuroscience, 3,* 14.

Glenberg, A. M., & Kaschak, M. (2002). Grounding language in action. *Psychonomic Bulletin and Review, 9*(3), 558–565.

Gollan, T. H., & Ferreira, V. S. (2009). Should I stay or should I switch? A cost–benefit analysis of voluntary language switching in young and aging bilinguals. *Journal of Experimental Psychology: Learning, Memory, and Cognition, 35,* 640–665.

Gollan, T. H., & Kroll, J. F. (2001) Lexical access in bilinguals. In B. Rapp (Ed.), *A handbook of cognitive neuropsychology: What deficits reveal about the human mind* (pp. 321–345). New York: Psychology Press.

Green, D. W. (1986). Control, activation and resource. *Brain and Language, 27,* 210–223.

Green, D. W. (1998a). Mental control of the bilingual lexico-semantic system. *Bilingualism: Language and Cognition, 1,* 67–81.

Green, D. W. (1998b). Bilingualism and thought. *Psychologica Belgica, 38*(3), 251–276.

Green, D. W. (2003). The neural basis of the lexicon and the grammar in L2 acquisition. In R. van Hout, A. Hulk, F. Kuiken, & R. Towell (Eds.), *The interface between syntax and the lexicon in second language acquisition.* Amsterdam: John Benjamins.

Grosjean, F. (1998). Studying bilinguals: Methodological and conceptual issues. *Bilingualism: Language and Cognition, 1,* 131–140.

Grosjean, F. (2001). The bilingual's language modes. In J. Nicol (Ed.), *One mind, two languages: Bilingual language processing* (pp. 1–22). Oxford, UK: Blackwell.

Hedden, T., Ketay, S., Aron, A., Markus, H. R., & Gabrieli, J. D. E. (2008). Cultural influences on the neural substrates of attentional control. *Psychological Science, 19,* 12–17.

Hermans, D., Bongaerts, T., de Bot, K., & Schreuder, R. (1999). Producing words in a foreign language: Can speakers prevent interference from their first language? *Bilingualism: Language and Cognition, 1,* 213–229.

Hernandez, A., & Li, P. (2007). Age of acquisition: Its neural and computational mechanisms. *Psychological Bulletin, 133,* 1–13.

Hernandez, A., Li, P., & MacWhinney, B. (2005). The emergence of competing modules in bilingualism. *Trends in Cognitive Sciences, 9,* 222–225.

Jones, B. C., DeBruine, L. M., Perrett, D. I., Little, A. C., Feinberg, D. R., & Law Smith, M. J. (2008). Effects of menstrual cycle phase on face preferences. *Archives of Sexual Behavior, 37,* 78–84.

Kaushanskaya, M., & Marian, V. (2009). The bilingual advantage in novel word learning. *Psychonomic Bulletin & Review, 16,* 705–710.

Kovács, A. M. (2009). Early bilingualism enhances mechanisms of false-belief reasoning. *Developmental Science, 12,* 48–54.

Kroll, J. F., Bobb, S. C., & Wodniecka, Z. (2006). Language selectivity is the exception, not the rule: Arguments against a fixed locus of selection in bilingual speech. *Bilingualism: Language and Cognition, 9,* 119–135.

Kroll, J. F., & Stewart, E. (1994). Category interference in translation and picture naming: Evidence for asymmetric connections between bilingual memory representations. *Journal of Memory and Language, 33,* 149–174.

La Heij, W. (2005). Selection processes in monolingual and bilingual lexical access. In J. F. Kroll & A. M. B. De Groot (Eds.), *Handbook of bilingualism: Psycholinguistic approaches* (pp. 289–307). Oxford, UK: Oxford University Press.

Lee, M-W., & Williams, J. N. (2001). Lexical access in spoken word recognition by bilinguals: Evidence from the semantic competitor priming paradigm. *Bilingualism: Language and Cognition, 4,* 233–248.

Levinson, S. C., Kita, S., Haun, D. B. M., & Rasch, B. H. (2002). Returning the tables: Language affects spatial reasoning. *Cognition, 84,* 155–188.

Li, P., & Farkas, I. (2002). A self-organizing connectionist model of bilingual processing. In R. Heredia & J. Altarriba (Eds.), *Bilingual sentence processing* (pp. 59–85). Amsterdam: Elsevier Science Publisher.

Li, P., & Green, D. W. (2007). Introduction to neurocognitive approaches to bilingualism: Asian languages. *Bilingualism: Language and Cognition, 10,* 117–119.

Li, P., Zhao, X., & MacWhinney, B. (2007). Dynamic self-organization and early lexical development in children. *Cognitive Science, 31,* 581–612.

Martin-Rhee, M. M., & Bialystok, E. (2008). The development of two types of inhibitory control in monolingual and bilingual children. *Bilingualism: Language and Cognition, 11,* 81–93.

Mechelli, A., Crinion, J. T., Noppeney, U., O'Doherty, J., Ashburner, J., Frackowiak, R. S., et al. (2004). Structural plasticity in the bilingual brain. *Nature, 431,* 757.

Meuter, R. F. I., & Allport, A. (1999). Bilingual language switching in naming: Asymmetrical costs of language selection. *Journal of Memory and Language, 40,* 25–40.

Miyake, A., Friedman, N. P., Emerson, M. J., Witzki, A. H., & Howerter, A. (2000). The unity and diversity of executive functions and their contributions to complex 'frontal lobe' tasks: A latent variable analysis. *Cognitive Psychology, 41,* 49–100.

Paradis, M. (2001). Bilingual and polyglot aphasia. In R. S. Berndt (Ed.),

Handbook of neuropsychology, 2nd edition, volume 3. Language and aphasia (pp. 69–91). Amsterdam: Elsevier Science.

Paradis, M. (2004). *A neurolinguistic theory of bilingualism.* Amsterdam/ Philadelphia: John Benjamins Publishing Company.

Paradis, M. (2009). *Declarative and procedural determinants of second languages.* Amsterdam: John Benjamins.

Philipp, A. M., & Koch, I. (2009). Inhibition in language switching; What is inhibited between languages in naming tasks? *Journal of Experimental Psychology: Learning, Memory and Cognition, 35,* 1187–1195.

Prior, A., & MacWhinney, B. (2010). A bilingual advantage in task switching. *Bilingualism: Language and Cognition, 13*(2), 253–262.

Romaine, S. (2004). The bilingual and multilingual community. In T. K. Bhatia & W. C. Ritchie (Eds.), *The handbook of bilingualism* (pp. 385–405). Oxford, UK: Blackwell.

Sandoval, T., Gollan, T., Ferreira, V., & Salmon, D. (2010). What causes the bilingual disadvantage in verbal fluency? The dual task analogy. *Bilingualism: Language and Cognition, 13*(2), 231–252.

Schwieter, J. W., & Sunderman, G. (2008). Language switching in bilingual speech production: In search of the language-specific selection mechanism. *The Mental Lexicon, 3,* 214–238.

Slobin, D. I. (2004). The many ways to search for a frog: Linguistic typology and the expression of motion events. In S. Strömqvist & L. Verhoeven (Eds.), *Relating events in narrative. Volume 2. Typological and contextual perspectives* (pp. 219–257). Mahwah, NJ: Lawrence Erlbaum Associates Inc.

Spivey, M. J., & Dale, R. (2006). Continuous dynamics in real-time cognition. *Current Directions in Psychological Science, 15,* 207–211.

Tan, L. H., Chan, A. H. D., Kay, P., Khong, P-K., Yip, L. K. C., & Luke, K-K. (2008). Language affects patterns of brain activation associated with perceptual decision. *Proceedings of the National Academy of Sciences USA, 105,* 4004–4009.

Thierry, G., Athanasopoulos, P., Wiggetta, A., Deringa, B., & Kuipers, J-R. (2009). Unconscious effects of language-specific terminology on preattentive color perception. *Proceedings of the National Academy of Sciences USA, 106,* 4567–4570.

Thierry, G., & Wu, J. Y. (2007). Brain potentials reveal unconscious translation during foreign-language comprehension. *Proceedings of the National Academy of Sciences USA, 104,* 12530–12535.

Ullman, M. T. (2001). The neural basis of lexicon and grammar in first and second language: The declarative/procedural model. *Bilingualism: Language and Cognition, 4,* 105–122.

Van Hell, J. G., & Mahn, A. C. (1997). Keyword mnemonics versus rote rehearsal: Learning concrete and abstract foreign words by experienced and inexperienced learners. *Language Learning, 47,* 507–546.

Vigliocco, G., Meteyard, L., Andrews, M., & Kousta, S. (2009). Toward a theory of semantic representation. *Language and Cognition, 1*(2), 215–244.

Vygotsky, L. S. (1960). The genesis of higher mental functions. In J. V. Wertson (Ed. & Trans.), *The concept of activity in Soviet psychology* (pp. 144–188). New York: M. E. Sharpe.

Wang, Y., Kuhl, P. K., Chen, C., & Dong, Q. (2009). Sustained and transient language control in the bilingual brain. *NeuroImage, 47,* 414–422.

Whorf, B. L. (1956). *Language, thought and reality: Selected writings of Benjamin Lee Whorf* (Ed. J. B. Carroll). Cambridge, MA: MIT Press.

Winawer J., Witthoft, N., Frank, M. C., Wu, L., Wade, A. R., & Boroditsky, L. (2007), Russian blues reveal effects of language on color discrimination. *Proceedings of the National Academy of Sciences USA, 104,* 7780–7785.

Zhao, X., & Li, P. (2007). Bilingual lexical representation in a self-organizing neural network. In D. S. McNamara & J. G. Trafton (Eds.), *Proceedings of the 29th Annual Cognitive Science Society Meeting* (pp. 755–760). Austin, TX: Cognitive Science Society.

11 Color and bilingual cognition

Panos Athanasopoulos

Color perception has been a traditional test-case of Whorf's principle of linguistic relativity (Whorf, 1940/1956), which states that speakers of different languages evaluate perceptual contrasts differently, influenced by language-specific partitions of reality. Early empirical studies showed that speakers of Zuni, a language that does not lexically separate the colors 'orange' and 'yellow' but instead uses a single term to describe them, do not distinguish the two colors as accurately or as frequently as English speakers in a recognition memory task (Brown & Lenneberg, 1954; Lenneberg & Roberts, 1956).

At the same time, the domain of color has also been used as a prime example of universality. In 1969, Berlin and Kay claimed that despite the wide cross-linguistic variation in how languages partition the color spectrum, underlying representation and perception must be universal, constrained by the physical characteristics of color itself, and the arguably common physiology of vision in humans with diverse cultural and linguistic backgrounds (Berlin & Kay, 1969; Kay & McDaniel, 1978).

The current chapter will argue that bilingual cognition has been, and continues to be, central to the universality versus relativity debate in the domain of color. There are various reasons for this, of which I will list four. First, researchers may overlook their participants' knowledge of another language apart from their native language when making cross-linguistic comparisons between groups. Berlin and Kay (1969) found that participants from diverse linguistic and cultural backgrounds displayed English-like color naming and prototype identification. They took this as evidence for universality, despite the fact that previous research had already shown that acquiring another language may lead to a shift in naming and prototype identification (Ervin, 1961). Berlin and Kay (1969) admitted that the speakers in their sample were for the most part US immigrants with various levels of acculturation and English proficiency, yet they '... find it hard to believe that English could so consistently influence the placement of the foci in these diverse languages' (Berlin & Kay, 1969, p. 12).

Second, due to its dynamic nature, bilingualism presents an ideal opportunity to test a fundamental question of human cognition, namely whether cognitive representation of entities such as colors is innate and fixed from birth, or whether it is a learned sociocultural construct that overrides presumably universal perceptual mechanisms. Studies in first language (L1) acquisition may go some way in answering this question, but bi- or multilingualism provides an ideal empirical tool because it allows researchers to investigate variables that would have been impossible to investigate through monolingual development alone. For example, one cannot deprive an infant of language input to test the role of maturational constraints in acquisition of color categories, but one can easily find bilinguals who learned the other language at various points in time. Variables such as frequency of language use, amount of language exposure, and degree of immersion in a particular culture, to name a few, are readily observable in the study of bilingual cognition and have the potential to offer researchers invaluable information about language and cognitive processing in humans.

Third, bilingualism was a basic tenet of Whorf's formulation of the linguistic relativity principle, as he firmly believed '. . . that those who envision a future world speaking only one tongue, whether English, German, Russian, or any other, hold a misguided ideal and would do the evolution of the human mind the greatest disservice' (Whorf, 1941/1956, p. 244). The revival of Whorf's hypothesis in the 1990s among psychologists was also inspired by bilingualism. Most notably, Hunt and Agnoli, in their seminal 1991 article, which questioned the prevalent universalist paradigm of the time and called for a fresh look at the Whorfian hypothesis from the perspective of cognitive psychology, state:

> the idea that language is a module in the service of thought is not compatible with the phenomenological experience of people who go back and forth from one language to another [. . .] We believe that this discrepancy between academics and bilinguals tells us something. It is time to take another look at theWhorfian hypothesis, making use of the progress that has been made in psychology and linguistics since Whorf's day.
>
> (Hunt & Agnoli, 1991, p. 377).

Finally, these statements resonate with scholars in the field of bilingualism itself, who emphasize the need to study bilinguals in their own right rather than as imperfect versions of a monolingual native speaker ideal. For example, Cook's (1991, 1992, 1999, 2003) multi-competence hypothesis views the person who speaks more than one language as an independent speaker/hearer/thinker, with linguistic and cognitive representations and abilities which are qualitatively distinct from those of a monolingual person. Similarly, Grosjean (1982, 1989, 1992, 1998) has repeatedly argued that the bilingual person is not two monolinguals in the same body, but a unique language user with a complete language system. Thus this chapter will demonstrate that there is a reciprocal benefit in studying bilingualism and thought in the context of linguistic relativity. On the one hand, bilingualism can serve as a test-case helping to shed light on important questions in linguistic relativity research. On the other hand, the study of bilingual cognition requires methods that go beyond mere observation of linguistic performance, i.e., methods that aim to investigate the influence of specific linguistic categories on cognition itself. These methods are readily available in the current methodological designs of linguistic relativity research, as advocated by Lucy (1992), Roberson (2005), Levinson (Majid, Bowerman, Kita, Haun, & Levinson, 2004), and others.

Here I will review two recent studies that have attempted to answer the question of whether bilinguals do indeed think differently from monolinguals in the domain of color. The vast majority of empirical research to date shows that color categories are essentially language derived (see Roberson, 2005, and Roberson & Hanley, 2007, for recent reviews). This makes the color domain an ideal testing ground of central issues in bilingual cognition. Given that speakers of different languages perceive the color spectrum differently, how do bilinguals with languages that partition the spectrum in contrasting ways reconcile these contrasts in their mind? Several proposals concerning bilinguals' minds have been made in recent theoretical accounts (see e.g., Cook, 2002, 2003; Jarvis & Pavlenko, 2008; Pavlenko, 2005). One possibility is that representation is L1 based, such that bilinguals' processing of color is based on the distinctions made in the language first acquired. Another possibility is that there is some, potentially quantifiable, cognitive restructuring of pre-existing L1-based categories. In such cases, do bilinguals shift completely towards the L2 system; are their representations an amalgamation of those of monolinguals speakers of their respective languages; do they form completely novel representations that do not resemble either monolingual pattern; or do they maintain two separate representations shifting back and forth depending on context and task demands? The current chapter will show that bilinguals may exhibit all or most of these possibilities depending on several factors, such as proficiency in their respective languages, length of cultural immersion in the L2-speaking country, and frequency of language use, thus demonstrating the dynamic and flexible nature of bilingual, and by extension human, cognition.

This chapter is organized as follows: First I will review attempts to investigate semantic representation of color, exploring whether there is reverse transfer (from L2 to L1) in the way bilinguals map their L1 color category prototypes on color space. Then I will focus on a particular aspect of higher-level cognition, namely categorical perception, to see how bilinguals judge the similarity between color distinctions lexicalized in the L1 but not in the L2. Finally, I will consider the implications of this preliminary research for the fields of linguistic relativity and bilingual cognition, concluding that bilingual concepts and categories may be much more complex constructs than traditionally assumed in models of bilingual memory, primarily due to the dynamic and flexible nature of the bilingual mind.

SEMANTIC SHIFT IN BILINGUALISM: ERVIN REVISITED

Early studies showed shifts of bilinguals' color categories and foci (best examples) towards those of monolingual speakers of their L2 (Caskey-Sirmons & Hickerson, 1977; Ervin, 1961; Lenneberg & Roberts, 1956). For example, Caskey-Sirmons and Hickerson (1977) demonstrated that the color category prototypes of native speakers of five different L1s who had English as their L2 shifted from the L1 monolingual pattern towards the prototypes displayed by English monolinguals. Ervin (1961) showed a similar shift towards the L2 in Navajo–English bilinguals. Prototype identification tasks typically require participants to select a 'best example' among many different variants of a category. In the domain of color, participants are presented with an array of different color squares arranged in different hues (e.g., blue, bluish green, green, yellowy green, yellow, etc.) and lightness steps (usually eight steps from dark to light in the Munsell system, see below), and are asked to point to the best example of a particular color category.

The most commonly used color chart is based on the Munsell color system (Heider & Olivier, 1972; Roberson, Davies, & Davidoff, 2000; Roberson, Davidoff, Davies, & Shapiro, 2005). The chart consists of 160 fully saturated Munsell color chips varying in hue and lightness. They are usually mounted on a sheet of stiff white cardboard and they are arranged to represent hue levels 5 and 10 of ten equally spaced steps around the Munsell circle (Munsell dimension Hue R, YR, Y, YG, G, BG, B, PB, P, RP) each at eight lightness levels (Munsell dimension Value 9/, 8/, 7/, 6/, 5/, 4/, 3/, 2/). For a visual representation and precise coding details of the Munsell system see http://www.xrite.com/top_munsell.aspx.

Athanasopoulos (2009) used the Munsell color chart in a prototype identification task in order to replicate the early findings of bilingual semantic shift (Ervin, 1961). The researcher looked at semantic representation of native color terms in Greek–English bilinguals. Greek divides the blue region of color space into two distinct regions, a darker shade called *ble*, and a lighter shade called *ghalazio* (Androulaki et al., 2006). Athanasopoulos (2009) wanted to establish the semantic representation of *ble* and *ghalazio* prototypes, and see to what extent knowledge of a second language that does not make a systematic lexical distinction between light and dark blue (i.e., English) would influence representation of L1 categories in Greek–English bilinguals.

Participants

Ten native speakers of Greek with intermediate-level English proficiency and 10 native speakers of Greek with advanced English proficiency took part. The group with advanced English proficiency consisted of adult individuals who were students at a UK university and were tested in the UK. English proficiency was measured by means of performance on an English vocabulary test (Nation, 1990; for a more detailed description of the test see Athanasopoulos, 2009). Advanced participants' mean score was 85/90 (*SD* = 3, range 80–90). Their age range was 21–31 years, seven were female and three male. The mean age at which they started to learn English was 8 years (*SD* = 3), ranging from 5 to 13 years. Their mean length of stay in the UK was 30 months (*SD* = 14), ranging from 9 to 48 months. The group with intermediate English proficiency were students attending non-English-related university courses in Greece who had never lived in an English-speaking country before. They were tested in Greece. Their mean score on the Nation test was 64 (*SD* = 4, range = 60–69). Their age-range was 19–26 years, eight were female and two male. Their mean age of L2 acquisition was 9 years (*SD* = 2, range 5–13).

Materials and procedure

The Munsell stimuli used for elicitation of category prototypes were identical to the ones used by Heider and Olivier (1972) and Roberson et al. (2000, 2005), as described earlier. Each participant was tested individually. They were shown the full array of Munsell chips and they were asked to indicate which chips were the best examples of *ble* and *ghalazio* (counterbalanced within each group, such that half of the participants were asked to identify the *ble* focus first, and half were asked to identify the *ghalazio* focus first). Participants received instructions in Greek from a Greek native speaker. Upon completion of this task, participants completed a personal information questionnaire and then the Nation test was administered.

Results and discussion

Figure 11.1 represents the bluish portion of Munsell color space. It shows the modal prototype placement for *ble* and *ghalazio* by advanced- and intermediate-level bilinguals, alongside prototype placement data for *blue* in English native speakers as reported in the studies by Roberson et al. (2000, 2005).

As Figure 11.1 shows, intermediate bilinguals place the best example of *ble* one step away from the *blue* focus, in both lightness and hue. Advanced bilinguals, on the other hand, tend to shift the *ble* focus towards *blue*. This finding is in line with previous results from Ervin (1961) and

	10BG	5B	10B	5PB	10PB
9					
8			◊		
7		♦			
6					
5					
4			o □		
3				■	
2					

Key: ■ Intermediate bilingual *ble* prototype, ♦ Intermediate bilingual *ghalazio* prototype,
o English monolingual blue prototype, □ Advanced bilingual *ble* prototype,
◊ Advanced bilingual *ghalazio* prototype

Figure 11.1 Distribution of advanced- and intermediate-level bilingual modal prototypes for *ble* and *ghalazio*, and English modal prototype for *blue* reported in Roberson et al. (2000, 2005). The three-dimensional Munsell system is shown as a two-dimensional projection of hue (horizontal axis, BG = BlueGreen, B = Blue, PB = PurpleBlue) against lightness (vertical axis, value 2 being the darkest, 9 the lightest).

Caskey-Sirmons and Hickerson (1977) showing semantic shift towards the L2 values. The best example of *ghalazio*, on the other hand, presents an interesting case. In the dimension of hue, advanced bilinguals exhibit focus shift towards the L2 for this category as well but, in the dimension of lightness, advanced bilinguals seem to be shifting away from the L2, and select an exemplar that is even lighter than the one selected by their intermediate-level counterparts. This suggests that bilingual semantic shift of color prototypes need not always occur in the direction of the L2. In this particular case advanced bilinguals shift their prototypes for *ble* towards *blue*, but they also maintain the perceptual distance in lightness between *ble* and *ghalazio* prototypes by shifting the latter away from *blue*. This is evidence that advanced bilinguals have established a category prototype that is unique and dissimilar to that displayed by lower-proficiency bilinguals. This supports Cook's and Grosjean's claims that bilinguals are unique language users with their own distinct language system and way of representing reality.

In this light, future studies may attempt to gather prototype data not only for the categories of interest but also for a broader set of categories to see whether shift in one category dimension may influence semantic representation of other categories. In addition, we cannot know from the current data the relative influence of language proficiency per se and length of cultural immersion in the L2-speaking country. The advanced bilinguals here had all been living in the UK while the intermediate bilinguals had all been living in Greece. Future studies may attempt to dissociate language proficiency and length of immersion by gathering data from groups of equal proficiency but different lengths of stay, and vice versa. Correlational analyses would also shed considerable light on the relative influence of such variables on bilingual semantic representation. However, in the case of prototype identification such analyses are very difficult, or indeed impossible, to carry out due to the qualitative nature of the data gathered. The next section presents data from similarity judgments of light and dark blue color squares and rests on correlational analyses in order to shed light on the relative influence of variables such as proficiency, length of immersion, age of L2 acquisition, etc. on bilingual cognition. More specifically, it moves away from semantic representation, which was the concern of this section, and looks at cognitive processing of native color categories in Greek–English bilinguals. The aim is to see whether bilinguals think about their native categories differently as a function of several characteristics of the bilingual person. The area of cognition under investigation is categorical perception: People's tendency to perceive perceptual continua such as color as discontinuous discrete categories, resulting in finer discriminations across category boundaries than within category boundaries (Harnad, 1987, 2005).

BILINGUAL COGNITION: THE CASE OF GREEK BLUES

The second experiment in Athanasopoulos (2009) sought to establish whether the previously observed shift in semantic representation would also be observed in Greek–English bilinguals' categorical perception. Bilinguals may shift their category prototypes towards the L2 or may establish new ones, but underlying cognition of the difference between *ble* and *ghalazio* may remain unchanged. On the other hand, using a second language that does not lexically mark the boundary between two native categories may lead to cognitive restructuring of perception of those categories. Previous research shows that participants rate two colors to be more similar if they fall within a category boundary than if they cut across the boundary (Roberson et al., 2000, 2005). In the case of Greek speakers, Athanasopoulos (2009) asked participants to rate the perceptual similarity between pairs of stimuli that are within the *ble* or *ghalazio* boundary, and pairs of stimuli that crossed the boundary. Participants' ratings were then correlated with their semantic memory for *ble*, *ghalazio*, and *blue*, their general L2 proficiency, their length of stay in the L2-speaking country, their age of L2 acquisition, and the degree to which they used their L2 in their everyday lives. Given that previous studies in other domains (number, time, motion events) had shown independent effects of some of those variables on bilingual cognitive shift (see e.g., Athanasopoulos, 2006; Bassetti, 2007; Boroditsky, 2001; Boroditsky, Ham, & Ramscar, 2002; Cook, Bassetti, Kasai, Sasaki, & Takahashi, 2006), the aim of these correlations was to help elucidate the precise impact of each of these variables on bilingual cognition.

Participants

Participants were 30 adult native speakers of Greek who had not taken part in the previous experiment (20 female, 10 male, age range 19–32 years). They were all bilingual in English and were studying at a UK university. Their mean score on the Nation vocabulary test was 75/90 (SD = 9), with scores ranging from 61 to 90. Their mean length of stay in the UK was 33 months (SD = 27 months), ranging from 2 to 96 months. Their mean age of L2 acquisition was 7 years (SD = 3 years), ranging from 1 to 13 years. They reported using English for 9 hours per day on average (SD = 4), ranging from 3 to 17 hours.

   In addition to all the measures above, Athanasopoulos (2009) asked participants to write down all the color names they could think of, first in one language and then, after an intervening filler task, in the other (counterbalanced across the whole sample). This task was given in order to measure availability of the relevant color terms in the bilingual lexicon. The higher up the list a term appears, the more available it is in bilingual memory. The aim was to correlate the semantic saliency of each term (i.e., how high it appears in the list) with participants' similarity judgments. On average, *ble* was placed sixth on the list (SD = 4, range 1–17), *ghalazio* was placed twelfth (SD = 7, range 2–28), and *blue* was placed fifth (SD = 3, range 1–13).

Materials and procedure

The stimuli were individual 10 × 20 mm glossy Munsell chips, mounted on 40-mm square pieces of white card. Five pairs of within-category stimuli and three pairs of cross-category stimuli were created by asking 20 native Greek participants who did not take part in this experiment to name several chips from the blue area of Munsell space. Within-category stimuli were constructed so that both members were within the same category (i.e., both were named *ble* or both *ghalazio*), and cross-category stimuli were created so that members cut across the *ble*/*ghalazio* boundary (i.e., one was named *ble* and the other *ghalazio*). The Munsell designations of the stimuli used are expressed in the form Hue/Lightness (Munsell Value)/Saturation) (Munsell Chroma). The within-category pairs were 10B/2/6–10B/4/10,

5PB/2/8–5PB/4/12, 5B/6/8–5B/8/4, 10B/6/10–10B/8/6, and 5PB/6/10–5PB/8/6. The cross-category pairs were 5B/4/10–5B/6/8, 10B/4/10–10B/6/10, and 5PB/4/12–5PB/6/10. All stimuli were perceptually equidistant, meaning that the perceptual distance between each stimulus was maintained at two lightness levels.

Participants were asked to judge 'how different or similar these two colors are' using a 10-point scale where 10 represents maximum dissimilarity and 1 represents maximum similarity. Each pair was shown twice, counterbalancing the position of each individual chip in the pair. All participants were tested in the UK. After the similarity judgment task, participants completed a personal information questionnaire, then the color list for one language was elicited, then the Nation test was administered, and finally the color list for the other language was elicited. The similarity judgment task was also given to a group of English monolinguals of comparable age and socioeconomic background. Instructions were given to all participants in their native language by a Greek–English bilingual speaker.

Results and discussion

The analysis first focused on comparing bilinguals' similarity judgments to those of English monolinguals (see Table 11.1). A 2 (Group: English vs. Greek) × 2 (Pair type: Within vs. Cross) mixed ANOVA showed that the main effects of Group and Pair type were not significant, $F(1, 50) = .513$, $p > .05$, and $F(1,50) = .448$, $p > .05$ respectively. The Group × Pair type interaction approached significance, $F(1, 50) = 3.247, p = .08$.

Correlational analyses were then performed to examine to what degree bilingual cognition is influenced by general L2 proficiency as measured by the Nation test, length of stay in the L2 country, age of L2 acquisition, amount of L2 use, and semantic saliency of *ble*, *blue*, and *ghalazio*, as measured by the position of each term on each participant's list of color terms. For this purpose, a new variable was calculated, hereafter called the Categorical Perception Index (CPI), by subtracting each participant's mean similarity judgment score for within-category pairs from their mean similarity judgment score for cross-category pairs. The greater the remaining score, the more distinction is made between within- and cross-category

Table 11.1 Mean similarity judgments (and standard deviations) of *ble* and *ghalazio* in within- and cross-category pairs

Pair type	Greek–English bilinguals	English monolinguals
Within-category	4.08 (0.99)	4.08 (0.86)
Cross-category	4.34 (1.07)	3.96 (1.22)

Figures are rounded to the nearest two decimal places.

pairs. CPI was then correlated with each of the aforementioned variables, while partialling out all the other variables. This would ensure that any significant correlation obtained reveals a true relationship between two variables, eliminating all other potentially confounding or mediating variables.

The strongest significant correlation was obtained for semantic saliency of *ble* ($r = -0.53, p < .01$). This means that the further down *ble* appears on the color list (and thus the greater its number on the list), the less bilinguals distinguish between within- and cross-category pairs. There was also a moderate correlation with semantic saliency of *blue* ($r = 0.41, p < .05$), such that the higher *blue* appears in each participant's color list (and thus the smaller its number on the list), the less distinction is made between within- and cross-category pairs. Finally, the weakest significant correlation was obtained for length of stay in the UK ($r = -0.39$), such that the more bilinguals have stayed in the L2 country, the less they distinguish between within- and cross-category pairs. None of the rest of the variables correlated significantly with CPI.

These findings show that a systematic analysis of the relationship between several linguistic and extra-linguistic variables and bilingual cognition reveals that *both* specific linguistic knowledge (measured here by color lists) as well as cultural immersion (measured by length of stay in the L2-speaking country) may independently affect the way bilinguals think about categorical distinctions made in their L1. The significant relationship between the availability of specific terms in the bilingual lexicon and bilingual cognition shows a direct link between specific linguistic items (in this case color terms) and categorical perception. The significant relationship between length of stay and bilingual cognition shows that bilinguals may think differently not only as a function of linguistic experience per se, but also as a function of immersion into the L2-speaking environment. The novelty of this particular study is the fact that these variables were individually correlated with bilingual cognition while controlling for the effects of all the other variables. This means that linguistic knowledge can independently affect bilingual cognition, and, conversely, that cultural immersion in the L2-speaking country can also independently affect bilingual cognition. More importantly, perhaps, the link between the weakening of an L1 color term in semantic memory and bilingual cognition shows that it might not just be acquisition of novel linguistic categories that may influence the way bilinguals behave in cognitive tasks, but also attrition of the original L1 term in semantic memory.

Finally, the finding of a persistent effect of length of stay in the L2 country, but not of general L2 proficiency as measured by the Nation vocabulary test, suggests one of two things. One possibility is that socio-cultural factors like length of stay exert a stronger influence on bilingual cognition than general language proficiency, at least for the domain of color. The other possibility is that the Nation test alone is not an accurate reflection of true language proficiency, as it is designed to test vocabulary knowledge only. Future studies across different domains could use a range of other available proficiency tests in addition to the Nation test in order to obtain a more informed measure of overall language proficiency. For example, some studies on grammatical number and object classification show effects of length of stay and not of general L2 proficiency as indicated by the Nation test (Cook et al., 2006), while other studies in the same domain demonstrate robust effects of L2 proficiency as indicated by another test, the Oxford Quick Placement test, which measures performance on a range of language features including grammar, syntax and vocabulary (Athanasopoulos, 2006, 2007).

Studies to date have shown that, because of the dynamic nature of bilingualism, it is possible to directly investigate effects of several types of variables on the changing linguistic and cognitive state of the bilingual person. Studies from other domains point to the synergistic influence of both linguistic and sociocultural variables on the bilingual mind. For example, a study of grammatical gender and picture similarity judgments in a group of Spanish–German bilinguals revealed a strong relationship between similarity scores and language proficiency, age of acquisition, and length of language use (Boroditsky, Schmidt, & Phillips, 2003; see also Bassetti, 2007; Kousta, Vinson, & Vigliocco, 2008). Brown and Gullberg (2008) showed that Japanese–English bilinguals shifted their gesture behavior towards the English pattern even when they were living and tested in Japan. Dewaele (2004) found that self-rated proficiency in a language and frequency of use of a language significantly predicted perception of emotional force of swearwords in multilinguals. These studies point to the conclusion that the precise relationship between language and bilingual cognition might be more complex than previously thought. To probe this relationship further, Athanasopoulos, Damjanovic, Krajciova and Sasaki (in press) conducted a study that looks into the way Japanese–English bilinguals evaluate perceptual distinctions of dark and light blue stimuli, to be described in the next section.

THE CASE OF JAPANESE BLUES

Like Greek, Japanese divides the blue region of color space into a darker shade called *ao* and a lighter shade called *mizuiro* (Uchikawa & Boynton, 1987). Athanasopoulos et al.'s (in press) goal was to see to what degree bilingual cognition remains flexible in bilinguals who have advanced proficiency in both their languages. Thus the study tested categorical perception of color in late bilinguals who have attained a high level of proficiency in the L2 and who live and study in the L2-speaking country. The hypothesis was that advanced bilinguals may display cognitive flexibility, indicating that they can 'behave' in an L1-like or L2-like way depending on linguistic and/or sociocultural variables. Thus the study kept L2 proficiency constant and tested the effects of length of stay in the L2-speaking country, frequency of L1 and L2 use, and testing context, such that some bilinguals were tested in Japanese by a Japanese native speaker, and some were tested in English by a non-Japanese speaker.

Participants

The participants were 12 monolingual Japanese speakers (8 females, 4 males, mean age 26 years, $SD = 4$), 15 monolingual English speakers (8 females, 7 males, mean age 24 years, $SD = 5$), and 27 Japanese–English bilingual speakers (19 females, 8 males, mean age 27 years, $SD = 5$). The Japanese monolingual participants were all university students in Japan, studying non-English language-related subjects. They were selected from a larger pool of potential participants who had just arrived in the UK to attend an English summer school. None of them had stayed in the UK or another English-speaking country for more than 2 weeks. In addition, their mean score on the Nation test was 49/90, $SD = 3$, which is usually indicative of low English proficiency. The majority of these participants self-reported that their proficiency in English was 'Poor' or 'Basic' on a 4-point scale that included the categories 'Poor', 'Basic', 'Intermediate', and 'Advanced'.

The Japanese–English bilingual participants were undergraduate or postgraduate students in the UK and all had Japanese as their native language. They had started learning English as a second language at a mean age of 12, $SD = 0.6$, range 10–13 years. Their mean score on the Nation test was 76/90 ($SD = 4$, range 70–88). Their mean length of stay in the UK was 38 months ($SD = 33$ months, range 2–114 months). They reported that they used English 57% of the time, on average, in their daily activities ($SD = 22$, range 15–100) and Japanese 43% of the time ($SD = 22$, range 0–85).

The English monolingual participants were undergraduate and postgraduate students in the UK. All participants reported that they had normal color vision, and were rewarded for their participation.

Materials and procedure

A total of 10 color stimuli were used from a range supplied by the Color-Aid Corporation (www.coloraid.com). The Coloraid system is commonly used in color research (e.g., Laws, Davies, & Andrews, 1995) and it is used here mainly for ecological validity purposes. While Athanasopoulos (2009) used the Munsell system, it is desirable to be able to demonstrate robust effects of language on bilingual cognition using a range of different stimuli. The selected stimuli came from the Blue (B) and Cyan Blue (C) Hue range, and varied across six levels of lightness, called 'Hue', 'Tint 1' (T1),

'Tint 2' (T2), 'Tint 3' (T3), 'Tint 4' (T4), and 'Light Tint' (LT), going from darkest to lightest. Color-aid codes for each stimulus are expressed in the form Hue/Lightness. The stimuli we used were: B/T1, B/T2, B/T3, B/T4, C/Hue, C/T1, C/T2, C/T3, C/T4, and C/LT. These stimuli were consistently named *ao* or *mizuiro* by 17 Japanese monolinguals in a naming database compiled by Athanasopoulos, Sasaki, and Cook (2004). The stimuli were mounted on 40-mm square pieces of white card. They were then organized into within- and cross-category pairs. Within-category pairs were constructed so that both members were named either *ao* or *mizuiro*. Cross-category pairs were constructed so that one member of the pair was called *ao* and the other *mizuiro*. Stimuli within the pair were perceptually equidistant with a perceptual distance of two lightness steps. The within-category pairs constructed were C/T2–C/T4 and C/T3–C/LT. The cross-category pairs were C/Hue–C/T2, and C/T1–C/T3.

Pairs of stimuli were presented to each participant one at a time in random order. Participants were asked to judge 'how different or similar these two colors are' using a 10-point scale where 10 represents maximum dissimilarity and 1 represents maximum similarity. Each pair was shown twice, counterbalancing the position of each individual stimulus in the pair. All participants were tested in the UK. Bilinguals were given a linguistic/sociocultural background questionnaire and the Nation test to complete after the similarity judgment task. All monolinguals received instructions in their native language: 11 bilinguals were given instructions in Japanese by a native Japanese speaker, and 16 bilinguals were given instructions in English by a near-native English speaker who did not speak Japanese.

Results and discussion

Figure 11.2 shows the mean similarity judgments of cross-category and within-category pairs of stimuli for the three groups. A 3 (Group: English monolinguals vs. Japanese monolinguals vs. Bilinguals) × 2 (Pair type: Within vs. Cross) mixed ANOVA showed that the main effect of Group was not significant, $F(2, 51) = 0.502, p < .05$, while there was a significant main effect of Pair type, $F(1, 51) = 5.917, p < .05$. Crucially, the interaction was statistically significant, $F(2, 51) = 3.788, p < .05$. This means that there are differences between the groups in how they judge the difference between within- and cross-category pairs.

Planned comparisons *t*-tests showed that Japanese monolinguals distinguished more between cross-category than within-category pairs, $t(11) = -3.36, p < .01$, while English monolinguals did not, $t(14) = 0.88, p > .05$. For the Japanese–English bilinguals, the difference between within- and cross-category pairs approached but did not reach significance, $t(26) = -1.94$, $p = .06$. This finding shows that the Japanese–English bilingual group pattern seems to be between that of the two monolingual groups. Following Athanasopoulos (2009), correlations between similarity judgments and all

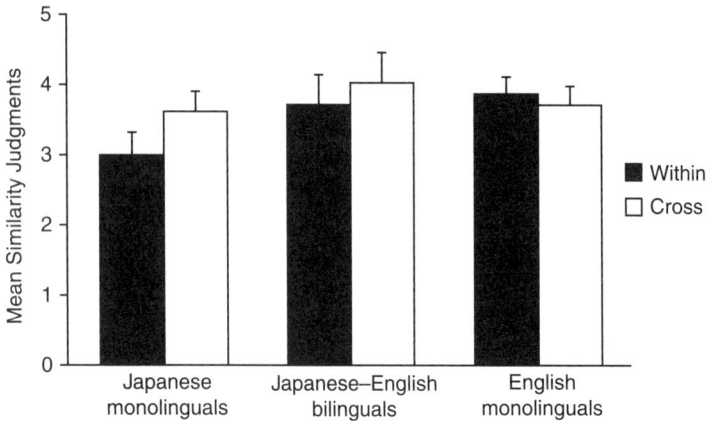

Figure 11.2 Mean similarity judgments of within- and cross-category pairs across the three groups.

the linguistic and sociocultural variables that were measured for the bilinguals were conducted.

As in Athanasopoulos (2009), a new variable was created for the correlational analyses called the Categorical Perception Index (CPI) by subtracting each participant's mean similarity judgment score for within-category pairs from their mean similarity judgment score for cross-category pairs. The greater the resulting score, the more distinction is made between within- and cross-category pairs. This was correlated with each bilingual's score on the Nation vocabulary test, their length of stay in the L2 country, their amount of L2 use (the amount of L1 use was 1 minus the amount of L2 use, since participants were asked what proportion of their daily activities is conducted in the L2 and what proportion in the L1), and the experimental setting that participants were in (i.e., whether they were given task instructions in Japanese by a native Japanese speaker or in English by a near-native English speaker who did not speak any Japanese). CPI correlated significantly only with amount of L2 use, $r = -.54$, $p < .01$. This means that the more bilinguals use English in their daily interactions (and the less they use Japanese), the less distinction they make between within- and cross-category pairs.

This study, then, shows that individuals who have reached an advanced level of proficiency in the L2 may still display cognitive flexibility, behaving in an L1-like or L2-like way depending on linguistic and/or sociocultural variables. Specifically, the degree to which advanced bilinguals resembled monolingual speakers of their L2 when they evaluated perceptual distinctions of colors depended on which language they used most frequently in their daily activities. Bilinguals who used predominantly English performed more similarly to English monolinguals, while bilinguals who used predominantly Japanese resembled more Japanese monolinguals. There was no effect of length of stay in the UK or of testing context. These findings may suggest that it is ultimately language rather than cultural exposure that drives the observed shift in bilingual cognition. However, length of stay in the L2 country is likely to be mediating this relationship, since living in the UK and immersing oneself in its culture would potentially facilitate English use for these bilinguals.

GENERAL DISCUSSION

Taking early studies of semantic representation of color categories in bilinguals (Caskey-Sirmons & Hickerson, 1977; Ervin, 1961) as well as current methods used in linguistic relativity research as points of departure, the studies by Athanasopoulos (2009) and Athanasopoulos et al. (in press) reviewed here took first steps in addressing categorical perception of color in bilinguals. The study by Athanasopoulos (2009) asked whether cognitive processing of L1 color categories would be influenced by a number of variables that characterize the bilingual person. First, Athanasopoulos (2009) replicated the early findings of bilingual semantic shift, showing that advanced bilinguals shift the focus of one of their L1 categories towards the L2 category focus. However, Athanasopoulos (2009) also showed that bilinguals may also create entirely new category prototypes, as demonstrated by the case of *ghalazio*, which advanced bilinguals shifted towards the L2 in the dimension of hue, but away from the L2 in the dimension of lightness. Data from a similarity judgment task of dark and light blue squares showed that categorical color perception in bilinguals is influenced by availability of specific color terms in the lexicon, as well as length of stay in the L2 country. Thus, in addition to the established semantic shift of color categories in bilinguals, Athanasopoulos's (2009) study revealed that a core component of higher-level cognition, categorical perception, is also affected.

The subsequent study by Athanasopoulos et al. (in press) asked whether bilingual cognition fossilizes once bilinguals reach an advanced level of proficiency in the L2, or whether it is still flexible. Results from a categorical perception task showed that Japanese–English bilinguals' similarity judgments were in between those of monolinguals of either language, and that frequency of language use correlated with the degree to which bilinguals resembled either monolingual pattern. This demonstrates the dynamic and flexible nature of bilingual cognition even when advanced levels of L2 proficiency have been reached.

These first studies on color and bilingual cognition, then, demonstrate that the study of bilingual cognition in the context of linguistic relativity research may yield benefits for both fields. For example, one of the major issues in the study of language and thought is whether the cognitive differences between different populations are due to language differences per se, or due to extra-linguistic cultural differences. Because bilingual cognitive patterns can be examined at various stages of development, it is possible to measure the relative impact of both linguistic and extra-linguistic variables in 'real time'. Thus the finding by Athanasopoulos (2009) that availability of specific color terms in the bilingual lexicon, as well as length of stay in the L2-speaking country, could independently predict cognitive shift suggests a synergistic influence of language and culture on human cognition. Athanasopoulos et al. (in press) further elucidated the intricate relationship between language, culture, and thought, by showing that frequency of language use can affect categorical perception patterns in advanced bilinguals. Obviously, frequency of language use itself is indirectly contingent on the culture of residence. So living in the L2-speaking country provides more opportunity to socialize with native speakers of the L2, and thus facilitates increased usage of the L2. Thus, investigating linguistic relativity through bilingualism shows that the language/culture dichotomy may not be as rigid as previously thought. Rather it seems that both language and culture may affect human cognition in the domain of color.

Aside from the language/culture debate, the findings from the study of bilingual cognition demonstrate that bilingualism is a variable that researchers can no longer ignore. For example, Berlin and Kay (1969) interpreted the finding that speakers of different languages had color prototypes similar to those of English speakers as evidence for universality, and explicitly stated that they believed their participants' bilingualism could not have influenced the results (see the first section of this chapter). Given the findings of prototype shift by Ervin (1961), Caskey-Sirmons and Hickerson (1977), and Athanasopoulos (2009), Berlin and Kay's (1969) findings could be attributed to bilingual semantic shift rather than universal tendencies. Other studies that have overlooked their participants' bilingualism have yielded inconsistent results. Laws et al. (1995) found no differences in categorical perception of blue between Russian and English speakers, but a more recent study by Winawer et al. (2007) reported significant differences between populations. In both studies Russian participants were bilingual in English, with varying degrees of L2 proficiency, yet no measures controlled for any possible influence of their bilingualism on the results. Some studies rule out the possibility of any effect of a second language on cognition by making a priori assumptions about their participants' proficiency or cultural immersion. For example, in Munnich, Landau, and Dosher's (2001) study of spatial cognition, the authors claim that knowledge of L2 English would play no role in their non-native English participants' cognition because 'even with substantial exposure to English, participants would not be expected to gain a native-like proficiency in English' (p. 180). The studies of bilingual cognition reviewed here have shown that it is not necessary for participants to have 'native-like' proficiency of the other language for the other language to influence their cognitive dispositions. Furthermore, exposure to the L2-speaking culture as well as frequency of language use can also have profound effects. Therefore rather than dismissing or ignoring bilingualism in their studies, researchers would do better to rigorously study its effects and the variables that may influence bilingual cognition.

Turning now to the benefits of linguistic relativity research for bilingualism, several scholars have long argued that to investigate conceptual representation in bilinguals one needs to triangulate evidence both from linguistic tasks and, crucially, from non-linguistic reasoning tasks (Green, 1998; Pavlenko, 1999). Tasks that measure higher-level cognitive processes such as categorical perception have been shown to be particularly useful in elucidating underlying conceptual representation of the perceived world (Jarvis & Pavlenko, 2008). In the case of bilingualism, non-linguistic tasks can be used to address a range of possibilities regarding conceptual representation. For example, the studies reviewed here suggest that bilinguals at lower levels of proficiency, or with little experience in the L2-speaking culture, may use L1-based representations when processing color distinctions. This is in line with Jarvis and Pavlenko's (2008) suggestion that L1-based transfer is usually observable at early stages of foreign language learning. As expertise with the L2-speaking culture and language increases, pre-existing representations also seem to undergo some degree of restructuring, with bilinguals typically exhibiting behavior that is 'in between' that of monolinguals of either language.

Finally, the findings from color perception in bilinguals have important implications for modeling the bilingual lexicon because they provide information about mental representations, thus contributing to the question of whether bilinguals have integrated or separated conceptual categories. The current findings suggest that bilinguals may have a much more complex conceptual organization than previously thought, and may exhibit the full range of possibilities proposed (with total separation and total integration of/across/between? the two poles of a continuum, see e.g., Cook, 2002) depending on several dynamic variables like proficiency, cultural immersion, and frequency of language use, highlighting the multi-competent nature of the bilingual mind. This implies that the task of L2 learners is not only to map new words onto pre-existing concepts, as has been traditionally assumed in models of lexical retrieval and conceptual access (see e.g., Kroll, 1993; Kroll & De Groot, 1997), but also to create new concepts either by internalizing concepts that are specific to the L2, or by merging existing concepts with new ones.

CONCLUSION

This chapter has provided a review of recent attempts to investigate semantic representation and cognitive processing of color in bilinguals.

Data from prototype identification and categorical perception tasks revealed semantic and cognitive shifts which were attributed to increasing expertise with the second language and culture, as well as to availability of specific color terms in the mental lexicon and the frequency of use of either language in the daily activities of bilinguals. Due to the exploratory nature of the studies, conclusions drawn from them remain tentative, and invite further research in order to arrive at a more nuanced picture of representation of color categories in the bilingual mind. Such a picture will be informed by examining several variables in detail, as well as using more recent techniques that study real-time processing, utilizing advances in online cognitive paradigms (see e.g., Roberson, Pak, & Hanley, 2008; Winawer et al., 2007) as well as neurophysiological techniques that may reveal very early perception of color in the visual processing stream (see e.g., Athanasopoulos, Wiggett, Dering, Kuipers, & Thierry, 2009; Thierry, Athanasopoulos, Wiggett, Dering, & Kuipers, 2009). The findings presented here do, however, lend considerable support to Cook's multi-competence hypothesis, highlighting the dynamic and flexible nature of the bilingual mind. Any theoretical model of language processing and cognition would need to accommodate the changing nature of both, paying particular attention to the variables that modulate the link between them, and the mechanisms that are involved in their interaction.

REFERENCES

Androulaki, A., Gomez-Pestana, N., Mitsakis, C., Jover, J. L., Coventry, K., & Davies, I. (2006). Basic colour terms in Modern Greek: Twelve terms including two blues. *Journal of Greek Linguistics, 7,* 3–45.

Athanasopoulos, P. (2006). Effects of the grammatical representation of number on cognition in bilinguals. *Bilingualism: Language and Cognition, 9,* 89–96.

Athanasopoulos, P. (2007). Interaction between grammatical categories and cognition in bilinguals: The role of proficiency, cultural immersion, and language of instruction. *Language and Cognitive Processes, 22,* 689–699.

Athanasopoulos, P. (2009). Cognitive representation of colour in bilinguals: The case of Greek blues. *Bilingualism: Language and Cognition, 12,* 83–95.

Athanasopoulos, P., Damjanovic, L., Krajciova, A., & Sasaki, M. (in press). Representation of colour concepts in bilingual cognition: The case of Japanese blues. *Bilingualism: Language and Cognition.*

Athanasopoulos, P., Sasaki, M., & Cook, V. J. (2004). *Do bilinguals think differently from monolinguals?* Paper presented at the 14th European Second Language Association Conference, San Sebastian, Spain, 8–11 September.

Athanasopoulos, P., Wiggett, A., Dering, B., Kuipers, J., & Thierry, G. (2009). The Whorfian mind: Electrophysiological evidence that language shapes perception. *Communicative & Integrative Biology, 2,* 332–334.

Bassetti, B. (2007). Grammatical gender and concepts of objects in bilingual children. *International Journal of Bilingualism, 11,* 251–273.

Berlin, B., & Kay, P. (1969). *Basic color terms: Their universality and evolution.* Berkeley: University of California Press.

Boroditsky, L. (2001). Does language shape thought? English and Mandarin speakers' conceptions of time. *Cognitive Psychology, 43,* 1–22.

Boroditsky, L., Ham, W., & Ramscar, M. (2002). What is universal about event perception? Comparing English and Indonesian speakers. In W. D. Gray & C. D. Schunn (Eds.), *Proceedings of the 24th Annual Meeting of the Cognitive Science Society.* Mahwah, NJ: Lawrence Erlbaum Associates Inc.

Boroditsky, L., Schmidt, L., & Phillips, W. (2003). Sex, syntax, and semantics. In D. Gentner & S. Goldin-Meadow (Eds.), *Language in mind: Advances in the study of language and thought* (pp. 61–79). Cambridge, MA: MIT Press.

Brown, A., & Gullberg, M. (2008). Bidirectional crosslinguistic influence in L1–L2 encoding of manner in speech and gesture: A study of Japanese speakers of English. *Studies in Second Language Acquisition, 30,* 225–251.

Brown, R., & Lenneberg, E. (1954). A study in language and cognition. *Journal of Abnormal and Social Psychology, 49,* 454–462.

Caskey-Sirmons, L., & Hickerson, N. (1977). Semantic shift and bilingualism: Variation in the color terms of five languages. *Anthropological Linguistics, 19,* 358–367.

Cook, V. J. (1991). The poverty-of-the-stimulus argument and multi-competence. *Second Language Research, 7,* 103–117.

Cook, V. J. (1992). Evidence for multi-competence. *Language Learning, 42,* 557–591.

Cook, V. J. (1999). Going beyond the native speaker in language teaching. *TESOL Quarterly, 33,* 185–209.

Cook, V. J. (2002). Background to the L2 user. In V. Cook (Ed.), *Portraits of the L2 user* (pp. 1–31). Clevedon, UK: Multilingual Matters.

Cook, V. J. (2003). The changing L1 in the L2 user's mind. In V. Cook (Ed.), *Effects of the second language on the first* (pp. 1–18). Clevedon, UK: Multilingual Matters.

Cook, V. J., Bassetti, B., Kasai, C., Sasaki, M., & Takahashi, J. (2006). Do bilinguals have different concepts? The case of shape and material in Japanese L2 users of English. *International Journal of Bilingualism, 10,* 137–152.

Dewaele, J. M. (2004). The emotional force of swearwords and taboo words in the speech of multilinguals. *Journal of Multilingual and Multicultural Development, 25,* 204–222.

Ervin, S. (1961). Semantic shift in bilingualism. *American Journal of Psychology, 74,* 233–241.

Green, D. W. (1998). Bilingualism and thought. *Psychologica Belgica, 38,* 253–278.

Grosjean, F. (1982). *Life with two languages: An introduction to bilingualism.* Cambridge, UK: Cambridge University Press.

Grosjean, F. (1989). Neurolinguists, beware! The bilingual is not two monolinguals in one person. *Brain and Language, 36,* 3–15.

Grosjean, F. (1992). Another view of bilingualism. In R. Harris (Ed.), *Cognitive processing in bilinguals* (pp. 51–62). Amsterdam: North Holland.

Grosjean, F. (1998). Studying bilinguals: Methodological and conceptual issues. *Bilingualism: Language and Cognition, 1,* 131–149.

Harnad, S. (1987). *Categorical perception: The groundwork of cognition.* Cambridge, UK: Cambridge University Press.

Harnad, S. (2005). Cognition is categorization. In C. Lefebvre & H. Cohen (Eds.), *Handbook of categorization* (pp. 719–737). Amsterdam: Elsevier.

Heider, E. R., & Olivier, D. C. (1972). The structure of the colour space in naming and memory for two languages. *Cognitive Psychology, 3,* 337–354.

Hunt, E., & Agnoli, F. (1991). The Whorfian hypothesis: A cognitive psychology perspective. *Psychological Review, 98,* 377–389.

Jarvis, S., & Pavlenko, A. (2008). *Crosslinguistic influence in language and cognition.* New York: Routledge.

Kay, P., & McDaniel, C. K. (1978). The linguistic significance of the meanings of basic colour terms. *Language, 54,* 610–646.

Kousta, S. T., Vinson, D. P., & Vigliocco, G. (2008). Investigating linguistic relativity through bilingualism: The case of grammatical gender. *Journal of Experimental Psychology: Learning, Memory, and Cognition, 34,* 843–858.

Kroll, J. (1993). Accessing conceptual representations for words in a second language. In R. Schreuder & B. Weltens (Eds.), *The bilingual lexicon* (pp. 53–81). Amsterdam: John Benjamins.

Kroll, J., & De Groot, A. M. B. (1997). Lexical and conceptual memory in the bilingual: Mapping form to meaning in two languages. In A. M. B. De Groot & J. Kroll (Eds.), *Tutorials in bilingualism: Psycholinguistic perspectives* (pp. 169–199). Mawhah, NJ: Lawrence Erlbaum Associates Inc.

Laws, G., Davies, I., & Andrews, C. (1995). Linguistic structure and non-linguistic cognition: English and Russian blues compared. *Language and Cognitive Processes, 10,* 59–94.

Lenneberg, E. H., & Roberts, J. M. (1956). The language of experience: A study in methodology. *Memoir 13*: Supplement to *International Journal of American Linguistics, 22,* 13.

Lucy, J. A. (1992). *Grammatical categories and cognition. A case study of the linguistic relativity hypothesis.* Cambridge, UK: Cambridge University Press.

Majid, A., Bowerman, M., Kita, S., Haun, D. B. M., & Levinson, S. C. (2004). Can language restructure cognition? The case for space. *Trends in Cognitive Sciences, 8,* 108–114.

Munnich, E., Landau, B., & Dosher, B. (2001). Spatial language and spatial representation: A cross-linguistic comparison. *Cognition, 81,* 171–207.

Nation, P. (1990). *Teaching and learning vocabulary.* New York: Newbury House/ Harper Row.

Pavlenko, A. (1999). New approaches to concepts in bilingual memory. *Bilingualism: Language and Cognition, 2,* 209–230.

Pavlenko, A. (2005). Bilingualism and thought. In A. M. B. De Groot & J. F. Kroll (Eds.), *Handbook of bilingualism: Psycholinguistic approaches* (pp. 433–453). Oxford, UK: Oxford University Press.

Roberson, D. (2005). Color categories are culturally diverse in cognition as well as in language. *Cross-Cultural Research, 39,* 56–71.

Roberson, D., Davidoff, J., Davies, I., & Shapiro, L. (2005). Colour categories: Evidence for the cultural relativity hypothesis. *Cognitive Psychology, 50,* 378–411.

Roberson, D., Davies I., & Davidoff, J. (2000). Colour categories are not universal: Replications and new evidence from a Stone-Age culture. *Journal of Experimental Psychology: General, 129,* 369–398.

Roberson, D., & Hanley, J. R. (2007). Color categories vary with language after all. *Current Biology, 17,* 605–606.

Roberson, D., Pak, H. S., & Hanley, J. R. (2008). Categorical perception of colour in the left and right visual field is verbally mediated: Evidence from Korean. *Cognition, 107,* 752–762.

Thierry, G., Athanasopoulos, P., Wiggett, A., Dering, B., & Kuipers, J. (2009). Unconscious effects of language-specific terminology on pre-attentive colour perception. *Proceedings of the National Academy of Sciences, 106,* 4567–4570.

Uchikawa, K., & Boynton, R. M. (1987). Categorical color perception of Japanese observers: Comparison with that of Americans. *Vision Research, 27,* 1825–1833.

Whorf, B. L. (1940/1956). Linguistics as an exact science. In J. B. Carroll (Ed.), *Language, thought, and reality: Selected writings of Benjamin Lee Whorf* (pp. 220–232). Cambridge, MA: MIT Press.

Whorf, B. L. (1941/1956). Languages and logic. In J. B. Carroll (Ed.), *Language, thought, and reality: Selected writings of Benjamin Lee Whorf* (pp. 233–245). Cambridge, MA: MIT Press.

Winawer, J., Witthoft, N., Frank, M. C., Wu, L., Wade, A. R., & Boroditsky, L. (2007). Russian blues reveal effects of language on colour discrimination. *Proceedings of the National Academy of Sciences, 104,* 7780–7785.

12 Spatial language and second language acquisition

Kenny R. Coventry,
Pedro Guijarro-Fuentes, and
Berenice Valdés

Spatial language is important. It serves the basic function of enabling people to describe where objects are in the world, thereby directing hearers to objects and locations that they might otherwise be unable to find efficiently. Given this basic function, it is perhaps surprising that languages differ quite widely with respect to how spatial language is structured. For example, it is well known that containment and support relations are associated with different numbers of spatial prepositions (and their equivalents) across languages (see Bowerman, 1996). Spanish has a single term, *en*, that maps onto the use of *in* and *on* in English. Dutch more finely differentiates support relations, with one term (*aan*) for situations such as 'a handle on a door' and another (*op*) corresponding to situations such as 'a book on a shelf'. This presents a problem for second language learners/ bilinguals when learning second languages and switching between them.

In this chapter we first review experimental work that has identified the constraints that operate on spatial language comprehension in English and other languages. We then consider how spatial terms are acquired in the first language, and whether this learning may affect memory for spatial arrays and non-linguistic spatial judgments across different languages. Finally, we present an overview of a large-scale study examining spatial language in L1/bilingualism in English and Spanish. This study took the parameters identified as important for L1, and tested whether bilinguals at different levels of proficiency in English and Spanish differ in their mastery of these individual parameters. We show that L1 and bilingual acquisition share a number of similarities.

SPATIAL LANGUAGE AND THE FUNCTIONAL GEOMETRIC FRAMEWORK IN ENGLISH

Spatial language in English contains a wide range of terms across syntactic categories. Spatial prepositions such as *in*, *on*, and *over* in particular have received much attention in both linguistic analyses and empirical studies. With respect to the latter, there is now quite an extensive body of work that has examined the comprehension and production of spatial language in English using controlled experimental techniques. The main goal of this type of research is to understand how spatial language and the spatial world covary—a necessary precursor to the identification of the component lexical representations for specific prepositions (if there are any at all; see Elman, 2009). Here we briefly review some of the experimental data, which will also serve to motivate the manipulations in the large-scale study of L1 and bilingual English and Spanish acquisition we overview below.

Spatial prepositions indicate where one object (the located object, LO) is located with respect to a second (usually known) object (the reference object, RO), thus allowing hearers to narrow a search for an object (Landau & Jackendoff, 1993; Talmy, 1983). For example, *The apple is in the bowl* locates the apple with respect to the bowl, guiding the hearer to the bowl first and then directing attention to the region denoted by the preposition. According to the 'functional geometric framework' (see Coventry & Garrod, 2004), the situation-specific meaning of these terms in English is associated with three sets of interlocking constraints: geometric routines, dynamic-kinematic routines, and object/situational knowledge. We take each of these in turn.

To begin with, spatial prepositional use maps onto the geometric relations in the visual scenes (real or imaged) being described. Two examples will illustrate this. First, the so-called 'topological' term *in* is associated with containment, and *on* is associated with a support relation. Second, *above* and *over*, examples of so-called 'projective' prepositions (the set of prepositions that also include terms such as *to the left of*, *in front of*, etc.) share the same geometric constraints (at least in part); for these terms to be acceptable to describe a scene the LO—that is, the object located—must be located higher than the RO, that is, the reference object. So prepositions are associated with different geometric relations. However, it is important to note that these relations are graded, not absolute. For instance, it has been shown that *in* becomes less appropriate when the containment relation becomes weaker. Thus *the apple is in the bowl* becomes less acceptable as a description of the location of the apple the further away the apple is from the rim of the bowl (see Figure 12.1a). For higher placements, other prepositions (*on top of*, *over*, *above*, etc.) in turn become increasingly acceptable (see Garrod, Ferrier, & Campbell, 1999; Richards, Coventry, & Clibbens, 2004). In studies examining *above*, this term is preferred/rated as being more acceptable when the LO is located directly higher than the RO (see Figure 12.1b). As the LO is positioned progressively leftwards or rightwards with respect to the RO and/or downwards, acceptability ratings for this term go down incrementally (Hayward & Tarr, 1995; Logan & Sadler, 1996).

In addition to geometric relations, two further sets of constraints have been shown to be important for spatial language comprehension. These

(i)

(ii)

(iii)

(iv)

(a)

A	A	A	G	A	A	A
A	A	A	G	A	A	A
A	A	A	G	A	A	A
B	B	B		B	B	B
B	B	B	B	B	B	B
B	B	B	B	B	B	B
B	B	B	B	B	B	B

(b)

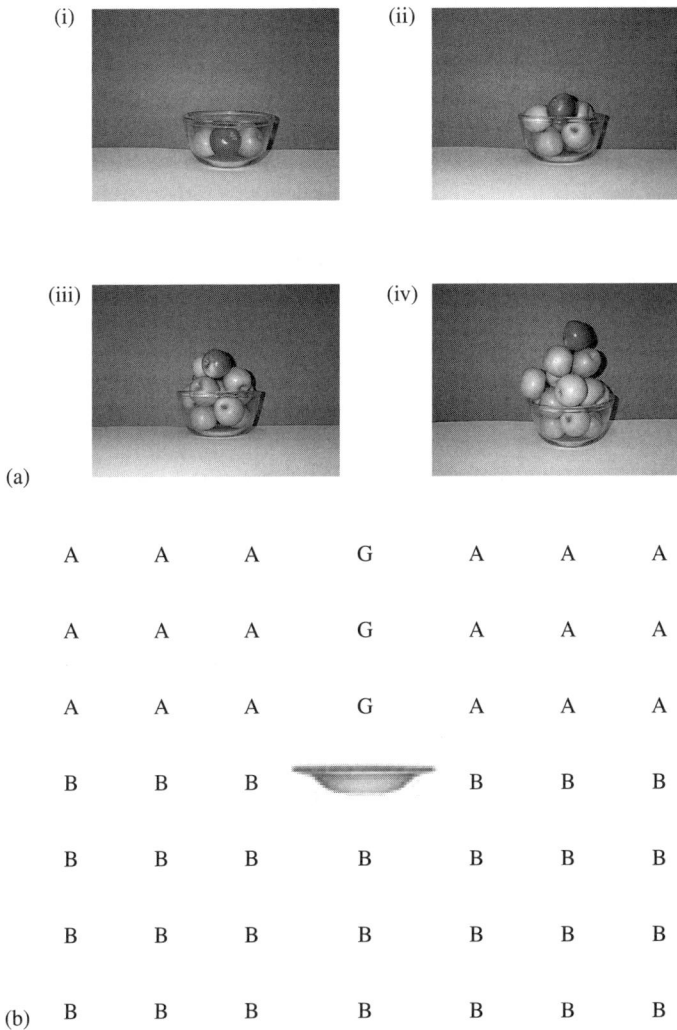

Figure 12.1 (a) Is the red apple in the bowl? As the height of pile increases ((i) to (iv)) *in* becomes a less-preferred description of where the red apple is located. (b) Gradedness for *above* (Logan & Sadler, 1996). When is an object above a bowl? G = good above relation, A = acceptable, B = bad.

so-called 'extra-geometric' constraints are what Coventry and Garrod classify as 'dynamic-kinematic routines' and 'object and situational knowledge' (Coventry & Garrod, 2004). 'Dynamic-kinematic' routines involve 'knowledge' of how objects interact in context. *A bottle above a glass* is usually associated with the situation where a bottle is not only positioned higher than a glass (geometry), but also where the bottle is in the correct position for the contained liquid to reach the glass when pouring. Several studies have shown that participants rate spatial descriptions as more appropriate to describe spatial scenes that illustrate such functional relations between objects, even when the scenes do not always show the best 'geometric' relations (e.g., Carlson-Radvansky, Covey, & Lattanzi, 1999; Carlson-Radvansky & Tang, 2000; Coventry et al., 2010c; Coventry, Prat-Sala, & Richards, 2001). In one study, Carlson-Radvansky et al. (1999) presented pictures of a coin positioned higher than a piggy bank. When the slot on the piggy bank was misaligned with the center of mass of the piggy bank, participants rated *the coin is above the piggy bank* as more appropriate when the coin was aligned with the slot rather than when the coin was aligned with the center of mass. In another study, Coventry et al. (2001) got participants to rate the appropriateness of sentences of the form *The person is PREPOSITION the object* to describe pictures that varied in both geometric relations and functional relations. The pictures showed a person holding an object with a protecting function (e.g., umbrella, shield) and the shown position of the object was crossed with the degree to which the object was shown to be fulfilling its protecting function (see Figure 12.2). In non-functional scenes, falling objects were shown missing the protecting object (bottom row, Figure 12.2), in functional scenes the objects were shown protecting the person holding the object (middle row), and in control scenes no falling objects were presented (top row). Coventry et al. (2001) found that the position of the falling objects affected judgments just as much as the position of the protecting object, even though the falling objects were never mentioned in the sentences to be rated.

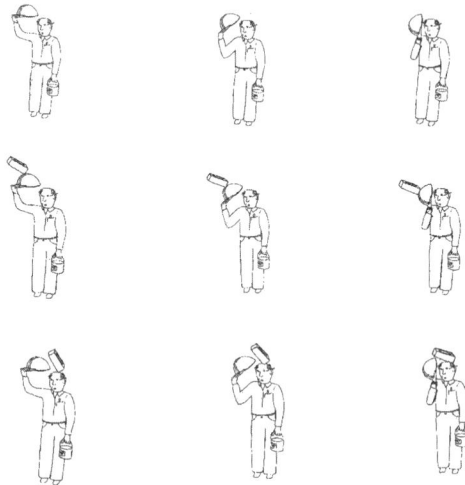

Figure 12.2 Example scenes from Coventry et al. (2001).

More recently Coventry et al. (2010c) have shown that people look at the potential end-point of falling objects when they are making judgments regarding whether an object is *over, under, above,* or *below* another object. Participants were asked to judge how appropriate sentences involving these prepositions were to describe pictures that followed. The pictures showed static images of containers, such as bottles, beginning to pour liquid/objects with a second container (e.g., a glass) underneath in various positions. Participants' eye fixations were measured using an eyetracker (Eyelink II) while they performed the task. Eye tracking works on the assumption that where people look corresponds with what they are attending to and what they are processing (see for example, Hoffman, 1998; Just & Carpenter, 1980; Rayner, 1998). Coventry et al. found that participants looked at the potential end-point of falling objects before they made their judgments, suggesting that participants mentally animate the static scene in order to establish whether falling objects will end up in the recipient container.

Another example of dynamic-kinematic routines is 'location control' which has been shown to underlie the comprehension and production of *in* and *on*. Location control is the case where an RO constrains the location of an object over time—the primary function of containers and supporting surfaces. Garrod et al. (1999) got participants to rate how appropriate sentences containing *in* were to describe pictures showing the location of a ball with reference to a container. The position of the ball with respect to the container was manipulated, but so was whether the ball and container would remain in the same relative location over time. This was achieved through the presence/absence of a string connected to the ball from above. The idea was that a string attached to a ball 'in' a bowl would compromise the control the container has over the location of the ball. One group of participants rated how appropriate *The ball is in the bowl* was to describe the scenes. A second group of participants rated the likelihood that the ball and bowl would remain in the same relative positions if the bowl were to be moved (judgments of degree of location control). Garrod et al. (1999) found a correlation between ratings of *in* from one group and the (non-linguistic) likelihood ratings from the other group, showing a strong association between judgments of location control and spatial language judgments. In another study, Richards et al. (2004) showed participants (adults and children) videos of plates, bowls, and objects placed in various configurations with respect to these supporting surfaces and containers. The task was to freely describe the location of an object marked with a colored star. In addition to manipulating the geometry of the scenes, degree of location control was manipulated by showing videos of movement. In the strong location control condition, RO plus LO (and other contents) were shown moving together from side to side at the same rate over time. In the weak location control condition the LO was shown wobbling side to side independently of the container/supporting surface and other contents. A further static (no movement) condition was also used as an experimental control condition (between strong and weak location control). Both children and adults described the LO as being *in* the RO (as first or only mention; see Richards et al., 2004, for more detail) most frequently in the strong location control condition and least frequently in the weak location control condition. These results show that the success with which an RO is shown to control the location of an LO over time directly impacts on spatial language choice to describe those scenes (and in particular on the choice of *in* and *on*).

The final constraint on the comprehension and production of spatial prepositions in the functional geometric framework is 'situational knowledge'. According to Coventry and Garrod (2004), geometric and dynamic-kinematic routines are driven by knowledge of objects and of how those objects typically interact, gleaned from past learned interactions. Coventry, Carmichael, and Garrod (1994) originally reported object-specific effects on the comprehension of *in* and *on*. Although a plate usually possesses a containing space (by virtue of its concave shape) it is usually conceptualized as a supporting object, and *on* is therefore the preposition associated with plates. However, the same object can be called a *dish*, and under those circumstances *in* becomes the appropriate preposition to use.

In addition to specific objects having associations with specific function and associated spatial relations, associations between objects also affect spatial prepositional choice. For example Carlson-Radvansky et al. (1999) found that prepositional choice was affected by functional relations between objects. Participants were asked to position (by sticking) a picture of an object in the location in accordance with an instruction. For example, they were asked to *Place a toothpaste tube above a toothbrush*. It was found that placements for objects that were associated with each other were between the center of mass (the midpoint) and the functional part (e.g., the bristles for the toothbrush). However, when the objects were not associated, such as a tube of paint and the toothbrush, placements were nearer the center of mass than the functional part. This suggests that object association affects the relative extent to which geometric or functional placements are expected.

In summary there are three interconnected sets of constraints associated with spatial preposition comprehension and production in English, namely 'geometric routines', 'dynamic-kinematic routines', and 'object/situational knowledge'. Moreover, these constraints individually are shared to some degree across prepositions. For example, as we have already seen, the 'dynamic-kinematic' routine of 'location control' is shared by *in* and *on*. What distinguishes them is geometric routines (and perhaps the strength of location control). *Over*, *under*, *above*, and *below* also exhibit different degrees of reliance on types of constraints. Coventry et al. (2001) found that ratings for sentences containing *over* and *under* (to describe pictures of the type shown in Figure 12.2) were more affected by functional relations between objects (e.g., the position of falling objects in Figure 12.2) than the ratings for *above* and *below*. And conversely ratings for sentences containing *above* and *below* were more affected by the position of the protecting object (e.g., the position of the hat in Figure 12.2) than the ratings for *over* and *under*. While the position of the object and the functional manipulation both influenced appropriateness ratings, this experiment produced the first evidence that *over/under* versus *above/below* are differentially influenced by geometric and extra-geometric information.

To sum up, the 'functional geometric framework' maintains that geometric and extra-geometric relations together affect the comprehension of spatial prepositions in English. There is also mounting evidence that the parameters in the functional geometric framework may well apply across a wide range of languages. Vandeloise (1991, 1994), in his analyses of French spatial prepositions, has recognized the importance of extra-geometric constraints. For example, he identifies the relation 'container/ contained' as underlying the semantics of *dans*, and this is in essence the location control routine similarly identified for *in* and *on* by Garrod and Sanford (1989). In Spanish there is also evidence that functional relations affect the comprehension of the prepositions *sobre/encima de/debajo de/ bajo*. In a series of experiments, Coventry and Guijarro-Fuentes (2004) compared acceptability ratings for *over/under/above/below* to ratings for these related Spanish prepositions using similar materials to those used by Coventry et al. (2001; see Figure 12.2). For the superior terms *sobre* and *encima de*, the results mirrored the findings for *over* and *above*. Acceptability ratings for *sobre* were more affected by functionality (e.g., whether the umbrella is shown to fulfill its function or not) than ratings for *encima de*. However, no differences in the influence of functionality and geometry were found for the inferior terms *debajo de* and *bajo*; ratings for both terms were strongly influenced by 'dynamic-kinematic' routines. Finally, the influence of the manipulation of geometry for superior and inferior prepositions in Spanish was weaker than for the equivalent terms in English (see also Regier & Carlson, 2002, for a related discussion of differences between German and English).

More generally, recently Feist (2008) has shown that the components of the 'functional geometric framework' apply across a much wider range of languages. She tested small groups of speakers of 24 languages across 11 different language families (e.g., Indo-European, Afro-Asiatic, Uralic, Dravidian, Austronesian, and Altaic). Speakers of these languages had to describe spatial relationships in static (line drawn) pictures adapted from Bowerman and Pederson (2010). The pictures illustrated varying degrees of enclosure, connectivity, and adhesion. Feist found that spatial relational terms spanning various degrees of specificity are influenced by geometric relations and extra-geometric relations. Although there is still much work to be done to examine the relative extent to which the parameters matter across a range of languages, it appears that the functional geometric framework may well be generally applicable as a means of capturing the relationship between spatial language and the spatial world.

ACQUIRING SPATIAL LANGUAGE IN THE FIRST LANGUAGE

Spatial terms start to appear in the lexicon of the child in the second year of life (e.g., Tomasello, 1987), but the development of spatial language continues through the first 8 years or so (Sinha, Thorseng, Hayashi, & Plunkett, 1994). Across languages the order in which spatial prepositions are first understood is very consistent (Bowerman, 1996; Piaget & Inhelder, 1956), beginning with the so-called 'topological' prepositions *in*, *on*, and *under* (in the second and third years) with proximity terms such as *next to* and *beside* occurring from the fourth year, followed by projective terms such as *behind* (*in back of*) and *in front of*. When projective prepositions are first used (around 5 years of age), they tend to be used only for objects that have identifiable intrinsic front and back sides. This corresponds with the child's ability to identify the sides of objects (e.g., Harris & Strommen, 1972; Kuczaj & Maratsos, 1975). Later these prepositions begin to be used for objects that do not have identifiable sides, requiring the child to project sides onto the object (as is the case, for example, where the front of an object is determined by direction of motion, as in the case of a moving train or ball). The last prepositions to appear in the lexicon are *between*, *over*, *above*, *left*, and *right* (e.g., Johnston, 1984, 1985; Johnston & Slobin, 1979; Sinha et al., 1994).

There has been much debate regarding the mapping between spatial language and non-linguistic spatial concepts during learning. Specifically, one can ask whether spatial knowledge structures the acquisition of spatial language, or alternatively whether spatial language plays a part in structuring (non-linguistic) spatial knowledge.

Pre-linguistically (i.e., before spatial language shows signs of presence) the infant already has quite sophisticated knowledge about spatial relations mapping onto both geometric and dynamic-kinematic routines. With regards to the former, it has been shown that infants at a very young age are able to make quite fine-grained geometric distinctions. Infants exhibit a general tendency to look longer at new stimuli than at familiar stimuli, and this has been used as a means of testing whether infants are able to distinguish between different spatial relations. At only a few months old, infants can distinguish between a whole range of spatial relations, including *left* and *right* (e.g., Behl-Chadha & Eimas, 1995) and *above*, *below*, and *between* (e.g., Quinn, Cummins, Kase, Martin, & Weissman, 1996).

With regards to extra-geometric relations, knowledge of physical relations is also in place prior to evidence that spatial language is present. This includes knowledge of containment and support relations, of gravity, and about how objects function (stereotypical function). For example, knowledge of containment and support relations beyond geometric relations has been found in infants only a few months old. Hespos and Baillargeon (2001) found that infants at age 2½ months appear to understand that when an object is placed inside a container the object is expected to move when the container moves. Infants were either shown an object being lowered inside a container or behind a container; when the container was moved, infants looked longer at the object still in its original location when it had been lowered inside the container compared to when it had been placed behind the container.

Although one would expect that spatial concepts in the early months of life develop equivalently across cultures, there are many differences in the ways in which languages map onto the spatial world. It is therefore natural to ask if the language that is being acquired packages spatial concepts as language learning unfolds, or alternatively whether the spatial knowledge pre-linguistic infants possess remains (and perhaps develops independently) during language learning. Differences between Korean and English have afforded careful testing between these alternatives.

English is a satellite language, expressing path using a constituent that is separate to the main verb, while Korean is a verb-framed language which expresses the path in the verb directly (see Talmy, 1985; see also Cadierno, 2008; Hasko, 2010). For example, in English one can say that the object was put out of the box, into the box, etc. Here the path is denoted by the preposition. In contrast, in verb-framed languages, such as Korean and Spanish, path is expressed in the verb itself. In English *a video cassette is put in/into a video case, a lid is put on a kettle, a pear is put in/into a bowl*, and *a glass is put on a table*, but in Korean the verb *kkita* is used for tight-fit path events (e.g., put video cassette in video case/put lid on kettle), *nehta* is used for loose-fit containment relations (e.g., put pear in bowl), and *nohta* is used for loose-fit support relations (e.g., put glass on table) (Bowerman, 1996). So English carves up containment and support relations based on geometric routine differences (recall that both *in* and *on* involve location control), while Korean carves up the spatial world according to degrees of fit/location control between objects. Such distinctions have allowed direct testing as to when these differences become salient during learning for first language learners of these languages.

Originally Choi and Bowerman (1991) tested whether children learning English and Korean extend meanings of terms based on the semantic structure of the language being learned. They found that English children produced *in* for paths into both tight- and loose-fit containers and extended their use of *in* accordingly, whereas Korean children produced *kkita* for putting objects into tight places, *nehta* for putting objects into loose containers, and extended their use accordingly. A follow-up study by Choi, McDonough, Bowerman, and Mandler (1999) employed a preferential looking task to assess the generalizations made by children learning either English or Korean. Children as young as 1½ to 2 years of age were found to spend more time looking at the language-appropriate aspects of spatial relations; Korean children looked more at tight-fit scenes than loose-fit scenes when hearing *kkita*, while English children looked more at containment scenes than non-containment scenes on hearing *in*. These results suggest that, at an early stage, the language being learned affects spatial categorization. However, two further studies suggest that, prior to this, both groups of children actually exhibit the same patterns of spatial distinctions. McDonough, Choi, and Mandler (2003) and Hespos and Spelke (2004) have provided evidence that 9- to 14-month-old Korean and English infants possess the same conceptual readiness for learning tight-fit/loose-fit relations. Both groups categorized tight and loose containment and tight and loose support, suggesting that language in fact reduces focus on an earlier distinction rather than producing a new one.

While the parameters required for spatial language understanding are available pre-linguistically (although they are packaged during development for the specific language), one can ask if the mapping between these parameters and spatial language itself unfolds through development. More specifically, one can ask if children focus on some aspects of knowledge relevant for spatial language before others. Two studies have tested spatial language in different age groups of children in English. Richards et al. (2004) tested children aged from 3;3 to 7;8 using the videos of containment and support described above. The task was to freely describe the position of an object marked with a star in each video. Critically the videos varied the degree of containment and support afforded in two ways: through the height of the pile of objects on which the LO was positioned (geometry), and through location control (the whole scene moving together from side to side, the LO moving on its own, no movement). Richards et al. found that children across age groups altered the word order in their spatial descriptions in order to highlight the functional salience of an object's location when describing such scenes. The effect of location control was present even for the youngest children. However, there was an interaction between the geometric manipulation and age group. Older children (and adults) changed their spatial language when talking about the location of objects based on the distance between the LO and the container/supporting surface, while younger children's spatial language was less influenced by height of pile. In contrast, children and adults similarly changed the way in which they described spatial location based on location control. Thus, it is possible that making graded geometric distinctions using language is something that continues to develop even when children have a command of spatial language.

In another study, Monrouxe, and Coventry (2010) asked children (aged from 6;7 to 11;5) and adults to describe the locations of objects which were presented along the vertical axis. The pictures were similar to those used by Coventry et al. (2010c), described above, and displayed static shots of teapots pouring tea with a cup below. The scenes manipulated the relative positions of teapot and cup (among other materials), and the extent to which the tea from the teapot ended up in the cup. Monrouxe and Coventry found that all participants—from the youngest to the adults— changed their spatial language in response to the presence/absence of a functional relation in the picture. However, when participants were required to produce an inferior description (e.g., to describe where the cup is in relation to the teapot) there were no effects of geometry (the relative positions of teapot and cup) on spatial description. So again this study suggests the primacy of functional relations over geometric relations, at least for situations involving objects that normally interact.

SPATIAL LANGUAGE AND LINGUISTIC RELATIVITY

As language learning unfolds, and children come to learn about the parameters that are relevant for their language, one can ask whether the differences in the way in which languages carve up the spatial world are associated with corresponding differences in non-linguistic spatial judgments. In other words, if a language makes certain distinctions and not others, does this affect the speaker's ability to make non-linguistic distinctions?

There is now much work that has asked the basic question whether the language one speaks affects how one makes non-linguistic distinctions— the so-called 'linguistic relativity' hypothesis. In order to test various versions of linguistic relativity, much work has examined whether differences in color perception are associated with differences in color terms across languages (see, for example, Athanasopoulos, Chapter 11, this volume; Regier, Kay, & Cook, 2005; Roberson, Davidoff, Davies, & Shapiro 2005), whether those who speak languages without extensive number terms have problems with number (e.g., Gelman & Butterworth, 2005; Gordon, 2004) and finally whether speakers of languages that differ in the spatial language distinctions they make also exhibit corresponding non-linguistic differences. The evidence for spatial terms is somewhat mixed.

One of the spatial language differences across languages that has received much attention in relation to linguistic relativity involves reference frame use differences across languages. In English the projective spatial prepositions, such as *to the left of*, *in front of*, and *above*, are dependent on reference frame selection in order to establish the direction in which the spatial relation applies. Levinson (1996) distinguishes between three basic types of reference frames: intrinsic, relative, and absolute. The intrinsic frame locates an object with respect to the salient axes of the RO; *to the left of the dog* is on the dog's left. The relative frame locates an object with respect to the position of the viewer or speaker; *to the left of the dog* is the region to the left of the dog from the viewer's perspective. Finally, the absolute frame locates an object with reference to salient fixed dimensions of the environment, as is the case with the use of cardinal directions. Now, while English and similar languages use the relative and intrinsic frames with which to locate objects in small-scale (tabletop) space, other languages such as Tzeltal use the absolute frame for small-scale space (e.g., the equivalent of the cup is north of the plate on the table). Pederson et al. (1998) have tested whether these differences in reference frame use affect performance across a range of 'non-linguistic' tasks. Imagine, for example, looking at a table on which several objects are placed. On your left is a pencil, on your right is a cup, and in between these objects, but further away from you, is a book. Imagine now turning 180 degrees. Now in front of you is a second table, and you are now asked to arrange the three objects so that the arrangement matches the arrangement you have just seen. Using variants of this basic task (for example, seeing a card on the first table with an arrangement of dots on it, and then selecting the matching card on the second table), Pederson et al. (1998) found that speakers of languages that use the absolute frame predominantly chose the card/arranged objects in the same location in the absolute frame, while speakers of languages such as Dutch and English chose the card with the dots in the same location within the relative frame. So the language one speaks appears to affect memory for spatial location.

One interpretation of these results is that they support a strong version of the linguistic relativity hypothesis—perhaps the language one speaks is associated with quite different spatial distinctions that speakers of those languages simply cannot avoid making. Alternatively, the data may support a weaker version of linguistic relativity—Slobin's thinking-for-speaking hypothesis—which maintains that language directs attention to some aspects of a visual scene while diminishing attention to other aspects (see Slobin, 1996). However, evidence for the effect of linguistic encoding on spatial memory and spatial categorization is not always forthcoming.

Coventry, Guijarro-Fuentes, and Valdés (2010a) tested whether differences between Spanish and English with respect to containment and support relations are associated with differing abilities for L1 Spanish and English speakers to immediately remember levels of concavity of containers and supporting surfaces. Using an on-line computer-based task, L1 Spanish and English speakers were shown an initial scene together with a sentence. For example, one of the scenes showed a hand with objects in/on it (see Figure 12.3). In English one can say that *the objects are in the hand* or *the objects are on the hand*. However, in Spanish *en* is appropriate for containment and support relations. A second picture was then presented which showed either the same level of concavity as the initial picture, or a lesser or greater degree of concavity (see Feist & Gentner, 2007, for results in English using this methodology). Participants were asked to indicate if this image was identical to or different from the previously seen image. We

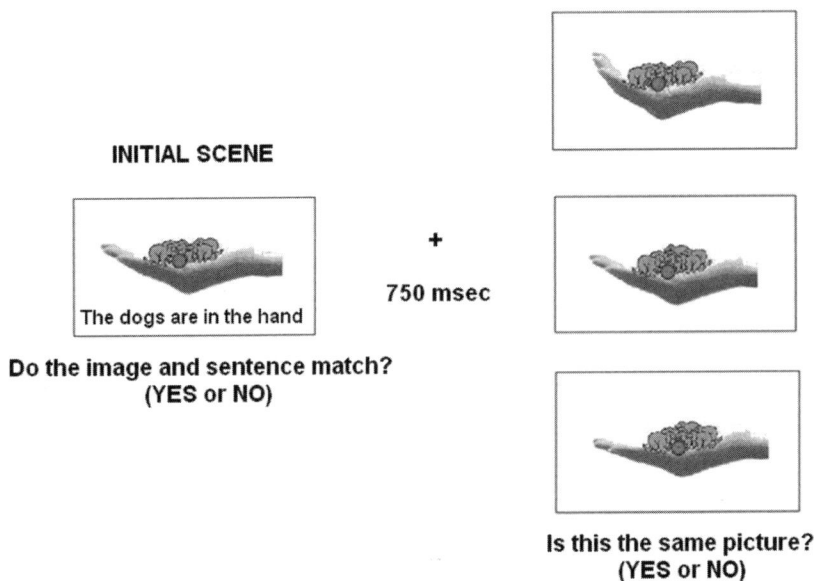

INITIAL SCENE

The dogs are in the hand

+

750 msec

Do the image and sentence match?
(YES or NO)

Is this the same picture?
(YES or NO)

Figure 12.3 Examples of scenes from Coventry et al. (2010a).

reasoned that the language distinctions participants have might bias memory for spatial scenes, and hence the extent to which they think they have seen pictures that they have in fact never seen before (false alarms). So it was predicted that a scene presented with *on* would result in false alarms (indicating 'same' when pictures were different) towards the lesser degree of concavity, and vice versa for scenes presented with *in* for English speakers. For Spanish speakers (where *en* was always presented), we expected no systematic pattern of false alarms given that *en* covers both containment and support relations. The results across a series of studies were somewhat surprising. There was a failure to find any evidence for an effect of language on immediate recognition of spatial relations. Coventry et al. argue that the failure to find any effects could be due to the short time interval between the prime and probe scenes, thus participants still have an active memory for the visual scene and do not get confused between memory for linguistic coding and memory for the spatial relation in the scene shown. These results do not discount the possibility that language can be used to facilitate memory (at encoding and retrieval) for spatial information, but they do question the stronger view that languages narrow or sharpen up non-linguistic spatial distinctions for speakers of those languages.

SPATIAL LANGUAGE AND BILINGUALISM

We have thus far outlined the functional geometric framework for spatial language comprehension and production, how components in the framework map onto first language learning, and whether languages that differ in these components might be associated with different underlying 'conceptual' representations. We now turn to consider spatial language in bilinguals at varying levels of proficiency.

One can ask whether the components in the functional geometric framework are equally hard to master over time in bilingual acquisition, and whether it is the case that bilinguals focus initially on single components, determined either by the most important distinctions made in their own first language, or alternatively mirroring the components that may be acquired earlier in first language acquisition. Coventry and Guijarro-Fuentes (2008) distinguish between several possibilities:

1   A single dimension is used for L2 learning (either geometric or extra-geometric dimensions), but weightings for this dimension from L1 are not used.
2   A single dimension is used for L2 learning and weightings from L1 are used.
3   Both geometric and extra-geometric dimensions are used to acquire L2, but weightings from L1 are not used.
4   Both dimensions are used to acquire L2, and weightings from L1 are used.

Possibilities (1) and (2) are consistent with data from artificial language learning, where it has been shown that participants have a tendency to focus on one cue at a time when learning (see Ellis, 2006, for discussion). These possibilities are also consistent with L1 acquisition of spatial prepositions where it has been found that children modify their spatial descriptions as a function of extra-geometric information in the scenes being described more than geometric information in the scenes to be described at an early stage of spatial prepositional use (Monrouxe & Coventry, 2010; Richards et al., 2004).

There is some existing evidence for L1 to L2 transfer across a range of languages for spatial language. With respect to motion events, quite a bit of attention has been paid to comparing L1 speakers of so-called 'verb-framed' versus 'satellite-framed' languages (Talmy, 1985; see Cadierno, 2008, for discussion). Specifically, researchers have asked if it is easier to acquire path expressions in L2 if one is moving from a language that is satellite-framed to another satellite-framed language than if one is learning an incongruent L2 (i.e., an L2 with the other type of path motion event structure). Cadierno and Ruiz (2006; see also Cadierno, 2004) tested how native speakers of Danish (a satellite-framed language) learning

Spanish (a verb-framed language) and native speakers of Italian (a verb-framed language) learning Spanish expressed motion events in both their first and second languages compared to a group of Spanish native speakers. Data were collected using elicited narratives based on the frog story (Berman & Slobin, 1994). The researchers found no substantive differences between groups with respect to the frequency of use of manner of motion verbs, suggesting limited support for the view that there is L1 to L2 transfer with respect to talking about motion events. These data are also supported by the results of L1-English advanced learners of L2 Spanish (Navarro & Nicoladis, 2005), and by a previous study by Cadierno testing L1 Danish—L2 Spanish speakers (Cadierno, 2004). The evidence for an advantage based on similarity between L1 and L2 for motion events is therefore currently somewhat equivocal (Cadierno, 2008).

A number of other studies have examined spatial expressions from a transfer perspective (e.g., Carroll, 1997; Harley, 1989; Ijaz, 1986; Jarvis & Odlin, 2000; Mukattash, 1984; Pavesi, 1987; Schumann, 1986), using a range of methodologies. For example, Jarvis and Odlin (2000) tested Swedish and Finnish speakers in L2 English. Swedish, like English, has nominative and genitive cases for nouns alone plus the accusative for pronouns. In contrast Finnish is much more complex, with 15 productive nominal cases expressed as agglutinative suffixes on nouns and their modifying adjectives. Moreover, Finnish also has a complex subject–verb agreement system in comparison with both Swedish and English. Jarvis and Odlin (2000) instructed participants in English to watch part of a silent movie of which they then had to write a description. The narrative descriptions participants produced showed some differences between Swedish and Finnish speakers consistent with L1 transfer. For instance, consistent with descriptions of the same movie segments in L1 Swedish and Finnish, Swedish speakers in L2 English exhibited a preference for using *on* while Finnish speakers showed a preference for using *in*. Finnish speakers in L2 English also produced more spatial expressions omitting prepositions than Swedish speakers, and a different range of prepositions, consistent again with L1 differences between Swedish and Finnish. This study and others (e.g., Carroll, 1997; Harley, 1989; Ijaz, 1986; Mukattash, 1984; Pavesi, 1987; Schumann, 1986), across a variety of different L1–L2 combinations and methodologies support various degrees of L1 to L2 transfer (see Coventry & Guijarro-Fuentes, 2008, for discussion). However, these studies are not grounded in what is known about the components of spatial language, so it is often hard to know what is and is not transferred. Arguably one first needs to know what spatial language involves before one can tackle whether transfer occurs or not.

Coventry, Guijarro-Fuentes, and Valdés (2010b) conducted a large-scale study investigating the comprehension of spatial prepositions in L1 and L2 English and Spanish. The primary purpose of this study was to test the relative importance of geometric and extra-geometric constraints on the comprehension of spatial prepositions across a wide range of spatial relations and levels of attainment in L2 English and Spanish. The materials employed were finer grained than those used previously, allowing a comprehensive test of the mapping between spatial terms and geometric and extra-geometric relation understanding across a wide range of spatial relations (see below). Participants in the study were 324 students in Spain (from the Universities of Cadiz, Valencia, and Madrid) and 130 students in England (from the Universities of Durham, Newcastle, Northumbria, Leeds, and Plymouth) studying Spanish at various proficiency levels. The Spanish sample comprised 189 students of English, 88 students of psychology with some knowledge of English, and 47 students with no knowledge of English (who therefore completed the L1 Spanish version of all the materials). Of the students in England, 15 were monolinguals who completed the materials in English.

Each participant completed a set of questionnaires including a range of measures to establish language proficiency. A modified version of the on-line Oxford Placement test (http://www.lang.ox.ac.uk/courses/tst_english_placement.html) was used to assess language proficiency level in L2. This is a language test created by Oxford University Language Centre (OULC), containing 50 questions with optional answers designed to measure language proficiency. With permission from the OULC we used slightly modified versions of their Spanish and English placement tests in order to classify our participants into proficiency levels. A self-report measure of language-learning history and proficiency was also used, together with a 'preposition identification test' to establish participants' recognition of spatial prepositions in L2. The main materials comprised a large battery of sentence–picture mapping tasks (using 120 pictures) adapted from previous studies (including those described above). For the majority of materials, participants had to rate how appropriate each of a set of given spatial prepositions was to complete sentences to describe the given pictures. The rating scale ranged from 0 (not appropriate) to 7 (very appropriate). Materials were also included where participants had to rank order a given set of prepositions to describe pictures; some free response sentence completions were also used.

The materials used were designed to measure the use of spatial prepositions (*above, below, over, under, in, on, at, in front of, behind, to the right, to the left, facing*) both in English and Spanish across a range of spatial situations. Specifically, across eight different experiments we manipulated geometrical and functional properties of the scenes being described. The body of this work is reported in Coventry et al. (2010b). Here we do not exhaustively cover the results of all of these experiments, but instead examine some general themes across these data sets due to space limitations.

One set of materials adapted the umbrella materials used previously by Coventry et al. (2001)—similar to the images displayed in Figure 12.2, the orientation of the umbrella was manipulated, and this was crossed with the extent to which falling objects (rain) were shown hitting the lady or missing the lady holding the umbrella (or no rain was present). Another set of materials showed a can at various positions higher than a bowl, and this geometric manipulation was crossed with peanuts falling from the can shown either missing the bowl (non-functional condition) or ending up in the bowl (functional condition), or no peanuts were shown (control condition).

Another set of materials manipulated an object in/on a hand or bowl similar to the materials displayed in Figure 12.3. Animacy of the located object was manipulated (it was either an insect or a padlock) and the level of concavity of the reference object was also manipulated.

Data from participants in both L2 Spanish and L2 English were partitioned as a function of scores on the Oxford Placement test. These scores correlated both with self-reported language-level ability and with other measures of proficiency, so we felt this was a valid and robust means with which to separate speakers into proficiency-level groups. Doing so, we were then able to examine the extent to which geometric versus extra-geometric parameters affect the ratings and free productions of participants in L2 at different levels of proficiency (and in turn, in comparison with L1 speakers of those languages).

Coventry et al. (2010b) conducted a number of different analyses, including analyses of non-target-like performance in L2 (prepositions rated as appropriate by L2 speakers when they were considered as inadmissible descriptions by native speakers) and analyses examining the degree to which appropriate prepositions are influenced by the components of the functional geometric framework. Here we focus on the latter data, which are informative regarding how the components of the functional geometric framework influence spatial language comprehension in L2 acquisition.

For each experiment, analyses of variance on the acceptability rating data were conducted in order to establish whether acceptability ratings were sensitive to the geometric and extra-geometric information in the scenes described. As an example, we can consider the results from the umbrella pictures described above, which manipulated both position of rain (function) and position of umbrella. Based on the Oxford Placement test scores, participants were divided into proficiency levels in their L2—beginners, intermediate, advanced—and acceptability ratings were compared to a group of native speakers in each language. The rating data were submitted to a 4 (group: beginners, intermediate, advanced, native) × 4 (preposition: *over, under, above, below*) × 3 (geometry) × 3 (function) analysis of variance. All four groups in both English and Spanish were indistinguishable in their ratings of *over, under, above,* and *below* for different degrees of functional relations. Acceptability ratings for *over, under, above,* and *below* were highest across all groups when rain was shown hitting the umbrella, and lowest when the rain was shown missing the umbrella and instead wetting the person holding it. There was no inter-action between group and function, showing that speakers at all levels of proficiency were equally sensitive to making linguistic distinctions based on functional information. However, there was a reliable group by geom-etry interaction for each language, indicating that speakers at different proficiency levels do not distinguish geometric relations to the same extent (see Figure 12.4). Native speakers exhibited more marked gradedness in geometry than the other less-proficient groups overall. Moreover, as is shown in Figure 12.5, this was particularly the case for *below* in English, where beginners in L2 English failed to show significant geometric dis-tinctions for this term, in contrast with native speakers who demonstrated marked gradedness in responses.

Similar interactions between proficiency level and geometry were found for a range of spatial relations (though not all relations—see Coventry et al., 2010b, for more detail). Overall this suggests a similarity in the pattern of L1 and L2 acquisition with respect to components of the func-tional geometric framework, at least for these relations. The finding that sensitivity to functional relations occurs earlier than sensitivity to fine-grained geometric relations seems to characterize both L1 and L2 spatial language learning. Moreover, the results also show that speakers are none-theless sensitive to several interlocking parameters when they map lan-guage onto the visual world even when they do not have an advanced proficiency in L2.

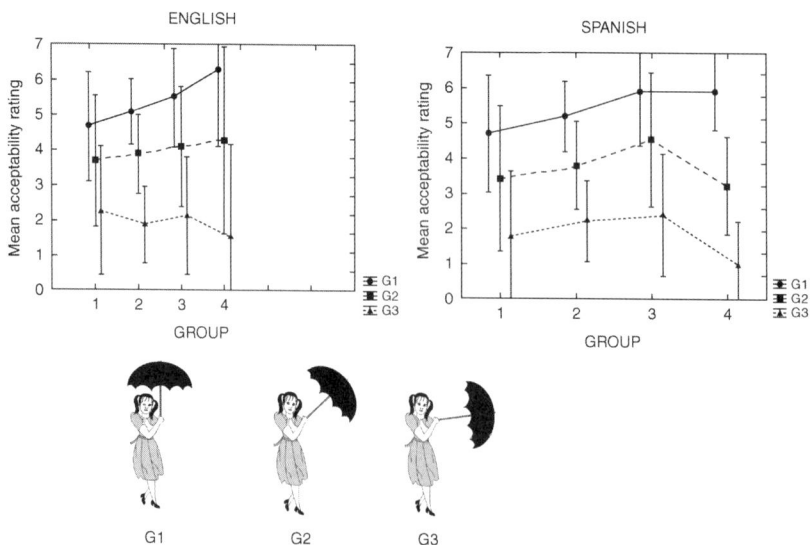

Figure 12.4 Some results from Coventry et al. (2010b). Group key: 1 = beginners, 2 = intermediate, 3 = advanced, 4 = native speakers. Bars denote 95% confidence intervals. The levels of geometry, denoted G1–G3, are shown below the graphs.

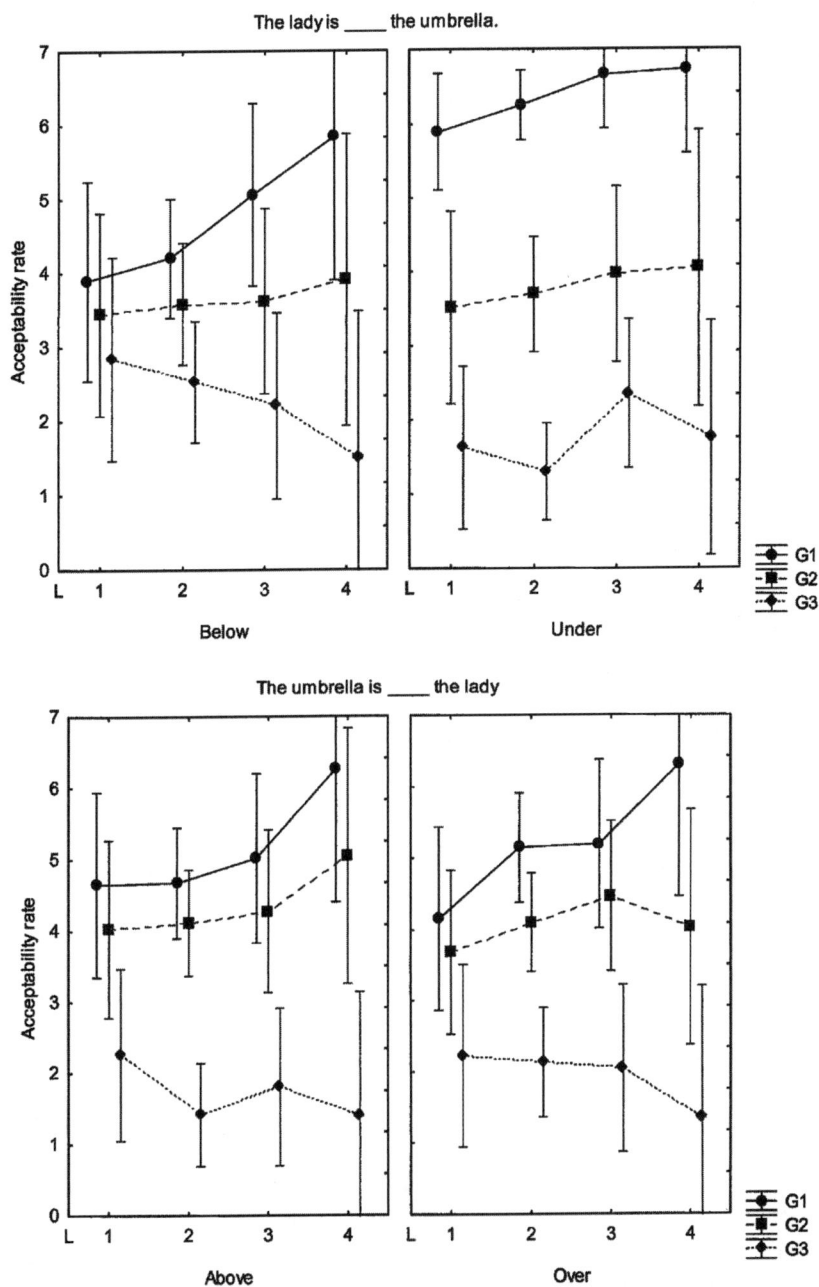

Figure 12.5 Three-way interaction between geometry, preposition and group in Coventry et al. (2010b). Bars denote 95% confidence intervals.

CONCLUSIONS

In this chapter we have considered spatial language comprehension and production in first and second language learning. First, we argued that it is necessary to understand the components of spatial language comprehension in languages prior to tackling the issues of how these languages are acquired in first and second language acquisition. We overviewed the functional geometric framework for spatial language (cf. Coventry & Garrod, 2004) which identifies three sets of constraints that characterize spatial language understanding—constraints that appear to generalize across languages (Feist, 2008). Considering the three sets of constraints, we then examined the first language acquisition of spatial prepositions. Although this is a relatively sparsely researched topic, we identified the general trend that the gradedness of geometric relations appears to become more marked with age. In the final section of the chapter we showed a similar pattern comparing L2 speakers of English and Spanish at varying levels of proficiency. It would appear that both L1 and L2 learners hook onto distinctions in language that map closely onto important distinctions in the scenes being described.

Language learning involves grasping three sets of constraints. First, language learners need to learn how words in a language co-occur with other words. For example, that the word *liquid* co-occurs with the words *in* and *bottle*. Second, language learners have to grasp how words map onto the non-linguistic world—that the word *bottle* maps onto perceptual representations for bottle, and bottles in the world being described. Third, language learners need to know how non-linguistic entities co-occur with other non-linguistic entities—that bottles are usually found near glasses, keep liquids in predictable places, pour into bottles to quench thirst, etc. These last two constraints are already well developed prior to and during first language acquisition. Therefore it is perhaps not surprising that bilinguals at all levels of proficiency in L2 make distinctions based on salient functional distinctions in the scenes being described. However, theories of transfer do not often cleanly separate out these three sets of constraints. Far from being a unitary notion, the notion of transfer needs to consider the status of distinctions made in L1 that may be transferred. The distinctions that may be transferred the most are those perhaps that emerge from the first set of constraints—how words co-occur with other words—but in cases where the other constraints are weaker. For example, with respect to spatial language, whether one describes objects as *in* or *on* large objects, such as buses or planes, is somewhat arbitrary across languages. A bus both contains and supports the passengers traveling on it, making this distinction very much reliant on how nouns and prepositions co-occur alone. In such cases one expects that errors as a function of transfer may be at a premium.

While second language acquisition/bilingualism research has focused on error patterns in L2 and on whether the similarity between L1 and L2 affects language production and comprehension in L2, the approach we have adopted here illustrates that language proficiency level maps onto differences in comprehension even for terms which are correctly identified as applicable to describe scenes. What is not currently known is just how sensitive these respective measures are in differentiating speakers at different levels of proficiency. Future research in this area would do well to focus not just on errors in L2 as a function of possible transfer from L1, but also on gradedness in the applicability of terms that are in the lexicon, but none the less show development as proficiency increases.

ACKNOWLEDGMENTS

The research reported in this chapter was funded by an Arts and Humanities Research Council grant (grant no. 112211) awarded to Coventry and Guijarro-Fuentes.

REFERENCES

Behl-Chadha, G., & Eimas, P. D. (1995). Infant categorization of left–right spatial relations. *British Journal of Developmental Psychology, 13,* 69–79.

Berman, R. A., & Slobin, D. I. (1994). *Relating events in narrative*. Hillsdale, NJ: Lawrence Erlbaum Associates Inc.

Bowerman, M. (1996). Learning how to structure space for language: A cross-linguistic perspective. In P. Bloom, M. A. Peterson, L. Nadel, & M. F. Garrett (Eds.), *Language and space* (pp. 385–436). Cambridge, MA: MIT Press.

Bowerman, M., & Pederson, E. (2010). *Cross-linguistic perspectives on topological spatial relationships*. Manuscript in preparation.

Cadierno, T. (2004). Expressing motion events in a second language: A cognitive typological perspective. In M. Archard & S. Niemeier (Eds.), *Cognitive linguistics, second language acquisition, and foreign language teaching* (pp. 13–49). Berlin: Mouton de Gruyter.

Cadierno, T. I. (2008). Learning to talk about motion in a foreign language. In P. Robinson & N. Ellis (Eds.), *Handbook of cognitive linguistics and second language acquisition* (pp. 239–275). New York/London: Routledge.

Cadierno, T. I., & Ruiz, L. (2006). Motion events in Spanish L2 acquisition. *Annual Review of Cognitive Linguistics, 4,* 183–216.

Carlson-Radvansky, L. A., Covey, E. S., & Lattanzi, K. M. (1999). 'What' effects on 'where': Functional influences on spatial relations. *Psychological Science, 10,* 516–521.

Carlson-Radvansky, L. A., & Tang, Z. (2000). Functional influences on orienting a reference frame. *Memory and Cognition, 28*(5), 812–820.

Carroll, M. (1997). The acquisition of English. In A. Becker & M. Carroll (Eds.), *The acquisition of spatial relations in a second language* (pp. 35–78). Amsterdam: Benjamins.

Choi, S., & Bowerman, M. (1991). Learning to express motion events in English and Korean: The influence of language-specific lexicalization patterns. *Cognition, 41,* 83–121.

Choi, S., McDonough, L., Bowerman, M., & Mandler, J. M. (1999). Early sensitivity to language-specific spatial categories in English and Korean. *Cognitive Development, 14,* 241–268.

Coventry, K. R., Carmichael, R., & Garrod, S. C. (1994). Spatial prepositions, object-specific function and task requirements. *Journal of Semantics, 11,* 289–309.

Coventry, K. R., & Garrod, S. C. (2004). *Saying, seeing and acting: The psychological semantics of spatial prepositions.* Hove & New York: Psychology Press.

Coventry, K. R., & Guijarro-Fuentes, P. (2004). Las preposiciones en español y en inglés: la importancia relativa del espacio y función. *Cognitiva, 16*(1), 73–93.

Coventry, K. R., & Guijarro-Fuentes, P. (2008). Spatial language learning and the functional geometric framework. In P. Robinson & N. Ellis (Eds.), *Handbook of cognitive linguistics and second language acquisition.* London: Routledge.

Coventry, K. R., Guijarro-Fuentes, P., & Valdés, B. (2010a). Thinking for speaking and immediate memory for spatial relations. In Z-H. Han & T. Cadierno (Eds.), *Linguistic relativity in SLA* (pp. 84–101). Clevedon, UK: Multilingual Matters.

Coventry, K. R., Guijarro-Fuentes, P., & Valdés, B. (2010b). *Talking about space in first and second languages: The case of Spanish and English.* Manuscript in preparation.

Coventry, K. R., Lynott, D., Cangelosi, A., Monrouxe, L., Joyce, D., & Richardson, D. C. (2010c). Spatial language, visual attention, and perceptual simulation. *Brain and Language, 112*(3), 202–213.

Coventry, K. R., Prat-Sala, M., & Richards, L. (2001). The interplay between geometry and function in the comprehension of 'over', 'under', 'above' and 'below'. *Journal of Memory and Language, 44,* 376–398.

Ellis, N. C. (2006). Selective attention and transfer phenomena in L2 acquisition: Contingency, cue competition, salience, interference, overshadowing, blocking and perceptual learning. *Applied Linguistics, 27,* 164–194.

Elman, J. L. (2009). On the meaning of words and dinosaur bones: Lexical knowledge without a lexicon. *Cognitive Science, 33,* 1–36.

Feist, M. I. (2008). Space between languages. *Cognitive Science, 32*(7), 1177–1199.

Feist, M. I., & Gentner, D. (2007). Spatial language influences memory for spatial scenes. *Memory and Cognition, 35*(2), 283–296.

Garrod, S., Ferrier, G., & Campbell, S. (1999). *In* and *on*: Investigating the functional geometry of spatial prepositions. *Cognition, 72,* 167–189.

Garrod, S. C., & Sanford, A. J. (1989). Discourse models as interfaces between language and the spatial world. *Journal of Semantics, 6,* 147–160.

Gelman, R., & Butterworth, B. (2005). Number and language: How are they related. *Trends in Cognitive Science, 9*(1), 6–10.

Gordon, P. (2004). Numerical cognition without words: Evidence from Amazonia. *Science, 306,* 496–499.

Harley, B. (1989). Transfer in the written compositions of French immersion students. In H. Dechert & M. Raupach (Eds.), *Transfer in language production* (pp. 3–19). Norwood, NJ: Ablex.

Harris, L. J., & Strommen, E. A. (1972). The role of front–back features in children's 'front', 'back', and 'beside' placements of objects. *Journal of Child Development, 18,* 259–271.

Hasko, V. (2010). Unidirectional and multidirectional motion events in the speech of L2 learners of Russian. In Z-H. Han & T. Cadierno (Eds.), *Linguistic Relativity in SLA* (pp. 34–58). Clevedon, UK: Multilingual Matters.

Hayward, W. G., & Tarr, M. J. (1995). Spatial language and spatial representation. *Cognition, 55*, 39–84.

Hespos, S. J., & Baillargeon, R. (2001). Reasoning about containment events in very young infants. *Cognition, 78*, 207–245.

Hespos, S. J., & Spelke, E. S. (2004). Conceptual precursors to language. *Nature, 430*, 453–456.

Hoffman, J. E. (1998). Visual attention and eye movements. In H. Pashler (Ed.), *Attention* (pp. 119–154). Hove, UK: Psychology Press.

Ijaz, H. (1986). Linguistic and cognitive determinants of lexical acquisition in a second language. *Language Learning, 36*, 401–451.

Jarvis, S., & Odlin, T. (2000). Morphological type, spatial reference, and language transfer. *Studies in Second Language Acquisition, 22*, 535–556.

Johnston, J. R. (1984). Acquisition of locative meanings: *Behind* and *in front of. Journal of Child Language, 11*, 407–422.

Johnston, J. R. (1985). Cognitive prerequisites: The evidence from children learning English. In D. I. Slobin (Ed.), *The cross-linguistic study of language acquisition, volume 2: Theoretical issues* (pp. 961–1004). Hillsdale, NJ: Lawrence Erlbaum Associates Inc.

Johnston, J. R., & Slobin, D. I. (1979). The development of locative expressions in English, Italian, Serbo-Croatian and Turkish. *Journal of Child Language, 6*, 529–545.

Just, M. A., & Carpenter, P. A. (1980). A theory of reading: From eye fixation to comprehension. *Psychological Review, 87*, 329–354.

Kuczaj, S. A., & Maratsos, M. P. (1975). On the acquisition of front, back and behind. *Child Development, 46*, 202–210.

Landau, B., & Jackendoff, R. (1993). 'What' and 'where' in spatial language and cognition. *Behavioural and Brain Sciences, 16*(2), 217–265.

Levinson, S. C. (1996). Frames of reference and Molyneux's question. In P. Bloom, M. A. Peterson, L. Nadel, & M. F. Garrett (Eds.), *Language and space* (pp. 109–169). Cambridge, MA: MIT Press.

Logan, G. D., & Sadler, D. D. (1996). A computational analysis of the apprehension of spatial relations. In P. Bloom, M. A. Peterson, L. Nadel, & M. F. Garrett (Eds.), *Language and space* (pp. 493–530). Cambridge, MA: MIT Press.

McDonough, L., Choi, S., & Mandler, J. M. (2003). Understanding spatial relations: Flexible infants, lexical adults. *Cognitive Psychology, 46*(3), 229–259.

Monrouxe, L. V., & Coventry, K. R. (2010). *When above becomes near: Functional constraints on how adults and children talk about spatial relations.* Manuscript submitted for publication.

Mukattash, L. (1984). Errors made by Arab university students in the use of English prepositions. *Glottodidactica, 17*, 47–64.

Navarro, S., & Nicoladis, E. (2005). Describing motion events in adult L2 Spanish narratives. In D. Eddington (Ed.), *Selected proceedings of the 6th conference on the acquisition of Spanish and Portuguese as first and second languages* (pp. 102–107). Somerville, MA: Cascadilla Proceedings Project.

Pavesi, M. (1987). Variability and systematicity in the acquisition of spatial prepositions. In R. Ellis (Ed.), *Second language acquisition in context* (pp. 73–82). Englewood Cliffs, NJ: Prentice Hall.

Pederson, E., Danziger, E., Wilkins, D., Levinson, S. C., Kita, S., & Senft, G. (1998). Semantic typology and spatial conceptualisation. *Language, 74*(3), 557–589.

Piaget, J., & Inhelder, B. (1956). *The child's conception of space.* London: Routledge & Kegan Paul.

Quinn, P. C., Cummins, M., Kase, J., Martin, E., & Weissman, S. (1996). Development of categorical representations for above and below spatial relations in 3- to 7-month-old infants. *Developmental Psychology, 32,* 942–950.

Rayner, K. (1998) Eye movements in reading and information processing: 20 years of research. *Psychological Bulletin, 124,* 372–422.

Regier, T., & Carlson, L. A. (2002). Spatial language: Perceptual constraints and linguistic variation. In N. Stein, P. Bauer, & M. Rabinowitz (Eds.), *Representation, memory, and development: Essays in honor of Jean Mandler* (pp. 199–221). Mahwah, NJ: Lawrence Erlbaum Associates Inc.

Regier, T., Kay, P., & Cook, R. (2005). Focal colors are universal after all. *Proceedings of the National Academy of Sciences, 102*(23), 8386–8391.

Richards, L. V., Coventry, K. R., & Clibbens, J. (2004). Where's the orange? Geometric and extra-geometric factors in English children's talk of spatial locations. *Journal of Child Language, 31,* 153–175.

Roberson, D., Davidoff, J., Davies, I. R., & Shapiro, L. R. (2005). Color categories: Evidence for the cultural relativity hypothesis. *Cognitive Psychology, 50*(4), 378–411.

Schumann, J. (1986). Locative and directional expressions in Basilang speech. *Language Learning, 36,* 277–294.

Sinha, C., Thorseng, L. A., Hayashi, M., & Plunkett, K. (1994). Comparative spatial semantics and language acquisition: Evidence from Danish, English, and Japanese. *Journal of Semantics, 11,* 253–287.

Slobin, D. (1996). From 'language and thought' to 'thinking for speaking'. In J. J. Gumperz & S. C. Levinson (Eds.), *Rethinking linguistic relativity* (pp. 70–96). Cambridge, UK: Cambridge University Press.

Talmy, L. (1983). How language structures space. In H. Pick & L. Acredolo (Eds.), *Spatial orientation: Theory, research and application* (pp. 225–282). New York: Plenum Press.

Talmy, L. (1985). Lexicalization patterns: Semantic structure in lexical forms. In T. Shopen (Ed.), *Language typology and syntactic description, Volume 3: Grammatical categories and the lexicon* (pp. 36–149). Cambridge, UK: Cambridge University Press.

Tomasello, M. (1987). Learning how to use prepositions: A case study. *Journal of Child Language, 14,* 79–98.

Vandeloise, C. (1991). *Spatial prepositions. A case study from French.* Chicago: University of Chicago Press.

Vandeloise, C. (1994). Methodology and analyses of the preposition 'in'. *Cognitive Linguistics, 5–2,* 157–184.

13 Perception of motion by Polish–English bilinguals

Natalia Czechowska and Anna Ewert

In this chapter we focus on bilinguals' and monolinguals' non-verbal perceptions of motion. We assume that the way people perceive motion events is modulated by the languages they know and use.

Whorf (1941/1956, p. 137) claimed that 'the cue to a certain line of behavior is often given by the analogies of the linguistic formula in which the situation is spoken of, and by which to some degree it is analyzed, classified and allotted its place in that world'. The implication of this statement is that language modulates the way its speakers categorize and perceive reality in that linguistic structures serve as a tool of directing attention to specific aspects of reality. According to Whorf, the effect of language can be either permanent, taking place at the deep level of everyday 'habitual thought', or temporary, present at the moment of language use. The latter case can be treated as synonymous with Slobin's (1987) idea of 'thinking for speaking', according to which speakers depend on categories introduced in language to partition reality at the moment of speaking, reading, listening, and writing. Both these theoretical positions implicate that there are two levels of organization at which events are represented in people's minds and at both levels the representations are shaped by language.

Talmy (2008) emphasizes the role of attention, maintaining that specific linguistic mechanisms assign different degrees of salience to different aspects of reality, thus increasing or decreasing speakers' attention. Talmy in fact claims that language is an attentional system of its own. Since bilinguals know more than one language, it follows that their attentional systems must be different from monolingual systems. There are two neurophysiological studies that explicitly point to the role of attention in bilinguals' non-verbal perceptions of reality. Hedden, Ketay, Aron, Markus, and Gabrieli (2008) demonstrate that people can be trained to make visuo-spatial distinctions that are unusual in their culture to the point that they do not differ behaviorally from members of that other culture, but their brains show increased activation in the regions responsible for attentional control while performing the task. An ERP study by Thierry, Athanasopoulos, Wiggett, Dering, and Kuipers (2009) shows that bilinguals may differ from monolingual speakers of their second language at the level of pre-attentive, i.e., non-linguistic, processing while making visual distinctions. The results of these two studies also point to the existence of different levels of representation in bilingual processing, but even at the deepest levels representations are shaped by language. Moreover, attending to task demands can change bilinguals' perceptual judgments.

LANGUAGES AND CONCEPTS IN THE BILINGUAL MIND

The relationship between two languages in the bilingual mind has for decades been the focus of second language acquisition research. The possible influence of one language on another has been conceptualized as 'transfer' (see e.g., Gass & Selinker, 1983). More recent research has revealed that linguistic transfer is bidirectional (see Pavlenko & Jarvis, 2002), i.e., apart from native language influences on the second language, second language knowledge also influences native language structures. Moreover, proficient second language users can show hypersensitivity to certain features of their first language, as compared to monolingual native speakers (Cook, Iarossi, Stellakis, & Tokumaru, 2003; Ewert, in press; Ewert & Bromberek-Dyzman, 2008), in a sense performing in a more native-like way than the monolingual native speakers of their first language on a variety of linguistic tasks. Research on pragmalinguistic aspects of language use, concerning the use of language in social communication, indicates that this increased sensitivity of the proficient L2 user is not limited to the first language and, in certain tasks, L2 users may perform in a more native-like way than monolingual native speakers in their second language as well (Ewert, Bromberek-Dyzman, & Singleton, 2008), so they can be hypersensitive to cues from either the L1 or the L2.

There is a growing body of evidence that transfer takes place not only at the linguistic, but also at the conceptual level (cf. Jarvis & Pavlenko, 2008; Pavlenko, 2005, 2009). Since we believe that transfer is a cognitive phenomenon in nature, we expect to find the same kind of changes described above, i.e., bidirectionality and hypersensitivity, in bilinguals' conceptual representations.

For the purpose of the present study, we define concepts following Pavlenko (2005, p. 435) as 'mental representations that affect individuals' immediate perception, attention, and recall and allow members of specific language and culture groups to conduct identification, comprehension, inferencing, and categorization along similar lines'. This definition allows us to operationalize any differences between the behavior of monolinguals and bilinguals as instances of conceptual change.

Pavlenko (2005, p. 438) distinguishes the following types of conceptual change:

1   coexistence of L1 and L2 conceptual domains,
2   L1-based conceptual transfer,
3   internalization of new concepts,
4   shift from L1 to L2 conceptual domain,
5   convergence of L1 and L2 conceptual domains,
6   restructuring of a conceptual domain,
7   attrition of previously learned concepts.

As far as the non-linguistic perceptions of balanced bilinguals are concerned, shift, convergence and restructuring are the types of conceptual change to be expected. Shift is defined as a unidirectional change of category prototypes or boundaries in the direction of L2 values, hence a quantitative change. Conceptual restructuring is a qualitative change affecting the internal structure of a concept. Convergence is defined as 'a particular kind of restructuring . . . whereby a unitary conceptual category is created that incorporates both L1 and L2 features' (Jarvis & Pavlenko, 2008, p. 164). To date, there are a number of studies that provide evidence for both quantitative change (Athanasopoulos, 2009; Athanasopoulos & Kasai, 2008; Cook, Bassetti, Kasai, Sasaki, & Takahashi, 2006) as well as qualitative change (Ameel, Storms, Malt, & Sloman, 2005; Bassetti, 2007; Brown & Gullberg, 2008; Hohenstein, Eisenberg, & Naigles, 2006) in bilingual conceptual representations.

MOTION

Cross-linguistic studies of motion in monolinguals

The experience of motion seems to be universal among human beings due to the biologically determined perceptual mechanisms that we all share. As far as language is concerned, it has been found that this universal experience underlies similar semantic representations of motion events across different languages. Dimitrova-Vulchanova, Martinez, and Edsberg (in press) found that in spontaneous descriptions of motion events speakers of English, Norwegian, and Bulgarian all encode motion primarily in basic-level verbs, such as *walk, run, climb*, and *crawl*, rather than specific, e.g., *trudge, strut*, etc. or general verbs, e.g., *go, come*, etc. Their study revealed that, when talking about motion events, speakers conform to one pattern based on depicting basic features of human motion, which seem to be most transparent. However, at the same time the study showed that the three languages differ in the size of inventory of more specific motion verbs. In comparison to Bulgarian speakers, English and Norwegian speakers were found to use specific verbs more frequently. Following Slobin's (2003) argument that motion lexicalization patterns have an impact on non-linguistic representation of motion, the tendency of English and Norwegian speakers to resort to specific verbs more frequently than Bulgarian speakers can translate into greater salience and, consequently, richer imagery of manner in speakers of those two languages.

Therefore it is possible that although the basic experience of human motion is universal, perception of motion events by speakers of different languages can be modulated by linguistic structures used to encode motion. And motion, due to its high level of abstractness, is a domain that shows vast cross-linguistic variation. According to Talmy (1985, 2000), languages can be divided into two groups on the basis of how they encode two aspects of motion—manner and path. The group of 'satellite-framed' languages, e.g., the Germanic group, conveys primarily manner of motion, which is encoded in a main verb in a sentence, while path of motion is expressed by a preposition or a particle, i.e., a satellite. The group of 'verb-framed' languages, e.g., the Romance group, conveys primarily path of motion, which is encoded in a main verb in a sentence, while manner of motion is expressed only additionally in an adverbial phrase or other verbs (for details see Table 13.1).

Apart from the two elements of motion mentioned above, i.e., manner and path, there are also other structures in which motion descriptions are embedded both in speech and gesture. As indicated by von Stutterheim (2003) and von Stutterheim and Nüse (2003), as well as Brown (2008), features such as speaker's viewpoint and grammatical aspect can influence the overall perception of motion events and of events in general to the same extent as the motion lexicalization strategies proposed by Talmy (1985, 2000). Additionally, in bilinguals, differences in types of information organization according to which motion is described can lead to conceptual change in the representation of motion. In the present chapter we are interested in the way speakers of Polish and English categorize motion on the basis of two aspects only: path and manner.

Slobin (2003) suggested that these lexicalization strategies have cognitive consequences for speakers of a given language group: Speakers of 'satellite-framed' languages pay more attention to manner of motion, while speakers of 'verb-framed' languages pay more attention to path of motion. In other words, the way in which a particular language encodes

Table 13.1 Strategies for lexicalizing motion

	Satellite-framed languages	*Verb-framed languages*
Manner of motion	Conveyed by verbs (e.g., English *run, walk, jump, crawl*, etc.)	Expressed optionally in independent constituents, i.e., adverbial phrases or other verbs
Path of motion	Conveyed by prepositions/ particles (satellites) (e.g., English *into, out, under*, etc.)	Conveyed by verbs (e.g., Spanish *entrar* 'enter', *salir* 'exit', *ascender* 'ascend', *cruzar* 'go across')

motion might influence how one conceptualizes actions, attracting the speaker's attention to the feature that is encoded more saliently in language, i.e., either manner or path.

The support for these assumptions comes from Slobin's (2000) experiment on mental imagery of motion events, in which English and Spanish speakers were given a fragment of a novel to summarize. While the English speakers, specifying the actions of the protagonist, reported the story using a number of manner verbs, only a few Spanish speakers did so. Although clear descriptions of the scenes were provided in the story, the Spanish speakers reported the events in a static manner. This finding indicates that language lexicalization strategy focuses speakers' attention on different aspects of motion. As far as the bilingual participants are concerned, their use of manner verbs in the reports was found to depend on the language of the retelling. Again, this suggests that language does play a role in how one thinks about motion events, focusing the speaker's attention on those aspects that are encoded in language more saliently.

Addressing the same issue of the relation between language and thought, Billman, Swilley, and Krych (2000) examined whether specific verb primes may change the participants' perception of motion events. In their experiment the participants saw a series of video-taped events that were either not labeled (non-priming condition), or labeled with either manner or path verbs (priming condition). In all conditions there were unlabeled events for which the participants were asked to give a description. On the next day, the participants saw another series of video-taped events and were asked to judge whether those were identical to the ones they had been shown on the previous day. The question addressed in the task was whether specific verb primes would change the participants' perception of motion events. The results indeed showed that errors on manner verbs were related to the types of primes used on the first day of the experiment. Furthermore, the participants were found to be primed by specific labels in the instances where they were asked to produce their own descriptions. Similar to Slobin's (2000) experiment, the findings of this study indicate that if particular language aspects are made more salient than others in language comprehension and production, this can enable access to specific dimensions of a given language domain, in this case motion. In other words, manipulating language structures can change the focus of speakers' attention.

Coming back to cross-linguistic differences in how Germanic and Romance languages encode motion events, taking the above-mentioned evidence into account, a critical question is whether the non-linguistic behavior of speakers from these language groups differs in line with the linguistic patterns of their languages. To answer this question, Malt, Sloman, and Gennari (2003) asked Spanish and English speakers to watch short films portraying motion events. These were organized into triads in which one video showed a motion event, e.g., 'walking into a room', and two others showed manner and path alternates, e.g., 'walking out of the room', and 'striding into the room'. There were three conditions in the task: In the first condition the participants were instructed to repeat non-sense syllables while watching the videos to inhibit language processing, in the second they simply watched the films, and in the third they were asked to describe the scene while watching it. Later, during a memory task, the participants judged whether a presented action was the one they saw pre-viously or not. Second, they were asked to point to two out of three pictures of actions that seemed most similar to each other. It was expected that the Spanish speakers would confuse actions with the same path, judging them as identical although they presented different manners of motion. Nevertheless, no such effect of language-specific lexicalization strategy on visual memory recognition was found in either the English or Spanish speakers, which could suggest that linguistic and non-linguistic behaviors are not dependent on each other in a strong sense of the lin-guistic relativity hypothesis. Nonetheless, the influence of language on performance was found for the Spanish speakers in the similarity task. When these participants had named actions while watching them, they chose same-path alternates more frequently than when they had watched the videos in the other conditions. This finding shows that language can serve as a tool of directing thought in order to solve a non-linguistic task, which supports the weaker version of the Sapir-Whorf hypothesis as well as Slobin's (1987) 'thinking for speaking'.

Motion research with bilinguals

If Spanish and English speakers encode the manner and path of motion with different salience, which can have an effect on their perception of events (Malt et al., 2003; Slobin, 2000), bilinguals whose two languages differ in lexicalization strategies should exhibit conceptual shift in the rep-resentation of motion towards the L2 pattern. To verify this hypothesis, Hohenstein et al. (2006) asked Spanish–English bilinguals to name actions seen in videos. The participants were interviewed twice in both their lan-guages to check whether their patterns of motion description change together with language. The actions portrayed in the films were instances of different paths of motion, presented with alternate manners, e.g., 'entering a building' versus 'twirling out of a building' and 'walking out of a build-ing'. The results of the interviews were quite striking, since when tested in English the bilinguals used more path verbs than English monolinguals (the Spanish pattern), but when tested in Spanish they used more manner verbs than Spanish monolinguals (the English pattern). In other words, as concluded by Hohenstein et al. (2006, p. 257), 'speakers' Spanish is dimin-ishing their manner use in English while their English is enhancing their manner use in Spanish'. Hence, it is hard to state whether such an effect is an instance of bidirectional transfer or a general influence of bilingualism, which resulted in hypersensitivity to linguistic cues from both their languages. Nevertheless, it is quite clear that the participants in this study are somewhere in between the monolinguals of both of their languages as far as the perception of motion events is concerned. This finding, in turn, shows that the acquisition of another language may lead to qualitative changes in bilingual conceptual representation, i.e., convergence.

Similarly, Brown and Gullberg (2008) investigated the representation of motion events by Japanese–English bilinguals in speech and gesture in comparison to monolinguals of their respective languages and found evidence in support of conceptual convergence. The participants were asked to retell stories presented in a film. Their narratives were analyzed for the number of motion verbs and gestures portraying motion that accompanied speech. In line with earlier reports (McNeill, 2001, 2005) that manner might be alternatively expressed in gesture in verb-framed languages like Spanish and Japanese, Brown and Gullberg (2008) found that speakers of English, a satellite-framed language, encoded manner of motion more frequently in speech than Japanese participants, while Japanese speakers compensated for the lack of information on manner in speech with gestures. Bilingual participants, on the other hand, exhibited bidirectional transfer and convergence of their linguistic and, possibly, conceptual systems. Namely, in both their L1 and L2 the bilinguals adopted some elements of the Japanese as well as English systems of representing motion, expressing manner in speech similarly to the Japanese monolinguals (Japanese pattern), but slightly less in accompanying gestures (English pattern). Thus, their performance was the same irrespective of the language used in the narratives, but differed significantly from monolinguals of their respective languages. Hence, on the whole, the bilinguals expressed manner of motion less frequently than the Japanese monolinguals, which indicates that manner became less perceptually salient to them under the influence of their second language.

In contrast to the previous studies discussed in this section, which show that language structures used to encode and describe motion both in speech and gesture have their cognitive consequences, Pavlenko's (2010) study, concerning motion lexicons in the narratives of late Russian–English bilinguals, offers scant evidence in support of cross-linguistic influence in language and conceptual representation in the domain of motion. Although there are clear-cut differences between how Russian and English speakers encode motion events with respect to aspect, directionality, manner, and path, with Russian being a more complex language, Pavlenko found little evidence for simplification of motion representation in Russian–English bilinguals under the influence of L2. A few instances of L2 influence concerned the substitution of perfective verbs with imperfective ones, use of lexical verbs instead of prefixes, and simplification of lexical verbs under the influence of high-frequency English verbs like *come* and *go*. Interestingly, the bilingual groups exhibited greater lexical diversity of motion lexicon than monolinguals of their respective languages, which could suggest cross-linguistic influence and interconnection between the bilinguals' mental lexicons. Pavlenko's results demonstrate that the distinctions present in the L1 may sometimes be hard to obliterate. They also suggest that conceptual change under the influence of the L2 may enrich the bilinguals' perception of motion events instead of impoverishing it. The difference between this and the previous studies points to a clear need to distinguish between L2 effects in the conceptual and the linguistic domains. There is a possibility that change in bilingual perceptions takes place even if no differences are to be found in the linguistic domain.

Motion lexicalization strategies in English and Polish

According to Talmy (1985, 2000), Polish and English belong to the same group of satellite-framed languages that encode manner of motion more saliently than its path. Nevertheless, despite many similarities in motion lexicalization, there are some crucial differences between these two languages:

1   In contrast to Polish, English has a variety of path verbs, similarly to verb-framed languages like Spanish and French, e.g., *enter, exit, descend, ascend, rise, arrive, cross*, etc., that do not specify the manner of motion. Polish, in contrast, has few path verbs, e.g., *przybyć* ('arrive') or *wyruszyć* ('depart').

2   English has at least three generic verbs, frequently used for expressing motion, which are not specified for manner, i.e., *go, come*, and *get* (Pavlenko, 2010). In contrast, in Polish, similarly to Russian, motion is rarely expressed by verbs that are unmarked for manner, e.g., *przybyć* ('arrive') or *wyruszyć* ('depart'). When talking about the activities expressed by English verbs *go, come*, and *get*, a speaker of Polish needs to specify whether a person is walking or driving.

3   English motion events are conveyed by verb phrases in which a preposition or a particle, a free morpheme, expresses path, which is thus more salient than in Polish. In comparison, in Polish, satellites are inseparable prefixes of verbs (Talmy, 1985, 2000), not so perceptually salient as in English, e.g.,
    we-jść ('walk **into**') – *wy-jść* ('walk **out**'),
    w-biec ('run **into**') – *wy-biec* ('run **out**'),
    w-skoczyć ('jump **into**') – *wy-skoczyć* ('jump **out**'), etc.
    Polish motion verbs are frequently followed by prepositions, e.g., *we-jść do* 'walk **into**', where both the prefix *we-* and the preposition *do* indicate path, similarly to English verb phrases.

In the study that follows, we hypothesize that the above-mentioned differences in motion lexicalization between Polish and English will have cognitive consequences, in that speakers of English will pay additional attention to path of motion in comparison to speakers of Polish. We would also like to address the issue of bilingual conceptual representation of motion, hypothesizing that Polish–English bilinguals will shift towards L2-based conceptual representation, paying more attention to the path of motion. Additionally, we hypothesize that bilinguals' conceptual representations will be affected by L2 proficiency, and quality and quantity of exposure to the L2.

THE STUDY

The present study consists of two experiments whose aim is to investigate the influence of linguistic structures encoding motion on perception of two aspects of motion: manner and path. Both experiments make use of non-linguistic materials in order to avoid examining the influence of language on language, i.e., linguistic transfer (Lucy, 1992).

Participants

The same five groups of participants, 123 people altogether, took part in both Experiment 1 and Experiment 2 (see Table 13.2). There were two groups of monolingual speakers of Polish and English respectively, and three groups of Polish–English bilinguals: two groups of L2 learners and one group of L2 users. Such a distinction was made following Cook (2002) who defines L2 learners as people who acquire L2 for future use and L2 users as people who use their L2 for real-life purposes on a daily basis. In the present study L2 learners and L2 users differed with respect to L2 proficiency as well as the amount and quality of exposure to the L2.

The L2 learners in this study were two groups of students in a language school in Poznań, preparing for the University of Cambridge examinations in English: First Certificate in English (FCE) and Certificate in Advanced English (CAE) respectively. The FCE group, henceforth called intermediate ESL learners, consisted of 20 participants (mean age = 22; 6 females, 14 males), the CAE group, henceforth advanced ESL learners,

Table 13.2 Summary of participants' details

	Polish monolinguals	English monolinguals	Intermediate ESL learners	Advanced ESL learners	L2 users
N (=123)	30	22	20	21	30
Mean age (range)	44 (21–58)	36 (22–58)	22 (17–39)	23 (16–28)	22 (20–24)
Gender	17 F/13 M	4 F/18 M	6 F/14 M	14 F/7 M	23 F/7 M

numbered 21 participants (mean age = 23; 14 females, 7 males). All the L2 learners attended the school for 90-minute sessions twice a week.

The L2 users (N = 30; mean age = 22; 23 females, 7 males) were undergraduate students in the English Studies program at Adam Mickiewicz University. With a few exceptions, all the courses the students take in this program are taught through the medium of English. The use of an L2 as a means of obtaining education is considered a real-life use (Cook, 2007).

The monolingual participants were 22 English-speaking adults (mean age = 36; 4 females, 18 males) and 30 Polish-speaking adults (mean age = 44; 17 females, 13 males). At the time of the study, none of the English monolingual participants knew Polish or could communicate in it fluently. Both English and Polish monolinguals reported having studied other foreign languages, yet their competence in those languages was minimal. Due to the fact that truly monolingual populations of university students and graduates are virtually non-existent in Poland nowadays, the monolingual samples were recruited from people who were on average older than the bilingual participants and who reported no knowledge of English.

Experiment 1

Materials and procedure

The aim of Experiment 1 was to find out which aspect of motion appears more salient to the participants in the study—manner or path. To this end, we designed a similarity judgment task consisting of 78 triads of pictures portraying everyday actions performed by the same actor. The triads were each placed in one row on the computer screen. In the whole set, three groups of items displaying activities can be further distinguished (see Table 13.3).

Table 13.3 Types of motion events used in Experiments 1 and 2

	Group 1 *(13 items)*			Group 2 *(6 items)*		Group 3 *(8 items)*	
	Entering/exiting a room		*Getting over a box*	*Descending/ascending steps*		*Getting over/ under a table*	
Walking	into	out	over	down	up	over	–
Running	into	out	–	down	up	–	–
Jumping	into	out	over	–	–	over	–
Crawling on all fours	into	out	over	down	up	over	under
Crawling	into	out	–	–	–	over	under

Each triad consisted of one double-paired item (e.g., walking into) and two alternates: same path alternate (e.g., jumping into) and same manner alternate (e.g., walking out) (see Figure 13.1). Thus, two items can be paired together in one of two possible ways: Either on the basis of the same path, but different manner criterion, or the same manner, but different path criterion. For example, in the above-mentioned triad, either 'walking into' and 'walking out' items can be paired together on the basis of the same manner criterion, or 'walking into' and 'jumping into' items can be paired together on the basis of the same path criterion. Each triad appeared on the screen with all pictures in a row in the center of the screen. The order of the triads was the same for all participants. The position of the pictures within each triad was semi-randomized (see Appendix 13-A).

The participants were instructed to choose two out of three pictures that, in their opinion, were most similar to each other. No other criteria for selection were given to the participants. Apart from the instructions given to the participants in their mother tongue at the beginning of the experiment, no other linguistic cues were used in the whole study. The triads stayed on the computer screen until a participant pressed the space bar. The participants were asked to say their answers ('ab' or 'bc' or 'ac') out loud so that the experimenter could code them in questionnaire forms provided for the study. The results were coded separately for manner and path as 1 or 0, i.e., a response was coded as 1 if the criterion (manner or path) had been selected by a participant as the basis for similarity judgment, 0 if it had not been selected. Only in 3.4% of all the responses did the participants choose the double-paired item, which indicated that they chose other criteria for their similarity judgments than manner or path of motion.

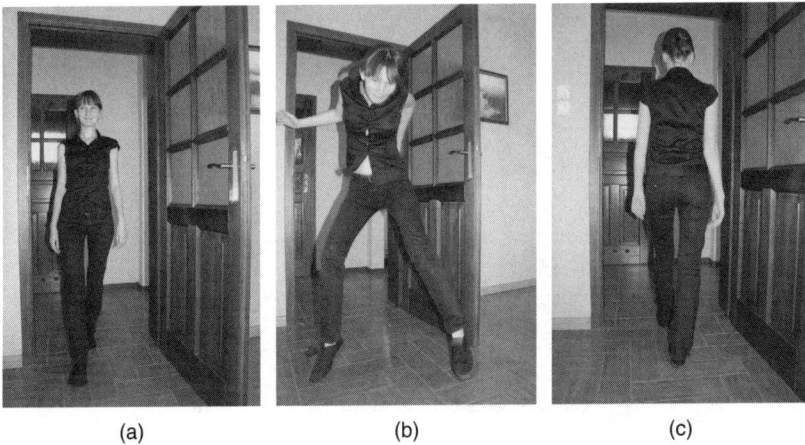

(a)   (b)   (c)

Figure 13.1 An example of a triad from Experiment 1 (see Appendix 13-A).

Results

A comparison of the mean numbers of same path and same manner responses (Figures 13.2 and 13.3) shows that the participants chose the same manner alternates approximately 3.5 times more often than the same path alternates. This indicates that manner is a more salient domain of motion than path for all the participants tested in Experiment 1.

Tests for equal or given proportions between five groups (see Newcombe, 1998a, 1998b; Wilson, 1927) were used to compare path and manner preferences from each of the five groups. Since the results were coded

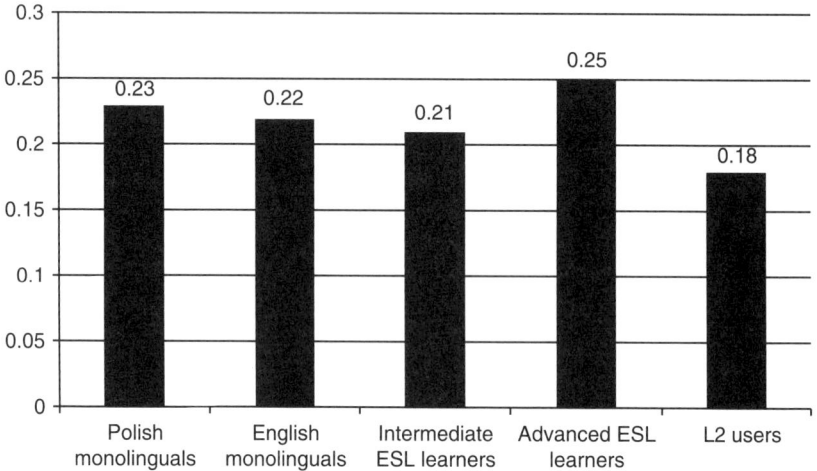

Figure 13.2 The results of the same path condition in Experiment 1 (mean scores).

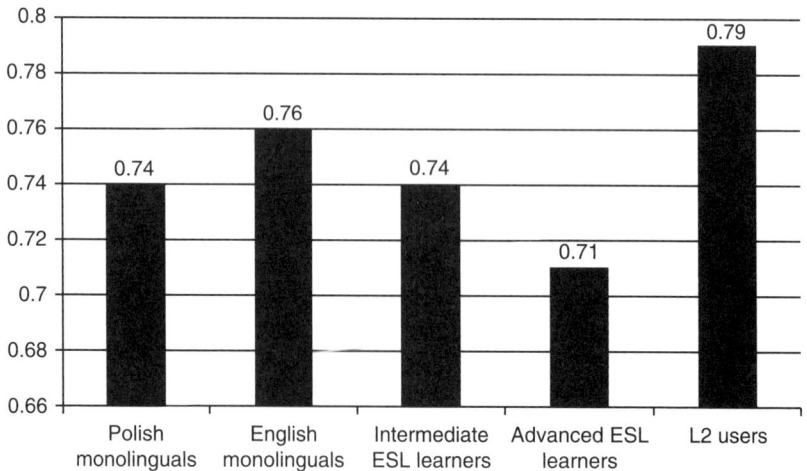

Figure 13.3 The results of the same manner condition in Experiment 1 (mean scores).

as either 0 or 1 values, i.e., lack or presence of a criterion in a response (path or manner), a test for equal or given proportions was used as it tests the probability of occurrence of a criterion in a number of groups. The results of the tests indicate that there is a significant difference between the groups tested in both conditions of Experiment 1 (the same path condition: $\chi^2 = 32.4755$, $df = 4$, $p < .000005$, the same manner condition: $\chi^2 = 34.6873$, $df = 4$, $p < .000001$).

Multiple comparisons (post-hoc tests) were used to specify which groups differ at the .05 level of significance (see Tables 13.4 and 13.5). In the same path condition (Table 13.4), post-hoc tests did not reveal any statistically significant difference between the monolingual groups ($p > .05$). The intermediate ESL learners were found to behave like Polish and English monolinguals (both $p > .05$). However, the L2 users and advanced ESL learners, i.e., the groups with highest L2 proficiency, differed from all the remaining groups tested in Experiment 1 in the same path condition ($p < .05$) (with the difference between L2 users and intermediate ESL learners approaching significance). Finally, all the bilingual groups tested in Experiment 1 differed from one another, with the advanced ESL learners choosing the same path alternates most frequently of all the groups ($M = 0.25$, i.e., 25% of all the responses, see also Figure 13.2) and the L2 users least frequently of all the groups ($M = 0.18$).

In the same manner condition (Table 13.5), similarly to the same path condition, post-hoc tests did not reveal any statistically significant difference between the monolingual groups ($p > .05$). Again, the intermediate ESL learners behaved like the Polish and English monolinguals (both $p > .05$). Advanced ESL learners and L2 users, i.e., the groups with highest L2 proficiency, behaved in a specific manner that was different from all the remaining groups tested in Experiment 1 in the same manner condition ($p < .05$). All the bilingual groups tested in

Table 13.4 Probability (*p*) for post-hoc tests for the same path condition in Experiment 1

	Polish monolinguals	English monolinguals	Intermediate ESL learners	Advanced ESL learners	L2 users
Polish monolinguals	–	0.38870	0.13920	0.04803*	0.00019*
English monolinguals	0.38870	–	0.57450	0.00777*	0.01111*
Intermediate ESL learners	0.13920	0.57450	–	0.00143*	0.06918
Advanced ESL learners	0.04803*	0.00777*	0.00143*	–	0.00000*
L2 users	0.00019*	0.01111*	0.06918	0.00000*	–

* $p < .05$

Table 13.5 Probability (*p*) for post-hoc tests for the same manner condition in Experiment 1

	Polish monolinguals	English monolinguals	Intermediate ESL learners	Advanced ESL learners	L2 users
Polish monolinguals	–	0.21800	0.97030	0.02148*	0.00027*
English monolinguals	0.21800	–	0.29600	0.00096*	0.03756*
Intermediate ESL learners	0.97030	0.29600	–	0.03171*	0.00140*
Advanced ESL learners	0.02148*	0.00096*	0.03171*	–	0.00000*
L2 users	0.00027*	0.03756*	0.00140*	0.00000*	–

* $p < .05$

Experiment 1 in the same manner condition differed from one another—advanced ESL learners chose the same manner alternates least frequently of all the groups ($M = 0.71$, i.e., 71% of all the responses, see also Figure 13.3) while the L2 users chose them most frequently of all the groups ($M = 0.79$).

Experiment 2

Materials and procedure

The aim of Experiment 2 was to investigate the degree of salience of both aspects of motion, i.e., manner and path, at the same time. In this way it was possible to find out how salient the domain of motion rejected in Experiment 1 was. While in Experiment 1 the participants had to choose between two criteria, manner and path, in Experiment 2 they had to focus on one criterion at a time, and rate its importance. Thus a similarity rating task was designed, consisting of 46 pairs of pictures portraying everyday activities performed by the same actor. The pictures were paired according to one of two criteria—the same manner or the same path of motion (see Appendix 13-B). The same set of pictures as in Experiment 1 served as stimuli in Experiment 2: a total of 13 pairs displayed same manner alternates with a different path (e.g., 'walking into' and 'walking out'), and the remaining 33 showed same path alternates with a different manner (e.g., 'walking into' and 'running into') (see Figure 13.4). The pairs of pictures were placed in a row on the computer screen together with a 5-point scale. The order of the pairs of pictures was the same for all the participants. The participants were instructed to rate the similarity between pictures on the scale.

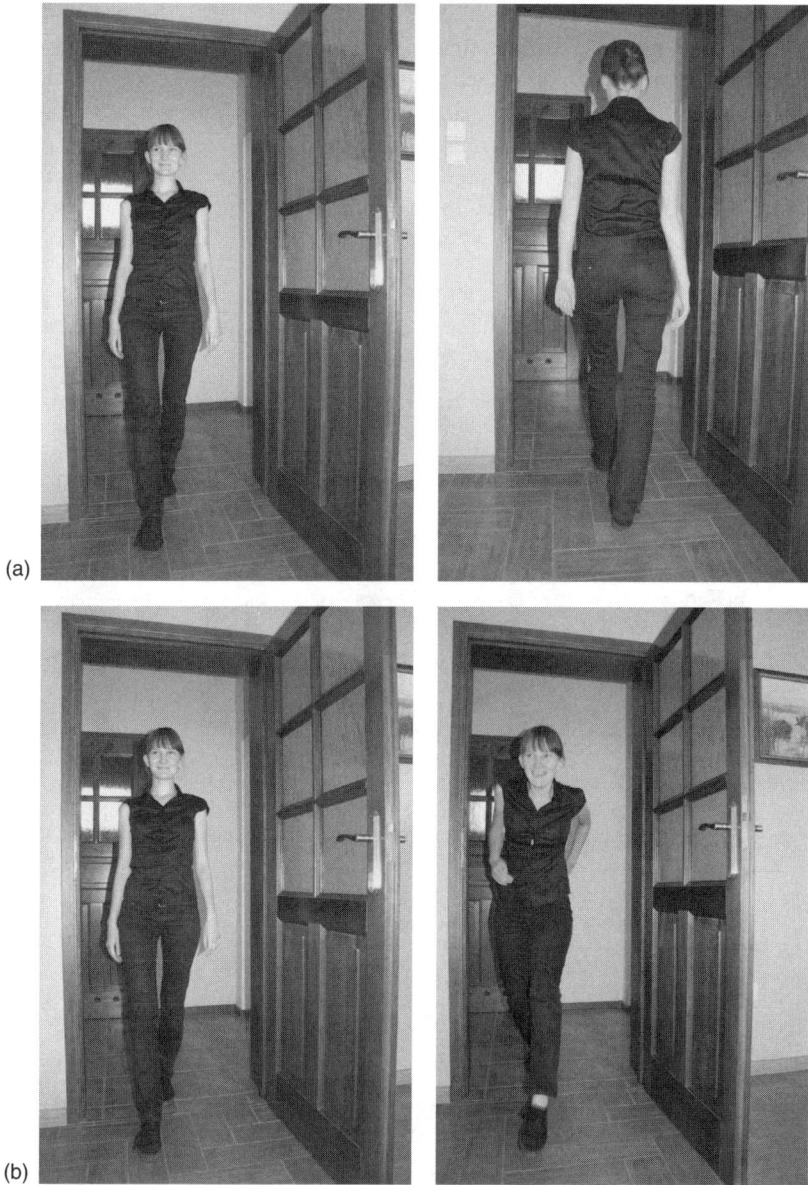

Figure 13.4 Examples of same manner (a) and same path (b) alternates from Experiment 2 (see Appendix 13-B).

Results

Mean ratings provided by the participants in both experimental conditions (path and manner) are presented in Figures 13.5 and 13.6 (with 5 = most similar). The analysis of similarity ratings indicated that the participants rated the same manner alternates as more similar than the same path alternates. This finding suggests that manner is a more salient domain of motion for all the groups tested in Experiment 2.

Two Kruskal-Wallis one-way analyses of variance (ANOVA) showed

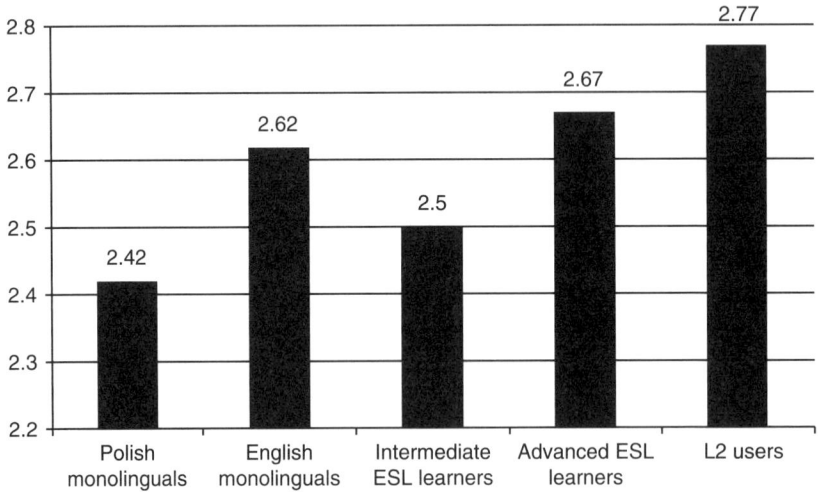

Figure 13.5 The results of the same path condition in Experiment 2 (mean scores).

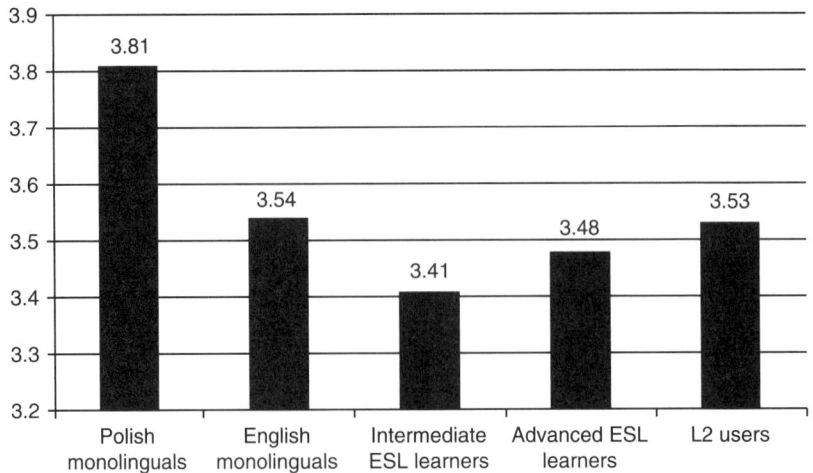

Figure 13.6 The results of the same manner condition in Experiment 2 (mean scores).

the effect of group (English monolinguals, Polish monolinguals, inter-mediate ESL learners, advanced ESL learners, L2 users) on similarity ratings for both the same path of motion condition, $H(4, N = 4059) = 56.12822$, $p < .0001$, and the same manner of motion condition, $H(4, N = 1599) = 36.17530$, $p < .0001$. Multiple comparisons (post-hoc tests) were used to specify which groups differ at the .05 level of significance (Tables 13.6 and 13.7).

The Kruskal-Wallis one-way ANOVA conducted in Experiment 2 revealed further differences between individual groups not found in Experiment 1. First, in both conditions in Experiment 2, post-hoc tests revealed a statistically significant difference between monolingual groups (Tables 13.6 and 13.7). English monolinguals rated path of motion as more similar than Polish monolinguals ($p < .001$) and Polish monolin-guals rated manner of motion as more similar than English monolinguals ($p < .005$).

In the same path condition (Table 13.6), as far as bilingual groups are concerned, intermediate ESL learners did not differ from Polish and English monolinguals ($p > .05$). Advanced ESL learners and L2 users did not differ from English monolinguals ($p > .05$) and differed from Polish monolinguals ($p < .0001$). Advanced ESL learners and L2 users, i.e., the two groups with highest L2 proficiency, rated the same path alternates as more similar in comparison to other groups, and even as more similar than English monolinguals. Moreover, although there was no difference between intermediate ESL learners and advanced ESL learners ($p > .05$), nor between advanced ESL learners and L2 users ($p > .05$), L2 users differed significantly from intermediate ESL learners ($p < .0001$).

In the same manner condition (Table 13.7), all the bilingual groups, i.e., intermediate ESL learners, advanced ESL learners and L2 users, were found to follow the English, but not the Polish, pattern of behavior. All the bilingual groups differed significantly from the Polish monolinguals

Table 13.6 Probability (p) for post-hoc tests for Kruskal-Wallis one-way analysis of variance (ANOVA) for the same path condition in Experiment 2

	Polish monolinguals	English monolinguals	Intermediate ESL learners	Advanced ESL learners	L2 users
Polish monolinguals	–	0.000758*	1.000000	0.000071*	0.000000*
English monolinguals	0.000758*	–	0.266437	1.000000	0.297588
Intermediate ESL learners	1.000000	0.266437	–	0.064141	0.000073*
Advanced ESL learners	0.000071*	1.000000	0.064141	–	1.000000
L2 users	0.000000*	0.297588	0.000073*	1.000000	–

* $p < .05$

Table 13.7 Probability (*p*) for post-hoc tests for Kruskal-Wallis one-way analysis of variance (ANOVA) for the same manner condition in Experiment 2

	Polish monolinguals	English monolinguals	Intermediate ESL learners	Advanced ESL learners	L2 users
Polish monolinguals	–	0.002349*	0.000006*	0.000301*	0.000240*
English monolinguals	0.002349*	–	1.000000	1.000000	1.000000
Intermediate ESL learners	0.000006*	1.000000	–	1.000000	1.000000
Advanced ESL learners	0.000301*	1.000000	1.000000	–	1.000000
L2 users	0.000240*	1.000000	1.000000	1.000000	–

* $p < .05$

(all $p < .0005$) but did not differ from the English monolinguals (all $p > .05$). In other words, when rating the similarity between the same manner alternates, the bilingual groups behaved more like native speakers of their L2 than native speakers of their L1.

DISCUSSION

Two experiments were designed to test the hypothesis that differences in motion lexicalization between Polish and English have cognitive consequences in that speakers of English will pay additional attention to path of motion in comparison to speakers of Polish. Experiment 1 was designed to check which aspect of motion appears more salient to the participants; thus in choosing one domain of motion, the participants had to reject the other one. Experiment 2 was a more controlled task which asked the participants to rate the salience of only one aspect of motion at a time. In this way it was possible to find out how salient the domain of motion rejected in Experiment 1 was. The results obtained from the monolingual and the bilingual groups of participants will be discussed below.

Monolingual groups

In the monolingual groups the results of both Experiment 1 and Experiment 2 showed that manner is the primary domain by which speakers of both Polish and English categorize motion. Experiment 1, in which the participants had to choose one criterion to judge similarity between action events, showed no differences in the preferences of Polish and English monolinguals. Both groups chose the same manner alternates three times more frequently than the same path alternates. A similar tendency could be observed in Experiment 2, in which both monolingual groups rated the same manner alternates higher than the same path alternates. This finding is in line with Talmy's (1985, 2000) classification of languages into satellite- and verb-framed, which places Polish and English in the same overall group of satellite-framed languages that encode manner of motion more saliently than its path.

Nevertheless, the results of Experiment 2, which made use of a more controlled task, revealed differences in the perception of motion by Polish and English monolinguals. These results show that, although both languages belong to the same group of satellite-framed languages (Talmy, 1985, 2000) that primarily encode manner of motion, English monolinguals pay additional attention to path of motion, as they rated the same path alternates higher than Polish monolinguals. An additional finding that had not been anticipated in our research hypotheses is that, in comparison to English monolinguals, Polish monolinguals pay more attention to manner of motion, which again shows that despite some morpholexical similarities, those two languages differ in weights they assign to two aspects of motion, i.e., path and manner. The finding that Polish monolinguals rate motion events with the same manner as more similar than English monolinguals can be explained by Polish grammatical structures. It seems that the fact that Polish rarely leaves its verbs unmarked for manner can contribute to a different imagery of motion events in Polish speakers, making them pay more attention to manner of motion than speakers of English. More importantly, it seems that differences in the linguistic encoding of motion between Polish and English pointed out at the beginning of this chapter are reflected in non-linguistic preferences of speakers of those languages. More specifically, speakers of English, which encodes path of motion in a separable prefix and has a variety of path and generic verbs which do not specify manner of motion, seem to categorize motion events on the basis of its path more frequently than speakers of Polish. In other words, the conceptualization of motion by English monolinguals appears to be influenced by linguistic structures of their language. The same holds true for Polish monolinguals who, in comparison to speakers of English, do not pay so much attention to path, as this aspect of motion seems not to be encoded so saliently in Polish as it is in English. These findings confirm our first research hypothesis that differences in motion lexicalization between Polish and English have cognitive consequences for speakers of these languages.

The results obtained from both groups of monolingual speakers in Experiments 1 and 2 indicate that, although the main assumptions of Talmy's (1985, 2000) classification of languages are confirmed for Polish and English as satellite-framed languages, the difference in how speakers of those two languages perceive motion is visible. Our interpretation of this phenomenon is that differences in the categorization of motion events are rooted in morpholexical structures encoding motion in both languages.

Therefore the classification of languages introduced by Talmy (1985, 2000) seems more like a scale or a continuum than a clear-cut distinction into two different groups.

Bilingual groups

The results of Experiments 1 and 2 for the bilingual groups indicate that bilinguals undergo conceptual change under the influence of the L2 that is both quantitative and qualitative in nature.

The group with lowest L2 proficiency and exposure, i.e., intermediate ESL learners, behaved just like Polish and English monolinguals in Experiment 1. However, in Experiment 2, in which Polish and English monolinguals were found to differ, intermediate ESL learners displayed signs of conceptual change taking place. Rating the salience of path of motion, they did not differ significantly from either Polish or English monolinguals, which means that their ratings fell somewhere between the mean values assigned by the monolinguals of the two languages. On the other hand, rating the salience of manner of motion, they behaved just like English, and differently from Polish, monolinguals. In other words, Experiment 2 revealed that intermediate ESL learners are somewhere in between Polish and English monolinguals, when it comes to the conceptualization of path of motion, and closer to the English pattern as far as manner of motion is concerned. Such results can be interpreted as an instance of conceptual shift towards L2 values that is quantitative in nature. This finding shows that even bilinguals with relatively low L2 proficiency and exposure mostly in a formal setting can undergo conceptual change in the process of second language acquisition.

The most proficient bilingual groups, i.e., advanced ESL learners and L2 users, behaved in a specific manner in both Experiments 1 and 2. In Experiment 1 they differed from all the other groups tested and from each other in their choices of the same manner alternates. With regard to same path alternates, they differed from all the other groups (with the difference between L2 users and intermediate ESL learners approaching significance), as well as from each other. Advanced ESL learners chose the same path alternates most frequently of all the groups and more frequently than English monolinguals, and the same manner alternates least frequently of all the groups and less frequently than English monolinguals. On the other hand, L2 users chose the same manner alternates most frequently of all the groups and more frequently than Polish monolinguals, and the same path alternates least frequently of all the groups and less frequently than the Polish monolinguals. Since no differences have been found between the monolinguals of the respective languages in the same experimental task, this finding should be interpreted as a manifestation of hypersensitivity to one of the domains of motion, either manner or path, in the most proficient L2 speakers. Since, as the results of Experiment 2 have shown, manner and path figure differently in the perception of motion by Polish and English monolinguals, this untypical behavior of the most proficient bilinguals points to cognitive reorganization taking place in their perceptions of motion. The differences between the two most proficient bilingual groups require further comment. Paying more attention to path of motion, advanced ESL learners behaved in a more English-like fashion, and the L2 users behaved in a more Polish-like fashion, paying more attention to manner of motion. If the way motion is encoded in language influences speakers' non-verbal perceptions, then advanced ESL learners seem to be paying more attention to cues from their L2, while the L2 users seem to be paying more attention to cues from their L1. Considering the differences between the two groups of participants, this differential development can only be explained by their different experiences of using the two languages, particularly differences in the amount and quality of exposure to the L2. This interpretation of the results is supported by previous research with L2 users with a similar background (Ewert, 2010; Ewert & Bromberek-Dyzman, 2008), which also showed hypersensitivity to L1 cues in a variety of tasks.

Experiment 2 helped to reveal further differences between the bilingual groups. In the same path condition, intermediate ESL learners showed a pattern of behavior that was intermediate between the monolingual Polish and monolingual English patterns. Advanced ESL learners and L2 users responded like monolingual native speakers of English and differently from monolingual Poles. Hence, the participants' ratings of path salience show a clear shift towards L2 values with increasing proficiency. In the same manner condition, all the bilingual groups differ from Polish monolinguals and follow the English pattern of responses. Again, the perceptions of manner of motion show shift towards the L2.

CONCLUSION

The results of the present study with Polish and English monolinguals as well as the three groups of Polish–English bilinguals with different L2 proficiency and exposure supported our research hypotheses.

Our first research hypothesis assumed that although Polish and English belong to one group of satellite-framed languages (Talmy, 1985, 2000) in categorizing motion events, monolingual speakers of English will focus on the path of motion more than monolingual speakers of Polish. This hypothesis was confirmed by the results of the rating task (Experiment 2), but not of the triad task (Experiment 1). This result indicates that, although manner is more salient than path to speakers of both languages, speakers of English pay additional attention to path when their attention is focused on more than one attribute of motion at the same time. An additional finding is that, focusing on more than one attribute of motion at the same time, monolingual speakers of Polish pay additional attention to manner. Those non-verbal differences in categorization of motion between the two groups of monolinguals are rooted in language. Therefore the results of our study indicate that the group of satellite-framed languages is not homogeneous and should be seen as a spectrum along which languages falling within the same group encode two features of motion, i.e., manner and path, with different saliency.

Our second hypothesis stated that Polish–English bilinguals will shift towards L2-based conceptual representations, paying more attention to path of motion. This hypothesis was borne out by the results of Experiment 2, in which all the bilingual participants behaved like monolingual speakers of English, attending to path. Additionally, Experiment 2 has shown that the bilinguals are rapidly desensitized to manner of motion, behaving differently from monolingual Poles. Moreover, the results of Experiment 1 suggest that attentional restructuring is taking place in the conceptual domains of the most proficient bilinguals, making them hypersensitive to path and manner cues.

The third research hypothesis concerned the relationship between bilinguals' perceptions of motion and L2 proficiency and amount and quality of exposure to the L2. The results of Experiment 2 revealed an almost linear relationship between L2 proficiency and perception of motion events, thus clearly pointing to a shift towards L2 values. However, the results of Experiment 1 indicate that the change taking place in bilingual conceptual representations is more complex than shift in perception. The most-proficient bilinguals demonstrate hypersensitivity to either path or manner cues. Since manner has been additionally salient to Polish monolinguals and path has been additionally salient to English monolinguals in our study, it may be said that the L2 users behave more in a Polish-like manner, demonstrating hypersensitivity to cues from Polish, and the advanced ESL learners behave more in an English-like manner, demonstrating hypersensitivity to cues from English. In the light of our data, this differential development in the two most-proficient bilingual groups can only be explained by the different experiences they have using their languages. It seems that each of the groups is more sensitive to cues from the language they use less: Advanced ESL learners are more sensitive to cues from English, with which they have only limited contact, while the L2 users attend more to cues from Polish, which they use less frequently than the other bilingual groups.

All in all, using Pavlenko's (Jarvis & Pavlenko, 2008; Pavlenko, 2005) classification of conceptual change, our data show conceptual shift towards the L2 in the least-proficient bilinguals and restructuring of the conceptual domain in the two most-proficient groups. Hypersensitivity to cues from either the L1 or the L2 should be taken as evidence of conceptual restructuring, since it points to different allocation of attention to perceptual cues. In sum, while the bilinguals in our study become more

English-like with increased proficiency, they differ qualitatively from the monolinguals of their respective languages.

ACKNOWLEDGMENTS

The authors are grateful to Agnieszka Skrzypek for useful suggestions concerning data analysis. We would also like to thank Dr. Waldemar Wołyński from the Faculty of Mathematics and Statistics, Adam Mickiewicz University, for assistance with the statistical analyses. We are also indebted to the editors of this volume, whose comments on the manuscript allowed us to report the results of our study with greater precision and clarity.

REFERENCES

Ameel, E., Storms, G., Malt, B. C., & Sloman, S. A. (2005). How bilinguals solve the naming problem. *Journal of Memory and Language, 52*, 309–329.

Athanasopoulos, P. (2009). Cognitive representation of colour in bilinguals: The case of Greek blues. *Bilingualism: Language and Cognition, 12*, 83–95.

Athanasopoulos, P., & Kasai, C. (2008). Language and thought in bilinguals: The case of grammatical number and nonverbal classification preferences. *Applied Psycholinguistics, 29*, 105–123.

Bassetti, B. (2007). Bilingualism and thought: Grammatical gender and concepts of objects in Italian–German bilingual children. *International Journal of Bilingualism, 11*, 251–273.

Billman, D., Swilley, A., & Krych, M. (2000). Path and manner priming: Verb production and event recognition. In L. R. Gleitman & A. K. Joshi (Eds.), *Proceedings of the twenty-second annual conference of the Cognitive Science Society* (pp. 615–620). Mahwah, NJ: Lawrence Erlbaum Associates Inc.

Brown, A. (2008). Gesture viewpoint in Japanese and English: Cross-linguistic interactions between two languages in one speaker. *Gesture, 8*, 256–276.

Brown, A., & Gullberg, M. (2008). Bidirectional crosslinguistic influence in L1–L2 encoding of manner in speech and gesture: A study of Japanese speakers of English. *Studies in Second Language Acquisition, 30*, 225–251.

Cook, V. J. (2002). Background to the L2 user. In V. Cook (Ed.), *Portraits of the L2 user* (pp. 1–18). Clevedon, UK: Multilingual Matters.

Cook, V. J. (2007). The nature of the L2 user. In L. Roberts, A. Gürel, S. Tatar, & L. Marti (Eds.), *EUROSLA yearbook 7* (pp. 205–220). Amsterdam: John Benjamins.

Cook, V. J., Bassetti, B., Kasai, C., Sasaki, M., & Takahashi, J. A. (2006). Do bilinguals have different concepts? The case of shape and material in Japanese L2 users of English. *International Journal of Bilingualism, 10*, 137–152.

Cook, V. J., Iarossi, E., Stellakis, N., & Tokumaru, Y. (2003). Effects of the L2 on the syntactic processing of the L1. In V. Cook (Ed.), *Effects of the second language on the first* (pp. 193–213). Clevedon, UK: Multilingual Matters.

Dimitrova-Vulchanova, M., Martinez, L., & Edsberg, O. (in press). A basic level category for the encoding of motion. In J. Hudson, C. Paradis, & U. Magnusson (Eds.), *Conceptual spaces and the construal of spatial meanings: Empirical evidence from human communication*. Oxford, UK: Oxford University Press.

Ewert, A. (in press). *L2 users' L1*. Bristol, UK: Multilingual Matters.

Ewert, A., & Bromberek-Dyzman, K. (2008). L2 users' sociopragmatic and pragmalinguistic choices in L1 acts of refusal. In L. Roberts, F. Myles, & A. David (Eds.), *EUROSLA yearbook 8* (pp. 32–51). Amsterdam: John Benjamins.

Ewert, A., Bromberek-Dyzman, K., & Singleton, D. (2008). *Understanding conversational implicatures in two languages*. Poster presented at the EUROSLA 18 Conference, Aix en Provence, 10–13 September.

Gass, S. M., & Selinker, L. (Eds.). (1983). *Language transfer in language learning*. Rowley, MA: Newbury House.

Hedden, T., Ketay, S., Aron, A., Markus, H. R., & Gabrieli, J. D. E. (2008). Cultural influences on neural substrates of attentional control. *Psychological Science, 19*, 1–17.

Hohenstein, J., Eisenberg, A., & Naigles, L. (2006). Is he floating across or crossing afloat: Cross-influence of L1 and L2 in Spanish–English bilingual adults. *Bilingualism: Language and Cognition, 9*, 249–261.

Jarvis, S., & Pavlenko, A. (2008). *Crosslinguistic influence in language and cognition*. New York: Taylor & Francis.

Lucy, J. A. (1992). *Grammatical categories and cognition: A case study of the linguistic relativity hypothesis*. Cambridge, UK: Cambridge University Press.

Malt, B. C., Sloman, S. A., & Gennari, S. (2003). Speaking versus thinking about objects and actions. In D. Gentner & S. Goldin-Meadow (Eds.), *Language in mind: Advances in the study of language and thought* (pp. 81–111). Cambridge, MA: MIT Press.

McNeill, D. (2001). Imagery in motion event description: Gestures as part of thinking-for-speaking in three languages. *Proceedings of the twenty-third annual meeting of the Berkeley Linguistics Society* (pp. 255–267). Berkeley, CA: Berkeley Linguistics Society.

McNeill, D. (2005). *Gesture and thought*. Chicago, IL: University of Chicago Press.

Newcombe, R. G. (1998a). Two-sided confidence intervals for the single proportion: Comparison of seven methods. *Statistics in Medicine, 17*, 857–872.

Newcombe, R. G. (1998b). Interval estimation for the difference between independent proportions: Comparison of eleven methods. *Statistics in Medicine, 17*, 873–890.

Pavlenko, A. (2005). Bilingualism and thought. In J. F. Kroll & A. M. B. de Groot (Eds.), *Handbook of bilingualism: Psycholinguistic approaches* (pp. 433–453). Oxford, UK: Oxford University Press.

Pavlenko, A. (2009). Conceptual representation in the bilingual lexicon and second language vocabulary learning. In A. Pavlenko (Ed.), *The bilingual mental lexicon: Interdisciplinary approaches* (pp. 125–160). Bristol, UK: Multilingual Matters.

Pavlenko, A. (2010). Verbs of motion in L1 Russian of Russian–English bilinguals. *Bilingualism: Language and Cognition, 13*(1), 49–62.

Pavlenko, A., & Jarvis, S. (2002). Bidirectional transfer. *Applied Linguistics, 23*, 190–214.

Slobin, D. I. (1987). Thinking for speaking. In J. Aske, N. Beery, L. Michaelis, &

H. Filip (Eds.), *Proceedings of the thirteenth annual meeting of the Berkeley Linguistics Society* (pp. 435–444). Berkeley, CA: Berkeley Linguistics Society.

Slobin, D. I. (2000). Verbalized events: A dynamic approach to linguistic relativity and determinism. In S. Niemeier & R. Dirven (Eds.), *Evidence for linguistic relativity* (pp. 107–138). Amsterdam: John Benjamins.

Slobin, D. I. (2003). Language and thought online: Cognitive consequences of linguistic relativity. In D. Gentner & S. Goldin-Meadow (Eds.), *Language in mind: Advances in the study of language and thought* (pp. 157–191). Cambridge, MA: MIT Press.

Talmy, L. (1985). Lexicalization patterns: Semantic structure in lexical forms. In T. Shopen (Ed.), *Language typology and syntactic description* (Vol. 3, pp. 56–149). Cambridge, UK: Cambridge University Press.

Talmy, L. (2000). *Towards a cognitive semantics* (Vol. 2). Cambridge, MA: MIT Press.

Talmy, L. (2008). Aspects of attention in language. In P. Robinson & N. C. Ellis (Eds.), *Handbook of cognitive linguistics and second language acquisition* (pp. 27–38). New York: Routledge.

Thierry, G., Athanasopoulos, P., Wiggett, A., Dering, B., & Kuipers, J-R. (2009). Unconscious effects of language-specific terminology on pre-attentive color perception. *Proceedings of the National Academy of Sciences, 106,* 4567–4570.

von Stutterheim, C. (2003). Linguistic structure and information organization: The case of very advanced learners. In S. Foster-Cohen & S. Pekarek Doehler (Eds.), *EUROSLA yearbook 3* (pp. 183–206). Amsterdam: John Benjamins.

von Stutterheim, C., & Nüse, R. (2003). Processes of conceptualization in language production: Language-specific perspectives and event construal. *Linguistics, 41*(5), 851–881.

Whorf, B. L. (1941/1956). The relation of habitual thought and behavior to language. In L. Spier (Ed.), *Language, culture and personality*. [Reprinted in J. B. Carroll (Ed.), *Language, thought, and reality: Selected writings of Benjamin Lee Whorf* (pp. 134–159). Cambridge, MA: MIT Press.]

Wilson, E. B. (1927). Probable inference, the law of succession, and statistical inference. *Journal of the American Statistical Association, 22,* 209–212.

APPENDIX 13-A

The full experimental design consisted of triads of pictures depicting motion events displayed in the following manner:

No.	Picture a Double-paired item	Picture b Same path alternate	Picture c Same manner alternate
1	walk into	run into	walk out
2	run into	jump into	run out
3	jump into	crawl on all fours into	jump out
4	crawl on all fours into	crawl into	crawl on all fours out
5	walk into	jump into	walk out
6	run into	crawl on all fours into	run out
7	jump into	crawl into	jump out
8	walk into	crawl on all fours into	walk out

No.	Picture a	Picture b	Picture c
	Double-paired item	*Same path alternate*	*Same manner alternate*
9	run into	crawl into	run out
10	walk into	crawl into	walk out
	Same path alternate	*Double-paired item*	*Same manner alternate*
11	crawl on all fours into	crawl into	crawl out
12	jump into	crawl on all fours into	crawl on all fours out
13	run into	jump into	jump out
14	walk into	run into	run out
15	jump into	crawl into	crawl out
16	run into	crawl on all fours into	crawl on all fours out
17	walk into	jump into	jump out
18	run into	crawl into	crawl out
19	walk into	crawl on all fours into	crawl on all fours out
20	walk into	crawl into	crawl out
	Double-paired item	*Same path alternate*	*Same manner alternate*
21	crawl on all fours into	crawl into	crawl on all fours over
22	walk into	run into	walk over
23	jump into	crawl on all fours into	jump over
24	walk into	jump into	walk over
25	jump into	crawl into	jump over
26	walk into	crawl on all fours into	walk over
27	walk into	crawl into	walk over
	Same path alternate	*Double-paired item*	*Same manner alternate*
28	walk into	crawl on all fours into	crawl on all fours over
29	jump into	crawl on all fours into	crawl on all fours over
30	walk into	jump into	jump over
	Double-paired item	*Same path alternate*	*Same manner alternate*
31	walk out	run out	walk into
32	run out	jump out	run into
33	jump out	crawl on all fours out	jump into
34	crawl on all fours out	crawl out	crawl on all fours into
35	walk out	jump out	walk into
36	run out	crawl on all fours out	run into
37	jump out	crawl out	jump into
38	walk out	crawl on all fours out	walk into
39	run out	crawl out	run into
40	walk out	crawl out	walk into
	Same path alternate	*Double-paired item*	*Same manner alternate*
41	crawl on all fours out	crawl out	crawl into
42	jump out	crawl on all fours out	crawl on all fours into
43	run out	jump out	jump into
44	walk out	run out	run into
45	jump out	crawl out	crawl into
46	run out	crawl on all fours out	crawl on all fours into
47	walk out	jump out	jump into
48	run out	crawl out	crawl into
49	walk out	crawl on all fours out	crawl on all fours into
50	walk out	crawl out	crawl into
	Double-paired item	*Same path alternate*	*Same manner alternate*
51	crawl on all fours out	crawl out	crawl on all fours over
52	walk out	run out	walk over
53	jump out	crawl on all fours out	jump over
54	walk out	jump out	walk over
55	jump out	crawl out	jump over
56	walk out	crawl on all fours out	walk over
57	walk out	crawl out	walk over

	Same path alternate	*Double-paired item*	*Same manner alternate*
58	walk out	crawl on all fours out	crawl on all fours over
59	jump out	crawl on all fours out	crawl on all fours over
60	walk out	jump out	jump over

	Double-paired item	*Same path alternate*	*Same manner alternate*
61	walk down	crawl on all fours down	walk up
62	crawl on all fours down	run down	crawl on all fours up
63	walk down	run down	walk up

	Same path alternate	*Double-paired item*	*Same manner alternate*
64	walk down	crawl on all fours down	crawl on all fours up
65	crawl on all fours down	run down	run up
66	walk down	run down	run up

	Double-paired item	*Same path alternate*	*Same manner alternate*
67	walk up	crawl on all fours up	walk down
68	crawl on all fours up	run up	crawl on all fours down
69	walk up	run up	walk down

	Same path alternate	*Double-paired item*	*Same manner alternate*
70	walk up	crawl on all fours up	crawl on all fours down
71	crawl on all fours up	run up	run down
72	walk up	run up	run down
73	walk over	crawl on all fours over	crawl on all fours under
74	jump over	crawl on all fours over	crawl on all fours under

	Double-paired item	*Same path alternate*	*Same manner alternate*
75	crawl on all fours over	crawl over	crawl on all fours under

	Same path alternate	*Double-paired item*	*Same manner alternate*
76	walk over	crawl over	crawl under
77	jump over	crawl over	crawl under
78	crawl on all fours over	crawl over	crawl under

	Double-paired item	*Same path alternate*	*Same manner alternate*
79	crawl on all fours under	crawl under	crawl on all fours over

	Same path alternate	*Double-paired item*	*Same manner alternate*
80	crawl on all fours under	crawl under	crawl over

APPENDIX 13-B

The full experimental design consisted of pairs of pictures depicting motion events displayed in the following manner:

No.	Picture a	Picture b
	Same path alternates	
1	walk into	run into
2	run into	jump into
3	jump into	crawl on all fours into
4	crawl on all fours into	crawl into
5	walk into	jump into
6	run into	crawl on all fours into
7	jump into	crawl into
8	walk into	crawl on all fours into
9	run into	crawl into
10	walk into	crawl into

No.	Picture a	Picture b
	Same manner alternates	
11	walk into	walk out
12	run into	run out
13	jump into	jump out
14	crawl on all fours into	crawl on all fours out
15	crawl into	crawl out
16	go into	go over
17	jump into	jump over
18	crawl on all fours into	crawl on all fours over
	Same path alternates	
19	walk out	run out
20	run out	jump out
21	jump out	crawl on all fours out
22	crawl on all fours out	crawl out
23	walk out	jump out
24	run out	crawl on all fours out
25	jump out	crawl out
26	walk out	crawl on all fours out
27	run out	crawl out
28	walk out	crawl out
29	walk down	crawl on all fours down
	Same manner alternates	
30	run down	run up
	Same path alternates	
31	crawl on all fours down	run down
	Same manner alternates	
32	walk down	walk up
	Same path alternates	
33	walk down	run down
	Same manner alternates	
34	crawl on all fours down	crawl on all fours up
	Same path alternates	
35	walk up	crawl on all fours up
36	crawl on all fours up	run up
37	walk up	run up
38	go over	jump over
39	jump over	crawl on all fours over
40	crawl on all fours over	crawl over
41	crawl on all fours under	crawl under
	Same manner alternates	
42	crawl on all fours over	crawl on all fours under
	Same path alternates	
43	walk over	crawl on all fours over
	Same manner alternates	
44	crawl over	crawl under
	Same path alternates	
45	jump over	crawl over
46	walk over	crawl over

14 Expressing voluntary motion in a second language: English learners of French

Henriette Hendriks and
Maya Hickmann

Space is of utmost importance in our lives and all languages provide an inventory of linguistic means to represent spatial information. Given its universal importance, space is an ideal domain in which to explore the following questions regarding the relationship between language and thought: Are the linguistic and the conceptual systems entirely independent? Does our conceptualization of the world determine the structure of linguistic systems? Or, conversely, does language partially determine our cognitive organization? And from the point of view of language acquisition does cognition drive language acquisition or is cognition mainly shaped by the language to be acquired?

Given the need for all human beings to construct spatial representations, one might expect a strong link between universal properties of linguistic systems and of human spatial cognition. With respect to the expression of motion, which will be at the center of the present study, one might therefore expect that linguistic systems would treat motion events in a universal way. Many studies in the last 25 years, however, have disconfirmed this hypothesis, showing that languages actually vary a great deal in how they express motion. Such variation has generated a large number of studies (Gentner & Goldin-Meadow, 2003; Gumperz & Levinson, 1996; Hickmann & Robert, 2006; Levinson, 2003; Lucy, 1992), many of which have revived the 'linguistic relativity' hypothesis.

Studies in this area are typically of a cross-linguistic nature, aiming at identifying the scope of variation that can be found across different languages and the possible effect of the language-specific differences on behavior (Levinson, 1996). Significant projects went well beyond the traditionally researched European languages (see, for example, research by the Language and Cognition group of the Max-Planck Institute for Psycholinguistics, Nijmegen).

As regards language acquisition, a large number of studies have examined the expression of motion in the context of first language acquisition (as discussed in some detail below), but very few have done so for second language (L2) acquisition (but see Cadierno, 2004; Cadierno & Lund, 2004; Carroll, Murcia-Serra, Watorek, & Bendiscoli, 2000; von Stutterheim,

2003; von Stutterheim & Lambert, 2005; and our own work as published in Hendriks, 2005; Hendriks, Hickmann, & Demagny, 2008). L2 acquisition, however, provides a most interesting context to pursue this line of questioning. Thus, if we assume that language has an influence on thought, and if we follow Slobin's proposal (1996) that the native speaker learns over time how to 'think for speaking', then learning a second language that organizes the linguistic expression of motion in a different way at a later stage in life (adulthood) should lead to considerable difficulties for learners: In this view, they have to learn not only new linguistic means to express motion, but also a new way of thinking for the purposes of communication in discourse.

In the present chapter we will therefore study the productions of adult learners of a second language who are confronted with typologically different source and target languages, and we will identify their developmental path as they learn to speak about motion and/or to think for speaking about motion.

THE TYPOLOGY OF MOTION EVENTS IN A COGNITIVE LINGUISTIC FRAMEWORK

Since the 1970s, researchers have sought to classify languages according to their expression of motion and location. Leonard Talmy's work (1983, 2000) is seminal in this domain. Talmy proposes that languages can be classified according to the locus at which they express the most basic information component of motion events, i.e., Path, or the trajectory taken by the moving object (for a detailed description of Talmy's framework in this volume, see Evans, Chapter 4). According to Talmy's classification, languages belong to two main groups, 'verb-framed' languages that express Path in the verb, and 'satellite-framed' languages that express Path in satellites (verb particles for example). Note that not all languages can be easily classified accordingly, possibly showing the need for more than two categories, or need for a continuum of languages (Italian, Greek, and Chinese for example (cf. Ji, 2009), are thought to be somewhere midway on the continuum). For the source and target languages studied in this chapter, however, there is general consensus that English is satellite-framed and that (contemporary) French is predominantly verb-framed.

Although Talmy's classification concerns first and foremost the expression of Path, the locus of other relevant information (such as Manner e.g., *walking*, *running*, and Cause of motion, e.g., *pulling*, *pushing*) is influenced as well. Thus, in French, where Path is expressed in the verb, Manner may not be expressed at all, or, when expressed, it is frequently placed outside the main clause, in subordinate constructions, as in example 1. In English, where Path is expressed in the satellite, the verb is free for the expression of Manner, and this is indeed where Manner is most often expressed in English (as is Cause of motion), as in example 2.

(1) Le garçon **traverse** [Path] la rue **en courant** [Manner].
(2) The man **runs** [Manner] **across** [Path] the street.

Finally, previous studies have pointed out that one more fairly systematic difference between satellite-framed and verb-framed languages concerns the ease with which multiple types of information can be expressed simultaneously. For example, given typological differences across languages, the stacking of Path information (example 3) is quite straightforward and common in satellite-framed languages such as English (resulting in highly informative utterances), whereas it requires more complex syntactic structures (such as subordinate clauses) in verb-framed languages such as French or Spanish (example 4).

(3) The bird **flew down from out of** the hole in the tree.
(4) El pájaro **salió** del agujero del árbol **volando hacia abajo**.
     The bird **exited** of the hole of the tree **flying towards below**.
                                        (Slobin, 1996, p. 83, bold added)

We have explored this phenomenon of density in more depth for a number of European verb-framed and satellite-framed languages. With respect to first language acquisition, a large and varied database shows that density is systematically higher in satellite-framed languages (English and German) than in verb-framed languages (French) in both children and adult native speakers (Hendriks, 2005; Hickmann, Hendriks, & Roland, 1998; Hickmann, Taranne, & Bonnet, 2009). Further studies discuss second language acquisition by adults (Hendriks et al., 2008), which will be the focus of the present study. We turn to this type of learners to examine in detail the questions that have arisen in relation to L2 acquisition.

THINKING FOR SPEAKING AND ITS IMPLICATIONS FOR L2 ACQUISITION

The current debate regarding the interrelation between language and conceptualization finds its roots in ideas put forward in the nineteenth and early twentieth centuries (works by Humboldt, Boas, Sapir, and Whorf). In the context of this debate, some studies claim to have found a clear influence of language on non-linguistic thinking, i.e., on recall memory, recognition memory, transitive inference, and possibly even visual recall and gesture (Levinson, 1996). Others, using different methodologies such as eye-tracking and categorization tasks, argue that no effects of language on cognition can be found (Papafragou, Massey, & Gleitman, 2002), thus implying that the first set of findings must be the result of a methodological artefact (i.e., even though the task was meant to test non-linguistic behavior, speakers make use of 'internal' language that contaminates their performance).

Initially studies claimed a very strong link between language and thought, a view that Lucy (1992, p. 3) summarizes as follows: 'a self-conscious speaker can never be free of constraints imposed by [language]'. Most researchers now propose a much more carefully worded hypothesis, such that 'there may be some identifiable cognitive correlates (outside of the specifically linguistic realm) associated with using a particular language' (Lucy, 1992, p. 3). In this study we will work with a yet different formulation of the hypothesis by Slobin, who argues that language may influence thought when thinking is carried out while speaking. According to this view there is a special kind of thinking that is intimately related to language, namely the thinking that is carried out on-line during the process of speaking (Slobin, 1996). This type of thinking, according to Slobin, 'involves picking those characteristics of objects and events that (a) fit some conceptualization of the event, and (b) are readily encodable in language' (1996, p. 76). When formulated in this way, the hypothesis focuses on thinking as it takes place during the act of communicating.

Assuming that language has an influence on cognitive processes, several types of predictions are possible. According to one (extreme) view, speakers of different languages might construct rather different mental representations of the same events. For example, their verbal and underlying non-verbal representations of someone running down a hill would contain Manner information in English but not in French. As a result, English speakers should be able to remember how the motion was carried out (lexicalized in the main verb, e.g., *run*), but not French speakers (Manner peripheral and/or not at all expressed). More reasonably, another type of prediction is that speakers might differentially weigh the salience of various types of information, despite the fact that they may all include the same types of information in their mental representations. According to this view, English speakers should remember Manner information better than French speakers. Yet a third view would be that all speakers might be equally good at remembering all aspects of the event, despite the fact that they may differentially focus on different types of information for the purposes of speaking.

Turning to first language acquisition, the main question is whether cognition drives language acquisition or, conversely, whether cognition is shaped by the language to be acquired. If the latter were true, one would expect that children's developmental course would be influenced by whether their language more naturally expresses Manner and Path in one clause (satellite framing) or whether it tends to express either Manner or Path but not both in one clause (verb framing). However, if we assume that conceptualization has an influence on language and that the conceptualization of space is universally fundamental to survival, one would expect it to be very similar for all human beings. Under this assumption, then, language-specific influences should be negligible and all children should focus on similar types of spatial information. In this respect, studies in first language acquisition show contradictory results. On the one hand, some evidence shows that children have quite an extensive amount of knowledge about space very early on in life, well before they start producing language (Baillargeon, 1995; Mandler, 1998; Spelke, 1998). Accordingly, some results show that children follow a very similar developmental course, for example in acquiring spatial prepositions, irrespective of their language (Johnston & Slobin, 1979). On the other hand, the same study also shows cross-linguistic differences in developmental rhythms, and recent research (Bowerman & Choi, 2001; Choi & Bowerman, 1991, among others) further claims that children's perceptual and cognitive behaviors are influenced by their surrounding language as early as the pre-linguistic period.

Slobin proposes that one of the main tasks faced by children consists of learning the thinking for speaking that is specific to their mother tongue. In a given language anything can be expressed but not everything is as easily expressed, so that children have to acquire the typical patterns that characterize information focus and locus for their specific language. Once acquired, it should constitute an intricate part of the language production process, since knowing how to think for speaking will become automatized with age and speed up language production, making it error free.

We propose that one can also address the question of the role of language and cognition in acquisition by studying adult second language acquisition. Thus, if language and cognition are largely independent, one would expect the learner of a second language to have an easier task of shaking off the linguistic system of the L1 and finding a new L2 system to fit the motion events observed in a language-neutral way. If, however, language and cognition get intricately related during L1 acquisition, one would expect some of the spatial conceptualization of an adult speaker to mirror the features of their native language. This should lead to some difficulty in acquiring a language that requires both different linguistic spatial means, and a different way of conceptually organizing space. In Slobin's framework, if thinking for speaking is an intricate part of language production, one may wonder what happens when speakers learn a second language in which space is not organized in the same way as in their first language.

Whereas it seems obvious that there may be interference from the type of 'thinking for speaking' that is specific to the L1 during the acquisition of the L2, interference (or transfer) phenomena until recently have only been measured at particular levels of language, i.e., syntax, semantics, lexicon. But just as important is the question of whether and how L2 learners acquire a *different way of thinking*. Recent studies of the latter type (Carroll et al., 2000; Hendriks et al., 2008; von Stutterheim, 2003) show that reorganizing information in discourse following the patterns of the target language may be one of the last things acquired by L2 learners (cf. work on near-natives by Carroll et al., 2000, and von Stutterheim et al., 2003).

In the present study we will address precisely this question: How do adult learners of a second language adjust their thinking for speaking, particularly if this second language is typologically different from their first language? We will address this question by examining how native speakers of English learning French deal with the expression of motion. Some evidence as to the developmental course of such speakers is already available from our previous research (Hendriks et al., 2008). In that study we looked at how English learners of French expressed Caused motion situations in the L2. Participants were presented with short cartoons involving a little man (Hoppy) who PUSHED or PULLED objects (Cause and Manner of cause) such that they ROLLED or SLID (Manner) along various Paths (ACROSS, INTO, UP, or DOWN). English native speakers typically reported on such events in a very systematic way, expressing Manner and/ or Cause of motion in the verb, and Path in the satellite. In contrast, French native speakers typically resorted to syntactically complex structures to talk about such events. In addition, semantic components were not systematically coded by particular linguistic means, but rather showed a highly variable distribution. As for English learners of French, they initially expressed only part of the information in the target language (mostly the Cause of motion). With proficiency they managed to express more information, but initially relied on an English organizational pattern, resulting in idiosyncratic uses of French linguistic devices. Only when learners had acquired complex syntactic structures did their language start to look grammatically correct, but even then the information organization (caused by a different way of thinking for speaking) remained non-target-like.

The present study follows up these results by extending the research to other types of motion events. In particular, we examine how the same set of learners described displacements intentionally carried out by agents. After a description of the methodology, we present results based on two sets of analyses. We first examine the semantic information that was expressed by participants (hereafter 'focus') and the total number of semantic components in their responses (hereafter 'density'), then the particular means used to encode this information in the response (hereafter 'locus').

METHODOLOGY

Several groups of participants took part in the study (12 per group): (1) two groups of native speakers of English and French who provided the baseline for comparison with the L2 data; (2) three groups of (mostly

American) English learners of French at different levels of proficiency. L2 learners had been studying and living in Paris for a period ranging between 2 months and approximately 2 years. They were enrolled in the American University of Paris, and were learning French as a second language in that context. They can therefore be classified as semi-guided learners of the language. At the time of the experiment, the learners were at three levels of proficiency: Low Intermediate, High Intermediate, and Advanced. Levels of proficiency were determined on the basis of an independent in-house language test administered by the American University of Paris. The information regarding proficiency levels was complemented by a socio-linguistic questionnaire including information about the amount of time spent learning French, the time spent in French-speaking contexts, contact with French native speakers, etc.

Participants were seen individually in a quiet room. They were shown animated cartoons representing voluntary motion carried out by a variety of agents in a variety of locations. Twelve cartoons corresponded to the target items (see Appendix). Six involved agents moving upwards and then downward (hereafter UP and DOWN items) in relation to a ground (e.g., a tree, the stem of a plant, a telegraph pole), while six others involved agents crossing a boundary (hereafter ACROSS items) represented by a spatial entity (e.g., a street, river, railroad crossing). In all cases Manner varied across all items (e.g., walk, climb, jump, swim). Cartoons were chosen as the mode of presentation because they allow for total control of the elicited information. Great care was taken to make the cartoons as 'realistic' as possible with the help of a professional artist, and all agents represented human beings or familiar animals that allowed for a natural range of Manners of motion. Items were semi-randomly ordered in six different experimental sets that were randomly assigned to participants within each proficiency level. Each set was preceded by a training item that allowed learners to get used to the task and to the experimental set-up.

After each cartoon was shown, the experimenter invited the participants to say 'what happened'. They were asked to narrate for a 'naive' interlocutor who was not present in the situation and would not have access to the cartoon material. This set-up encouraged participants to rely maximally on speech (avoiding pointing gestures, etc.).

All data were transcribed in CHAT format (MacWhinney, 1995) and coded for semantic information, parts of speech, and utterance type. Data were coded with respect to information focus and locus. With respect to focus, Manner and Path information was identified in all parts of speech. With respect to locus, a distinction was made between main verbs and all other linguistic means used for the expression of this information. As illustrated below, the latter include satellites as defined by Talmy (notably verb particles) but also other parts of the utterance such as prepositions, adverbials, nouns, subordinate clauses, etc.

(5) Le **nageur** traverse la rivière.
    'The **swimmer** crosses the river.'
(6) Le bébé traverse **à quatre pieds**.
    'The baby crosses **on all fours**.'
(7) Elle traverse **en courant**.
    'She crosses **running**.'

One further coding concerned target utterances, particularly in cases where participants produced more than one utterance in response to a given item. In these cases we identified only one of these utterances as the target response according to the following criteria: (1) the 'richness' criterion was first applied, i.e., the utterance that expressed most information was considered to be the target response; (2) if utterances were equally rich, the 'relevance' criterion was used, according to which Path was considered to be the most basic and therefore the most relevant information. For example, the first utterance in example 8 expresses both Manner and Path and is therefore richer than the second utterance, which expresses only Path. The two utterances in example 9 are equally rich (one semantic component) and the first one was taken to be the target response (Path component).

(8) Le chat **grimpe** (Path + Manner) le poteau. Il **monte** (Path) pour aller au nid.
    'The cat **climbs** the pole. He **goes up** to get to the nest.'
(9) The boy **goes across** (Path) the street. He is **running** (Manner).

RESULTS

We present below two types of analyses for both native speakers and L2 learners. The first analysis examines the semantic information expressed by participants and the resulting semantic density of their responses. The cartoons were meant to elicit two types of semantic information, Manner and Path. Therefore maximum response density was 2 (both Manner and Path expressed simultaneously), and responses expressing only one type of information (either only Manner or only Path, but not both simultaneously) had density 1. Density was measured for the target utterance only. In those cases where participants produced several utterances in response to a given item (e.g., 8 and 9 above), we return to the content of all utterances in more detail below. Given previous studies, we expected native speakers of English to produce utterances of higher density than French native speakers.

In a second analysis we examined information locus, i.e., the particular means used to encode the information in the response. A different locus was expected in the two languages. In particular, we expected Path to be encoded by satellites in English but by verbs in French. We will examine whether findings for native speakers follow expectations based on the literature and how these findings may influence the L2 learners' progression towards the target. More specifically, the discussion regarding the L2 learners focuses on the influence of lexicalization and thinking for speaking patterns in the source language on the acquisition of the expression of motion in a second, typologically different language. We first present the native speaker data, then the L2 data.

Native speakers

Type of information expressed and resulting density

Since all test items specifically showed an agent moving along a certain Path in a certain Manner, a full account of what happened for a naive interlocutor should provide information about both Path and Manner. Figures 14.1a and 14.1b show the semantic information that was expressed by English and French native speakers. English native speakers provided both Path and Manner (P+M) more frequently (82%) than French native speakers (63%). In English, Path (15%) and Manner (3%) are seldom expressed in isolation. In contrast, Path was more frequently the only type of semantic information found in utterances of French native speakers (34%).

Typical examples of native speakers' responses are shown in example 10 for English, and in 11 and 12 for French. Note that when both Manner and Path are expressed in French, this often (although not necessarily) involves the use of subordinate structures, as illustrated in 11.

    (10) [. . .] **swam across** the river.
    (11) il **a traversé** la route **en marchant à quatre pattes**.
        'he **has crossed** the road **walking on all fours**.'
    (12) une souris qui heu, **monte** le long d'un pied, du pied de, d'une table [. . .] et qui **redescend**.

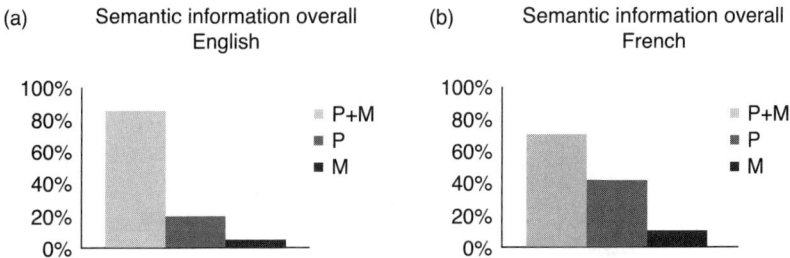

Figure 14.1 Semantic information expressed by native speakers of English and French.

'A mouse, who **goes up** [literally: **ascends**] along the leg of a table [. . .], and who **comes back down** [literally: **descends**].'

Figures 14.2a and 14.2b display these data in more detail as a function of event type (UP, DOWN, or ACROSS). They show that the type of experimental item had an influence on responses. Thus, in both languages UP items most frequently elicited Path+Manner responses. In English ACROSS items also frequently elicited Path+Manner responses. DOWN events, however, more frequently elicited Path only. Recall that downward motion always occurred after upward motion in these items, making it perhaps possible for speakers to leave it to the listener to infer Manner from the UP event. Note also that in French Path+Manner responses for UP motion typically resulted from the use of the verb *grimper* ('to climb up'), which is an exception among French verbs in that it lexicalizes both types of information together.

This distribution of information leads to the following typical responses to our experimental items:

(13) [. . .], and he's coming back down.
(14) [. . .] elle a grimpé tout en haut vers une feuille [. . .] et puis elle a redescendu.
    '[. . .] she climbed all the way up to a leaf [. . .] and then she came back down.'
(15) A girl was cycling on a bicycle across the track, railroad track.
(16) [. . .] il traverse à la nage la petite rivière.
    '[. . .] he crosses the little river swimming.'

Locus of information

Figures 14.3a and 14.3b display the locus of information in our native speaker data. They show that the distribution of information was very systematically organized in English: Manner was always expressed by the main verb and Path by other linguistic means (example 17). In French

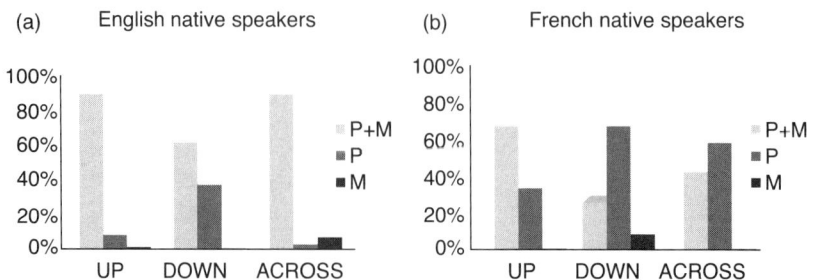

Figure 14.2 Semantic information expressed by native speakers of English and French as a function of event type.

(a)   Locus of information English   (b)   Locus of information French

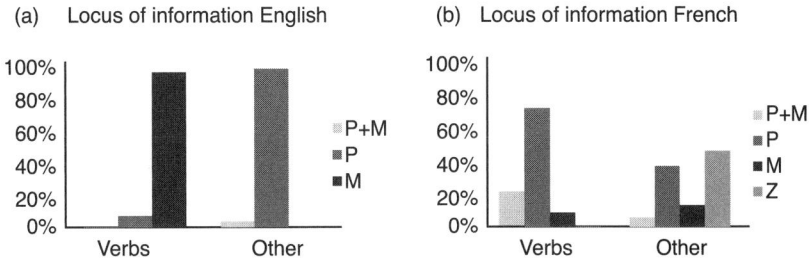

Figure 14.3 Locus of information in native speakers of English and French. Z = no semantic information expressed.

the expression of Manner and Path was less systematically organized. Path was mostly expressed in the main verb, but up to 40% of other linguistic means also expressed path. French also provides a verb that expresses Manner and Path simultaneously (see above), and Manner can be expressed both in the main verb and elsewhere. Finally, a large percentage of other linguistic means do not express any Path or Manner in French. Such cases do not occur in English. In short, the French language is more flexible in terms of the locus of semantic information, and adult native speakers fully used this flexibility, as illustrated in examples 18–20 below.

(17)   A girl with red hair and green skirts and hat **skated across** a pond with big trees all around it.

(18)   [. . .] cette chenille **monte** sur la tige, [. . .], **redescend**.
'[. . .] this caterpillar **goes up** the stem, [. . .], **comes down again**.'

(19)   on a une **patineuse** [. . .] elle **fait quelques petites glissades** pour **arriver** sur le ponton gauche.
'We have a **skater** [. . .] she does **a few little slides** in order **to get to** the bridge on the left.'

(20)   [. . .] en fait on a un un **joggeur** donc [. . .] qui **court** et qui **traverse** la route.
'[. . .] in fact we have a **jogger** [. . .] who **runs** and who **crosses** the road.'

Summary of results for native speakers

The main differences between English and French native speakers can be summarized as follows: English speakers typically express both Manner and Path simultaneously and they do so more frequently than French speakers, therefore providing denser utterances than the French native speakers. In English Path+Manner responses, speakers systematically express Manner in the verb and Path in other linguistic devices (mainly verb particles and prepositional phrases). This result is in line with many earlier findings in the literature and reflects the typical pattern expected for satellite-framed languages. French native speakers provide utterances that are not only less dense overall, but also lack a systematic pattern with respect to locus. Although Path is mainly expressed in the verb, it also occurs in other linguistic means. As a result, the picture is less transparent than one would expect based on the typological descriptions of French in the literature. We now examine whether this lack of transparency has an influence on the L2 results.

English L2 learners of French

Given the above findings, we would expect the following for the English learner of French: English native speakers may attempt to express the same level of density in French as in their source language and encounter problems finding the best way of organizing that information using French linguistic means and constructions. In particular, English speakers have to acquire a much less transparent system with respect to locus in French L2 than the one they know in their L1.

Several hypotheses are possible in terms of learners' course of acquisition. First, adult learners may follow a course that is similar to child L1 learners of French, who were found to express often just one type of information (located in the verb) at younger ages (Path or Manner, depending on item), and only at later ages acquire the means to express both Path and Manner (cf. Hickmann et al., 2009). In that case we would expect an increase in density with proficiency level, as well as a focus on Path information initially for most items. Second, adult learners may be guided by a universal cognitive understanding of the situations and express only Path because it is universally basic in these types of situations. In that case, we would again expect an increase in density with proficiency level. Third, they may start out with the pattern of the source language, which simultaneously expresses Manner and Path in the utterance, and transpose the source system to French. They might encounter problems in this case, since French does not offer the speaker many satellites to express changes of location. Such an attempt might thus result in utterances expressing only Manner at lower proficiency levels, since learners will express Manner in the verb and then run into trouble. Finally, they may show a developmental course which is different from the one in French L1 acquisition, but that cannot be explained through the learners' source language pattern either.

If thinking for speaking is deeply embedded in the language production process, the third and fourth possibilities should be more likely than the first two. And depending on the 'resistance' of the source system to restructuring during adult second language acquisition, the third option may be more or less likely than the fourth one.

Type of information expressed and resulting density

Figure 14.4 shows the types of information that were expressed by English learners of French in the three proficiency groups: Low Intermediate (LOW), High Intermediate (HIGH), and Advanced (ADV). At all three levels learners struggled to express Path and Manner information simultaneously within one utterance when speaking French. Only 15% of the responses in the Low Intermediate learners, 23% in the High Intermediate Learners, and 22% in the Advanced learners were of this type. Most frequently, L2 learners just provided Path information in their target utterances (78%, 68%, and 67% respectively). The pattern was slightly more pronounced in the Low Intermediate learners, but stayed very much the same across proficiency levels.

Thus, English L2 learners of French produced target utterances that provided less information than one might expect from an adult in this type of experiment, which invited speakers to express both Path and Manner. However, they respected the typical pattern of the target language in which Path was more prominent than Manner. A major reason for learners' lower density in comparison to native speakers may lie in the fact that French frequently relies on more complex syntactic structures to express Path and Manner simultaneously, and that such structures have to be acquired over time.

In a small number of occurrences, the learners' target utterances were accompanied by another utterance that presented another type of semantic information (cf. example 9 above). We found a total of 7% of such 'disjoint' responses across the Low Intermediate, High Intermediate, and Advanced groups. Most of these responses occurred with ACROSS items.

To illustrate these responses, consider example 21, typical for our French native speaker data. It includes a main Path verb and a subordinate clause

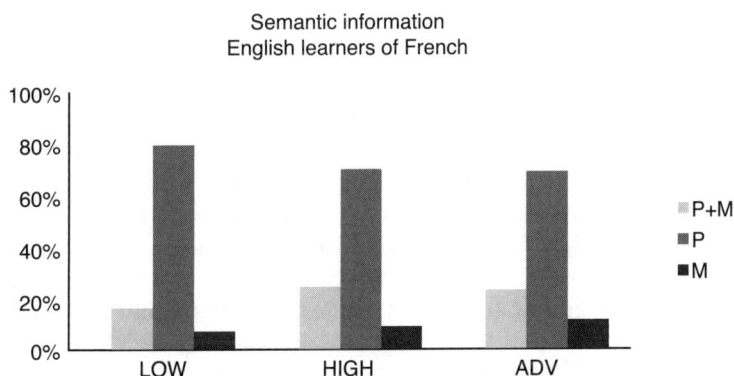

Figure 14.4 Type of semantic information by proficiency (LOW = Low Intermediate; HIGH = High Intermediate; ADV = Advanced).

expressing Manner. Examples 22–24 are taken from the English learners of French (proficiency level indicated). As can be seen, both types of information are expressed but in two separate utterances which are not syntactically related.

> (21) Une petite fille, hum, qui heu, qui donc qui **traverse** en fait une rivière gelée **en glissant**.
> 'A little girl who ehm who **crosses** well a frozen river **sliding**.'
> (22) Il y a une homme et il **faire du jogging** et **traverser** une rue. (Low Intermediate)
> 'There is a man and he **jog** [sic] and **cross** [sic] a road.'
> (23) Il y a un homme qui run euh qui qui **faire du jogging** et i(l) **traverse** une une auto-stop autoroute. (High Intermediate)
> 'There is a man who run who **jog** [sic] and he **crosses** a a highway.'
> (24) Ça c'est une p(e)tit fille et elle **fait d(e) le patinage** et elle **traverse** un lac gelé. (Advanced)
> 'That's a little girl and she **does skating** and she **crosses** a frozen lake.'

When learners provided this type of disjoint responses, the majority provided Manner information in the first utterance (as in the examples above). This pattern was quite stable across proficiency levels (Low Intermediate 12/14, High Intermediate 5/10, and Advanced 9/11). Example 25 shows a learner providing path information in the first utterance.

> (25) il **est—a traversé** la rue et il **est courir**.
> 'He **is—has crossed** the road and he **is run** [sic].'

In this small subset of cases, then, learners clearly seemed to provide spatial information in the order in which it would occur in the source language, that is, first Manner (encoded by the verb in English), and then Path (encoded in satellites after the verb).

In sum, the density of information in the learners is clearly lower (mostly just one information component per utterance). The fact that this component mainly consists of Path could be explained in two ways: Either Path is the most basic component for motion (universal explanation) or learners are sensitive to a different focus in English (Manner) and French (Path). In some cases learners express semantic components across two main clauses, rather than integrating them by means of more complex syntactic structures. In these cases they mostly start out with Manner information, suggesting a focus on Manner information in these learners at all proficiency levels.

A closer look at responses expressing Path+Manner simultaneously showed that the across items attracted most of these responses at all proficiency levels (91% at the Low Intermediate level, 90% at High

Intermediate level, and 83% at Advanced level). Recall that this response type occurred in English with both ACROSS and UP items, but only with UP items in French. The learner data therefore reflect neither source nor target language, but deviate more clearly from target than from source language.

Locus of information

As mentioned above, a main typological difference is the locus of Path information, which is typically expressed by satellites in satellite-framed languages and by the verb in verb-framed languages. We hypothesized that this difference in organizing information (i.e., thinking for speaking) might confront L2 learners with difficulties, especially since French presents a highly opaque system, as shown in our native speaker data.

Figure 14.5a and 14.5b present the information expressed by the learners in main verb versus other linguistic devices as a function of proficiency. As can be seen in these figures, verbs mainly express Path information, as one would expect in verb-framed languages. Very few verbs in our data encode both Manner and Path (possible in French but only for a small set of specific verbs such as *grimper*) and only approximately 10–15% of the verbs encode Manner alone (typical in the source language English). Semantic information in other linguistic means is even less frequent in our data with rare occurrences of utterances combining both Path+Manner information, and mostly no information is expressed in other linguistic means at all. The cases in which Manner is encoded in the verb mostly resulted from utterances that encoded Path+Manner. In order to examine this type of utterance in more detail, Table 14.1 shows what was expressed in the verb (Path, Manner or both) in responses that encoded Path+Manner simultaneously.

Most Path+Manner responses express Path in the verb as one would expect in a verb-framed language (but recall that the French native speaker data do not actually look as systematic as the typology would have predicted). Looking more closely at these 'path-in-verb' responses, we found that at the Low Intermediate level, learners mainly give Manner

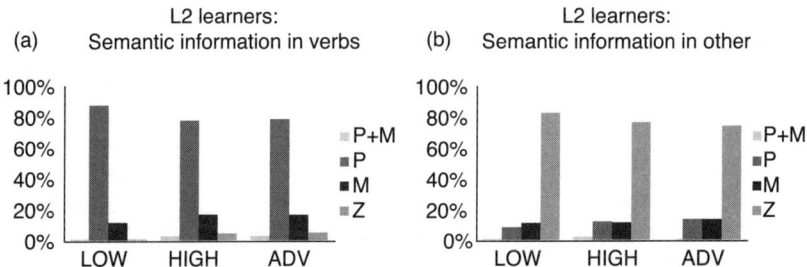

Figure 14.5 Locus of information (verbs versus other devices) by proficiency level. Z = no semantic information expressed.

Table 14.1 Information expressed in the main verb of Path+Manner responses and total number of responses, by proficiency level

	Manner only	Path only	Path+Manner	Total
Low Intermediate	29%	65%	6%	34
High Intermediate	41%	49%	10%	41
Advanced	27%	59%	14%	37

information in a prepositional construction (*avec* 'with', *sur* 'on', *dans* 'in') which was intended to indicate an instrument, as in example 26. The prepositions used for this type of construction at this proficiency level are often non-target-like. Other cases expressed Manner using non-target-like subordinating constructions, as illustrated in 27 and 28. At the High Intermediate level, again non-target-like subordinate clauses and prepositional phrases expressing instruments were used. Finally, at the Advanced level, more target-like subordinate clauses were used, as well as prepositional phrases introducing objects as instruments (with the use of target-like prepositions). In most of these cases Path precedes Manner as the verb precedes prepositional phrases in French. Interestingly, however, in some cases learners actually pre-posed Manner information by creating, for example, a presentational construction as in 29, thereby recreating the same order of information as in the source language (Manner first).

(26) Le femme traverse les rails **dans** le bicyclette.
'The woman crosses the tracks **in** a bicycle.'
(27) Ça c'est une garçon qui traverse le rivière **par glisser** sur le glace.
'That's a boy who crosses the river **by sliding** on the ice.'
(28) Il a traversé le rue **par marchant** sur ses mains.
'He has crossed the road **by walking** on his hands.'
(29) une fème [sic] **dans un vélo** a crossé des rails du train.
'A woman **in a bike** has crossed the tracks of the train.'

In 27% to 41% of the Path+Manner cases English L2 learners of French produced utterances that seem to follow the very systematic type of organization found in the source language, i.e., 'manner-in-verb'. When we examine these cases in more detail, we find the following cases represented in that group:

a. About one third of these (across all proficiency levels) involve target-like expressions of motion as in examples 30 and 31, mainly involving the satellites *jusqu'à* 'until/up to' and *d'un côté à l'autre* 'from one side to the other'.
b. One third involves a Manner verb followed by an idiosyncratic satellite, often close to the verb *traverser* ('to cross'), for example *à travers*,

à traverse, *à croissé*, as illustrated in examples 32 and 33. Often these idiosyncratic satellites are existing French expressions that have been given a different meaning to serve as a marker of a location change for the learner. Thus, *à travers* exists but does not mean 'across'. Similar expressions were found in our Hoppy task in which the French preposition *entre* ('between') was used to express 'into'. Both expressions have a close formal relationship with the French verbs that do indeed express the change of location the learner is looking to express.

c. Finally, one third involves attempts to subordinate some information by means of different subordinate markers, such as *pour V* 'in order to V', *pendant que V* 'while V-ing', and *en V-ant* 'V-ing', as illustrated in examples 34 and 35.

Interesting from a 'relativistic' point of view is the fact that both response categories (b) and (c) are non-target-like, but for different reasons. The examples in (b) (32–33) show idiosyncratic linguistic means, or lexical inventions, to force the target language system into a source language mold. The examples in (c) (34–35), however, are grammatically very close to the target language, but are non-target-like in that they subordinate Path information. The latter is not likely to be found in our French native speaker data.

(30) la fille patine de **de le côte droite à le côte gauche** (Low Intermediate).
      'The girl skates **from the right side to the left side**.'
(31) un garçon qui court **jusqu' à** le aut(re) côté de le rue (High Intermediate).
      'A boy who runs **all the way to** the other side of the road.'
(32) un vrai homme court **à travers** une route (High Intermediate).
      'A real man runs **across** a road.'
(33) et il a glissé **à travers** la rivière (Advanced).
      'And he has slid **across** the river.'
(34) et puis il nage **en traversant** le la fleuve (Advanced).
      'And then he swims **crossing** the river.'
(35) il a fait une petite peu de piscine **pour traverser** <la rive [= rivière]> le fleuve (Low Intermediate).
      'He has done a little bit of swimming pool **in order to cross** the river.'

Summary of results for L2 speakers

In sum, English learners of French have clear difficulties expressing the same level of density (P+M) in their second language as they would in their source language. Being adult speakers of the language, they are well aware that information regarding both Manner and Path is required in the experimental situation, but they do not have the linguistic means to integrate both types of information in syntactically complex constructions, frequently used in the target language. Occasionally, learners remedy this problem by producing two separate utterances, one providing Manner, the other Path. This situation does not change much across proficiency levels. A more qualitative look at such 'disjoint' responses showed that overall the first utterance provides Manner information, which could be considered a trace of the thinking-for-speaking pattern of the source language.

Cases in which both types of information are expressed simultaneously mostly occur with ACROSS events. We identified two types of responses in this category. The first type places Path information in the verb and adds Manner information either in prepositional phrases (in an attempt to indicate an instrument) or in subordinate clauses, both of which become more target-like with proficiency. In this type of response the order of information is mainly target-like except for some cases in which learners manage to pre-pose Manner information, thereby conveying Manner first. The second type of response encodes Manner in the verb, thereby adhering more closely to the organization pattern that is preferred in the source language. Some of those responses are target-like (French allows many different patterns of encoding), some use idiosyncratic satellite-type expressions, and some are grammatically close to the target language, but differ from it with respect to information organization.

DISCUSSION AND CONCLUSION

Analyses of how native speakers of English and French describe voluntary motion in our production task clearly show very different ways of organizing information. First, as expected, responses show a higher level of density in English as compared to French. Furthermore, the patterns identified mostly confirm the literature, although they also show some more complex results. The English native speakers indeed express Manner in the verb along with Path in satellites. In contrast, the French data show more variation than expected on the basis of Talmy's typology. Although French speakers express most Path information in the verb, some Path is also expressed by other linguistic means. Furthermore, Manner can also be expressed in the main verb (whether lexicalized with Path as in *grimper* ('to climb') or alone as in *patiner* ('to skate'), in nouns, and in subordinate clauses with Path expressed in other linguistic means.

One can then hypothesize that English learners of French will be faced with a number of acquisition challenges. Are learners just learning new linguistic devices to express familiar spatial information? Or do they have to acquire a different way of focusing on the information, a different thinking-for-speaking, in order to sound like native speakers? We would suggest that part of the problem is purely linguistic. One needs a minimal lexicon to express a variety of Manners and Paths when representing motion in a second language. And learners clearly show insufficient lexical items particularly to express the required Manners (French verbs equivalent to *sliding*, *hopping*, etc. or related adverbial expressions, such as *à quatre pattes* 'on all fours'), sometimes leading them to resort to code switching. In addition, they do not always express Path in target-like ways (*il ascende le arbre* 'he ascends the tree'), even though the number of verbs to be acquired as part of their lexicon is reduced in this case.

French native speakers most frequently resorted to a system of complex clauses to express both Path and Manner information. Constructing such clauses involves the acquisition of appropriate markings of subordination, i.e., the marking of gerunds, knowing when to use different forms of a given verb, knowing what connectives to use and when. The data show that choosing between an inflected (gerund) form and an infinitival form (**pour **marchant*** versus *pour **marcher***; **en **marcher*** versus *en **marchant***), as well as selecting the appropriate connective (*pour*, *par*, *en*, *parce que*) are not obvious tasks for the learner (*il court *par traverser* versus *pour traverser*). Many attempts at subordination are not well formed especially at earlier levels of proficiency. Moreover, subordination is sometimes just not attempted at all, or attempted and given up, thereby preventing the combined expression of Path and Manner.

However, our main interest in this chapter was not so much with the acquisition of the linguistic means per se, but rather with the use of the available linguistic means to organize information appropriately and with the different ways of conceptualizing the task that may result from this repertoire. As regards focus, many of the target utterances identified in the learner data, at all levels of proficiency, only express one of the two semantic components shown in the stimuli. And Path is the component that is most often expressed. There are two possible explanations for this finding: Either learners express only Path because this information is most basic to motion and it is therefore the most efficient way of expressing a change of location; or they provide Path only because they are sensitive to the fact that it constitutes the most salient focus of information in French.

Let us now compare our present findings with those reported in our earlier study of Caused motion among the same English learners of French. In the Caused motion task learners minimally expressed the Cause of motion, which was indeed the most basic and important common denominator of all events presented in that experiment. This most efficient choice corresponds to what has been called a 'minimal response to the task' ('*traitement minimal / prototypique*'; Watorek, 1996, among others). It constitutes a highly efficient way of dealing with the task of communicating complex information in a second language with only a minimal amount of linguistic means at one's disposal. The focus of information (in both tasks), then, may well result from universal strategies linked to efficiency in communication from the very start of L2 acquisition. Such strategies are available to adult learners who have a fully developed cognitive system and therefore a good understanding of the discourse requirements in such a communicative task.

With respect to the locus of information, two patterns occurred, depending on whether target responses expressed Path alone (most frequent cases) or Manner and Path together (infrequent cases). In the majority of cases, learners only expressed Path, and encoded this information in the verb. Although Path verbs are highly typical for verb-framed languages, the French native speakers in our experiment actually showed evidence for a more complex type of organization, in which Path (as well as Manner) occurred in different parts of speech. The learners therefore relied on a more systematic way of organizing information than the target language speakers.

One explanation for this finding might be that learners chose to express only one type of information and placed it in the verb, where it is expected to be encoded in French. When there is less of an emphasis on providing full information for a naive interlocutor than there is in this experiment (i.e., in normal speech), this will be the prevailing pattern in the input. However, it seems unlikely that these learners would have failed to process Manner information, given the systematic marking of that information in their L1. Indeed we found that when target utterances expressed Path alone, some (7%) were accompanied by another utterance expressing Manner, suggesting that learners had processed this information. Moreover, a minority of learners' responses expressed both Manner and Path in the target utterance, thereby showing that both types of information were processed. In the cases where both types of information were expressed, Path was still mainly expressed in the verb, but learners' utterances also showed (less frequently) an attempt to present the information in the order imposed by their source language (Manner before Path). Note that learners adhered more strongly to the organization of their source language when expressing Caused motion as compared to voluntary motion. In particular, they expressed Cause in the main verb and Path elsewhere (Caused motion), whereas they prevailingly expressed Path in verb and Manner elsewhere in the voluntary motion task.

Therefore the two tasks do not reveal the same strategy of adaptation to the target language with regards to the locus of information. It was hypothesized that the complexity of the Caused motion task (in which no fewer than six semantic components had to be expressed) may have led learners to rely heavily on their source language, because English allows for more information to be expressed in a more compact way. Thus, although it cannot be excluded that learners are sensitive to the organization of the target language, it seems that they choose to rely on a system that is most efficient for them independently from the target language. In other words, they are content to flout some of the target language rules to get their message across as completely as possible. If we are correct in this assumption, then 'thinking for speaking' is not entirely imposed by the source language, but this language does provide the learner with a convenient additional array of organizational options to choose from.

Task therefore seems to have an effect on the degree to which the organization of information might be transferred. In particular, our learners fell back on a familiar type of organization when the information to be expressed was complex (Caused motion), but not when the task was simpler (voluntary motion). Similar results in other studies (Carroll et al., 2000; von Stutterheim, 2003; von Stutterheim & Lambert, 2005) also show that even at a near-native level of proficiency L2 speakers do not fully organize information according to patterns of the target language. The data elicited in many of these studies were based on complex verbal tasks, in which many information components had to be organized for speaking. It seems, then, that there are two possible explanations for the differences found between our voluntary and Caused motion results. It may be that, at a given level of complexity, L2 learners look for the most efficient way of presenting information, rather than for the most target-like pattern. It may also be that at such level of complexity they automatically fall back on the system provided by their source language. If the latter hypothesis is correct, one would not expect French learners of English to adhere to a French-like organization in the Caused motion task. This question is currently under investigation (Engemann, 2010).

We started this chapter by asking a number of questions regarding the relation between language and cognition, arguing that, if language and cognition are largely independent, one would expect second language learners to have an easier task of shaking off the linguistic system of the L1 and finding new L2 lexical and structural means to fit the motion events observed in a language-neutral way. If, however, language and cognition are intricately related during L1 acquisition, one would expect some of the spatial conceptualization of adult speakers to mirror the features of their native language. This should lead to some difficulty in acquiring a language that requires both different linguistic spatial means and a different way of conceptually organizing space. The findings presented in this chapter (concerning voluntary motion, in comparison to Caused motion from a previous study) seem to point to the following conclusions. In the voluntary motion task, English speakers of French seem to adapt easily to the information focus and locus of the target language. In fact, they look more French than the French in some sense, and seem to follow the pattern predicted by Talmy for verb-framed languages more precisely that the native speakers. However, in the Caused motion task, English learners of French seem to have much difficulty shaking off their source language pattern. We propose that there is language-independent spatial conceptualization, which allows all speakers and learners to identify the semantic components that should or could be expressed when describing given motion events and to decide what information is minimally required for such descriptions to be adequate. In this sense, different languages do not constrain the content of speakers' internal event conceptualization per se. However, languages introduce a great deal of variation in terms of the typical linguistic means they provide for event descriptions, thereby influencing the relative salience of incoming information and its relative focus in communication.

In the L2 learner, then, there will be competition between, on the one hand, the need to be explicit, and, on the other hand, the need to be target-like. The L2 learner will choose the optimal encoding of information and, when need be, will override the organization of the target language, especially when the linguistic means in the target language involve more complex linguistic structures (i.e., subordination in this case). When, on the other hand, all necessary information can be expressed in a more straightforward way by adhering to the target language pattern, learners have no problem shaking off their L1 linguistic means and adapting to the target language system. Thus, the Caused motion task strongly invites participants to express Cause, Manner of cause, and Path to minimally describe the target events, and English provides the most cost-effective way of expressing the combination of these information components. Hence learners adhere to the English pattern. In the voluntary motion task, however, the most basic information to be expressed is Path, and Path can very well be expressed in French in a target-like manner. Hence, the L1 pattern is shaken off and the L2 pattern adopted.

In conclusion, all speakers share some general language-independent way of conceptualizing space, despite the fact that they think-for-speaking in different ways. As a result, L2 learners are not completely trapped by their L1 mode of thinking-for-speaking. Rather, their L1 mode may provide them with a welcome 'escape' from the L2 mode, particularly in cases where it allows them to solve problems in organizing information in L2. Learners can therefore flout some of the target language rules if this strategy allows them to get their message across more efficiently for communication. In order to sound entirely native-like, learners will have to enter completely into the L2 mode and 'switch off' the L1 mode of thinking-for-speaking.

REFERENCES

Baillargeon, R. (1995). A model of physical reasoning in infancy. In C. Rovee-Collier & L. Lipsitt (Eds.), *Advances in infancy research Vol. 9,* (pp. 305–371). Norwood, NJ: Ablex.

Bowerman, M., & Choi, S. (2001). Shaping meanings for language: Universal and language-specific in the acquisition of spatial semantic categories. In M. Bowerman & S. Levinson (Eds.), *Language acquisition and conceptual development* (pp. 475–511). Cambridge, UK: Cambridge University Press.

Cadierno, T. (2004). Expressing motion events in a second language: A cognitive typological perspective. In M. Achard & S. Niemeyer (Eds.), *Cognitive linguistics, second language acquisition, and foreign language teaching* (pp. 13–49). Berlin: Mouton de Gruyter.

Cadierno, T., & Lund, K. (2004). Cognitive linguistics and second language acquisition: Motion events in a typological framework. In B. vanPatten, J. Williams, S. Rott, & M. Overstreet (Eds.), *Form–meaning connections in second language acquisition* (pp. 139–154). Mahwah, NJ: Lawrence Erlbaum Associates Inc.

Carroll, M., Murcia-Serra, J., Watorek, M., & Bendiscoli, A. (2000). The relevance of information organization to second language studies: The descriptive discourse of advanced learners of German. *Studies in Second Language Acquisition, 22*(3), 441–466.

Choi, S., & Bowerman, M. (1991). Learning to express motion events in English and Korean: The influence of language-specific lexicalization patterns. *Cognition, 41,* 83–121.

Engemann, H. (2010). *The expression of motion in simultaneous and successive bilinguals acquiring English and French.* PhD in progress, University of Cambridge, UK.

Gentner, D., & Goldin-Meadow, S. (2003). *Language in mind: Advances in the study of language and thought.* Cambridge, MA: MIT Press.

Gumperz, J. J., & Levinson, S. C. (1996). *Rethinking linguistic relativity.* Cambridge, UK: Cambridge University Press.

Hendriks, H. (2005). Structuring space in discourse: A comparison of Chinese, English, French and German L1 and English, French and German L2 acquisition. In H. Hendriks (Ed.), *The structure of learner varieties* (pp. 111–156). Berlin: Mouton de Gruyter.

Hendriks, H., Hickmann, M., & Demagny, A. C. (2008). How adult English learners of French express caused motion: A comparison with English and French natives. *Acquisition et interaction en langue étrangère, 27,* 15–41.

Hickmann, M., Hendriks, H., & Roland, F. (1998). Référence spatiale dans les récits d'enfants français: Perspective inter-langues. *Langue Française, 118,* 104–123.

Hickmann, M., & Robert, S. (2006). *Space in languages: Linguistic systems and cognitive categories.* Amsterdam: John Benjamins.

Hickmann, M., Taranne, P., & Bonnet, P. (2009). Motion in first language acquisition: Manner and Path in French and English child language. *Journal of Child Language, 36*(4), 705–742.

Ji, Y. (2009). *The expression of voluntary and caused motion events in Chinese and in English: Typological and developmental perspectives.* PhD Thesis, University of Cambridge, UK.

Johnston, J., & Slobin, D. (1979). The development of locative expressions in English, Italian, Serbo-Croatian and Turkish. *Journal of Child Language, 6,* 531–547.

Levinson, S. C. (1996). Frames of reference and Molyneux's question: Cross-linguistic evidence. In P. Bloom, M. A. Peterson, L. Nadel, & M. F. Garrett (Eds.), *Language and space* (pp. 109–170). Cambridge, MA: MIT Press.

Levinson, S. C. (2003). *Space in language and cognition.* Cambridge, UK: Cambridge University Press.

Lucy, J. A. (1992). *Language diversity and thought.* Cambridge, UK: Cambridge University Press.

MacWhinney, B. (1995). *The CHILDES project: Tools for analyzing talk* (2nd ed.). Hillsdale, NJ: Lawrence Erlbaum Associates Inc.

Mandler, J. M. (1998). Representation. In W. Damon, D. Kuhn, & R. S. Siegler (Eds.), *Handbook of child psychology Vol. 2.* (pp. 255–308). New York: Wiley.

Papafragou, A., Massey, C., & Gleitman, L. (2002). Shake, rattle, 'n' roll: The representation of motion in language and cognition. *Cognition, 84,* 189–219.

Slobin, D. I. (1996). From 'thought and language' to 'thinking for speaking'. In J. J. Gumperz & S. C. Levinson (Eds.), *Rethinking linguistic relativity* (pp. 70–96). Cambridge, UK: Cambridge University Press.

Spelke, E. S. (1998). Nativism, empiricism, and the origins of knowledge. *Infant Behavior and Development, 21,* 181–200.

Talmy, L. (1983). How languages structure space. In H. Pick & L. Acredolo (Eds.), *Spatial orientation: Theory, research and application* (pp. 225–282). New York, London: Plenum Press.

Talmy, L. (2000). *Towards a cognitive semantics.* Cambridge, MA: MIT Press.

von Stutterheim, C. (2003). Linguistic structure and information organization: The case of very advanced learners. In S. Foster-Cohen & S. Pekarek-Doehler (Eds.), *EUROSLA yearbook* (pp. 183–206). Amsterdam: John Benjamins.

von Stutterheim, C., & Lambert, M. (2005). Cross-linguistic analyses of temporal perspectives in text production. In H. Hendriks (Ed.), *The structure of learner varieties* (pp. 203–230). Berlin: Mouton de Gruyter.

Watorek, M. (1996). *Conceptualisation et représentation linguistique de l'espace en italien et en français, langue maternelle et langue étrangère.* PhD, University of Paris VIII.

APPENDIX

The experimental design consisted of cartoons displaying the following information:

UP/DOWN items

Mouse: A mouse tiptoes (on her hind legs) towards a table leg, climbs up the table leg, takes the cheese, slides back down carrying the cheese on her back, and tiptoes away.

Bear: A bear walks up to a tree (on his hind legs), climbs up the tree, puts his paw in the bees' nest, climbs back down, stops under the tree to lick the honey off his paw, and walks off.

Monkey: A monkey walks towards a tree, climbs the tree, takes a banana, comes back down, and walks away holding the banana.

Cat: A cat runs up to a telegraph pole, climbs the pole, puts one paw in a nest and throws an egg out of the nest which splits open on the pavement under the pole. He climbs back down to eat the egg yolk and runs away.

Caterpillar: A caterpillar crawls up to a stem of a leaf, crawls up to the leaf, nibbles part of the leaf, and crawls back down.

Squirrel: A squirrel comes running up to a tree, climbs up the tree to a hole, disappears in the hole and comes out again, and runs down.

ACROSS items

Boy swimming: A boy swims across a river.
Girl cycling: A woman cycles across the railroad tracks.
Boy sliding: A boy slides across a frozen river on his feet.
Girl skating: A girl skates across a lake.
Man running: A man runs across a road.
Baby crawling: A baby crawls across a big crossroads.

15 Chinese–English bilinguals' sensitivity to the temporal phase of an action event is related to the extent of their experience with English

Jenn-Yeu Chen and Jui-Ju Su

An event consists of several components and properties such as the manner and path of motion or the temporal phases of an action. Languages tend to employ different linguistic devices to encode these components and properties, resulting in their differential codability. For example, manner of motion in a motion event is highly codable in English because it is carried by the main verb (e.g., *walk* versus *run*), and every clause requires a verb. In French, manner is an optional addition to a clause that is already complete. For example, in English, Sentence (1a) can be expressed as Sentence (1b) by using the verb *run*, which encodes the manner of entering. In contrast, the corresponding sentence in French can only be expressed as Sentence (2), which encodes the manner by adding an adverbial phrase (Slobin, 2003, p. 162).

(1a) The dog went into the house by running.
(1b) The dog **ran** into the house.
(2) *Le chien est entré dans la maison **en courant.***
'The dog entered the house **by running**.'

Slobin (2003, p. 162) stated that:

> French speakers indicate manner when it is at issue, but otherwise do not mention it. As a consequence, English speakers would make widespread communicative and cognitive use of this dimension, whereas French speakers would be less sensitive to this dimension overall.

Likewise, the temporal relations in an event are encoded differently in different languages. Aksu-Koç and von Stutterheim (1994) suggested that 'the lexical as well as the morphological options available in a given language appear to have a close bearing on the ability to attend to and conceptualize different types of temporal relations, . . .' (p. 455). The present study focused on the temporal phase of an action event and examined how its perception might be related to the language used to encode it.

In many languages, there are three basic temporal relations in an event: Simultaneity, before, and after (Aksu-Koç & von Stutterheim, 1994). 'Simultaneity' represents present or present progressive aspect. 'Before' refers to past or perfective aspect. 'After' points to future or imperfective aspect. Different languages encode these relations with different devices. English, for example, marks verbs for tense and aspect by inflection (*walked, walking*) or by a combination of inflection and grammatical words (***will** walk, **has** walked, **had** walked, **is going to** walk*). Modern Hebrew is said to mark verbs for tense, but not aspect (Slobin, 2003).

Mandarin Chinese is different from both English and Hebrew. It contains no verb markings for tense or aspect. Although some morphemes have been identified as aspect markers (e.g., *le5, zai4, zhe5, guo4*), they do not carry that function and meaning exclusively. For example, *guo4* is also used as a verb to mean 'to pass' and *zai4* can serve as a verb ('to exist') or a preposition for location.

Tense and aspect are most often inferred from contexts in Chinese, so much so that the so-called aspect markers can be left out. For example, the verb *chi1* ('eat') in Sentence (3) can be interpreted as referring to future/imperfective or past/perfective.

> (3) *zhong1-wu3 chi1 she2-me5*
>   noon   eat   what
>   'What did you eat for lunch?' or 'What are you going to eat for lunch?'

Even when an aspect marker is present, the time of an event is usually jointly determined by the aspect marker and the situation type of the verb (Chang, 1998; Lin, 2002, 2003), or by other factors such as viewpoint, aspect, verbal semantics, temporal adverbials, the definite/indefinite distinction, quantifier raising, informational status, pragmatics, and people's knowledge of the world (Lin, 2006). For example, both Sentence (4) and Sentence (5) employ the aspect marker *le5*, which is commonly characterized as a perfective marker. However, although Sentence (4) clearly describes a past event, Sentence (5) actually implicates a present ongoing situation (Lin, 2003).

> (4) *Ta1 chi1-le5 yi1-tiao2 yu2*
>   he eat-Asp one-Classifier fish
>   'He ate a fish.'
> (5) *Ta1 yang3-le5 yi1-tiao2 yu2*
>   he raise-Asp one-Classifier fish
>   'He is raising a fish.'

We were interested in knowing whether the lack of distinction between past and present events in Mandarin Chinese tense and aspect, as contrasted with English, could predict a different behavioral pattern when Chinese speakers viewed an action event.

In a previous study (Chen, Su, & O'Seaghdha, 2010), we presented Chinese and English speakers with a set of pictures, each depicting a person at a different temporal phase of performing an action, e.g., a woman is about to throw a frisbee, is throwing a frisbee, or has thrown a frisbee. For convenience, we will refer to these temporal phases as future (meaning 'not occurred yet'), present (meaning 'currently occurring'), and past (meaning 'has occurred'). For a given action event, participants saw a single picture representing one of the three temporal phases. Their task was simply to describe each action event with one sentence in their language. Results show that the English participants were more likely than the Chinese participants (88% versus 64%) to produce sentences whose temporal meanings matched those of the pictures. When the three temporal phases were examined separately, we found that the Chinese participants often described the past and the future phases as present ones. This tendency towards the present disappeared when the participants were told ahead of time that each action could assume one of the three temporal phases. We interpreted the participants' verbal descriptions of action events as reflecting their habitual ways of viewing these action events, which correlated interestingly with the different ways of coding tense and aspect in the two languages.

Chen et al.'s (2010) findings are consistent with those of Boroditsky, Ham, and Ramscar (2002), as well as those of Alloway and Corley (2004). Boroditsky et al. (2002) studied English and Indonesian, the latter being a tenseless language. In a similarity judgment task they found that English speakers tended to judge two pictures with the same time of action but different actors as more similar than two pictures with the same actor but different times of action. Indonesian speakers tended to make the opposite judgments. In a memory task, English speakers could distinguish events that took place at different times better than Indonesian speakers. Alloway and Corley (2004) studied Tamil and Mandarin Chinese, the former being a tensed language. In a similarity judgment they found that Chinese speakers spent much longer time than Tamil speakers evaluating the similarity of two action pictures differing in tense (i.e., time of action), but not as long time as Tamil speakers when evaluating two action pictures differing in theme. The authors interpreted their findings as suggesting that 'considering tense in Mandarin is not "automatic" and requires extra work, possibly because it is not intrinsic to the verb' (p. 341). The interpretation was in agreement with the proposal by Hunt and Agnoli (1991) that having a direct lexical entry (i.e., usually a word) for a concept speeds up speakers' processing time.

The purpose of the present study was twofold. First, we wanted to know if Chinese participants' tendency towards the present might vary with their experience with English. Second, we wanted to seek converging evidence from a non-linguistic task, as opposed to the linguistic task employed in our previous study. The task involved initially showing participants a prime sentence depicting an action event in one of three temporal phases, followed by two pictures. The participants were then asked to decide which picture matched the sentence just shown. We measured participants' performance (response time and hit rate) on picture matching, which was non-linguistic.

We hypothesized that the bilinguals' sensitivity to the temporal phase of an action event might be higher if their English proficiency was high rather than low. High English proficiency bilinguals should therefore be more likely to choose the matching pictures than low-proficiency bilinguals, particularly for pictures depicting past and future phases.

Two experiments were conducted. Experiment 1 presented the prime sentences in Chinese and involved two groups of Chinese–English bilinguals with high and low levels of English proficiency. Experiment 2 presented the prime sentences in English and involved only high English proficiency bilinguals.

EXPERIMENT 1: SENTENCES PRESENTED IN CHINESE

Method

Participants

A total of 22 native Chinese speakers with high English proficiency (scoring at or beyond the 88th percentile on the English element of the Taiwan College Entrance Exam, which includes vocabulary, grammar, reading comprehension, sentence translation, and composition; CE-High-C) and 27 with low English proficiency (scoring at or below the 12th percentile; CE-Low-C) participated in this experiment. The high-proficiency participants were recruited from National Cheng Kung University and were not majoring in English, while the low-proficiency ones were seniors of a local high school having taken the 2009 College Entrance Exam. They were paid for their participation.

Materials and equipment

We chose 18 action events as target events (blowing up a balloon, erasing something on a whiteboard, crossing a log, cutting a rope, throwing a frisbee, drinking tea, folding a piece of colored paper, sliding down a slide, eating a banana, lighting a candle, peeling an orange, walking on a balance beam, cutting up a lettuce, doing a puzzle, walking up the stairs, tearing a piece of paper, kicking a ball, and pouring dark liquid into a glass). One woman performed all the actions. A snapshot was taken of each of the three temporal phases of an action event (e.g., is about to cut a rope, is cutting a rope, has finished cutting a rope). Therefore three pictures were taken for each action event, resulting in a total of 54 pictures (see Figure 15.1 for an example). For each picture a Chinese sentence was constructed that described the action in a given temporal phase. The 54 targets were divided into three sets of 18. Each set covered all the 18 action events, with each action event appearing in only one of the three temporal phases and each temporal phase appearing equally often. (See Table 15.1, left column for a list of all the target sentences.)

Each participant received only one set (18) of the target sentences and pictures. Another 62 sentences and pictures describing people of different occupations or objects were also prepared and served as fillers (non-targets) (e.g., 'this is a teacher', 'this is a ballpoint pen', etc.).

All the materials were presented on a 19-inch color screen connected to an ASUS personal computer. E-prime (Psychology Software Tools, Inc.) was used to program the experimental procedure.

Procedure

The experiment was run individually in a small room. Before the experiments, participants were given instructions and eight practice trials. For the experiment trials, each participant saw 80 Chinese sentences, including one set of 18 target sentences together with 62 non-targets, in randomized order. Each sentence was shown on the screen one Chinese character at a time, moving from left to right and for 200 ms per character. Before a sentence was shown, a cross appeared for 1000 ms to the left of the first character of the sentence to signal the position where the sentence would appear. All sentences ended with a period (full stop). Immediately after the period of each sentence disappeared, two pictures appeared on the screen. One matched the sentence just shown. The other either depicted the same action but in a different temporal phase, if the trial involved a target, or it depicted a different object or occupation, if the trial involved a non-target.

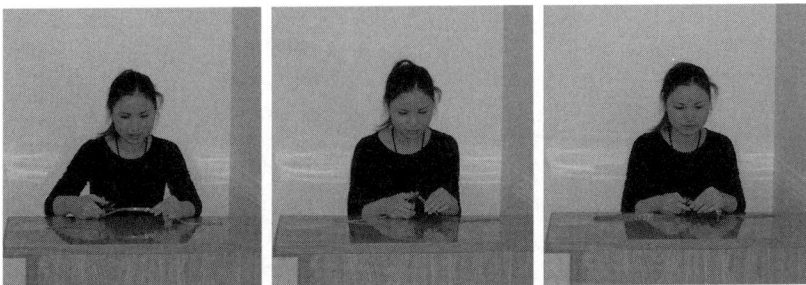

Figure 15.1 Action pictures at three different temporal phases (from left to right: future, present, past).

Table 15.1 Action events

Event		Chinese sentence		English sentence	
1	她	正在吹 剛剛吹完 準備要吹	氣球	She is blowing has just blown is about to blow	a balloon
2	她	正在擦掉 剛剛擦掉 準備要擦掉	白板上的東西	She is erasing has just erased is about to erase	something on a white- board
3	她	正在跨過 剛剛跨過 準備要跨過	橫木	She is crossing over has just crossed over is about to cross	a log
4	她	正在剪 剛剛剪斷 準備要剪	一條繩子	She is cutting has cut is about to cut	a rope
5	她	正在丟 剛剛把飛盤丟出去 準備要丟	飛盤	She is now throwing has just thrown is about to throw	a frisbee
6	她	正在喝 剛剛喝完 準備要喝	飲料	She is drinking has just finished drinking is about to drink	a cup of tea
7	她	正在摺 剛剛摺完 準備要摺	紙	She is making has just finished is about to make	an origami
8	她	正在溜 剛剛溜下 準備要溜	滑梯	She is sliding down has just slid down is about to slide down	the slide
9	她	正在吃 剛剛吃完 準備要吃	香蕉	She is eating has just eaten is about to eat	a banana
10	她	正在點 剛剛點燃 準備要點	蠟燭	She is lighting has lit is about to light	a candle

11	她	正在剝	橘子	She is peeling	an orange
		剛剛剝好		has peeled	
		準備要剝		is about to peel	
12	她	正在走	平衡木	She is walking on	a log
		剛剛走		has walked towards the end of	
		準備要走		is about to step on	
13	她	正在切	菜	She is cutting	a lettuce
		剛剛切完		has cut	
		準備要切		is about to cut	
14	她	正在拼	拼圖	She is doing	a puzzle
		剛剛完成了		has just finished	
		準備要拼		is about to begin doing	
15	她	正在走	樓梯	She is walking up	the stairs
		剛剛走完		has walked to the top of	
		準備要走上		is about to step on	
16	她	正在撕	一張紙	She is ripping	a piece of
		剛剛把紙撕破		has ripped	paper
		準備要撕		is about to rip	
17	她	正在踢	球	She is kicking	a ball
		剛剛把球踢出去		has just kicked	
		準備要踢		is about to kick	
18	她	正在倒	可樂	She is pouring	Coke into a
		剛剛倒完		has poured	glass
		準備要倒		is about to pour	

The 18 events described in Chinese (Experiment 1) and English (Experiment 2) sentences with respect to the three temporal aspects (future, present, past).

The participants had to choose the one which matched the sentence they just read, by pressing the designated left or right key on the computer keyboard. The response keys were counterbalanced across participants.

Measurement and data analysis

Participants' response times were measured by E-Prime from the onset of the pictures to their key-press on the keyboard. Response hits were also recorded. Analysis of variance and *t*-tests were employed for data analysis. *T*-tests were conducted for planned comparisons between the high- and the low-proficiency participants on each of the three temporal phases.

Results

Response times

Table 15.2 (left panel) presents the mean response times to the target pictures and the non-target pictures for the high-proficiency participants (CE-High-C) and the low-proficiency participants (CE-Low-C). Overall, the mean response times to the non-target pictures were shorter than those to the target pictures: $F(1, 47) = 372.79$, $MSe = 8986.49$, $p < .001$. This is the only significant effect in the analysis of variance. The mean response times of the high-proficiency participants were no different from those of the low-proficiency participants, and this is regardless of whether the pictures were targets or non-targets, both $Fs < 1$.

Hit rates

The right panel of Table 15.2 presents the mean hit rates. Overall, the hit rates were higher for the non-target pictures than for the target pictures: $F(1, 47) = 130.37$, $MSe = 0.001$, $p < .001$. High-proficiency participants (CE-High-C) responded with higher hit rates than low-proficiency participants (CE-Low-C): $F(1, 47) = 9.18$, $MSe = 0.008$, $p = .004$. The significant two-way interaction indicates that the high-proficiency participants responded with somewhat higher hit rates than the low-proficiency participants to the non-target pictures (.98 versus .96), but responded with much higher hit rates to the target pictures (.84 versus .75): $F(1, 47) = 6.39$, $MSe = 0.006$, $p = .015$.

Table 15.3 presents the mean response times and the mean hit rates for the target pictures separately for the three temporal phases. Analysis of variance of the response times reveals no significant main effects (both

Table 15.2 Response times and hit rates: Targets and non-targets

	Response time		Hit rate	
	Non-target pictures	Target pictures	Non-target pictures	Target pictures
CE-High-C	626 (19.89)	1001 (39.80)	.98 (.0004)	.84 (.023)
CE-Low-C	642 (16.64)	1008 (41.22)	.96 (.0006)	.75 (.0231)
CE-High-E	678 (20.78)	1322 (56.71)	.98 (.0004)	.81 (.021)

Mean response times in milliseconds and mean proportions of hit rates for the target and the non-target pictures by the high-proficiency (CE-High-C) and the low-proficiency (CE-Low-C) bilinguals tested in Chinese in Experiment 1, and by the high-proficiency bilinguals tested in English (CE-High-E) in Experiment 2 (standard errors of the means in parentheses).

Table 15.3 Response times and hit rates: Targets

	Response time			Hit rate		
	Future	Present	Past	Future	Present	Past
CE-High-C	1020	1014	969	.80	.82	.95
	(48.49)	(50.00)	(36.91)	(.04)	(.03)	(.03)
CE-Low-C	997	1017	1009	.70	.75	.85
	(48.04)	(43.21)	(40.23)	(.03)	(.04)	(.03)
CE-High-E	1354	1243	1369	.76	.91	.76
	(71.05)	(55.99)	(69.08)	(.04)	(.02)	(.03)

Mean response times in milliseconds and mean proportions of hit rates for the target pictures by the high-proficiency (CE-High-C) and the low-proficiency (CE-Low-C) bilinguals tested in Chinese in Experiment 1, and by the high-proficiency bilinguals tested in English (CE-High-E) in Experiment 2. The means were calculated separately for the three temporal phases (standard errors of the means in parentheses).

Fs < 1) or interaction effect (p = .059). Analysis of the hit rates reveals two significant main effects but no significant interaction: $F(1, 47)$ = 8.22, MSe = 0.04, p = .006 for the proficiency main effect; $F(2, 94)$ = 4.12, MSe = 0.025, p = .019 for the temporal phase main effect; F < 1 for the interaction. Although the interaction effect was not reliable, the pattern that emerged from planned comparisons was interesting and worth noting. It showed that the lower hit rate in the low-proficiency participants (CE-Low-C) relative to the high-proficiency participants (CE-High-C) came mainly from their responses to the past phases (.85 versus .90, p = .008 on a t-test) and the future phases (.70 versus .80, p = .06), but not so much from their responses to the present phases (.75 versus .82, p = .221).

Discussion

Having read a Chinese sentence describing an action event, Chinese–English bilinguals with a high level of English proficiency (CE-High-C) could access the temporal phase of the action more readily than those with a low level of English proficiency (CE-Low-C). The advantage appeared for the past and the future phases, but not for the present.

The low English proficiency bilinguals in the present study performed similarly to the monolinguals in our previous study (Chen et al., 2010). Both groups of participants showed the same tendency to miss the future and the past phases of an action event. We suggest the tendency is more likely perceptual or conceptual rather than merely linguistic in both studies. In the case of our previous study, even though Chinese does not have verb markings for tense and aspect, there are still ways to express future and past phases of action events—by using aspectual words (e.g., *guo4*, *wan2* for past or completion) and adverbial words and phrases (e.g., *gang1-gang1* for past, *zhun3-bei4-yao4* for future). Therefore the tendency to describe the future and the past phases of an action event found in the previous study was unlikely to be due to the lack of appropriate linguistic devices in Chinese to encode these temporal phases. In fact, our previous study also showed that Chinese participants could describe these phases if their attention had been directed towards making a distinction among the different temporal phases. Thus, although the tendency was verbal, the origin of the tendency, we think, was non-linguistic.

In the case of the present experiment the main task involved processing pictures and choosing one—a non-linguistic task. Therefore the fact that the low-proficiency participants tended to miss the matching pictures more often than the high-proficiency participants when the previously read sentences referred to the past or the future phases could be interpreted as reflecting their perceptual or conceptual insensitivity to these temporal phases. However, the possibility remains that the low-proficiency participants' lower sensitivity in the present experiment could be linguistic in origin. That is, it could have been brought about by the limited time allowed to process the prime sentences.

The finding that high English proficiency bilinguals showed higher levels of sensitivity is important. It implies that extensive exposure to a language that marks tense and aspect explicitly on the verb might serve to modify the conceptual system of the Chinese–English bilinguals such that the initially blurred boundaries between the present and the past phases as well as between the present and the future have become distinctive enough to allow for a somewhat different perception of an action event. The fact that the prime sentences in the present experiment were presented in Chinese suggests that the modification most likely has taken place in the conceptual system. This is consistent with Boroditsky's (2001) finding that training on the use of vertical metaphors changed English speakers' conceptualization of time.

EXPERIMENT 2: SENTENCES PRESENTED IN ENGLISH

The purpose of Experiment 2 was to test the hypothesis that high English proficiency bilinguals who read the sentences in English would perform similarly to bilinguals with the same levels of English proficiency tested in Chinese.

Method

Participants

A total of 24 native Chinese speakers with high English proficiency (scoring at or beyond the 88th percentile on the English subject of the Taiwan

College Entrance Exam, CE-High-E) participated in this experiment. None of them was an English major and none had participated in Experiment 1. They were paid for participation.

Materials, procedure, and analysis

The experimental materials were the same as those used in Experiment 1, except that all the target and non-target sentences were in English (see the right-hand column of Table 15.1 for the target sentences). The Chinese sentences were translated into English and back-translated into Chinese to ensure the comparability of contents. Some of the English translations were reworded, following the advice of a native speaker, to make them more natural English (e.g., *She has just finished drinking a cup of tea* instead of *She has just drunk a cup of tea*). The procedure was the same except that each sentence was displayed word by word, and each word was shown for 500 ms. The analysis of response times and hit rates included the data from Experiment 1 for comparison.

Results

Overall, response times of the CE-High-E participants (see Table 15.2) for the target and the non-target pictures were longer than those of the CE-High-C and the CE-Low-C participants: $F(2, 70) = 10.90$, $MSe = 48,210.79$, $p < .001$. Target pictures took longer to respond to than non-target pictures: $F(1, 70) = 574.53$, $MSe = 13,433.68$, $p < .001$. The interaction effect was significant, reflecting the greater difference between the CE-High-E participants and the other two groups (CE-High-C and CE-Low-C) for the target pictures than for the non-target pictures: $F(2, 70) = 22.52$, $MSe = 13,433.68$, $p < .001$.

The differences in hit rates among the three groups of participants (see Table 15.2) were significant: $F(2, 70) = 5.86$, $MSe = 0.008$, $p = .005$. A close examination of the differences reveals that the hit rates of the CE-High-E participants for the target and non-target pictures were comparable to those of the CE-High-C participants ($p > .5$), and together they were higher than those of the CE-Low-C participants ($p < .002$). The hit rates for the target pictures were generally lower than those for the non-target pictures: $F(1, 70) = 195.42$, $MSe = 0.006$, $p < .001$. The two-way interaction effect was also significant: $F(2, 70) = 3.41$, $MSe = 0.006$, $p = .039$, reflecting a larger group difference for the target pictures than for the non-target pictures. The difference was particularly evident on the target pictures, as CE-Low-C participants showed a lower hit rate than the two high English proficiency groups.

When the analyses focused on the target pictures and included temporal phases as a factor, the following results emerged. With respect to response times, the CE-High-E participants produced longer response times than the CE-High-C and the CE-Low-C participants (see Table 15.3). This is supported by the significant overall main effect: $F(2, 70) = 14.99$, $MSe = 162187.17$, $p < .001$; the significant contrast between the CE-High-E participants and the CE-High-C participants, as well as between the CE-High-E participants and the CE-Low-C participants: both $ps < .001$; but not between the CE-High-C participants and the CE-Low-C participants: $p > .9$. Response times to the different temporal phases were not significantly different, $p = .367$. However, the two-way interaction was significant: $F(2, 140) = 2.89$, $MSe = 19540.94$, $p = .024$.

With respect to response hit rates (see Table 15.3), both main effects and the interaction effect were significant: $F(2, 70) = 4.87$, $MSe = 0.037$, $p = .01$ for the group main effect; $F(2, 140) = 4.57$, $MSe = 0.025$, $p = .012$ for the temporal phase main effect; $F(2, 140) = 3.47$, $MSe = 0.025$, $p = .01$ for the interaction effect. When analyzed separately for different temporal phases, the results show no significant group effect for the future phases ($p = .157$), but a significant effect for the present and the past phases (both $ps < .01$). For the present phases, the CE-High-E participants performed with a higher hit rate than the CE-High-C ($p = .056$) and the CE-Low-C participants ($p = .001$), while the latter two groups performed equally ($p = .161$). For the past phases, the CE-High-E participants performed similarly to the CE-Low-C participants ($p = .647$), both of whom responded with lower hits than the CE-High-C participants ($p = .01$ and $.004$ respectively).

Discussion

When the sentences were in English, the Chinese–English bilinguals with a high level of English proficiency (CE-High-E) seemed to perform similarly to those with comparable English proficiency reading Chinese sentences (CE-High-C). However, a close inspection of their responses with respect to the different temporal phases revealed striking differences. Compared to the CE-High-C participants, the CE-High-E participants responded with a higher hit rate to the present phases, with an equal hit rate to the future phases, and with a lower hit rate to the past phases. In fact, their performance on the past phases was similar to those with low English proficiency receiving Chinese sentences (CE-Low-C). Thus, the results were not entirely consistent with our prediction.

One possible explanation for the peculiar performance of the CE-High-E participants may be found in the English sentences they read. To perform the task, the participants had to rely on some linguistic cue(s) in the sentences to quickly determine whether they described a future, a past, or a present phase. For instance, *is about to* signals a future phase, *is V-ing* signals a present phase, and *V-ed* a past phase. The much slower responses of the CE-High-E participants relative to the CE-High-C and the CE-Low-C participants indicate that reading and comprehending the English sentences was not as easy and efficient as reading and comprehending the

Chinese sentences. Accordingly, it is likely that the CE-High-E participants adopted the strategy of searching for the critical cues in the sentences (e.g., linguistic forms such as *is about to*, *is V-ing*, and *V-ed*) in order
to meet the demand of the task. The finding that the CE-High-E participants responded with a very high hit rate to the present phases is also an
indication that they adopted this strategy for the task. It turns out that the
linguistic cue was fairly obvious and consistent for the present phases,
being in the form of *be V-ing* as in English. This could explain why the CE-
High-E participants' hit rates to the present phases were especially high.
The linguistic cue for the future phases was also obvious and consistent,
being in the form of *is about to*. In contrast, for past phases, the linguistic
cue was in the form of words and phrases, which tend to take longer to
process than a simple verb marking like *-ing*. Moreover, the cue was inconsistent across sentences. In most sentences the past was expressed in the
form of *has just V-ed*. However, in some sentences it had been re-worded
by a native speaker of English we consulted as *has finished V-ing*. The
V-ing form in these sentences may have caused confusion. Additionally,
some of the verbs had irregular past participles, such as *cut*, *thrown*, *slid*,
and *eaten*. The inconsistency in the linguistic cues for the past phases
might have led to misreading the sentences and, as a consequence, to lower
hits in the responses to the pictures.

Another factor that could contribute to the unexpected performance of
the CE-High-E participants, especially with respect to the past phases, was
that they were not native speakers of English, and the sentences had been
presented with limited inspection time. That is, their English language
system could not operate as automatically as their Chinese system.
Accordingly, accessing the conceptual system would not be as efficient
when done through English as when done through Chinese. This factor
could contribute to the use of the strategy described in the last paragraph.

A model is proposed to illustrate the above explanations and to account
for the data of both experiments. Figure 15.2 shows that the CE-High-C
and the CE-High-E bilinguals share the same conceptual system, which
has been adapted to become time-sensitive regardless of the language
being used. The conceptual system of the CE-Low-C bilinguals has not
been adapted to the same extent, and remains time-insensitive. In addition,
the Chinese language system is a mature system, whereas the English system is a developing system that is not mature and automatized enough to
allow for fast lexical access and access to the conceptual system. The CE-
High-C bilinguals accessed their time-sensitive conceptual system by
means of the mature Chinese language system. The CE-High-E bilinguals
accessed the same conceptual system, but by means of their immature
English language system, as well as by employing a search strategy when
reading the English sentences. The CE-Low-C bilinguals used the same
Chinese language system as the CE-High-C bilinguals, but accessed the
time-insensitive conceptual system. According to this model, the particular

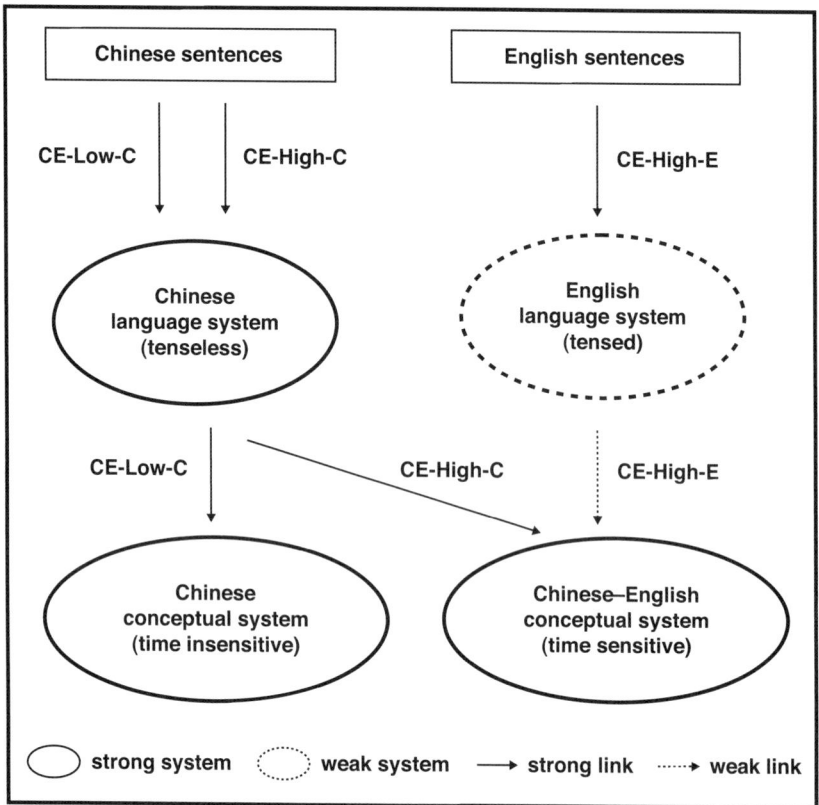

Figure 15.2 A conceptual model for explaining the different performances of the high English proficiency bilinguals reading Chinese and English sentences (CE-High-C and CE-High-E) and the low English proficiency bilinguals reading Chinese sentences (CE-Low-C).

performance of the CE-Low-C bilinguals was due to their time-insensitive conceptual system, which reflects the characteristics of the Chinese language. The particular performance of the CE-High-E bilinguals, on the other hand, was due to their imperfect English language system.

GENERAL DISCUSSION AND CONCLUSION

The key finding of the present study is that Chinese–English bilinguals with a high level of English proficiency perceive the future and the past phases of an action event, as encoded in a picture, more readily than bilinguals with a low level of proficiency. With respect to their perception of the present phase, the two groups of bilinguals did not differ. This is in line with our previous finding that Chinese and English monolinguals can describe an action event in the same way when it relates to the present phase but, unlike the English monolinguals, the Chinese monolinguals tend to describe the past and the future phase of an action as present. The current study adds to the previous one by showing that long-term experience with English may be linked to a change in Chinese speakers' perception of the temporal phases of an action event. Whether the change is merely linguistic, or whether it may also be conceptual, will need to be established by further research.

The findings of the present study and those of the previous one (Chen et al., 2010) suggest that people's perception of the temporal phases of an action event may be closely related to how the temporal relations are encoded in the language they speak. The mechanism through which this relation develops and becomes established may be attentional. That is, an explicit marking on the verb for tense and aspect could serve to direct speakers' attention to that component of an action event. Long-term experience with a language that carries such markings could then lead to a perceptual system that becomes sensitive at discriminating the different temporal relations in an action event.

An alternative explanation for our findings is cultural. Extensive research has shown that when viewing a scene, westerners (e.g., Americans) tend to pay attention to the focal object, while easterners (e.g., Chinese) tend to pay attention to the background context (Nisbett, 2003). Easterners are inclined to adopt a holistic perspective and view an action event as continuous, while westerners are accustomed to an analytic perspective and tend to view an action event as consisting of discrete components. The tendency to focus on the figure instead of the ground, and the analytic perspective, could lead to automatic event segmentation and render the different temporal components of an action event more distinct and identifiable for English speakers. The tendency to attend to the context and the holistic perspective could encourage Chinese speakers to view an action event as a non-segmentable whole, and to include the near future and the recent past as part of the extended present of the action event.

The linguistic explanation and the cultural explanation may be difficult to distinguish. However, our bilingual participants with high English proficiency were all local residents of Tainan, Taiwan; they had learned English in school as one of the many subjects in their curriculum; they were unlikely to have had experience of living in the American or British culture; accordingly, their better performance on the task of the present study is more likely to reflect their linguistic experience than their cultural experience, because of their lack of experience of English-speaking culture.

To conclude, people's sensitivity to the temporal aspect of an action event is related to their language experience, and that sensitivity might be modified by exposure to a second language.

ACKNOWLEDGMENTS

The work reported here was supported by the NSC-96-2752-H-006-001-PAE grant of the National Science Council of Taiwan, the Republic of China, as well as by an internal grant (D16-B0045) of National Cheng Kung University. We thank the editors for their very helpful suggestions regarding the revision of this chapter.

REFERENCES

Aksu-Koç, A. A., & von Stutterheim, C. (1994). Temporal relations in narrative: Simultaneity. In R. A. Berman & D. I. Slobin (Eds.), *Relating events in narrative: A crosslinguistic developmental study* (pp. 393–455). Hillsdale, NJ: Lawrence Erlbaum Associates Inc.

Alloway, T. P., & Corley, M. (2004). Speak before you think: The role of language in verb concepts. *Journal of Cognition and Culture, 4*(2), 319–345.

Boroditsky, L. (2001). Does language shape thought? Mandarin and English speakers' conceptions of time. *Cognitive Psychology, 43*(1), 1–22.

Boroditsky, L., Ham., W., & Ramscar, M. (2002). What is universal about event perception? Comparing English and Indonesian speakers. In W. D. Gray & C. D. Schunn (Eds.), *Proceedings of the 24th annual meeting of the Cognitive Science Society*. Mahwah, NJ: Lawrence Erlbaum Associates Inc.

Chang, J. P. (1998). *Situation types and their temporal implicatures in Chinese.* Ph.D. thesis, University of Kansas.

Chen, J-Y., Su, J-J., & O'Seaghdha, P. G. (2010). *Tense and speakers' perception of time in English and Chinese*. Manuscript submitted for publication.

Hunt, E., & Agnoli, F. (1991). The Whorfian hypothesis: A cognitive psychology perspective. *Psychology Review, 98*(3), 377–389.

Lin, J. W. (2002). Selectional restrictions of tenses and temporal reference of Chinese bare sentences. *Lingua, 113,* 271–302.

Lin, J. W. (2003). Temporal reference in Mandarin Chinese. *Journal of East Asian Linguistics, 12,* 259–311.

Lin, J. W. (2006). Time in a language without tense: The case of Chinese. *Journal of Semantics, 23,* 1–53.

Nisbett, R. E. (2003). *The geography of thought: How Asians and Westerners think differently . . . and why*. New York: The Free Press.

Slobin, D. I. (2003). Language and thought online: Cognitive consequences of linguistic relativity. In D. Gentner & S. Goldin-Meadow (Eds.), *Language in mind: Advances in the study of language and thought* (pp. 157–192). Cambridge, MA: MIT Press.

16 The grammatical and conceptual gender of animals in second language users

Benedetta Bassetti

GRAMMATICAL GENDER AND MONOLINGUAL COGNITION

Languages that have a grammatical gender system assign all nouns to one of two or more classes called 'genders'. 'Grammatical gender' (GG) is reflected in 'agreement', i.e., the GG of a noun determines changes in the form of constituents that refer to the noun or accompany it (for an overview, see Corbett, 1991, 2006). In many Indo-European languages grammatical gender (GG) has two or three categories: Italian has two, 'masculine' and 'feminine', German has three, the previous two plus 'neuter'. In both languages gender agreement shows in determiners (e.g., articles *il/lo* and *la* in Italian; *der*, *die*, and *das* in German), in adjectives, and in anaphoric pronouns. For instance, a German speaker asking for a knife, a spoon, or a fork has to use a male, female, or neuter pronoun (*Gib ihn/sie/ es mir mal herüber*, 'pass (masculine/feminine/neuter) it to me'). An Italian speaker would use a masculine *lo* for 'knife' and 'spoon', and feminine *la* for 'fork' (*passame lo* vs *passame la*). The grammatical gender of a noun is determined by 'gender assignment', a system of semantic and/or formal rules for grammatical gender. In Italian and German, assignment is partly semantic (male referents are mostly grammatically masculine and female referents are mostly grammatically feminine) and partly formal (depending on the form of the noun rather than on the sex of the referent). In these languages therefore gender assignment partly reflects biological sex, being used for female and male beings (like 'natural', or 'semantic', gender); however, gender is assigned not only to nouns of sexed beings, but also to nouns of artifacts, natural kinds, and abstract concepts. Thus, 'assignment rules' are semantically arbitrary (albeit largely formally justified). In both Italian and German there are phonological and morphological rules. In Italian, most masculine nouns end in *-o* (plural *-i*) and most feminine ones end in *-a* (plural *-e*), although there are nouns ending in *-e* as well as exceptions. In German, some endings regularly co-occur with masculine or feminine gender (e.g., 90% of nouns ending in schwa /ə/ are feminine; 65% of those ending in *-el/en/er* are masculine). While German gender assignment depends on declensional class, the system is complicated because nouns are also marked for number and case. The German gender system is therefore less transparent than the Italian one.

The issue of interest here is the relationship between the morphosyntactic feature of grammatical gender and the masculinity and femininity of nouns' referents. In GG languages, besides the semantic core of nouns that refer to male and female beings, all other nouns (the semantic residue) are also assigned a gender, which is semantically arbitrary. Referents of feminine nouns include not only female referents (e.g., Italian *moglie*, 'wife', and *gallina*, 'hen'), but also male referents (*guardia*, 'guard'), asexual referents (*finestra*, 'window'), and referents of either sex (*aquila*, 'eagle', used for both male and female eagles), as well as referents with feminine connotations (e.g., *gonna*, 'skirt'), and referents with masculine connotations (e.g., *cravatta*, 'tie'). The same applies to the masculine gender.

The semantic arbitrariness of most assignment rules in GG languages is evident from cross-linguistic comparisons: Although it is possible to identify some semantic rules for assignment within a single language (e.g., in German, predators are masculine; see Zubin & Köpcke, 1986, for an overview), cross-linguistic comparisons reveal little agreement on gender assignment across languages and especially across language families (Foundalis, 2002). For instance, the following words are feminine in Italian and masculine in German: 'faith' (*la fede, der Glaube*); 'butterfly' (*la farfalla, der Schmetterling*); 'armchair' (*la poltrona, der Sessel*); the following words are masculine in Italian and feminine in German: 'sin' (*il peccato, die Sünde*), 'spider' (*il ragno, die Spinne*), 'mattress' (*il materasso, die Matrazze*).

Grammatical gender therefore creates categories of entities that have nothing in common in the real world, but whose nouns belong to the same morphosyntactic class. For this reason it is a good test-bed for research on the effects of language on thought, since there is no reason why a fox should be considered similar to a woman and a cat to a man. It is therefore not surprising that researchers interested in the effects of language on thought have investigated the effects of grammatical gender.

Sapir ruled out the possibility that grammatical gender might affect mental representations of entities: 'It goes without saying that a Frenchman has no clear sex notion in his mind when he speaks of *un arbre* ("a-masculine tree") or of *une pomme* ("a-feminine apple")' (1921/2004, p. 77). However, there is evidence that grammatical gender affects real-life behaviors: Anthropomorphized objects and animals in German children's stories follow the grammatical gender of their referent (Mills, 1986); Spanish-speaking consumers prefer brand names with masculine or feminine endings depending on the gender connotations of the product (e.g., *Aizo* for a beer, which is perceived as a 'masculine' drink, and *Aiza* for a fruit cocktail; Yorkston & De Mello, 2005).

Experimental research then tried to establish whether GG affects the conceptualization of artifacts, animals, natural kinds, and abstract concepts. Effects were found in a variety of tasks, although not consistently. In some of these tasks, effects could be due to the strategic use of GG, but in other tasks this is not a possible explanation. GG affects performance in *name attribution tasks* and *voice attribution tasks*, where participants choose a male or female voice or name for animals and objects, in French and Spanish adults and children (Sera et al., 2002) and in French, German and Spanish adults, but not in English or Japanese controls (Flaherty, 1999; Mills, 1986). When targets have opposite gender in two languages, speakers of these languages make the opposite choice of voice, and effects are stronger with natural kinds than artifacts (Sera et al., 2002). GG also affects performance in 'semantic similarity rating' tasks. In some studies, participants matched pictures of animals and objects with pictures of female or male humans, and GG effects were found with objects, animals, and natural kinds in French and Spanish adults (Flaherty, 1999), and with objects in Spanish and German speakers (Phillips & Boroditsky, 2003). Guiora's (1983) study found no overall effects of GG, but one third of sortings of objects with no gender connotations were consistent with GG, and none was inconsistent. In these tasks GG could be used strategically. Other similarity rating tasks involve matching two animals or artifacts out of a triad (therefore hiding the link between the task and gender assignment), and predict that participants will match targets with the same grammatical gender. Results show that Spanish GG affects adult and child speakers of French, German, and Spanish, but not English or Japanese controls (Flaherty, 1999; Martinez & Shatz, 1996; Vigliocco, Vinson, Paganelli, & Dworzynski, 2005). In these studies, GG is not used strategically—sortings are never entirely consistent with GG, and some items are sorted in the same way across languages (Flaherty, 1999), showing that GG is only one of the factors affecting performance in these tasks.

Various factors modulate the effects of grammatical gender: Age of participants, language of testing, and stimuli (whether materials are linguistic or not; whether referents are animate or not). First, GG effects only appear in children above the age of 8, at least in those languages where this variable has been tested (Flaherty, 2001; Mills, 1986; Nicoladis & Foursha-Stevenson, 2010; Sera et al., 2002)—this could be due to linguistic development, cognitive development or both. Second, effects are consistently found with speakers of Spanish and French (e.g., Sera et al., 2002), but not with speakers of German (e.g., Flaherty, 1999, and Imai, Saalbach, & Shalk, 2009, found effects, but Vigliocco et al., 2005, did not). It has been proposed that German grammatical gender has weaker effects because animate nouns are sometimes neuter, thus weakening the link between GG and biological sex (Vigliocco et al., 2005); a more likely explanation is that German has a more complex GG system than Spanish, both in terms of actual number of GG markers and of the regularity of the relation between a noun's GG and its ending. Third, effects are stronger with pictures accompanied by a linguistic label than with unlabeled pictures (Sera et al., 2002), or only show up with words but not with pictures (Vigliocco et al., 2005). This could be evidence of linguistic rather than conceptual effects. Also, while some researchers found GG effects with artifacts (Martinez & Shatz, 1996; Nicoladis & Foursha-Stevenson, 2010), others found effects with animals but not with artifacts (Vigliocco et al., 2005). This shows that GG interacts with characteristics of concepts— animals are attributed gender characteristics or connotations more than inanimate objects. Since objects and abstract concepts do not have bio- logical sex, perhaps these entities are attributed feminine or masculine connotations, so that speakers of one language can consider 'love' a femi- nine emotion while speakers of another language consider it masculine.

In conclusion, research has found effects of grammatical gender on monolinguals' performance in a variety of tasks, although these findings are not consistent and are affected by other factors. Different explanations have been proposed for these effects. One possibility is that GG affects conceptual representations of entitites, which are then perceived as being more or less masculine or feminine, or having masculine or feminine conno- tations. Alternative explanations include: the strategic use of GG, *thinking for speaking*, and category learning. One explanation is that GG is used as a strategy. Some tasks used to study the effects of GG on concepts in fact rely on gender attribution (e.g., voice attribution, name attribution, object– human similarity judgment), and participants might use GG as a strategy (but see Bassetti, 2007, for evidence that child participants do not report strategic use of GG). A second explanation is purely linguistic. GG lan- guage speakers are likely to make choices that allow them to talk about the referent without a conflict between the referent's GG and its name or voice. It is better to call an apple *Patricia* rather than *Patrick* because in speaking it will be necessary to refer to the apple as *she*, and this would be awkward if the apple was called *Patrick*. A third explanation is that GG effects are effects of category learning. Having found GG effects on object–human similarity ratings with a connectionist simulation, Eberhard, Scheutz, and Heilman (2005) argue that categorization tasks only show that objects belong to the same category as human males or human females, not that objects are perceived as masculine or feminine. However, just because computers perform a learning task that leads to the same learning out- comes as in humans, it does not follow that humans learn in the same way. In conclusion, since the results reported above can be explained in different ways, in order to test whether GG affects perception of masculin- ity and femininity, it is necessary to use tasks that measure masculinity/ femininity connotations—such as the semantic differential task.

GRAMMATICAL GENDER AND MONOLINGUALS' PERFORMANCE IN SEMANTIC DIFFERENTIAL TASKS

The *semantic differential* emerged in the 1950s as a technique for measuring the connotative meaning of concepts (Osgood, Suci, & Tannenbaum, 1957). Concepts are presented as words (or phrases) or pictures. Participants rate each concept on a series of scales between bipolar adjective pairs, such as 'big–small' or 'cold–hot'. Ratings on adjectival scales provide a measure of three factors: 'evaluation' (e.g., 'good–bad'), 'potency' (e.g., 'weak–strong'), and 'activity' (e.g., 'active–passive'). Participants' scores then create a representation of meaning in a geometric space that represents the direction of the rating (positive or negative) and its intensity (distance from the middle of the scale).

The semantic differential task (SDT) has been repeatedly used to test the effects of grammatical gender on the perceived masculinity and femininity of entities. Some studies used a straightforward masculinity–femininity scale. Two early studies that used nouns of objects as targets found effects of GG in Arabic speakers (Clarke, Losoff, Dickenson, McCracken, & Still, 1981), but not in Hebrew speakers (Guiora & Acton, 1979; Guiora & Sagi, 1978); in a more recent study (Sera et al., 2002), GG affected the ratings of artifacts and natural kinds in Spanish speakers but not in English controls. Since rating on a masculine–feminine scale is an explicit task, this type of research was criticized for testing participants' responses to words rather than to referents, and for measuring differences in strategies rather than in perception of reality (Herold, 1982). However, if GG was used strategically, participants should always give GG-consistent answers, and should rate targets at the ends of the scales, i.e., as masculine or feminine, rather than somewhere along the scale, i.e., as more or less masculine/feminine. Since this is not the case, either GG is not used as a strategy, or at least it is not the only one.

Other studies used various scales associated with masculinity and femininity, rather than a straightforward masculinity–femininity scale. A study of Chinese speakers (Tong, Chiu, & Fu, 2001) found that pseudowords that contained the semantic radical for 'woman' were rated lower on potency and activity, compared with pseudowords with the radical 'human being'. This study reveals a relationship between grammatical and conceptual gender as measured in SDTs, since the mere presence of a feminine gender marker in a linguistic label leads to higher femininity rating of its unknown referent. In Konishi (1993), German and Spanish monolinguals rated nouns of objects that have opposite GG in their languages (e.g. masculine *Äpfel* and feminine *manzana*, 'apple'). The two groups gave opposite ratings to the same referent, with masculine nouns of artifacts rated higher in scales measuring potency (but not evaluation or activity). Mills (1986) compared German- and English-speaking adults and children who rated animals and artifacts on 15 semantic differential scales. For

German speakers the ratings of grammatically feminine referents ('cat', 'mouse', and 'clock') correlated with the rating of 'woman' and the ratings of grammatically masculine and neuter referents correlated with 'man'. The English controls showed the same pattern of results, which reflected English speakers' choice of pronouns for referring to these entities in a cloze test, again showing the relationship between language and semantic differential ratings. In a study that looked at abstract concepts (Zubin & Köpcke, 1984), German speakers rated affect nouns such as 'sadness' and 'courage'. Grammatically feminine affect nouns were rated higher on introversion (a feminine characteristic), and grammatically masculine ones were higher on extroversion, although results are marred by the absence of a control group with a different language background. Finally, Hofstätter (1963) compared German and Italian monolinguals' concepts of 'sun' and 'moon' using 24 scales and found no differences. Concepts of sun and moon are affected by culture (e.g., in Italian visual arts the sun is represented as male and the moon as female, and vice versa in German arts), so the absence of effects in this study shows that GG effects do not consistently show in SDTs.

While all the studies reported above used words as targets, other studies used pictures. Flaherty (1999) found GG effects on French and Spanish adults' ratings of pictures of objects and animals on various 2-point scales; no effects were found in English and Japanese controls. Flaherty (2001) replicated the study with English and Spanish children, and found GG effects only above age 10, i.e., later than in gender assignment tasks such as name attribution, where effects are established at age 8 (see above).

In conclusion, grammatical gender seems to affect semantic differential ratings, although some studies found no effects. GG effects appear mostly on scales measuring potency (Konishi, 1993; Tong et al., 2001), are weaker compared with tasks such as voice attribution tasks (Flaherty, 1999), and appear at a later age than in other tasks (Flaherty, 2001).

The results of SDT studies cannot be ruled out as a consequence of the strategic use of GG, or as linguistic effects or categorization effects. It appears that GG affects perceptions of entities, which are then perceived as masculine or feminine. For animate entities, one possibility is that they are assigned their grammatical gender as default gender—for instance, an Italian speaker would consider a fox as female by default, unless there is reason to believe that it is a male fox, and a mouse as male, unless there is reason to believe that it is a female mouse. An alternative explanation is that entities are perceived as having masculine or feminine connotations—Germans might think that a mouse is a feminine animal, and Italians might consider it a masculine animal. This explanation has the advantage of accounting for ratings of inanimate entities, such as 'love'—love cannot be attributed a gender, but it can be considered a masculine or feminine emotion. Since the SDT is supposed to measure connotations, this is probably the correct explanation.

The question is, then, how could a feature of grammar affect mental representations of entities in the real world? Researchers have suggested that when children learn language, the categorizations reflected in language could affect the categorization of entities in the real world. For instance, Bowerman wrote: 'children are prepared from the beginning to accept linguistic guidance as to which distinctions—from among the set of distinctions that are salient to them—they should rely on in organizing particular domains of meaning' (1985, p. 1285). There is indeed some evidence that children think there is a link between the grammatical gender of a noun and the gender of its referent. Chini (1995) reports the case of a 3-year-old Italian girl who refused to accept that *vestito* ('dress') is masculine, because the dress belonged to her doll, and *vestito* 'is for men' (i.e., *vestito* belongs to men because it is grammatically masculine). With older children, the association between GG and referents' gender could even be reinforced by explicit teaching. French parents correct children's GG errors by referring to the nouns' referents as *garçon* and *fille* ('boy' and 'girl'; Nicoladis & Foursha-Stevenson, 2010). What is presumably a trick to make grammar understandable to children could in fact reinforce children's intuition that GG is related to gender. There is evidence that German children associate grammatical gender with semantic rules before they learn formal GG rules, and, when the two conflict, children choose the former, for instance using the female pronoun *sie* for *Rotkäppchen* (Little Red Riding Hood) rather than the correct neuter pronoun, because *Rotkäppchen* is a girl (Wegener, 2000). Finally, adults might look for logical explanations of the gender assignment of their mother tongue. For instance, Clarke, Losoff, and Rood (1982) report cases of Arabic speakers who explain that 'beard', a typical male attribute, is grammatically feminine because it is soft and pliable. The conflict between properties of the word (feminine GG) and properties of the referent (male connotation) is rationalized by concluding that there is something feminine about beards. It appears that there are many ways grammatical gender can creep into people's perception of entities. The next question is, then, what happens to those who speak two languages that assign opposite gender to the same entity?

GRAMMATICAL GENDER AND BILINGUAL COGNITION

Anecdotal and observational evidence shows conceptual effects of learning or knowing more than one GG language. Adult speakers of two GG languages sometimes show a preference for the gender assignment of one or the other language for a specific entity. For instance, the German poet Rainer Maria Rilke preferred to talk about a masculine sun and a feminine moon, choosing the gender assignment of L2 French over L1 German (Hofstätter, 1963). In the other direction, the Italian–German bilingual daughters of Traute Taeschner forcefully insisted that the sun is a 'girl', in line with their L2 gender assignment, rather than a 'boy' as in their L1 Italian (Taeschner, 1983). Child L2 learners might try to rationalize why some entities are masculine or feminine in the L2, as in the case of a 7-year-old speaker of a grammatical genderless language who rejected L2 French gender assignments when these contrasted with the perceived masculine or feminine connotations of objects such as ribbons and stains (Kenyeres, 1938).

Experimental research on the effects of grammatical gender on bilinguals' cognition began with a pioneering study by Ervin (1962; Chapter 9, this volume). Ervin asked Italian–English bilinguals to rate Italian pseudowords with masculine or feminine endings on four scales. Italian-dominant bilinguals rated grammatically feminine pseudowords as more feminine than grammatically masculine ones. However, English-dominant bilinguals, who had acquired English before age 6, were not affected by Italian gender markers. This study shows that a second language learnt early in life can eliminate L1 GG effects, even if the L2 is grammatical genderless. However, this study used pseudowords as stimuli, so it shows that speakers of grammatical gender languages relate GG to gender, not that GG affects conceptual gender. In a recent study that used linguistic stimuli and a linguistic task, L2 learners and users assigned a masculine or feminine gender to L1 neuter words (Andonova, Gosheva, Schaffai, & Janyan, 2007). Users and learners of a grammatical gender L2 mostly followed the L2 assignment, whereas users and learners of a semantic gender L2 (English) performed randomly. The meaning of these results is unclear, as L2 learners and users might have used L2 GG strategically to perform this unusual task.

Other studies used non-linguistic stimuli. Two studies looked at bilinguals with a grammatical gender L1 and a semantic gender L2, tested in the L2 (English). Boroditsky and Schmidt (2000) used a paired associate learning task performed in English, and found that participants learnt proper names for objects and animals better when the English name was consistent with the object's L1 GG. In a second experiment, participants described entities using three adjectives in L2 English; they produced more stereotypically feminine adjectives for referents whose nouns was feminine in their L1, and vice versa. Testing participants in L2 English reduces the possibility that effects are due to thinking-for-speaking, so results support the hypothesis of conceptual effects. Furthermore, since all items had opposite GG in the two languages, these are language effects rather than effects of referents' characteristics. L1 GG effects therefore appear in bilinguals whose L2 is grammatically genderless. Unfortunately no information is provided about the L2 age of acquisition or proficiency of participants. Nicoladis and Foursha-Stevenson (2010) also found that L1 grammatical gender affects French–English bilingual children when tested in English. The children, who were bilinguals from birth, had to decide whether a toy (an animal or an artifact) was a boy or a girl. The bilingual children aged 8 to 10 were affected by L1 French GG, while English controls and younger bilinguals were not. These two studies of bilinguals tested in a semantic gender language show that GG effects are not artifacts of the language of testing, and are not reduced by knowledge of a semantic gender L2. On the other hand, one study looked at the effects of learning a grammatical gender L2 on native speakers of a semantic gender L1 (Kurinski & Sera, in press). English-speaking learners of L2 Spanish performed a voice attribution task with objects as targets. Results show that voice attribution is affected by the grammatical gender of the objects in L2 Spanish, and this is linked to L2 proficiency. It appears that learning a grammatical gender second language might negatively affect cognition, leading to a misrepresentation of reality that does not exist in monolingual speakers of a semantic gender first language.

While bilinguals with a grammatical gender L1 and a semantic gender L2 are influenced by L1 grammatical gender, bilinguals whose L2 is also a GG language appear to differ from monolingual speakers of their L1. Phillips and Boroditsky (2003) tested bilinguals' concepts of entities that have opposite gender in their two languages. A group of Spanish–German and German–Spanish bilinguals performed a picture similarity task in L3 English. The L1 grammatical gender effect was negatively correlated with self-rated L2 fluency, showing that higher proficiency in a language that assigns opposite gender to the same entity reduces the conceptual effects of L1 grammatical gender. Bassetti (2007) compared Italian monolingual and Italian–German bilingual children using a voice attribution task with pictures of artifacts that had opposite gender in Italian and German. Italian monolingual children preferred female voices for grammatically feminine objects; Italian–German bilinguals were not affected by Italian GG. The bilingual children did not prefer female voices for grammatically feminine referents even though they were being tested in Italian, a language in which referring to these referents as masculine would be awkward. This shows that the effects of GG on voice attribution tasks cannot be dismissed as 'thinking for speaking'. It appears that knowledge of two GG languages reduces the effects of L1 grammatical gender.

Finally, two studies tested the effects of learning an artificial language. In Boroditsky, Schmidt, and Phillips (2003), English-speaking adults learnt a series of object nouns in an artificial language. Nouns belonged to one of two categories, one comprising objects and male humans, and one comprising objects and female humans. After learning the objects' nouns, participants rated the similarity of the objects with female or male humans. Their similarity judgments were influenced by the two-gender system they had learnt. Adult speakers of a semantic gender language who learn the grammatical gender system of an artificial language show effects in their similarity judgment tasks in line with the effects found in native speakers of GG languages, at least in tests immediately following the learning task. A connectionist network trained with words in two languages, English and either Spanish or German, also produced similarity ratings that were affected by GG (Dilkina, McClelland, & Boroditsky, 2007).

The above two studies on bilinguals with two GG-languages (Phillips & Boroditsky, 2003, and Bassetti, 2007) show that grammatical gender effects on cognition differ between monolinguals and bilinguals whose two languages assign opposite genders to the same entities. The main limitation of the above studies is that grammatical gender could have been used as a strategy to perform the tasks (object–human similarity ratings and voice attribution). The present study aims at testing the conceptual effects of knowing two GG languages through a task that measures connotative meaning.

GRAMMATICAL AND CONCEPTUAL GENDER OF ANIMALS IN MONOLINGUALS AND BILINGUALS

Aims and hypotheses

This study aimed at comparing the effects of grammatical gender on the perceived masculinity and femininity of animals in monolinguals and bilinguals using a semantic differential task. Italian monolinguals, German monolinguals, and Italian users of German as a second language (GSL) rated a series of animals on various semantic differential scales. Animals were used as targets because GG effects appear more consistently with animals than artifacts (Sera et al., 2002), and were presented as drawings without linguistic labels to avoid the potential confound of grammatical gender marking. All animals had opposite grammatical gender in the two languages. It was predicted that GG would affect performance on the SDT, but it would not determine it, i.e., answers would not be entirely due to GG. It was predicted that the Italian and German monolinguals would give opposite ratings, as all targets had opposite gender in the two languages. Italians who know L2 German were expected to differ from Italian monolinguals, because of their knowledge of two languages that assign opposite grammatical gender to the same referent.

This is the first study to look at the effects of grammatical gender in users of two grammatical gender languages using a semantic differential task (SDT). Previous research that tested grammatical gender effects on the representation of entities in bilinguals used voice attribution (Bassetti, 2007), object–human similarity rating (Phillips & Boroditsky, 2003) or other gender attribution tasks (e.g., Andonova et al., 2007; Nicoladis & Foursha-Stevenson, 2010). Since the SDT is intended to measure connotative meaning, differences between bilinguals and monolinguals on this task might be better evidence of a conceptual effect of bilingualism. In the only previous study of GG effects in bilinguals that used the SDT (Ervin, 1962), targets were pseudowords, and the bilinguals' L2 did not have grammatical gender. This study instead compared bilinguals with two GG languages who were rating concepts of real-world entities.

Participants

There were 48 participants: 16 German monolinguals, 16 Italian mono-linguals, and 16 Italian users of German as a second language (GSL). The groups were similar in age (Italians: $M = 30$, range: 22–64; Germans: $M = 29$, range 20–62; Italian GSL users: $M = 31$, range 21–41) but differed in gender composition (number of males: Germans 7, Italians 10, Italian GSL users 4).

The Italian GSL users were native speakers of Italian who had started learning German mostly between age 10 and 15 ($M = 13$, $SD = 5$, with one age of onset of acquisition of 6 and one of 26) and had been L2 users of German for 19 years on average ($SD = 6$). They rated their own knowledge of German as 'intermediate' or 'advanced' on a 5-point scale (88% and 12% respectively).

Most participants in all groups spoke English and reported an inter-mediate or advanced proficiency level (88% of Germans, 81% of Italians, 69% of Italian GSL users). Knowledge of English was not expected to influence the results of this study because bilinguals with L2 English are affected by L1 grammatical gender (Boroditsky et al., 2003), unless they are English-dominant immigrants with an early age of arrival (Ervin, 1962). While none of the Italian monolinguals had been exposed to any Germanic languages, all the German participants had learnt a Romance language (mostly French), since age 12–14, but mostly rated themselves as beginners (69%), with a few intermediates (31%).

Procedure

Participants filled in an online questionnaire. Each animal was evaluated using a 7-point semantic differential scale consisting of seven adjective pairs measuring evaluation and potency. Items were always presented in the same order. Participants made their rating by clicking on a scroll-down list. They were instructed to rate the animal rather than the drawing (e.g., they had to rate the beauty of 'mice' rather than the beauty of the mouse picture on the questionnaire). The SDT was followed by a questionnaire. Participation was voluntary and unpaid.

Materials

The web questionnaire contained: instructions; 14 items, each consisting of the drawing of an animal followed by seven 7-point semantic differential scales; a questionnaire about biographical and linguistic background; and space for providing feedback. There were two versions, one written in German and one in Italian. Both had been translated from English by qualified and experienced translators. Participants only saw the questionnaire in their first language (i.e., bilinguals saw the Italian questionnaire).

The 14 animals were presented using line drawings (which are displayed in the Appendix). Pictures were used rather than words to avoid effects of gender marking. Drawings were black-and-white in order to avoid the gender connotations of colors (Flaherty, 2001), and were selected from royalty-free collections published in the UK to avoid cultural effects on the visual representation of animals. All animals had opposite grammatical gender in Italian and German. The seven 'masculine animals' had a noun that is masculine in Italian and feminine in German, and the seven 'feminine animals' were feminine in Italian and masculine in German. The Italian nouns had the appropriate phonological ending for their grammatical gender (/a/ for feminine nouns, /o/ for masculine nouns), except for two male and two female animals that ended in /e/—'pigeon' (M), 'snake' (M), 'tiger' (F), and 'fox' (F). The grammatical gender of nouns in German was established using a dictionary, and confirmed with a pilot study in which five German native speakers wrote down a (gender-marked) definite article and a noun for each of the drawings. Only items that elicited 100% consistent responses were selected.

Below each animal drawing there were seven 7-point semantic differential scales. Five scales used the following adjective pairs: 'good–bad'; 'weak–strong'; 'clean–dirty'; 'beautiful–ugly'; 'soft–rough'. Due to difficulties in finding antonyms, and therefore difficulties in ensuring linearity between two polar opposites, two scales were presented as 7-point Likert-type scales evaluating one adjective ('disgusting' and 'dangerous'). The scales had sufficient reliability, Chronbach's α = .69. The adjectives were not obviously related to masculinity and femininity, so that the purpose of the study was masked. The scales also met the criterion of relevance to the concept being measured, as most of them had been used to measure, or had been shown to correlate with, masculinity–femininity in previous SDT studies ('Beautiful': Ervin, 1962; Konishi, 1993; Mills, 1986; Osgood et al., 1957; Zubin & Köpcke, 1984. 'Good': Ervin, 1962; Konishi, 1993; Osgood et al., 1957. 'Clean': Osgood et al., 1957. 'Soft': Mills, 1986; Zubin & Köpcke, 1984. 'Weak': Ervin, 1962; Konishi, 1993; Mills, 1986; Zubin & Köpcke, 1984). The scales measured evaluation (ugly, bad, dirty, and disgusting) and potency (strong, rough, and dangerous). In order to facilitate the task, each scale was presented as a scroll-down list, and cells were labeled with the format 'very x', 'x', 'rather x', 'neither x nor y', 'rather y', 'y', 'very y'. The scales varied in polarity direction: In two scales the masculine end was at the top of the list and in three at the bottom.

Results

Ratings were scored from −3 to +3, with 0 being the midpoint and −3 denoting 'masculine', so that higher scores indicate higher levels of femininity. For each participant, mean scores were calculated for each animal on each scale. Table 16.1 and Figure 16.1 show the mean ratings of grammatically masculine and grammatically feminine animals on each scale by group.

With regards to grammatically feminine animals, in scales measuring evaluation they were rated by all groups as being on the feminine half of all scales (above 0, on the right-hand side in the profiles), and overall as more feminine than grammatically masculine animals. On potency scales, Germans rated grammatically feminine animals as more masculine than did Italians, and overall as more masculine than masculine animals. Italians and Italian GSL users rated feminine animals as more feminine on two scales and as more masculine on the strong–weak scale, possibly reflecting characteristics of the animals (feminine animals included 'eagle',

Table 16.1 Mean rating of grammatically masculine and feminine animals by scale and group

Scale	Germans			Italian GSL users			Italians		
	F	M	Diff.	F	M	Diff.	F	M	Diff.
Ugly *Brutto* *Häßlich*	1.30	0.07	1.23	1.25	−0.24	1.49	1.84	−0.19	2.03
Dirty *Sporco* *Schmutzig*	1.05	0.48	0.57	1.13	0.21	0.92	0.91	−0.19	1.10
Bad *Cattivo* *Schlecht*	1.33	0.72	0.61	0.28	−0.03	0.31	0.78	0.44	0.34
Disgusting *Disgustoso* *Eklig*	2.65	1.28	1.37	2.24	0.51	1.73	2.15	0.30	1.85
Strong *Forte* *Stark*	−0.36	0.24	−0.60	−0.39	0.07	−0.46	−0.12	0.27	−0.39
Rough *Ruvido* *Hart*	0.02	0.21	−0.19	0.29	−0.14	0.43	0.72	−0.12	0.84
Dangerous *Pericoloso* *Gefährlich*	1.49	1.30	0.19	1.32	0.74	0.58	1.08	0.57	0.51

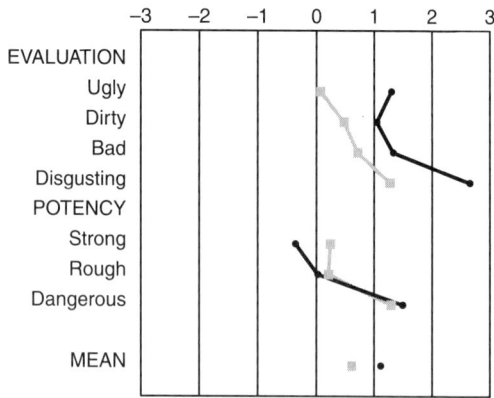

(a)

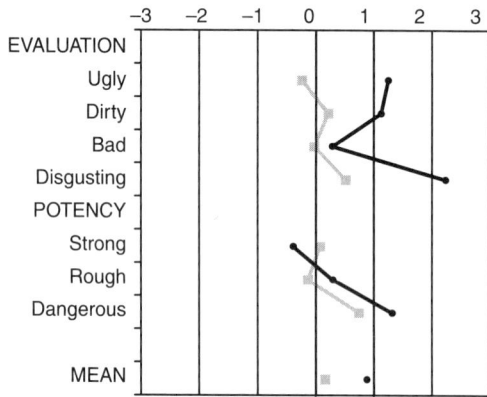

(b)

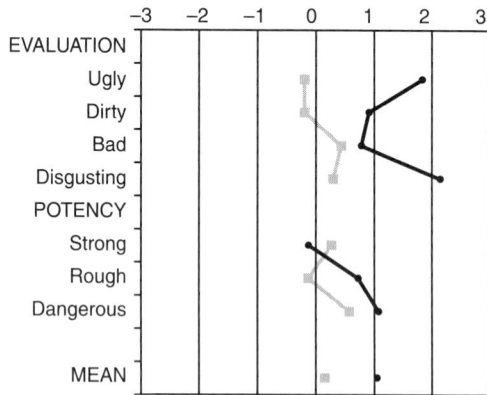

(c)

Figure 16.1 Profiles of masculine (gray line) and feminine (black line) animals on the seven scales, and mean across all scales, by group. (a) German monolinguals; (b) Italian users of German as a second language; (c) Italian monolinguals.

'tiger', and 'fox', whereas the only strong masculine animal was 'snake'). The difference between feminine and masculine animals was larger in the Italian monolingual group than in the Italian GSL users group.

With regards to masculine animals, the German monolingual group rated them on the feminine half of all the scales, probably because these animals are feminine in their language. The Italian and Italian–German bilingual groups rated masculine animals around the midpoint of all scales, slightly more masculine on some scales and slightly more feminine on others. The ratings of Italian and Italian–German participants could reflect the fact that the female gender is marked in Italian, and therefore leads Italian speakers to categorize grammatically feminine referents as more feminine, whereas masculine gender is unmarked and its referents are not considered either masculine or feminine. This is in line with findings by Bassetti (2007) that Italian children attribute a female voice to grammatically feminine referents but do not choose a male voice for masculine referents.

Table 16.2 shows the mean ratings for feminine and masculine animals by group. For each participant, the mean difference in rating between feminine and masculine animals was calculated by subtracting the mean rating for grammatically masculine animals from the mean rating for grammatically feminine animals. While all groups rated grammatically feminine animals as more feminine than masculine ones, the mean difference between the perceived femininity of feminine and masculine animals was largest among Italian monolinguals and smallest among German monolinguals, with the Italian–German bilinguals in between.

A mixed $3 \times (2)$ ANOVA was performed with language background (German monolingual; Italian GSL user; Italian monolingual) as a between-group factor, and grammatical gender (grammatically masculine; grammatically feminine) as a within-group factor. There was a main effect of grammatical gender, $F(1, 45) = 179.23$, $p < .001$, $r = .89$, showing that grammatically feminine animals were rated as more feminine across groups. The effect of language background, $F(2, 45) = 4.87$, $p = .012$, $r = .31$ was qualified by the interaction, $F(2, 45) = 6.26$, $p = .004$, $r = .35$.

Table 16.2 Mean femininity rating of grammatically feminine and masculine animals and mean difference between the two ratings, by group

Language background	Feminine animals	Masculine animals	Difference
Germans	1.07	0.62	0.45
	(0.42)	(0.43)	(0.33)
Italian GSL users	0.87	0.16	0.71
	(0.27)	(0.36)	(0.36)
Italians	1.06	0.16	0.90
	(0.22)	(0.37)	(0.38)

Bonferroni *t*-tests revealed that the difference in rating between feminine and masculine animals was larger in the Italian monolingual group than in the German monolingual group ($p = .003$), whereas the Italian–German bilinguals did not differ from either the Italian or German monolinguals ($p = .458$ and $.134$ respectively).

Mean evaluation and potency were then computed for masculine and feminine animals for each participant. Evaluation was a composite of 'ugly', 'bad', 'dirty', and 'disgusting'; potency was a composite of 'strong', 'rough', and 'dangerous'. Figure 16.2 shows the mean difference between ratings of feminine and masculine animals on potency and evaluation scales by groups. On evaluation scales, feminine animals were rated as more feminine than masculine ones across groups, but the Italians had the largest difference, the Germans had the smallest difference, and the Italian GSL users were in between. Italian and German monolinguals gave opposite ratings on potency scales, as Italians rated feminine animals as more feminine than masculine ones (above 0), while Germans rated them as more masculine than masculine ones (below 0).

Two mixed $3 \times (2)$ ANOVAs were performed on potency and evaluation. For potency there were no main effects of grammatical gender, $F(1, 45) = 2.62$, $p = .112$, or language background, $F(2, 45) = 2.54$, $p = .090$, but the

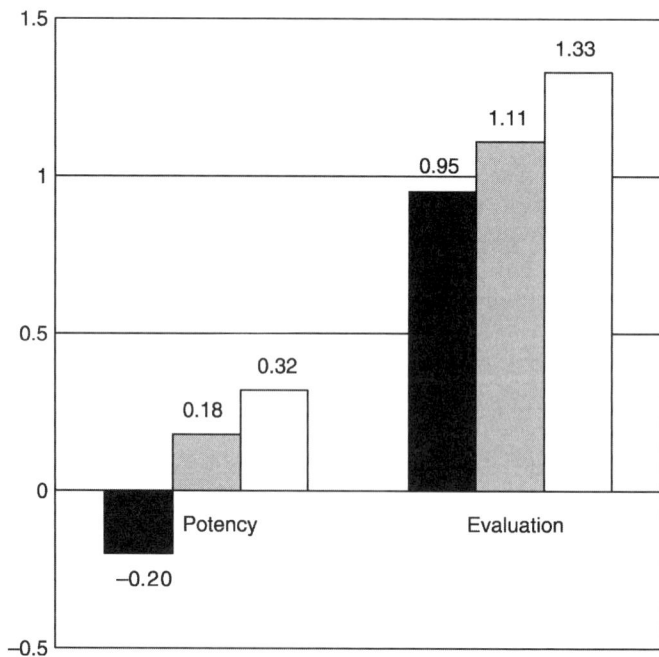

Figure 16.2 Mean differences between the ratings of grammatically feminine and masculine animals on potency and evaluation scales by group (black = Germans, gray = Italian GSL users, white = Italians).

interaction was significant, $F(2, 45) = 6.33$, $p = .004$, $r = .35$. Bonferroni post-hoc tests revealed that the difference in potency between feminine and masculine animals was smaller in the German group than in the Italian group ($p = .004$) and in the Italian GSL users group ($p = .047$), but the Italian monolinguals and Italian GSL users did not differ ($p = 1.000$). For evaluation, there were main effects of grammatical gender, $F(1, 45) = 270.70$, $p < .001$, $r = .93$, and language background, $F(2, 45) = 3.61$, $p = .035$, $r = .27$, but no interaction, $F(2, 45) = 2.61$, $p = .085$.

An item analysis was performed to test whether specific animals were rated differently across groups. For each participant, the mean rating across all animals was subtracted from the rating for each animal. Results are shown in Table 16.3 (a negative figure indicates that the animal was rated as more masculine than the mean rating for participants in that group, and vice versa). A series of ANOVAs was then performed to compare the three groups' differences in rating from the mean for each of the animals. Animals whose ratings differed across groups were: mouse, toad, snake, fox, starfish, butterfly, and stork. Germans differed from Italians because they rated mouse, toad, and snake as more feminine, and butterfly and stork as more masculine, in line with the German grammatical gender of these animals. There were no differences between Germans and Italian GSL users. Italian GSL users differed from Italians because they rated starfish and butterfly as more masculine, in line with the German GG. Fox was rated as more masculine by Germans than either of the Italian groups,

Table 16.3 Distance from the mean by item by group (a positive figure indicates that the animal was rated as more feminine than the group's mean for all animals), ANOVA significance and Bonferroni post-hoc significance (De = German monolinguals, It = Italian monolinguals, GSL = Italian GSL users).

Animal	German monolinguals	Italian GSL users	Italian monolinguals	Sig.	Post-hoc sig.
Spider	−.95	−.89	−.83	.956	
Mouse	.34	−.22	−.10	.011*	De–It = .011
Crab	−.58	−.26	−.60	.108	
Pigeon	−.06	.33	.27	.118	
Toad	−.24	−.65	−.78	.034*	De–It = .034
Owl	.06	−.17	−.28	.982	
Snake	−.33	−.70	−1.08	.001**	De–It < .001
Frog	.10	−.05	−.36	.115	
Tiger	.15	.31	.13	.275	
Eagle	−.16	.20	.00	.300	
Fox	−.19	.33	.36	.031*	
Starfish	.21	.01	.64	.025*	It–GSL = .027
Butterfly	.87	.94	1.58	.013*	De–It = .018
Stork	.19	.35	.68	.002*	De–It = .002
					It–GSL = .046

but the post-hoc tests did not reach significance ($p = .06$ for Italian GSL users and $.073$ for Italians).

DISCUSSION AND CONCLUSIONS

A semantic differential task was used to measure the effects of grammatical gender on the perceived masculinity–femininity of animals in German monolinguals, Italian monolinguals, and Italian native speakers with knowledge of German as a second language. Although participants were expected to rate animals on the basis of non-linguistic considerations, language effects were expected. It was predicted that the two monolingual groups would give opposite ratings, and that the Italian GSL users would differ from Italian monolinguals. Results show effects of grammatical gender on conceptual gender in all groups, but differences are mostly evident in the intensity rather than the directionality of ratings. As predicted, effects are weaker in those who know a grammatical gender second language, compared with monolingual speakers of their first language.

Effects of grammatical gender on monolinguals

Overall, results reveal effects of grammatical gender on conceptual gender, although as expected GG was not the only or indeed the main factor affecting ratings. Italian monolinguals appear to be strongly affected by Italian grammatical gender. They rated feminine animals about one point above the midpoint, with an average difference of almost one point in femininity rating between grammatically feminine and masculine animals. Italians rated masculine animals at the midpoint rather than in the male half of the scale. This contradicts predictions, but it is in line with previous findings. Bassetti (2007) found that Italian children prefer female voices for grammatically feminine referents and show no preference for male or female voices for grammatically masculine referents. The researcher argued that the feminine gender is marked in Italian and could therefore be associated with femininity more than the masculine gender is associated with masculinity. Since fewer nouns have feminine than masculine gender, it follows that a higher proportion of referents of feminine nouns are female, compared with the proportion of referents of masculine nouns that are male. Since the masculine gender is unmarked, and it covers many nouns that were neuter in Latin, it is a less reliable clue to the gender of the referent compared with the feminine gender, and therefore GG effects do not appear in either voice attribution or semantic differential rating tasks.

The results also show GG effects in German speakers. While previous research often found GG effects in speakers of Romance languages, evidence from German speakers is inconsistent (e.g., Imai et al., 2009; Vigliocco et al., 2005). While the present study provides more evidence of

GG effects in German speakers, these are evident from comparisons with Italian monolinguals, rather than on their own, and are evident more in the intensity than in the directionality of ratings. There is a difference between Germans and Italians in the directionality of rating of masculine animals, which Germans rated on average in the feminine half of the scale, arguably because these animals are feminine in German. However, German speakers rated grammatically feminine animals on average one point above the midpoint, like Italian monolinguals. Since these animals were masculine in German, they should have been rated around the mid-point or in the masculine half of the scale. With regards to the difference between femininity of feminine and masculine animals, Germans rated animals that were grammatically feminine as more feminine. However, the difference was about half a point in the German group, compared with almost one point in the Italian group, i.e., it was exactly half the size (.45 vs .90). Thus the direction of rating in both monolingual groups is consistent with Italian grammatical gender, as both groups rated grammatically feminine animals closer to the feminine end of scales than grammatically masculine animals. The effects of German GG are then evident not in the directionality, but in the intensity of rating. It appears that effects of GG show in German speakers, but are weak. Effects are only apparent in comparison with Italian speakers, and then only in intensity and not in directionality.

The weak effects of German GG could have a linguistic explanation, for instance because German has three rather than two gender classes (Vigliocco et al., 2005), or because it has a more complex GG system, with a larger number of endings that provide less-reliable clues to GG, compared with Italian or Spanish. While it is possible that GG affects German speakers less than speakers of Romance languages for linguistic reasons, a non-linguistic explanation is also possible. Italian GG assignment might reflect universals of perception of masculinity–femininity. Overall, all participants regardless of L1 rated those animals that were grammatically feminine in Italian on the feminine half of the scale, and as more feminine than grammatically masculine animals. The feminine rating of feminine animals across groups, both in absolute terms and in comparison with masculine animals, might reflect a general agreement between the Italian gender assignment and universally perceived characteristics of its referents. Sera et al. (2002) argued that the Spanish gender assignment is more widespread than the German one. Since Italian and Spanish gender assignments are very similar (Foundalis, 2002), it is possible that animals that are feminine in Italian but masculine in German are generally perceived as more feminine. If this is indeed the case, then part of the GG effects in Romance speakers would be in fact due to universals of masculinity–femininity perception, and vice versa the effects of German GG would be weaker with targets that have opposite gender in Romance languages and in German. German GG would then appear stronger in those items that have the same grammatical gender as in Romance languages, as the latter effects would not be reduced by universals of femininity–masculinity perception. This would then not be a linguistic explanation, linked to characteristics of the gender systems of different languages, but a cognitive explanation, linked to universals of perception of masculinity–femininity. Future research could investigate this possibility by comparing items that have opposite gender in the two languages with items that have the same gender. Future research should also test participants from other cultural backgrounds. Although previous researchers used English speakers as controls (e.g., Martinez & Shatz, 1996; Mills, 1986), these controls still share similar cultural backgrounds with speakers of Romance and Germanic languages. In order to rule out possible effects of European culture, more research should look at participants with non-European cultural backgrounds (as done by Flaherty, 1999). Finally, many German participants in this study had learnt a Romance language, and this might have reduced the effects of German GG in their ratings. Future research might look at Germans with no knowledge of Romance languages.

The prediction that Germans and Italians would give opposite ratings to the same referents was not confirmed by overall ratings, but it was confirmed by ratings on potency scales. On evaluation scales both groups gave higher ratings to feminine than masculine animals, and the difference was only in intensity. On the other hand, on potency scales the difference between feminine and masculine animals was positive in the Italian group and negative in the German group. This shows that Germans rated grammatically feminine animals as more masculine than masculine ones on potency scales. Ratings on these scales then reveal effects of GG, as the same items received opposite ratings by the two monolingual groups, in line with the GG of referents in their languages. It is not surprising that the predicted differences should only show in potency scales. Previous research had consistently found effects of GG on potency scales (Konishi, 1993; Tong et al., 2001; the latter found no effects on evaluation scales). Furthermore, masculinity–femininity was associated with potency in Osgood et al. (1957). Future research that compares GG effects across groups of speakers of different languages could concentrate on potency ratings.

The item analysis reveals that Italians' and Germans' ratings differed significantly on just over one third of animals. Germans rated mouse, toad, and snake as more masculine than Italians, and stork and butterfly as less feminine. All these differences are in line with predictions based on participants' L1 gender assignment, confirming that these are probably language effects.

Finally, results confirm that the semantic differential task is a suitable tool for measuring the effects of grammatical gender on conceptual gender. First of all, grammatical gender was not used strategically to perform the task: The task was not obviously related to gender, participants did not rate animals at the ends of scales as would happen if they were relying on GG, GG affected but did not determine ratings, and Italian and German monolinguals did not give opposite ratings. Furthermore, ratings were affected by the animal's characteristics as well as by GG. For instance, all participants rated snakes as masculine, although 'snake' is feminine in German (*Die Schlange*). All participants also considered frogs more feminine than toads, although in German 'frog' is masculine (*Der Frosch*) and 'toad' is feminine (*Die Kröte*). This means that participants were performing the task in a meaningful way, rating animals on the basis of their characteristics and connotations.

The use of the semantic differential task also helps shed light on the nature of GG effects. Results from this task cannot be explained in terms of category learning. While nouns and voices can be associated with animals that belong to the same category 'masculine' or 'feminine', the category learning hypothesis could not explain why some animals are rated as more feminine than others. Also, these effects cannot be due to thinking-for-speaking. When speaking Italian it is necessary to refer to foxes as females and mice as males, which makes it sensible to choose a female voice or name for a fox and a male one for a mouse. However, thinking-for-speaking cannot explain differences in femininity ratings. The SDT therefore seems a suitable task to test the effects of grammatical gender on conceptual gender, because it measures the perceived masculine and feminine connotations of entities, especially if researchers focus on potency measures.

Grammatical gender and bilingualism

As predicted, the Italian native speakers who knew German as a second language differed from Italian monolinguals. As is the case with Germans, the difference was not in the direction of rating, but in the intensity. Like Italian monolinguals, Italian GSL users rated feminine animals in the feminine half of the scale, masculine animals around the midpoint, and feminine animals as more feminine than masculine ones. However, the Italian GSL group was in between the two monolingual groups: (1) the difference in overall femininity rating between feminine and masculine animals in the bilingual group was in between the two monolinguals' groups, and there was no statistically significant difference with either group; (2) the difference in potency rating between feminine and masculine animals in the bilingual group was about half of the Italian group's difference, although it differed significantly from the Germans' difference (which was negative); (3) the difference in evaluation rating was about halfway between the two monolingual groups' differences, and no statistical differences were found with either group. Overall, on all measures the difference between grammatically feminine and masculine animals was largest among Italians and smallest among Germans, with the Italian GSL group's ratings in between.

All the differences between Italian GSL users and the two monolingual groups were in the direction predicted by their language combination. GSL users considered animals that are grammatically feminine in Italian and masculine in German as more masculine than the Italian group and more feminine than the German group. Across all measures, the difference between Italian GSL users and the two monolingual groups was in intensity of rating. With potency ratings, animals that are feminine in Italian and masculine in German were rated as less potent by Italians and more potent by Germans. On these scales, the two monolingual groups have a difference in directionality, whereas the Italian monolingual and Italian GSL users groups differ in intensity. This is the only measure on which Italian GSL users differ from German monolinguals in directionality. Finally, the item analysis reveals that Italian GSL users differ from Italian monolinguals on only two animals, compared with the five animals that were rated differently by the two monolingual groups. However, both differences were in line with predictions (both animals were feminine in Italian and masculine in German, and were rated as more masculine by Italian GSL users than Italian monolinguals), and there were no differences between Italian GSL users and German monolinguals, again confirming that Italian GSL users differ from Italian monolinguals.

Results confirm the hypothesis that speakers of a GG L1 who learn a GG L2 with different gender assignment differ in their performance on semantic differential tasks from Italian monolinguals. It is argued that learning a GG L2 affects conceptual gender as reflected in STD ratings that are likely to be measures of masculine and feminine connotations. This could be an overall effect of learning a GG second language, as learning a new GG assignment system might reveal the semantic arbitrariness of L1 grammatical gender assignments; alternatively, effects might be limited to those entities that have opposite grammatical gender in the bilinguals' two languages. Future research could compare ratings of entities that have opposite gender in the two languages and entities that have the same gender. This would clarify whether learning a grammatical gender L2 has a general effect of reducing the effects of L1 grammatical gender, or simply affects the perception of masculinity–femininity for the individual referents that have opposite GG in the two languages.

An interesting aspect of this study is that all (but one) bilinguals had learnt L2 German after age 8, which is the age when L1 grammatical gender effects appear in monolingual children (Flaherty, 2001; Mills, 1986; Nicoladis & Foursha-Stevenson, 2010; Sera et al., 2002). This might mean that conceptual gender can be affected by experiences in later life. Future research could compare bilinguals from birth with bilinguals with ages of onset of acquisition above 8 years, to see whether those who learnt a GG L2 during the period of concept formation are more affected than late learners. Furthermore, future research could try to link L2 GG effects to proficiency (as in Phillips & Boroditsky, 2003), frequency of use, or other variables that have been found to correlate with effects of second languages on bilingual cognition (see Bassetti & Cook, Chapter 7, this volume).

Finally, these findings might have implications for second language learning research. In general, learning L2 grammatical gender assignment is not easy (Holmes & Dejean de la Bâtie, 1999; Rogers, 1987). Tight (2006) demonstrated that with unknown L2 words, learners assign gender based on their perception of the gender connotations of the word's referent. If therefore the referent is perceived as masculine or feminine due to the influence of L1 GG assignment, this could interfere with gender assignment in the second language. Indeed, White, Valenzuela, Kozlowska-MacGregor, and Leung (2004) report in an aside to their results section that French learners of Spanish make more gender errors when the referent has opposite gender in their first language (Dewaele & Véronique, 2000, found no L1 GG effects, but the L1 gender system of their participants does not have masculine or feminine classes). Future research could then look at the specific effects of L1 on L2 grammatical gender acquisition by focusing on specific items that have opposite grammatical gender in learners' L1 and L2, rather than on generic effects of knowing a gender L1 on L2 GG acquisition.

In conclusion, it is argued that bilingualism can affect concepts, at least when the bilingual's two languages represent the same entity or event differently. When the bilingual's two grammatical gender systems are in conflict, grammatical gender ceases to constitute a reliable clue, either overall or at least for those entities that have opposite gender in the two languages. Bilingualism therefore might eliminate a language-induced bias in the perception of entities. This means that the more languages people learn, the closer they might get to an understanding of reality that is not affected by the biases induced by their first language.

ACKNOWLEDGMENTS

I am grateful to Dagmar Schulte for translating the materials into German.

REFERENCES

Andonova, E., Gosheva, A., Schaffai, J. S., & Janyan, A. (2007). Second language gender system affects first language gender classification. In I. Kecskes & L. Albertazzi (Eds.), *Cognitive aspects of bilingualism* (pp. 271–300). London: Springer.

Bassetti, B. (2007). Bilingualism and thought: Grammatical gender and concepts of objects in Italian–German bilingual children. *International Journal of Bilingualism, 11*(3), 251–273.

Boroditsky, L., & Schmidt, L. A. (2000). Sex, syntax, and semantics. In L. R. Gleitman & A. K. Joshi (Eds.), *Proceedings of the 22nd conference of the Cognitive Science Society* (pp. 42–47). Mahwah, NJ: Lawrence Erlbaum Associates Inc.

Boroditsky, L., Schmidt, L. A., & Phillips, W. (2003). Sex, syntax and semantics. In D. Gentner & S. Goldin-Meadow (Eds.), *Language in mind: Advances in the study of language and thought* (pp. 61–78). Cambridge, MA: MIT Press.

Bowerman, M. (1985). What shapes children's grammar. In D. I. Slobin (Ed.), *The cross-linguistic study of language acquisition* (Vol. 2, pp. 1257–1319). Hillsdale, NJ: Lawrence Erlbaum Associates Inc.

Chini, M. (1995). *Genere grammaticale e acquisitione. Aspetti della morfologia nominale in italiano L2*. Milano, Italy: Franco Angeli.

Clarke, M. A., Losoff, A., Dickenson, M., McCracken, J., & Still, A. (1981). Gender perception in Arabic and English. *Language Learning, 31*, 159–169.

Clarke, M. A., Losoff, A., & Rood, D. S. (1982). Untangling referent and reference in linguistic relativity studies: A response from Clarke et al. *Language Learning, 32*(1), 209–217.

Corbett, G. G. (1991). *Gender*. Cambridge, UK: Cambridge University Press.

Corbett, G. G. (2006). Grammatical gender. In K. Brown (Ed.), *The encyclopaedia of language and linguistics* (2nd ed., pp. 749–756). Oxford, UK: Elsevier.

Dewaele, J-M., & Véronique, D. (2000). Relating gender errors to morphosyntactic and lexical systems in advanced French interlanguage. *Studia Linguistica, 54*(2), 212–224.

Dilkina, K., McClelland, J. L., & Boroditsky, L. (2007). How language affects thought in a connectionist model. In D. S. McNamara & J. G. Trafton (Eds.), *Proceedings of the 29th annual conference of the Cognitive Science Society* (pp. 215–220). Austin, TX: Cognitive Science Society.

Eberhard, K. M., Scheutz, M., & Heilman, M. (2005). An empirical and computational test of linguistic relativity. In B. B. Bara, L. Barsalou, & M. Bucclarell (Eds.), *Proceedings of the 27th annual conference of the Cognitive Science Society* (pp. 618–623). Mahwah, NJ: Lawrence Erlbaum Associates Inc.

Ervin, S. M. (1962). The connotations of gender. *Word, 18*, 249–261.

Flaherty, M. (1999). The influence of a language gender system on perception. *Tohoku Psychologica Folia, 58*, 1–10.

Flaherty, M. (2001). How a language gender system creeps into perception. *Journal of Cross-Cultural Psychology, 32*(1), 18–31.

Foundalis, H. (2002). Evolution of gender in Indo-European languages. In W. D. Gray & C. D. Schunn (Eds.), *Proceedings of the 24th annual conference of the Cognitive Science Society* (pp. 304–309). Mahwah, NJ: Lawrence Erlbaum Associates Inc.

Guiora, A. (1983). Language and concept formation: A cross-lingual analysis. *Behavior Science Research, 18*(3), 228–256.

Guiora, A. Z., & Acton, W. R. (1979). Personality and language behavior: A restatement. *Language Learning, 29*(1), 193–204.

Guiora, A. Z., & Sagi, A. (1978). A cross-cultural study of symbolic meaning: Developmental aspects. *Language Learning, 28*(2), 381–386.

Herold, A. L. (1982). Linguistic relativity: Transforming the relative into the insensible: A reply to Clarke et al. *Language Learning, 32*(1), 201–207.

Hofstätter, P. R. (1963). Über Sprachliche Bestimmungsleistungen: Das Problem des grammatikalischen Geschlechts von Sonne und Mond. *Zeitschrift für experimentelle und angewandte Psychologie, 10*, 91–108.

Holmes, V. M., & Dejean de la Bâtie, B. (1999). Assignment of grammatical gender by native speakers and foreign learners of French. *Applied Psycholinguistics, 20*, 479–506.

Imai, M., Saalbach, H., & Shalk, L. (2009). *Mrs. Giraffe and Mr. Elephant: The influence of grammatical gender on German children's deductive reasoning about biological properties of animals.* Paper presented at the 31st annual meeting of the Cognitive Science Society. Amsterdam: The Netherlands, 29 July–1 August 2009.

Kenyeres, A. (1938). Comment une petite Hongroise de sept ans apprend le Français. *Archives de Psychologie, 26*(104), 321–366.

Konishi, T. (1993). The semantics of grammatical gender: A cross-cultural study. *Journal of Psycholinguistic Research, 22*, 519–534.

Kurinski, E., & Sera, M. (in press). Does learning Spanish grammatical gender change English-speaking adults' categorization of inanimate objects? *Bilingualism: Language and Cognition.*

Martinez, I., & Shatz, M. (1996). Linguistic influences on categorization in preschool children: A crosslinguistic study. *Journal of Child Language, 23*, 529–545.

Mills, A. E. (1986). *The acquisition of gender: A study of English and German.* Berlin: Springer-Verlag.

Nicoladis, E., & Foursha-Stevenson, C. (2010). *Is a skife a boy or a girl? How grammatical gender in French influences bilingual children's conceptualizations in English.* Manuscript submitted for publication.

Osgood, C. E., Suci, G. J., & Tannenbaum, P. H. (1957). *The measurement of meaning.* Urbana, IL: University of Illinois.

Phillips, W., & Boroditsky, L. (2003). Can quirks of grammar affect the way you think? Grammatical gender and object concepts. In R. Alterman & D. Kirsh (Eds.), *Proceedings of the 25th annual conference of the Cognitive Science Society.* Boston: Cognitive Science Society.

Rogers, M. A. (1987). Learners' difficulties with grammatical gender in German as a foreign language. *Applied Linguistics, 8*, 48–74.

Sapir, E. (1921/2004). *Language: An introduction to the study of speech.* New York: Dover Publications.

Sera, M., Elieff, C., Forbes, J., Burch, M. C., Rodríguez, W., & Dubois, D. P. (2002). When language affects cognition and when it does not: An analysis of grammatical gender and classification. *Journal of Experimental Psychology: General, 131*(3), 377–397.

Taeschner, T. (1983). *The sun is feminine. A study of language acquisition in bilingual children.* Berlin: Springer.

Tight, D. G. (2006). The relationship between perceived gender in L1 English and grammatical gender in L2 Spanish. In C. A. Klee & T. L. Face (Eds.), *Selected proceedings of the 7th conference on the acquisition of Spanish and Portuguese as first and second languages.* Somerville, MA: Cascadilla Proceedings Project.

Tong, Y.-y., Chiu, C.-y., & Fu, H-y. (2001). Linguistic gender is related to psychological gender: The case of 'Chinese characters'. *Hua ren xin li xue bao* [*Journal of Psychology in Chinese Societies*], 2(1), 107–117.

Vigliocco, G., Vinson, D., Paganelli, F., & Dworzynski, K. (2005). Grammatical effects of gender on cognition: Implications for language learning and language use. *Journal of Experimental Psychology, 134*(4), 501–520.

Wegener, H. (2000). German gender in children's second language acquisition. In B. Unterbeck & M. Rissanen (Eds.), *Gender in grammar and cognition* (pp. 511–544). The Hague: Mouton de Gruyter.

White, L., Valenzuela, E., Kozlowska-MacGregor, M., & Leung, Y-K. I. (2004). Gender and number agreement in nonnative Spanish. *Applied Psycholinguistics, 25*(1), 105–133.

Yorkston, E., & De Mello, G. E. (2005). Linguistic gender marking and categorization. *Journal of Consumer Research, 32*, 224–234.

Zubin, D. A., & Köpcke, K. M. (1984). Affect classification in the German gender system. *Lingua, 63*, 41–96.

Zubin, D. A., & Köpcke, K. M. (1986). Gender and folk taxonomy: The indexical relation between grammatical and lexical categorization. In C. G. Craig (Ed.), *Noun classes and categorization: Proceedings of a symposium on categorization and noun classification* (pp. 139–180). Amsterdam: Benjamins.

APPENDIX

List of items used in the semantic differential task

Masculine animals (masculine in Italian and feminine in German)

Picture	Italian noun	German noun	English translation
	Il ragno	Die Spinne	Spider
	Il topo	Die Maus	Mouse
	Il granchio	Die Krabbe	Crab
	Il piccione	Die Taube	Pigeon
	Il rospo	Die Kröte	Toad
	Il gufo	Die Eule	Owl
	Il serpente	Die Schlange	Snake

Feminine animals (feminine in Italian and masculine in German)

Picture	Italian noun	German noun	English translation
	La rana	Der Frosch	Frog
	La tigre	Der Tiger	Tiger
	L'aquila	Der Adler	Eagle
	La volpe	Der Fuchs	Fox
	La stella marina	Der Seestern	Starfish
	La farfalla	Der Schmetterling	Butterfly
	La cicogna	Die Storch	Stork

17 The interpretation of emblematic gestures in second language users of Italian

Giuliana Salvato

In second language acquisition (SLA) research, the attention of scholars has traditionally focused more on verbal language than on non-verbal language such as gestures. It is only in the last few years that the relationship between gestures and speech in second language (L2) oral communication has interested a number of scholars, as the topic introduces a new way to investigate L2 development and acquisition (see discussion in Gullberg, 2006, 2009). People around the world perceive and interpret the form, meaning, and function of gestures in distinctive ways, whether gestures occur in combination with verbal language or by themselves (Gullberg, 1998, 2006; Gullberg & McCafferty, 2008; Jungheim, 2006; Kendon, 2004; McCafferty & Gullberg, 2008; McCafferty & Stam, 2008; McNeill, 1992, 2000, 2005). In this chapter we will discuss the interpretation of L2 gestures by L2 learners with different linguistic and cultural backgrounds in order to offer insights towards the understanding of how bilingual and multilingual speakers organize concepts and meanings in their minds and in their language.

As a way to contribute to this area of research, we asked 329 university students of Italian at two Canadian universities to interpret a selection of gestures of the Italian language. We expected the exercise to be quite challenging for the following reasons. In the first place, the activities that form part of our study are not usually present in L2 syllabi. Also, the gestures that we chose have a specific meaning within the Italian culture and the bodily movement involved in their performance may suggest different interpretations to people belonging to other world cultures. The gestures of our study are known as *emblematic gestures* and are distinguished from those that, in strict relation with speech, physically illustrate the content expressed by the words or stress the rhythm of their enunciation. Emblematic gestures do not need speech to convey meaning. They can occur either by themselves as silent expressions or in association with speech, exercising a complementary function. Unlike gestures of other types, emblematic gestures have a conventional form. They can assume iconic features, which describe or imitate concrete objects or actions (e.g., the 'drink' gesture reproduces the action of drinking), or characteristics that do not obviously reproduce the referent (e.g., the 'hand purse' gesture is conventionally used in Italy to mean 'what do you want?' or 'what are you doing?'). In both cases, however, the meaning of emblematic gestures can be rendered into words (Ekman & Friesen, 1969; Kendon, 2004; McNeill, 1992).

For our study, we chose 6 of the 100 Italian emblematic gestures described in Diadori (1990), seen in Figure 17.1. These gestures reflect the conceptualization of their referent in the following way. Gesture 1 (G1) conveys the meaning of 'agreement' by showing two index fingers coming together and tapping repeatedly on their inner side. The Italian verbal expression that defines G1 is *andare d'accordo* ('to get along'). G2 indicates the meaning of 'good food' by rotating the tip of an index finger against one's cheek. The cheek stands for the mouth, the place where food is tasted. The Italian verbal expression that describes G2 is *buono* ('good'). G3 conveys the meaning of 'perfect' by means of the thumb and the index finger of one hand joining together in a ring and sliding to the outer side as if they were pulling a thread. In Italian, one of the verbal expressions that describe G3 includes the word *filo* ('thread', *tutto fatto per filo e per segno*, literally 'everything done by thread and sign', idiomatic 'everything is done perfectly'). G4 conveys the meaning of 'money' by acting out the gesture of handling paper money between thumb and index finger of the same

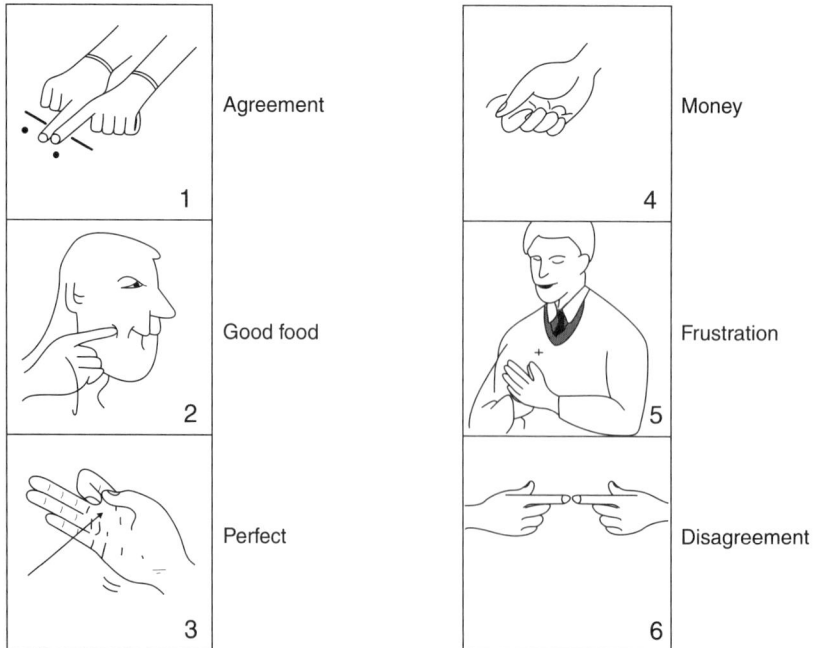

Figure 17.1 The gestures and their meanings.

hand. The Italian verbal expression used for G4 is *soldi* ('money'). G5 indicates 'frustration' by showing an up-and-down movement of two hands joined in prayer position at the chest level. G5 conceptualizes the verbal meaning of *ti prego* (literally 'I beg you', idiomatic 'do me a favour'). Finally, G6 conveys the meaning of 'disagreement' by tapping the tips of two index fingers one against the other. In Italian, the verbal expression that describes G6 is *non andare d'accordo* ('to not get along'). As we can see from this description, G4 (= money) establishes a direct link between the bodily movement that it performs and the meaning that it conveys. The movement of pulling a thread in G3 (= 'perfect') establishes a direct link with the word *filo* ('thread') of the Italian phrase that defines G3. On the other hand, G1 (= 'agreement'), G2 (= 'good food'), G5 (= 'frustration'), and G6 (= 'disagreement') demand a more complex interpretation of their bodily movement: joining fingers implies agreement whereas tapping fingers one against the other implies disagreement; rotating an index finger against a cheek indicates not only eating but also the appreciation of food; hands in prayer position express an emphatic request for something to change.

Having described the conceptual relationship that the six gestures of our study create with their meaning, we organized our investigation in order to inquire how L2 learners would respond to these gestures. Particularly, we wanted to see whether: (a) there is any correlation between the language(s) that the learners know and their interpretation of Italian L2 gestures; (b) Italian L2 verbal language facilitates the interpretation of Italian L2 gestures; (c) context created in mini-dialogues can help the interpretation of Italian L2 gestures. Since the sample in our study is made up of learners of Italian at two universities in Ontario, where Italian is not only a foreign or a second language, but also one of the heritage languages for many, we wanted to investigate the impact of language background and language proficiency on the interpretation of Italian emblematic gestures. We assumed that learners whose language background includes a number of languages (i.e., multilingual speakers), or prior knowledge of Italian (i.e., learners with an Italian family background), or knowledge of a language historically related to Italian (i.e., a Romance language), would be in a more favorable position to interpret Italian emblematic gestures. We also assumed that when gestures are accompanied by Italian verbal language and a context of occurrence, such as a dialogue, L2 learners are facilitated in the interpretation of the L2 non-verbal language of our study. Ultimately, the testing of these hypotheses will give us some insights into what meanings and concepts L2 learners relate to Italian emblematic gestures, and how different, or how similar, they are from the meanings and concepts attributed to the same gestures by Italian native speakers. In addition, in the evaluation of the differences and similarities, we will have to take into account that the L2 learners in our study may have been exposed to non-standard varieties of Italian verbal and non-verbal languages.

GESTURES IN SLA: APPROACHES AND PERSPECTIVES

Introducing gestures to L2 learners is not a new approach in language education. In the last few decades language educators have made the concept of language competence and performance include more and more of the aspects that characterize language used in oral communication. One example of this is found in the principles of Total Physical Response (TPR) (Asher, 1965), the neurolinguistic approach that advocates the key role of body language in order to facilitate the comprehension of L2 input and the language acquisition process.

Similarly, but with a different perspective in mind, the communicative approach maintains that we need to help learners become good communicators in the languages that we teach. Since gestures occupy an important role in L2 oral interaction, the communicative approach advocates integrating them into the L2 syllabus (Canale & Swain, 1980; Hymes, 1972; Savignon, 1998).

Nevertheless, the point of view of SLA researchers has traditionally been to regard gestures as a compensatory strategy in L2 learning. In other words, when unable to retrieve target verbal language, L2 learners communicate their appeal for help typically through gestures (see discussion in Gullberg, 1998). As a consequence of this tradition, scholars have not granted to gesture the rank of communicative strategy for purposes other than as an appeal for help (see taxonomies in Dörnyei & Scott, 1997; Faerch & Kasper, 1983; Tarone, 1977; Yule & Tarone, 1997).

Thanks to the work by Bialystok (1990) and Poulisse (1990), today's research on L2 communication strategies no longer considers the verbal result alone, but also the process behind the linguistic outcome. This requires, on the one hand, an examination of the concept that language learners intend to communicate and, on the other hand, the examination of the form or means of expression that they choose in order to communicate with another person. Communication strategies can thus take various shapes, one of which is non-verbal language such as gestures.

SLA scholars have studied gestures from a socio-cultural point of view. For example, they have inquired about the understanding of culturally specific meanings in L2 gestures. This area of investigation is interested in L2 learners' interpretations of L2 non-verbal language as well as in finding evidence as to whether the acquisition of cultural meanings encoded in L2 non-verbal language is possible in SLA. With respect to emblematic gestures, Gullberg (2006) says that little is known about whether L2 speakers can learn to understand and use L2 emblematic gestures. Research so far suggests that L2 speakers benefit from explanation and teaching of emblematic gestures, especially when their form does not reproduce the referent in obvious ways. This applies to natural settings as well as to the classroom setting. Jungheim (2006) found that the interpretation of the Japanese 'hand fan' refusal gesture by adult L2 learners in Japan was not in line with the interpretation provided by Japanese L1 speakers. Jungheim (1991) also demonstrated that explicit teaching of American emblems to Japanese L2 learners is a more effective methodology than implicit teaching. Similarly, Allen (1995) showed the advantage of using emblems in the teaching of French. The author found that learning emblematic gestures simultaneously with French expressions promotes vocabulary retention.

One other approach to gesture studies in SLA has considered the typological characteristics that differentiate the languages of the world (see Talmy, 1991). This perspective focuses on the concept of cross-linguistic influence when languages with or without the same historical origin are in contact (Jarvis & Pavlenko, 2008; Kellerman & Sharwood Smith, 1986) as well as on the concept of thinking for speaking (Slobin, 1996). Scholars working in this area have researched which parts of speech are typically accompanied by gestures in different languages. For example, gestures expressing motion path occur with path verbs in verb-framed languages such as Italian (e.g., *scendere*) whereas they occur with particles in satellite-framed languages such as English (e.g., *to go down*). Scholars have also studied whether the path and manner of motion are expressed in speech or in gestures across languages. They have found that speakers of satellite-framed languages can convey path and manner together in one gesture (e.g., to express the meaning of 'rolling down') whereas speakers of verb-framed languages are more likely to use two gestures. Scholars have then investigated the evolution of gestures from L1-like to more target-like uses by considering the timing of gesture with respect to speech and the information that L2 speakers are more likely to express in speech and in gesture in their L2 performance. Speakers of verb-framed languages typically express manner in gesture because their L1 verbs do not always specify manner (e.g., Italian *entrare saltellando*, 'to go in jumping') whereas speakers of satellite-framed languages can express manner in speech through phrases accompanying verbs (e.g., English *hopping in*). Research has found that L2 speakers may transfer gesture and speech patterns from their L1 into their L2 (see review of studies in Gullberg, 2006, 2009).

Among the most recent studies, Pika, Nicoladis, and Marentette (2006) worked with Spanish and French, two high-frequency gesture languages, in relationship to English, a low-frequency gesture language, and analysed the gestural behavior of bilingual and monolingual speakers in their study. The authors found that knowledge of a high-frequency gesture language is likely to produce an increase of gestures in the low-frequency gesture language. Kellerman and van Hoof (2003) found evidence of L1 gesture patterns in L2 speakers' performance. As a consequence of this, the authors propose to redefine proficiency and bilingualism to account for the non-verbal characteristics that L2 speakers have, or have not yet, acquired. However, the analysis of L2 speakers' non-verbal behavior can pose quite a challenge. For example, Negueruela, Lantolf, Rehn Jordan, and Gelabert (2004) investigated the concept of thinking for speaking in the use of motion verbs by advanced English and Spanish L2 speakers and found that both groups expressed manner in gestures, which could be interpreted to mean that there are no differences between the two groups. Conversely, Negueruela et al. explained that the Spanish speakers of English continued to rely on gestures in the expression of manner by transferring a pattern from the L1 into the L2. The English speakers of Spanish, instead, did not express manner in speech because they did not find the verbal means to do so. Since they were used to encode manner, they relied on gestures as a compensatory strategy. Negueruela et al.'s study shows that the encoding of meaning in speech or in gestures depends not only on the linguistic habits that we transfer from one language into another but also on the verbal and non-verbal possibilities available in different languages.

Although SLA research has made progress towards integrating gestures into the study of language development, use, and comprehension, also for pedagogical purposes (see section V in McCafferty & Stam, 2008), language teaching and learning still seem to give priority to linguistic competence of the verbal type. For example, an analysis of textbooks used in Italian classes in Canada suggests that the introduction of L2 gestures lags behind compared to verbal language (Salvato, 2008). Above everything else, learners are expected to acquire target sounds; to recognize and use verbal meanings; to construct phrases and sentences; and to coordinate sentences in discourse. In the case of Italian, this finding is quite striking given the fact that the Italian language has been traditionally classified as a gesture-rich language (de Jorio, 1832/1979; Diadori, 1990; Graham & Argyle, 1975; Kendon, 2004; Morris, Collett, Marsh, & O'Shaughnessy, 1979).

We believe that the recent interest in gesture studies in SLA has nonetheless opened the prospect of discovering new insights into the process of learning a new language. It has also created an opportunity for second language education to draw valuable guidelines for the implementation of more effective practices in language teaching and learning.

GESTURES IN THE ACQUISITION OF ITALIAN AS A SECOND LANGUAGE

Introduction

The theoretical background introduced in the previous sections has inspired the development of the following study. A total of 329 learners of Italian at the University of Toronto and at McMaster University in Hamilton, Ontario, Canada, were asked to recognize and interpret a selection of emblematic gestures typically used by Italian native speakers today. The main purpose of this task was to draw the attention of learners of

Italian to the meanings and functions of emblematic gestures in Italian oral communication. Figure 17.1 shows the gestures chosen for our study, which are taken from Diadori (1990).

A three-page questionnaire was distributed to show the sketches of the Italian gestures, and to collect information about the participants' language background and their understanding of the gestures of our study. The gestures were performed in front of each class by the main researcher, a native speaker of Italian.

We chose these gestures on the basis of their characteristic features. G1 and G6 have opposite meanings. G2 and G5 involve bodily parts in addition to the hands. This combination of gesture types was expected to correlate with interpretation difficulties of different kinds. In line with previous studies, we assumed that the more bodily parts participate in the performance of a gesture, the more clues are made available for its interpretation and for the interpretation of a communicative exchange (see Graham & Argyle, 1975; Kellerman, 2001; Ricci Bitti, 1992; Rimé & Schiaratura, 1991). Diadori (1990) says that the gestures in her collection are used in different communicative contexts and by different media (e.g., newspapers, TV). For this reason, it is expected that Italian native speakers understand their meaning although their use may vary across regions, social classes, and individuals. Moreover, all six gestures can be explained with a single word or a short phrase. Finally, we limited our selection to six gestures because we needed to take into account the time available to conduct our research in class and the fact that six gestures can be clearly reproduced all together on one page.

Participants

There were 329 participants from 20 classes. All participants belonged to the beginners' level of proficiency in Italian. The 100-level students ($N = 258$) were absolute beginners from St. George campus (University of Toronto), Mississauga campus (University of Toronto), and Hamilton (McMaster University). The 101-level students ($N = 59$) were beginners with an Italian background or with less than 4 years of high-school training in Italian. The 152-level students ($N = 12$) were beginners with 4 years of high-school training in Italian. The last two groups were both from St. George campus. This distribution of students indicates that different proficiency profiles are found among beginners of the Italian language at the universities.

In order to understand the impact of language background on the interpretations provided, we asked the participants to indicate their mother tongue and the other languages that they knew at the time of our visit. Participants were native speakers of a variety of languages: English ($N = 217$), Polish ($N = 10$), Spanish ($N = 10$), Italian ($N = 8$), and speakers with various other languages and language combinations, including Albanian,

Arabic, and Mandarin Chinese, among others. This shows that, apart from being a heritage language for some, Italian is a foreign language for the majority of the participants in our study. Typically Italian is learned after English and French, the two official languages of Canada. In this case, Italian is a third language (L3). At the time of their enrollment in their Italian class, 71 participants had prior knowledge of Italian, whether active or passive, and 258 participants did not have any prior knowledge of Italian.

We then streamlined the characteristics of the language background (i.e., mother tongue and other languages known) by creating four categories: language class one (i.e., monolinguals, N = 53), language class two (i.e., bilinguals, N = 112), language class three (trilinguals, N = 104), and language class four or more (i.e., multilinguals, N = 60). The majority of the participants in our study were speakers of two or more languages (whenever this was the case, we included Italian as one of the languages). Only a minority of participants (16%) could be defined as monolingual (i.e., speakers of one language, their mother tongue, which in our study most likely means English), whereas 84% of them were at least bilinguals. Of these, 32% were trilinguals and 18% knew four languages or more.

We classified our data in this way in order to be able to correlate the interpretations of the six gestures with prior knowledge of Italian and the language class of our participants. We expected the participants with an Italian family background, or with knowledge of Italian from high school, or with knowledge of more than one language, or knowledge of a language related to Italian, to be in a favorable position when they had to interpret the gestures of our study. These expectations are in line with the literature in second and third language acquisition that claims a positive influence of the language background in the learning of second and third or additional languages, especially when the languages are historically related (see Cenoz, Hufeisen, & Jessner, 2001; Ringbom, 1987, 2007). We also expected that participants with a higher number of languages in their background would be facilitated in the performance of the activities of our study, because we assumed that people who learn or know more than one language are likely to develop multicompetence (Cook, 1992, 2002) and abilities such as language awareness to a greater extent than monolingual speakers (Jessner, 2006). Finally, we expected the data of this study to help us understand whether the Italian emblematic gestures suggest some relationship between language and thought. Particularly, we may find that our participants' interpretations indicate that speakers of languages different from Italian conceptualize meaning either in similar or in distinctive ways. On the one hand, we may find some universal patterns; on the other hand, we may note some divergent conceptualizations.

Methodology

Data collection took place in three steps. Participants were asked to carry out the following activities:

1   identify and interpret six Italian gestures without verbal commentary;
2   identify and interpret the same gestures in a multiple-choice exercise with the help of a verbal commentary in the form of short sentences or phrases or single words;
3   identify and interpret the same gestures in a matching exercise with the help of a verbal commentary in the form of mini-dialogues.

Participants were asked to fill out the three-page questionnaire by completing one page at a time, and they were not given the opportunity to change their responses. The questionnaire is reproduced in Figure 17.2. In the first activity, the participants were asked to describe the meaning of the six gestures on the page, either in English or in Italian. Since no language description was provided for each sketch, the gestures substituted for verbal language. We expected participants to rely only on their perception and on their prior linguistic and cultural knowledge during the completion of this exercise. No foils or controls were used in any of the steps of the study. The second activity consisted of a multiple-choice exercise. This time four verbal options were provided. The participants were asked to recognize both the gestures and the verbal language of the exercise and to interpret gestures in combination with verbal language, that is to say, in their clarifying function. The third activity consisted of a matching exercise, where each gesture was to be matched to the most appropriate mini-dialogue randomly organized on the side of the page. The participants were asked to recognize and interpret the gestures in association with verbal language, that is, in a complementary function with verbal language.

Results

In general, participants reported some difficulty in interpreting the gestures of our study. Of the 71 participants with prior knowledge of Italian, 63% said that their language and culture background helped them interpret the gestures, whereas only 32.6% of the 258 participants with no prior knowledge of Italian said that their language and culture background helped them interpret the gestures. Moreover, 12.5% of the former group and 16% of the latter group said that their language and culture background helped them interpret only some of the gestures.

More specifically, Table 17.1 shows what gestures posed the greatest difficulty and at what step. We counted the occurrences of wrong or no interpretations for each gesture and we compared them to the total participants in our study. The highest ratios suggest difficulty of interpretation.

(a)

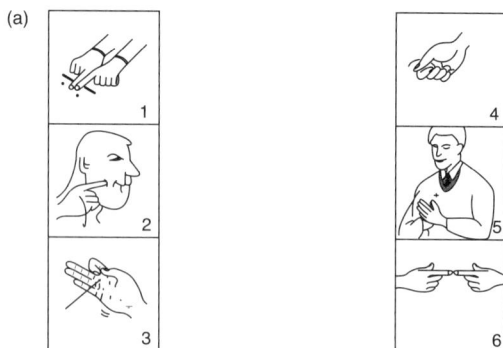

a) What is your native tongue and what other languages do you know?
b) Do you find that your language and cultural background help you in interpreting the gestures in the pictures? Please briefly explain why and how.
c) Would you consider these gestures typically Italian? Please explain.

(b)

1
a) Quei due non vanno d'accordo
b) Quei due vanno d'accordo
c) Numero 2
d) *I don't know*

4
a) Che caldo!
b) Per favore/Per piacere
c) Soldi/Denaro
d) *I don't know*

2
a) Ho male ai denti ('*toothache*') . . .
b) Numero 1
c) Buono!
d) *I don't know*

5
a) Che freddo!
b) Numero 10
c) Come faccio ora!/Cosa posso fare?
d) *I don't know*

3
a) Numero 3
b) Che difficile!
c) Perfetto!
d) *I don't know*

6
a) Numero 2
b) Quei due non vanno d'accordo . . .
c) Che brutto!
d) *I don't know*

a) Do you find that the phrases accompanying the pictures facilitate your interpretation of the meanings of the gestures? Please briefly explain why and how.

(c)

Mamma: Hai riordinato la tua stanza?
Elisabetta: Sì, *è tutto a posto*!
Mamma: Bene!

Gianni: Ho visto Lucia in compagnia di Carlo.
Cristina: Sì, *sono assieme* da tre mesi e sono contenti.

Giovanna: Vuoi dei biscotti?
Paolo: *Umm, che buoni!*
Giovanna: Li ho preparati io!
Paolo: Brava!

Alice: Giulio e Roberto giocano ancora nella stessa squadra di pallavolo ('*volleyball team*')?
Elisa: No, non giocano più insieme.
Alice: Eh…Giulio e Roberto *sono come cane e gatto*.
Elisa: Me lo immaginavo…

Enrico: Vorrei una macchina nuova…
Paolo: Compratela!
Enrico: Eh…non ho *questi*!/*non posso permettermelo*…

Luigi: Cosa fai lì fuori casa?
Maurizio: *Ho perso le chiavi e non so come entrare*…
Luigi: Aspetta, chiamo la polizia.
Maurizio: Grazie!

a) Did you encounter any difficulties in understanding the situation and the language of the mini-dialogues? If so, please briefly explain why.
b) In your search for the best gesture to combine with each dialogue, did the situation and the language provided facilitate your choices? Please briefly explain why and how.

Figure 17.2 (a) Step 1: Gestures without verbal commentary. (b) Step 2: The multiple-choice exercise. (c) Step 3: The matching exercise.

Table 17.1 Number and percentage (in brackets) of participants (N = 329) who gave incorrect or no interpretation, by gesture and type of context

Gestures	Step 1 (gesture only)	Step 2 (sentences)	Step 3 (mini-dialogues)
G1 agreement	290 (88%)	123 (37%)	162 (49%)
G2 good food	277 (84%)	120 (36%)	180 (55%)
G3 perfect	296 (89%)	78 (24%)	175 (53%)
G4 money	59 (18%)	45 (14%)	130 (40%)
G5 frustration	227 (69%)	70 (21%)	155 (47%)
G6 disagreement	306 (93%)	156 (47%)	109 (33%)

As we can see, participants provided better interpretations when moving from step 1 to step 2 and from step 1 to step 3. They did not provide better interpretations when moving from step 2 to step 3. Therefore the verbal language in the mini-dialogues of step 3 was not as effective as the verbal language in the multiple-choice exercise of step 2.

These data suggest that the presence of Italian verbal language played a significant role in helping the participants provide correct interpretations of the Italian gestures, especially in the case of G1, G3, and G6, which at step 1 were revealed to be the most difficult gestures to interpret. The participants themselves explained the reasons for this result. They seemed to be in agreement in saying that the verbal language in the multiple-choice exercise (i.e., at step 2) helped them make up their minds about the most likely interpretation. In addition, a number of participants said that some verbal commentaries given at step 2 made more sense than others. Therefore they concentrated on the verbal options that they regarded as the most meaningful. For example, the verbal commentary that indicates a number, such as *numero 1* ('number 1'), *numero 3* ('number 3'), etc., was not convincing enough for them to be selected as the correct meaning. It is interesting to note that not all the participants with Italian as their mother tongue (N = 8) scored 100% on the multiple-choice exercise. This fact suggests that they may have not been exposed to Italian emblematic gestures in the same way as native speakers living in Italy. Integration into the dominant Anglophone culture and its influence on the codification of meaning in ways other than the Italian emblematic gestures could be the reasons for this case of reverse transfer from the L2 into the L1 (see Efron, 1972; Jarvis & Pavlenko, 2008).

When asked the question 'Did you encounter any difficulties in understanding the situation and the language of the mini-dialogues?', a higher percentage (53%) of participants in the group with no prior knowledge of Italian expressed difficulty, compared with the group with prior knowledge of Italian (5%). This result suggests that language proficiency made a difference in the completion of the activities of this study. The mini-dialogues posed comprehension difficulties but proved useful to both groups: 46.3% of the participants with no prior knowledge of Italian said that the situation and the mini-dialogues facilitated their choices; 67% of the participants with prior knowledge found the mini-dialogues helpful.

Participants were then asked to express their opinion about whether the gestures of this study were typical of the Italian language and, if so, which ones were the most typical. Overall the gestures of this study were perceived as typically Italian. Across all levels, G5 (= 'frustration') and G3 (= 'perfect') were ranked as the most typical. The absolute beginners considered G4 (= 'money') typically Italian whereas the beginners with prior knowledge of Italian regarded G2 (= 'good food') as typically Italian. Unlike the absolute beginners, the latter group thought that the gesture that indicates 'money' is international, as it is also used in Canada. This opinion suggests that higher proficiency levels helped the participants make better observations based on the characteristics that distinguish their native language and the Italian target language, not only with respect to verbal language but also with respect to the gestures of this study.

Across language levels, then, G1 and G6 were regarded as the least typical gestures. This view may depend on how frequently participants had seen G1 and G6, whether performed by Italians or by other cultural groups. Alternatively, these gestures may be considered as the least typical because using fingers is a universal way to express meaning in a gestural form (see, for example, the discussion of the universality of the pointing finger in Kita, 2003). On the other hand, the combination of fingers with other bodily parts may be viewed as a more specific way to create meaning through gestures. By engaging different bodily parts, G2, G3, and G5 are not only more obviously noticeable, but perhaps more likely to receive the status of typicality. Answers to the question 'Would you consider these gestures typically Italian?' reveal that overall 31% of participants considered these gestures typically Italian, while 18% answered 'no', 10% answered 'some', 23% provided either no answer or a non-readable answer, and 18% indicated what gestures they regarded as typical Italian. Table 17.2 shows the percentage of participants who considered each of the six gestures as typically Italian.

Table 17.2 Percentage of participants (*N* = 329)
who explicitly said what gestures are typically
Italian

G1 = agreement	4%
G2 = good food	11%
G3 = perfect	7%
G4 = money	6%
G5 = frustration	15%
G6 = disagreement	3%

Statistical analysis of the data

Our study tested three hypotheses. The first hypothesis explored whether language background affects the correct interpretation of emblematic gestures. The second hypothesis was that contextual mini-dialogues facilitate the interpretation of emblematic gestures. The third hypothesis was that knowledge of Italian helps one interpret the gestures correctly. The independent variables in our analysis are: the number of languages known (i.e., language classes); the three steps of our study (i.e., only gestures; gestures with sentences; gestures with mini-dialogues); and the groups of learners distributed in three campuses (i.e., St. George 100, 101, 152; Mississauga, 100; McMaster 100). The response variable is a dichotomous variable (i.e., correct or incorrect). We carried out logistic regression analysis, which typically compares one of the classes of an independent variable (i.e., the reference group) to the rest of the classes, and it interprets the odds ratios. Testing such comparisons reveals the significance of our hypotheses. Multilingual speakers, step 3, and St. George 101-level group, were chosen as the reference groups for the three independent variables in our study. Moreover, in order to take into account that data collected on the same units (i.e., the six gestures) across successive points in time (i.e., three steps) are correlated over time, we used a generalized logistic regression model with random effects (Allison, 2003). Odds ratios and their 95% confidence intervals as well as *p*-values are reported in Table 17.3.

Table 17.3 reveals that the number of languages in our participants' background does not facilitate a correct interpretation of the Italian gestures, $F(3, 5591) = 1.01$, $p = .3856$. None of the language classes (i.e., monolinguals, bilinguals, trilinguals, and multilinguals) exhibited a significant probability of interpreting the gestures correctly. The odds ratios and confidence intervals are not significant.

Although the number of languages in the participants' background was not a significant factor, we need to inquire further into this variable. Particularly, we would like to investigate the role of historical relations among languages in order to see if the presence of one or more Romance

Table 17.3 Summary of the results of logistic regression with the variables of interest

Variables of interest	Odds ratio	p-value	95% confidence interval for odds ratio
Language class (ref: multilinguals, N = 60)			
monolingual (N = 53)	0.807	.2260	(0.570, 1.142)
bilingual (N = 112)	0.774	.0869	(0.577, 1.038)
trilingual (N = 104)	0.843	.2607	(0.627, 1.135)
Step (ref: step 3, gestures with dialogues)			
step 1 (only gestures)	0.264	<.0001**	(0.229, 0.305)
step 2 (gestures with sentences)	2.162	<.0001**	(1.883, 2.483)
Group (ref: St. George 101, N = 59)			
McMaster 100 (N = 41)	0.442	<.0001**	(0.303, 0.645)
Mississauga 100 (N = 113)	0.339	<.0001**	(0.251, 0.458)
St. George 152 (N = 12)	0.975	.9337	(0.539, 1.764)
St. George 100 (N = 104)	0.427	<.0001**	(0.315, 0.578)

* indicates significance.

languages in the participants' background had an impact on their inter-pretation of the six gestures. Knowledge of more than one language in combination with prior knowledge of Italian may be shown to help the interpretation of Italian emblematic gestures. Both hypotheses are based on the fact that at step 1 no verbal commentary was provided with the gestures. Table 17.3 also reveals that step was a significant independent variable, $F(2, 5591) = 387.10$, $p < .001$. Participants were less likely to interpret gestures correctly at step 1 than at step 3. The best interpretation results were obtained at step 2.

These data confirm that knowledge of Italian made a significant differ-ence, while the mini-dialogues were not as helpful as the phrases of the multiple-choice exercise. This may have been due to the more complex task entailed in the exercise of step 3, where participants were expected to put together the meaning of the mini-dialogues with the meaning of the six gestures. Alternatively, it is also possible that the mini-dialogues were not perceived as real-life situations. Yet the verbal language in the mini-dialogues enabled better interpretations than were possible at step 1, when no verbal language was involved. The participants themselves found the verbal language of the mini-dialogues meaningful at this point of the study.

Finally, Table 17.3 shows that all groups except for St. George 152 ($p = .9337$) exhibited less likelihood of interpreting gestures correctly when compared to St. George 101 (i.e., the reference group): McMaster 100 ($p < .0001$), Mississauga 100 ($p < 0001$), and St. George 100 ($p <$

.0001). Since St. George 101 and 152 included participants with an Italian family background and participants with some or with 4 years of high-school training in Italian, this finding suggests that prior exposure to the Italian language, whether within a family context or a classroom context, made our participants better prepared to interpret the gestures correctly. Group is a significant independent variable and this is confirmed by $F(4, 5591) = 14.47, p < .0001$.

Conclusion

In this study we found that Italian emblematic gestures are, and are perceived to be, a difficult type of non-verbal language for Italian learners in Canada. However, this difficulty is partly reduced by two factors: presence of target verbal language (sentences or mini-dialogues versus only gestures) and proficiency levels in the target language (participants with prior knowledge of Italian compared to participants with no prior knowledge of Italian). We also found that emblematic gestures pose different degrees of difficulty. The greatest difficulties were associated with the gestures that played a substitutive function with respect to verbal language (i.e., at step 1). Fewer difficulties were encountered when gestures had a clarifying or a complementary function with respect to verbal language.

Moreover, the gestures that involved use of the hands only (i.e., G1 'agreement', G3 'perfect', and G6 'disagreement') were ranked as the most difficult. This fact supports the assumption that when fewer bodily parts are involved in the performance of a gesture, the gesture is more difficult to interpret. We can argue that the other three gestures of our study were less difficult to interpret because either they involved other bodily parts besides the hands (i.e., G2 'good' and G5 'frustration') or their meaning was known by some participants (i.e., G4 'money'). This ranking of difficulty may also depend on the frequency of gesture occurrences that our participants have witnessed through personal experience and mass media. It is likely that non-native speakers notice the more frequent gestures of another culture although they may have no clue about the meaning to attribute to them.

In the light of these conclusions, L2 emblematic gestures need to be explained to L2 learners especially when they play a substitutive function in oral communication, that is, when they are not accompanied by any verbal commentary. Participants who were not familiar with the meaning of the emblematic gestures of our study, but tried to reconstruct their meaning anyway, described the movement involved in their performance (e.g., G3 was interpreted to mean 'pulling something' because the thumb and the index finger perform an outward movement similar to pulling a thread). In so doing the participants provided iconic interpretations which do not correspond to the meaning conveyed by the gestures under

Table 17.4 The emblematic gestures and their meaning vs iconic interpretations

Emblematic gestures	Iconic interpretations at step 1
G1 = agreement	Moving; Being in close proximity; Being similar, alike, identical; Fitting together; Coming together; Two people or things meeting; 'Together' with no specification
G2 = good food	Toothache; Cuteness; Signs of affection; Being poked
G3 = perfect	Pulling something; Sewing
G4 = money	Thinking; Feeling the thickness of textures; Come on; Come here
G5 = frustration	Praying; Thanking; Asking for forgiveness; Pleading; Begging; Bowing
G6 = disagreement	Anything indicating togetherness; Getting together; Meeting

examination. Table 17.4 shows the most common iconic interpretations exhibited at step 1.

DISCUSSION

The main topic of this chapter has been the role of gestures in the acquisition of an L2. We have assumed a close relationship between gestures and verbal language in the creation of meaning. We have commented on the interpretation strategies that 329 Italian learners in Canada adopted when asked to explain the meaning of six emblematic gestures of the Italian language, whether combined or not with Italian verbal language.

This chapter has tackled the question of how speakers of different linguistic and cultural backgrounds perceive the dimension of meaning conveyed by six emblematic gestures of the Italian language. As our investigation suggests, L2 learners need to be made aware of the meanings and functions of L2 emblematic gestures, especially when these substitute for verbal language. In the absence of such an explanation, L2 learners tend to interpret emblematic gestures iconically, that is, they describe the movement involved in the performance of the gestures. This can be defined as a strategy of L2 gesture learning.

This study also provides some insights into the relationship between language and thought in the area of codification of meaning through emblematic gestures. The emblematic gestures of our study reveal that Italian native speakers encode meaning in ways that are specific to their culture and their language. The majority of the L2 learners in our study attributed different meanings or no meaning at all to most of our gestures.

Learners may express the concepts conveyed by the gestures in our study either through speech only or through bodily movements of a different kind. The learning of Italian emblematic gestures demands, therefore, that they understand the mechanisms through which Italian native speakers establish a connection between concepts and gestural movements. We found that only the 'money' gesture was recognized across the L2 learners in our study, regardless of their language background. For this reason, the 'money' gesture can be said to use the same way of encoding meaning in Canada as in Italy.

From a pedagogical perspective, our study suggests that receptive and interpretative skills are to be promoted in L2 classes as they allow learners to develop abilities that they will not explore otherwise. One of these skills is language awareness. The Italian learners who were asked to perform the three exercises of our study were given the opportunity to reflect on their language background in relation with the language that they were learning. Moreover, they were presented with material that is not usually part of Italian L2 syllabi. The combination of target verbal language and target emblematic gestures is rarely made the topic of exercises in Italian L2 classes in Canada. We believe that by doing the exercises of our study, the participants became better aware of what Italian oral communication entails. Indeed, L2 learners need to understand emblematic gestures before they can interpret and produce them in interaction exchanges.

The use of verbal language along with the emblematic gestures of the Italian language is an important suggestion that our study can offer to language educators. When introducing Italian emblematic gestures, language educators need to consider the clues that the target language can offer in the interpretation of the gestures. For instance, the difference in meaning between G1 and G6 (i.e., 'agreement' vs 'disagreement') in our study can be explained by looking at the movement involved in their performance along with their verbal meaning. Language educators can point out that when index fingers come together one on the side of the other (i.e., G1), the movement is suggestive of agreement. When the index fingers, instead, tap their tips one against the other (i.e., G6), the movement performed suggests that there is a contrast between two things or people.

This chapter has also considered the role of cross-linguistic influence in the interpretation of L2 gestures. We found that L2 learners rely on their background languages and cultures when they have to interpret L2 gestures. Specifically, we noted that L2 learners with prior exposure to the Italian language were in a more favorable position than the participants with no prior knowledge. Although we did not find evidence that knowledge of more than one language is a determining factor in helping the interpretation of Italian emblematic gestures, we believe that the combination of this factor with prior knowledge of Italian or with knowledge of a language related to Italian may have played a role. For this reason, we are currently exploring the extent of cross-linguistic influence when the participants in our study know languages related to Italian from an historical point of view (i.e., learners with a Romance language background). In so doing, we aim to expand the concept of cross-linguistic influence by considering its application to areas beyond the ones concerned with verbal language, and we want to provide further insights into the nature of L2 gesture learning.

ACKNOWLEDGMENTS

I would like to thank Prof. Domenico Pietropaolo from the University of Toronto for his continuous encouragement during the time when the investigation discussed in this chapter was being carried out. I would also like to thank Prof. Camilla Bardel from the University of Stockholm, and Prof. Giulio Lepschy from University College London, for their very helpful comments on previous versions of this chapter. I am grateful to my research assistants at the University of Windsor, Alyssa Daichendt and Stacey Hamilton, for helping me file and organize the linguistic data reported in this chapter. I also want to thank Prof. Lori Buchanan from the University of Windsor for her suggestions and insights, and I acknowledge the contribution of the Department of Mathematics and Statistics of the University of Windsor to the interpretation of the linguistic data of this chapter. Finally, I would like to thank Bonacci editore for permission to include in this chapter diagrams from Diadori, Pierangela (1990). *Senza parole. 100 gesti degli italiani.* Roma: Bonacci editore.

REFERENCES

Allen, L. (1995). The effect of emblematic gestures on the development and access of mental representations of French expressions. *Modern Language Journal, 79*(4), 521–529.

Allison, P. D. (2003). *Logistic regression using the SAS system: Theory and application.* New York: John Wiley. [Production GLIMMIX procedure with SAS 9.1.3. Available HTTP: <http://support.sas.com/rnd/app/da/glimmix.html> (accessed April 10, 2009).]

Asher, J. J. (1965). The strategy of the Total Physical Response: An application to learning Russian. *International Review of Applied Linguistics, 3,* 292–299.

Bialystock, E. (1990). *Communication strategies. A psychological analysis of second-language use.* Oxford, UK: Basil Blackwell.

Canale, M., & Swain, M. (1980). Theoretical bases of communicative approaches to second language teaching and testing. *Applied Linguistics, 1,* 1–47.

Cenoz, J., Hufeisen, B., & Jessner, U. (Eds.). (2001). *Cross-linguistic influence in third language acquisition: Psycholinguistic perspectives* Clevedon, UK: Multilingual Matters.

Cook, V. J. (1992). Evidence for multicompetence. *Language Learning, 42*(2), 557–592.

Cook, V. J. (Ed.). (2002). *Portraits of the L2 user.* Clevedon, UK: Multilingual Matters.

de Jorio, A. (1832/1979). *La mimica degli antichi investigata nel gestire napoletano.* Bologna: Arnaldo Forni Ed.

Diadori, P. (1990). *Senza parole. 100 gesti degli italiani.* Roma: Bonacci Ed.

Dörnyei, Z., & Scott, M. L. (1997). Communication strategies in a second language: Definitions and taxonomies. *Language Learning, 47*, 173–210.

Efron, D. (1972). *Gesture, race and culture.* The Hague: Mouton.

Ekman, P., & Friesen, W. (1969). The repertoire of nonverbal behaviour: Categories, origins, usage and coding. *Semiotica, 1*, 49–98.

Faerch, C., & Kasper, G. (Eds.). (1983). *Strategies in interlanguage communication.* London: Longman.

Graham, J. A., & Argyle, M. (1975). A cross-cultural study of the communication of extra-verbal meaning by gestures. *International Journal of Psychology, 10*(1), 57–67.

Gullberg, M. (1998). *Gesture as a communication strategy in second language discourse.* Lund: Lund University Press.

Gullberg, M. (Ed.). (2006). Special issue 'Gesture and second language acquisition'. *International Review of Applied Linguistics, 44*, 2.

Gullberg, M. (2009). Why are gestures relevant to the bilingual lexicon. In A. Pavlenko (Ed.), *The bilingual mental lexicon. Interdisciplinary approaches* (pp. 161–184). Clevedon, UK: Multilingual Matters.

Gullberg, M., & McCafferty, S. G. (2008). Introduction to gesture and SLA: Toward an integrated approach. *Studies in Second Language Acquisition, 30*, 133–146.

Hymes, D. H. (1972). On communicative competence. In J. Pride & J. Holmes (Eds.), *Sociolinguistics: Selected readings* (pp. 269–293). Harmondsworth: Penguin.

Jarvis, S., & Pavlenko, A. (2008). *Cross-linguistic influence in language and cognition.* New York: Routledge.

Jessner, U. (2006). *Linguistic awareness in multilinguals. English as a third language.* Edinburgh, UK: Edinburgh University Press.

Jungheim, N. O. (1991). A study on the classroom acquisition of gesture in Japan. *Journal of Ryutsu Keizai University, 27*(1), 61–68.

Jungheim, N. O. (2006). Learner and native speaker perspectives on a culturally-specific Japanese refusal gesture. *International Review of Applied Linguistics, 44*(2), 125–142.

Kellerman, E. (2001). New uses for old languages: Cross-linguistic and cross-gestural influence in the narratives of non-native speakers. In J. Cenoz, B. Hufeisen, & U. Jessner (Eds.), *Cross-linguistic influence in third language acquisition: Psycholinguistic perspectives* (pp. 170–191). Clevedon, UK: Multilingual Matters.

Kellerman, E., & Sharwood Smith, M. (Eds.). (1986). *Cross-linguistic influence in second language acquisition.* Elmsford, NY: Pergamon.

Kellerman, E., & van Hoof, A-M. (2003). Manual accents. *IRAL: International Review of Applied Linguistics in Language Teaching, 41*(3), 251–269.

Kendon, A. (2004). *Gesture. Visible action as utterance.* Cambridge, UK: Cambridge University Press.

Kita, S. (Ed.). (2003). *Pointing: Where language, culture and cognition meet.* Mahwah, NJ: Lawrence Erlbaum Associates Inc.

McCafferty, S. G., & Gullberg, M. (Eds.). (2008). Special issue 'Gesture and SLA: Toward an integrated approach'. *Studies in Second Language Acquisition, 30, 2.*

McCafferty, S. G., & Stam, G. (Eds.). (2008). *Gesture: Second language acquisition and classroom research.* London: Routledge.

McNeill, D. (1992). *Hand and mind. What gestures reveal about thought.* Chicago, IL: University of Chicago Press.

McNeill, D. (Ed.). (2000). *Language and gesture.* Cambridge, UK: Cambridge University Press.

McNeill, D. (2005). *Gesture and thought.* Chicago, IL: University of Chicago Press.

Morris, D., Collett, P., Marsh, P., & O'Shaughnessy, M. (1979). *Gestures: Their origins and distribution.* London: Jonathan Cape.

Negueruela, E., Lantolf, J. P., Rehn Jordan, S., & Gelabert, J. (2004). The 'private function' of gesture in second language speaking activity: A study of motion verbs and gesturing in English and Spanish. *International Journal of Applied Linguistics, 14*(1), 113–147.

Pika, S., Nicoladis, E., & Marentette, P. F. (2006). A cross-cultural study on the use of gestures: Evidence for cross-linguistic transfer? *Bilingualism, 9*(3), 319–327.

Poulisse, N. (1990). *The use of compensatory strategies by Dutch learners of English.* Dordrecht: Foris.

Ricci Bitti, P. E. (1992). Facial and manual component of Italian symbolic gestures. In F. Poyatos (Ed.), *Advances in nonverbal communication. Sociocultural, clinical, esthetic and literary perspectives* (pp. 187–196). Amsterdam: John Benjamins.

Rimé, B., & Schiaratura, L. (1991). Gesture and speech. In R. S. Feldman & B. Rimé (Eds.), *Fundamentals of nonverbal behaviour* (pp. 239–281). Cambridge, UK: Cambridge University Press.

Ringbom, H. (1987). *The role of the first language in foreign language learning.* Clevedon, UK: Multilingual Matters.

Ringbom, H. (2007). *Cross-linguistic similarity in foreign language learning.* Clevedon, UK: Multilingual Matters.

Salvato, G. (2008). The representation of gestures in Italian textbooks and workbooks. *Italica, 85*(1), 1–26.

Savignon, S. J. (1998). *Communicative competence: Theory and classroom practice.* New York: McGraw-Hill.

Slobin, D. (1996). From 'thought and language' to 'thinking for speaking'. In J. Gumperz & S. Levinson (Eds.), *Rethinking linguistic relativity* (pp. 70–96). Cambridge, UK: Cambridge University Press.

Talmy, L. (1991). Path to realisation: A typology of event conflation. In L. Sutton, C. Johnson, & R. Shields (Eds.), *Proceedings of the 17th annual meeting of the Berkeley Linguistics Society* (pp. 480–519). Berkeley, CA: Berkeley Linguistics Society.

Tarone, E. (1977). Conscious communicative strategies in interlanguage: A progress report. In H. D. Brown, C. A. Yorio, & R. H. Crymes (Eds.), *On TESOL '77* (pp. 194–203). Washington, DC: TESOL.

Yule, G., & Tarone, E. (1997). Investigating communication strategies in L2 reference: Pros and cons. In G. Kasper & E. Kellerman (Eds.), *Communication strategies. Psycholinguistic and sociolinguistic perspectives* (pp. 17–30). Harlow, UK: Longman.

18 *Yo no lo tiré, se cayó solito,* 'I did not throw it, it just fell down': Interpreting and recounting accidental events in Spanish and English

Debbie S. Cunningham, Jyotsna Vaid,
and Hsin Chin Chen

In recent years a number of studies have begun to explore how structural characteristics of different languages shape language users' cognitive processing (Green, 1998; Levinson, Kita, Haun, & Rasch, 2002; Yoshida & Smith, 2005). Whereas the majority of studies on this issue have focused on monolingual users, an increasing number have begun to use second language learners or bilinguals (e.g., Bassetti, 2007; Cook, Bassetti, Kasai, Sasaki, & Takahashi, 2006). Kousta, Vinson, and Vigliocco (2008) advocate studies that include both monolinguals and bilinguals as a new way of approaching the topic of the link between language and thought. They note that if language indeed affects cognition, then one could hypothesize an effect of the second language on the 'cognitive dispositions' associated with a first language (Kousta et al., 2008, p. 844), or vice versa. Use of monolinguals and bilinguals in the same study could also, it is proposed, offer a way of investigating the degree to which semantic representations of the bilingual's two languages are functionally autonomous. An autonomous view would be supported if bilinguals' performance in each of their languages is indistinguishable from that of monolingual counterparts. By contrast, an interactionist view would be supported if bilinguals' performance is influenced by their knowledge of the other language and, thus, differs from the performance of monolingual counterparts.

Several recent cross-linguistic studies have begun to explore how systematic differences between languages in the coding of such things as number (Athanasopoulos, 2006), grammatical gender (Bassetti, 2007; Kousta et al., 2008), or motion (Slobin, 2003) affect the way in which speakers perceive, attend to, describe, or remember objects, individuals, or events. With respect to the lexicalization of motion events, for example, Spanish and English speakers stand at different ends of a continuum. The pattern favored in Spanish, a so-called 'verb-framed' language, is for path of movement to be expressed primarily by the main verb, whereas the pattern favored in English, a so-called 'satellite-framed' language, is for path of movement to be expressed as a satellite (i.e., as a particle or preposition). Thus, a bottle moving on top of the water past a rock would be described by an English speaker as *The bottle floated past the rock* but the same event would be described by a Spanish speaker as *La botella pasó por la piedra, flotando*/*The bottle passed by the rock, floating* (Cifuentes-Férez & Gentner, 2006). Although the evidence is mixed as to whether these linguistic differences give rise to differential event memory in English and Spanish speakers, clear differences have been found in how Spanish and English speakers describe motion events (Slobin, 1996), and in the mental images of motion events evoked by the same text presented in English and Spanish (Slobin, 2003). Moreover, differences in the naming of motion events in Spanish and English extend even to novel motion verbs (Cifuentes-Férez & Gentner, 2006). To the extent that in verb-framed languages the action rather than the doer of the action appears to be foregrounded, one may ask if agents tend to be mentioned less often in descriptions of events by speakers of verb-framed languages vs satellite-framed ones. The present research addressed this question experimentally in monolingual and bilingual speakers of Spanish and English.

The same scene or event may be described differently by different speakers depending on the speaker's point of view or conceptualization of the event, and on the communicative intention in the discourse context. A given event could be conceptualized in terms of an underlying notion of causation in which there is a fully specified agent responsible for precipitating the actions described in the event. Alternatively, the same event could be described as 'just happening' without a particular causal agent implicated. Cross-linguistic analyses indicate that languages differ in the structural options they provide for expressing causation (Song & Wolff, 2003). Although all languages can convey direct and indirect causes of events, speakers of some languages, such as English, are more inclined to specify agents whereas speakers of other languages, such as Spanish, are less inclined to do so. For example, in English, depending on the emphasis one wants to convey, one can talk about an event either by explicitly associating it with a causal agent, as in *Mary broke a glass*, in which case the emphasis is presumably on Mary as the responsible party, or by not overtly identifying an agent, e.g., through use of the passive voice (*The glass was broken*) or use of an active voice with an intransitive verb (*When Mary was reaching for her napkin, her glass tipped over, fell, and broke*). In Spanish, likewise, one can highlight the agent by using an active voice with a fully specified agent and a transitive verb, e.g., *Ana olvidó las llaves de Pedro* 'Ana forgot Pedro's keys' or one can de-emphasize the agent by using a passive construction comparable to the English one, e.g., *Las llaves fueron olvidadas* 'The keys were forgotten'. However, a more common way of de-emphasizing agency in Spanish is by using the reflexive pronoun *se*, also known as the impersonal *se*. So, for example, for the English sentence *Ana forgot Pedro's keys* a non-agentive form of expressing it in Spanish would be *A Ana se le olvidaron las llaves de Pedro* 'The keys were forgotten unto Ana'. In the Spanish impersonal *se* form of the sentence, which has no real equivalent in English, the emphasis is presumed to be on the fact that the keys were not remembered; there is no implicit fault intended to be inferred, such as that this was due to Ana's forgetfulness (Rivero, 2004).

Whereas the Spanish reflexive passive and reflexive impersonal both show the sequence *se* V DP, they differ syntactically. In the reflexive passive, the *se* checks accusative case, and the internal argument (DP) bears nominative case and triggers agreement on the verb; in the reflexive impersonal construction the *se* checks nominative case and the internal argument bears accusative case (Tremblay, 2005).

There is also a passive impersonal *se* construction, in which one uses *se* with a verb in the third person singular or plural to de-emphasize the subject, as in *Se habla español*, 'Spanish is spoken here', or *Se reparan coches*, 'Cars are repaired here'. Intransitive verbs use *se* + the third person singular to express passive meaning, e.g., *Se sale por aquí*, 'You go out this way' or 'This is the way out' (Bradley & MacKenzie, 2004).

The impersonal *se* has long been considered by scholars as an indicator of an indeterminate subject (Babcock, 1970), or a device that serves to 'defocus' or take attention away from the agent (García, 1975, p. 197). The impersonal *se* in Spanish provides a way of talking about things that occur when the agent is either unknown or else considered unimportant, relative to the action described. In such cases, although reference may be made to a human participant, he or she is not necessarily described as causing the event (Haverkate, 2004).

Indeed, an acknowledged use of *se* is for unplanned or accidental occurrences. In this use the speaker seeks to avoid responsibility for an action; for example, a speaker may say *no lo rompí, patrón. Se me rompió* (lit: 'I did not break it, Sir. It broke to me') to reflect that he/she did not break a glass but that it just broke by itself (Bull, 1965, cited in Schmitz, 1966). Aside from the use of the reflexive *se* for accidental or unpremeditated occurrences, Schmitz (1966) identifies two other uses of the *se me*, *se le* construction, based on an analysis of literary texts: for involuntary physiological or emotional reactions over which the speaker has little or no control (e.g., *Se me hace agua la boca*, 'My mouth is watering'; *Se me sube la sangre a la cabeza*, 'My blood is going to my head') and for figurative expressions of catastrophic events (e.g., *Se los tragó la tierra*, 'The earth swallowed them up'). Whereas events in the latter case are always unplanned from the speaker's perspective, those in the first category (reflexive for unplanned, unpremeditated occurrences) are somewhat different in that they could change from a deliberate to an accidental pattern (*Rompí el vaso/Se me rompió el vaso*, 'I broke the glass /The glass broke unto me').

Given that the polysemous *se* clitic in Spanish offers an explicit way of de-emphasizing agency and that an equivalent structure is not present in English, one may well ask if agenthood is less prominent psychologically for Spanish than for English speakers when characterizing or remembering events. We are using the term 'agent' here to refer to the participant described in a sentence that acts in an intentional or voluntary manner to initiate the action; 'patient' here refers to the participant affected by the action of the agent. A further question of interest is whether the source of a difference in the prominence of agency lies in linguistic or cultural conventions (e.g., Slobin, 2003). Although important, it is not necessary at this stage to resolve whether language or culture undergirds an individual's choice of agent or agentless expressions to describe events. The aim of the present research was simply to establish (1) if there is a greater preference for non-agentive conceptualization of events in Spanish than in English among Spanish–English bilinguals when describing unplanned or accidental occurrences, and (2) whether prior knowledge of Spanish contributes to a lower overall incidence of agentive conceptualizations even when events are being described in English.

Linguistic analyses attest to the many varied functions of the 'multiply ambiguous' *se* clitic in Spanish (Babcock, 1970; Bello & Cuervo, 1960; Hidalgo, 1994; Roldán, 1971). Not only does it mark direct and indirect objects, it also can indicate two types of co-reference—reflexivity and reciprocality, as well as a broad range of so-called middle voice functions, that is, where the focus is on a specific part of an event, such as its abruptness or accidentality (these functions are described further below). Given its many and varied uses, it is not surprising that a grammaticality judgment study found that the impersonal *se* construction was not fully mastered even by fairly advanced second language learners of Spanish, as compared to native speakers (Tremblay, 2005).

Two corpus studies provide insights into the relative frequency of occurrence of different impersonal forms in standard written Spanish texts. Hidalgo (1994), examining news stories from the Madrid newspaper *El Pais*, found a high frequency of use of the passive *se* and impersonal *se* constructions, indicating that these are fairly common in formal registers. More recently, an extensive corpus study of 450,000 words extracted from books, magazines, and newspapers in Spanish across an array of genres found 2395 occurrences of the word *se* (Meseguer, Acuna-Farina, & Carreiras, 2009). Of these, the vast majority of occurrences (over 60%) involved the aspectual use, that is, co-occurrences of *se* with specific verbs, such as *ir* ('go'), as in *Juan se fue*, 'John left', or middle uses of verbs such as *secar* ('dry') as in *la ropa se secó rápidamente*, 'the clothes dried quickly'. Only 14% were reflexive uses, 7.4% were impersonal uses, and 8.0% were passive uses, with the remainder being indirect or reciprocal uses.

Jackson-Maldonado, Maldonado, and Thal (1998) conducted a developmental study of the acquisition of the *se* construction in native speakers of Mexican Spanish, based on recordings of naturalistic language samples. Whereas traditional grammars (e.g., Bello & Cuervo, 1960) have regarded all occurrences of *se* as either derived from a type of reflexive or as an unanalyzed, memorized form, the study by Jackson-Maldonado et al. (1998) found that the earliest uses of *se*, from around 3 years of age, show a clear differentiation between a reflexive and a middle usage. In contrast to reflexives, in middle-marking systems the initiator of the action cannot be distinguished from the undergoer. Of the total number of utterances in which *se* was used in the language samples by the children, Jackson-Maldonado et al. (1998) found that the vast majority of uses (87%) were middle forms (that is, forms in which there was not a clear differentiation of the agent and the patient thematic roles), with only 9% being true reflexive forms. The most frequently occurring middle forms they noted were those referring to motion (32%) and unexpected change (30%), and change of state—whether physical or emotional—accounted for 10% of the uses of *se*. These findings led Jackson-Maldonado et al. (1998) to propose that the earliest uses of *se* involve a strategy of focusing on change: 'the *se* marker functions as an aspectual marker of inceptivity, inchoativity, abruptness and even pragmatic factors related to accidentality and unexpectedness' (p. 404). The authors further note that 'focusing on the pivotal moment of change also allows elimination of subject responsibility' (p. 408). Use of *se* to mark avoidance of responsibility has also been observed in two previous studies of Spanish-speaking children (López-Ornat, 1994; Martínez, 2000).

There are few studies of actual *use* of the various impersonal forms by Spanish-speaking adults. Jisa, Reilly, Verhoeven, Baruch, and Rosado (2002) conducted a cross-linguistic study of the use of the passive voice construction in written texts produced by native speakers of Spanish, Dutch, English, French, and Hebrew from four age groups (9–10 years, 12–13, 15–16, and adults). They hypothesized that languages such as Hebrew and Spanish, which allow null subject constructions in simple clauses, have rich subjectless impersonal constructions that provide an alternative to passive constructions, and have productive morphological means for middle voice constructions, should show fewer use of passives than languages that mark subjects and lack middle voice constructions. Their results showed that, as hypothesized, passive constructions were used significantly less by Spanish and Hebrew speakers relative to Dutch, English, and French speakers.

Two additional studies with Spanish speakers are of particular relevance to the present research. The first is a study by Berk-Seligson (1983), who examined whether Spanish speakers use non-agentive constructions to describe adverse events and whether they do so deliberately as a way of avoiding attributing responsibility to an agent. Respondents, who were high-school students in Costa Rica, were shown two sets of line drawings depicting accidental or adverse events. The first drawing, for example, showed a boy reaching for his back pants pocket; something that looked like a handkerchief dangled from the pocket and a large coin fell from the pocket to the ground. Participants were to answer in a single sentence what happened, then explain more fully what happened, and then write an imaginary dialogue between the actors in the drawings and their respective mothers. Using this approach, Berk-Seligson was able to study not just how the adverse incidents were characterized (the relative use of agentive versus non-agentive forms) but also whether use of non-agentive constructions was intended by speakers and interpreted by hearers as a way of avoiding attributing responsibility to an agent. Indeed, Berk-Seligson concludes that her findings support the existence of a 'culturally prominent mode of discourse in Costa Rican Spanish, namely, one which avoids both the mention of agents and the use of active voice in adverse situations' (1983, p. 145).

The second study of relevance to the present research is reported in an unpublished manuscript by Fausey and Boroditsky (in press), who examined elicited descriptions by English and Spanish speaking monolingual adults of videotaped portrayals of intentional and accidental events. Participants included 113 English-speaking monolinguals and 109 Chilean Spanish-speaking monolinguals. Fausey and Boroditsky found no differences between the two groups in the description of intentional events but, when describing accidental events, agentive language was used much more often by the English than by the Spanish speakers. The authors further tested whether differences in use of agentive constructions differentially affected participants' memory for the agents of intentional versus accidental actions. Memory was tested after presentation of a brief distractor task following videotapes of the events. Participants' memory for agents of accidental events was better among English than Spanish speakers, whereas memory for agents of intentional events did not differ between the two groups (Fausey & Boroditsky, in press). This study extends the previous findings by Berk-Seligson (1983) in indicating that there is a clear de-emphasis of agents on the part of Spanish speakers when describing scenes involving accidental events which, in turn, lowers participants' accuracy of recalling the agents of the events.

The studies reviewed above were on monolingual speakers of Spanish and English. We were able to find only two published studies of use of impersonal Spanish forms in Spanish–English fluent bilinguals. Morales (1995) observed the use of Spanish impersonal forms in the spontaneous discourse of 47 Spanish–English bilingual Americans originally from Puerto Rico and Spanish-speaking monolinguals living in Puerto Rico. Respondents were recorded talking about their happiest or saddest experiences in Spanish. It was found that, in contrast to monolinguals, the bilinguals tended not to use *se* for inclusive reference, that is, to refer to situations that involved the speakers. The distinction between inclusive and exclusive use of a form is thought to provide an indication of the degree of involvement of the speaker in the events or ideas expressed. Morales suggested that the lack of use of *se* by bilinguals to convey inclusive reference may reflect a process of simplification and/or an influence of English schooling.

Gervasi (2007) investigated the use of various Spanish impersonal forms in conversation. Her data were drawn from a corpus of 30-minute interviews with 19 third-generation Mexican Spanish–English speakers in the American southwest and 5 Spanish-speaking monolingual speakers in Mexico City. Similar to Morales (1995), Gervasi (2007) found subtle discourse differences between her bilingual and monolingual samples' use of *se*, which she interpreted as a possible effect of linguistic convergence, i.e., the influence of exposure to English on the Spanish language use of the bilinguals. While intriguing, these largely observational studies are based on fairly small samples and do not, therefore, permit firm generalizations. They, do, however, point to the possibility of cross-language influence in ways of linguistically signaling and interpreting agency.

THE PRESENT STUDY

The present research used an experimental approach, seeking to replicate and extend previous empirical findings of a de-emphasis of agency, that is, a less-frequent use of agentive constructions, in Spanish speakers' characterizations of accidental events by considering how Spanish–English bilingualism affects the relative marking of agency in each language. Specifically, the study aimed at determining not only if agency is de-emphasized in Spanish relative to English in bilingual speakers, but also whether the availability of the impersonal *se* construction in Spanish has carry-over effects, leading bilingual users of Spanish to de-emphasize the agent when summarizing a passage describing an accidental occurrence even in English.

Two experiments were conducted to study the influence of language on judgments of agency in descriptions of unplanned occurrences. In each experiment there were three groups of participants—English monolinguals, Spanish monolinguals (tested in Mexico), and English–Spanish proficient bilinguals (tested in the US). Participants in Experiment 1 read scenarios and had to select an agentive or an agentless characterization of the event (choice-based response). In Experiment 2 participants read the same scenarios as in Experiment 1 but had to produce their own one-sentence summaries of the event (free production procedure). Monolinguals were tested in their first language, bilinguals in both languages. The dependent measure was percent choice (Exp. 1) or use (Exp. 2) of agentive responses. This was examined for bilinguals as a function of language of the event, and for each language as a function of group (bilingual versus English monolingual or Spanish monolingual).

Predicted outcomes

Three hypotheses were tested. The first was that narratives of accidental events in Spanish would elicit a higher percentage of non-agentive constructions than depictions of the same events in English; thus, Spanish-speaking monolinguals should show a higher selection or production of agentless constructions than English monolinguals, and bilinguals should show more agentless constructions in response to the Spanish than the English version of the narratives. Our second hypothesis was that non-agentive responses in Spanish should be more frequent for items presented in Spanish first than for those items in Spanish that were preceded by a block of items in English. Similarly, we expected a higher incidence of non-agentive responses in English for English narratives that followed a block of items in Spanish than for items that appeared in English first. Our third hypothesis was that knowledge of Spanish should lead to a lowering of agentive responses in bilinguals as compared to the level manifested in English-speaking monolinguals. That is, bilinguals in the English trials should show a lower incidence of agentive constructions than that exhibited by English-speaking monolinguals. We also examined the possibility that knowledge of English would have a corresponding effect of increasing the level of agentive constructions in Spanish in bilinguals relative to that in Spanish-speaking monolinguals

METHOD

Participants

Participants were college-age students tested in the US and Mexico. They ranged in age from 18 to 21 years. In Experiment 1 there were 30 English-speaking monolinguals, 30 Spanish-speaking bilinguals, and 32 Spanish–English bilinguals. Experiment 2 tested a new set of participants, consisting of 30 Mexican American bilingual speakers of English and Spanish, 22 English-speaking monolinguals, and 25 Spanish-speaking monolinguals. The English monolinguals and the bilinguals for both experiments were recruited from the psychology participant pool and from students enrolled in Hispanic Studies at Texas A&M University; Spanish-speaking monolinguals were recruited from students enrolled in various disciplines at the Escuela Normal in Guanajuato, Mexico.

All participants completed a brief language background questionnaire. Answers were used to classify them as monolingual or bilingual. Participants who were classified as English monolinguals had been schooled in English and, although they had studied Spanish for an average of 2 years in high school, they did not consider themselves to be at all fluent in it. Similarly, participants classified as Spanish monolinguals had been schooled in Spanish and had studied English for an average of 2 years but did not consider themselves to be fluent in it. By contrast, participants classified as bilingual rated themselves as highly fluent in both Spanish and

English. For all the bilinguals, Spanish was their first language, and the language spoken at home. English was acquired in childhood and was the language of schooling.

Materials

The test instrument, developed for the purposes of the study, consisted of a set of 16 narratives in each language and their equivalents in the other language. The narratives depicted unplanned or accidental occurrences. They included such events as a glass being knocked down, a passport lost, or a flight missed. The way in which the events were described in the narratives was generally non-agentive. Although for a subset of the items in Spanish the non-agentive wording used in the narratives was echoed in the wording of the non-agentive choice, for the majority of the items the phrasing in the narrative was not similar in the response choices, so as to prevent participants from choosing merely on the basis of what resembled an actual sentence in the narrative. As an example, one of the Spanish items (narrative and two response choices) is given below, followed by its English translation:

> Luisa se va de compras. Al salir del coche ella cierra la puerta detrás de ella. Después de ir de compras, al regresar al coche, se da cuenta que las llaves están adentro del coche.
> ¿Qué oración mejor capta lo que pasó?
> A. Las llaves se quedaron en el coche.
> B. Luisa dejó las llaves dentro del coche.

> *English translation:*
> Luisa goes shopping. After getting out of the car, she shuts the door behind her. She returns from shopping and realizes the keys are inside the car.
> Which sentence better captures what happened?
> A. The keys remained in the car.
> B. Luisa locked her keys in the car.

(Note that no agent is expressed in the scenario itself with regard to who lost the keys.)

The same set of 16 narratives per language were used across the two experiments; Experiment 2 also contained six filler narratives that were inserted to prevent participants from guessing the purpose of the study. See the Appendix for a complete list of the scenarios presented per language across the two experiments, as well as the response choices provided in Experiment 1.

Procedure and scoring

Monolinguals were tested in their respective language (Spanish or English). Bilinguals were administered the task once in each language with the order counterbalanced. Thus, for half of the bilinguals the scenarios were presented in English first (i.e., for the first block of eight critical items), followed by Spanish (for the remaining block of eight), whereas for the remainder the scenarios were first presented in Spanish followed by English.

Participants' task was to summarize the action depicted in each scenario either by choosing one of two response options per scenario (Experiment 1—choice-based response mode) or by generating a one-line summary in the language of the scenario (Experiment 2—free production response mode).

The choice-based version of the test (Exp. 1) contained 16 scenarios followed by an agentive and a non-agentive one-line summary of each scenario (see the Appendix for the list of scenarios). For half of the items the agentive summary preceded the non-agentive one, and for the remainder the non-agentive statement was presented first. As previously noted, the free production version (Exp. 2) contained the same 16 scenarios used in Experiment 1 and six filler scenarios.

The dependent measure was mean percent choice of an agentive response (Exp. 1) and mean percent use of an agentive response (Exp. 2). The coding of responses as agentive or non-agentive was relatively straightforward in both experiments. In Exp. 1 the choices were constructed such that one option was clearly agentive and the other clearly non-agentive (as in the example provided earlier). In Exp. 2 participants' free responses were coded as agentive or as non-agentive based on their use of an active voice and transitive verbs (agentive) or the passive voice, intransitive verbs, or (in the case of Spanish), the *se* clitic. Sample agentive and non-agentive responses provided by participants are listed below for the following scenario (presented in English and in Spanish versions):

> Sample scenario in English:
>   Mr. Smith is out of town on business and is staying in a hotel. He prepares to leave for a meeting, and as he steps out into the hall, the door shuts behind him, and he realizes he does not have his keys.

> Examples of responses coded as 'agentive':
>   Mr. Smith left his keys in the room.
>   Mr. Smith forgot his keys.

> Examples of responses coded as 'non-agentive':
>   Mr. Smith's keys were left in the room.
>   The keys got locked in the room.
>   The keys were left behind.

Sample scenario in Spanish:
El. Sr. Ramírez está fuera de la ciudad por el negocio y se está quedando en un hotel. Él se prepara para irse a una reunión y al entrar al pasillo, la puerta se cierra detrás de él. Se da cuenta que no trae las llaves.

Examples of responses coded as 'agentive':
El Sr. Ramírez olvidó las llaves en la habitación.
El Sr. Ramírez dejó las llaves en la habitación.

Examples of responses coded as 'non-agentive':
Se le olvidaron las llaves en la habitación al Sr. Ramírez.
Al Sr. Ramírez se le quedaron las llaves en la habitación.

As can be seen from these examples, non-agentive responses in Spanish typically used the *se le* expression, whereas non-agentive responses in English were typically in the passive voice.

Three sets of analyses were performed for each experiment. The first analysis was conducted on the monolinguals only and compared the mean percent choice of agentive response in English versus Spanish monolinguals as a function of primary language and stimulus block. The second analysis was conducted on the bilinguals' data and compared percent choice of agentive response in bilinguals by language and language order. The third set of analyses compared the response of bilinguals in English with that of English-speaking monolinguals, and the response of bilinguals in Spanish versus that of Spanish-speaking monolinguals.

RESULTS

Experiment 1: Choice-based responses

Monolinguals

Percent choice of agentive constructions was entered into a 2 × 2 analysis of variance as a function of Group (English versus Spanish monolinguals) and Stimulus Block (first eight scenarios versus last eight scenarios). There was only a significant effect of Group, indicating that the agentive response was favored more by English- than Spanish-speaking monolinguals, $F(1, 58) = 26.81$, $p < .001$, $\eta_p^2 = .32$. See Figure 18.1.

Bilinguals

Bilinguals' percent choice of agentive constructions was analyzed in a 2 × 2 analysis of variance as a function of Language of Narrative (English versus Spanish) and Language Order (English presented first versus Spanish presented first). The analysis revealed a main effect of Language of

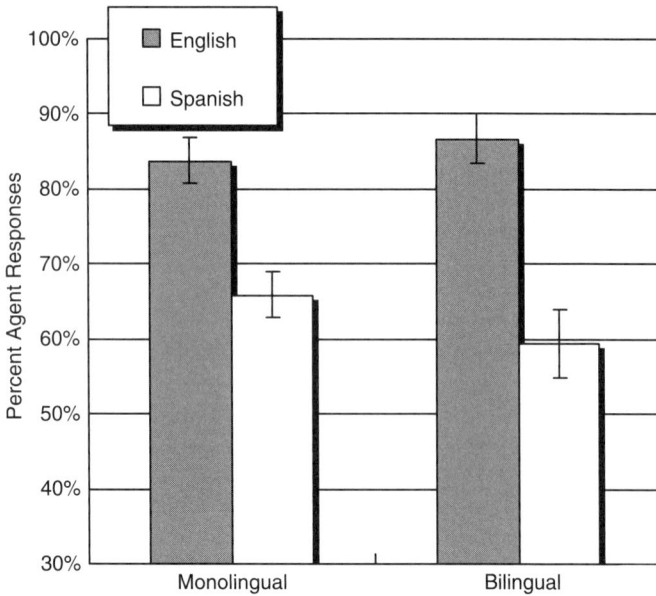

Figure 18.1 Mean percent preference for agentive versus agentless responses by monolinguals and bilinguals as a function of language of scenario (Exp. 1).

Narrative, $F(1, 30) = 42.98$, $p < .001$, $\eta_p^2 = .59$, indicating a significantly higher incidence of agentive response choices in English than in Spanish (86.7% versus 59.4%, respectively). The Language Order variable did not reach an acceptable level of significance, $F(1, 30) = 2.64$, $p = .12$, $\eta_p^2 = .08$. See Figure 18.2.

Bilinguals versus monolinguals

These analyses were conducted as four separate *t*-tests that compared bilinguals with English monolinguals on English (in each block) and bilinguals versus Spanish monolinguals on Spanish (in each block). Across all four analyses there were no differences between groups; that is, bilinguals behaved like English monolinguals on the English scenarios, showing a high degree of selection of agentive responses, and behaved like Spanish monolinguals on the Spanish scenarios, showing a high degree of selection of non-agentive responses.

Experiment 2: Free production responses

Mean percent of agent-based characterizations on the free production version of the test instrument were analyzed in three separate sets of analyses.

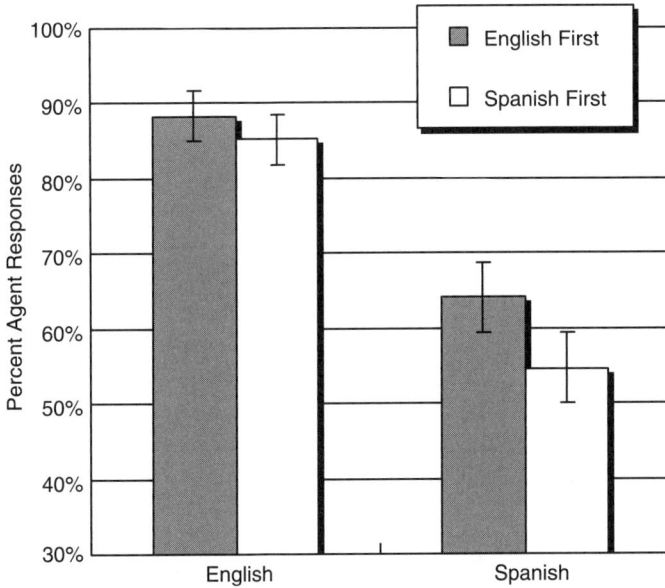

Figure 18.2 Mean percent selection of agentive responses by bilinguals as a function of language and language order (Exp. 1).

Monolinguals

The monolinguals-only analysis revealed a main effect of Stimulus Block, $F(1, 45) = 7.12$, $p < .01$, $\eta_p^2 = .14$, a main effect of Group, $F(1, 45) = 44.11$, $p < .001$, $\eta_p^2 = .50$, and a Group × Block interaction, $F(1, 45) = 19.43$, $p < .001$, $\eta_p^2 = .30$. Agentive responses were significantly more common in the English- than in the Spanish-speaking monolinguals' responses. Analyses of simple main effects for the significant interaction indicated that whereas the use of agentive responses for English monolinguals was uniformly high across blocks (78.81% in Block 1 and 84.06% in Block 2), $F(1, 45) = 1.42$, $p = .24$, $\eta_p^2 = .03$, it decreased substantially for Spanish monolinguals from Block 1 to Block 2 (67.92% in Block 1 versus 46.59% in Block 2), $F(1, 45) = 26.75$, $p < .001$, $\eta_p^2 = .37$. See Figure 18.3.

Bilinguals

A 2(Language of Narrative) × 2(Language Order) ANOVA conducted on the bilinguals' responses revealed a main effect of Language, $F(1, 28) = 4.38$, $p < .05$, $\eta_p^2 = .14$, indicating a higher incidence of agentive responses for scenarios presented in and responded to in English than for those in Spanish (68.26% in English versus 56.28% in Spanish). Incidence of agentive constructions was not affected by whether narratives were presented in English first or Spanish first. See Figure 18.4.

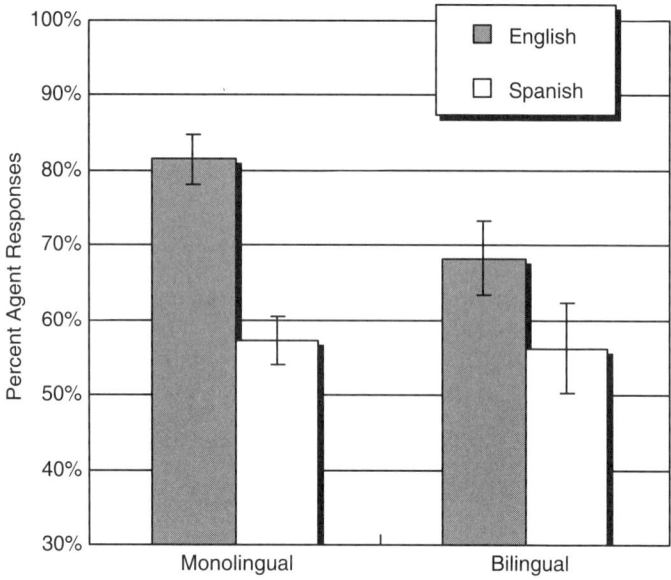

Figure 18.3 Mean percent production of agentive responses by monolinguals and bilinguals as a function of language of scenario (Exp. 2).

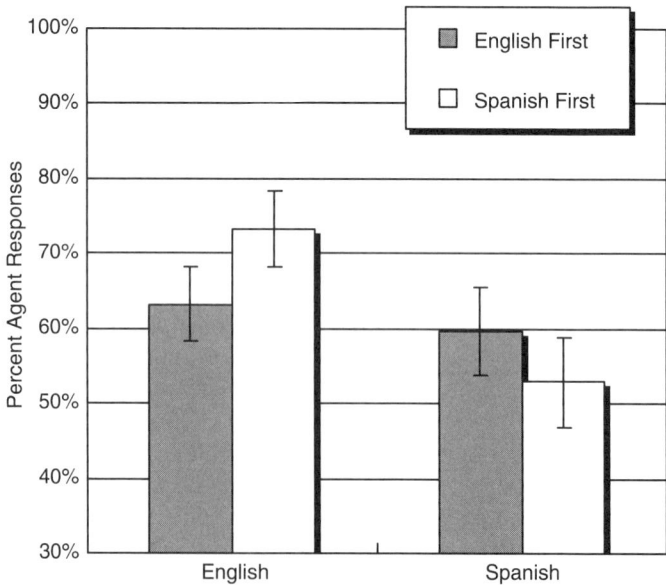

Figure 18.4 Mean percent production of agentive responses by bilinguals as a function of language of scenario and language order (Exp. 2).

Bilinguals versus monolinguals

A direct comparison of bilingual versus monolingual data using *t*-tests showed that, for English language narratives, bilinguals made significantly fewer agentive responses than did English monolinguals, for both Block 1, $t(35) = 2.87$, $p < .01$, $d = .99$; 63.26% versus 78.81%, respectively, and Block 2 items, $t(35) = 2.33$, $p < .05$, $d = .80$. For Spanish language narratives, bilinguals made significantly fewer agentive responses than monolinguals but only in Block 1; $t(38) = 2.17$, $p < .05$, $d = .73$. Block 2 items in Spanish showed a near significant trend for an opposite pattern, namely, a higher incidence of agentive responses in bilinguals than in Spanish-speaking monolinguals, $t(38) = 1.94$, $p = .06$, $d = .65$ (see Figure 18.3).

In other words, it appears that knowledge of Spanish in bilinguals was associated with an overall lowering of English agentive responses relative to the level of agentive responses characterizing monolinguals in English. However, bilinguals' Spanish performance relative to that of Spanish-speaking monolinguals showed a mixed pattern, with a lower level of agentive responses in bilinguals relative to those produced by mono-linguals for items in Block 1 but a higher level of agentive responses than those of monolinguals for items in Block 2.

GENERAL DISCUSSION

The present research sought to test whether the option available in Spanish of omitting or de-emphasizing the agent of an action makes Spanish users less likely to attribute agency relative to users of English when characterizing verbal narratives involving unfortunate or accidental events or unforeseen consequences of actions.

Our first hypothesis, that knowledge of Spanish would be associated with a reduced use of agentive responses when describing accidental occurrences, was strongly supported across both experiments. There was a clear effect of the language of the narrative. For narratives presented in English, participants showed a higher level of agentive responses than for the same narratives presented in Spanish. As such, our findings corroborate those based on monolinguals previously obtained by Fausey and Boroditsky (2009) and Berk-Seligson (1983).

Our second hypothesis, that lower agency should be found in the Spanish-first than English-first condition in bilinguals, was not supported in either experiment, as bilinguals showed the same pattern of choice of agentive responses for English-first as for Spanish-first conditions. Thus we found no evidence for transient effects due to language presentation order in the marking of agency.

Our third hypothesis, that bilinguals would show a lower incidence of agentive responses in English relative to English monolinguals and a higher level of agentive responses in Spanish relative to Spanish monolinguals, was partially supported. When the task involved choosing between an agentive versus an agentless response (Exp. 1), bilinguals behaved like English monolinguals on the English items and like Spanish monolinguals on the Spanish items. However, when the task involved participants coming up with their own characterization of the scenarios (Exp. 2), bilinguals' relative use of agentive constructions was heightened or lessened relative to that of monolinguals, reflecting an interaction between the bilinguals' two languages. Specifically, bilinguals responding in English were less agentive than English monolinguals in both blocks, whereas bilinguals responding in Spanish gave more agentive responses than Spanish monolinguals (in Block 2, $p = .06$), but significantly fewer agentive responses in Block 1.

Taken together, our findings demonstrate a clear effect of language structure on bilinguals' perceptions of agency for actions involving accidental or unplanned occurrences as a function of whether they are depicted in Spanish versus English. Spanish–English bilinguals are less inclined to use agentive constructions in Spanish than in English and show a lower level of agentive constructions in English relative to that of English monolinguals, suggesting that the agency-reducing effect of Spanish carries over to English use in bilinguals.

One limitation of the present research is that in our analysis of participants' responses, particularly the open-ended responses in Experiment 2, we did not consider the relative frequency with which participants used particular ways of de-emphasizing agency (e.g., the passive versus the intransitive versus the reflexive impersonal *se*, etc.). In future research it would be instructive to do more fine-grained analyses of specific forms to capture possible differences in the nuances between different impersonal forms.

Our findings generally concur with previous ethnomethodological reports across a range of language users that suggest that adverse or unhappy incidents tend to be described in terms of events that happened rather than in terms of actions performed by actors/agents (Berk-Seligson, 1983). However, the extent to which this is the case appears to vary across languages, as we found a greater tendency for agentive construals in English than Spanish for such types of events. Further, our findings add to the body of evidence (e.g., Grosjean, 2008) that suggests that bilinguals do not behave like the sum of two monolinguals, inasmuch as we found that bilinguals' pattern of responses reflected an interactive effect of knowing another language and did not completely mirror the pattern observed in monolingual speakers of each language.

Finally, the present findings add to a growing body of research on similarities and differences across languages in ways of expressing causation. Following Song and Wolff (2003), we concur that linguistic theories of causality can be experimentally tested by creating and manipulating instances of direct and indirect causation and examining elicited spontaneous descriptions of the events. By studying the range of expressions that are used to talk about these two types of events, it will become possible to test theories of causal meaning and hypotheses about the linguistic level at which directness of causation is encoded. Finally, it is important to remember that issues of causality are of importance beyond their theoretical significance for linguistic and psycholinguistic models. One practical domain in which these issues are of particular importance is eyewitness testimony. A recent study comparing police transcripts of original Spanish language with English translations of court testimony by Spanish-speaking witnesses (Filipovic, 2007) indicates that differences between languages in ways of marking agency and causality may have very real consequences for such issues as the process of interviewing witnesses and interpreting their answers.

ACKNOWLEDGMENTS

An earlier version of this research was presented at the 2007 International Symposium on Bilingualism held at Hamburg. This research was supported in part by funding from the Melbern G. Glasscock Center for Humanities Research at Texas A&M University. We would like to thank Caitlin Fausey for providing us with important references of relevance, including her own, and Belem Lopez for proofreading assistance.

REFERENCES

Athanasopoulos, P. (2006). Effects of the grammatical representation of number on cognition in bilinguals. *Bilingualism: Language and Cognition, 9,* 89–96.

Babcock, S. S. (1970). *The syntax of Spanish reflexive verbs: The parameters of the middle voice.* The Hague: Mouton.

Bassetti, B. (2007). Bilingualism and thought: Grammatical gender and concepts of objects in Italian–German bilingual children. *International Journal of Bilingualism, 11*(3), 251–273.

Bello, A., & Cuervo, R. (1960). *Gramática de la lengua española* (6th ed.). Buenos Aires: Editorial Sopena.

Berk-Seligson, S. (1983). Sources of variation in Spanish verb construction usage: The active, the dative, and the reflexive passive. *Journal of Pragmatics, 7,* 143–168.

Bradley, P. T., & MacKenzie, I. (2004). *Spanish: An essential grammar.* London: Routledge.

Cifuentes-Férez, P., & Gentner, D. (2006). Naming motion events in Spanish and English. *Cognitive Linguistics, 17,* 443–462.

Cook, V. J., Bassetti, B., Kasai, C., Sasaki, M., & Takahashi, J. A. (2006). Do bilinguals have different concepts? The case of shape and material in Japanese L2 users of English. *International Journal of Bilingualism, 10,* 137–152.

Fausey, C., & Boroditsky, L. (in press). Who dunnit? Cross-linguistic differences in eye-witness memory. *Psychonomic Bulletins & Review.*

Filipovic, L. (2007). Language as a witness: Insights from cognitive linguistics. *The International Journal of Speech, Language and the Law, 14*(2), 245–267.

García, E. (1975). *The role of theory in linguistic analysis: The Spanish pronoun system.* Amsterdam: North-Holland.

Gervasi, K. (2007). The use of Spanish impersonal forms in monolingual and bilingual speech. *Hispania, 90,* 342–253.

Green, D. (1998). Bilingualism and thought. *Psychologica Belgica, 38,* 251–276.

Grosjean, F. (2008). *Studying bilinguals.* Oxford, UK: Oxford University Press.

Haverkate, H. (2004). Gramática y pragmática: Categorías desfocalizadoras en español. *Spanish in Context, 1*(1), 21–40.

Hidalgo, R. (1994). The pragmatics of de-transitive voice in Spanish: From passive to inverse? In L. Talmy (Ed.), *Voice and inversion* (pp. 169–186). Amsterdam: John Benjamins.

Jackson-Maldonado, D., Maldonado, R., & Thal, D. (1998). Reflexive and middle markers in early child language acquisition: Evidence from Mexican Spanish. *First Language, 18,* 403–429.

Jisa, H., Reilly, J., Verhoeven, L., Baruch, E., & Rosado, E. (2002). Passive voice constructions in written texts: A cross-linguistic developmental study. *Written Language and Literacy, 5,* 163–181.

Kousta, S. T., Vinson, D., & Vigliocco, G. (2008). Investigating linguistic relativity through bilingualism: The case of grammatical gender. *Journal of Experimental Psychology, 34*(4), 843–858.

Levinson, S. C., Kita, S., Haun, D. B. M., & Rasch, B. H. (2002). Returning the tables: Language affects spatial cognition. *Cognition, 84,* 155–188.

López-Ornat, S. (1994). *La adquisicion de la lengua Espanola.* Madrid: Siglo XXI.

Martínez, I. (2000). The effects of language on children's understanding of agency and causation. *Dissertation Abstracts International, 61(10),* 3976A. (UMI No. 9990936)

Meseguer, E., Acuna-Farina, C., & Carreiras, M. (2009). Processing ambiguous Spanish *se* in a minimal chain. *Quarterly Journal of Experimental Psychology, 62,* 766–788.

Morales, A. (1995). The loss of the Spanish impersonal particle *se* among bilinguals: A descriptive profile. In C. Silva-Corvalan (Ed.), *Spanish in four continents: Studies in language contact and bilingualism* (pp. 148–162). Washington, DC: Georgetown University Press.

Rivero, M. L. (2004). Spanish quirky subjects, person restrictions, and the person–case constraint. *Linguistic Inquiry, 35*(3), 494–502.

Roldán, M. (1971). Spanish constructions with *se. Language Sciences, 18,* 15–29.

Schmitz, J. R. (1966). The *se me* construction: Reflexive for unplanned occurrences. *Hispania, 49*(3), 430–433.

Slobin, D. (1996). Two ways to travel: Verbs of motion in English and Spanish. In M. Shibatani & S. A. Thompson (Eds.), *Grammatical constructions: Their forms and meaning* (pp. 195–220). Oxford, UK: Clarendon Press.

Slobin, D. (2003). Language and thought online: Cognitive consequences of linguistic relativity. In D. Gentner & S. Goldin-Meadow (Eds.), *Language in mind: Advances in the study of language and thought* (pp. 157–192). Cambridge, MA: MIT Press.

Song, G., & Wolff, P. (2003). Linking perceptual properties to linguistic expressions of causation. In M. Achard & S. Kemmer (Eds.), *Language, culture, and mind* (pp. 1–13). Stanford, CA: CSLI Publications.

Tremblay, A. (2005). The L2 acquisition of Spanish passive and impersonal *se* by French and English speaking adults. In L. Dekeydtspotter, R. Sprouse, & A. Liljestrand (Eds.), *Proceedings of the 7th generative approaches to second language acquisition conference* (pp. 251–268). Somerville, MA: Cascadilla.

Yoshida, H., & Smith, L.B. (2005). Linguistic cues enhance the learning of perceptual cues. *Psychological Science, 16,* 90–95.

APPENDIX

Experiment 1: Narratives and response options per language

English

For each of the following situations, choose the sentence that best captures the essence of the situation, according to your point of view.

1. Monica went to Florida to visit her boyfriend. The morning of her return flight, she did not wake up on time, and because of this, she arrives late to the airport. The airline agent tells her that it is too late to board her flight, and that she will have to take a later one. Monica calls her friend who is going to pick up her in College Station, and tells her:
   A. I missed my plane, and I am going to arrive late.
   B. The plane left me behind, and I am going to arrive late.

2. David is a businessman, and he is carrying a briefcase full of many documents. Upon entering the elevator, David runs into another man, the briefcase falls and the documents spread out all over the floor. Which sentence best captures the situation?
   A. David dropped the briefcase.
   B. The briefcase fell from David's hand to the floor.

3. Mark is going on vacation with some friends for five days, and he brings $200. He has been spending a lot of money on food and drinks. On the third day, he has no money left. He plans on calling his Dad to ask him for more money. What will he say to his Dad?
   A. All my money is gone.
   B. I've spent too much and I ran out of money.

4. María is washing dishes when the phone rings. She goes to answer it, and in the process a glass is broken. Which sentence best captures the situation?
   A. A glass was broken while María was answering the telephone.
   B. María broke a glass while answering the telephone.

5. John is going out to Northgate, and he becomes intoxicated. A friend lets him stay at his apartment to sleep. The next day, John cannot find his keys. What would John say to his friend?
   A. I lost my keys.
   B. My keys are missing.

6. You and I are roommates and we are going to a concert in Houston. We leave College Station and arrive at the concert. You realize you do not have the tickets. What would you tell me?
   A. I forgot the tickets.
   B. The tickets were left at the house.

7. Laura is cooking when her kids come into the kitchen playing with a soccer ball. She gets angry and slams a plate on the kitchen table, and the plate breaks. Which sentence best captures the situation?
   A. A plate was broken while Laura was cooking.
   B. Laura broke a plate.

8. Mrs. Lawson is very busy with work, and she forgets to pay the cable bill. Two weeks later, when she gets home and turns on the television, there is no cable. Which sentence best captures the situation?
   A. The cable was turned off.
   B. Mrs. Lawson did not pay her bill and they turned off her cable.

9. Charlie and Rick are going to a party at some friends' house. It is the first time they will go to this house. Before the party, one of their friends gives them directions so they can find the house. Charlie asks Rick to bring the directions before they get into the car. When they get close to the neighborhood where the friends' house is located, Charlie asks Rick for the directions. Rick looks for them, and he doesn't have them. He says he's sorry, and tells him:
   A. I forgot the directions at home.
   B. The directions were left at home.

10. Richard is drinking a cup of coffee when a friend comes up behind him and scares him. The cup of coffee drops and spills. Which sentence best captures the situation?
   A. Richard dropped the coffee cup.
   B. The coffee cup fell.

11. Lisa is going shopping. As she gets out of the car, she leaves her keys in the car, and locks the door behind her. After shopping, she returns to her vehicle, and realizes that she has locked her keys in the car. Which sentence best captures the situation?
   A. The keys were locked in the car.
   B. Lisa locked her keys in the car.

12. Robert is playing outside in his front yard, and he climbs a tree. His friends distract him, and he falls and breaks his arm. Which sentence best captures the situation?

A. Robert's arm was broken when he fell out of the tree.
B. Robert broke his arm when he fell out of the tree.

13. The Millers have been out of town on vacation. When they return home, they find their telephone has been disconnected. Mr. Miller asks Mrs. Miller if she paid the bill. Mrs. Miller responds that she thought he said he was going to pay it. Which sentence best captures the situation?
    A. The Millers did not pay the bill and they disconnected the telephone.
    B. The telephone was disconnected.

14. Travis is making spaghetti. After he boils the pasta, he takes it to the sink to drain it. The steam from the pasta burns his hand, and he drops the pot, and the spaghetti spills into the sink. Which sentence best captures the situation?
    A. Travis spilled the spaghetti.
    B. The spaghetti was spilled.

15. Jack is traveling to Arizona on a bus. His friend is picking him up to give him a ride to the bus station. Jack's friend arrives, and as they leave Jack's house, Jack realizes he does not have his bus ticket. They return to Jack's house, and set out for the bus station again. Jack arrives at the station, and realizes he is running late. The bus company representative tells him that it is too late, and that he will have to wait for the next bus. Which sentence best captures the situation?
    A. Jack missed the bus.
    B. The bus left Jack behind.

16. Carl is working on his final papers for the semester, and has been printing a lot of pages. His last paper is 30 pages long, and he realizes he does not have enough paper left to print the document at his house. He decides to go to the school to print the document. Which sentence best captures the situation?
    A. There is not enough paper left to print the document.
    B. Carl ran out of paper.

Spanish

Por cada de las situaciones siguientes, escoja la oración que mejor contesta la pregunta según su punto de vista.

1. Monica se fue al D. F. para visitar a su novio. Por la mañana del día de su vuelo de regreso, ella no se despertó a tiempo y por eso llega tarde al aeropuerto. El agente le dice que ya es demasiado tarde para abordar y tendrá que tomar otro vuelo. Monica le llama a una amiga que la iba a recoger del aeropuerto y le dice:
    A. Perdí el avión y voy a llegar tarde.
    B. Me dejó el avión y voy a llegar tarde.

2. David es hombre de negocios y lleva un portafolio lleno de muchos documentos. Al entrar al ascensor, choca con otro hombre y el portafolio cae al suelo y los documentos se dispersan por todos lados. ¿Qué oración mejor capta lo que pasó?

    A. David dejó caer el portafolio.
    B. El portafolio se le cayó a David.

3. Marco se está pasando las vacaciones con algunos amigos por 5 días y trae $3000 pesos para los gastos. Él ha estado gastando mucho dinero por las bebidas y la comida. Al tercer día no le queda nada de dinero. Él piensa llamar a su papá para pedirle más dinero. ¿Qué le diría a su papá?
    A. Se me acabó el dinero.
    B. Gasté todo el dinero.

4. María está lavando los traste cuando suena el teléfono. Al irse para contestarlo se rompe un vaso. ¿Qué oración mejor capta lo que pasó?
    A. Se rompió un vaso mientras María contestaba el teléfono.
    B. María rompió un vaso mientras contestaba el teléfono.

5. Juan se va al jardín y se pone borracho. Un amigo lo deja quedarse con él en su departamento para dormir. Al día siguiente Juan no puede encontrar sus llaves. ¿Qué le diría Juan a su amigo?
    A. Se me perdieron las llaves.
    B. Perdí las llaves.

6. Tú y yo somos compañeros de casa y vamos a un concierto en el D. F. Salimos de Guanajuato y llegamos al concierto. Te das cuenta que no tienes los boletos para el concierto. ¿Qué me dirás?:
    A. Se me olvidaron los boletos en casa.
    B. Dejé los boletos en la casa.

7. Laura está cocinando cuando sus hijos entran a la cocina jugando con una pelota de fútbol. Laura se enoja y pone un plato muy fuertemente en la mesa y el plato se rompe. ¿Qué oración mejor capta lo que pasó?
    A. Se rompió un plato mientras Laura cocinaba.
    B. Laura rompió un plato mientras cocinaba.

8. La Señora Castro está muy ocupada con su trabajo y se le olvida pagar la cuenta del cable para la televisión. Dos semanas después, cuando llega a su casa, prende el televisor pero no hay cable. ¿Qué oración mejor capta lo que pasó?
    A. Se le olvidó pagar la cuenta y se le apagó el cable.
    B. La Sra. Castro no pagó su cuenta y por eso le cortaron el cable.

9. Jorge y Miguel se van a una fiesta en la casa de algunos amigos. Es la primera vez que van a esta casa. Antes de la fiesta, uno de sus amigos les da direcciones para que encuentren la casa. Jorge le dice a Miguel que traiga las direcciones antes de que suban al coche. Cuando llegan al vecindario donde se encuentra la casa, Jorge le pregunta a Miguel por las direcciones. Miguel las busca pero no las tiene. Le dice perdón y:
    A. Olvidé las direcciones en casa.
    B. Se me olvidaron las direcciones en casa.

10. Ricardo está tomando un café cuando se le acerca un amigo y lo asusta. Se le cae el café. ¿Qué oración mejor capta lo que pasó?
   A. Ricardo dejó caer el café.
   B. Se le cayó el café a Ricardo.

11. Luisa se va de compras. Al salir del coche ella cierra la puerta detrás de ella. Después de ir de compras, al regresar al coche, se da cuenta que las llaves están adentro del coche. ¿Qué oración mejor capta lo que pasó?
   A. Las llaves se quedaron en el coche.
   B. Luisa dejó las llaves dentro del coche.

12. Roberto, un niño de 10 años, está jugando afuera de su casa y sube a un árbol. Un amigo lo distrae y Roberto se cae y se le rompre un brazo. ¿Qué oración mejor capta lo que pasó?
   A. Se le rompió un brazo a Roberto cuando se cayó del árbol.
   B. Roberto se rompió el brazo al caer del árbol.

13. Los Ortiz han estado fuera por las vacaciones. Cuando regresan a casa se dan cuenta que se ha desconectado el teléfono. El Sr. Ortiz le pregunta a la Sra. Ortiz si ella pagó la cuenta. Ella dice que ella pensó que él iba a pagarla. ¿Qué oración mejor capta lo que pasó?
   A. Los Ortiz no pagaron la cuenta y por eso les desconectaron el teléfono.
   B. Se desconectó el teléfono.

14. Raul está cocinando espagueti. Después de hervir la pasta, la lleva al fregadero para escurrirla. El humo de la pasta le quema su mano y él deja caer la olla y el espagueti se tira al fregadero. ¿Qué oración mejor capta lo que pasó?
   A. Raul dejó caer el espagueti.
   B. Se le cayó el espagueti a Raul.

15. Carlos está viajando a Guadalajara en camión y ya compró su boleto en la agencia. Su amigo lo va a recoger para llevarle a la central. Su amigo llega a la casa para recogerlo y al salir de la ciudad, Carlos se da cuenta que no tiene su boleto. Regresan a la casa de Carlos por el boleto y salen otra vez para la central. Carlos llega a la central y el agente le dice que ya es demasiado tarde y que tendrá que salir en otro camión en una hora. ¿Qué oración mejor capta lo que pasó?
   A. Carlos perdió el camión.
   B. El camión se le fue a Carlos.

16. Antonio está terminando sus trabajos finales para el semestre y ha imprimido muchas hojas. El último trabajo es de 15 páginas y él se da cuenta que le va a faltar papel para imprimir todo el documento. Él decide imprimirlo en la universidad. ¿Qué oración mejor capta lo que pasó?
   A. No le queda suficiente papel a Antonio para imprimir el documento.
   B. Se le acabó el papel a Antonio.

19 Theory of Mind and bilingual cognition

Michael Siegal, Chiyoko Kobayashi Frank, Luca Surian, and Erland Hjelmquist

Possession of a 'Theory of Mind' (ToM) permits us to reason about the mental states of others—their beliefs, desires, and intentions—and to understand and anticipate how these can differ from our own and from reality. A lack of ToM would be a formidable obstacle to all sophisticated forms of human social interaction. Without the recognition that our beliefs and those of others can be true or false, it would very often be impossible to avoid misunderstandings and to overcome conflict or mistrust.

There has been a large surge in ToM research over the past 30 years. This work has extended to tests of ToM reasoning in individuals with autism (Peterson & Slaughter, 2009; Tager-Flusberg, 2007), in non-human primates (Penn, Holyoak, & Povinelli, 2008) and even in birds (Dally, Emery, & Clayton, 2010). However, the large majority of investigations of ToM reasoning have been concerned with children's understanding of false beliefs. These have often used a form of the 'Sally–Anne' task involving changed locations for hidden objects (Baron-Cohen, Leslie, & Frith, 1985). In the standard 'changed location' story task, children are told about Sally, a story character with a false belief about the location of a marble. The character is described as having placed the marble in a box but, while she is away, another story character called Anne moves it into a different location. The test question concerns where Sally—who has not witnessed the deceptive change of location and therefore has a false belief—will look for the marble. There are also 'changed contents' tasks in which a box that typically contains candies in reality contains objects such as pencils (Perner, Leekam, & Wimmer, 1987). The test question in this case concerns what the character with a false belief will think he or she will find in the box.

Such story-based measures require children to have an appreciable vocabulary and verbal comprehension abilities, and so it is not surprising that performance on false belief ToM tasks clearly improves with age. However, the extent to which children of different ages can be said to display ToM reasoning is controversial. One position is that, despite variations in culture and family background, most typically developing

4-year-olds respond correctly whereas most 3-year-olds do not (Callaghan et al., 2005). Nevertheless, there has been a range of studies indicating that children's responses to ToM test questions on changed location and changed contents tasks are influenced by linguistic and cultural factors that may accelerate or delay their performance on measures of ToM reasoning, though possibly not their underlying competence. Moreover, research has started to emerge suggesting that bilingual children who are exposed to two languages in the early years show advanced performance on ToM false belief tasks compared to their monolingual counterparts (Goetz, 2003; Kovács, 2009). Other research from the area of cognitive neuroscience has used fMRI to explore neural systems involved in bilinguals' performance on ToM tasks with the finding that individual patterns of brain activation on ToM reasoning tasks are associated with language/culture (Kobayashi, Glover, & Temple, 2006, 2007a, 2007b, 2008). In this chapter, on the basis of cognitive developmental and neuro-imaging studies, we examine accounts of changes with age in successful ToM task performance and how access to one or more languages may come to influence the ontogenesis of ToM, particularly in terms of the awareness that others' beliefs may be different from reality.

LANGUAGE AND ToM: TWO ACCOUNTS

At present, two main accounts have been proposed to characterize the origin and development of the expression of ToM reasoning in children. One is that ToM undergoes a fundamental conceptual change in the pre-school years (Perner et al., 1987; Wellman, Cross, & Watson, 2001)—a change that has been hypothesized by Milligan, Astington, and Dack (2007) to come about through the child's language development. The conceptual change or 'theory-theory' view is compatible with research indicating that performance change on false belief tasks between 3 and 4 years is linked to children's acquisition of words and semantics (Slade & Ruffman, 2005). In keeping with a conceptual change account, it has also been maintained that mastery of the grammatical rules for embedding tensed complement clauses under verbs of speech or cognition enables ToM reasoning (de Villiers & Pyers, 2002; Schick, de Villiers, de Villiers, & Hoffmeister, 2007). In embedded complements of this kind (e.g., 'Sally—who has a false belief—thinks that the marble is in the basket'), the truth value of the embedded clause (prefaced by 'that . . .') is independent of that of the main argument ('Sally thinks . . .').

It may be that acquisition of a certain level of semantics and syntax is necessary for success on standard story-based ToM reasoning tasks. Nevertheless, on current evidence, a link between understanding of sentence complements and ToM reasoning has not been established (Harris, de Rosnay, & Pons, 2005; Tardif, So, & Kaciroti, 2007). Young children are often proficient in the semantics and syntax of language but still do not respond correctly on ToM tasks. Many 3-year-olds who do poorly on such tasks are nevertheless able to produce and comprehend sentence complements that take the structure [person]-[pretends]-[that x] (e.g., 'He pretends that his puppy is outside').

The second main proposal is that ToM is present very early in development owing to a specialized module that allows children to compute and predict behavior based on an understanding of others' mental states. According to this account, the improvements in responses on ToM false belief tasks that occur around the age of 3–4 years can be explained with reference to various performance factors such as a strengthening of inhibitory processes and pragmatic skills. Leslie, Friedman, and German (2004) argue that success on false belief measures depends on a dedicated attentional mechanism for mental state reasoning termed a 'selection processor.' This mechanism involves general purpose 'executive functioning' (EF) abilities that enable children to inhibit the usual state of affairs in which a person's beliefs do correspond to reality and to recognize instead that beliefs may be false (for reviews of EF in children, see Garon, Bryson, & Smith, 2008; Zelazo, Carlson, & Kesek, 2008). Development of the selection processor mechanism underpins children's selection of the correct alternative on Sally–Anne type ToM tasks based on Sally's false belief about where the object that she has hidden is now located.

It is important to recognize that this analysis is based on a cognitive modularity framework rather than other conceptions of modularity. For instance, although Perner and Aichhorn (2008, p. 124) describe modularity theory as assuming that ToM is 'prespecified in a genetic code awaiting maturation', modules may not need their own sets of genes. As Barrett and Kurzban (2006) point out, there is a strong overlap between the genes that build arms and legs. The same logic applies to the construction of cognitive modules. According to this view, modularity can be best conceptualized in terms of a functional specialization that permits effective problem solving. This is in contrast to an earlier and perhaps more complex view (Fodor, 1983) that modules are 'encapsulated' and 'automatic' in so far as their information-processing properties are mandatory and are not influenced by outside information apart from their relevant 'bottom-up' inputs.

The functional specialization view is supported by evidence that, under certain conditions, even 3-year-olds can be enticed to reason successfully on Sally–Anne type changed location tasks. For example, as 3-year-olds are not yet advanced in their acquisition of pragmatics/discourse, they may interpret the test questions such as 'Where will Sally look for her marble?' that are characteristically used in many ToM tasks to mean, straightforwardly, 'Where should Sally go, or where must Sally go, in order to find the marble?' They may not recognize that the intended meaning of the test question is 'Where will Sally look first for the marble?' based on the desire of a speaker to determine what children know about false beliefs. For the most part, 3-year-olds in many cultures perform well when the test question is made explicit in this way (Bloom & German, 2000; Surian & Leslie, 1999; Yazdi, German, Defeyer, & Siegal, 2006). According to this account, by the age of 4 years children have achieved a pragmatic understanding founded on a developing selection processor that permits them to interpret non-explicit test questions correctly (e.g., 'Where will Sally look for the marble?' as 'Where will she look first?') and refrain from being guided by default strategies that compute the content of belief as corresponding to the actual state of affairs. In doing so, they can base their response on the proposition that a story character's belief about the location of an object may be false rather than true and inhibit the response that the character will look for the object in its real location. They then reveal a ToM competence that is actually present considerably earlier.

In recent support of this position, Onishi and Baillargeon (2005) have examined infants' performance on non-verbal looking tasks designed to examine differential attention to situations in which a false belief has been created in a person who has not been party to a deception. In these experiments even preverbal 15-month-olds display patterns of attention that appear to reflect expectations about the behavior of a person with a false belief. A rich interpretation of such results to suggest that infants possess the capacity for false belief understanding remains controversial (Perner & Ruffman, 2005). However, Onishi and Baillargeon's findings are in line with those from an increasing number of studies indicating that infants can indeed attribute true and false beliefs to others as indicated by infants' looking preference (Song & Baillargeon, 2008; Song, Onishi, Baillargeon, & Fisher, 2008; Southgate, Senju, & Csibra, 2007; Surian, Caldi, & Sperber, 2007) or communicative pointing gestures (Liszkowski, Carpenter, Striano, & Tomasello, 2006).

Whatever the preferred account, there seems little doubt that performance on story-based ToM tasks does depend on early experience in conversational exchanges which provides children with the insight that others have beliefs that can differ from reality. Evidence comes from research on ToM reasoning in deaf children with different language backgrounds. Deaf children with deaf parents acquire a sign language as their native language in the same way as hearing children acquire the spoken language of their parents (Petitto & Marentette, 1991). Deaf children in sign language environments have early opportunities to be exposed to conversations about the beliefs of others and to the way to formulate an understanding of how these can be false. Such children can be regarded as 'native signers' and often display ToM—both on standard verbally based story tasks and on 'thought-picture' tasks designed to minimize the need for verbal story comprehension—at the same time as hearing children (Courtin & Melot, 2005; Peterson & Siegal, 1999; Peterson, Wellman, & Liu, 2005; Remmel,

Bettger, & Weinberg, 2001; Siegal & Peterson, 2008; Woolfe, Want, & Siegal, 2002). By contrast, since deaf children of hearing parents are commonly not exposed to a language until they go to school, they do not have early opportunities for exposure to conversations about beliefs. These children have difficulties on ToM tasks that persist throughout childhood and even later in development. For example, Morgan and Kegl (2006) report that Nicaraguan deaf adults without early access to language show persistent difficulties on ToM thought-picture tasks although, as in previous studies (Marschark, Green, Hindmarsh, & Walker, 2000), they do display a good degree of proficiency on other measures of 'mentalizing' ability such as is involved in accurately characterizing the mental states of characters in cartoon stories. Other studies have been carried out in Sweden where there is legislation to provide deaf children with access to Swedish Sign Language from the age of 2 years. Even when provided with this early access, Swedish deaf children with hearing parents still show protracted difficulties on a range of ToM false belief tasks (Falkman, Roos, & Hjelmquist, 2007). These difficulties appear to be specific to the representation of false beliefs and do not generalize to other areas of cognitive development. Therefore research with deaf children is consistent with the view that some minimal exposure to conversation in very early communicative exchanges is necessary to trigger a core ToM understanding in young children (Siegal, 2008; Siegal & Peterson, 2008; Siegal & Varley, 2002).

ACCESS TO LANGUAGE AND CONVERSATION AND THE ORIGINS OF ToM

On this basis, it is conceivable that even preverbal infants profit through access to conversational input about beliefs and other mental states in order to express ToM, at least as shown on measures to date that have been designed to examine false belief understanding (Siegal, 2008). Preschoolers' ToM proficiency has often been linked to infants' and toddlers' exposure to mothers' talk about the mental states of others (Dunn & Brophy, 2005; Hughes & Leekam, 2004; Meins et al., 2002; Slaughter, Peterson, & Mackintosh, 2007). Thus the increase with age in children's performance on ToM measures involving understanding of false beliefs appears to reflect two processes. First, very early conversational input conveys to infants and children the notion that others have beliefs that may be false representations of reality. Second, the increase with age in ToM performance reflects a pragmatic development that enables children to inhibit a response based on a canonical situation where beliefs are a true representation of reality and to recognize instead that the test question refers to how a person with a false belief will be initially misled as to the location of an object.

Although both processes critically facilitate the expression of ToM, these are not sufficient to explain why children in different cultures apparently show variable performance on ToM tasks. One important consideration is that languages differ in the explicitness of verbs for which there is a connotation that a person's belief may be false. The degree of explicitness can lead children to judge that a story character will initially fail to retrieve a desired object because his or her actions will be misguided by a false belief. For example, in Chinese, the verbs *yiwei* or *dang* are more explicit and less neutral than *xiang* in implying that a belief may be false. When either *yiwei* or *dang* are used in ToM tasks, Chinese children answer more correctly than with *xiang* (Lee, Olson, & Torrance, 1999). Similar findings come from other languages in which there is lexical explicitness in verbs used in tests of children's false belief understanding such as Greek, Turkish and Puerto Rican Spanish (Maridaki-Kassotaki, Lewis, & Freeman, 2003; Shatz, Diesendruck, Martinez-Beck, & Akar, 2003). For example, in a recent study, Matsui, Rakoczy, Miura, and Tomasello (2009) compared 3-year-old Japanese-speaking children and German children on false belief measures. Japanese children were tested using grammaticalized particles of speaker (un)certainty, characteristic of everyday Japanese utterances, and German children were tested in their native language that does not have grammaticalized epistemic concepts. On such measures, Japanese children responded more accurately to explicit statements marked with the sentence final particle *yo* ('sure') that in Japanese connotes the certainty of a protagonist holding a false belief than when the sentence final particle *kana* that connotes uncertainty or 'maybe' was used. German children, in contrast, did not similarly profit from ungrammaticalized counterparts in German, i.e., *sicher* ('sure') and *vielleicht* ('maybe'). Matsui et al. interpret this result to reflect the need for Japanese children to process such marking routinely in their daily discourse—a practice not present in German.

Moreover, even if the verbs and particles used in the language of false belief tests are non-explicit as to the possibility that a person may hold a false belief, children's incorrect responses may not necessary reflect a lack of ToM competence. In extensive testing in Japan, Naito and Koyama (2006) have documented Japanese children's responses on ToM false belief tasks. They note that, in Japanese, *omou* is a belief verb that corresponds to the English verb 'think' and, unlike Chinese verbs, it has no connotation with beliefs as true or false. Compared to Western children, Japanese children were considerably delayed on false belief tests using *omou* and did not generally succeed until 6 or 7 years of age. Naito and Koyama point out that these responses might well reflect the attitudes of Japanese children rather than their ToM competence. In response to unfamiliar 'scholar-like' questions, children may strive toward the perceived expectation that an adult questioner would favor a realistic answer that is behaviorally correct. When asked to provide the justifications for the correct response that a protagonist with a false belief about the location of a person or an object would look in the initial location, children in Western countries commonly give internal justifications in terms of ignorance such as 'He thinks the object is still there' (Bartsch & Wellman, 1989; Wimmer & Mayringer, 1998). In stark contrast, Naito and Koyama report that many Japanese children justify their responses in terms of a simple descriptive statement such as 'The person (or object) was there first.' These results are compatible with longstanding findings (Kashima, Siegal, Tanaka, & Kashima, 1992; Kashima et al., 1995; see also Lillard, 1998; Vinden, 1999) that, in Japanese and several other non-Western societies compared to the West, individuals are less likely to be seen as agents acting as autonomous individuals rather than as members of group or community. While Western children may conceptualize ToM as being personal and intentional, non-Western children may conceptualize ToM as being mostly situational and constrained by group or community influences (Naito & Koyama, 2006).

BILINGUALISM AND ToM: EVIDENCE FROM COGNITIVE DEVELOPMENTAL RESEARCH

Given limitations in the interpretation of cross-linguistic and cross-cultural research on ToM in which false belief tasks are given in different cultures and languages, it is not surprising that a fully coherent account of bilinguals' performance on ToM tasks has remained elusive. To date, two studies with hearing children have appeared, suggesting tentatively that bilingual children are advanced in their ToM reasoning compared to monolingual children. In an initial investigation, Goetz (2003) gave Sally–Anne type tasks to three groups of children aged 3 and 4 years: English monolinguals, Mandarin Chinese monolinguals, and Mandarin–English bilinguals. The monolinguals were tested in their native language whereas the bilinguals were tested in both English and Mandarin Chinese in two sessions separated by a week interval with half tested in English first and Mandarin Chinese second and the remainder in the reverse order. An attempt to match different groups on socio-economic status was done by making sure that all children had at least one college-educated parent. The children who were bilingual in Mandarin and English outperformed either group of monolinguals on measures of their false belief reasoning and the level of their performance was similar in both languages. As Goetz observes, the advantage shown by bilinguals could be due to more advanced sociolinguistic interactions with interviewers, metalinguistic understanding, or inhibitory control, all of which have been seen to be advanced in bilingual children (see, for example, Bialystok & Martin, 2004; Bialystok & Senman, 2004; Carlson & Meltzoff, 2008; Cromdal, 1999; Martin-Rhee & Bialystok, 2008).

More recently, Kovács (2009) compared the performance of 3-year-olds who were either bilingual in Romanian and Hungarian or monolingual in Romanian. The bilingual children were tested in their language of instruction, with 17 receiving the tasks in Hungarian and the remaining 15 tested in Romanian. The 32 monolingual children were tested in their native Romanian. All children were given two ToM tasks. In a changed location task (Wimmer & Perner, 1983), they were told a story about a boy who puts his chocolate in a cupboard. When he leaves the room, his mother moves it into another cupboard. The test question was 'Where will the boy look for the chocolate when returning to the room?' Children were scored as answering correctly if they identified the false location and also gave correct answers to two memory questions: 'Where did the boy put the chocolate in the beginning?' and 'Where is the chocolate now?' They were also given a modified 'language-switching' ToM task that was structurally similar to the standard task. In this task the children were required to identify a false belief by taking account of story characters' understanding of different languages. In the story two characters, represented by a monolingual Romanian puppet and a bilingual Romanian–Hungarian puppet, are shown in the process of buying ice-cream. There are two 'stands', one selling ice-cream and the other selling sandwiches. The ice-cream vendor is portrayed as calling out to the characters in Hungarian that he no longer has ice-cream and that they should go to the sandwich stand. It was pointed out to the children that the Romanian monolingual character did not understand Hungarian and they were asked to respond to the question, 'Where will the monolingual (Romanian speaking) puppet go to buy ice-cream?'

Compared to the monolingual children, the bilinguals were significantly more successful on both ToM tasks. However, this result should be considered with caution. On the standard task 59% of the 32 bilinguals were correct compared to only 25% of the 32 monolinguals. Comparable percentages on the modified task were 47% and 19%. Thus in either case, although individual bilingual children may have been advanced in their ToM performance, the bilinguals as a group performed no better than at a 50% level that would be expected by chance. There was also no specific information on the social class background of the children in terms, for example, of years of parental education, that has been shown to influence differences between bilingual and monolingual children on cognitive measures (Morton & Harper, 2007), and no information on the bilinguals' actual proficiency in their two languages and how this influenced their task performance. As in the Goetz study, again there was no actual measure of inhibition or other executive functioning measures given to the children.

Further evidence on bilingualism and ToM comes from an investigation of deaf children in Estonia, Italy, and Sweden (Meristo et al., 2007). This study sought to examine the effects of bilingualism in a spoken and sign language in the performance of deaf children aged 4 to 16 years on a range of ToM and related mentalizing tasks. With similar home language environments, bilingually instructed native signers who had access to both sign and spoken language as the medium of instruction outperformed those instructed in oralist schools where access to a sign language is absent. This result indicates that the expression of ToM, as well as related aspects of mentalizing such as emotion understanding, may also depend on native-signing deaf children's continuing exposure to a sign language, and that the expression of ToM in native signers may be maintained through practice and automatization specifically in a bilingual environment where they have access to their native language both at home and school. Under these circumstances, children may have optimal opportunities for monitoring the nature of conversational input about mental states and its implications for evaluating beliefs and other mental states as true or false.

In a follow-up study, Meristo and Hjelmquist (2009) sought to investigate the relation of memory and executive functioning to deaf children's performance on ToM tasks. Deaf, native-signing children and late-signing children, either bilingually or orally instructed, from Experiment 2 in Meristo et al.'s investigation were given a range of measures. These included (1) a backward digit span task, (2) a Corsi block task involving visuo-spatial memory in which the child is required to repeat pointing to a series of blocks in the same sequence as that demonstrated by an experimenter, (3) the Wisconsin Card Sorting Task (WCST) in which the task is to follow a rule in sorting a series of cards by color (or shape) and to switch when the rule is changed to one that involves sorting by shape (or color), and (4) a go–no-go and conflict task. For go–no-go, the child was told to press a button on the keyboard when presented with two squares on a computer screen and not to press when presented with one square. For conflict, the child was told to press once when presented with two squares on the screen and twice when presented with one square.

In contrast to the significant difference in ToM performance that favored the early signers in a bilingual instruction environment, there were no consistent differences between the groups of children on these four tests. This pattern is similar to that reported by Woolfe et al. (2002) who found no differences between early and late signers on a child-adapted version of the WCST. Across groups, digit span correlated significantly with ToM but, when chronological age and mental age were partialed out, there were no significant correlations between ToM scores and performance on the Corsi blocks or WCST, or accuracy in the go–no-go and conflict task.

In related research with hearing children, Siegal, Iozzi, and Surian (2009) sought to examine the relation of executive functioning to the ability of bilingual and monolingual children in recognizing appropriate responses in conversation—an ability that has been seen to be closely related to performance on ToM tasks as it relies on identifying a speaker's intentions and beliefs (Siegal & Surian, 2007). Two groups of children from the Italian–Slovenian border area near Trieste were tested in Italian: One group was monolingual in Italian and the other bilingual in Slovenian (L1) and Italian (L2). The children were given two executive functioning measures. As in Woolfe et al. (2002) and Meristo and Hjelmquist (2009), one of these was a child-adapted version of the WCST. The other was the Day–Night Task (Gerstadt, Hong, & Diamond, 1994). On this measure, children are shown pictures of a sun and a moon and are required to respond 'day' when they see a moon picture and 'night' when they see a sun picture. The children also received a Conversational Violations Test (CVT) based on Grice's (1989) proposal that appreciation of certain conversational maxims provides the foundation for pragmatic competence. These maxims enjoin speakers to 'say no more or no less than is required for the purpose of the (talk) exchange' (maxims of 'quantity'), 'tell the truth and avoid statements for which there is insufficient evidence' (maxims of 'quality'), 'be relevant' (maxim of 'relation'), and 'avoid ambiguity, confusion, and obscurity' (maxims of 'manner'). Using a laptop computer, children were shown a DVD in which short conversational exchanges were staged by three doll speakers, one male and two female. For each episode, one of the two female speakers asked a question to the other two speakers who each gave a short answer. One answer violated a conversational maxim and the other did not (see examples in Figure 19.1). The children were asked to 'point to the doll that said something silly or rude'.

It is well documented that bilingual children are often delayed in vocabulary comprehension in their individual languages compared to monolinguals, though not necessarily in total vocabulary (Bialystok, Luk, Petts, & Yang, in press). Despite delay in their L2 vocabulary development, children who were bilingual in Italian and Slovenian (with Slovenian as the dominant language L1 spoken at home) generally outperformed those who were monolingual in either Italian or Slovenian on utterances that violated the maxims of quantity, quality, relation, and politeness with five items for each type of maxim violation. However, there was no significant relation between the executive functioning measures and performance on the Conversational Violations Test. Very similar findings have come from studies carried out in Italian with children bilingual in German and Italian compared to Italian monolinguals and with children bilingual in English and Japanese compared to Japanese monolinguals (Siegal et al., 2009, 2010). In the latter case, bilingual children were tested in both English and Japanese and displayed a similar advantage on the CVT.

In both the Meristo and Hjelmquist (2009) and Siegal et al. (2009, 2010) studies there was a tendency for a ceiling effect on the executive functioning measures. Most children performed at a high level that may have precluded finding a significant difference between bilingual and monolingual groups. Nevertheless, as previously mentioned, using a broader range of executive functioning measures with both children and adults, it has often been reported that bilingual children outperform their monolingual counterparts. One suggestion is that the flexibility in attention and

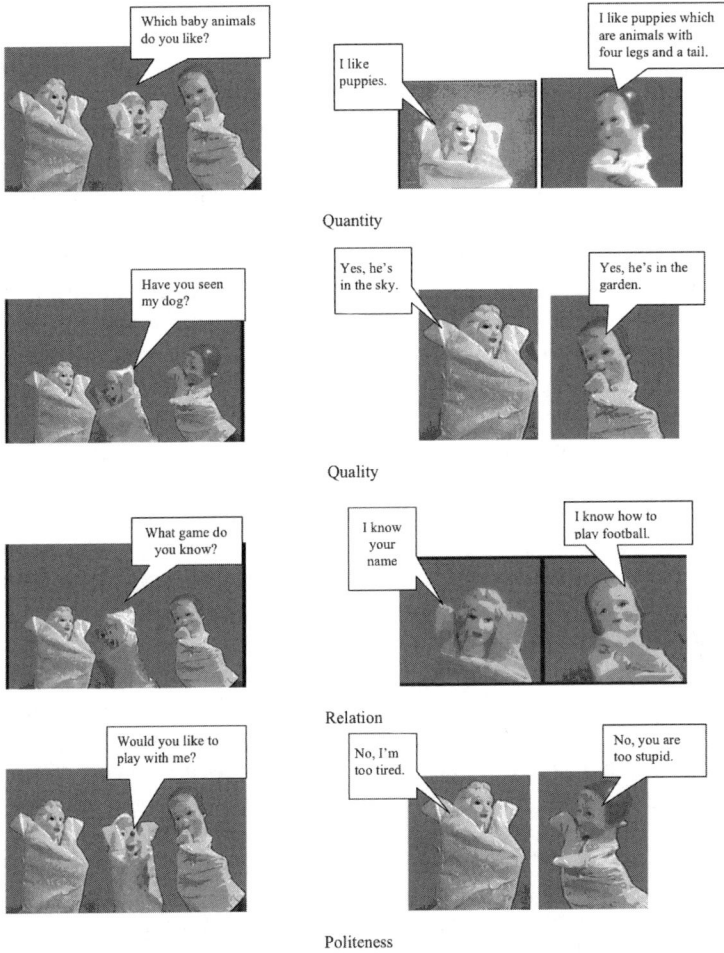

Figure 19.1 Examples of items in the quantity, quality, relation, and politeness maxim components of the Conversational Violations Test (Siegal et al., 2009, 2010) in English translation selected from those given to children in Italian/Slovenian/Japanese.

inhibition that accounts for a bilingual advantage on ToM and related measures may not be easily tapped by heterogeneous executive functioning but may be investigated, for example, with specifically language-based measures of response inhibition and reaction time (German & Hehman, 2006; Mäntylä, Carelli, & Forman, 2007). These may involve language-switching tasks aimed to determine the extent to which bilinguals are balanced in their language proficiency—tasks that provide a measure of whether the switch to a first language is inhibited by the effect needed to process in a second language (see Philipp & Koch, 2009).

ToM AND BILINGUALISM: EVIDENCE
FROM NEUROIMAGING

An important direction for research on bilingualism and ToM is in neuro-imaging. As age of exposure, age of acquisition, and degree of proficiency are all liable to contribute to the effects of bilingualism in cognitive and neuroimaging research, investigation of such effects requires comparisons of persons who have acquired two languages early or who have acquired one of their languages later in their development (Birdsong, 2006). In this connection, there is a need to separate linguistic effects from those that pertain specifically to culture (Han & Northoff, 2008).

According to Ervin and Osgood (1954), an individual who as a child has acquired two languages in the same context such as in the home with his or her parents can be seen to have one representation for a verbal label and its translation equivalent. This would be a case of 'compound bilingualism'. An individual who acquires a second language in a different context has a distinct representation for each language. This would be a case of 'coordinate bilingualism'. Usually, compound bilinguals acquire their languages simultaneously while coordinate bilinguals acquire theirs consecutively, and coordinates are often weaker in their second language than are compound bilinguals.

This analysis is compatible with both findings from research on bilingual cognition and neuroimaging. Ji, Zhang, and Nisbett (2004) investigated whether attributes are categorized in terms of a thematic relationship between objects based on time, space, or causality or in terms of a taxonomic categorization based on perceptual similarities. For example, if given three items such as 'seagull', 'squirrel', and 'tree', a thematic categorization would be to place squirrel and tree together whereas to place seagull and squirrel together would be to categorize taxonomically. Ji et al. found that bilingual Chinese who learned Chinese and English as compound bilinguals categorize objects in a more thematic way than do European Americans regardless of the language in which they are tested. However, the categorizations of Chinese who learned Chinese and English as coordinate bilinguals were more thematic when tested in Chinese than in English. Converging support for the distinction between the two types of bilinguals from neuroimaging has shown that, for bilinguals who are exposed to two languages simultaneously as young children, both languages are represented in common cortical regions. By contrast, for late bilinguals who acquired their second language as adults, native and second languages activate spatially separate regions (Hernandez & Li, 2007; Kim, Relkin, Lee, & Hirsch, 1997; Ullman, 2001). These findings suggest that type of bilingualism (compound vs coordinate) can influence important aspects of cognition such as categorization.

As already noted, considerable evidence indicates that conversational input contributes to the triggering of ToM reasoning, at least as shown on story-based tasks. Does activation associated with ToM reasoning in bilinguals correspond to a pattern in which similar responses on cognitive tasks and common regions of activation are shown for early bilinguals, regardless of the language of testing, and a dissimilar response pattern and separate regions of activation for late bilinguals?

In a recent series of studies, Kobayashi et al. (2006, 2007a, 2007b, 2008) examined the effects of language and culture on ToM reasoning and its neural substrates. Their bilingual adult participants had Japanese as their first language and had acquired English as a second language after the age of 15. They thus could be regarded as coordinate bilinguals. The bilingual child participants were aged between 8 and 12 years. They had acquired Japanese and English simultaneously before the age of 5 and spoke Japanese as their L1 and English as their L2. They thus could be regarded as compound bilinguals. These groups were compared to monolingual English-speaking American children and adults on 'second-order' ToM tasks that were more complex than first-order 'Sally–Anne' tasks in that these involved responses to a story character who is thinking about what another story character is thinking. For example, 'Anne, Bob and Cathy play a hiding game. Bob and Cathy watch while Anne hides a marble inside a red can. When Cathy is not watching, Anne takes a marble out of the red can. Then Anne hides the marble in a green can' (test question: 'Bob thinks that Cathy thinks that the marble is . . . A. in the red can. B. in the green can'). These second-order tasks were given to the bilingual groups in a text-based version in Japanese and to both American English-speaking monolinguals and bilinguals in Japanese and English in a text-based English version as well as in a cartoon-based version.

Both Japanese and American groups activated a set of brain regions that have been repeatedly implicated in previous ToM imaging literature such as the medial prefrontal cortex (mPFC) and anterior cingulate cortex (Kobayashi et al., 2006). However, there were also differences in the ToM task-specific brain activity between the two groups in several regions, most notably in the temporoparietal junction (TPJ) in that there was significantly greater TPJ-specific activation in the American monolingual children than in the Japanese bilingual children (Kobayashi et al., 2007b). Moreover, in a comparison of the responses of bilingual Japanese children to stories presented in their L1 and L2, ToM-related activity converged in the mPFC (Kobayashi et al., 2008). This finding is consistent with the commonality found for early bilinguals in brain activation regardless of the language in which the experimental stimuli are presented. For Japanese adults who were late bilinguals, there was convergence of neural activation that included the TPJ region, but only at a lenient threshold of significance.

The TPJ area has been implicated in recent ToM imaging studies (Kobayashi et al., 2007a; Saxe & Kanwisher, 2003; Saxe & Wexler, 2005).

Increasing evidence indicates that a key function of the TPJ is to distinguish self-agency from other-agency (Blakemore & Frith, 2003; Decety & Grézes, 2006; Jackson & Decety, 2004). Compared to people in Western cultures, Japanese and other Asians may display a greater ability to recognize the perspective and influence of others on an individual's behavior (Cohen & Gunz, 2002; Wu & Keysar, 2007). As we have noted in relation to Naito and Koyama's findings discussed above, Japanese may make less distinction between the self and others than do people in Western cultures and be more likely to embrace the conception of a relational or interdependent self (Kashima et al., 1992, 1995; Markus & Kitayama, 1991). In this respect, greater overlap in the activation in mPFC has consistently been implicated in self-referential processing (Ochsner et al., 2004, 2005), and was evident when Chinese participants judged self-related and intimate other-related adjectives in comparison to Americans (Zhu, Zhang, Fan, & Han, 2007). Similarly, in Kobayashi et al. (2007a), stronger right mPFC activity in Japanese–English bilingual children than English monolingual children was found during the English story condition. In contrast, stronger right TPJ activity was found in English-speaking American monolingual children than Japanese–English bilingual children during the cartoon condition. Thus, to process second-order ToM tasks that require a consideration of a story character's desires and beliefs, it is possible that Japanese and other Asians employ greater self-reflection than American children who focus more on agency detection that has been suggested as a primary function of TPJ (Blakemore & Frith, 2003; Decety & Grézes, 2006; Jackson & Decety, 2004).

In addition, Kobayashi et al. (2008) found that neural representation of ToM in bilingual children who had acquired their two languages early and simultaneously is more circumscribed in the mPFC than that in adults who had acquired their second language after childhood. This is consistent with the previous results indicating a positive relation between age of acquisition and the degree of separation between the neural correlates of L1 and L2. The finding of age differences in the pattern of mPFC activation is also consistent with the recent proposal that the mPFC plays a role in the recruitment of executive functions in ToM-related tasks that involve responses to social and affective stimuli (Harris, McClure, van den Bos, Cohen, & Fiske, 2007). In second-order ToM tasks there is the need to inhibit not only the first story character's mental state, but also that of the second character which is doubly embedded in the story. Such tasks may require more inhibitory executive control for children than for adults. In this respect, resources such as executive functioning and syntax may be seen as systems that are recruited or 'co-opted' by a core ToM processing system to compute accurate responses (Siegal & Varley, 2002, 2006).

CONCLUSIONS

Research to date on bilingualism and ToM has been largely limited to 'first-order' false belief tasks in a Sally–Anne format. There is a need to extend findings to research on other types of more subtle and complex, first- and second-order tasks (Miller, 2009; Rutherford, 2004). Beyond the more specific definition of ToM in terms of false belief understanding, a related and still largely uninvestigated issue is whether children with bilingual exposure in various languages are advantaged compared to monolinguals in their word learning or language learning more generally because of their enhanced understanding of speaker intentions based on a sophisticated conception of other minds.

Given the few results so far that have shown bilingualism to have a positive effect on first-order ToM reasoning, it seems premature to claim that bilingualism confers a ToM advantage, at least in terms of children's performance on first-order false belief tasks involving changed locations and changed contents. The studies of Kobayashi and her colleagues represent an initial effort to dissociate universal from culturally variant components of ToM but, in contrast to the abundant studies in adults, data from brain-imaging studies of ToM in children are still scarce. As biological underpinnings are clearly necessary but not sufficient for the expression of ToM reasoning, new cognitive and neuro-developmental evidence is required to advance a model of ToM that accounts for continuity, universality, and linguistic/cultural effects. To establish the specific effects of bilingualism on the neural correlates of ToM as it has been investigated on second-order tasks requires further research to compare early and late bilinguals of the same age. As in Ji et al.'s research that involved Chinese on the mainland, Hong Kong, Singapore, and Taiwan, there is a need also to compare bilinguals who have learned their languages in different contexts.

In any event, although Perner and Aichhorn (2008) claim, for example, that the Kobayashi et al. results are inconsistent with a modular account owing to differences in ToM-related brain activity that are related to culture and language, this sort of argument does not undermine a cleanly defined 'functional specificity' view of cognitive modularity in which spatial discreteness—the notion that a given mechanism is located in a particular area of the brain—is unnecessary (Barrett & Kurzban, 2006). That functions can occur and develop in more than one brain location, apparently in response to cultural and linguistic inputs, does not falsify the claim that there exists in humans a core modular ToM system that is function-specific, universal, and present early in development. Since results of a further conjunction analysis by Kobayashi (2008) do indicate significant overlap between Japanese bilingual and American monolingual children and adults in the prefrontal cortex and the TPJ for ToM-specific brain activity, it can still be maintained that the 'core' component of

ToM may indeed be universal and relatively unchanging throughout development.

Nevertheless, even if there may ultimately be seen to be no direct, specific link between bilingualism and first-order or even second-order ToM, it is reasonable to expect that bilingualism can influence how ToM can be used in conversational understanding in terms of a recognition of what it means to communicate effectively through a mechanism that involves enhanced executive functioning and inhibitory control. As Scholl and Leslie (1999) point out, specific beliefs may differ across language and culture, though not the core concept that a belief may be true or false. Even though a universal core to ToM may be present early in life in terms of first-order false belief understanding following exposure to conversation with others, the proficient expression of first- and second-order ToM reasoning and the adoption of specific beliefs and attitudes often vary cross-culturally and cross-linguistically. For bilinguals, the use of ToM reasoning may be linked to the contexts in which languages are simultaneously or consecutively acquired. Performance on ToM tasks can also be influenced by explicitness in pragmatics and verb semantics in mental state discourse concerning the possibility that persons may hold false beliefs.

ACKNOWLEDGMENTS

This chapter was prepared with support from an EU 6th Framework Marie Curie Chair (Project ALACODE—Contract MEXC-CT-2005-024061), and grants from the Fondazione Benefica Kathleen Foreman-Casali, the Italian Ministry of Education FIRB and PRIN programs, and the Swedish Council for Working Life and Social Research.

REFERENCES

Baron-Cohen, S., Leslie, A., & Frith, U. (1985). Does the autistic child have a 'Theory of Mind'? *Cognition, 21,* 37–46.

Barrett, H. C., & Kurzban, R. (2006). Modularity in cognition: Framing the debate. *Psychological Review, 113,* 628–647.

Bartsch, K., & Wellman, H. (1989). Young children's attribution of action to beliefs and desires. *Child Development, 60,* 946–964.

Bialystok, E., Luk, G., Petts, K. F., & Yang, S. (in press). Receptive vocabulary differences in monolingual and bilingual children. *Bilingualism: Language and Cognition.*

Bialystok, E., & Martin, M. (2004). Attention and inhibition in bilingual children: Evidence from the dimensional change card sort task. *Developmental Science, 7,* 325–339.

Bialystok, E., & Senman, L. (2004). Executive processes in appearance–reality tasks: The role of inhibition of attention and symbolic representation. *Child Development, 75,* 562–579.

Birdsong, D. (2006). Age and second language acquisition: An overview. In M. Gullberg & P. Indefrey (Eds.), *The cognitive neuroscience of second language acquisition* (pp. 9–49). Malden, MA: Blackwell.

Blakemore, S-J., & Frith, C. D. (2003). Self-awareness and action. *Current Opinion in Neurobiology, 13,* 219–224.

Bloom, P., & German, T. P. (2000). Two reasons to abandon the false belief task as a test of Theory of Mind. *Cognition, 77*(1), B25–B31.

Callaghan, T. C., Rochat, P., Lillard, A., Claux, M. L., Odden, H., Itakura, S., et al. (2005). Synchrony in the onset of mental-state reasoning. *Psychological Science, 16,* 378–384.

Carlson, S. M., & Meltzoff, A. N. (2008). Bilingual experience and executive functioning in young children. *Developmental Science, 11,* 282–298.

Cohen, D., & Gunz, A. (2002). As seen by the other . . .: Perspectives on the self in the memories and emotional perceptions of Easterners and Westerners. *Psychological Science, 13,* 55–59.

Courtin, C., & Melot, A-M. (2005). Metacognitive development of deaf children: Lessons from the appearance–reality and false belief tasks. *Developmental Science, 8,* 16–25.

Cromdal, J. (1999). Childhood bilingualism and metalinguistic skills: Analysis and control in young Swedish–English bilinguals. *Applied Psycholinguistics, 20,* 1–20.

Dally, J. M., Emery, N. J., & Clayton, N. S. (2010). Avian Theory of Mind and counter espionage by food-caching western scrub-jays (*Aphelocoma californica*). *European Journal of Developmental Psychology, 7,* 17–37.

de Villiers, J. G., & Pyers, J. E. (2002). Complements to cognition: A longitudinal study of the relationship between complex syntax and false-belief understanding. *Cognitive Development, 17,* 1037–1060.

Decety, J., & Grézes, J. (2006). The power of simulation: Imaging one's own and other's behavior. *Brain Research, 1079,* 4–14.

Dunn, J., & Brophy, M. (2005). Communication relationships and individual differences in children's understanding of mind. In J. W. Astington & J. A. Baird (Eds.), *Why language matters for Theory of Mind* (pp. 50–69). New York: Oxford University Press.

Ervin, S. M., & Osgood, C. E. (1954). Second language learning and bilingualism. *Journal of Abnormal and Social Psychology, 49,* 139–146.

Falkman, K., Roos, C., & Hjelmquist, E. (2007). Mentalizing skills of non-native, early signers: A longitudinal perspective. *European Journal of Developmental Psychology, 4,* 178–197.

Fodor, J. A. (1983). *The modularity of mind.* Cambridge, MA: Bradford/MIT Press.

Garon, N., Bryson, S. E., & Smith, I. M. (2008). Executive function in preschoolers: A review using an integrative framework. *Psychological Bulletin, 134,* 31–60.

German, T. P., & Hehman, J. A. (2006). Representational and executive selection resources in 'Theory of Mind': Evidence from compromised belief–desire reasoning in old age. *Cognition, 101,* 129–152.

Gerstadt, C., Hong, Y. J., & Diamond, A. (1994). The relationship between cognition and action: Performance of children 3.5–7 years old on a Stroop-like day–night task. *Cognition, 53,* 129–153.

Goetz, P. J. (2003). The effects of bilingualism on Theory of Mind development. *Bilingualism: Language and Cognition, 6,* 1–15.

Grice, H. P. (1989). *Studies in the way of words.* Cambridge, MA: Harvard University Press.

Han, S., & Northoff, G. (2008). Culture-sensitive neural substrates of human cognition: A transcultural neuroimaging approach. *Nature Reviews Neuroscience, 9,* 646–654.

Harris, L. T., McClure, S., van den Bos, W., Cohen, J., & Fiske, S. T. (2007). Regions of MPFC differentially tuned to social and nonsocial affective evaluation. *Cognitive, Affective, & Behavioral Neuroscience, 7,* 309–316.

Harris, P. L., de Rosnay, M., & Pons, F. (2005). Language and children's understanding of mental states. *Current Directions in Psychological Science, 14,* 69–73.

Hernandez, A. E., & Li, P. (2007). Age of acquisition: Its neural and computational mechanisms. *Psychological Bulletin, 133,* 638–650.

Hughes, C., & Leekam, S. (2004). What are the links between Theory of Mind and social relations? Review, reflections and new directions for studies of typical and atypical development. *Social Development, 13,* 590–619.

Jackson, P. L., & Decety, J. (2004). Motor cognition: A new paradigm to study self–other interactions. *Current Opinion in Neurobiology, 14,* 259–263.

Ji, L. J., Zhang, Z., & Nisbett, R. E, (2004). Is it language or is it culture? Examination of language effects in cross-cultural research on categorization. *Journal of Personality and Social Psychology, 87,* 57–65.

Kashima, Y., Siegal, M., Tanaka, K., & Kashima, E. S. (1992). Do people believe that attitudes are consistent with behavior? Towards a cultural psychology of attribution processes. *British Journal of Social Psychology, 31,* 111–124.

Kashima, Y., Yamaguchi, S., Kim, U., Choi, S-C., Gelfand, M. J., & Yuki, M. (1995). Culture, gender, and self: A perspective from individualism–collectivism research. *Journal of Personality and Social Psychology, 69,* 925–937.

Kim, K., Relkin, N., Lee, K., & Hirsch, J. (1997). Distinct cortical areas associated with native and second languages. *Nature, 388,* 171–174.

Kobayashi, C. (2008). *Language and thought: Cultural and linguistic influence on developmental neural bases of Theory of Mind.* Saarbrücken, Germany: VDM Verlag.

Kobayashi, C., Glover, G. H., & Temple, E. (2006). Cultural and linguistic influence on neural bases of 'Theory of Mind': An fMRI study with Japanese bilinguals. *Brain and Language, 98,* 210–220.

Kobayashi, C., Glover, G. H., & Temple, E. (2007a). Children's and adults' neural bases of verbal and nonverbal 'Theory of Mind'. *Neuropsychologia, 45,* 1522–1532.

Kobayashi, C., Glover, G. H., & Temple, E. (2007b). Cultural and linguistic effects on neural bases of 'Theory of Mind' in American and Japanese children. *Brain Research, 1164,* 95–107.

Kobayashi, C., Glover, G. H., & Temple, E. (2008). Switching language switches mind: Linguistic effects on developmental neural bases of 'Theory of Mind'. *Social, Cognitive, and Affective Neuroscience, 3,* 62–70.

Kovács, Á. M. (2009). Early bilingualism enhances mechanisms of false belief reasoning. *Developmental Science, 12,* 48–54.

Lee, K., Olson, D. R., & Torrance, N. (1999). Chinese children's understanding of false beliefs: The role of language. *Journal of Child Language, 26,* 1–21

Leslie, A. M., Friedman, O., & German, T. P. (2004). Core mechanisms in 'Theory of Mind'. *Trends in Cognitive Sciences, 8,* 528–33.

Lillard, A. (1998). Ethnopsychologies: Cultural variations in theories of mind. *Psychological Bulletin, 123,* 3–32.

Liszkowski, U., Carpenter, M., Striano, T., & Tomasello, M. (2006). 12- and 18-month-olds point to provide information for others. *Journal of Cognition and Development, 7,* 173–187.

Mäntylä, T., Carelli, M. G., & Forman, H. (2007). Time monitoring and executive functioning in children and adults. *Journal of Experimental Child Psychology, 96,* 1–19.

Maridaki-Kassotaki, K., Lewis, C., & Freeman, N. H. (2003). Lexical choice can lead to problems: What false belief tests tell us about Greek alternative verbs of agency. *Journal of Child Language, 30,* 1–20.

Markus, H. R., & Kitayama, S. (1991). Culture and the self: Implications for cognition, emotion, and motivation. *Psychological Review, 98,* 224–253.

Marschark, M., Green, V., Hindmarsh, G., & Walker, S. (2000). Understanding Theory of Mind in children who are deaf. *Journal of Child Psychology and Psychiatry, 41,* 1067–1073.

Martin-Rhee, M. M., & Bialystok, E. (2008). The development of two types of inhibitory control in monolingual and bilingual children. *Bilingualism: Language and Cognition, 11,* 81–93.

Matsui, T., Rakoczy, H., Miura, Y., & Tomasello, M. (2009). Understanding of speaker certainty and false-belief reasoning: A comparison of Japanese and German preschoolers. *Developmental Science, 12,* 602–613.

Meins, E., Fernyhough, C., Wainwright, R., Gupta, M., Fradley, E., & Tuckey, M. (2002). Maternal mind-mindedness and attachment security as predictors of Theory of Mind understanding. *Child Development, 73,* 1715–1726.

Meristo, M., Falkman, K. W., Hjelmquist, E., Tedoldi, M., Surian, L., & Siegal, M. (2007). Language access and Theory of Mind reasoning: Evidence from deaf children in bilingual and oralist environments. *Developmental Psychology, 43,* 1156–1169.

Meristo, M., & Hjelmquist, E. (2009). Executive functions and theory-of-mind among deaf children—different routes to understanding other minds? *Journal of Cognition and Development, 10,* 67–91.

Miller, S. A. (2009). Children's understanding of second-order mental states. *Psychological Bulletin, 135,* 749–773.

Milligan, K., Astington, J. W., & Dack, L. A. (2007). Language and Theory of Mind: Meta-analysis of the relation between language ability and false-belief understanding. *Child Development, 78,* 622–646.

Morgan, G., & Kegl, J. (2006). Nicaraguan Sign Language and Theory of Mind: The issue of critical periods and abilities. *Journal of Child Psychology and Psychiatry, 47,* 811–819.

Morton, J. B., & Harper, S. N. (2007). What did Simon say? Revisiting the bilingual advantage. *Developmental Science, 10,* 719–726.

Naito, M., & Koyama, K. (2006). The development of false-belief understanding in Japanese children: Delay and difference? *International Journal of Behavioral Development, 30,* 290–304.

Ochsner, K. N., Beer, J. S., Robertson, E. R., Cooper, J. C., Gabrieli, J. D. E., Kihsltrom, J. F., & D'Esposito, M. (2005). The neural correlates of direct and reflected self-knowledge. *Neuroimage, 28*, 797–814.

Ochsner, K. N., Kieran, K., Ludlow, D. H., Hanelin, J., Ramachandran, T., Glover, G., et al. (2004). Reflecting upon feelings: An fMRI study of neural systems supporting the attribution of emotion to self and other. *Journal of Cognitive Neuroscience, 16*(10), 1746–1772.

Onishi, K. H., & Baillargeon, R. (2005). Do 15-month-old infants understand false beliefs? *Science, 308*, 255–258.

Penn, D. C., Holyoak, K. J., & Povinelli, D. J. (2008). Darwin's mistake: Explaining the discontinuity between human and nonhuman minds. *Brain and Behavioral Sciences, 31*, 109–178.

Perner, J., & Aichhorn, M. (2008). Theory of Mind, language and the temporoparietal junction mystery. *Trends in Cognitive Sciences, 12*, 123–126.

Perner, J., Leekam, S., & Wimmer, H. (1987). Three-year-olds' difficulty with false belief: The case for a conceptual deficit. *British Journal of Developmental Psychology, 5*, 125–137.

Perner, J., & Ruffman, T. (2005). Infants' insight into the mind: How deep? *Science, 308*, 214–216.

Peterson, C. C., & Siegal, M. (1999). Representing inner worlds: Theory of Mind in autistic, deaf, and normal hearing children. *Psychological Science, 10*, 126–129.

Peterson, C. C., & Slaughter, V. (2009). Eye reading and false belief understanding in children with autism, deafness or typical development. *Research in Autism Spectrum Disorders, 3*, 462–473.

Peterson, C. C., Wellman, H. M., & Liu, D. (2005). Steps in theory-of-mind development for children with deafness or autism. *Child Development, 76*, 502–517.

Petitto, L. A., & Marentette, P. F. (1991). Babbling in the manual mode: Evidence for the ontogeny of language. *Science, 251*, 1493–1496.

Philipp, A. M., & Koch, I. (2009). Inhibition in language switching: What is inhibited when switching between languages in naming tasks? *Journal of Experimental Psychology, 35*, 1187–1195.

Remmel, E., Bettger, J. G., & Weinberg, A. M. (2001). Theory of Mind development in deaf children. In M. D. Clark, M. Marschark, & M. Karchmer (Eds.), *Context, cognition, and deafness* (pp. 113–134). Washington, DC: Gallaudet University Press.

Rutherford, M. D. (2004). The effect of social role on Theory of Mind reasoning. *British Journal of Psychology, 95*, 1–13.

Saxe, R., & Kanwisher, N. (2003). People thinking about thinking people: The role of the temporo-parietal junction in 'Theory of Mind.' *Neuroimage, 19*, 1835–1842.

Saxe, R., & Wexler, A. (2005). Making sense of another mind: The role of the right temporo-parietal junction. *Neuropsychologia, 43*, 1391–1399.

Schick, B., de Villiers, P., de Villiers, J., & Hoffmeister, R. (2007). Language and Theory of Mind: A study of deaf children. *Child Development, 78*, 376–396.

Scholl, B. J., & Leslie, A. M. (1999) Modularity, development and 'Theory of Mind.' *Mind and Language, 14*, 131–153.

Shatz, M., Diesendruck, G., Martinez-Beck, I., & Akar, D. (2003). The influence of language and socioeconomic status on children's understanding of false belief. *Developmental Psychology, 39*, 717–729.

Siegal, M. (2008). *Marvelous minds: The discovery of what children know*. New York: Oxford University Press.

Siegal, M., Iozzi, L., & Surian, L. (2009). Bilingualism and conversational understanding in young children. *Cognition, 110*, 115–122.

Siegal, M., & Peterson, C. C. (2008). Language and Theory of Mind in atypical children: Evidence from studies of deafness, blindness, and autism. In C. Sharp, P. Fonagy, & I. Goodyer (Eds.), *Social cognition and developmental psychopathology* (pp. 79–110). New York: Oxford University Press.

Siegal, M., & Surian, L. (2007). Conversational understanding in young children. In E. Hoff & M. Shatz (Eds.), *Blackwell handbook of language development* (pp. 304–323). Oxford, UK: Blackwell.

Siegal, M., Surian, L., Matsuo, A., Geraci, A., Iozzi, L., Okumura, Y., et al. (2010). Bilingualism accentuates conversational understanding. *PLoS ONE, 5*, 2, e9004. doi:10.1371/journal.pone.0009004

Siegal, M., & Varley, R. (2002). Neural systems involved in 'Theory of Mind'. *Nature Reviews Neuroscience, 3*, 463–471.

Siegal, M., & Varley, R. (2006). Aphasia, language and Theory of Mind. *Social Neuroscience, 1*, 167–174.

Slade, L., & Ruffman, T. (2005). How language does (and does not) relate to Theory of Mind: A longitudinal study of syntax, semantics, working memory and false belief. *British Journal of Developmental Psychology, 23*, 117–141.

Slaughter, V., Peterson, C. C., & Mackintosh, E. (2007). Mind what mother says: Narrative input and Theory of Mind in typical children and those on the autism spectrum. *Child Development, 78*, 839–858.

Song, H., & Baillargeon, R. (2008). Infants' reasoning about others' false perception. *Developmental Psychology, 44*, 1789–1795.

Song, H., Onishi, K. H., Baillargeon, R., & Fisher, C. (2008). Can an actor's false belief be corrected by an appropriate communication? Psychological reasoning in 18.5-month-old infants. *Cognition, 109*, 295–315.

Southgate, V., Senju, A., & Csibra, G. (2007). Action anticipation through attribution of belief by 2-year-olds. *Psychological Science, 18*, 587–592.

Surian, L., Caldi, S., & Sperber, D. (2007). Attribution of beliefs by 13-month-old infants. *Psychological Science, 18*, 580–586.

Surian, L., & Leslie, A. M. (1999). Competence and performance in false belief understanding: A comparison of autistic and normal 3-year-old children. *British Journal of Developmental Psychology, 17*, 141–155.

Tager-Flusberg, H. (2007). Evaluating the theory-of-mind hypothesis of autism. *Current Directions in Psychological Science, 16*, 311–315.

Tardif, T., So, C. W-C., & Kaciroti, N. (2007). Language and false belief: Evidence for general, not specific, effects in Cantonese-speaking preschoolers. *Developmental Psychology, 43*, 318–340.

Ullman, M. (2001). A neurocognitive perspective on language: The declarative/procedural model. *Nature Reviews Neuroscience, 2*, 717–726.

Vinden, P. G. (1999). Children's understanding of mind and emotion: A multiculture study. *Cognition & Emotion, 13*, 19–48.

Wellman, H. M., Cross, D., & Watson, J. (2001). Meta-analysis of Theory of Mind development: The truth about false-belief. *Child Development, 72,* 655–684.

Wimmer, H., & Mayringer, V. (1998). False belief understanding in young children: Explanations do not develop before predictions. *International Journal of Behavioral Development, 22,* 403–422.

Wimmer, H., & Perner, J. (1983). Beliefs about beliefs: Representation and constraining function of wrong beliefs in young children's understanding of deception. *Cognition, 13,* 103–128.

Woolfe, T., Want, S. C., & Siegal, M. (2002). Signposts to development: Theory of Mind in deaf children. *Child Development, 73,* 768–778.

Wu, S., & Keysar, B. (2007). The effect of culture on perspective taking. *Psychological Science, 18,* 600–606.

Yazdi, A. A., German, T. P., Defeyer, M., & Siegal, M. (2006). Competence and performance in belief–desire reasoning across two cultures: The truth, the whole truth, and nothing but the truth about false belief? *Cognition, 100,* 343–368.

Zelazo, P. D., Carlson, S. M., & Kesek, A. (2008). The development of executive function in childhood. In C. Nelson & M. Luciana (Eds.), *Handbook of developmental cognitive neuroscience, second edition* (pp. 553–574). Cambridge, MA: MIT Press.

Zhu, Y., Zhang, L., Fan, J., & Han, S. (2007). Neural basis of cultural influence on self-representation. *Neuroimage, 34,* 1310–1316.

20 Bilingualism and the impact of emotion: The role of experience, memory, and sociolinguistic factors

Hugh Knickerbocker and
Jeanette Altarriba

There is an increasing interdependence and connectivity between the people and nations of the world which has led to a greater amount of communication across cultures and languages. Bilingualism, the use of two languages on a regular basis, has become increasingly common in today's world (see e.g., Altarriba & Santiago-Rivera, 1994; Santiago-Rivera & Altarriba, 2002). But what effect, if any, does bilingualism have on the memory and emotions of individuals? How does knowledge of multiple languages influence the perception of language? Is there an interaction between personality factors and language? Researchers have used numerous methodologies in order to study different aspects of emotional experience, perception, memory, and personality in bilinguals.

Bilinguals do not necessarily have equal abilities in both of their languages and can exhibit dominance and preference for one of their known languages. It has been proposed that balanced bilinguals are fluent in both languages and have no true dominant language, while unbalanced bilinguals are more fluent in one language and make more use of one language on a daily basis (Kroll & Stewart, 1994). It is important to note that the dominant language is not necessarily the bilinguals' first language (L1) and can be an individual's second language (L2) under some circumstances. Language dominance is dependent on the fluency and daily usage of both languages. The pattern of language usage over a lifetime is what determines language dominance in bilinguals. Some bilinguals segregate their languages and have language preferences depending on the environment they are in or the specific people they are talking to. This pattern of usage will most likely lead to a clear preference for one language and the development of a dominant language. Language dominance can have a large impact on studies using emotionally charged words, as bilinguals may activate the emotional associations of words in their dominant language more strongly than words in their non-dominant language.

In the literature, language dominance has been measured and operationally defined in several different ways, including age of acquisition, daily usage, self-reported preference, and self-reported ability and fluency.

These different measures all have varying assumptions of what constitutes language dominance. For example, age of acquisition measures define language dominance in chronological terms and assume that the first language learned is the dominant language, while daily usage measures assume that the most often utilized language is the dominant language. In contrast, using measures of self-rated abilities in language assumes that perception of ability is linked to language dominance. In the current chapter, research using all of these operational definitions of language dominance is explored.

The aims of the current chapter are to discuss existing data and present new data on the influence of the perception of emotion on the bilingual speaker. This chapter will outline the influence of emotion on automatic processing by discussing data from affective priming, the Emotional Stroop Task, and physiological measure paradigms. The influence of emotion on more complex cognitive tasks will be explored through a presentation of studies on recall, autobiographical memory, sociolinguistic variables, and frame switching. The interaction of language dominance and emotion will also be highlighted. Finally, this chapter will present data and findings of a study, conducted by the current authors, focusing on the repetition blindness effect (RB) and emotion across languages.

INFLUENCE OF EMOTION ON
AUTOMATIC PROCESSING

The investigation of the relationship between the perception of emotion and cognitive processes begins with an examination of lower-level and automatic processes such as the early recognition of emotion words. This line of research has used methods previously established by cognitive psychologists including affective priming, the Emotional Stroop Task, and skin conductance response (SCR), a physiological measure. Researchers have studied the impact of the perception of emotion on bilinguals' cognitive processing in situations with brief stimulus presentation times and the recording of participants' reaction time (RT) in milliseconds (ms).

Affective priming

In the word-priming paradigm, word pairs are created and presented to participants individually in sequential order. Participants perform a lexical decision task (LDT) where they indicate whether the second word, or target, is a word or nonword. When the first word, or prime, is related to the target, participants generally exhibit a priming effect evidenced by faster reaction time (RT) in the LDT (e.g., responses to *cheese* would be faster after *mouse* than after *cloud*). This effect has also been established when the prime and target are similarly emotionally charged (e.g., when both have negative or positive emotional connotations, such as *hate–fear* or *kiss–happy*; Fazio, Sanbonmatsu, Powell, & Kardes, 1986). Altarriba and Canary (2004) used the word-priming paradigm to investigate the effect of 'word arousal', an emotional component of words, on the priming effect in bilinguals. English monolinguals and fluent Spanish–English bilinguals were tested for RT differences in a LDT. Emotion words used were selected from the University of South Florida Word Norms database (Nelson, McEvoy, & Schreiber, 1998). The researchers created the following three prime–target categories: high arousal (e.g., *prisoner–jail*), moderate arousal (e.g., *criminal–jail*), and unrelated (e.g., *guitar–jail*). Participants viewed prime–target and prime–nonword pairs in English and used a key press mechanism to make a lexical decision for each target.

Evidence of affective priming was found in both groups, but monolinguals were faster to identify the target words than bilinguals. When compared to monolinguals, bilinguals had longer reaction times (bilingual overall RT mean = 640 ms, monolingual overall RT mean = 606 ms) and smaller priming effects in the high arousal (bilingual = 25 ms, monolingual = 63 ms) and moderate arousal conditions (bilingual = 29 ms, monolingual = 62 ms). The reduced affective priming in bilinguals provided evidence that word arousal had a different effect on bilinguals than monolinguals. The differences between affective priming in monolinguals and bilinguals may be explained by the different contexts in which the bilinguals had learned and used the English emotion terms. Bilinguals may have learned and used English in educational and work-oriented environments. Using English in only these limited settings reduced the emotional connotations for those words and reduced affective priming (Altarriba & Canary, 2004).

Emotional Stroop Task

Continuing the investigation of lower-level cognitive processes, Sutton, Altarriba, Gianico, and Basnight-Brown (2007) and Eilola, Havelka, and Sharma (2007) used the Emotional Stroop Task to investigate bilingual participants for differences in processing emotion words. The Emotional Stroop Task is similar to the traditional Stroop Task in which participants report the color of a word while ignoring the meaning of the word, which labels a color (e.g., the word *red* appears in blue ink, and the correct response is to say 'blue' aloud). A Stroop effect is exhibited when participants take longer to report the color of a word when there is a mismatch between the color the word appears in and the color the word labels, in comparison to when these two factors are matched (Stroop, 1935). While the task is the same, the words in the Emotional Stroop Task do not label colors, but instead have emotional definitions and associations. Again, participants are to report the color of emotional and neutral words instead of the actual words (e.g., reporting that the words *grief* or *seat* appear in the color red). Emotional associations tend to have an interference effect and result in an increase in the time required for the color-naming task, similar to the interference found in a traditional Stroop Task (Sutton et al., 2007).

Sutton et al. (2007) sampled Spanish–English bilinguals. Participants were proficient in English and Spanish and used English more often in daily speaking. The Affective Norms for English Words (ANEW) database (Bradley & Lang, 1999) was used to select negative emotion words with low valence and high arousal ratings (e.g., *nervous*, *fear*, and *angry*). As defined by Bradley and Lang (1999), valence is a measure of the strength and direction of the emotional charge of words (low ratings indicate negative emotional associations, moderate ratings indicate few emotional associations, and high ratings indicate positive emotional associations). Arousal is a rating of the amount of excitement and energy associated with words (low ratings indicating lower levels of associated excitement and high ratings indicating higher associated excitement). Neutral words were selected from a list of boat parts (e.g., *engine*, *boom*, and *propeller*). Emotion and neutral words were matched on frequency and length. The participants viewed emotion and neutral words in both English and Spanish. The words were presented in either blue or green, and participants made a key press to indicate word color. The authors found evidence of interference for emotion words on the Emotional Stroop Task in bilinguals. In both languages, participants had shorter RTs with neutral words as compared to emotion words. Emotion words captured attention regardless of the language in which they appeared. Furthermore, participants were able to respond significantly faster when the words were presented in English. However, the size of the interference effect was similar in both languages (Spanish = 28 ms, English = 48 ms).

Eilola et al. (2007) followed an Emotional Stroop procedure similar to the procedure used by Sutton et al. (2007). The authors sampled Finnish–English participants who were proficient in Finnish and English, and were late learners of English. The study found a word type effect where participants had longer RTs on the Emotional Stroop Task when presented with taboo (e.g., *bastard* and *slut*) and negative words (e.g., *rape* and *agony*). When the results are considered along with those of Sutton et al. (2007), it appears that language proficiency had a larger influence on bilingual performance on the Emotional Stroop Task. In both studies, bilinguals had high levels of proficiency in their first language (L1), as well as their second language (L2), despite learning L2 later in life. Sutton et al. (2007) and Eilola et al. (2007) found that similar levels of proficiency resulted in no differences in Emotional Stroop Task interference when presenting words in participants' L1 or L2. These findings suggest that emotional content in different languages does not result in processing differences in bilinguals when they have equal levels of proficiency in both languages.

Physiological measures

Studies on the perception of emotion words have used psychophysiological measures, including skin conductance response, to measure autonomic nervous system reactions to emotion and neutral words (Gray, Hughes, & Schneider, 1982; McGinnies, 1949). More recent studies have measured the extent to which different types of emotion words presented in participants' L1 and L2 influence the response of the autonomic nervous system (Harris, 2004; Harris, Ayçiçeği, & Berko-Gleason, 2003). One component of the physical response to perceived danger is an increase of sweat on the fingertips and palms, which in turn increases skin conductance. Skin conductance response (SCR) measures the conductivity of the skin to determine if the autonomic nervous system has begun to activate in response to a perceived threat (Harris, Berko-Gleason, & Ayçiçeği, 2005).

Harris et al. (2003) recruited Turkish–English bilingual participants who were late learners of English and had greater fluency in Turkish. Neutral words (e.g., *box* and *name*), positive words (e.g., *happy* and *love*), aversive words (e.g., *anger* and *poison*), taboo words (e.g., *breast* and *pee*), and reprimands (e.g., *Don't do that!* and *Shame on you!*) were selected from the *Handbook of Semantic Word Norms* (Toglia & Battig, 1978) and a previous study (Gonzalez-Regiosa, 1976). Reprimands were expressions commonly used with children, for example 'Go to your room!'. Participants viewed half of the trials in English and half in Turkish. The Davicon C2A Custom Skin Conductance Monitor was used to measure participants' skin conductance response (SCR). Electrodes were attached to the index and middle fingers of each participant's dominant hand, and SCRs were measured for a 10-second interval. A single word was presented during this entire 10-second interval, and participants rated the word on a pleasantness scale. The rating task ensured that participants attended and processed the target words during the entire SCR measurement interval (Harris et al., 2003).

The researchers found that language and word type had a significant impact on SCR scores. In general, Turkish words evoked higher SCR scores than English words. Taboo words and reprimands resulted in higher SCR scores than neutral words. However, only Turkish reprimands resulted in significantly higher SCR scores than their English translations. Emotional reactivity to childhood reprimands was limited to Turkish. During debriefing, several participants commented that the Turkish reprimands led to a memory of being reprimanded by a family member. Hearing reprimands in Turkish activated associated memories of the context in which those reprimands were originally heard. This was strong evidence for the existence of language-specific memories and of the notion that context of use influences the formation of associations in memory (Harris et al., 2003).

Harris (2004) shifted focus onto language proficiency and the age of acquisition of bilingual participants. Spanish–English bilinguals were sampled and divided into early and late learners of English. Early learners were more proficient in English, while late learners were more proficient in Spanish. Several Spanish and English words were presented while participants underwent a SCR measurement procedure similar to Harris et al. (2003). In both languages, early and late learners had higher SCR scores for taboo words. In late learners, reprimands resulted in higher scores only when presented in Spanish, while early learners had higher SCR scores for reprimands in both languages. Early learners had similar SCR patterns in both languages, while late learners exhibited higher SCR in L1. Harris (2004) provided evidence that L1 is not inherently more emotional than L2 (but see Altarriba, 2003) and that language proficiency, age of acquisition, and context of usage all influence the experienced emotional intensity of a language.

INFLUENCE OF EMOTION ON MEMORY AND PERSONALITY

The study of more complex cognitive processes has included various procedures in addition to the methods more traditionally used in cognitive research. Some investigators have used more qualitative paradigms in order to determine the influence of the perception and production of emotional stimuli on bilingual participants. Processes, such as recall, have been investigated utilizing more traditional methodologies. Meanwhile, other constructs, including autobiographical memory, sociolinguistic variables, personality factors, and frame switching, have been analyzed using newly developed methods. These methods tend to focus on the creation of a natural situation or environment, as in the research on autobiographical memory, which allows participants to give detailed accounts of actual, personal memories.

Memory

Researchers have investigated the influence of emotion in bilingual participants using recall and recognition tasks. This line of research has provided evidence of language-specific advantages in a free recall task. Anooshian and Hertel (1994) measured bilinguals' ability to recall neutral and emotional words in both their L1 and L2. Neutral words included *box*, *part*, and *salt*. Emotional words were both positive and negative terms, including *laugh*, *kiss*, *death*, and *fight*. The authors selected bilinguals who spoke Spanish and English and were late learners of their second language. All participants were fluent in both languages, but half were native Spanish speakers and half native English speakers. The participants viewed neutral and emotional words in Spanish and English and performed one of three distracter rating tasks. After completing the rating task, participants were given an unexpected free recall test, where they were instructed to write down as many of the words as they could remember.

A memory advantage for emotion words, where emotion words were recalled more often than neutral words, was found in the participants' native language but not in their second language. The advantage of L1 over L2 was the same regardless of specific language (Anooshian & Hertel, 1994). The recall advantage can be explained by the differences in the contexts in which participants learned and used their languages. The different contexts in which words are used influence the development of associations between words and concepts. Late learning of L2 reduced the use and associations in memory of L2 emotion words and hindered the effective use of recall strategies for words present in participants' L2.

Autobiographical memory

The methods utilized by Anooshian and Hertel (1994) allowed for the controlled empirical study of memory and emotion, but created artificial situations that do not allow for the study of the natural formation of memories. Javier, Barroso, and Muñoz (1993) suggested that autobiographical memory allows for a more natural study of memory that does not attempt to control the meaning of memories as traditional experimental methods do. This line of research assumes that memory can be assessed through an analysis of verbalizations, and that language serves an encoding function to aid in the organization and retrieval of memories. The study of autobiographical memory has focused on cued memories that contain personal information about the self and events related to the self (e.g., having participants describe personal memories associated with the cuing word *store*).

Javier et al. (1993) investigated this theory of linguistic organization of memory by interviewing five Spanish–English bilinguals. Participants were asked to speak for 5 minutes about life experiences using the language in which the event took place. Participants also described the event again in their second language. The first monologue had more detail and elaboration than the second monologue, which was less imaginative and more abbreviated. Regardless of language, the first monologue was more vivid than the second monologue, as measured by the amount of detail, elaboration, and imagery. The study provided evidence that memory of personal events is organized using linguistic information from the event, and retrieving a memory may be hindered by using a language other than the original encoding language (see Marian & Neisser, 2000).

Schrauf and Rubin (1998, 2000, 2001) conducted several empirical studies on autobiographical memory and the linguistic organization of memories and experiences in immigrants who moved from primarily Spanish-speaking nations to primarily English-speaking nations. Their studies shifted focus to the 'reminiscence bump'. The reminiscence bump refers to the time period between the ages of 10 and 30. There are typically a greater number of memories from the reminiscence bump than from other time periods of participants' lives.

Schrauf and Rubin (1998) sampled Spanish–English bilinguals, who had emigrated from Spanish-speaking to English-speaking cultures. Participants were divided into the following three groups: early immigration (ages 20 to 24), middle immigration (26 to 30), and late immigration (34 to 35). The researchers utilized a word-cuing paradigm where participants were presented with a single word and associated the word with a specific personal memory (e.g., having participants describe personal memories related to the cue *car*). Participants were presented with 50 different words during separate, 2-hour, English and Spanish cuing sessions. Participants had to write their memories in the language of the session. After each session, participants were asked if they experienced any memories in their 'other' language. At the end of the second session, the participants dated each of the 100 memories.

The authors found that the reminiscence bump shifted with the immigration period in each of the immigration groups. The early immigration group had a relatively typical reminiscence bump, but the bump was shifted in both the middle and late immigration groups (Schrauf & Rubin, 1998). Rather than remaining in the typical time period, the reminiscence bump shifted with the emigration time period of the participants, and occurred later in participants who emigrated later in life. The reminiscence bump shift was also found by Schrauf and Rubin (2001), who had participants freely recount their life stories, rather than cuing memories. Again, the reminiscence bump shifted with the immigration period of the participants.

Schrauf and Rubin (1998) found additional evidence of language-specific memories as approximately 20% of participants' memories did not occur in the cuing language. These memories occurred in participants' other language (the cue was in English and the memory was in Spanish, or the cue was in Spanish and the memory was in English). Language-specific Spanish memories tended to be from pre-immigration periods (mean age = 29.69), while English memories tended to be from post-immigration periods (mean age = 46.52). The mean age of the memories with Spanish as a cuing language was 39.79 and with English as a cuing language was 40.55. The authors found evidence that language served an encoding function in autobiographical memory. Schrauf and Rubin (2000) found additional evidence for linguistic encoding. The authors had Spanish–English bilinguals label memories as non-linguistic, congruent (cue and retrieval language were the same), crossover (cue and retrieval language were different), or dual language (cue and retrieval occurred in both languages) memories. Spanish congruent and crossover memories tended to be from pre-immigration periods (mean age = 27.74), while English congruent and crossover memories tended to originate from post-immigration periods (mean age = 50.55). Utilizing a similar cuing paradigm with Polish–Danish bilingual immigrants, Larsen, Schrauf, Fromholt, and Rubin (2002) also reported evidence of linguistic encoding. They found pre-immigration memories were more likely to be retrieved in participants' L1, and post-immigration memories were more likely to be retrieved in L2.

Schrauf and Hoffman (2007) studied emotional intensity and valence in autobiographical memories. The authors studied the 'fade effect bias', which predicts that pre-immigration memories (formed during younger ages) will be less emotionally intense than post-immigration memories (formed during older ages). Furthermore, this fading effect should influence negative memories more than positive memories. The authors also studied the 'positivity bias', which predicts pre-immigration memories will be recalled as more pleasant than post-immigration memories. A cuing method similar to Schrauf and Rubin (1998, 2000) was used, and memories were coded for emotional intensity and valence. Memories from youth were recalled with less emotional intensity than memories from old age, and negatively valenced memories were rated as less intense than positively valenced memories. There was also evidence of a positivity bias, as earlier memories were recalled with more positive valence than more recent memories.

The evidence reported by this line of autobiographical memory research supports the notion that the cognitive associations formed with languages vary greatly depending on the context of use. In the studies reported above, the immigration event created separate contexts of usage for participants' L1 and L2. These vastly different contexts, literally distinct geographic and social locations, led to the formation of different associations between bilinguals' languages and their autobiographical memories.

Frame switching and biculturals

Luna, Ringberg, and Peracchio (2008) have begun a relatively new line of inquiry into personality, language use, and culture. This line of research is related to the previous investigations of autobiographical memory, as it also analyzes the influence of culture and language usage. While autobiographical research has focused on the reminiscence bump, 'frame switching' emphasizes changes in personality and judgments as a result of activating different mental frameworks containing different connotations and associations for the same concepts. The authors defined biculturals as bilingual individuals who have fully internalized two separate cultures. The full internalization of both cultures leads to the formation of separate culture specific mental frameworks and identities, which are linked to the different languages biculturals have mastered. Biculturals are able to utilize language cues and frame switch, alternating between culturally defined identities which lead to different interpretations of specific concepts and stimuli. Monocultural bilinguals have not fully identified with both cultures and have only internalized a single culture. For a more thorough discussion see Luna (Chapter 25, this volume).

Sociolinguistic approaches

Researchers have also focused on sociolinguistic factors that influence bilingual language use and speech production, including personality factors, demographic variables, and language history variables. Several authors have published articles highlighting the personality factor 'extraversion' as important in the perception and production of speech (Dewaele & Furnham, 1999, 2000; Dewaele & Pavlenko, 2002). Dewaele (2004, 2008) conducted studies on bilinguals' use of emotion and emotionally charged words in speech. Here, sociobiographical variables were used to study the perception of emotionally charged words and phrases, including the phrase *I love you* and taboo words.

In defense of extraversion as a sociolinguistic factor, Dewaele and Furnham (1999) emphasized that research has indicated that extraversion influences speech production through its impact on arousal, stress resistance, and immediate recall. Research has established that extraverts tend to be under-aroused by events, while introverts tend to be over-aroused (Eysenck, 1981). Extraverts, as compared to introverts, also show greater resistance to stress and have an increased ability in short term recall, which is influential in verbal task performance (Shapiro & Alexander, 1969). Taken together, this evidence suggests that extraverts have several advantages over introverts in speech production.

Dewaele and Furnham (2000) investigated the relationship between L2 production and extraversion by sampling 25 Flemish students with several years of classroom instruction in French. A sociobiographical questionnaire and the Eysenck Personality Inventory (EPI; Eysenck & Eysenck, 1964) were used as extraversion measures. Each participant had a stressful conversation, focused on evaluating lingual proficiency, and a casual conversation. Introverts appeared unable to produce speech at the same level of automaticity as extraverts in stressful, formal situations. Introverted participants may have been more concerned with searching lexical memory stores and utilizing vocabulary in stressful, formal situations. Extraverts appeared more focused on fluency and used shorter high-frequency words to produce shorter and better-understood responses.

Dewaele and Pavlenko (2002) provided additional evidence of the influence of extraversion, language proficiency (as measured by linguistic errors), and gender on the production of L2 speech and the use of emotion words in the second language. The researchers had relaxed, informal, one-on-one conversations with participants in their second language. Similar to Dewaele and Furnham (2000) the EPI was used to measure extraversion. All of the conversations were coded for the use of emotion words, as well as lexical and morphological errors. The authors found that extraversion, language proficiency, and gender all had significant effects on the use of emotional speech in a second language. Extraverts utilized a wider range of emotions in L2 conversation than introverts. Building on Dewaele and Furnham (2000), extraverts' wider expression of emotion may be linked to their increased use of more simplistic and easily expressed vernacular vocabulary. Extraverts may be more comfortable expressing themselves and self-edit less often than introverts when speaking in their second language (Dewaele & Pavlenko, 2002).

Dewaele (2008) collected information on multilinguals' perception of *I love you* in their different languages using a web questionnaire. Data on several sociobiographical variables, L2 learning history, recent use of L2, and lingual proficiency (self-report measures of competence in each language, including reading, writing, speaking, and comprehension) were also collected. Participants perceived the phrase *I love you* as more emotional in their L1 as compared to L2. Although no significant influence of sociobiographical variables on the perception of *I love you* was found, L2 learning history, recent use of L2, and self-perceived proficiency in L2 did have significant influences on the perception of *I love you*. The study found increased perception of emotional weight was related to increased fluency and use of a specific language. Dewaele (2004) utilized a similar web questionnaire paradigm when studying multilinguals' perception of swearwords and taboo words (S-T words). Similar to Dewaele (2008), it was discovered that the perceived emotional force of S-T words was typically highest in participants' L1. Furthermore, the perception of emotionality of S-T words decreased in L1 when L1 was no longer the dominant language (L2 had higher self-rated proficiency than L1) and increased in L2, as L2 proficiency increased. Both studies provided evidence that bilinguals, as well as multilinguals, experience greater emotional weight for emotionally charged words in their more fluent and dominant language. Presumably, the more dominant language was used in a greater range of contexts than the non-dominant language, and this increased use of the dominant language led to greater semantic and emotional meanings being associated with the dominant language.

Summary of bilingual emotion studies

Thus far, the articles reviewed on the cognitive research on bilingual participants provided several lines of convergent evidence. The research data have also supported the notion that bilinguals process emotionally charged stimuli differently when the stimuli are presented in the dominant versus the non-dominant language. Participants tested with an affective priming paradigm (Altarriba & Canary, 2004), an Emotional Stroop Task (Eilola et al., 2007; Sutton et al., 2007), physiological measures (Harris, 2004; Harris et al., 2003), and a recall memory task (Anooshian & Hertel, 1994) all provided empirical evidence of differences in processing emotional stimuli in dominant and non-dominant languages. These studies also provided evidence that language fluency and age of acquisition had a significant influence on language dominance and the performance of L1 and L2 on the various cognitive tasks.

Furthermore, research on autobiographical memory encoding and retrieval has shown that languages can cue memories from separate time periods (Javier et al., 1993; Larsen et al., 2002; Schrauf & Rubin, 1998, 2000, 2001). Luna et al. (2008) provided evidence that language stimuli can produce changes in personality and judgments, an effect they labeled 'frame switching'. The differences in autobiographical memory and personality frame are both related to the contextual use of language. Sociolinguistic personality factors, such as extraversion, have also been implicated in the perception and production of emotional speech (Dewaele, 2004, 2008; Dewaele & Furnham, 1999, 2000; Dewaele & Pavlenko, 2002).

In general, previous research has supported the view that bilinguals process L1 and L2 emotional stimuli differently based on language dominance. Participants tended to view emotional phrases and words as having greater emotional weight when presented in their dominant language. Inquiry into differences in the cognitive processing of emotional stimuli has continued with the use of the rapid serial visual presentation (RSVP) methodology. This topic forms the basis of the remainder of the present chapter.

RECENT RESEARCH UTILIZING RAPID SERIAL VISUAL PRESENTATION

Often when reading, words appear more than once within a single sentence. For example, the sentence *They arrived early for the play though the play had been canceled* contains a repetition of the word *play*. An interesting question posed by several researchers has been whether these repetitions of the same word are processed similarly or differently by the reader. The RSVP (rapid serial visual presentation) procedure has been used to present sentences, and other word stimuli, to participants to determine if there are differences in the cognitive processing of a repeated word as compared to unrepeated words.

Repetition blindness

Words in the RSVP paradigm are presented to participants for extremely brief periods of time, approximately 70 ms to 110 ms per word. As mentioned earlier, when investigating 'repetition blindness' (RB), target words can be repeated or unrepeated and are typically embedded within streams of distracter stimuli. These distracter stimuli can be symbols or other words. Targets are also embedded in strings of words that form entire sentences. Researchers have found that when words are presented in the RSVP paradigm, repeated words are actually recalled less accurately than unrepeated words. That is, participants are often 'blind' to the second repetition of a word. Kanwisher (1987) found that repetition blindness occurred even when the repeated target words were presented in different cases. This degraded recall suggested that RB is not a visual phenomenon but a cognitive processing phenomenon. Kanwisher and Potter (1990) found RB did not occur when targets were synonyms, and concluded RB must occur prior to semantic coding. The authors did find RB with orthographically similar words (e.g., *cap/cape* or *barn/bar*), words that were part of compound nouns (e.g., *dog/hot-dog* or *heart-attack/attack*) and orthographically identical words with semantic differences—for example, *(the) rose/(she) rose* or *(to) watch/(the) watch*. These results suggest that RB occurs at the orthographic level, rather than at the semantic level. Differences and similarities in orthographic information appeared to influence the RB effect, while semantic repetition did not result in a significant RB effect, and semantic differences did not hinder RB in orthographically identical words. Research focused on RB with bilingual participants may be able to provide insight into the connections between L1 and L2 words and their similar, conceptual representations.

Repetition blindness in bilinguals

Altarriba and Soltano (1996) investigated the level of processing at which repetition blindness (RB) occurs through the study of RB in bilingual participants. Fluent bilinguals are uniquely able to provide insight into whether or not RB occurs at the semantic level because they have L1 and L2 lexical representations of the same semantic concept. For example, Spanish–English bilinguals have the words *sobrino* and *nephew* linked to a semantic concept representing the son of one's sibling. The researchers selected Spanish–English bilinguals from the Florida International University community, in Miami, Florida, to participate in two studies. Miami provided an environment where participants had a high likelihood of speaking and reading Spanish and English on a daily basis. The sample used in both studies included participants who were fluent in reading and writing both Spanish and English as measured by responses to a language history questionnaire (LHQ; Altarriba & Mathis, 1997).

The authors designed two studies to investigate RB at the semantic level. Participants in the first study were presented with sentences on a computer screen, one word at a time. Participants in the second study were presented with words embedded within symbol streams (e.g., *door* and *nephew*). The sentences and word–symbol strings were presented following the RSVP methodology and participants were asked to identify which words they had viewed after each trial. Both studies utilized two targets embedded within distracters. In the first study two of the words in the sentence were target words (e.g., *I like steak but this steak tastes awful*), while in the second study two of the words were targets and a third word was presented between the two targets as a distracter:

%%%%%/*****/nephew/duck/nephew/?????/%%%%%.

Altarriba and Soltano (1996) found that RB was eliminated when the sentences and word–symbol strings were presented in mixed languages. When the participants viewed sentences that were half English and half Spanish, recall was virtually identical in the repeated and unrepeated target sentences. The second study found significant RB within each language condition (recall was 30% poorer in repeated trials than unrepeated trials), where participants viewed word–symbol strings in only a single language. However, in the mixed language conditions, where one target was in Spanish and the other in English, recall was significantly facilitated (recall was 12.5% better in repeated trials than unrepeated trials). These findings were in line with the conclusion reached by Kanwisher and Potter (1990) that RB does not occur at a semantic or conceptual level. The recall facilitation in the Spanish–English repeated targets occurred despite the common conceptual representation that the repeated Spanish–English target activated. These findings provide further evidence that RB occurs at the lexical and orthographic levels of processing (see also MacKay, Hadley, & Schwartz, 2005, and MacKay, James, & Abrams, 2002 for similar results). Moreover, these data suggest that semantic information influences language processing, even in situations that are highly constrained in terms of presentation time (e.g., RSVP tasks).

THE PRESENT STUDY

The current study continues the investigation of repetition blindness (RB) in bilingual participants, while expanding the experimental design to include not only different language conditions, but also different types of emotion words. Silvert, Naveteur, Honoré, Sequeira, and Boucart (2004) used the rapid serial visual presentation (RSVP) methodology to investigate differences in the recall of repeated and unrepeated words with different levels of emotional valence. The authors found that recall of emotionally weighted words was higher than neutral words in the unrepeated condition. However, emotionally weighted words exhibited lower recall than neutral words in the repeated condition resulting in a larger RB effect. Silvert et al. (2004) created a single emotion word category, which mixed together different types of emotion words possibly influencing their results. The current study expands the comparisons made by Silvert et al. (2004) by including separate emotion word (e.g., *depression* and *angry*) and emotion-laden word (e.g., *blackmail* and *feeble*) conditions. Different conditions were created for the emotion word categories to determine if various types of emotionally weighted words had differential influences on processing. The purpose of the current study was to determine whether emotion, emotion-laden, and neutral words exhibit similar RB effects when presented in Spanish and English following the RSVP paradigm. Do Spanish–English bilinguals process emotion, emotion-laden, and neutral words differently in Spanish and English?

Method

Participants

A total of 32 Spanish–English bilingual participants were selected from the University at Albany, State University of New York. Participants were awarded credit or payment for completing the study. The language background of the participants was measured with the Language History Questionnaire (LHQ; Altarriba & Mathis, 1997). Several LHQ measures are presented in Table 20.1. Anxiety levels could potentially influence

Table 20.1 Participant responses to the Language History Questionnaire

	Mean	*Standard deviation*
Mean years in US schools	12.66	5.36
Mean age began speaking English	6.16	4.76
Mean age began reading English	6.84	3.84
Mean age began speaking Spanish	1.26	1.44
Mean age began reading Spanish	6.58	3.59
Mean self-ratings* of ability on:		
Spoken English	9.31	0.90
Written English	9.22	0.94
Conversation skills English	9.22	1.01
Spoken Spanish	8.94	1.19
Written Spanish	8.31	1.51
Conversation skills Spanish	8.72	1.33
Daily use (%):		
English	78.63	13.72
Spanish	20.66	13.74

* Self-ratings were made on a 10-point scale, with 1 indicating low or poor language abilities and 10 indicating high or excellent language abilities.

participants' perception of stimuli, as previous studies have shown that high-anxiety individuals are more likely to perceive and respond to negative stimuli, as compared to neutral stimuli (Trippe, Hewig, Heydel, Hecht, & Miltner, 2007). Therefore, the Beck Depression Inventory II (BDI-II; Beck, Steer, & Brown, 1996) and the State Trait Anxiety Inventory (STAI; Spielberger, Gorsuch, Lushene, Vagg, & Jacobs, 1983) were used as measures of trait and state anxiety. Participants who surpassed predetermined cut-off scores on either the BDI-II or STAI were eliminated from the study.

Design

The design included the following three within-participants factors: language (Spanish and English), repeatedness (repeated and unrepeated targets), and emotion word type (emotion, emotion-laden, and neutral).

Materials

The Affective Norms for English Words database (Bradley & Lang, 1999) was used to select 120 English words. Valance and arousal measures were used as indicators of the emotional weight of a word. Emotion words (which label a specific emotion or feeling, e.g., *fear* and *hate*) and emotion-laden words (which have emotional associations but do not actually refer to a specific emotional state, e.g., *disaster* and *funeral*) had low valence ratings, indicating strong negative emotional connotation, and high arousal ratings, indicating increased ability to capture attention. Neutral words (which have no emotional associations, e.g., *cabinet* and *tool*) had moderate valence ratings and moderate arousal ratings.

The selected emotion, emotion-laden, and neutral words were all normed on several measures, including length, frequency, orthographic neighborhood, mean naming reaction time (RT), and lexical decision task RT (Balota et al., 2002). The emotion and emotion-laden words had comparable valence and arousal ratings. The emotion and emotion-laden words had significantly lower valence and higher arousal ratings than the neutral words. The English words were translated into Spanish by a fluent Spanish–English bilingual, and the Spanish translations were normed on length and frequency.

Word–symbol string trials were created for the emotion, emotion-laden, and neutral words. The word–symbol strings contained target words and distracter symbols. Repeated and unrepeated target trials contained two target words, while filler trials contained only a single target word. The first target word appeared in the third position and the second target word appeared in the fifth position. The second target word could be either a new word or a repetition of the first target word. In the filler trials, the fifth position was filled by distracter symbols. For an example of the word–symbol streams see Figure 20.1.

The study included 54 experimental trials, which were split into two blocks of 27 trials, one Spanish block and one English block. Each block contained nine repeated target trials, nine unrepeated target trials, and nine filler trials. Each block also contained nine emotion words (three emotion repeated, three emotion unrepeated, and three emotion filler), nine emotion-laden words (three emotion-laden repeated, three emotion-laden unrepeated, and three emotion-laden filler) and nine neutral word trials (three neutral repeated, three neutral unrepeated, and three neutral filler). The order of these trials was randomized within each of the two blocks. Eight unique and counterbalanced lists of stimuli were created, such that each block appeared in the first and second positions, each trial occurred in Spanish and English, and each non-filler trial appeared as repeated and unrepeated. Each participant viewed a single, unique list. Eighteen practice trials were split into two equally sized Spanish and English blocks, which were counterbalanced following a similar procedure.

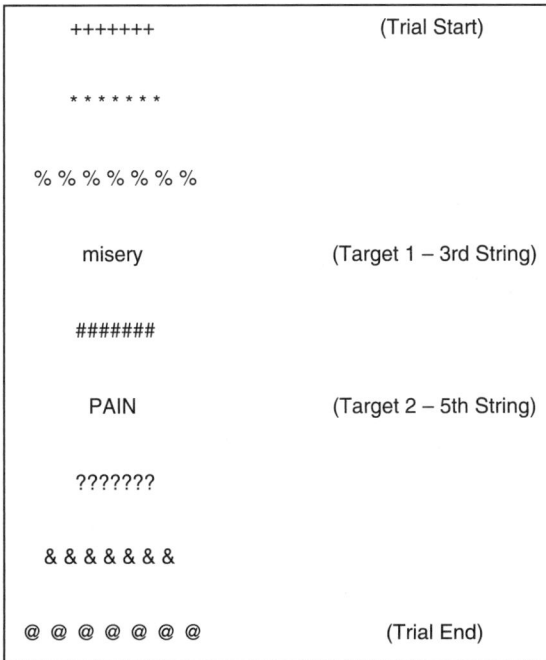

```
+++++++                        (Trial Start)


* * * * * *


% % % % % % %


misery                         (Target 1 – 3rd String)


#######


PAIN                           (Target 2 – 5th String)


???????


& & & & & & &


@ @ @ @ @ @ @                  (Trial End)
```

Figure 20.1 Sample trial for the current study (unrepeated trial). In repeated trials, the fifth string was a repetition of Target 1. In filler trials, the fifth string was filled with symbols.

Procedure

Participants were tested individually. The length of the study was approximately 30 minutes. Participants completed the BDI-II and STAI before the beginning of the experimental trials. The Language History Questionnaire (LHQ) was completed after the experimental trials. The BDI-II, STAI, and LHQ required a total of approximately 15 minutes to complete. The bilingual RSVP experiment also required approximately 15 minutes. The experiment was presented to participants on a Dell Optiplex GX240 PC running Superlab 4.0.

Participants viewed a practice block for one language, and an experimental block for that same language, followed by a practice block for the second language, and an experimental block for the second language. Each trial began with the presentation of a fixation row, +++++++, for 1000 ms. Targets and symbol rows were presented for 100 ms each. Every trial ended with a row of @@@@@@@, which signaled the end of the trial and that participants were to report the target words they recalled perceiving. Participant responses were recorded with a Memorex Personal Cassette Recorder, model MB1055.

Results and discussion

Language history measures are reported in Table 20.1. Participant self-ratings of written, spoken, and comprehension abilities in English and Spanish were analyzed as a 2 (Spanish or English) × 3 (spoken, written, and comprehension abilities) ANOVA. A significant main effect of language was found, $F(1, 31) = 5.49, p < .05$, indicating that participants rated themselves as significantly higher in English abilities (9.25) than Spanish abilities (8.66). Despite being native Spanish speakers, participants rated themselves as having higher abilities in English than Spanish. Pairwise comparisons revealed that participants rated English written abilities as higher than Spanish written abilities, $t(31) = 3.00, p < .01$. This is particularly important for the current study, as the RSVP task required the ability to read and understand the written word in English and in Spanish. Further, analyzing the self-reported ages of learning to speak and read Spanish and English revealed that participants did learn to speak Spanish earlier in life, $t(31) = 5.76, p < .0005$, but there were no significant age differences in learning to read English and Spanish, $t(31) = .32, p > .05$. Finally, participants reported using English significantly more in their daily lives than Spanish (79% vs 21%, respectively), $t(31) = 11.99, p < .0005$.

The results of the current study can be found in Figure 20.2. A repeated measures ANOVA was run, including a 2 × 2 × 3 design with the following three, within-participants variables: language (English and Spanish), repeatedness (repeated and unrepeated), and emotional word

Trial Recall Accuracy

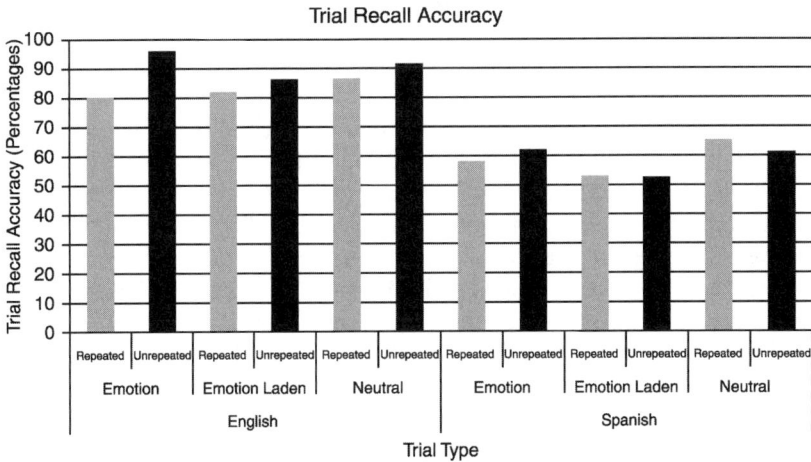

Figure 20.2 Accuracy of recall of trials (percentages). A clear pattern of repetition blindness (RB) was observed in the English emotion, emotion-laden, and neutral trials. The RB effect was more robust in the emotion trials than either the emotion-laden and neutral trials. No consistent pattern of RB was observed in the Spanish trials.

type (emotion, emotion-laden, and neutral). In all of the following analyses, the dependent variable measured was the average percentage of correct trials under each condition of the three independent variables.

The main effect of language was significant, $F(1, 31) = 33.37, p < .001$. The significant main effect of language highlighted a generally lower recall of Spanish words compared to English words. In all conditions of repeatedness and emotion word type, English words had significantly higher recall than Spanish words. There was also a significant main effect of emotion word type, $F(2, 62) = 4.90, p < .01$ The significant main effect of emotion word type provided evidence of differences in the perception of the different emotion word types.

The interaction between language and repeatedness was significant, $F(1, 31) = 5.58, p < .05$. Spanish and English trials had different response patterns when repeated and unrepeated trials were compared. English trials evidenced a typical RB effect, with lower accuracy in reporting target words in repeated trials than unrepeated trials. However, in Spanish, the typical RB effect was not observed, and there were minimal differences between repeated and unrepeated trials. Each of these findings will be further explored below.

Pairwise comparisons between the average percentages of correct trials in the different conditions were conducted using a series of repeated measures *t*-tests. In line with the significant main effect of language, differences between the repeated English and Spanish word conditions were significant, $t(31) = 4.46$, $p < .001$, and differences between unrepeated English and Spanish word conditions were also significant, $t(31) = 5.98$, $p < .001$. Comparisons between English and Spanish repeated emotion word conditions were significant, $t(31) = 3.48$, $p < .01$, as were comparisons between repeated emotion-laden word conditions, $t(31) = 4.63$, $p < .001$, and repeated neutral word conditions, $t(31) = 3.40$, $p < .01$. Similarly, differences between English and Spanish unrepeated emotion word conditions were significant, $t(31) = 5.75$, $p < .001$, as were differences between unrepeated emotion-laden word conditions, $t(31) = 5.11$, $p < .001$, and unrepeated neutral word conditions, $t(31) = 4.37$, $p < .001$. Each of these comparisons supported the finding that English words were recalled with greater accuracy than Spanish words. English words had significantly higher recall under both of the repeatedness conditions, as well as all of the emotion word type by repeatedness conditions.

Comparisons between English word conditions yielded several interesting outcomes. First, the repeated word condition was recalled with significantly lower accuracy than the unrepeated word condition, $t(31) = 2.35$, $p < .05$. Dividing the English words into emotion, emotion-laden, and neutral words, also allowed for several intriguing comparisons. The difference between the repeated emotion word and unrepeated emotion word conditions was significant, $t(31) = 2.79$, $p < .01$. Repeated English words, specifically repeated emotion English words, showed a typical RB effect. However, emotion-laden and neutral English words did not exhibit significant RB effects. The differences between repeated and unrepeated emotion-laden and neutral English word conditions reflected the typical RB effect. A larger RB effect in emotion words than neutral words does support the previous findings of Silvert et al. (2004). Emotion-laden and neutral English words exhibited small, non-significant differences between repeated and unrepeated conditions as compared to the emotion words. Emotion-laden words may have resulted in accuracy rates similar to the neutral words because they were perceived as less emotionally weighted when presented intermixed with emotion words. This interpretation of the findings is supported by Harris et al. (2003) and Harris (2004) where typical negative emotion words were intermixed with taboo words and reprimands. Similar to the current study, typical negative emotion words did not elicit significant SCR scores, while the taboo words and reprimands did elicit significantly raised SCR scores.

Overall, the Spanish word trials did exhibit slightly higher recall in the unrepeated condition when compared to the repeated condition, although this comparison was not significant ($p > .05$). Differences between the emotion, emotion-laden, and neutral repeated and unrepeated Spanish words were all non-significant. In the emotion word condition, unrepeated words were more accurately recalled than repeated emotion words, however the difference in means was not significant ($p > .05$).

GENERAL DISCUSSION

The results of the current study suggest that bilingual individuals process and experience emotional words differently in English and in Spanish. Under the repeated emotion word condition, English trials exhibited a significant repetition blindness (RB) effect while Spanish trials did not. This same pattern of results was found when word type was ignored; overall, English words evidenced a significant RB effect while Spanish words did not. These results can be explained by language dominance and participants' differing daily usage of English and Spanish.

Despite the fact that Spanish was the earliest-learned language, participants reported higher levels of English proficiency, learned to read English and Spanish at about the same age, and utilized English more heavily on a daily basis (no participant reported using Spanish more often on a daily basis, and only three participants reported a perfect 50–50 split in daily language usage). Spanish may have been the first language learned, but it appears that English was actually the dominant language of the participants. The higher accuracy of English trials overall, compared to Spanish trials, was further support for the argument that participants were more dominant in English than in Spanish. The dramatic increase in the daily use of English compared to Spanish suggested that the participants used English in most of their daily interactions. The participants generally reported utilizing Spanish at home with family and English in school and work settings. However, the participants were college students who were constantly in the school and work environment and were no longer in their home and family environments. It appears that Spanish was only used in specific situations and English was generally the language of choice. Thus, participants may have used English more often across all situations, including in more personal and emotional situations, as well as more social and professional situations. In contrast, Spanish was used only occasionally at home or with specific friends and family members. Due to the different patterns of daily usage, participants may have been more familiar with the general and emotional connotations and denotations of English words than Spanish words. This increased familiarity and comfort with English words would naturally result in English being experienced more emotionally than Spanish for the current set of bilinguals.

The results of this study support the views of several of the authors and studies presented in the automatic processing section of the current chapter. The prevailing theme of those studies was that emotion had a larger impact on automatic and lower-level processing when emotionally weighted words were presented and processed in the dominant language of the bilingual participants (Altarriba & Canary, 2004; Eilola et al., 2007; Sutton et al., 2007). Emotional words and phrases also had a larger impact on skin conductance response scores and autonomic nervous system response when they were presented in the dominant language of the bilingual participants (Harris, 2004; Harris et al., 2003). Furthermore, the investigation into the perception of emotionally weighted phrases has found that specific phrases are perceived more emotionally when they are presented in the dominant language of bilinguals (Dewaele, 2004, 2008). Interpreting the findings of all of these studies together, the emotional weight of words has a larger impact on automatic, lower-level, and even some higher-level cognitive processes when those words are presented in the dominant language of bilinguals.

The current results mirrored the findings of experiments focused on memory and personality. The emotional weight of words was found to increase the recall of dominant language words (Anooshian & Hertel, 1994). Several authors were able to provide evidence that language served encoding and retrieval functions in the autobiographical memories of immigrants who moved from a Spanish-speaking culture to an English-speaking culture (Javier et al., 1993; Larsen et al., 2002; Schrauf & Hoffman, 2007; Schrauf & Rubin 1998, 2000, 2001). As a result of the very different contexts in which Spanish and English were used over the lifetime of this specific population of bilinguals, each language had become associated with memories from different time periods.

The current study is supported by research into the use of language as a personality cue conducted by Luna et al. (2008). When bilinguals have fully internalized both cultures, suggesting high fluency in both languages and the possibility of shared language dominance, language can have a cuing or priming effect and influence the personality and judgments of those individuals. Language can cue a specific cultural background and system of judgments which influences individuals' interpretation of the content of the message. Furthermore, research has found evidence that extraverts are more likely to produce emotional speech in L2 than introverts (Dewaele & Furnham, 2000; Dewaele & Pavlenko, 2002). Due to limited experience with the nuance of non-dominant language emotional terms, introverts are less likely to use emotional speech in their subordinate language. Extraverts, with their increased confidence and comfort in expressing themselves have less trouble utilizing emotional speech in their non-dominant language. In general, all of the findings in memory, personality, and sociolinguistic research support a model where context of language usage and language dominance affect the perception and processing of language. If languages can be associated with different memories and personality trends, then they may also be associated with different emotional connotations.

In conclusion, the different experiences and daily routines that people experience can influence the perception and processing of emotional language in bilinguals. These different routines and patterns of language usage can lead to different memory structures and associations which will influence the processing of language in the immediate present, as well as in the future. These differences in the stored associations of words can lead to language-processing differences that are observed in controlled cognitive studies and language production differences in more qualitative studies. Future research should focus on systematically examining language dominance and its influence on cognitive tasks involving emotion stimuli for bilingual speakers.

REFERENCES

Altarriba, J. (2003). Does cariño equal 'liking'? A theoretical approach to conceptual nonequivalence between languages. *The International Journal of Bilingualism, 7*, 305–322.

Altarriba, J., & Canary, T. M. (2004). The influence of emotional arousal on affective priming in monolingual and bilingual speakers. *Journal of Multilingual and Multicultural Development, 25*, 248–265.

Altarriba, J., & Mathis, K. M. (1997). Conceptual and lexical development in second language acquisition. *Journal of Memory and Language, 36*, 550–568.

Altarriba, J., & Santiago-Rivera, A. L. (1994). Current perspectives on using linguistic and cultural factors in counseling the bilingual Spanish-speaking client. *Professional Psychology: Research and Practice, 25*, 388–397.

Altarriba, J., & Soltano, E. G. (1996). Repetition blindness and bilingual memory: Token individuation for translation equivalents. *Memory and Cognition, 24*, 700–711.

Anooshian, L. J., & Hertel, P. T. (1994). Emotionality in free recall: Language specificity in bilingual memory. *Cognition and Emotion, 8*, 503–514.

Balota, D. A., Cortese, M. J., Hutchinson, K. A., Neely, J. H., Nelson, D. L., Simpson, G. B., et al. (2002). *The English Lexicon Project: A web-based repository of descriptive and behavioral measures for 40,481 English words and non-words.* (Available at http://elexicon.wustl.edu)

Beck, A. T., Steer, R. A., & Brown, G. K. (1996). *BDI-II: Beck Depression Inventory manual* (2nd ed.). Boston, MA: Harcourt, Brace.

Bradley, M. M., & Lang, P. J. (1999). *Affective norms for English words (ANEW).* Gainesville, FL: The NIMH Center for the Study of Emotion and Attention, University of Florida.

Dewaele, J. M. (2004). The emotional force of swearwords and taboo words in the speech of multilinguals. *Journal of Multilingual and Multicultural Development, 25*, 204–222.

Dewaele, J. M. (2008). The emotional weight of *I love you* in multilinguals' languages. *Journal of Pragmatics, 40*, 1753–1780.

Dewaele, J. M., & Furnham, A. (1999). Extraversion: The unloved variable in applied linguistic research. *Language Learning, 49*, 509–544.

Dewaele, J. M., & Furnham, A. (2000). Personality and speech production: A pilot study of second language learners. *Personality and Individual Differences, 28*, 355–365.

Dewaele, J. M., & Pavlenko, A. (2002). Emotion vocabulary in interlanguage. *Language Learning, 52*, 263–322.

Eilola, T. M., Havelka, J., & Sharma, D. (2007). Emotional activation in the first and second language. *Cognition and Emotion, 21*, 1064–1076.

Eysenck, H. J., & Eysenck, S. B. G. (1964). *Manual of the Eysenck personal inventory*. London: Hodder & Stoughton.

Eysenck, M. W. (1981). Learning, memory, and personality. In H. J. Eysenck (Ed.), *A model for personality* (pp. 169–209). Berlin, Germany: Springer Verlag.

Fazio, R. H., Sanbonmatsu, D. M., Powell, M. C., & Kardes, F. R. (1986). On the automatic activation of attitudes. *Journal of Personality and Social Psychology, 50,* 229–238.

Gonzalez-Regiosa, F. (1976). The anxiety arousing effect of taboo words in bilinguals. In C. D. Spielberger & R. Diaz-Guerrero (Eds.), *Cross-cultural anxiety* (pp. 89–105). Washington, DC: Hemisphere.

Gray, S. G., Hughes, H. H., & Schneider, L. J. (1982). Physiological responsivity to a socially stressful situation: The effect of moral development. *Psychological Record, 32,* 29–34.

Harris, C. L. (2004). Bilingual speakers in the lab: Psychophysiological measures of emotional reactivity. *Journal of Multilingual and Multicultural Development, 25,* 223–247.

Harris, C. L., Ayçiçeği, A., & Berko-Gleason, J. B. (2003). Taboo words and reprimands elicit greater autonomic reactivity in a first language than in a second language. *Applied Psycholinguistics, 24,* 561–579.

Harris, C. L., Berko-Gleason, J. B., & Ayçiçeği, A. (2005). When is a first language more emotional? Psychophysiological evidence from bilingual speakers. In A. Pavlenko (Ed.), *Bilingual minds: Emotional experience, expression, and representation* (pp. 257–283). Clevedon, UK: Multilingual Matters.

Javier, R. A., Barroso, F., & Muñoz, M. A. (1993). Autobiographical memory in bilinguals. *Journal of Psycholinguistic Research, 22,* 319–338.

Kanwisher, N. G. (1987). Repetition blindness: Type recognition with token individuation. *Cognition, 27,* 117–143.

Kanwisher, N. G., & Potter, M. C. (1990). Repetition blindness: Levels of processing. *Journal of Experimental Psychology: Human Perception and Performance, 16,* 30–47.

Kroll, J. F., & Stewart, E. (1994). Category interference in translation and picture naming: Evidence for asymmetric connections between bilingual memory representations. *Journal of Memory and Language, 33,* 149–174.

Larsen, S. F., Schrauf, R. W., Fromholt, P., & Rubin, D. C. (2002). Inner speech and bilingual autobiographical memory: A Polish–Danish cross-cultural study. *Memory, 10,* 45–54.

Luna, D., Ringberg, T., & Peracchio, L. A. (2008). One individual, two identities: Frame switching among biculturals. *Journal of Consumer Research, 35,* 279–293.

MacKay, D. G., Hadley, C. B., & Schwartz, J. H. (2005). Relations between emotion, illusory word perception, and orthographic repetition blindness: Tests of binding theory. *Quarterly Journal of Experimental Psychology: Human Experimental Psychology, 58A,* 1514–1533.

MacKay, D. G., James, L. E., & Abrams, L. (2002). Cross-language facilitation, repetition blindness, and the relation between language and memory: Replications of Altarriba and Soltano (1996) and support for a new theory. In R. Heredia & J. Altarriba (Eds.), *Bilingual sentence processing* (pp. 89–109). Amsterdam: Elsevier Science Publishers.

Marian, V., & Neisser, U. (2000). Language-dependent recall of autobiographical memory. *Journal of Experimental Psychology: General, 129,* 361–368.

McGinnies, E. (1949). Emotionality of perceptual defense. *Psychological Review, 56*, 427–433.

Nelson, D. L., McEvoy, C. L., & Schreiber, T. A. (1998). *The University of South Florida word associations, rhyme, and word fragment norms.* (Available at http://w3.usf.edu/FreeAssociation)

Santiago-Rivera, A. L., & Altarriba, J. (2002). The role of language in therapy with the Spanish–English bilingual client. *Professional Psychology: Research and Practice, 33*, 30–38.

Schrauf, R. W., & Hoffman, L. (2007). Effects of revisionism on remembered emotion: The valence of older, voluntary immigrants' pre-migration autobiographical memories. *Applied Cognitive Psychology, 21*, 895–913.

Schrauf, R. W., & Rubin, D. C. (1998). Bilingual autobiographical memory in older adult immigrants: A test of cognitive explanations of the reminiscence bump and the linguistic encoding of memories. *Journal of Memory and Language, 39*, 437–457.

Schrauf, R. W., & Rubin, D. C. (2000). Internal languages of retrieval: The bilingual encoding of memories for the personal past. *Memory & Cognition, 28*, 616–623.

Schrauf, R. W., & Rubin, D. C. (2001). Effects of voluntary immigration on the distribution of autobiographical memory over the lifespan. *Applied Cognitive Psychology, 15*, S75–S88.

Shapiro, K. J., & Alexander, I. E. (1969). Extraversion–introversion, affiliation, and anxiety. *Journal of Personality, 37*, 387–406.

Silvert, L., Naveteur, J., Honoré, J., Sequeira, H., & Boucart, M. (2004). Emotional stimuli in rapid serial visual presentation. *Visual Cognition, 11*, 433–460.

Spielberger, C. D., Gorsuch. R. L., Lushene, R., Vagg, P. R., & Jacobs, G. A. (1983). *Manual for the State-Trait Anxiety Inventory (Form Y).* Palo Alto, CA: Consulting Psychologist Press.

Stroop, J. R. (1935). Studies of interference in serial verbal reactions. *Journal of Experimental Psychology, 18*, 643–662.

Sutton, T. M., Altarriba, J., Gianico, J. L., & Basnight-Brown, D. M. (2007). The automatic access of emotion: Emotional Stroop effects in Spanish–English bilingual speakers. *Cognition and Emotion, 21*, 1077–1090.

Toglia, M. P., & Battig, W. F. (1978). *Handbook of semantic word norms.* Hillsdale, NJ: Lawrence Erlbaum Associates Inc.

Trippe, R. H., Hewig, J., Heydel, C., Hecht, H., & Miltner, W. H. R. (2007). Attentional blink to emotional and threatening pictures in spider phobics: Electrophysiology and behavior. *Brain Research, 1148*, 149–160.

21 Emotions in bilingual life narratives

Mary Besemeres

PERSONAL NARRATIVES BY BILINGUALS AS A FORM OF INQUIRY INTO BILINGUALISM

A premise of this chapter is that bilingual life narratives constitute more than raw data for scholars' research on language and cognition. The authors discussed here—Eva Hoffman, Luc Sante, Judith Ortiz Cofer, and others—reflect actively in their own right on questions that concern scholars of bilingualism, such as the central question explored in this chapter, whether bilinguals experience emotions differently in their respective languages. They reflect, however, with respect to their own experience and in a personal, and often literary rather than technical, academic language.

Indeed, I would argue that we can learn at least as much about the relationship of bilingualism to emotions from personal reflections by articulate bilingual writers as from standard methods of research used in disciplines like psychology and psycholinguistics, such as tests or rating and categorization tasks. This point of view has a forceful advocate in cognitive psychologist Merlin Donald (2001), who contends that we can discover more about human consciousness from a novel by Henry James than from clinical psychology:

> The best writers have pushed the subjective exploration of the mind much further than would be permissible in clinical ... psychology. [Their] portrayals of it ... are possibly the most authoritative descriptions we have. ... [S]uch testimony constitutes our primary ethological database.
>
> (Donald, 2001, pp. 78–85)

At least one linguist concurs, arguing that bilingual writers shed more light on bilingual cognition than researchers who rely exclusively on impersonal methods of eliciting data. The linguist Aneta Pavlenko cites the writer Alice Kaplan's complaint that, in reading 'scholarly disquisitions on second language learning' as preparation for writing her own language memoir, *French Lessons* (Kaplan, 1994), she found:

methods and statistics and the occasional anecdote but nothing, really, about what is going on inside the head of the person who suddenly finds herself passionately engaged in new sounds and a new voice, who discovers that '*chat*' is not a cat at all, but a new creature in new surroundings.

(Kaplan, cited in Pavlenko, 2005, p. 195)

Pavlenko argues that the contribution of bilingual writers like Kaplan to the field has in some respects gone further than the work of researchers on second language acquisition, counter to linguist John H. Schumann's view that such writers are 'naive about psychological issues in SLA':

The literature in SLA and bilingualism still ignores such intrinsic aspects of bilingual lives as bilingual selves, bilingual emotions, or the incompatibility between the *chat* and the cat. It is possible, then, that it is research that remains naïve about the language learning process, not bilingual writers and literary scholars, many of whom produced some of the most insightful and inspired writing there is on language, learning and emotions, making connections that have not yet been made in the scholarly literature (Hoffman, 1989; Kellman, 2000; Pérez Firmat, 2003).

(Schumann, cited in Pavlenko, 2005, p. 195)

In this chapter I shall be focusing on what writers like these have to say about aspects of bilingual emotions, but also relating this to what Pavlenko here calls bilingual selves, or in Polish-born author Eva Hoffman's term, bilinguals' 'self-translation' (cf. Besemeres, 2002). The special contribution of such texts is their reflection on, in Kaplan's phrase, 'what is going on inside the head of the person' who finds themselves negotiating new ways of thinking—and feeling—about the world.

In treating bilingual life narratives as sources of insight into bilingual lives, I do not mean to present them as transparent, unmediated records of experience, a 'through-the-clear-crystal recital of something univocally given', as Jerome Bruner (1987, p. 13) puts it in his seminal essay, 'Life as Narrative'. Like any representation in words, life narratives are necessarily selective, and inevitably impose a particular, culturally and historically conditioned, shape on the life they represent. As Bruner and auto-biography theorists like Sidonie Smith have shown, autobiographers are guided by culturally salient, generic conventions that frame their life stories in certain familiar ways. For example, many twentieth-century American life writers frame their story as either a quest or a conversion narrative (cf. Couser, 2004, pp. 72, 101; Smith & Watson, 2001, pp. 70–71), and in doing so omit aspects of their lives that fail to fit into the relevant frame. However, as Paul John Eakin (1992, 1999) and David Parker (2007), among others, argue, autobiography is still best thought of as a mode of reflection on experience, a mode which is also reflective of aspects of that experience: 'Narrative in autobiography is always a retrospective imposition on remembered experience, but the choice of narrative is justified by its roots in that experience' (Eakin, 1992, p. 197). If autobiography is a culturally shaped narrative rather than a record it still, integrally, reflects something of an author's life because, as Bruner argues, that life is itself shaped by the same culture and, I'd add, like the written narrative, bears the unique stamp of his or her own take on that culture. As thoughtful interpretations of personal bilingual experience, the narratives I discuss are a significant resource for researchers aiming to better understand the relationship between human emotions and life in two languages.

The bilingual authors discussed here—Eva Hoffman, Luc Sante, Judith Ortiz Cofer, Julia Alvarez, Ilan Stavans, Irina Reyn, Irene Ulman, Andrea Witcomb, Anna Gladkova, Jock Wong—may not, at first glance, look representative of bilinguals in general. They are all tertiary educated, and most work in language-related fields. Several are linguists by profession; one is a journalist and translator, another, a cultural historian. Several are acclaimed creative writers.

I would argue, however, that the practice of thinking and writing about language and one's own bilingual experience does not disqualify a person from offering reflections on bilingualism and emotion that might be, at least in part, valid for others. The close parallels between the reflections of these authors, who are of widely different cultural backgrounds and significantly different socio-economic backgrounds—Luc Sante's parents working-class Belgians, Eva Hoffman's parents born into artisan families in a Ukrainian shtetl, becoming lower middle class in postwar Poland, then working-class immigrants in Canada, Ortiz Cofer's father a US Navy man and her mother the daughter of a builder (both Puerto Rican), Julia Alvarez's family belonging to the Dominican elite—strongly suggest that what they say about bilingualism and emotions carries a relevance beyond their own individual cases.

RESEARCH ON EMOTION IN BILINGUAL NARRATIVES

Before turning to the treatment of emotions in these narratives, I offer below a brief review of the scholarly literature on bilingualism and emotion in life narratives written in English. A growing number of bilingual or 'translingual' (Kellman, 2000) memoirs have appeared in the 20 years since the 1989 publication of one of the earliest and perhaps the most influential, Hoffman's *Lost in Translation*, and many have been discussed by scholars (e.g., Beaujour, 1989; Besemeres, 1998; Eakin, 1992; Kellman, 2000; Pavlenko, 2001). The study of their representation of language and emotions (as opposed to ethnic identity, or gender), however, is still at a relatively early stage.

In her essay 'On language memoir' (Kaplan, 1994), the first critical work to identify the genre, Alice Kaplan writes of the emotions that motivate language learning, contending that they more often involve 'desire and fear and greed and the need to escape' than a wish to communicate or to achieve empathy (1994, p. 60). '[S]uch positive, altruistic motives', she writes, 'cannot possibly take into account the variety of contexts in which languages are learned' (p. 60). In support of this claim she offers persuasive readings of the memoirs of New York Jewish intellectual Alfred Kazin, *Walker in the City* (1951), and Mexican American writer Richard Rodriguez, *Hunger of Memory* (1981), and a memorable excerpt from her own memoir, *French Lessons* (Kaplan, 1993).

In a more recent article on the same phenomenon of language desire (Piller & Takahashi, 2006) in bilingual narratives, Celeste Kinginger (2004) sheds light on the emotional history of Canadian-born French writer Nancy Huston's complex transition from English to French. She argues that Huston's autobiographical writings demonstrate that 'study of a foreign language can be driven by emotional investment and by richly nuanced imagination' and 'can also emerge from desire for new and more complex ways to live' (Kinginger, 2004, p. 160).

Two key monographs in the field are Gustavo Pérez Firmat's *Tongue Ties: Logo-Eroticism in Anglo-Hispanic Literature* (2003) and Aneta Pavlenko's *Emotions and Multilingualism* (2005). Pérez Firmat's study explores the affective connections or, as his punning title has it, 'tongue ties' to Spanish and English of a series of prominent bilingual Spanish–American and US Latino writers, including George Santayana, Guillermo Cabrera Infante, Maria Luisa Bombal, Richard Rodriguez, and Sandra Cisneros. He argues that their 'careers are shaped by a linguistic family romance' that forces them to negotiate 'the competing claims . . . of Spanish and English' (p. 5). I'll return in more detail to his argument on page 491 below.

Pavlenko's book examines a number of bi- and multilingual narratives, alongside experimental data, surveys, and interviews. She considers such central questions as whether the first language always remains 'the language of emotions' and the second the 'language of distance and detachment' (Pavlenko, 2005, p. 30), and what part emotions play in narratives of language learning and attrition. One of her major findings is that autobiographical testimonies and interviews with bilingual respondents alike affirm that emotional investments in languages are subject to significant change. One of the most moving linguistic trajectories she explores is American historian Gerda Lerner's route from a visceral rejection of her native German, as a young Jewish refugee from Nazi Germany, to an eventual reconciliation with her childhood language in late middle age.

There are a number of edited volumes of translingual life writing (Besemeres & Wierzbicka, 2007; Danquah, 2000; de Courtivron, 2003; Kellman, 2003; Lesser, 2004; Novakovich & Shaphard, 2000; Ogulnick,

2000) whose editors' introductions touch, to varying degrees, on the theme of emotions and bilingualism. None focuses exclusively on the subject, although many of the collected essays in the volumes constitute significant autobiographical contributions to the field.

My book *Translating One's Self: Language and Selfhood in Cross-Cultural Autobiography* (Besemeres, 2002) looks at the representation of language-specific emotion words in several cross-cultural narratives, including the Polish *tęsknota* (a kind of nostalgic longing) in *Lost in Translation*, the English *embarrassment* in Hungarian-born Australian Andrew Riemer's memoir *Inside Outside*, and the recurrent use of *intimacy* in Rodriguez' *Hunger of Memory* as a form of transference from Spanish *intimidad*. The book concludes that these texts show that migrating into a new language means coming to live with significantly different conceptual and emotional worlds.

Elsewhere I discuss poet Stanisław Barańczak's comparison of *happy* with the Polish *szczęśliwy*, Hoffman's contrast between *boję się* (in Polish) and *I'm anxious*, Italian diminutives in English writer Tim Parks' *An Italian Education*, the Cantonese interjection *Aiyah* in Australian author Lilian Ng's *Silver Sister* and Italian forms of address in Canadian writer Nino Ricci's *The Book of Saints* (Besemeres, 2004a). An expanded, revised version of this article additionally discusses the role of the Polish *żal* in Australian poet Peter Skrzynecki's memoir *The Sparrow Garden*, and the Japanese term *morai-naki* in American novelist Kyoko Mori's *Polite Lies: On Being a Woman Caught Between Cultures* (Besemeres, 2006).

While not all of the studies reviewed above deal explicitly with the issue of the linguistic relativity of emotional life, they all affirm the centrality of emotional experience to bilingual life narratives. Whereas in my own previous research I addressed writers' accounts of emotion words like *tęsknota*, here I will look first at reflections on the emotions associated with the words *friend* and *friendship* in English and their counterparts in Polish, Russian, and Cantonese, and second at the extent to which English is represented in bilingual narratives as a comparatively 'cold' language, emotionally, and why this might be.

THE EMOTIONS OF 'FRIENDSHIP': POLISH, RUSSIAN, CANTONESE/MANDARIN, AND AUSTRALIAN AND AMERICAN ENGLISH

The words *friend* and *friendship* in English refer to a relationship rather than an emotion per se. But *friendship* clearly denotes an emotional tie, a human connection characterized by certain emotions. It is no accident that *friendship* frequently appears together with *love*. A Google search for the collocation *love and friendship* in March 2009 found 950,000 entries, as opposed to only 50,000 for the collocation *love and responsibility*, despite the fact that the word *responsibility* appears twice as often on the internet as *friendship*. In talking about the concept of 'friendship' in English we are talking about relationships prototypically characterized, like love, by good feelings towards another person.

This English-language concept is remembered by a number of bilingual commentators as an initial stumbling block to their acculturation into Anglophone ways. Aneta Pavlenko (2001) notes that the difficulty of translating understandings of 'friendship' is a recurrent theme of what she calls 'language learning memoirs': 'intimate relationships and friendships surface time and again as one of the most difficult areas for negotiation' (p. 151). My reading of bilingual life narratives confirms her observation.

I turn now to some telling examples of reflections on the translatability of 'friendship': one by a writer bilingual in Polish and English, three by Russian–English bilinguals, and one by a Singaporean whose family language is Cantonese. There are significant parallels between the comparisons of Russian and English, but also a striking overlap between these, as a group, and the passage comparing Polish and English. The undeniable congruence of all the discussions of the concept of 'friend' in English suggests some major continuities between attitudes to emotion reflected in Canadian, American, and Australian Englishes, for all the evident local variations between them.

In her memoir *Lost in Translation* (1989/1991), Eva Hoffman, who emigrated to Canada from Poland with her parents and sister when she was 13, in 1959, recalls her unease with applying the word *friend* to her Vancouver classmate Penny:

> We like each other quite well, though I'm not sure that what is between us is 'friendship'—a word which in Polish has connotations of strong loyalty and attachment bordering on love. At first, I try to preserve the distinction between 'friends' and 'acquaintances' scrupulously, because it feels like a small lie to say 'friend' when you don't really mean it, but after a while, I give it up. 'Friend', in English, is such a good-natured, easygoing sort of term, covering all kinds of territory, and 'acquaintance' is something an uptight, snobbish kind of person might say. My parents, however, never divest themselves of the habit, and with an admirable resistance to linguistic looseness, continue to call most people they know 'my acquaintance'—or, as they put it early on, 'mine acquaintance.'
>
> As the word is used here, Penny is certainly a friend, and we spend many hours together, gossiping about our classmates and teachers and futures.
>
> (Hoffman, 1989/1991, p. 148)

In Poland, Hoffman was used to having a choice between two words for girls with whom she associated: *przyjaciółka*, cognate with *przyjaźń* (the

Polish 'friendship') which, in her words, connotes 'strong loyalty' and 'border[s]' on 'love', and *znajoma*, loosely translatable as *acquaintance*. In Canada she found herself faced instead with the singular, undifferentiated *friend*. Whereas *znajoma* was colloquial, *acquaintance*, as the teenage Eva quickly recognized, was not, and she had to drop using it to avoid sounding snobbish to her peers. When they spoke of *acquaintances* her parents were using a literal calque from *znajomi*. In doing so they remained faithful to their previous social reality, whereas she adapted to using what 'fel[t] like a small lie'. Hoffman's gently ironic phrase 'an admirable resistance to linguistic looseness' identifies her parents' lack of receptivity to register, as older, psychologically less flexible immigrants. The detail that they continued to call most people they knew *acquaintance* highlights their isolation, and poignantly conveys the social costs for immigrants of not 'giv[ing] up' deeply ingrained ways of seeing and relating to others. (As we will see later, Hoffman's memoir is equally alert to the costs, for those who change languages, of giving up native ways of seeing.)

In her essay 'Recalling a Child of October', Irina Reyn (2000), who emigrated with her parents to the US from Russia at age 7 in 1981, recalls her early experiences of school in Brooklyn in terms that also foreground the strangeness to her of the new concept of 'friend':

> I enjoyed school, especially English class, but never understood American children's loyalties and friendships, which seemed to me to be arbitrary and ephemeral. I was awed by their command of space, but sensed that once claimed, the space was not to be shared. I was not able to formulate the impression that American children are raised with a certain degree of confidence, independence and self-reliance, that the degree to which relationships are needed seemed to be alleviated due to their ability to maneuver smoothly in their environment. Being born of a collective country, Russians' friendships take on the covenant of family and the relationships tend to be full of earnest ardour and vehement devotion.
>
> Not surprisingly, my shyness and intensity drove people away and I tended to gravitate to other immigrants like myself, who felt the same displacement.
>
> (Reyn, 2000, pp. 150–151)

Reyn is recalling schooldays from her first year or so after emigration, when, as a bright 7-year-old, she was quickly mastering English in a technical sense (winning the class spelling bee at the end of her first year) but struggling to grasp what she now sees were its underlying cultural norms: an emphasis on 'confidence, independence and self-reliance' contrary to the more collective emphases she had known in Russia. Reyn's description of Russian friendships as taking on 'the covenant of family' resonates with Hoffman's sense of *przyjaźń* as an 'attachment bordering on love'—an

unsurprising echo, perhaps, given the historical proximity between Polish-
and Russian-speaking cultures, but equally an implicit comment on seemingly superficial styles of friendship: 'easygoing' (Hoffman), 'ephemeral'
(Reyn). Reyn's remembered impression of 'space' not being shared even
among friends at her American school anticipates the description another
Russian–English bilingual, Anna Gladkova, gives of the 'lack of initiative
and overdependence' which her Australian friends read in her ways of
relating to them (Gladkova, 2007, p. 142) (a text to which I'll return).

   In 'Playgrounds and Battlegrounds' (Ulman, 2007), journalist and
translator Irene Ulman writes of coming to Australia with her parents
from Russia in 1976, aged 12, after 2 intervening years in Israel. She, too,
singles out for comment her disconcerting encounter, at school, with a new
set of rules for 'friendship' in English:

> I received a blow when a girl who said she was my friend renamed me
> Martha and talked about me, thinking that I didn't understand. Then
> a girl (whose name I thought was *Lorraaaahyne* until I saw it in writ-
> ing) asked me if I was her friend. I naturally said no. She said: 'Ough,
> why not?' I explained that I didn't know her well enough to be her
> friend, and she said: 'But you've known me all year!' Later, her friend
> (whose name I thought was *Treeeesa*) asked: 'Why did you tell
> Lorraine that you're not her friend? What's she done to you?'
>
>   It was hard to know how to use this word 'friend' in a way that
> would be helpful to me and would advance my social life, without
> compromising the principle behind words like 'friend' or the phrase
> 'being friends with' someone.
>
>   My idea of friendship came from a combination of the books I read
> and our own family values. Once, in Israel, my mother and I had a big
> laugh when our neighbour made gushingly enthusiastic comments
> about some newly acquired friends . . . She had said something like:
> 'Imagine! They're our newest friends!'—the implication being that the
> best thing about them was that they were new. In contrast, my
> mother's most valued friends were the old friends whom she'd just left
> behind in Russia, possibly forever, and this rapture over a totally new
> friend was very funny to both of us.
>
>   (Ulman, 2007, p. 48)

Like Reyn and Hoffman, Ulman is keenly aware of how, as a child, she did
not yet have the means to recognize her social troubles as symptoms of a
larger cross-cultural context ('As a child it's natural to think that whatever
you are experiencing is your own isolated, personal problem', p. 45). Her
memory of being at a loss for how to use *friend* in English in a socially
advantageous way 'without compromising the principle behind' the word
'friend' in Russian is closely akin to Hoffman's remembered attempt to
'preserve the distinction' between *friend* and *acquaintance* 'scrupulously'.

Both, at first, felt their adaptation to using the English *friend* involved betraying the values embedded in the concept they had lived with in their native language.

An interesting difference between Ulman's experience in 1970s Australia and Reyn's in the US of the 1980s is that whereas Reyn remembers confident command of space as the chief characteristic of children's interaction, Ulman's recollections highlight rather an egalitarian non-exclusivity which takes offence at the notion of friendship as special, one-on-one ('Why did you tell Lorraine she's not your friend? What's she done to you?'). Perhaps this emphasis is more typical of Australian culture with its concept of 'mateship'. (See Wierzbicka, 1997, for a comparison of the Australian term *mateship* with Polish, Russian, and English 'friendship' words.) Yet the sense that insisting on reserving *przyjaźń* for only a rare few looks snobbish in an English-language context (where the word *friend* 'cover[s] all sorts of territory') is equally salient in Hoffman's 1960s Canadian experience.

Given the parallels, then, with both Hoffman's and Reyn's accounts, the idea of 'friendship' that Ulman found so hard to translate into English and now describes as a mix of family values and books she had read, was clearly far from unique to her own family.

In her essay 'The journey of self-discovery in another language', Anna Gladkova (2007) reflects on her experiences as a Russian student and English teacher who moved to Australia in 2004 to pursue a doctorate in linguistics. Although she had previously read about the concept of personal autonomy in English she found the 'actual discovery of its invisible boundaries . . . quite painful' (p. 141). Given the 'friendly interactional style' that 'seemed to characterise Australian culture' she at first assumed that she could drop expressions like *would you . .?, could you . .?*, only to be brought up short:

> When wanting to show my closeness and appreciation of a person I would start dropping the . . . English 'politeness' terms of 'would you' and 'could you' and use a straight imperative and then realise that it was inappropriate. I once said to an Australian friend: 'Come here and look at it!' He remained motionless and said: 'Never say things like to this to people here unless they are close to you'. 'How close?' I inquired. 'Very close.'
>
> (Gladkova, 2007, p. 142)

She adds that after this exchange she made sure not to use the imperative with Australians again. As she renders it, her friend's reaction is quite forbidding although, ironically, he uses an imperative himself ('Never say . . .'). The scene helps us imagine how painfully disconcerting it is to learn that ways of relating with 'friends' in one's first language aren't acceptable in the new one.

In the same passage Gladkova recounts how she would forget to ask friends what their plans for the day were, on the assumption that they would want to spend the time together:

> I would forget about the need to keep asking whether someone would prefer to do something on his or her own rather than doing it 'to keep me company'—*za kompaniiu*, as we say in Russian. Similarly, my desire to express my friendly feelings to others by making it clear I want to keep them company would be perceived by English speakers as a lack of initiative and overdependence.
>
> (Gladkova, 2007, p. 142)

When translated literally, *za kompaniiu* is closer in meaning to *for company's sake* than to the idiomatic English expression *to keep someone company* which Gladkova uses to translate it. *To keep another person company* means to stay with them because of their particular (often, expressed) need. *Za kompaniiu*, by contrast, as Gladkova herself explains it here, implies a *shared* and taken for granted expectation that people will continue to do things together because of the value attached to being with one's friends. It is linked, therefore, with the Russian concept of *druz'ia*, which Gladkova goes on to discuss.

She reflects on the meanings of her current relationships with friends at her campus residential college in Canberra, and considers whether she thinks of them as *druz'ia* or not:

> Are they *druz'ia*—the most obvious Russian equivalent for the word 'friends' . . .? *Drug* (friend) is someone one knows for a long time and with whom one develops a very close bond. It is necessary to be in constant contact with a *drug*, to share each other's lives. Even though I get to know some residents at University House quite well, I can't call them *druz'ia* in Russian. We enjoy our time together, but we also know that this time will end, we will have to be in different parts of the world again . . . The English word 'friend' suits such a relationship because it reflects the reality of a mobile society, where people . . . have to find a way to enjoy their short-term relationships. In Russia most people are much less mobile; many live in one city for their whole lives and therefore establish . . . ties that are expected to be lifelong. . . . I want these people to be my *druz'ia*, but at the same time our reality stops me from thinking in these terms.
>
> (Gladkova, 2007, p. 147)

Gladkova's reflections on the differences between *druz'ia* and *friends*, particularly her emphasis on the depth and lifelong nature of the bond between *druz'ia*, compare interestingly with American journalist Hedrick

Smith's observations about Russian attitudes to friendship in his book *The Russians* (1975):

> Their [the Russians'] social circles are usually narrower than those of Westerners, especially Americans, who put such great stock in popularity, but relations between Russians are usually more intense, more demanding, more enduring and often more rewarding. . . .
> . . . Within the trusted circle, there is an intensity in Russian relationships that Westerners find both exhilarating and exhausting. . . . Russians are looking for a soul-brother, not a mere conversational partner. They want someone to whom they can pour out their hearts . . . As a journalist I sometimes found it ticklish because Russians want a total commitment from a friend.
> (Smith, 1975, pp. 109–110, cited in Wierzbicka, 1997, p. 55)

Whereas Smith presents the differences between Russian and American views of friendship in a style that generalizes freely, is faintly ironic (Russian friendship is 'exhausting'), and makes only marginal reference to his own feelings, Gladkova's reflections are much more deeply personal, as well as being those of a linguist explicitly concerned with how language relates to cross-cultural issues. Yet, for all that separates them in genre and approach to the subject, they are clearly addressing some common experiential realities, if from reverse cultural viewpoints. Gladkova's disappointment at not being able, finally, to call her Australian friends *druz'ia* because they do not 'share each other's lives' closely parallels Smith's perception that friendships in Russia are 'more enduring and often more rewarding'. Anthropologist Dale Pesmen (2000) is exploring the same territory when she comments on the Russian concept of '*obshchenie*' (literally, 'communion', but unlike communion in English, an entirely colloquial term for deep and close relations with others): 'I have discussed the importance to many people of memories of student days. People characterized such times . . . as connected with a circle of friends, *obshchenie* with whom you value more than anything' (Pesmen, 2000, p. 165).

While in her memoir *The Multilingual Self* (1997), Russian-born American language scholar Natasha Lvovich does not explicitly analyze differences between *druz'ia* and *friends*, the vocabulary she uses (in English) to describe friendships is clearly indebted to the same cultural values invoked by Reyn, Ulman, Gladkova, Hedrick Smith, and Dale Pesmen. Writing of her close friendship with a French woman whom she knew in Moscow, Lvovich exclaims: 'this friendship, *worshipped* over more than 15 years, was the best gift I ever received' (Lvovich, 1997, p. 24; emphasis added). The unidiomatic use of the word *worshipped* here sounds very like Reyn's phrase 'earnest ardour and vehement devotion'. It is a highly culturally revealing choice of word. Reyn's faintly ironic adjectives suggest a strong awareness, not present in Lvovich's text, of how *ardour* and *devotion* will sound to Anglophone ears; Lvovich's tone unselfconsciously embodies the emotional intensity Reyn remembers from her Russian childhood (and which Smith says Western visitors find 'exhilarating and exhausting').

I turn finally to Singaporean-born linguist Jock Wong's essay 'East meets West, or does it really?' (Wong, 2007). Wong first came to Australia in 1989 to do undergraduate studies, and returned a decade later to complete his doctorate. He writes of his deep discomfort with the 'politeness' routines used by Australians he regards as friends, which emphasize each person's personal space and autonomy. In Singapore, growing up in an extended family of 11 in a single apartment, he was used to identifying with the rest of his family 'more as a unit than as individuals' (Wong, 2007, p. 74). The Cantonese word for 'thank you' was reserved for receiving special gifts and 'even then only from someone younger to someone older'; he cannot recall his parents *ever* saying 'thank you' to him (p. 74). A Cantonese term for polite terms, *hak hei*, which Wong translates as 'reminiscent of a guest', suggests how alien rules of polite interaction must have appeared to him, in conversation with close friends in Australia.

Mandarin, Wong's second language, further reinforced some of the 'core Chinese values concerning human relations' he had assimilated via his family's Cantonese. He points out that in Mandarin, close male friends are called *xiongdi* ('brothers') or *shouzu* ('arm and leg'), and female friends *jiemei* ('sisters'). 'Above all,' he writes, 'a true mark of friendship is when people *bu fen bici* (. . . "to not distinguish between one another")' (2007, p. 74). He says he has tried to explain the principle of *bu fen bici* to some of his 'closest Anglo friends . . . in the hope that they would thank me less frequently and stop asking me what I want so routinely', talk which leaves him feeling alienated (p. 80). At the same time, he has at times experienced 'a curious sense of freedom', living in Australia, and has gradually become more accustomed to being accorded personal space, so that on returns to Singapore he has sometimes felt stifled (p. 78) when interacting with others in Chinese. (Wong also discusses salient differences between Australian English and the Singaporean English that is his third language, which I can't go into here.) His account of his ingrained reactions to the ubiquitous *thank you* among friends resonates with Gladkova's descriptions of feeling pushed away by Australian friends when she unconsciously translated into English the speech norms she was used to using with *druz'ia* in Russian.

The Polish *przyjaciółka* and *przyjaźń*, the Russian *drug* and *druz'ia*, the avoidance of politeness terms with close friends in Cantonese, and the Mandarin *bu fen bici* ('to not distinguish') and *shouzu* ('arm and leg', for male friendship), with its idea of inseparability, all encode expectations about human relating that are incompatible with the values underlying *friend* in English, which Hoffman, Gladkova, Ulman, Reyn, and Wong have found alien: broadly speaking, values of autonomy and self-reliance, as well as egalitarian non-exclusivity. To say this is not to imply the impossibility of deep and close friendships among native English speakers (and, after all, people do sometimes speak in English of friends who are inseparable). But it *is* to suggest that there is a cultural attitude to 'friendship'—or more precisely, to *being friends*—reflected in aspects of modern English as spoken in Australia and America (and arguably Britain, though that is beyond the scope of the present discussion) which is distinctive, and differs in important ways from the attitudes found in many other languages. *Friend* in English does *not* inherently connote an inseparable part of oneself as *shouzu* does; nor is there anything in the language, as there is in Russian (*obshchenie, za kompaniiu*) that discourages friends from going their own ways of an evening.

ENGLISH A 'COLD' LANGUAGE? REFLECTIONS BY POLISH, FRENCH, PORTUGUESE, AND SPANISH-SPEAKING IMMIGRANTS 'INTO' ENGLISH

Emotions are an integral part of cognition, of mental life, and hence of bilingual cognition, as is suggested by the title of Aneta Pavlenko's edited volume *Bilingual Minds: Emotional Experience, Expression and Representation* (Pavlenko, 2006). It is a commonplace of the literature on bilingualism that the mother tongue is the language of emotions, while acquired tongues are languages of distance and detachment (see Pavlenko, 2005, p. 30, for an approach that probes and extends this 'establish[ed]' view). Many bilingual writers who have moved into the sphere of a second language present their emotional connection to their mother tongue and relative detachment from their second in terms of the former's role as medium for their formative relationships and earliest engagements with the world. Hoffman eloquently evokes the interior images given to her by Polish and absent from English, and figures her entry into English as a 'radical disjoining between word and thing', 'the loss of a living connection' (Hoffman, 1989, p. 107). According to Andrew Riemer, only the language of childhood can express deeply personal experiences (1992, p. 178). American author Luc Sante, who moved to the US with his parents from Belgium as a child, portrays his relationship with French as an immigrant adolescent in terms of a painful intimacy, and that with English, in terms of artificiality: 'one is tissue and the other is plastic. One is a wound and the other is a prosthesis' (Sante, 1998, p. 263).

It could be argued that common perceptions of English among bilingual immigrants as a cold, unemotional language mistake this phenomenon of detachment from a second language for insight into aspects of English-language cultures. Yet not only do many narratives of migration 'into' English relay such a perspective, but several describing the reverse trajectory, 'away' from English into other languages, like Tim Parks's *An Italian Education*, suggest that English-speaking cultures may inhibit certain forms of emotional expression (see Besemeres, 2005, 2008). Texts like these testify in a personal way to the pervasive dampening of emotional intensity in modern English-speaking cultures which has been documented by historian of emotions Peter Stearns (1994), among others.

Sante's memoir *The Factory of Facts* (Sante, 1998) explores both what has been called the 'stepmother tongue' phenomenon (Novakovich & Shaphard, 2000) and what are arguably the intrinsically different emotional tonalities of French, Walloon, and English. Of the first phenomenon, he writes:

> To speak of my family, for example, I can hardly employ English without omitting an emotional essence that remains locked in French, although I can't use French either, unless I am willing to sacrifice my critical intelligence. . . . French is an archeological site of emotions, a pipeline to my infant self. It preserves the very rawest, deepest, least guarded feelings.
>
> (Sante, 2004, p. 265)

But in the following passage Sante reflects on some French words which are not only personal, Proustian emotional triggers like *Allons dire bonjour, une tasse de café* (p. 265), but inherently emotional words, specific to French or Walloon and virtually untranslatable, terms of endearment and expressions of anger or amused affection. He writes:

> In my family, the use of someone's first name was nearly always an indication of anger or the prelude to bad news. My parents addressed me as *fifi*, *chou* (cabbage), *lapin* (rabbit), *vî tchèt* (Walloon: old cat), *petit coeur* [little heart]. If I'd done something mischievous my father would laugh and call me *cûrêye* (Walloon for 'carcass' or 'spavined horse'—like saying 'you're rotten'). If my mother was . . . ang[ry] . . . she might call me a *vaurien* [worth-nothing] or . . . an *èstèné* (Walloon for 'idiot', literally 'bewildered') . . .
>
> (Sante, 1998, p. 266)

Chou, vî tchèt, èstèné and the rest convey attitudes that escape easy translation into English. Sante gives us an idea of the meaning of *cûrêye* by calling it 'like' the phrase *you're rotten*, but his father's laugh suggests a different feeling from even an affectionate use of this insult in English (cf. the post by Kim, 2009, 'You're rotten!', 7 March on American mother's blog 'Never a Dull Moment'). The habitual use of such words by Sante's parents in place of his name suggests a world of relations in which the parents' feelings for their child are at the fore, not his individual identity.

Hoffman writes poignantly of the gap between her mother's and her own emotional worlds as immigrants, her mother finding her new behavior cold:

My mother says I'm becoming 'English'. This hurts me, because I know she means I'm becoming cold. I'm no colder than I've ever been, but I'm learning to be less demonstrative. . . . I learn my new reserve from people who take a step back when we talk, because I'm standing too close, crowding them. . . . I learn restraint from Penny, who looks offended when I shake her by the arm in excitement, as if my gesture had been one of aggression instead of friendliness. . . .

Perhaps my mother is right, after all; perhaps I'm becoming colder. After a while, emotion follows action, response grows warmer or cooler according to gesture. I'm more careful about what I say, how loud I laugh, whether I give vent to grief. The storminess of emotion prevailing in our family is in excess of the normal here, and the unwritten rules for the normal have their osmotic effect.

(Hoffmann, 1989/1991, pp. 146–147)

I have discussed this passage at length elsewhere (Besemeres, 2004b) and so refrain from discussing it again in detail here, but quote it virtually in full because it speaks volumes about immigrant perceptions of English as a cold language. I will simply comment on its striking closeness to a passage in an essay by Andrea Witcomb, an Australian cultural historian born and partly brought up in Portugal, about her changed relationship to her father after the family's emigration to Australia (like Hoffman, Witcomb was 13 when she emigrated). Witcomb's father, whom she called *Pai*, was an Englishman, long settled in Portugal and deeply attached to his adopted homeland, who was forced by familial circumstances to move to Australia. In her essay 'Growing up between two languages/two worlds: Learning to live without belonging to a *terra*', Witcomb (2007) recounts how in Portugal he had always spoken with her and her brothers in Portuguese, but on arrival in Australia abruptly stopped using their shared language. In the months before he joined the family in Australia, he had written letters to her in Portuguese, which she now finds painful to reread.

Once he stepped off that plane he never once spoke in Portuguese to us again. Our relationship was now to be mediated through the English language. We lost our daily rituals, such as the little ditty he would say to us when we went to bed or the singing of Portuguese folk songs. I also lost a certain emotional landscape—a landscape in which he was an unquestioned figure of authority but which also allowed him to express emotion. For what those letters document is my father's ability to express, through the medium of written Portuguese, his love for me. It is, I know, trite to say that English is a cold language. But the language my father used in those letters has a higher intensity—it is there in his use of a string of adjectives, in his use of superlatives, in his attempt to comfort me over my experiences at school. . . . The emotional landscape I lost was also the ability to remember Portugal by talking about it in Portuguese. . . . And there is . . . no one else with whom I can share those memories and that language.

(Witcomb, 2007, pp. 93–94)

Like Luc Sante in the passage quoted earlier, Witcomb evokes both the stepmother tongue phenomenon here (the loss of the language of her childhood), and cultural aspects of English and Portuguese which she finds to be distinctive independently of her own chronological or bio-graphical relationship to them (the 'string of adjectives' and 'superlatives' that her father *could* use in Portuguese and not in English). In one respect, her experience appears to be the direct opposite of Hoffman's and Sante's: Whereas they recall the distance that their own use of English speech norms introduced between them and their parents (even when they spoke to them in their mother tongues), Witcomb portrays rather the distance that her father's *own* relinquishing of his beloved Portuguese and reversion to his native English brought about between them. Yet, clearly, the effects of the move into English from a language remembered as in certain ways warmer and emotionally more expressive, have been very similar.

In both her memoir, *Silent Dancing: A Partial Remembrance of a Puerto Rican Childhood* (Ortiz Cofer, 1991) and her autobiographical essay 'Rituals: A Prayer, a Candle, and a Notebook' (Ortiz-Cofer, 2000), Judith Ortiz Cofer recalls the Spanish voices she heard as a child, growing up between Puerto Rico and Paterson, New Jersey, as loud and strongly expressive. She contrasts them with more neutral-sounding speech charac-teristic of places where English was spoken. She evokes the vivid sounds of 'El Building', the Paterson tenement known as 'the vertical barrio' because it was home to Puerto Ricans who settled in the city. Her father, a Navy man during whose absences the family returned to Puerto Rico, moved them into an apartment above a store, a block away from 'El Building', to hasten their assimilation into American ways. From their apartment they could hear, but not participate, in the life of the barrio:

> Unlike El Building, where we had lived on our first trip to Paterson, our new home was truly in exile. There were Puerto Ricans by the hundreds only one block away, but we heard no Spanish, no loud music, no mothers yelling at children, nor the familiar *!Ay Bendito!*, that catch-all phrase of our people. Mother lapsed into silence herself, suffering from *La Tristeza*, the sadness that only place induces and only place cures. But Father relished silence, and we were taught that silence was something to be cultivated and practiced.
>
> (Ortiz Cofer, 1991, p. 64)

Of being taken shopping to the barrio, she remembers: 'The people in these bodegas shot Spanish at one another like machine-gun fire. So fast did they speak that I could barely understand what they were saying'

(Ortiz Cofer, 2000, p. 33). To the child's ear, in public, English is muted by comparison with Spanish. Ortiz Cofer contrasts not only English and Spanish, but also the atmosphere of the barrio and her father's strict imposition of quiet at their apartment. But, as I'll shortly discuss, she strongly suggests that her father's attitudes were unusual.

Texts like Sante's, Hoffman's, Witcomb's, and Ortiz Cofer's (and, conversely, Tim Parks') strongly suggest that the perception of English coldness, while reductive if used as a blanket generalization about English speakers, nevertheless has some basis in actual rules of interaction built into modern English. These 'unwritten rules for the normal' in Hoffman's phrase, or 'cultural scripts' (Goddard & Wierzbicka, 2004), encourage ways of speaking which reflect negative attitudes towards the expression of certain emotions and towards intensity of expression more generally (cf. Reyn, 2000; Stearns, 1994). No matter how warm an Anglophone individual may be, he or she must find ways to express warmth, verbally at least, within a framework that places no particular value on warmth, and limits its expression. Individual speakers can go beyond these limits by coining new words or borrowing foreign ones to convey their feelings, but this is a very different matter from being able to draw on available, and widely shared, linguistic resources. To the extent that Hoffman started to adapt her interactions with her mother *in Polish* to the cultural scripts she had picked up from her English-speaking environment, she was muting the expressions of feelings like the Polish *serdeczność* (cf. Wierzbicka, 1999) that so painfully marked her family out as foreigners.

Likewise, exploring contrasts between ways of expressing emotion in Spanish and those available in English as portrayed by US Latino writers like Ortiz Cofer need not translate into trading in stereotypes. Just as there is no denying the existence of warmly affectionate and gregarious speakers of English, there is no reason to imagine that Latin Americans are all equally comfortable with verbal and physical expressions of warmth (or rather, of *calor humano*, as discussed by Catherine Travis, 2006, in relation to Colombian culture). As Rosita D. Albert and In Ah Ha (2004) point out, while 'Latin American cultures are generally considered to be high contact. . . . [t]his is not to say that Latin Americans are *uniformly* "high contact" ' (emphasis added). Ortiz Cofer offers a memorable evocation of different personal attitudes to contact in this sense when she describes her parents' dissimilar attitudes to mingling with other Puerto Ricans in Paterson:

> A look of haughty indifference would settle over [my father's] face as he 'escorted' my mother up and down the aisles . . . She walked slowly, picking up cans and reading the labels, perhaps savoring the familiar smells of her culture, the sounds of sloppy Spanish as customers and clerks engaged in the verbal tag called *el gufeo* in barrio slang. It is a game of double entendre, of puns, semiserious insults, and responses

that are *tipicos*—the usual exchanges for Puerto Ricans in familiar settings. My father ignored the loud voices, the vulgar innuendos, and the uncontrolled laughter they incited. My mother obviously enjoyed it.

(Ortiz Cofer, 2000, p. 33)

In a very similar vein, in her book of essays *Something to Declare*, Dominican-American author Julia Alvarez portrays her father's discomfort with 'touching scenes':

> He hated touching scenes; they confused him. Perhaps as the last child of an older, disappointed woman, he was used to diffuse attention, not intimacy. To take hold of a hand, to graze a cheek and whisper an endearment were beyond him. Tenderness had to be mothered by necessity: he was a good doctor. Under cover of Hippocrates' oath, with the . . . bright examination light flushing out the personal and making any interchange completely professional, he was amazingly delicate.

(Alvarez, 1998, p. 58)

Tellingly, however, both Alvarez and Ortiz Cofer use words that suggest their father's emotional style and stance are not characteristic for Dominican and Puerto Rican cultures, respectively. Ortiz Cofer presents her father's style of speech as peculiar and foreign-sounding in either Spanish or English:

> He avoided using slang in both languages and sounded like a foreigner when he spoke either. It was the peculiar slowness of his speech and his insistence on the clarity of each word that made him seem cautious in the way he spoke.

(Ortiz Cofer, 2000, pp. 35–36)

She evokes his discomfort with forms of talk that were '*tipicos*' for barrio dwellers (like *el gufeo*) which makes him appear *atypical* of Puerto Rican migrants, in contrast to her mother, who enjoyed them. Alvarez explains her father's dislike of touching scenes with reference to his being the 'last child of an older, disappointed woman [. . .] used to diffuse attention, not intimacy', i.e., an unusual family dynamic, and says that small signs of familial tenderness were beyond him, presenting his behavior in terms of lack and loss rather than as normal or common. Writings like Ortiz Cofer's and Alvarez's suggest a vision of people as, at the same time, unique individuals and bearers of—or, perforce, reluctant negotiators with—widely shared cultural attitudes to emotions.

In his illuminating study of bilingual writers' emotional connections to their languages, *Tongue Ties*, Gustavo Pérez Firmat (2003) expresses skepticism about the reality of intrinsic cultural differences between languages. He concedes that there is 'much anecdotal evidence' for differences between Spanish and English, but regards the contrasts that are often drawn as stereotypical: 'All of us have heard (and sometimes repeated) the clichés: English is factual, Spanish is florid; English is plain, Spanish is ornate' (p. 10). He notes that US Latino writers 'often endorse the view that Spanish is more soulful than English' (p. 11) and thus de facto support a version of the Sapir-Whorf hypothesis of linguistic relativity according to which one's worldview is significantly shaped by one's language. As examples he mentions Ortiz Cofer and fellow Puerto-Rican American writer Rosario Ferré, whose respective descriptions of Spanish as 'passionate' and 'baroque' he allows 'contain a grain of truth', 'however reductive' they are. Having acknowledged that there is some experiential basis for what he nevertheless deems 'reductive clichés', he goes on to conclude that bilingual authors' views about their languages are, in the main, subjective, and that their significance lies in their influence on these authors' writing:

> For my purposes, ... the ultimate validity of the Sapir-Whorf hypothesis is irrelevant. What is crucial is that many bilinguals relate to their languages in ways that enact some version of this hypothesis. What may not be true for Spanish and English in any objectively demonstrable way may be true for an individual's apprehension of Spanish and English. Although the notion that Spanish is more 'passionate' or 'baroque' than English may not stand any sort of rigorous test, individual writers or speakers, believing this to be so, may use the two languages in ways that make it true for them.
>
> (Pérez Firmat, 2003, p. 13)

He emphasizes the idiosyncratic, deeply personal qualities of bilingual writers' perspectives on their languages:

> [W]riters' comments generally reveal more about the writer than the language [;] ... their assertions of difference tend to contradict one another, thereby undermining essentialist claims about the two languages. Ortiz Cofer and Ferré may regard Spanish as passionate and convoluted, but for Calvert Casey it is the medium for impassive, minimalist notation.
>
> (Pérez Firmat, 2003, p. 13)

Settling for a subjectivist argument about writers' intuitions of linguistic difference is an understandable move, given the apparent unverifiability of the linguistic relativity hypothesis. The objection that, as he puts it, 'the language of verification will necessarily "skew" the results' (p. 12) has been challenged by the development of a 'Natural Semantic Metalanguage' of simple concepts thus far found in all tested languages, which has been used to translate language-specific concepts (see for example Goddard & Wierzbicka, 1994). But whether or not one takes this methodology into account, a subjectivist position disregards the verifiable existence of lexical and grammatical categories which encode distinctive ways of thinking, including about emotions. Spanish demonstrably has a large fund of diminutives, for instance, that give speakers readymade tools for expressing emotions for which English has no readymade tools (cf. Besemeres, 2002; Gooch, 1967/1970; Travis, 2004, 2006; Wierzbicka, 1984). Julia Alvarez leaves words like *pobrecita* (literally 'little poorie') and *abuelita* (literally 'grandmotherie') in Spanish in her texts in part so as to convey to non-Hispanophone readers something of the culturally specific emotional attitudes they evoke. (See e.g., Alvarez, 1998, p. 136; 2007, p. 260.) In her memoir she tells of how an American editor once noted her overuse of the word *little*, which she realized was due to her unconsciously 'translating from the Spanish diminutive' (2000, p. 219). As Catherine Travis writes of (Colombian) Spanish:

> The use of terms of endearment such as *mi amor* 'my love', *gordo* 'fatty', fictive *mamita* 'mummy' and *papito* 'daddy' (e.g., to your spouse, a friend or a young girl or boy) and so on reflects the high value Colombian culture places on displaying affection for others, and on verbally affirming the tie that exists in relationships. Similar ideals are evident in the extensive use of the diminutive.
>
> (Travis, 2006, p. 199)

It seems likely that it is precisely these kinds of culture-specific expressive resources that motivate Ortiz Cofer's and Ferré's characterizations of Spanish as passionate and baroque.

A subjectivist position, then, fails to take account of the pervasive interconnections between language and culture, which affect writers no less than any other users of language. The language of writers is not completely idiosyncratic. Gifted and original writers may, like Nabokov, create a baroque type of literary English, or, like Calvert Casey, a pared-down, minimalist Spanish, but this doesn't negate the existence of contrary propensities in the language against whose grain they are writing. As for Casey, his sense of Spanish appears to be the exception that proves the rule: The others Pérez Firmat quotes here—Ortiz Cofer, Ferré, Luis Cernuda, Edmundo Desnoes, Rodriguez—as well as others he doesn't quote, such as Alvarez (1998), Ariel Dorfman (1998, pp. 18, 185) and Ilan Stavans (2001, pp. 223, 229), all view the relative emotional tonalities of English and Spanish in remarkably similar terms.

Nor need conflicting descriptions of the same language indicate that bilingual writers have nothing substantial to say about language and culture. For Mexican-born American writer Stavans, 'English is almost mathematical. Its rules manifest themselves in an iron fashion. This is in sharp contrast to Spanish, of course, whose Romance roots make it a free-flowing, imprecise language, with long and uncooperative words' (Stavans, 2001, p. 223). For Luc Sante, by contrast, French, despite also being a Romance language, is 'so much more rigorous and wilfully delimited than the sprawling mass of English, an elegantly efficient two-stroke engine to the latter's uncontainable Rube Goldberg mechanism' (Sante, 2004, p. 70). Sante elaborates:

> French does not necessarily have fewer sounds than English, but the protocols governing their order and frequency make their appearances predictable—hence the profusion of sound-alike phrases and sentences, which fueled Surrealism and ensure the ongoing appeal of Freudian and post-Freudian ideas in the French-speaking world: *Les dents, la bouche. Laid dans la bouche. Les dents la bouchent. L'aidant la bouche.* Etc. These phrases, which sound exactly alike, respectively mean 'the teeth, the mouth'; 'ugly in the mouth'; 'the teeth choke her'; 'helping her chokes her'. You don't need to have been psychoanalyzed by Jacques Lacan to see from these examples how language can assist thought in swiftly tunnelling from the mundane to the taboo.
>
> (Sante, 2004, p. 70)

Rather than dismissing the contrast between Stavans's and Sante's impressions of English as a matter of purely subjective difference, I'd argue there are two distinct issues involved here, which Pérez Firmat's discussion runs together—language as structure and language as meaning. Clearly, many aspects of a language's structure (e.g., rules of pronunciation) need not correspond in any obvious way to the social meanings the same language encodes, both lexically and grammatically (cf. Enfield, 2004; Morano, 2007; Travis, 2004; Wierzbicka, 1988). In its pronunciation, English is, as Sante wittily illustrates, less predictable than French, and in that sense less 'order[ly]', 'mess[ier]'. Yet as regards the emotional resonance of poetry, to the same ear, English has an opposite-sounding tendency to 'condensation and bluntness', while French is 'magic', 'lyric[al]' and its 'silken chains of prepositional phrases' give it an ' "incantatory power" ' (Sante, 2004, p. 78). As far as poetic diction is concerned, then, English is *more*, not less, 'containable' than French, for Sante.

In their study of language ideologies that they argue have been fundamental both to the emergence of modern English and of modern Western socio-political orders, Richard Bauman and Charles Briggs (2003) examine the sustained attack on rhetoric in John Locke's hugely influential *Essay Concerning Human Understanding* (1690):

> Rhetoric becomes the foe of rationality and knowledge through its connection with interest, passion, emotionality, and belief. Locke's

ideal discursive type—plain speech that conveys information with maximum economy through referentially stable signs—actively engages the rational capacity of the mind. Rhetoric and its devices (metaphor, figurative meaning, . . . and the like) rather renders the mind passive and *fosters an emotional attachment to the words of others.*

(Baumann & Briggs, 2003, p. 45, emphasis added)

Rhetoric is seen as suspect by Locke because of its link with emotions, or, in his own seventeenth-century discourse, *passions* (cf. Thomas Dixon, 2003, on how an English cultural discourse of *passions* has given way, historically, to one of *emotions*). The work of linguist Anna Wierzbicka (2006) on aspects of modern English like epistemic hedges substantially bears out Bauman and Briggs's claim for the continuing influence of Locke's language ideology on English as used in countries such as the UK and the US.

In view of this deep suspicion towards rhetoric built into modern English, it is no accident that Sante's epithets for French and English poetic discourse sound much closer to Stavans's 'mathematical' English and 'free-flowing' Spanish than his contrast between predictable French rules of pronunciation and unpredictable English ones. Cuban writer Edmundo Desnoes's comments on the rhetorical quality of Spanish are highly apposite here:

Its Latin matrix makes *Spanish highly rhetorical, in itself as well as compared to English; it lingers longer on words because language is cognitively more decisive within the culture*—it even takes longer to enunciate polysyllables than monosyllables. We spend more time in language, *feel its weight upon us*, and believe in throwing it around, as if words were weapons, stones, or limbs able to embrace.

(Desnoes, 1994, p. 264, emphasis added)

When Desnoes says that language is 'cognitively more decisive' in Spanish-speaking culture, he is elaborating on the rhetorical quality of Spanish, i.e., the emotional power of language beyond its practical or referential uses. Sante's comments on the difficulties of translating incantatory French poetry into blunt English suggest a very similar perception among French speakers, a sense of language as authoritative because it is resonant, not because it can impart information. Desnoes's simile 'as if words were weapons' is very close to Sante's when he writes, 'I was seduced by the French tendency to wrench words and phrases . . . from all context the better *to prize them as artefacts*' (p. 81, emphasis added). At the same time, both writers highlight the much more instrumental, anti-rhetorical attitude to language that each has found in English.

Although Stavans likely has a phonetic or morphological difference between Spanish and English in mind when he refers to Spanish as 'free-flowing' and with 'long, uncooperative' words (perhaps he is thinking of open vowels as against English diphthongs, or, like Desnoes, of polysyllabic words whose English counterparts are monosyllabic), again I suspect it is partly cultural attitudes to emotion that lead him to characterize English as bound by 'iron rules' and Spanish as 'free-flowing'. These are the same attitudes which Rosario Ferré conveys when she says that in her English writing, 'Locke is locked into every sentence' while her Spanish sentences 'are often as convoluted as a baroque *retablo*' (Ferré, 1997, p. 109). In calling them 'convoluted', Ferré is of course allowing us to view her Spanish sentences through an English language lens, as Stavans does when he calls Spanish words 'uncooperative'.

A more specifically psychological (or subjective) aspect of Stavans's account of Spanish and English, of the kind that Pérez Firmat (2003) brilliantly analyzes in relation to other US Latino writers, is his habit of putting English on a pedestal and disparaging Spanish. Stavans recalls his own atrocious accent in English, mockingly capturing the sound of himself reading *Moby Dick* out loud ('Som years agou—never maind jau long precaiseli', p. 222) and admits that he now prefers to read Cervantes and Marquez in English translation (p. 223). Of Spanish he writes:

> As a language, it is somewhat undeserving of the literature it has created ... Spanish, in spite of being the third-most important language on the globe, after Chinese and English, is peripheral. It is a language that flourishes in the outskirts of culture, more reactive than active.
>
> (Pérez Firmat, 2003, p. 223)

These evaluations of Spanish and English clearly betray the social power differential with which Stavans struggled as an immigrant writer striving to become fluent in the local language, which also happened to have the prestige of being the globally dominant language, and therefore all the more intimidating. He confesses to a sense of inferiority in English, and the effect of this on his attitude towards Spanish is conveyed unmistakably in the following, only half-humorous comment:

> I frequently felt uncomfortable when listening to my own voice, my appalling accent [in English], on the radio ... But my reaction was far stronger when, self-conscious as I was, I would hear myself talk on the phone long-distance to my parents ... Oh, that horrible melodiousness of Spanish. I couldn't stand it!
>
> (Pérez Firmat, 2003, p. 23)

Ironically, the 'horrible melodiousness' of Spanish seems to be the very quality celebrated by Judith Ortiz Cofer (among others) when she affirms in an interview that 'Spanish is lyrical. It is ... more poetic than English' (Ocasio & Ganey, 1992, p. 143).

Pérez Firmat (2003) writes that 'Spanish is the language of the soul no more than English is that of the wallet. Perceptions of difference emerge from personal history, not linguistic theory'. 'For Santayana,' he points out, 'English was renunciation; for Casey, bliss. For Salinas, Spanish was renunciation; for Cernuda bliss' (Pérez Firmat, 2003, p. 162). Yet to put these two epithets (Spanish 'the language of the soul' and English 'that of the wallet') on a par is to mistake their very different characters. One, however simplistically phrased, relates to a real cultural difference with English, whereas the other is a mere reductive slur. None of the bilingual texts I have discussed suggests that emotions are non-existent in English, but they do suggest that their expression is managed very differently than in many other languages, and that this can greatly intensify an immigrant's sense of emotional loss in coming to live in English as a second language.

These reflections by Hoffman, Sante, Ortiz Cofer, Alvarez, Stavans, and Witcomb show how resources for expressing emotions that were available to them in Polish, French, Spanish, and Portuguese, through diminutives, superlatives, special gestures or terms of endearment, have simply not been available to them in the sphere of English. While all of these authors write as immigrants to English-speaking countries, and hence their relationships to their mother tongues are to some extent colored by the experience of loss, in the case of both Ortiz Cofer and Alvarez English and Spanish were mingled early in their lives through American education and code switching between English and Spanish at home; Ortiz Cofer, moreover, moved between Puerto Rico and New Jersey on a regular basis throughout her childhood. These authors' bilingual testimonies indicate that emotional lives—and cognitive worlds—are significantly shaped by the particular languages we live with.

CONCLUSION

As Pérez Firmat (2003, p. 163) eloquently puts it, 'Before it becomes a political, social, or even linguistic issue, bilingualism is a private affair, intimate theatre.' Yet writers like Hoffman, Reyn, Ortiz Cofer, and Sante show us that it is not only the particular, idiosyncratic relationship to language which is intimate, but equally, one's relationship to the distinctive and widely shared *culture* encoded by that language, which is intimate, formative, and ongoing.

I've argued that bilingual narratives are important—pace Schumann on naive bilingual writers and Pérez Firmat on subjective ones—for what language and cognition scholars can learn from them about emotions and bilingualism. I'd like to end with the note that a still more significant contribution of bilingual narratives is the cultural work they can do to challenge and refine their wider readership's assumptions: about bilinguals, about speakers of foreign languages, and about how readers' own ways of thinking and feeling may relate to those of others.

REFERENCES

Albert, R. D., & Ha, I. A. (2004). Latino/Anglo-American differences in attributions to situations involving touch and silence. *International Journal of Intercultural Relations, 28*(3&4), 253–280.

Alvarez, J. (1998). *Something to declare*. Chapel Hill, NC: Algonquin Books.

Alvarez, J. (2000/2007). *Once upon a quinceañera: Coming of age in the USA*. New York: Viking.

Bauman, R., & Briggs, C. L. (2003). *Voices of modernity: Language ideologies and the politics of inequality*. Cambridge, UK: Cambridge University Press.

Beaujour, E. K. (1989). *Alien tongues: Bilingual Russian writers of the 'first' emigration*. Ithaca, NY: Cornell University Press.

Besemeres, M. (1998). Language and self in cross-cultural autobiography: Eva Hoffman's *Lost in Translation. Canadian Slavonic Papers, 40*(3&4), 327–344.

Besemeres, M. (2002). *Translating one's self: Language and selfhood in cross-cultural autobiography*. Oxford, UK: Peter Lang.

Besemeres, M. (2004a). Different languages, different emotions? Perspectives from autobiographical literature. *The Journal of Multilingual and Multicultural Development, 25*(2&3), 140–158.

Besemeres, M. (2004b). The family in exile, between languages: Eva Hoffman's *Lost in Translation*, Lisa Appignanesi's *Losing the Dead*, Anca Vlaspolos's *No Return Address. Auto/Biography Studies, 19*(1&2), 239–248.

Besemeres, M. (2005). Anglos abroad: Memoirs of immersion in a foreign language. *Biography, 28*(1), 27–42.

Besemeres, M. (2006). Language and emotional experience: The voice of translingual memoir. In A. Pavlenko (Ed.), *Bilingual minds: Emotional experience, expression and representation* (pp. 34–58). Clevedon, UK: Multilingual Matters.

Besemeres, M. (2008). Australian immersion narratives. In D. Deacon, A. Woollacott, & P. Russell (Eds.), *Transnational ties: Australian lives in the world* (pp. 245–257). Canberra: ANU E-Press.

Besemeres, M., & Wierzbicka, A. (Eds.). (2007). *Translating lives: Living with two languages and cultures*. St. Lucia, Queensland: University of Queensland Press.

Bruner, J. (1987). Life as narrative. *Social Research, 54*(1), 11–32.

Couser, G. T. (2004). *Vulnerable subjects: Ethics and life writing*. Ithaca, NY: Cornell University Press.

Danquah, M. N-A. (Ed.). (2000). *Becoming American: Personal essays by first generation immigrant women*. New York: Hyperion.

de Courtivron, I. (Ed.). (2003). *Lives in translation: Bilingual writers on language and creativity*. New York: Palgrave Macmillan.

Desnoes, E. (1994). Nacer en español. In A. Arteaga (Ed.), *An other tongue: Nation and ethnicity in the linguistic borderlands* (pp. 263–271). Durham, NC: Duke University Press.

Dixon, T. M. (2003). *From passions to emotions: The creation of a secular psychological category*. Cambridge, UK: Cambridge University Press.

Donald, M. (2001). *A mind so rare: The evolution of human consciousness.* New York: W. W. Norton & Co.

Dorfman, A. (1998). *Heading south, looking north: A bilingual journey.* New York: Farrar Straus & Giroux.

Eakin, P. J. (1992). *Touching the world: Reference in autobiography.* Princeton, NJ: Princeton University Press.

Eakin, P. J. (1999). *How our lives become stories: Making selves.* Ithaca, NY: Cornell University Press.

Enfield, N. J. (2004). *Ethnosyntax: Explorations in grammar and culture.* Oxford, UK: Oxford University Press.

Ferré, R. (1997). Writing in between. *Hopscotch: A Cultural Review, 1*(1), 102–109.

Gladkova, A. (2007). The journey of self-discovery in another language. In M. Besemeres & A. Wierzbicka (Eds.), *Translating lives: Living with two languages and cultures* (pp. 139–149). St. Lucia, Queensland: University of Queensland Press.

Goddard, C., & Wierzbicka, A. (1994). *Semantic and lexical universals: Theory and empirical findings.* Amsterdam: John Benjamins.

Goddard, C., & Wierzbicka, A. (2004). Cultural scripts: What are they and what are they good for? *Intercultural Pragmatics, 1*(2), 153–165.

Gooch, A. (1967/1970). *Diminutive, augmentative and pejorative suffixes in modern Spanish: A guide to their use and meaning.* Oxford, UK: Pergamon Press.

Hoffman, E. (1989/1991). *Lost in translation: A life in a new language.* London: Minerva.

Kaplan, A. Y. (1993). *French lessons.* Chicago: University of Chicago Press.

Kaplan, A. Y. (1994). On language memoir. In A. Bammer (Ed.), *Displacements: Cultural identities in question* (pp. 59–70). Bloomington, IN: Indiana University Press.

Kazin, A. (1951). *A walker in the city.* London: Victor Gollancz.

Kellman, S. G. (2000). *The translingual imagination.* Lincoln, NE: University of Nebraska Press.

Kellman, S. G. (Ed.). (2003). *Switching languages: Translingual writers reflect on their craft.* Lincoln, NE: University of Nebraska Press.

Kim. (2009, 7 March). You're rotten! Message posted to *Never a Dull Moment.* Available HTTP: <http://kim-neveradullmoment.blogspot.com/2009/03/youre-rotten.html> (accessed February 9, 2010).

Kinginger, C. (2004). Bilingualism and emotion in the autobiographical works of Nancy Huston. *The Journal of Multilingual and Multicultural Development, 25*(2&3), 159–178.

Lesser, W. (Ed.). (2004). *The genius of language: Fifteen writers reflect on their mother tongues.* New York: Pantheon Books.

Lvovich, N. (1997). *The multilingual self: An inquiry into language learning.* Mahwah, NJ: Lawrence Erlbaum Associates Inc.

Morano, M. (2007). *Grammar lessons: Translating a life in Spain.* Iowa City, IA: University of Iowa Press.

Novakovich, J., & Shaphard, R. (Eds.). (2000). *Stories in the stepmother tongue.* Buffalo, NY: White Pine Press.

Ocasio, R., & Ganey, R. (1992). Speaking in Puerto Rican: An interview with Judith Ortiz Cofer. *The Bilingual Review, 17*(2), 143–146.

Ogulnick, K. L. (Ed.). (2000). *Language crossings: Negotiating the self in a multi-cultural world*. New York: Teachers College Press, Columbia University.

Ortiz Cofer, J. (1991). *Silent dancing: A partial remembrance of a Puerto Rican childhood*. Houston, TX: Arte Publico Press.

Ortiz Cofer, J. (2000). Rituals: A prayer, a candle, and a notebook. In M. N-A. Danquah. *Becoming American: Personal essays of first generation women* (pp. 29–38). New York: Hyperion.

Parker, D. (2007). *The self in moral space: Life narrative and the good*. Ithaca, NY: Cornell University Press.

Parks, T. (1996/2001). *An Italian education*. London: Vintage.

Pavlenko, A. (2001). How am I to become a woman in an American vein? Transformations of gender performance in second language learning. In A. Pavlenko, A. Blackledge, I. Piller, & M. Teutsch-Dwyer (Eds.), *Multilingualism, second language learning, and gender* (pp. 133–174). Berlin: Mouton de Gruyter.

Pavlenko, A. (2005). *Emotions and multilingualism*. Cambridge, UK: Cambridge University Press.

Pavlenko, A. (2006). *Bilingual minds: Emotional experience, expression and representation*. Clevedon, UK: Multilingual Matters.

Pérez Firmat, G. (2003). *Tongue ties: Logo-eroticism in Anglo-Hispanic literature*. New York: Palgrave Macmillan.

Pesmen, D. (2000). *Russia and soul: An exploration*. Ithaca, NY: Cornell University Press.

Piller, I., & Takahashi, K. (2006). A passion for English: Desire and the language market. In A. Pavlenko (Ed.), *Bilingual minds: Emotional experience, expression and representation* (pp. 59–83). Clevedon, UK: Multilingual Matters.

Reyn, I. (2000). Recalling a child of October. In M. N-A. Danquah (Ed.), *Becoming American: Personal essays by first generation immigrant women* (pp. 146–155). New York: Hyperion.

Riemer, A. (1992). *Inside outside: Life between two worlds*. Pymble, NSW: Angus & Robinson.

Rodriguez, R. (1981). *Hunger of memory: The education of Richard Rodriguez*. Boston: David R. Godine.

Sante, L. (1998). *The factory of facts*. New York: Pantheon Books.

Sante, L. (2004). French without tears. In W. Lesser (Ed.), *The genius of language: Fifteen writers reflect on their mother tongues* (pp. 67–84). New York: Pantheon Books.

Smith, S., & Watson, J. (2001). *Reading autobiography: A guide for interpreting life narratives*. Minneapolis, MN: University of Minnesota Press.

Stavans, I. (2001). *On borrowed words: A memoir of language*. New York: Viking.

Stearns, P. N. (1994). *American cool: Constructing a twentieth-century emotional style*. New York: New York University Press.

Travis, C. E. (2004). The ethnopragmatics of the diminutive in conversational Colombian Spanish. *Intercultural Pragmatics, 1*(2), 249–272.

Travis, C. E. (2006). The communicative realization of *confianza* and *calor humano* in Colombian Spanish. In C. Goddard (Ed.), *Ethnopragmatics: Understanding discourse in cultural context* (pp. 199–229). Berlin: Mouton de Gruyter.

Ulman, I. (2007). Playgrounds and battlegrounds: A child's experience of migration. In M. Besemeres & A. Wierzbicka (Eds.), *Translating lives: Living with two languages and cultures* (pp. 45–55). St. Lucia, Queensland: University of Queensland Press.

Wierzbicka, A. (1984). Diminutives and depreciatives: Semantic representation for derivational categories. *Quaderni di Semantica, 5*, 123–130.

Wierzbicka, A. (1988). *The semantics of grammar*. Amsterdam: John Benjamin.

Wierzbicka, A. (1997). *Understanding cultures through their key words: English, Russian, Polish, German, and Japanese*. New York: Oxford University Press.

Wierzbicka, A. (1999). *Emotions across languages and cultures: Diversity and universals*. Cambridge, UK: Cambridge University Press.

Wierzbicka, A. (2006). *English: Meaning and culture*. New York: Oxford University Press.

Witcomb, A. (2007). Growing up between two languages/two worlds: Learning to live without belonging to a *terra*. In M. Besemeres & A. Wierzbicka (Eds.), *Translating lives: Living with two languages and cultures* (pp. 83–95). St. Lucia, Queensland: University of Queensland Press.

Wong, J. (2007). East meets West, or does it really? In M. Besemeres & A. Wierzbicka (Eds.), *Translating lives: Living with two languages and cultures* (pp. 70–82). St. Lucia, Queensland: University of Queensland Press.

Part C

Applications and implications of bilingual cognition research

The final part of this book relates the academic area of research into language and cognition to contexts where people with two or more languages are involved. It thus deals with more practical concerns such as: language teaching (Cook, Chapter 22), translation (House, Chapter 23), intercultural communication (Sercombe & Young, Chapter 24), and marketing (Luna, Chapter 25). It ends with an epilogue by Brooke discussing how science fiction writers have written about linguistic relativity and bilingualism.

22 Linguistic relativity and language teaching

Vivian Cook

If the people of the world differ in how they think as well as in how they speak, what does this mean for the teaching of second and foreign languages? The topic of linguistic relativity has been barely broached in language teaching yet it raises crucial issues concerning what language teaching is actually about, most of which are still necessarily speculative. This chapter starts by discussing various alternative relationships between linguistic relativity and teaching, in particular whether second language (L2) users are different from monolingual native speakers. These are then related to the main areas of language teaching, namely goals, syllabuses, methods, and examinations; these can only be sketched here as they are complex areas of education in their own right; a fuller account can be found in Cook (2008). As always, one has to be careful not to accept the simplistic discourse of language-teaching methodologies as necessarily reflecting more than a fraction of the complex realities of language-teaching classrooms (Swan, 2009): What methodologists suggest is often far removed from what actually happens in the class.

LINKS BETWEEN LINGUISTIC RELATIVITY AND LANGUAGE TEACHING METHODOLOGY

Before the days of Universal Grammar, linguists used to claim that '[L]anguages can differ from each other without limit and in unpredictable ways' (Joos, 1957, p. 96). If cognition varied in a similarly uncontrolled fashion, language teaching would be difficult, if not impossible. Acquiring another language would mean acquiring a complete new set of concepts, not just learning, say, the subjunctive tense in French but also its very meaning. Doubtless there are cases where both language and concept differ between languages. Every teacher of English encounters students who have problems with the present perfect tense *I have been to China* compared with the past tense *I went to China*; it is not just that the form of the auxiliary *have* + past participle *-en* is difficult, as the notion it expresses of 'contemporary relevance'. *I have been to China* shows something eternally true—it's a response to the question *Have you ever been to the Far East?;* *I went to China* describes a single past event, answering the question *Where did you go in East Asia?*

Some language teaching theorists have recognized that learning a language means not just learning the language but also the way of life that goes with it: Language teaching is the creation of intercultural competence (Byram, 1997). Indeed it was possible in the UK to give students a course on another culture without learning the language, or to get them to study a foreign literature only in translation. This takes language more as social customs, 'the possession of a community' rather than thought patterns, 'the knowledge in the mind of an individual' (Cook, 2010a).

If people who speak different languages don't think differently, language teaching is just a matter of teaching people aspects of language. This presumably is the consequence of any theory that insists on a strict separation of language and cognition, such as Chomsky's Minimalist Program with its interface between the computational system and the intentional-conceptual system (Chomsky, 1995): The conceptual component is independent from language and unvarying. If thinking is independent of knowledge of language, then language teachers can ignore cognition and concentrate on the language that connects to the concepts. In other words linguistic relativity has no bearing on their concerns.

The belief that there is a Chinese wall between the language component and the rest of the mind is probably the position with which most of the contributors to this volume have taken issue. Pace Chomsky, it is not just the language systems of the world that differ but also the concepts that are expressed through them, however much interpretations of these and of their origins may vary, as we see in the examples in the first chapter of this book.

Yet language teaching has essentially adopted the position that language is all that needs to be taught, with a nod in the direction of culture. Take the audiovisual teaching method popular in the 1960s and 1970s, based on the complex theory of structuro-globalism (Guberina, 1964); this emphasized the association of visual images of situations with complete sentences of the target language. For example, beginners had to repeat sentences in association with pictures, whether a film strip of cartoons projected on a screen or the equivalent in a book: a picture of a debonair man goes with 'Hello, Jim'; a picture of a town house with 'This is my house'; a pot of tea with 'Come and have a cup of tea' (Dickinson, Leveque, & Sagot, 1975). The student learns to associate the picture with the sentence by saying it over and over according to the model on a tape-recording. The difficulty, as Corder (1966) pointed out, is that a picture is inherently ambiguous: Does the man look debonair to you or just eccentric? Or is it indeed a man? In other words a practical illustration of Quine's famous 'gavagai' example of the problem learners face in knowing which attribute of an object a word refers to—if a native speaker of another language points to a rabbit and says *gavagai*, does this word refer to a rabbit, to a part of a rabbit, to food, or to what (Quine, 1964)? The assumption of audiovisualism is that pictures show concepts that are independent of language: Anybody who sees them will interpret them in the same way—arguably true of universal Roschian prototypes but hardly true of the 'visual grammar' used in some audiolingual course materials where a cross over the picture signifies negation, a speech balloon colored blue signifies the future.

The language-teaching fashion that succeeded audiovisualism in the 1970s was the communicative language teaching syllabus which saw the purpose of language teaching as getting students to communicate. The classroom was therefore a place to practice communication rather than to learn aspects of language directly. It assumed that the target the learner was aiming at could partly be described in terms of 'notions'—the ideas that people express through language (Wilkins, 1972, 1976), such as time, location, and quantity. Learning a second language means acquiring different 'exponents' for exactly the same ideas—how to express past time in French, German, or Chinese. Wilkins himself was cautious in insisting that he was dealing with European languages, thus at least ensuring some conceptual commonality. A Spanish-speaking teacher was, however, amused that the first item in Wilkins' classification of notions was 'time', not a priority for Spanish speakers in his view. The overall idea was that a universal set of ideas was expressed differently in different languages, not dissimilar to many linguistic relativity researchers who treat languages as choosing out of a universal set of concepts.

The more recent fashion is the Common European Framework of Reference (CEFR) for language teaching developed by the Council of Europe (Council of Europe, 2001), a cultural body not to be identified with the European Union and indeed not having the same membership. The CEFR calls for 'exponence of general specific notions' (p. 115), for example 'interlexical relations, such as: synonymy/antonymy, ... part–whole relations, componential analysis . . .' Nevertheless the CEFR insists:

> A problem arises when a particular conceptual field is differently organised in L1 and L2, as is frequently the case, so that correspondence of word-meanings is partial or inexact. . . . it is not simply a question of learning new words for old ideas.
>
> (Council of Europe, 2001, p. 132)

So while the CEFR sees language teaching as teaching people how to express certain common concepts, it recognizes some variation in the concepts. The CEFR is then the response to the recommendations of the Council of Europe 'To ensure, as far as possible, that all sections of their populations have access to effective means of acquiring a knowledge of the languages of other member states' (Council of Europe, 1982). The

CEFR division of language proficiency into six levels A1 to C2, measured by 'can-do' statements, is now being widely adopted in language-teaching education in Europe. It treats languages as discrete objective entities by adopting a creed of plurilingualism in which native speakers add another European language to their competence, rather than multilingualism in which they become part of multilingual communities. 'Plurilingualism differs from multilingualism, which is the knowledge of a number of languages, or the co-existence of different languages in a given society' (Council of Europe, 2001, p. 4). A more elaborated critique of the CEFR can be found in Cook (2010b).

The methodology of language teaching that has attracted most attention in the past decade is task-based learning. This sees second language learning as arising from particular tasks that students do in the classroom, i.e., goal-directed communicative exercises; in a sense it reconceptualizes communicative language teaching as tasks rather than as the language- or cognition-based syllabuses of communicative language teaching or the CEFR. To some extent this resembles a version of cognitive psychology that can be labeled 'cognitive behaviorism' (Anderson, 1993). It is concerned with language as processing, how the mind handles speech and listening through networks, connections, and the like, and how it learns to do this (Robinson, 2001). However, its remit seems not to extend to cross-linguistic comparison of concepts and categorization, perhaps because these differences are not relevant to its worldview. While task-based learning methodology draws on the research that shows the classroom advantages of teaching organized around tasks (Skehan, 1998), it has not gone on to discuss the cultural differences involved in tasks or to organize teaching around concepts and categories that may differ from one language to another.

ALTERNATIVE RELATIONSHIPS OF LINGUISTIC RELATIVITY AND LANGUAGE TEACHING

There are in the main two positions that can be taken about linguistic relativity and language teaching. If we accept that speakers of different languages think differently in some respects, second language teaching has first of all to have some idea what these may be, second to decide which of them may be teachable, and third to devise ways of teaching them. This can rely on the original cross-cultural approach showing differences between speakers of languages in thinking: If Japanese speakers classify some objects by material, and English speakers by shape (Imai & Gentner, 1997), then teaching Japanese to English speakers involves familiarizing them with the Japanese classification of objects and substances, possibly in relation to the grammatical differences that may connect with the categorization difference. So far this does not seem to have occurred in language teaching, apart from nods in the direction of 'culture'. The issue of what culture means in language teaching is vast and controversial; for more information see Kramsch (1994) and Byram (1994, 1997).

Most of the contributors to this book who are involved with bilingualism and second language acquisition, however, assume a different possibility: Neither language nor cognition is static in L2 users; not only the first and the second languages but also the cognition of the learner are affected by the presence of two languages and two ways of thinking in the same mind. Language evidence is presented for this in Cook (2003); evidence for the change in cognition is presented in this book and in many other places, say Athanasopoulos (2006) and Bassetti (2007). The claim is that the thinking of L2 users is distinct from that of monolingual native speakers; their concepts are not precisely the same as those of either language, whether first or second, but are something distinctive of their own; they occur in a 'third space', which is neither A nor B but something in between (Bassetti & Cook, Chapter 7, this volume); 'The "third place" of the language learner is an oppositional place where the learner creates meaning on the margins or in the interstices of official meanings' (Kramsch, 2009, p. 238). In this case L2 teaching should be concerned not so much with forcing the concepts of the second language on the learner, as allowing them to create their own unique blend of L1 and L2 ideas.

RELEVANCE TO LANGUAGE TEACHING

Despite the constant attempts to claim there is a single magic teaching method, there are many ways of teaching and learning second languages. Language teaching is not a global and unified pursuit; many teaching methods are in use, applied to the many aspects of the different language that are taught, the many situations in which teaching takes place, and the many types of students. The following sections discuss the areas of teaching goals, teaching methods, and examinations.

Goals of language teaching

At one level, why do we teach people second languages at all? In a sense this is as sensible as Benjamin Franklin's question, 'What is the use of a new-born baby?' Human beings have an infinite potential; language provides a tool for this. Teachers can no more determine what their students will eventually use the second language for than parents can determine what their children will do; one of my ex-students of English was exposed in a popular newspaper as an alleged torturer for the secret police in his home country. There are as many answers to the purposes of language teaching as there are educational systems and L2 learners. In most situations the implicit goal is to use the language like a monolingual native speaker, unachievable as this may be, rather than as an effective second language user, for example the CEFR's use of 'plurilingualism' rather than 'multilingualism'. Cook (2009) tries to split up the umbrella idea of L2 learners by looking at five different groups with very different purposes, partly based on the hierarchy in De Swaan (2001): L2 users of central languages such as Portuguese in Portugal; supercentral languages like Swahili in Africa; hypercentral languages like English used everywhere in the world as a second language; identity languages like Mandarin Chinese learnt as a heritage language by overseas Chinese, and personal languages used, e.g., between a married couple; plus a group of L2 classroom learners whose only purpose is to pass educational requirements. Many language students will join one or other of these groups of L2 users in due course, even if undoubtedly most of them see the purpose of language learning as a matter of getting as close as possible to the native speaker group; many classroom learners have no ambitions other than to emerge from their educational careers with the appropriate qualification, that is to say they are not L2 users except within the educational system of the school or college.

Recent national curricula insist that the goal of language students is not the native speaker but the L2 user, for instance the Israeli English curriculum starts: 'For Israelis, whatever other languages they may use, English is the customary language for international communication and for overcoming barriers to the flow of information, goods and people across national boundaries' (Israel Ministry of Education, 2002). In Japan there is an Action Plan to cultivate 'Japanese with English abilities' (MEXT, 2003). However, most other syllabuses such as the CEFR assume that people add their L2 to their L1, not that they create a new form of language that is like neither the L1 of the target L2 speakers nor their original L1; in other words that they become plurilinguals who resemble monolinguals in both languages, rather than multi-competent L2 users who resemble neither. In this case language teaching needs to take account of the different ways of thinking in the L1 and the L2 but not of the new combined knowledge of L1 and L2 as a third space.

If we take the view that L2 users are in fact different from monolingual native speakers (Grosjean, 1989), not only in language but also in thinking, then second language teaching can be seen in a different light. The objective of language teaching can be precisely the enhancements to cognitive processing that knowing another language brings—the greater cognitive flexibility (Ben Zeev, 1977), metacognitive awareness (Campbell & Sais, 1995), and indeed delay to onset of Alzheimer's (Bialystok, Craik, Klein, & Viswanathan, 2004). At present, however, national syllabuses, for instance in the UK, see the payoffs from language teaching as greater awareness of language, increased language learning skills, and better intercultural understanding.

Methods and techniques: Ways of executing teaching

The methods that are used for language teaching in principle depend on the different views of the relationship of the first and second language in the same mind. Does the teaching technique assume a simple carryover of L1 concepts to the L2, as in translation methods, mostly derided by methodologists for the past century, the acquisition of new distinctive L2 concepts as in direct method descendants, or the creation of a third space in between? The current orthodoxy of task-based learning, for example, sees students as learning by carrying out specific tasks designed by the teacher or course-book writer, and which rely on concepts and processes that come out of the native speaker world of thinking, not that of second language users.

The well-known differences between 'East' and 'West' in terms of the relative importance of background versus foreground (Nisbett, 2003) or in terms of collectivist versus individualist culture (Hofstede, 1980) have made no impact on the design of teaching methods or course materials. These differences would at least suggest that the use of pictures in the audiovisual teaching method or the use of pairwork in communicative language teaching would be very different for students who do not think in the same way as 'Western' students. If second language acquisition transforms someone into a different kind of person—a multi-competent L2 user—then teachers should encourage the use of novel L2 thinking rather than either the L1 or L2 models. That is ruled out for the hitherto respected monolingual native speaker teacher, but possible for teachers who are L2 users themselves. Students should not be restricted by teaching techniques that either force them into the mold of the L2 or keep them within the mold of the L1, but should be free to take advantage of the unique perspective of the L2 user.

Examinations

The measure of students' success in learning a second language is mostly treated by current examinations as approximation to a native speaker standard. Inasmuch as it is the business of language teaching to be concerned with the concepts that its students possess at the end of the day, implications of linguistic relativity could consist of measuring the extent to which they had assimilated the concepts of the second language, or of seeing whether they were cognitively different from their monolingual peers, or of testing whether they were using L2 user concepts rather than monolingual ones. The first approach would then use a test such as foreground/background from Nisbett (2003); the second would compare them with their peers on, say, cognitive flexibility such as the tasks in Ben Zeev (1977); the third would see whether, say, they were treating color perception in an L1/L2 way or an L2 user way. All of these are a far cry from existing ways of establishing people's command of a second language, such as the popular 'can-do' self-assessment statements in the Language Passport (Council of Europe, 2007) which ask people to rate themselves on their abilities to use language in various ways—'I can understand familiar words and very basic phrases concerning myself, my family and immediate concrete surroundings when people speak slowly and clearly.'

Overall, then, it cannot be said that language teaching has yet given a passing glance to linguistic relativity. To the extent that it bases itself on the idea of the independent L2 user rather than the monolingual native speaker, language teaching will have to take into account L2 learners' differences from monolinguals and explore ways of fostering students' distinctive ways of thinking; the pay-off from language teaching should not be limited to the ability to use the new language to communicate with others, but should be extended to the transformation of the mind that learning a second language involves for the individual.

REFERENCES

Anderson, J. (1993). *Rules of the mind*. Hillsdale, NJ: Lawrence Erlbaum Associates Inc.

Athanasopoulos. P. (2006). Effects of the grammatical representation of number on cognition in bilinguals. *Bilingualism: Language and Cognition, 9*(1), 89–96.

Bassetti, B. (2007). Bilingualism and thought: Grammatical gender and concepts of objects in Italian–German bilingual children. *International Journal of Bilingualism, 11*(3), 251–273.

Ben Zeev, S. (1977). The influence of bilingualism on cognitive strategies and cognitive development. *Child Development, 48,* 1009–1018.

Bialystok, E., Craik, F. I. M., Klein, R., & Viswanathan, M. (2004). Bilingualism, aging and cognitive control: Evidence from the Simon task. *Psychology and Aging, 19*(2), 290–303.

Byram, M. (1994). *Teaching-and-learning language-and-culture*. Clevedon, UK: Multilingual Matters.

Byram, M. (1997). *Teaching and assessing intercultural communicative competence*. Clevedon, UK: Multilingual Matters.

Campbell, R., & Sais, E. (1995). Accelerated metalinguistic (phonological) awareness in bilingual children. *British Journal of Developmental Psychology, 13,* 61–68.

Chomsky, N. (1995). *The minimalist program*. Cambridge, MA: MIT Press.

Cook, V. J. (Ed.). (2003). *The effects of the second language on the first*. Clevedon, UK: Multilingual Matters.

Cook, V. J. (2008). *Second language learning and language teaching* (4th ed.). London: Hodder Education.

Cook, V. J. (2009). Language user groups and language teaching. In V. J. Cook & L. Wei (Eds.), *Contemporary applied linguistics, Volume 1* (pp. 54–74). London: Continuum.

Cook, V. J. (2010a). Prolegomena to second language learning. In P. Seedhouse, S. Walsh, & C. Jenks (Eds.), *Conceptualising language learning*. London: Palgrave Macmillan.

Cook, V. J. (2010b). TEFL in Europe. In E. Hinkel (Ed.), *Handbook of research in second language teaching and learning, Volume 2*. London: Routledge.

Corder, S. P. (1966). *The visual element in language teaching.* London: Longman.

Council of Europe. (1982). *Recommendation R (82) 18 of the committee of ministers.* https://wcd.coe.int/com.instranet.InstraServlet?command=com. instranet.Cmd BlobGet&InstranetImage=601630&SecMode=1&DocId= 676400&Usage=2

Council of Europe. (2001). *Common European framework of reference for languages.* Cambridge, UK: Cambridge University Press. Available http:// www.coe.int/t/dg4/linguistic/CADRE_EN.asp (accessed January 15, 2009).

Council of Europe. (2007). *Language passport.* Available from Centre for Information on Language Teaching, http://www.cilt.org.uk/elp.htm

De Swaan, A. (2001). *Words of the world: The global language system.* Cambridge, UK: Polity Press.

Dickinson, A., Leveque, J., & Sagot, H. (1975). *All's well that starts well.* Paris: Didier.

Grosjean, F. (1989). Neurolinguists, beware! The bilingual is not two monolinguals in one person. *Brain and Language, 36,* 3–15.

Guberina, P. (1964). The audiovisual, global and structural method. In B. Libbish (Ed.), *Advances in the teaching of modern languages, Volume 1* (pp. 1–17). Oxford, UK: Pergamon.

Hofstede, G. (1980). *Culture's consequences: International differences in work-related values.* London: Sage.

Imai, M., & Gentner, D. (1997). A cross-linguistic study of early word meaning: Universal ontology and linguistic influence. *Cognition, 62,* 169–200.

Israel Ministry of Education. (2002). *English—Curriculum for all grades.* Jerusalem: Ministry of Education, http://www.education.gov.il/tochniyot_limudim/engl. htm

Joos, M. (Ed.). (1957). *Readings in linguistics: The development of descriptive linguistics in America since 1925.* Washington, DC: American Council of Learned Societies.

Kramsch, C. J. (1994). *Context and culture in language teaching.* Oxford, UK: Oxford University Press.

Kramsch, C. J. (2009). Third culture and language education. In V. J. Cook & L. Wei (Eds.), *Contemporary applied linguistics, Volume 1* (pp. 233–254). London: Continuum.

MEXT (Ministry of Education, Culture, Sports, Science and Technology, Japan). (2003). *Regarding the establishment of an action plan to cultivate 'Japanese with English abilities'.* http://www.mext.go.jp/english/topics/03072801.htm

Nisbett, R. E. (2003). *The geography of thought.* London: Nicholas Brealey Publishing.

Quine, W. (1964). *Word and object.* Cambridge, MA: MIT Press.

Robinson, P. (Ed.). (2001). *Cognition and second language instruction.* Cambridge, UK: Cambridge University Press.

Skehan, P. (1998). *A cognitive approach to language learning.* Oxford, UK: Oxford University Press.

Swan, M. (2009). We do need methods. In V. J. Cook & L. Wei (Eds.), *Contemporary applied linguistics, Volume 1* (pp. 117–136). London: Continuum.

Wilkins, D. A. (1972/1980). The linguistic and situational content of the common core in a unit/credit system. Reprinted in J. Trim, R. Richterich, J. Van Ek, & D. A. Wilkins (Eds.). (1980), *System development in adult language learning*. Oxford, UK: Pergamon.

Wilkins, D. A. (1976). *Notional syllabuses*. Oxford, UK: Oxford University Press.

23 Translation and bilingual cognition

Juliane House

In this chapter I first discuss the impact of linguistic relativity on translation, both in its strong deterministic version and its current version. Second, I present arguments for the theoretical possibility of translation, and propose the notion of 'linguistic–cultural relativity'. Finally I briefly touch on recent neurolinguistic research on the organization of two languages in the brain.

BILINGUAL COGNITION AND THE (IM)POSSIBILITY OF TRANSLATION

Linguistic determinism and translation

Broadly speaking, the hypothesis of linguistic determinism suggests that language strongly influences thought and behavior. Von Humboldt (1836) was the first influential propagator of the idea that languages as a priori frameworks of cognition determine their speakers' *Weltanschauung*, and he believed that languages have an 'inner form', a spiritual structure which corresponds to its users' thought processes. Languages therefore lie at the interface between objective reality and speakers' conceptualization of it and thus force speakers to perceive reality in language-specific ways.

Humboldt's ideas are, however, not as radically deterministic as they are often made out to be: His view of language as a creative entity also led him to suggest that the deep structure of all languages is the same—an idea later famously taken up by Chomsky. Language is no ready-made 'Ergon' (a static and fixed product), but rather 'eine Thätigkeit' (an activity) (1836, p. LVII), an immensely flexible system, open not only to new words but also to new concepts and ways of thinking transcending itself and its contexts of immediate use. This view of language foreshadows Jakobson's axiom of expressibility and the concomitant law of universal translatability, i.e., 'all cognitive experience and its classification is conveyable in any existing language' (Jakobson, 1959, p. 234).

Much later than Humboldt, the postulate of linguistic relativity was reconsidered by Sapir (1921) and his disciple Whorf (1956). In particular Whorf assembled a whole catalog of impressive data illustrating the differences between American Indian languages and what he called Standard Average European (SAE) languages, i.e., the undifferentiated collectivity of English, German, French, Italian, etc., and he inferred mental and behavioral differences from differences between languages on the levels of both lexis and grammatical structure, the latter being the crucial feature in the connection between language, thought, and the segmentation of reality.

While Whorf examined only such typologically distinct language groups as SAE and American Indian languages, it is not difficult to list many other instances of grammatical diversity among the languages of the world: Languages differ strikingly in the grammatical categories that are obligatorily represented. If languages display such grammatical differences, and if linguistic form has a truly 'tyrannical hold' (Sapir, 1931/2008, p. 498) on our way of thinking and perceiving, one might conclude that the theoretical possibility of translating is denied. If all our knowledge is mediated through our native language, translators, too, cannot rid themselves of that mediating influence.

Given Whorf's (implicit) mentalistic view of meaning as concepts in the human mind, it is logically impossible to know any foreign language, let alone translate: The cognitive differences between speakers of different languages result in different, unknowable concepts of the same referents in their minds. And since in translation grammatical form must necessarily change, the kind of grammatical meaning that Whorf imputed as being present in language users' minds is necessarily lost in translation. A translation, being thus formally different from its original, would no longer be a translation, but a 'transfiguration'. Put differently, linguistic relativity is the doctrine of untranslatability *par excellence*.

'Relativizing' linguistic relativity and its impact on translation

Following a long era of neglect, interest in linguistic relativity has recently revived, and numerous empirical studies have examined how language, thought, and reality are interconnected in clearly delimited areas. In studies comparing grammatical structures, observed differences between languages are taken as a starting-point for examining behavioral differences. An example is Slobin's (1997) finding that lexicalization patterns in different languages cause speakers to describe motions in typologically distinct ways, leading to different narrative styles in the languages involved. Other studies start from segments of experienced reality (e.g., space), investigating how different languages encode these segments, or they start from observed behavior in different cultures—following in essence Whorf's classic example of accidental fires attributed to linguistic usage. Lucy (1997, p. 303) gives an example, in which the higher rates of occupational accidents in Finnish-speaking contexts as compared to Swedish-speaking contexts are explained with reference to structural differences and differences in 'orienting meanings' (cf. Chafe, 2000, pp. 116ff) between Indo-European languages such as Swedish and Ural-Altaic ones such as Finnish.

Research such as the above supports the linguistic relativity postulate in narrowly specified ways. Structural differences are of central importance in any comparison of the meaning potential of two languages. Clearly, therefore, given that language structures necessarily change in translation, any argument concerning the feasibility of translation necessarily has to be located at some other linguistic level, i.e., the level of discourse. Since discourse is realized inside the social and cultural traditions in the two linguistic and cultural communities meeting in translation, and these can be analyzed and compared, a basis for translatability may be guaranteed. Recent attempts at examining differences between languages at the discourse level (e.g., Chafe, 2000) have pointed to differences in the conceptualization of certain domains and orientations to space, time, motion, to the reality of what is being said, and the interaction between speaker and hearer. Some languages have an elaborate apparatus of aspects—momentaneous, continuative, inceptive, cessative, durative, durative-inceptive, iterative, and so forth—while others do not. The category of number is not obligatory in Chinese; Fijian has a four-way number system for personal pronouns: singular, dual, paucal, multiple, and no number at all for nouns. Whether such differences amount to insuperable difficulties in translation or can be overcome will be discussed in the next section.

THE POSSIBILITY OF TRANSLATION

As mentioned above, the consequence of the linguistic relativity postulate for translation is the denial of its theoretical possibility—'theoretical' because the practice of translation flies in the face of this dictum, as translation practice has long been a thriving business. Why should we be confronted with such an apparent contradiction? One answer might be: Because of the nature of language and the nature of human beings. Arguing against the 'linguistically atomistic' nature of many early Whorfian studies, Longacre stated: 'Language is not utterly at the mercy of its own distinctions and categories, but has within itself resources for outstripping and transcending these categories' (1956, p. 304). This means that languages are not really that different from the viewpoint of the potential of the whole system, i.e., the differences between languages are not so much in kind as in the degree of explicitness and emphasis: What one language has built into the layers of its structure, another expresses only informally and sporadically, but all languages have the resources to express any experience or state-of-affairs.

Another argument relativizing linguistic relativism is language change (Ortega y Gasset, 1966, p. 60ff). Languages change constantly; so does our experience and conception of the world around us. But the two do not change in step with each other. Any language is full of fossils or anachronisms, and at any particular time much of language is conventionalized and automatic. The road from language forms to consciousness is still largely unknown and may be more complicated than is often assumed. Conclusions about direct correlations between language, thought, and reality, therefore, cannot easily be drawn.

Further, due to each language user's creativity, language cannot have an overpowering influence, so we might supplement the axiom of expressibility with an axiom of conceivability. Langacker has put this nicely:

> We are perfectly competent of forming and mentally manipulating concepts for which no word is available. We can make up imaginary entities at will, and if we so choose, proceed to name them. For example, imagine a unicorn with a flower growing out of each nostril.
> (Langacker, 1967, p. 40).

How well the influence of language on cognitive capacity, on the routes, rates, and quality of human thinking can be counteracted, is demonstrated by the fact that different philosophical positions have been expressed in the same language, and the same position has been expounded in structurally different languages: Descartes, Comte, and Bergson had essentially the same grammatical structure at their disposal, and Aristotelian metaphysics was developed by Arabic and Hebrew thinkers and by medieval Christian philosophers.

The idea of one single monolithic mother tongue as an instrument of powerful cognitive influence must also be relativized. There may be little justification in speaking of the speakers of any complex language community being similarly conditioned: Within one language community, contrasts in codability, grammatical structure, and discourse norms may be just as great as between different linguacultures. Subgroups may have developed highly differentiated vocabularies and grammatical and discoursal norms deviating from standard usage, and in any complex community a subsection may be found that shares the cognitive propensity of another supposedly very different linguaculture.

In a world which has always been multilingual, an overriding influence of 'the mother tongue' as a thought- and behavior-conditioning instrument seems highly unlikely. Second and foreign languages are acquired by individuals to admirable degrees of perfection, and the world is full of multilingual individuals, the monolingual person being something of an exception.

In sum, then, linguistic relativity, though clearly affecting cognitive behavior in specified areas, can always be counteracted. While it is undeniably true that differences in codability and obligatory structural distinctions in languages can have specifiable effects on perception, cognition, and behavior, these effects do not amount to impenetrable differences in worldview between different linguacultures. There is always an escape from the trap of one's language—through language itself, through the creativity, dynamism, flexibility, as well as the complexity and basic comparability of both individuals and languages. Translation is not in principle impossible.

TRANSLATABILITY: CULTURE AND CONTEXT

Such a positive approach to translatability also derives from linking linguistic diversity with external differences of historical, sociocultural background. If languages are seen to be structured in divergent ways because they embody different experiences, interests, conventions, values, then the importance of what may be called linguistic–cultural relativity emerges. Cultural knowledge, including knowledge of various subcultures, has long been recognized as indispensable for translation, as it is knowledge of the application that linguistic units have in particular situational and social contexts which makes translation possible. 'Application' refers to the relation holding between an expression and the cultural situation in which it is used; its pragmatic meaning. In establishing equivalences between linguistic structures in translation, the notion of 'application' is crucial: If sense and reference differ for two linguistic structures in two different languages—as they very frequently do—it is their 'application' in particular and knowable contexts that allows of translatability. For instance, the German expression *einen Schein machen* can only be explained and translated with reference to the current German university system, and might be translated into English as 'to get credit for a course'; however the German *Schein* is very different from the Anglo-Saxon concept of a 'credit'. Linguistic structures can never be fully understood in isolation from the particular sociocultural phenomena of which they are symbols. While differences in worldviews are not accessible to the translator, the intersubjectively experienceable application of words and structures in a particular situation certainly is. Even if the distance between languages is great, it can always be bridged via ethnographic knowledge and insights.

Conceptions of language in the context of culture, where meaning is contextually determined, are not recent developments (as suggested for instance by Gumperz & Levinson, 1996, p. 225) but go back to Russian Formalism, Prague School, and Firthian traditions (Firth, 1968) where it was claimed that the meaning of words and structures units cannot be fully captured unless their relation to 'the context of situation' is taken into account. Such a view of meaning has important consequences for the possibility of translation: Translation becomes 'rather the placing of linguistic symbols against the cultural background of a society than the rendering of words by their equivalents in another language' (Malinowski, 1935, p. 18).

For the theoretical possibility of translation the notion of 'context of situation' is important. Every time communication is possible between speakers of the same language, it is also possible between speakers of different languages, and for the same fundamental reason: It is possible to relate words and structures to the context of situation in which they occur, to analyze common or comparable situations, and to identify unfamiliar features that can be known, described, interpreted, and rendered in a different language. Such a view of language and of translation is adopted in a functional model of translation (House, 1997, 2000, 2009). Translation is here defined as the replacement of a text in one language by a functionally equivalent text in another in two different ways: overt and covert translation. An 'overt' translation is embedded in a new speech event in the target culture, with the translation also operating in a new cognitive frame, a new 'discourse world'. An overt translation is quite overtly a translation, not a 'second original'. The translation is clearly recognizable as a translation, but operates at the same time in the source discourse world such that recipients must co-activate both the target's and originals' discourse worlds. An example of an overt translation (produced in 1948) is a speech by Churchill given in 1942 in Bradford. Here the original is clearly source-culture linked and has independent status in the source language community.

A 'covert' translation, on the other hand, operates solely in the discourse world set up by the target text with no co-activation of the discourse world in which the original had unfolded. Examples are tourist brochures, advertisements, circulars issued by globally operating companies, all of which need to be adapted to different receptors when they are translated. Covert translations are psycholinguistically much less complex than overt translation, and more deceptive: The translator's task is to disguise the translation's origin and remain hidden behind this deception. To this end, the translator employs a 'cultural filter' with which to make allowances for sociocultural differences. These differences do not result from distinct and stable mental characteristics, let alone worldviews, but from variations in discourse conventions, obligatory grammatical forms, and degrees of lexical routinization. The possibility of translation arises in a necessary process of 're-contextualization', of taking a text out of its original frame and placing it into a new set of sociocognitive relationships (House, 2006). This is the essence of what one may call linguistic–cultural relativism. The distinction between overt and covert translation reflects different ways of re-contextualization: In overt translation the original's context is reactivated alongside the target text's context, such that two different discourse worlds and frames are juxtaposed in the medium of the target language; covert translation concentrates exclusively on the target context, employing a cultural filter to cater to the new addressees' habitual beliefs and values, and is thus more clearly affected by linguistic–cultural relativity. While the speech by Churchill mentioned above will be left intact—i.e., it will not be subjected to a cultural filter in the process of translation which would adapt it to the expectations of recipients in the target culture—advertisements will routinely be culturally filtered and adapted to better appeal to preferences and expectation norms assumed to hold in the target linguistic and cultural community.

TRANSLATABILITY: RECENT NEUROLINGUISTIC STUDIES

MacNamara's (1970) early *reductio ad absurdum* of the impossibility of bilingualism and translation as a logical consequence of linguistic relativity is still valid today. He argued that the 'Whorfian bilingual' would be unable to communicate with himself: In switching to language B, s/he would never be able to understand what s/he had just communicated in language A. Recent empirical neurolinguistic studies of bilingualism and translation (e.g., Altarriba, 1992; De Groot & Christoffels, 2006; Paradis, 2004; Price, Green, & von Studnitz, 1999) using modern technological means of neuroimaging such as fMRI, PET, and ERP can be taken to confirm MacNamara's necessarily more informal views. These studies suggest that in the bilingual's (and the translator's) brain a joint conceptual system can be accessed by different languages via different routes. Conceptual representations are language-independent, whereas lexico-semantic, morpho-syntactic, and phonological representations are language-specific. The two languages are organized in two separate subsystems, and these subsystems can be activated simultaneously, with the possibility of a supervisory attentional system exercising inhibiting control for the comprehension of the source text and the production of a target text. The two languages involved in the process of translation are therefore conceptualized as both interconnected and separate. If they are used simultaneously, as in translation, speakers are in a 'bilingual mode' (Grosjean, 2001), which enables them to understand, compare, and transfer expressions effectively and simultaneously in two different languages.

The importance of pragmatic meanings in translation referred to above is accounted for in the operation of two separate L1- and L2-related pragmatic systems that infer the text producer's intentions from given contexts and select the linguistic elements appropriate to the message to be expressed. The neuropsychological processes involved in the bilingual brain are believed to be identical for all languages, and there seems to be no mechanism in the bilingual's brain which is not also operative, at least to some extent, in the monolingual brain (Paradis, 2004, p. 229).

Neurolinguistic studies are an important and promising new line of research, and the hypotheses suggested in this paradigm may well provide plausible descriptions and explanations of why and how translation is made possible.

CONCLUSION

The relationship between translation and bilingual cognition, and the issues surrounding translatability were conceived differently over time depending on whether linguistic determinism or linguistic relativity was the dominant hypothesis. While linguistic determinism implied the doctrine of untranslatability *par excellence*, linguistic relativity, while clearly affecting perception, cognition, and behavior in specified areas, cannot be said to imply the impossibility of translation. Differences in codability and obligatory structural distinctions can always be overcome through the creativity and flexibility of individuals and their languages. Further, when one subscribes to the hypothesis of linguistic–cultural relativity, which emphasizes the importance of the context of situation for assessing the meaning of words and structures, translation is conceptualized not solely as a cognitive process but as a sociocognitive act of recontextualization. Recontextualization varies systematically in the two fundamental types of translation, overt and covert. In overt translation the translated text gives recipients access to the original's discourse world, whereas covert translations are culturally filtered and operate exclusively in the target text's discourse world, catering to the expectation norms of the new recipients. Recent neurolinguistic studies confirm the idea of universal translatability by suggesting a joint conceptual system accessible by different languages via different routes. At present, neurolinguistic work provides the most promising hypotheses with regard to the mechanisms involved in translation.

REFERENCES

Altarriba, J. (1992). The representation of translation equivalents in bilingual memory. In R. Harris (Ed.), *Cognitive processing in bilinguals* (pp. 157–174). Amsterdam: North Holland.

Chafe, W. (2000). Loci of diversity and convergence in thought and language. In M. Pütz & M. Verspoor (Eds.), *Explorations in linguistic relativity* (pp. 101–124). Amsterdam: Benjamins.

De Groot, A. M. B., & Christoffels, I. (2006). Language control in bilinguals: Monolingual tasks and simultaneous interpreting. *Bilingualism: Language and Cognition, 9*(2), 189–201.

Firth, J. R. (1968). Linguistics and translation. In F. R. Palmer (Ed.), *Selected papers of J. R. Firth 1952–1959* (pp. 84–95). London: Longman.

Grosjean, J. (2001). The bilingual's language modes. In J. Nicol (Ed.), *One mind, two languages: Bilingual language processing* (pp. 1–22). Oxford, UK: Blackwell.

Gumperz, J., & Levinson, S. (Eds.). (1996). *Rethinking linguistic relativity.* Cambridge, UK: Cambridge University Press.

House, J. (1997). *Translation quality assessment. A model revisited.* Tübingen: Narr.

House, J. (2000). Linguistic relativity and translation. In M. Pütz & M. Verspoor (Eds.), *Explorations in linguistic relativity* (pp. 69–88). Amsterdam: Benjamins.

House, J. (2006). Text and context in translation. *Journal of Pragmatics, 38*(3), 338–358.

House, J. (2009). *Translation.* Oxford, UK: Oxford University Press.

Jakobson, R. (1959). On linguistic aspects of translation. In R. Brower (Ed.), *On translation* (pp. 232–239). New York: Oxford University Press.

Langacker, R. W. (1967). *Language and its structure.* New York: Harcourt, Brace & World.

Longacre, R. E. (1956). Review of 'Language and Reality' by W. M. Urban and of 'Four Articles on Metalinguistics' by B. L. Whorf, *Language, 32*, 298–308.

Lucy, J. A. (1997). Linguistic relativity. *Annual Review of Anthropology, 26*, 291–312.

MacNamara, J. (1970) Bilingualism and thought. In J. Alatis (Ed.), *Monograph series on languages and linguistics* (pp. 25–40). Washington, DC: Georgetown University Press.

Malinowski, B. (1935). *Coral gardens and their magic (II).* London: Allen & Unwin.

Ortega y Gasset, J. (1966). *Miseria y esplendor de la traduccion: Elend und Glanz der Übersetzung* (3rd ed.). Ebenhausen, Germany: Langewiesche-Brandt.

Paradis, M. (2004). *A neurolinguistic theory of bilingualism.* Amsterdam: Benjamins.

Price, C., Green, D., & von Studnitz, R. (1999). A functional imaging study of translation and language switching. *Brain, 122*, 2221–2235.

Sapir, E. (1921). *Language.* New York: Harcourt, Brace & World.

Sapir, E. (1931/2008). Conceptual categories in primitive languages. In P. Swiggers (Ed.), *The collected works of Edward Sapir.* Berlin: Mouton De Gruyter.

Slobin, D. I. (1997). Mind, code, and text. In J. Bybee, J. Haiman, & S. A. Thompson (Eds.), *Essays on language function and language type* (pp. 437–467). Amsterdam: Benjamins.

von Humboldt, W. (1836). *Über die Verschiedenheit des menschlichen Sprachbaues und ihren Einfluß auf die geistige Entwicklung des Menschengeschlechts.* Bonn: Dümmler.

Whorf, B. L. (1956). *Language, thought and reality: Selected writings of Benjamin Lee Whorf* (J. B. Carroll Ed.). Cambridge, MA: MIT Press.

24 Culture and cognition in the study of intercultural communication

Peter Sercombe and Tony Young

This chapter considers issues in cognition with particular reference to intercultural communication (ICC). A focus is how coming from particular cultural and language backgrounds might impinge on people's thought processes and spoken interactions with people from separate cultural and linguistic backgrounds. Our reflections here are informed, in some measure, by our experiences of working closely with students following postgraduate programs of study in ICC, through English. We commence with a brief introduction to relevant basic issues and current thinking in cognition and ICC, and then link these to particular cultural, communicational, and linguistic considerations, in an attempt to provide an indication of ways in which cognition and culture combine to shape, influence, or affect interaction that can be considered intercultural.

CRITICAL ISSUES IN COGNITION AND INTERCULTURAL COMMUNICATION

Cognition

Much late twentieth-century psychological thinking held to the idea that fundamental cognitive processes, and ways in which they function, regardless of the kind of content to which they are exposed, appear to be universal (Nisbett & Norenzayan, 2002; see also Roberson, Davidoff, Davies, & Shapiro, 2006). Recently, within cross-cultural psychology in particular, this position has been challenged. For example, Nisbett and Norenzayan (2002, p. 562) claim that:

> some cognitive content is universal ... differences in cognitive processes are so tied to cultural differences in basic assumptions about the nature of the world that the traditional distinction between content and process begins to seem somewhat arbitrary.

Similarly, research into the patterns of performance of 'groups' (e.g.,

Mishra, 1997; Mishra, Sinha, & Berry, 1996) has provided some evidence for the existence of 'cognitive styles' which, it is suggested, can be reliably related to cultural, ecological, and acculturative characteristics of the groups under study. In this formulation, cultural cognitive styles are present when a group reacts in a systematic manner differently from the way other groups react to a cognitive stimulus. It has also been proposed that while 'cognition is fundamentally a biological phenomenon [. . .] our biological being, as realized in our human bodies [. . .] is a social and cultural construction at least as much as an individual one' (Foley, 1997, p. 12; see also Richerson & Boyd, 2005). Foley goes on to relate his suggestion to Bourdieu's (1977, 1990) concept of 'habitus', concerned with tacit knowledge and its transmission between generations, in the form of cultural practices; and about ways in which 'human organisms in a social system communicate with each other' (Foley, 1997, p. 14). An important corollary is that 'Cultural meanings are not in individual minds, but rather they are shared by the social actors' (Foley, 1997, p. 16).

Levinson (1995, p. 104) sees cognition as a 'system for organising the relation between organism and environment', bearing in mind that 'the environment is largely culturally constructed'. Language is a fundamental medium for representing certain facets of an individual's cognitive processes. However, that which is not said (but carried implicitly), can also be basic to socialization (Ochs & Schiefflin, 1990), acculturation and, more specifically, interaction, such that embedded, and often hidden, cultural perspectives may elude those from differing cultural and language backgrounds in interaction. Similarly, Sperber and Wilson (1995, p. 2) suggest, 'Even more important than the question of what is communicated is the question of how communication is achieved.' Sperber and Wilson go on to propose an alternative to the 'code model' of communication (whereby 'communication is achieved by encoding and decoding messages'): they suggest instead an 'inferential model', such that 'communication is achieved by producing and interpreting evidence' by and among those involved in communicative acts.

Possible links between a person's perceptions of the world and the (greater or lesser) extent to which these are influenced by a language have long been reflected in the debate over the linguistic relativity hypothesis, originally posited by Sapir and Whorf (e.g., Sapir, 1949; Whorf, 1956), which has enjoyed a resurgence of interest within applied linguistics in recent years (Kramsch, 2004). Clyne (1994), for example, notes that, regardless of the validity of the hypothesis, similar forms of determinism have emerged with regard to 'language and class', as well as 'language and gender', among others. What Clyne (1994, p. 6) does argue, however, is that the 'discourse level of language is inseparable from cultural behaviour.'

Cultural concerns in cognitive linguistics have been exemplified in the extensive investigation of metaphor, e.g., by Lakoff and Johnson (1980). More recently, Langacker (1997, p. 241) suggests that:

metaphor nicely illustrates the indissociability of cognitive and cultural considerations . . . [it is] likely that most cognitive domains are metaphorically structured to some extent, and it is quite evident that metaphor is a major factor in cultural construction.

Regarding bilingualism (seen here as including multilinguals), Pavlenko (2006) argues that this is not just an enlarged variety of monolingualism, but typologically different. Research previously conducted by Dewaele and Pavlenko, among bilinguals about 'different selves' (Pavlenko, 2006, p. 9), reveals that respondents state they can hold different cultural perspectives depending on the language being spoken (a finding distinct from those who are bidialectal), echoed across related studies that are referred to in Pavlenko (2006). More recently, Athanasopoulos (2009), in studies of color among Greek–English bilinguals, found that linguistic categories of color influenced cognitive representations of these, and that (p. 84) 'Since there is now a range of converging evidence to suggest the tight relationship between linguistic concepts and cognition, the issue of bilingualism becomes increasingly important.' In addition, Athanasopoulos's (2009) study indicates that the acquisition of a second language can affect conceptual representations, echoing Pavlenko (2006). Nonetheless, it is only relatively recently that explicit links between culture and cognition have been explored with reference to ICC (e.g., Wierzbicka, 1991), discussed in more detail below.

Intercultural communication

Relative to the study of cognition, ICC is an undeveloped field. Although emerging from second language acquisition study (e.g., Lado, 1957), Edward T. Hall's work on cross-cultural non-verbal communication in the 1940s (Hall, 1959) continues to reflect the predominant frames of reference for much 'cross-cultural' and 'intercultural' research, which have come from social psychology (cross-cultural communication tends to compare different cultural groups' styles of communication, while intercultural communication tends to consider communication that takes place between members of different cultural groups; however, the terms are often used synonymously). Social psychology has tended to explore group distinctiveness (cf. Barth, 1969/1998) rather than, say, communication among and between groups, although most communication takes place at the interpersonal level (e.g., Harwood, Giles, & Palomares, 2005).

The field of ICC also remains relatively ill defined and core terms can be used with little indication of their intended meanings. Žegerac (2007, p. 40) succinctly proposes that '*intra*-cultural communication could be characterized as communication between participants who share most cultural representations, and *inter*cultural communication, as communication between participants who share few cultural representations'. However, a question arises as to how similar cultural representations need to be for communication to be considered 'inter-' versus 'intra-cultural'. This issue can be notionally resolved by suggesting that cultural representations tend to be more or less salient 'to the extent they inform the beliefs and guide the actions of those who hold them' (Žegerac, 2007, p. 40). Certainly, all communication involves experience of 'otherness' (Schütz, 1972; see also Ma, 2004). In some contexts, for example, religious beliefs may shape or influence a person's communication style, while the cultural salience of clothes is likely to be less influential (notwithstanding issues such as dress codes). Furthermore, cultural knowledge shared by people may be relevant in certain situations but not others, so a university lecturer and a student may well have much in common regarding a particular academic subject but otherwise may share little. In addition, instances of miscommunication can occur just as much between those who are from similar cultural backgrounds as it may for those who are not (see Bonvillain, 2003). However, explanations for these instances are likely to be ascribed different reasons, such that 'those involved tend to over-emphasize differences between groups rather than within social groups' (Hamers & Blanc, 1983, p. 241).

Links between intercultural communicative ability, language learning, and language teaching have been the subject of little investigation to date (Young, Sachdev, & Seedhouse, 2009). Although the essential features of ICC competence have been proposed (e.g., Byram & Zarate, 1997), these remain untested. Bennett (1998, p. 21) suggests the purpose of education in ICC is to increase 'bistylistic competency' (discussed below). Hamers and Blanc (1983) suggest that Canadian bilinguals who had followed immersion programs tended to emerge as being more sensitive to sociolinguistic norms of behavior in their second language. Furthermore, there is an implicit understanding, informing many curricular guidelines dealing with the cultural dimension of language acquisition, that being interculturally effective is related to being linguistically and communicatively competent (e.g., Council of Europe, 2001). Overall, however, there was and still is little empirical evidence to confirm such an association (Young & Sachdev, 2009; see also Haugen, 1956), although an exception is discussed below.

Much of the popular ICC literature (e.g., Hofstede, 1997; Jandt, 2001) has tended to reduce the role of individual agency and over-emphasize cultural differences, without evidence to support this (Holliday, 1999). Despite a wealth of literature produced under the banner of ICC, the majority seems to lack an empirical basis, rhetoric being the norm. Much of the ICC literature also tends to advocate certain approaches, e.g., 'cognitive' (Gudykunst, 2003) and 'affective' (Stephan & Stephan, 2003), to ICC. However, there is a lack of rigor regarding conceptions of culture (failing to acknowledge, adequately, the complexity implicit within this term) and what can be meant by the idea of communication (a notable exception being Holliday, Hyde, & Kullman, 2004). Furthermore, while relatively few contextualized examples of ICC are provided, these few are often hypothetical rather than actual, although Young and Sachdev (2009) do provide empirical data from formal learning environments.

Cognition and intercultural communication

In so far as cognition and culture are of interest in ICC studies, this has, until very recently, tended to relate supposed culture-based value variations to particular sets of beliefs and types of behavior. Probably one of the most influential, yet controversial, figures in ICC remains Hofstede (e.g., 1997), who has made a number of widely publicized claims about groups' distinctive behaviors, based on apparently identifiable and quantifiable 'national' cultural characteristics, suggesting how people of a certain nationality view and interact with the world. From this perspective Hofstede developed five sets of cultural dimensions (emerging from work by Hall, 1959): power distance (the extent to which members of a culture accept inequalities in the distribution of power); individualism versus collectivism (the degree to which members are expected to be self-sustaining, rather than being part of unified groups that provide support in exchange for allegiance); masculinity versus femininity (the allocation of roles across gender); uncertainty avoidance (the extent to which cultural members can accept improbability); and long- or short-orientation (the degree to which people show values of prudence and determination vis-à-vis, for example, respect for tradition and social duties). These dyads have been used by Hofstede (1997) and Trompenaars and Hampden-Turner (1997) as measures to apply to whole nations and their purported tendencies. Hofstede's ideas have been heavily, if not widely, criticized (e.g., McSweeney, 2002; Søndergaard, 1994; and Young & Sercombe, 2010), yet remain seductive in their simplicity and continue to be extensively employed. Not actually referring to Hofstede, Foley (1997, p. 21), for example, makes the fairly obvious point that 'it is totally inappropriate to speak of a finite domain that constitutes, say, American culture, for it is equally apparent that it is impossible for every American to engage in intensive recurring social coupling with every other' (see also Clyne, 1994; nonetheless, Fox (2004) tentatively proposes, on the basis of her first-hand observation, a defining set of characteristics of Englishness).

The most useful ideas to emerge in relation to ICC have tended to derive from separate fields, otherwise implicitly linked to ICC, such as 'ethnography' (e.g., Bauman, 1996); and 'discourse analysis' (e.g., Rampton, 1995), in which scholars have paid much closer attention to the nuances of (inter- and intra-) cultural differences as well as people's simultaneous multiple memberships of different cultural groups, as evidenced from interaction in specific situations. Much of this research has not been explicitly linked to cognition. It is probably the work of Wierzbicka (e.g., 1991), and Goddard (e.g., 2006), that has most clearly linked cognitive processes to ICC; these are discussed further below.

Important initial considerations are the kinds of areas in which the cognitive make-up of someone from one cultural background can significantly affect the production and interpretation of her/his speech acts by someone from another cultural background. It would be impossible to produce a comprehensive taxonomy of speech acts affected by specific cognitive processes, besides also considering other fields in which cognition and intercultural communication interrelate, such as: literacy, oracy, learning styles, and multiple intelligences (i.e., the variation in people's abilities, in distinct fields, such as: music, mathematics, language, and interpersonal relationships), among others.

Examples of research linking cognition to culture include mainly studies related to linguistic relativity:

- Berlin and Kay (1969) looked at how color names are assigned across cultural groups and rejected the linguistic relativity hypothesis because their results were unaffected by speakers' mono- or bilingualism.
- More recently, Berlin (1992) showed cross-cultural similarities of plant and animal classification.
- Cognitive consequences of linguistic differences have been found in the categorization of spatial location, as well as number marking (Lucy, 1992) and this has repercussions for ways in which aspects of culture are mediated in thought.
- Levinson (1997) has revealed how speakers of certain Indo-European languages, including English, tend to prefer physical coordinates for the placing of objects, in contrast to speakers of an Australian Aboriginal language (Guugu Yimithirr) who lean towards the use of directional terms.
- Kasper and Rose (2001) have described how speech acts for apologies are realized through semantic formulas that comprise several common strategies across distinctly unrelated languages.

The links between thought patterns and their connections to (intercultural) pragmatics have received substantial coverage from Wierzbicka (1991). She suggests (p. 49): 'The complex of cultural attitudes which conditions every individual to be constantly aware of other people [. . .] leads to objectivism and anti-dogmaticism being regarded as important social and cultural values.' Wierzbicka (1991) maintains that the links between languages and cultural groups can be observed when speakers interact in non-first languages, while simultaneously operating under the constraints of first language and cultural background schemata. Consequently, Wierzbicka (1991, p. 398) argues that those learning English (as a second or foreign language) need, for example, rules to use various 'tautological constructions.'

Other research relating to cognition and bilingualism, such as Nishida (1999), proposes a primary set of schemata that help generate behavior in social interaction. Among these, the three most relevant for bilingualism appear to be:

- role schemas and knowledge about social roles and kinds of behaviour expected of people in particular social positions;
- context schemas which 'contain information about the situation and appropriate setting of behavioural parameters' (p. 758); and
- procedure schemas which 'are knowledge about the appropriate sequence of events in common situations' (p. 758).

These schemata relate to cultural knowledge and can be linked to ways in which speech is used to express or represent appropriate behaviors, for particular functions. However, we suggest that rules for such behaviors cannot be taught formulaically (cf. Kasper & Rose, 2001); one can only raise people's sense of awareness about issues of difference and similarity, in speech acts and their interpretation, whether this be through, for example, role-play, authentic interaction, and reflection about this (cf. Pavlenko, 2006), or through specific tasks including, for example, ways in which requests are often made in English, or how 'English . . . places heavy restrictions on the use of the imperative and makes extensive use of interrogative and conditional forms' (Wierzbicka, 1985, p. 145). The point is, as Kramsch (1993, p. 6) observes, 'learners have to discover that knowledge for themselves in order to internalize it.'

INTERCULTURAL REALIZATIONS AND IMPLICATIONS

Examples of empirical research linking cognition and culture, explicitly or implicitly, remain relatively few. For example, after a flurry of interest regarding culturally related learning and cognitive styles in the 1980s and 1990s among language-learning theoreticians (for a summary, see Oxford & Anderson, 1995), empirical research has become rarer. Young and Sachdev (2007) suggest this may be due to the confusion caused by the multiplicity of available definitions of, and approaches to, notions of both learning style and culture, few of which seem empirically related to underlying principles. In their own research Young and Sachdev found no evidence for the 'national–cultural' learning style differences indicated by much of the rhetorical literature on this matter. Also, in a study of mainland Chinese students undertaken by Sercombe (2003), it appeared that, with regard to learning styles and field-dependence, gender was a considerably more significant variable than nationality.

Despite this, the notion that nation equals culture remains influential in many applied fields (Dörnyei, 2005). Clyne (1994) undertook ICC research in work situations in Australia among a range of first-generation immigrants. He suggests: 'It is not even possible to suggest universal maxims concerning negotiation of meaning' (1994, p. 203). He also maintains that there is internal cultural variation concerning concepts of 'truth', 'harmony', 'uncertainty avoidance', and 'individuality', among others, besides differences he found based on social categories such as age and gender (cf. Francis, 2000; Paradis, 2000; Sercombe, 2003). Clyne (1994, p. 204) suggests, from his research, however: 'People on the periphery of a cultural area (e.g., Indonesians, Filipinos, Maltese) are often good intercultural communicators, because their own discourse patterns are more open.' It seems, too, that bilingual immigrants may merge features of different cultures (local and immigrant) and develop new distinct cultural groups (Agar, 1991; see also Bhabha, 1994; Hamers & Blanc, 1983), demonstrating the increasing salience of complexity and interculturality in considerations of cultural and cognitive difference.

More recently, Nisbett and Norenzayan (2002) suggest that cognition and culture can be linked to types of reasoning, arguing that: 'East Asians and Westerners reason in very different ways' (p. 579), with East Asians tending more towards holistic reasoning (an orientation towards the relevant context) versus analytic reasoning (which tends to detach the focus of attention from its context). Nisbett and Norenzayan also argue that Westerners organize the world into distinct categories more than East Asians do; consequently Westerners can better decontextualize content and structure than East Asians. When presented with apparent contradictions, Westerners resolve these by selecting, at least, a correct (for them) answer, while East Asians tend to see some truth in both positions (Hymes, 1996). Regarding the latter, we notice that some international postgraduate students (studying for the first time in the UK) are sometimes unfamiliar with or reluctant to criticize published sources in their own work, tending towards description, unsure of the purpose of evaluating ideas they see as authoritative by dint of being available in the public domain. This raises the possibility that 'Perhaps the most difficult aspect of cross-cultural discourse, whatever the medium' is 'the perception of relevance' (Pincas, 2001, p. 46). Scollon and Scollon (2001) also argue that some sources of miscommunication in intercultural contexts occur as a result of different discourse patterns, across diverse groups, arguing that Western discourse is dominated by a 'comment–topic' approach, while for many Asians 'topic–comment' is favored, leading to potential misunderstandings of what is most salient. (While it is beyond the remit of this chapter to discuss this, in detail at least, we do take issue with such broad-ranging categorizations as 'Western' and 'Asian', terms that carry notions of reductionism and essentialism which, we feel, tend to limit the credibility of ICC as a field of study.)

Goddard (2006, p. 2) maintains that 'ethnopragmatics is compatible with the insight from cultural psychology ... that people in different cultures speak differently because they feel differently, and relate differently to other people.' He works with the idea of cultural scripts 'framed ... within the non-ethnocentric metalanguage of semantic primes ... hypothesized to be widely known and shared among people of a given speech community' (p. 5), as in the following example:

A high-level Anglo cultural script connected with 'personal autonomy'
people think like this:
when a person does something, it is good if this person can think about it like this:
'I am doing this because I want to do it'

(Goddard, 2006, p. 6)

This example, Goddard argues, can be correlated with speech practices that are linked with this concept, and understood by speakers from the same background, even if not shared as a value. He further argues that 'cultural beliefs ... may be profoundly explanatory of aspects of communicative practice' (2006, p. 12), given that speech can be seen to act as an indicator of ways of thinking. A challenge that we feel remains unaddressed is the validity of such a claim among speakers of the same first language but from different cultural backgrounds, such as Malaysian versus British first language speakers of English, and that for Goddard's claims to be valid, these issues require further and more context-specific research (cf. Wierzbicka, Chapter 8, this volume).

Sercombe (2008) reports on problems of intercultural communication between Malay-speaking teachers and Penan–Malay bilingual pupils, in a rural primary school in Borneo. Observing Penan children's behavior at home, then in the school setting, Sercombe notes the contrast between the stratified and disciplined setting of the school compared to the informal, egalitarian environment of Penan communities, and the sad results that can ensue. Talk in their first language, for Penan children, is voluntary, such that non-participation (with other members of their ethnic community) is not equated with non-cooperation. When this kind of pupil behavior is manifested at school, teachers, who are all non-Penan, reported that they perceive Penan children's lack of overt participation as laziness, stupidity, and an indifference to learning; and they react negatively towards Penan children. It seems no accident that most Penan children leave school within 4 years of enrolling. Young and Sachdev (2007) consider numerous examples of 'style wars' between teachers and learners in classrooms worldwide, where disparities between belief systems about effective and appropriate learning tend to disadvantage learners from different cultural backgrounds to their teachers (South Africa being a particular case in point). In connection, Pincas (2001, p. 30) suggests that: 'Worldwide students encounter discourse problems rather than simple language difficulties.' Scollon and Scollon (2001) also claim that Western professional discourse (seemingly ever more globally influential) is primarily utilitarian and that this needs to be learned by those not from such a background but who wish to operate within it, if they are to be professionally successful.

A fundamental concern is whether an individual's degree of binguality can be associated with their degree of intercultural communicative effectiveness. In a personality-based study by Young and Sachdev (2009), correlational evidence suggests that cultural empathy, open-mindedness and, to a lesser extent, flexibility are associated with second language learning achievement (cf. Gao, 2000; Walker, 2005). However, there was insufficient evidence to confirm whether bi- or multilinguals necessarily have higher levels of ability in intercultural communication. The study does suggest, nonetheless, that associations between intercultural effectiveness and second language acquisition achievement are a fruitful area for further investigation. Obviously, misunderstandings rooted in cultural asymmetries cannot be totally alleviated or prevented but, as Wierzbicka observes: 'It seems clear that a linguistic study of culture-specific speech acts and speech styles has a great deal to contribute in this domain' (1991, p. 65).

CONCLUSIONS

This chapter has outlined current concerns in cognition studies and ICC and ways in which these two areas appear to intersect, as well as the implications of this intersection. While cognition studies are relatively mature, ICC is still in its infancy, especially in terms of models of effective ICC which are actually informed by empirical research. Nonetheless, the question of whether language background is responsible for the observed differences in cognitive performance across cultures remains open (Pincas, 2001). It would seem that cognitive style differences offer some support for the idea of 'deep' cultural differences, but that these may be as much to do with gender, for example, as other social factors. It is worth adding that the 'globalized' age in which we live means people are much more mobile, bi- or multicultural, and multilingual, and can maintain several (sometimes conflicting) cultural identities simultaneously. In this way, the 'Other is in Us and we are in the Other' (Kramsch, 2001, p. 205). However, this is perhaps less likely to be the case among those who are socioeconomically disadvantaged, about whom little research has been undertaken with regard to cognition and ICC. Further there is the inevitability of miscommunication, regardless of interlocutors' backgrounds (Young & Sercombe, 2010; see also Garner, 2004; Spencer-Oatey & Kotthoff, 2007). Finally, a fundamental dimension of all communication is context and 'The way in which talk itself both invokes context and provides context for other talk' (Goodwin & Duranti, 1992, p. 7), such that the act of communication itself is but one of many dimensions to take account of. To emphasize one point only: cognition and ICC seem to be intimately related but these relations cannot be easily defined, or corralled, in terms of national cultures (if these actually exist outside media or politics), or other large scale categorizations, but interact subtly in different contexts, in ways that remain insufficiently explored.

REFERENCES

Agar, M. (1991). The biculture in bilingual. *Language in Society, 20,* 167–181. [In Appel, R. (2000). Language, concepts and culture: Old wine in new bottles? *Bilingualism: Language and Cognition, 3*(1), 5–6.]

Athanasopoulos, P. (2009). Cognitive representation of colour in bilinguals: The case of Greek blues. *Bilingualism: Language and Cognition, 12*(1), 83–95.

Barth, F. (1969/1998). *Ethnic groups and boundaries.* Prospect Heights, IL: Waveland Press.

Bauman, G. (1996). *Contesting culture: Discourses of identity in multi-ethnic London.* Cambridge, UK: Cambridge University Press.

Bennett, M. J. (1998). Intercultural communication: A current perspective. In M. J. Bennett (Ed.), *Basic concepts of intercultural communication* (pp. 1–34). Boston, MA: Intercultural Press.

Berlin, B. (1992). *Ethnobiological classification: Principles of categorization of plants and animals in traditional societies.* Princeton, NJ: Princeton University Press.

Berlin, B., & Kay, P. (1969). *Basic color terms: Their universality and evolution.* Berkeley, CA: University of California Press.

Bhabha, H. (1994). *The location of culture.* London: Routledge.

Bonvillain, N. (2003). *Language, culture and communication: The meaning of messages* (4th ed.). Upper Saddle River, NJ: Prentice Hall.

Bourdieu, P. (1977). *Outline of a theory of practice.* Cambridge & New York: Cambridge University Press.

Bourdieu, P. (1990). *The logic of practice.* Stanford, CA: Stanford University Press.

Byram, M., & Zarate, G. (1997). Definitions, objectives and assessment of sociocultural competence. In M. Byram, G. Zarate, & G. Neuner (Eds.), *Sociocultural competence in language learning and teaching* (pp. 7–43). Strasbourg: Council of Europe.

Clyne, M. (1994). *Intercultural communication at work: Cultural values in discourse.* Cambridge, UK: Cambridge University Press.

Council of Europe. (2001). *Common European framework of reference for languages: Learning, teaching, assessment.* Strasbourg: Council of Europe/Cambridge University Press. Online HTTP: http://www.coe.int/t/dg4/linguistic/CADRE_EN.asp (accessed January 15, 2010).

Dörnyei, Z. (2005). *The psychology of the language learner: Individual differences in second language acquisition.* Mahwah, NJ: Lawrence Erlbaum Associates Inc.

Foley, W. (1997) *Anthropological linguistics: An introduction.* Oxford, UK: Blackwell.

Fox, K. (2004). *Watching the English: The hidden rules of English behaviour*. London: Hodder.

Francis, W. S. (2000). Clarifying the cognitive experimental approach to bilingual research. *Bilingualism: Language and Cognition, 3*(1), 13–15.

Gao, M. C. F. (2000). Influence of native culture and language on intercultural communication: The case of PRC student immigrants in Australia. *Journal of Intercultural Communication, 4*, n.p. Available HTTP: <http://www.immi.se/intercultural/nr4/gao.htm> (accessed January 15, 2010).

Garner, M. (2004). *Language: An ecological view*. Oxford, UK: Peter Lang.

Goddard, C. (2006). Ethnopragmatics: A new paradigm. In C. Goddard (Ed.), *Ethnopragmatics: Understanding discourse in cultural context* (pp. 1–30). Berlin: Walter de Gruyter.

Goodwin, C., & Duranti, A. (1992). Rethinking context: An introduction. In A. Duranti & C. Goodwin (Eds.), *Rethinking context* (preface). Cambridge, UK: Cambridge University Press.

Gudykunst, W. B. (2003). Intercultural communication theories. In W. B. Gudykunst (Ed.), *Cross-cultural and intercultural communication* (pp. 167–189). Thousand Oaks, CA: Sage.

Hall, E. T. (1959). *The silent language*. New York: Doubleday.

Hamers, J. F., & Blanc, M. H. A. (1983). *Bilinguality and bilingualism* (2nd ed.). Cambridge, UK: Cambridge University Press.

Harwood, J., Giles, H., & Palomares, N. A. (2005). Intergroup theory and communication processes. In J. Harwood & H. Giles (Eds.), *Intergroup communication: Multiple perspectives* (pp. 121–134). New York: Peter Lang.

Haugen, E. I. (1956). *Bilingualism in the Americas: A bibliography and research guide*. Baltimore, MD: American Dialect Society.

Hofstede, G. (1997). *Cultures and organizations: Software of the mind*. London: McGraw-Hill.

Holliday, A. (1999). Small cultures. *Applied Linguistics, 20*(2), 237–264.

Holliday, A., Hyde, M., & Kullman, J. (2004). *Intercultural communication: An advanced resource book*. London: Routledge.

Hymes, D. (1996). *Ethnography, linguistics, narrative inequality: Towards an understanding of voice*. London: Taylor & Francis.

Jandt, F. E. (2001). *Intercultural communication*. Thousand Oaks, CA: Sage.

Kasper, G., & Rose, K. R. (2001). Pragmatics in language teaching. In K. R. Rose & G. Kasper (Eds.), *Pragmatics in language teaching* (pp. 1–9). Cambridge, UK: Cambridge University Press.

Kramsch, C. (1993). *Context and culture in language teaching*. Cambridge, UK: Cambridge University Press.

Kramsch, C. (2001). *Intercultural communication*. In R. Carter & D. Nunan (Eds.), *The Cambridge guide to teaching English to speakers of other languages* (pp. 201–206). Cambridge, UK: Cambridge University Press.

Kramsch, C. (2004). Language, thought and culture. In A. Davies & C. Elder (Eds.), *The handbook of applied linguistics* (pp. 235–261). Oxford, UK: Blackwell.

Lado, R. (1957). *Linguistics across cultures*. Ann Arbor, MI: University of Michigan Press.

Lakoff, G., & Johnson, M. (1980). *Metaphors we live by*. Chicago: University of Chicago Press.

Langacker, R. W. (1997). The contextual basis of cognitive semantics. In J. Nuyts & E. Pederson (Eds.), *Language and conceptualization* (pp. 229–252). Cambridge, UK: Cambridge University Press.

Levinson, S. (1995). Cognitive anthropology. In J. Verscheuren, J-O. Ostman, & J. Blommaert (Eds.), *Handbook of pragmatics* (pp. 100–105). Amsterdam: John Benjamins.

Levinson, S. (1997). Language and cognition: The cognitive consequences of spatial description in Guugu Yimithirr. *Journal of Linguistic Anthropology, 7*(1), 98–131.

Lucy, J. (1992). *Language, diversity and thought: A reformulation of the linguistic relativity hypothesis.* Cambridge, UK: Cambridge University Press.

Ma, L. (2004). Is there an essential difference between intercultural and intracultural communication? *Journal of Intercultural Communication, 6.* Available HTTP: <http://www.immi.se/intercultural/nr6/lin.htm> (accessed January 14, 2010).

McSweeney, B. (2002). Hofstede's model of national cultural differences and their consequences: A triumph of faith—a failure of analysis. *Human Relations, 55*(1), 89–118.

Mishra, R. C. (1997). Cognition and cognitive development. In J. W. Berry, P. R. Dashen, & T. S. Sarawathi (Eds.), *Basic processes and human development.* Vol. II of *Handbook of cross-cultural psychology* (2nd ed., pp. 143–176). Boston, MA: Allyn & Bacon.

Mishra, R. C., Sinha, D., & Berry, J. W. (1996). *Ecology, acculturation and adaptation: A study of the Adivasi in Bihar.* New Delhi: Sage.

Nisbett, R. E., & Norenzayan, A. (2002). Culture and cognition (3rd ed., pp. 561–597). In D. L. Medin (Ed.), *Stevens' handbook of experimental psychology, Volume 3: Memory and cognitive processes.* New York: Wiley.

Nishida, H. (1999). A cognitive approach to intercultural communication based on schema theory. *International Journal of Intercultural relations, 23*(5), 753–777.

Ochs, E., & Schiefflin, B. (Eds). (1990). *Language socialization across cultures.* Cambridge, UK: Cambridge University Press.

Oxford, R. L., & Anderson, N. J. (1995). A crosscultural view of learning styles. *Language Teaching, 28,* 201–215.

Paradis, M. (2000). Cerebral representations of bilingual concepts. *Bilingualism: Language and Cognition, 3*(1), 22–24.

Pavlenko, A. (2006). Bilingual selves. In A. Pavlenko (Ed.), *Bilingual minds: Emotional experience, expression and representation* (pp. 1–33). Clevedon, UK: Multilingual Matters.

Pincas, A. (2001). Culture, cognition and communication in global education. *Distance Education, 22*(1), 30–51.

Rampton, B. (1995). *Crossing: Language and ethnicity among adolescents.* London: Longman.

Richerson, P. J., & Boyd, R. (2005). *Not by genes alone: How culture transformed evolution.* Chicago, IL: University of Chicago Press.

Roberson, D., Davidoff, J., Davies, I. R. L., & Shapiro, L. R. (2006). Colour categories and category acquisition in Himba and English. In N. J. Pitchford & C. P. Biggam (Eds.), *Progress in colour studies, Volume 2: Psychological aspects* (pp. 159–172). Amsterdam: John Benjamins.

Sapir, E. (1949). *The selected writings of Edward Sapir in language, culture, and personality*. Berkeley, CA: University of California Press.

Schütz, A. (Ed.) (1972). *Gesammte aufsätze* (Band 2). Den Haag: Nijhoff.

Scollon, R., & Scollon, S. W. (2001) *Intercultural communication: A discourse approach* (2nd ed.). Oxford, UK: Blackwell.

Sercombe, P. G. (2003). *A preliminary survey of learning styles among postgraduate mainland Chinese students*. Unpublished ms.

Sercombe, P. G. (2008). Small worlds: The language ecology of the Penan in Borneo. In A. Creese & P. W. Martin (Eds.), *Encyclopedia of language and education, Volume 9, Ecology of language* (2nd ed., pp. 183–193). Amsterdam: Kluwer.

Søndergaard, M. (1994). Research note: Hofstede's consequences: A study of reviews, citations and replications. *Organization Studies, 15*(3), 447–456.

Spencer-Oatey, H., & Kotthoff, H. (2007). Introduction. In H. Kotthoff & H. Spencer-Oatey (Eds.), *Handbook of intercultural communication* (pp. 1–6). Berlin: Mouton de Gruyter.

Stephen, C. W., & Stephan, W. G. (2003). Cognition and cross cultural relations. In W. B. Gudykunst & B. Moody (Eds.), *Handbook of international and intercultural communication* (pp. 127–142). Thousand Oaks, CA: Sage.

Sperber, D., & Wilson, D. (1995). *Relevance: Communication and cognition* (2nd ed.). Oxford, UK: Blackwell.

Trompenaars, F., & Hampden-Turner, C. (1997). *Riding the waves of culture: Understanding cultural diversity in business* (2nd ed.). London: N. Brealey Publishing.

Walker, N. N. (2005). Investigating the cognition behind the intercultural interactions of four Japanese teachers of English as a foreign language. *Electronic Journal of Contemporary Japanese Studies*, Article 4. Available HTTP: <http://www.japanesestudies.org.uk/articles/2005/Walker.html> (accessed January 15, 2010).

Whorf, B. L. (1956). *Language, thought, and reality: Selected writings of Benjamin Lee Whorf* (Ed. J. B. Carroll). Cambridge, MA: MIT Press.

Wierzbicka, A. (1985). Different cultures, different languages, different speech acts. *Journal of Pragmatics, 9,* 145–178.

Wierzbicka, A. (1991). *Cross-cultural pragmatics: The semantics of human interaction*. Berlin: Mouton de Gruyter.

Young, T. J., & Sachdev, I. (2007). Learning styles in the multicultural classroom. In Z. Hua, P. Seedhouse, L. Wei, & V. Cook (Eds.), *Language learning and teaching as social interaction* (pp. 235–249). Basingstoke, UK: Palgrave Macmillan.

Young, T. J., & Sachdev, I. (2009). Multicultural effectiveness: Issues in language learning and teaching. In S. K. Singh (Ed.), *Rethinking multilingualism* (pp. 85–104). Delhi, India: EBH Publishing.

Young, T. J., Sachdev, I., & Seedhouse, P. (2009). Teaching and learning culture on English language programmes: A critical review of the recent empirical literature. *Innovation in Language Learning and Teaching, 3*(2), 149–169.

Young, T. J., & Sercombe, P. (2010). Introduction: Communication, discourses and interculturality. In P. G. Sercombe & T. J. Young (Eds.), Special issue of *Language and Intercultural Communication, 10*(3), 181–188.

Žegerac, V. (2007). A cognitive pragmatic perspective on communication and culture. In H. Kotthoff & H. Spencer-Oatey (Eds.), *Handbook of intercultural communication* (pp. 31–53). Berlin: Mouton de Gruyter.

25 Advertising to the buy-lingual consumer

David Luna

The consensus seems to be that there are more bilingual individuals than monolinguals in the world (Tucker, 1999). However, perhaps because the field of consumer research developed largely in the US, where most adult individuals are monolingual (US Census, 2000), much of the research investigating people as consumers has not acknowledged the role of bilingualism in decision making, advertising, or in any other process within the consumption context. This chapter describes some recent advances in the area, most of which have been published in the last decade or so. The research outlined here shows a multiplicity of research traditions, which is a trait of the study of consumers. Consumer researchers often use a variety of theoretical paradigms to explain how individuals operate as consumers in the real world.

This chapter considers several factors that influence bilingual consumers' response to advertisements. Many of the studies described here utilize models from psycholinguistics and sociolinguistics, applying them to a consumer context. First, psycholinguistic factors will be discussed. The second part of the chapter examines the interaction of language and culture.

BILINGUALISM AND ADVERTISING

Ad content memory: The role of L2 proficiency, motivation, and pictures

In a series of studies (Bauman, Luna, & Peracchio, 2005; Luna & Peracchio, 2001, 2002) we found that, even for proficient bilinguals, first language (L1) texts, such as ads, lead to greater comprehension and memory than second language (L2) texts. Our research was based on the revised hierarchical model, or RHM (Kroll & De Groot, 1997). This model suggests that there exist two levels of representation in the bilingual's mind: the lexical (word) level and the conceptual (meaning) level. At the lexical level each language is stored separately. However, at the conceptual level there is a unitary system in which words in each language access a common semantic representation or meaning. The connections between words in different languages made at the lexical level are referred to as word associations or 'lexical links', while the connections in memory between lexical representations in either language and the meanings they represent are referred to as 'conceptual links'. The model specifies a stronger lexical link from individuals' L2 to their L1 than from individuals' L1 to their L2. Hence, words in L2 are closely associated with words in L1.

According to the RHM, bilinguals also have stronger conceptual links between the lexical representations in an individual's L1 and semantic representations in memory (concepts). Conceptual links to the individual's L2 are weaker than L1 links because it is only after individuals have achieved a high level of proficiency in their L2 that they rely less on their L1 to gain access to meaning. Thus, the strength of both lexical and conceptual links is a function of the L2 proficiency of the individual in question. However, even after the individual has become fluent in both languages there is a residual asymmetry in both lexical and conceptual links (Kroll & De Groot, 1997).

In summary, the RHM suggests that processing an L2 message at the conceptual level is less likely than processing an L1 message conceptually. Empirical testing of the RHM supports the proposition that semantic processing of L2 stimuli is less likely than processing equivalent L1 stimuli (e.g., Sholl, Sankaranarayanan, & Kroll, 1995). Therefore we argued and showed empirically that L1 ads result in greater memory and comprehension of the meaning conveyed in ad text. However, this finding was moderated by the use of pictures that supported the text and by whether the audience was motivated to process the ad.

As suggested by La Heij, Hooglander, Kerling, and Van Der Velden (1996), pictures could help make up for the weaker L2–conceptual store links. In our studies we found that if pictures that were highly supportive of the ad text were used in L2 ads, the ads did not have to be translated to result in relatively high memory of the ad claims, when targeting relatively fluent bilinguals. However, if the ads' pictures were not as congruent with the text, the ads would result in poor memory, even with relatively fluent bilinguals.

We also found that processing motivation is a factor that offsets some of the conceptual processing asymmetries between L1 and L2 in advertising text comprehension and memory. Luna and Peracchio (2002) again applied the revised hierarchical model to advertising and found that when consumers are extrinsically motivated to process the ad, those who have an intrinsic need to process information comprehensively (i.e., individuals with high need for cognition, see Cacioppo & Petty, 1982) tend to remember the text equally well regardless of whether it is in L1 or L2 (provided consumers are relatively proficient in both languages). Additional elaboration due to the increase in attentional focus can offset the L1–L2 conceptual processing asymmetry.

Code switching in advertising

Code switching, or using multiple languages in an utterance, is practiced every day in the lives of bilingual individuals. It also appears in advertising, which tries to mimic how bilinguals speak in order to create a bond with those consumers. The hope is that being able to relate to consumers in the language varieties that they use will lead to the purchase of the advertised brand. For instance, a California winery recently mixed Spanish and English in their slogan: 'Una latina with good taste', or 'Kick up your tacones', where *una* means 'a' and *tacones* means 'heels'. In a different example, the US Army, in an effort to recruit Hispanic individuals, used the slogan 'Yo soy el Army' (I am the Army). In a series of studies we investigated two aspects of code switching: The linguistic structural constraints of code-switched slogans, and the sociolinguistic implications of code switching for consumers' responses to code-switched slogans.

Structural constraints

Following up on Myers-Scotton's matrix language frame model, or MLF (Myers-Scotton, 1993), Luna, Lerman, and Peracchio (2005) examined whether breaking, versus following, some of the grammatical rules of code switching would have a negative impact on consumers' evaluations of advertising slogans. According to the MLF model, when bilingual individuals communicate with other bilinguals, they may choose to code switch. Whether or not they do depends on a variety of sociolinguistic factors, such as the meanings they wish to communicate or their attitudes toward the different languages they can use and toward code switching itself. A similar process applies to advertisers seeking to communicate with bilingual consumers. If bilinguals choose to code switch, their utterances follow certain grammatical rules.

Consider an advertiser who targets US Hispanics by placing an ad in *Latina* magazine, a publication that is printed primarily in English. The advertiser, to be consistent with the medium's language, chooses to use English for most of the ad but decides to insert certain elements in Spanish. Because, in that case, most of the text is in English, we can say that the 'matrix language' of the message is English and that the 'embedded language' is Spanish. The structure, or frame, of this message will be that of the matrix language (English), so the advertiser will draw from the matrix language to form the syntactic structure of the message. That is, the rules of English syntax will determine the organization and order of words in this ad.

The choice of which words to code switch is governed by the morphemes contained in the text. According to the MLF model, the frame for an utterance is formed by a particular type of morpheme called a system morpheme. System morphemes (e.g., quantifiers ·and determiners) are elements of speech that serve as the glue between the different elements of an utterance and indicate the relationships among them. Once this frame has been formed, content morphemes (e.g., nouns and verbs), the elements that convey the central meaning of the utterance, are inserted into appropriate slots to communicate the meanings intended by the speaker. Because the matrix language sets the frame for constructing a code-switched sentence, the MLF model specifies that system morphemes must come from the matrix language and not from the embedded language.

In addition to the general rule that system morphemes must come from the matrix language, the MLF model describes other, more specific rules in code-switched speech. These rules have been derived from observation and analysis of large corpora of speech (e.g., Myers-Scotton, 1993). The rules, or structural constraints, provide specific predictions that operationalize the MLF model's general rubric regarding the dominant role of the matrix language in code-switched speech. In our studies we investigated two of those rules, the morpheme order principle and the embedded language island hypothesis.

We expected that the constraints that the MLF model describes for code-switched language production would also influence language perception and, in particular, would influence bilinguals' evaluative responses to code-switched ads. That is, ads that follow the MLF model's rules should be preferred over ads that do not follow them. In several studies we indeed found that individuals evaluated slogans more favorably if they followed the rules set forth by Myers-Scotton. The effects were stronger if individuals processed the slogans in a data-driven mode, paying particular attention to the language of the slogans. This, in conjunction with the Luna and Peracchio (2002) finding regarding the effect of motivation mentioned earlier, suggests that at least some of the effects of language take place when particular attention is devoted to which language a message is written in.

Activating language schemas

Stimuli that stand out from their context become perceptually salient and therefore attract attention (Fiske & Taylor, 1984). Accordingly, Luna and Peracchio (2005a, 2005b) argued that the embedded language element in a code-switched utterance, for example, a word in Spanish in an otherwise English utterance, tends to direct an individual's attention to that element. By noticing the word in Spanish, individuals then tend to activate the associations that specific language has built over time. For instance, bilingual Hispanics in the US have developed a sense that the English language is used more often than Spanish to discuss technical, sophisticated matters. Instead, Spanish is connected to a sense of inferiority and prejudice. These associations, what we called the 'language schema', emerge when code-switched advertisements are encountered, and subsequently influence slogan evaluations. For instance, our studies found that, generally, English ad slogans in which a short phrase or word was switched to Spanish, thus attracting attention to that embedded term (e.g., 'In my *cocina* I would never make coffee with any other coffee maker'), resulted in lower slogan evaluations than slogans mostly in Spanish that switched a small component to English (e.g., '*En mi* kitchen *nunca haría café con ninguna otra cafetera*'). An analysis of the thoughts written down by respondents confirmed our theorizing: When Spanish was made salient by the code switch, respondents activated more thoughts about their minority culture (e.g., 'Hispanics would not like this product') and negative language-related thoughts (e.g., 'Spanish shouldn't be mixed with English'). Notice that in this research, when we switched to Spanish, we did not switch words or expressions traditionally associated with the 'maternal' culture of our respondents (Spanish-speaking, Hispanic cultures). For instance, we did not switch expressions of endearment, or culturally specific, or particularly emotional language. The switched terms were always common nouns that did not have a strong emotional content and were relatively culturally neutral. One could argue that if we had switched to Spanish more emotional or culturally bound terms, the reactions would not have been negative. This is an area ripe for further research.

The results of our code-switching research suggest that advertisers intending to use code switching in their ads need to ensure that their ads do not seem forced, but rather they should be the result of an organic process in which true speakers of the code-switching variety of interest generate the text of the message. If switching from English to Spanish in the US, advertisers must ensure that the switch seems natural and is done in the appropriate context—for example in an emotional, or family situation where Hispanics might use the language in their daily lives. Otherwise, advertisers run the risk of activating a negative language schema—as in our studies, where slogans switched to Spanish without considering such situational use of the language.

In fact, some advertisers who have not followed such advice have seen their efforts backfire, like the notorious case of the Volkswagen billboard targeting bilingual Hispanics in South Florida, whose text read 'Turbo-Cojones'. The billboard resulted in a public relations nightmare for VW and had to be withdrawn because of the inappropriateness of the word *cojones* in Spanish. The term does not have such negative connotations when borrowed in English, so it is likely that an English-speaking copywriter thought it might be a good idea to include it in the billboard to connote strength and power. Another awkward example of code-switching use was a Toyota Hybrid TV ad aired during the 2006 Superbowl. The ad included code switching from English to Spanish but seemed like a forced, gratuitous use of the practice. In that ad, a father and son traveling by car speak in English. As they converse, the father points at the car navigation system and, in a noticeably different voice, probably inserted from a different sound track, says '*Mira, mira aquí*' ('Look, look here'). On a more positive note, a McDonald's commercial recently used English-to-Spanish code switching very effectively in an advertisement in which a father and daughter discuss in English why she is saving a McNugget in the box. Later, in an emotional scene, the girl offers her mother, who has just returned from an Army assignment, the last (and best) chicken nugget, saying in Spanish: '*Es para ti*' ('It's for you'). The use of Spanish in a culturally appropriate emotional scene presumably prevents consumers from activating a negative language schema.

Price-oriented advertising

In a recently published paper, Luna and Kim (2009) followed up on numerical cognition and educational psychology research that found that mental arithmetic is intrinsically more difficult in some languages (e.g., Ellis & Hennelly, 1980). This increased difficulty occurs because the names of numbers in some languages (e.g., the word *five* in English) tend to be shorter than in others (*cinco* in Spanish). As a result, the phonological loop in working memory (Baddeley, 1986) is overtaxed when performing mental arithmetic in 'long' languages, relative to 'short' languages, so mental calculations have a greater chance of being wrong in long languages.

In a series of studies we found that when bilinguals were presented with texts that included a list of prices for several items, they were able to calculate and later recall the total price of the items in the text more accurately if the text was written in a language with shorter number names than if the numbers were written in a long language. Several of our studies were performed with bilingual participants, speakers of Korean (a short language) and English (a longer language). The results suggest that bilinguals are subject to certain cognitive limitations in one language but not the other, so it is possible that they could be 'better consumers' in one language than in the other—they could calculate running totals of how much their shopping cart is worth in one language but not in the other.

Biscriptal bilinguals

Many bilinguals are not just bilingual: They can use multiple writing systems. From a theoretical perspective, one of the most interesting cases of biscriptals are those individuals who can write in both an alphabetic and a character-based system such as Chinese. A number of consumer researchers have examined how such biscriptal bilinguals process information. For instance, Tavassoli and Han (2002) found that visual cues that support the verbal information in an ad, such as color logos, are most effective when the marketer uses the character-based Chinese style of writing, whereas auditory cues such as jingles or other sounds supporting the verbal information work better with the English alphabet. The authors theorize that the processing of words written in alphabetic scripts relies more heavily on the phonological loop of working memory. In contrast, the processing of words written in character-based scripts relies more on visual working memory. Therefore, a caveat emerges from another of the authors' articles (Tavassoli & Han, 2001): Auditory contextual interference (stimuli that are not related to the target verbal information) is higher for alphabetic words than for character-based words, and vice versa for visual distracters. This suggests, for example, that ads containing alphabetic words should be designed to minimize the use of distracting auditory information, which may potentially compete for the cognitive resources required in order to learn printed alphabetic information. In contrast, ads containing character-based words should be designed to minimize the use of distracting graphics or complex visual displays. Hence, different stimuli could interfere with bilingual/biscriptal individuals' ability to process an ad (or any other verbal stimulus), depending on the language/script in which it is written.

Ahn and La Ferle (2008) also investigated the case of biscriptals, but from a different perspective. They examined an extended practice in some Asian countries, where alphabetic writing is included in local-language print ads. They found that mixing scripts within one ad leads to greater memory, due to the deeper processing prompted by the inclusion of both scripts.

Linguistic relativity

The notion of linguistic relativity, typically embodied in the Whorfian hypothesis (Whorf, 1956), has been explored to some extent in consumer research. For instance, Schmitt and Zhang (1998), investigate how the use of classifiers influences cognitive processes like categorization. Classifiers are lexical items that depict perceptual and conceptual properties of objects in some languages. The authors found that the use of classifiers by speakers of a language that uses classifiers such as Chinese affects the perceived similarity of objects and the accessibility of classifier-related features, compared to speakers of languages that do not use classifiers such as English. In addition, they showed that classifiers are organized schematically and consumers use the conceptual knowledge associated with classifiers when they draw inferences about brands. Consumers also seem to use the conceptual knowledge represented in classifiers in judgments and choices. The authors argued that their results support the notion that language structure influences cognition, particularly in a cross-cultural context. This of course is the core of the Whorfian hypothesis of linguistic relativity (Whorf, 1956). In the last two decades the Whorfian hypothesis has been reconceptualized in terms of how linguistic forms are represented, how they operate in the mind, and how they affect the concepts and categories that denote objects and relations in the world (Hunt & Agnoli, 1991). Schmitt and Zhang's research is in line with this reformulation of the Whorfian hypothesis by demonstrating the influence of grammar-related differences on the fundamental process of categorization, judgment, and choice.

One possible extension of Schmitt and Zhang (1998) would involve the use of bilingual individuals, exposing them either to a language with classifiers or to a language without classifiers, to see if the linguistic relativity hypothesis also holds within-individual. Such a study would be related to the notions explored in the next section.

BICULTURALISM AND ADVERTISING

A growing number of consumer researchers have dedicated a great deal of effort in the last few years to studying biculturalism, in order to clarify some processes that involve both language and culture. Before further discussion, the notions of culture, biculturalism, and bilingualism should be defined. Culture can be seen as the beliefs, values, and norms of a specific sociocultural group (Brumbaugh, 2002). Bicultural individuals are those who have internalized two cultures (Lau-Gesk, 2003). Therefore, those cultures guide biculturals' thoughts, feelings, and behavior (Hong, Morris, Chiu, & Benet-Martínez, 2000; LaFromboise, Coleman, & Gerton, 1993; Ramírez-Esparza, Gosling, Benet-Martínez, Potter, & Pennebaker, 2006). Bilingualism, as used here, is the ability to communicate relatively well in two different languages, including the ability to speak, understand, read, and write in both languages (Luna & Peracchio, 2001). In the research described below, bilingualism is an essential property of being bicultural, so what is referred to as a bicultural is really a bicultural-bilingual.

Based on those definitions, several categories of individuals can be distinguished in addition to biculturals. Monocultural bilinguals are those individuals who never internalized the culture attached to their second language. They typically learned their second language in a classroom environment, without significant exposure to the corresponding culture. Biculturals and monoculturals differ from one another in several respects. Two key differences are important in our chapter: (1) compared to biculturals (e.g., Mexican American biculturals), the knowledge that monoculturals (e.g., Anglo Americans who have never lived immersed in a Mexican environment) have of the other culture (e.g., the Mexican culture) is not linked to self-relevant identity constructs. That is, their knowledge of the other culture, even if it stems from their temporary exposure to that culture, does not affect how they view themselves (Brumbaugh, 2002). Also, (2) biculturals and monoculturals differ regarding the complexity of their knowledge about the two cultures in question—biculturals have richer, more complex knowledge about what it means to be a member of each of the two cultures (Benet-Martínez, Lee, & Leu, 2006; Brumbaugh, 2002). That is, biculturals have two distinct and complete sets of knowledge structures for each culture. Monoculturals only have one set of structures for their own culture, and possess a collection of second-hand knowledge about the other culture.

Language, culture, and thoughts

In a recent article, Noriega and Blair (2008) examine how bilinguals' thoughts about an ad are influenced by the language of the ad. When the ad is in their native language, they tend to think more thoughts about the brand in relation to their family, home, friends, and/or homeland than if the ad is in a non-native language. In his dissertation work, Carroll (2008) takes this finding a step further, showing that when advertisers use a language other than the language typically used by consumers to discuss a particular topic (e.g., work or friendship), consumers' attitudes toward the message tend to be less positive than if the topic and the language match. Carroll found evidence to suggest that this effect was due to the increased accessibility of words in a given language when the topic at hand is typically discussed in that language. Such an increase in accessibility then leads to a fluency effect (Schwarz, 2004), which leads to more positive evaluations than if language and topic do not match.

Cultural frames: Switching in and out of ways of being

Recently, Arthur Laurents, the director of a new version of the Broadway musical *West Side Story*, in which Anglo and Latino characters speak in their respective languages, asserted that 'the scenes with the Spanish are wildly exciting because they are much less inhibited. I don't think many eyes are going to stray to the translation', referring to the English supertitles that appear whenever the characters speak Spanish (Bosman, 2008). Is it possible that Spanish leads to a less-inhibited behavior than English, as suggested by Laurents? How does such a switch in attitudes happen and does it have an influence on advertising perceptions? A great deal of research in cross-cultural psychology has investigated language-triggered switches in ways of being, calling them instances of 'frame switching'.

Mental frames

A mental frame is understood as 'an interpretation which is frequent, well organized, memorable, which can be made from minimal cues, contains one or more prototypic instantiations, and is resistant to change' (D'Andrade, 1992, p. 29). These mental frames, largely transparent and tacit to the individual, become mediating devices that organize and manage the comprehension of abstract processes (Holland & Quinn, 1993; Holland & Valsiner, 1988). The content of culture can be seen as a collection of mental frames that are internalized through individuals' socialization and participation in a cultural group (Brumbaugh, 2002). The notion of mental frames is very similar to that of schemas. Both are cognitive structures based on associations between mental representations. Therefore, even though one may refer to cognitive structures as either schemas (from a psycholinguistic perspective) or mental frames (from a sociolinguistic perspective), the term 'mental frames' is used here to be consistent with the literature on the topic.

It follows that biculturals, who by definition are exposed to two cultural value systems (often during upbringing), are likely to have identity constructs related to both cultures, whereas monoculturals only have identity constructs related to one culture. When two languages are linked to two different cultures (the case of biculturals), the languages are likely to tap into culture-specific identity frames.

Frame switching

Research in psycholinguistics has examined the possibility that words in two different languages activate different concepts from a cognitive perspective. For example, the conceptual feature model, or CFM (Kroll & De Groot, 1997), suggests that a word's translation is likely to have a different interpretation from the original. According to the CFM, words in each language known by a bilingual activate a series of conceptual features. Words are connected to a number of these features that represent the subjective interpretation of the word for each individual. Those conceptual features, if unified under a theme or category, could be considered distinct frames. Hence, bilinguals may possess two different culture-specific mental frames connected to what appears to be the same word translated to different languages (translation-equivalent words).

Figure 25.1, from Luna, Ringberg, and Peracchio (2008), depicts a hypothetical scenario derived from the CFM, and applied to both bicultural-bilinguals, and monocultural-bilinguals. The left side represents bicultural individuals and the right side represents monoculturals. The upper panels for both biculturals and monoculturals show the mappings between two words, 'masculine' and 'self-sufficient,' and the identity-related concepts they represent. The two words are contained in a language-specific memory store—the English lexicon. Their respective translation-equivalent words, 'masculino' and 'auto-suficiente,' are stored in the Spanish lexicon. The four words are linked to conceptual features which determine their meaning and are stored in a single conceptual store, which is common to both languages. Each translation-equivalent word is linked to different concepts. The lower panels of Figure 25.1 depict the conceptual mappings

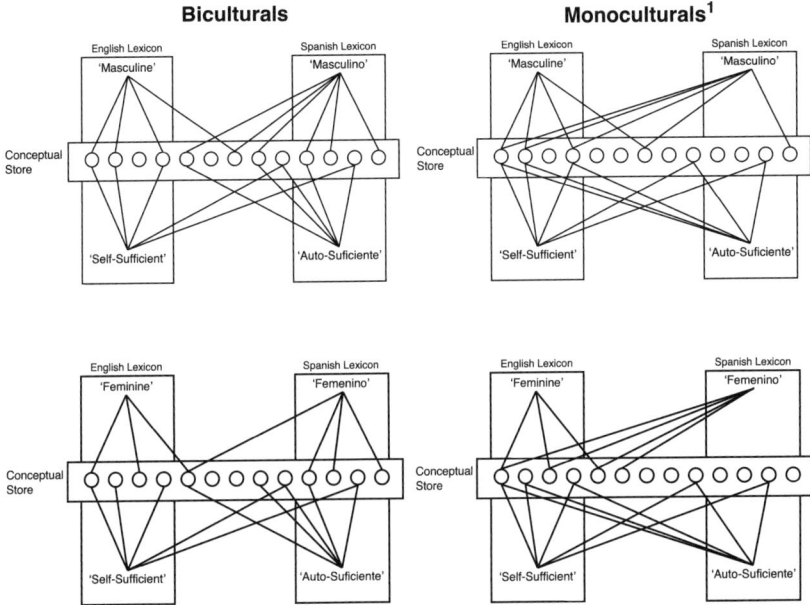

Figure 25.1 Mappings of words to concepts.

Note: Words are in quotations. Circles represent the conceptual, or semantic, nodes associated with each word.
[1]This column represents Anglo monoculturals who are proficient in Spanish.

between 'feminine' and 'self-sufficient' (and their translation-equivalents, 'femenino' and 'auto-suficiente') for biculturals and monoculturals. In a sense, then, Figure 25.1 represents different language- and culture-specific mental frames: the Spanish and the English frames, which differ in the associations to certain identity-related words (feminine and masculine).

Frame switching refers to the bicultural's act of switching from one mental frame to the other in response to certain cues. Researchers have found evidence of frame switching in several domains (e.g., Cheng, Lee, & Benet-Martínez, 2006; Ervin, 1964; Hong et al., 2000; Zou, Morris, & Benet-Martínez, 2008). Language-triggered frame switching has been found by several of these studies. For instance, differences in personality traits, like Extraversion, Agreeableness, and Conscientiousness, were found when bilingual-biculturals were shown the same questionnaire in different languages (Ramírez-Esparza et al., 2006).

Luna et al. (2008) attempted to shed some light on the frame-switching process by advancing a cognitive explanation, as implied in Figure 25.1. Our research provided some preliminary evidence of our framework. In a qualitative study we interviewed the same bicultural US Hispanic participants fluent in both Spanish and English first in one language

(Spanish or English) and then, 6 months later, in the other language. Their biculturalism was established by a series of scales and questionnaire items. During the interviews we showed them the same set of ads, with the text either in Spanish or English, depending on the language of the interview. We found that ad interpretations varied systematically between languages. One of the frames that consistently surfaced in the Spanish version of the ads was the 'self-sufficiency' frame. In English the frame did not emerge as readily. For instance, one of the ads portrayed a woman sitting alone atop a hill overlooking a lagoon (see Figure 25.2 for the English version). The advertisement was for a resort hotel and the major headline stated: 'For those who rarely find themselves at a loss for words, prepare to be left speechless.' The ad stated that the scenery was 'too unbelievable to describe', with pristine beaches, towering mountains and peaceful deserts. During the Spanish sessions, for example, informant Sara expressed: 'I think she is a positive person who takes risks, she can express herself, she is independent', but in the English session the same informant reported 'She feels, she looks, hopeless. . . . She looks lonely too and she looks very disturbed, confused like she's got something on her mind.' Similar comments were observed across the informants. We can only speculate as to the reason for the counterintuitive direction of this shift. Perhaps the Spanish language is associated with the culture of the immigrant, where self-sufficiency is a commonplace trait, or perhaps the language is associated with the trend in Hispanic women toward more assertiveness and activism (see Luna et al., 2008).

Two follow-up experiments confirmed that the self-sufficiency frame was more accessible than the other-dependence frame for bilingual-biculturals,

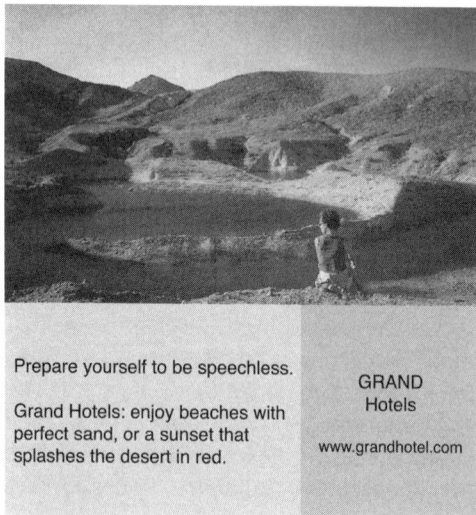

Prepare yourself to be speechless.

Grand Hotels: enjoy beaches with perfect sand, or a sunset that splashes the desert in red.

GRAND
Hotels

www.grandhotel.com

Figure 25.2 Hotel ad (English version).

but not for bilingual monoculturals. That is, bilinguals who were not true biculturals and thus had not incorporated 'Hispanic' frames into their repertoire of values and behaviors did not experience frame switching of the kind found in biculturals. However, we should emphasize that we did not seek to explore or experimentally test whether monoculturals can experience a change in their identity across situational contexts (e.g., coach, spouse, manager). Our research explored the activation of 'culture-specific' identity-related frames among biculturals and monoculturals; future research could explore whether identity-related frame switching might be triggered when different roles or situational contexts are made salient. Another direction for future research would be to examine biculturals who are not bilingual (e.g., individuals who have internalized both the South African and North American cultures but speak only one language—English).

CONCLUSION

Consumer research is characterized by a multidisciplinary approach to study topics that influence individuals in the marketplace. For instance, psycholinguistic theories could be the basis of a particular project, but often researchers need to inform their studies with principles from visual cognition, sociolinguistics, or even cultural studies, as profiled in this chapter. The result of inquiries in the domain of consumer research is therefore a rich exploration of the human experience. Bilingualism is no exception. In this chapter, we have seen how bilinguals—especially bilinguals who are bicultural, present an interesting case study in that they live in a world characterized by the interaction of a multitude of factors. Languages, writing systems, mental models, and imagery can present challenges that require the interaction of a variety of frameworks. The complexity of the marketplace can only be matched by the complexity of the multilingual mind. Understanding both requires a melding of paradigms and research traditions. The research presented here takes a step in the right direction, but much work is still needed to fill a multitude of gaps. For instance, regarding the notion of frame switching, studies could take a look at whether bicultural monolinguals are also able to switch cultural frames when cued by different accents or expressions. Similarly, bicultural-bilinguals may exhibit unique traits that distinguish them from monocultural monolinguals, such as enhanced creativity (e.g., Leung & Chiu, 2008). Many of these traits are important in a consumer-related context, or even in the business side—illuminating, for example, the question of whether ad agencies should employ more multicultural copywriters and art directors.

REFERENCES

Ahn, J., & La Ferle, C. (2008). Enhancing recall and recognition for brand names and body copy: A mixed-language approach. *Journal of Advertising, 37,* 107–118.

Baddeley, A. D. (1986). *Working memory.* Oxford, UK: Clarendon Press.

Bauman, C., Luna, D., & Peracchio, L. (2005). Improving tax compliance of bilingual taxpayers with effective consumer communication. *The IRS Research Bulletin, Proceedings of the 2005 IRS Research Conference, IRS Publication 1500,* 247–273.

Benet-Martínez, V., Lee, F., & Leu, J. (2006). Biculturalism and cognitive complexity. *Journal of Cross-Cultural Psychology, 37*(4), 386–407.

Bosman, J. (2008). Jets? Yes! Sharks? ¡Sí! in bilingual 'West Side'. *New York Times,* 17 July [electronic version].

Brumbaugh, A. M. (2002). Source and nonsource cues in advertising and their effects on the activation of cultural and subcultural knowledge on the route to persuasion. *Journal of Consumer Research, 29*(2), 258–270.

Cacioppo, J. T., & Petty, R. E. (1982). The need for cognition. *Journal of Personality and Social Psychology, 42,* 116–131.

Carroll, R. (2008). *The influence of language on communication and persuasion in advertising.* Unpublished dissertation, The Graduate Center, City University of New York.

Cheng, C. Y., Lee, F., & Benet-Martínez, V. (2006). Assimilation and contrast effects in cultural frame switching: Bicultural identity integration and valence of cultural cues. *Journal of Cross-Cultural Psychology, 37*(6), 742–760.

D'Andrade, R. (1992). Schemas and motivation. In R. D'Andrade & C. Strauss (Eds.), *Human motives and cultural models* (pp. 23–44). New York: Cambridge University Press.

Ellis, N. C., & Hennelly, R. A. (1980). A bilingual word-length effect: Implications for intelligence testing and the relative ease of mental calculation in Welsh and English. *British Journal of Psychology, 71,* 43–51.

Ervin, S. (1964). Language and TAT content in bilinguals. *The Journal of Abnormal and Social Psychology, 68*(5), 500–507.

Fiske, S. T., & Taylor, S. (1984), *Social cognition.* New York: McGraw-Hill.

Holland, D., & Quinn, N. (1993). *Cultural models in language and thought.* New York: Cambridge University Press.

Holland, D., & Valsiner, J. (1988). Cognition, symbols, and Vygotsky's developmental psychology. *Ethos, Journal of the Society for Psychological Anthropology, 16*(3), 247–272.

Hong, Y. Y., Morris, M. W., Chiu, C. Y., & Benet-Martínez, V. (2000). Multicultural minds: A dynamic constructivist approach to culture and cognition. *American Psychologist, 55*(7), 709–20.

Hunt, E., & Agnoli, F. (1991). The Whorfian hypothesis: A cognitive psychology perspective. *Psychological Review, 98,* 377–389.

Kroll, J. F., & de Groot, A. (1997). Lexical and conceptual memory in the bilingual: Mapping form to meaning in two languages. In A. de Groot & J. F. Kroll (Eds.), *Tutorials in bilingualism: Psycholinguistic perspectives* (pp. 169–199). Mahwah, NJ: Lawrence Erlbaum Associates Inc.

La Heij, W., Hooglander, A., Kerling, R., & Van Der Velden, E. (1996). Nonverbal context effects in forward and backward word translation: Evidence for concept mediation. *Journal of Memory and Language, 35,* 648–665.

LaFromboise, T., Coleman, H. L., & Gerton, J. (1993). Psychological impact of biculturalism: Evidence and theory. *Psychological Bulletin, 114*(3), 395–412.

Lau-Gesk, L. G. (2003). Activating culture through persuasion appeals: An examination of the bicultural consumer. *Journal of Consumer Psychology, 13*(3), 301–315.

Leung, A. K-Y., & Chiu, C. Y. (2008). Interactive effects of multicultural experiences and openness to experience on creative potential. *Creativity Research Journal, 20,* 376–382.

Luna, D., & Kim, H. M. (2009). Do you remember the price of your shopping basket? The role of linguistic number processing on total price recall. *Journal of Consumer Psychology, 19,* 346–355.

Luna, D., Lerman, D., & Peracchio, L. A. (2005). Structural constraints in codeswitched advertising. *Journal of Consumer Research, 32*(3), 416–423.

Luna, D., & Peracchio, L. A. (2001). Moderators of language effects in advertising to bilinguals: A psycholinguistic approach. *Journal of Consumer Research, 28,* 284–295.

Luna, D., & Peracchio, L. A. (2002). 'Where there is a will . . .': Motivation as a moderator of language processing by bilingual consumers. *Psychology and Marketing, 19*(7–8), 573–594.

Luna, D., & Peracchio, L. A. (2005a). Advertising to bilingual consumers: The impact of code-switching and language schemas on persuasion. *Journal of Consumer Research, 31*(4), 760–765.

Luna, D., & Peracchio, L. A. (2005b). Sociolinguistic effects on code-switched ads targeting bilingual consumers. *Journal of Advertising, 34*(2), 43–56.

Luna, D., Ringberg, T., & Peracchio, L. (2008). One individual, two identities: Frame-switching among biculturals. *Journal of Consumer Research, 35,* 279–293.

Myers-Scotton, C. (1993), *Dueling languages: Grammatical structure in code-switching.* Oxford, UK: Clarendon Press.

Noriega, J., & Blair, E. (2008). Advertising to bilinguals: Does the language of advertising influence the nature of thoughts? *Journal of Marketing, 72,* 69–83.

Ramírez-Esparza, N., Gosling, S. D., Benet-Martínez, V., Potter, J. P., & Pennebaker, J. W. (2006). Do bilinguals have two personalities? A special case of cultural frame switching. *Journal of Research in Personality, 40*(2), 99–120.

Schmitt, B. H., & Zhang, S. (1998). Language structure and categorization: A study of classifiers in consumer cognition, judgment, and choice. *Journal of Consumer Research, 25*(2), 108–123.

Schwarz, N. (2004). Metacognitive experience in consumer judgment and decision making. *Journal of Consumer Psychology, 14*(4), 332–348.

Sholl, A., Sankaranarayanan, A., & Kroll, J. F. (1995). Transfer between picture naming and translation: Test of asymmetries in bilingual memory. *Psychological Science, 6,* 45–49.

Tavassoli, N. T., & Han, J. K. (2001). Scripted thought: Processing Korean Hancha and Hangul in a multimedia context. *Journal of Consumer Research, 28*(3), 482–494.

Tavassoli, N. T., & Han, J. K. (2002). Auditory and visual brand identifiers in Chinese and English. *Journal of International Marketing, 10*(2), 13–29.

Tucker, G. R. (1999). *A global perspective on bilingualism and bilingual education.* Washington, DC: ERIC Clearinghouse on Languages and Linguistics.

US Census. (2000). *Language use and English-speaking ability: 2000.* Available <http://www.census.gov/prod/2003pubs/c2kbr-29.pdf> (accessed January 10, 2010).

Whorf, B. (1956). *Language, thought and reality: Selected writings of Benjamin Lee Whorf.* [Ed. J. B. Carroll.] Cambridge, MA: MIT Press.

Zou, X., Morris, M. W., & Benet-Martínez, V. (2008). Identity motives and cultural priming: Cultural (dis)identification in assimilative and contrastive responses. *Journal of Experimental Social Psychology, 44*(4), 1151–1159.

Epilogue: Bilinguals save the world

Keith Brooke

As the cover copy for Sheila Finch's *The Guild of the Xenolinguists* points out (Finch, 2007), human history shows that communicating with our own kind is hard enough, so just how much more challenging might it be to get across concepts such as peace, war, trade, territory, and so on to not only another species, but a species that has evolved in a completely different environment on some far-flung planet?

Science fiction (SF) is a genre of literature full of possibilities for thought experiments to explore and illustrate linguistic theory and speculation: The evolution of language into the far future, the challenges of communicating with artificial intelligences and alien species. Even where linguistic theory does not provide the principle novum in an SF tale, it must surely inform the extrapolations upon which these stories are based: How could it be possible to write a story about an encounter with an alien species without establishing how we might communicate with these fictional beings?

Much has been written about the scientific underpinnings of SF, but as Walter E. Meyers (1980) points out in his seminal study of linguistics in the genre, *Aliens and Linguists*, while attention has been devoted to physics, biology, economics, and political science in SF, the area of linguistics has been conspicuously neglected. Communication issues are far too frequently glossed over or tackled in haste, and only rarely feature prominently. One common method of dismissing the challenges of communicating with an alien species is to employ some kind of device as a universal translator, or 'magic decoder' as Meyers puts it—usually a form of mobile computer-translator, perhaps worn around the neck or as a jewel of some sort; or, as Douglas Adams memorably parodied, the 'Babel Fish', a small creature that, when inserted into the ear, converts sound waves into brain waves, neatly crossing the language divide between species (Adams, 1979). The magic decoder might at first appear to create the kind of implausibility that would undermine a story entirely—with the best will in the world it can be hard to believe in an alien who communicates in word-perfect American English—but Meyers takes a more generous perspective, pointing out that SF is full of conventions that, when viewed critically, would destroy the reader's necessary suspension of disbelief, but which have come to be regarded as acceptable genre furniture. Time travel and faster-than-light travel come into this category, both highly implausible in any scientific worldview and yet staples of the genre; Meyers puts the magic decoder in the same category, a somewhat dubious device which nonetheless opens up many opportunities for fine stories.

Putting aside the types of SF that sidestep a realistic portrayal of the language challenges in encountering the alien, some genre authors have produced deep and thoughtful explorations of the subject. Indeed, one of the linguists who has had most influence in SF started to formulate his theories through the writing of a science-fiction novel. In 1924 Benjamin Lee Whorf wrote *The Ruler of the Universe*; the novel was never published, but it was during the writing of this that he began to consider the relationship between language and thought, culminating in the theory of linguistic relativity (Meyers, 1980). Whorf's theories have been seized on by those authors intent on using the genre to explore ideas of language. Sheila Finch is a writer whose work tends to revolve around linguistic what-ifs, as in her Nebula Award-winning novelette 'Reading the Bones' which has perhaps the perfect opening line for a linguistic SF story: 'Someone was trying to tell him something.' She explores such Whorfian questions as 'Does our perception of "reality" shape our language, or does our language shape the reality that we are able to perceive?' (Finch, 1998/2007, p. 277). Learning another language forces us to see things differently:

> If learning another human language can be compared to opening a window on the world, then learning an alien language may open the door on the universe. We will never be the same again.
>
> (Finch, 1998/2007, p. 281)

Opening these alien doors will not necessarily be easy, though. Finch's protagonists bear the mental and emotional scars of their vocation, often ending up addicted to the substances that help them open the doors of language, and when they succeed in so drastically changing their perception of reality in order to see and code the world as aliens do, they find that they will 'never be able to find the words in our stunted languages to describe what they have come to know'.

Samuel R. Delany's 1966 novel *Babel-17* makes similar reference to the extreme changes in what, and how, we see when we shape our thoughts in a language that is truly *other*:

> Well most textbooks say language is a mechanism for expressing thought, Mocky. But language *is* thought. Thought is information given form. The form is language. . . . when you learn another tongue, you learn the way another people see the world, the universe . . . And as I begin to see into this language, I begin to see . . . too much.
>
> (Delany, 1966/1987, p. 21)

Speculating on just how challenging it might be to communicate with the alien, Finch argues that, if Chomsky's Universal Grammar, the notion that the human brain is hard-wired for language, is truly universal, then we're in luck. 'On the other hand, the possibility exists that the concept only reveals the limitations of our very human brains. It may be, as J.B.S. Haldane said of the universe, that these alien languages are not only queerer than we imagine, but queerer than we *can* imagine.' (Finch, 2007, p. 279). Is it really conceivable that there may be an all-pervasive universal grammar? Both humankind and any aliens we encounter have evolved in the same universe, presumably with the same imperatives to communicate and survive and prolong our lines. Just as biology displays convergent evolution, with species developing in isolation on separate continents turning out to be very similar in form and function, might there be a convergent evolution in language, towards a universal grammar that works to describe the universe?

Ian Watson argues for exactly this, suggesting that 'there may be "a topological grammar of the universe, which reflects itself in the grammars of actual languages"—Chomsky writ very large indeed' (1975, quoted in Nicholls, 1993, p. 359). This view is exemplified in Watson's 1973 novel *The Embedding*, where he speculates that the human brain's innate capacity for learning the languages of our own species might extend to those of others. Combining this with Whorfian speculations about the mapping of language to reality, Watson tells a three-stranded story: One story-line centers on a secret project where war refugee children are taught artificial languages to probe what the human mind can accept as real; in another, an Amazonian tribe with a unique language is threatened by a project to flood their jungle home; and in the third strand, an alien race called the Signal Traders approaches Earth for a first encounter. The aliens travel from planet to planet collecting languages, which they can imprint directly into the mind as long as they conform to the Universal Grammar. Through these collected languages the Signal Traders are mapping reality itself; with each language they acquire another door on the universe (to use Finch's terminology): They see themselves as trading in realities, rather than in languages. Finch's Xenolinguists, the Lingsters, have a mantra: 'I am a channel ... Through me flows the meaning of the Universe.' Through language, and languages, they're closer to reality, just as Watson's Signal Traders seek to understand reality by seeing it from as many different linguistic perspectives as possible.

The Signal Traders would have understood the experience of Rydra Wong, protagonist of Samuel R. Delany's *Babel-17*. Poet and former military linguist Wong is brought in to investigate a series of accidents that look like sabotage, each associated with a rush of indecipherable radio exchanges, which at first appear to be some kind of coded communication. Wong soon realises that the messages are actually in a previously unknown language, one far richer with meaning than any she has previously encountered. As she immerses herself in the language, starting to think in it, she realizes that it is 'not only a language but a flexible matrix of analytical possibilities' allowing her to analyze an array of hostile spaceships, or the tensions and yearnings in a human face, all in an instant (Delany, 1966, pp. 122–123).

Science fiction is all about extrapolating a what-if question to a logical conclusion—taking ideas to their extremes. One such extrapolation of linguistic relativity theory argues that if language reflects the worldview, or reality, of its speaker, then control of language is one way to exert control over those who speak that language and think in it. In Philip José Farmer's 1961 story *Prometheus* an explorer teaches intelligent bird-like aliens a form of English, prompting him to speculate about what impact that will have on their identity, and to wonder about their social and political development if he were to teach groups different languages. Robert Heinlein's *Gulf* (1949) tells of a future where a super-intelligent elite has developed a language called Speedtalk, where complex syntax combines with limited vocabulary to create an efficient, highly-compressed language that only the elite can understand. But how rich would a rigidly limited language such as this be? In *1984* George Orwell (1949) suggests that such a rigid, constricted language, with a greatly reduced vocabulary and grammar (getting more reduced every year, by design) could be used to control how people think: If something can't be said then it can't be thought.

Jack Vance's *The Languages of Pao* (Vance, 1958/1974) is perhaps the science-fiction novel which pursues ideas of language shaping thought, and therefore society, to the greatest and most carefully detailed extreme, and which, by doing so, most powerfully demonstrates the potential of bilingualism to avoid this problem. The world of Pao has long been stable and virtually stagnant, its culture reflected in, and shaped by, its main language:

> The [Paonese] language contains no verbs, adjectives, or word comparisons such as good, better, and best. The lack of verbs encourages indolence and inaction among the Paonese, whereas the lack of word comparisons and adjectives produces a culture devoid of conflict and ambition.
>
> (Bee, 2008)

Such a world is a soft target for Pao's powerful neighbors; it is invaded, occupied, and a puppet government installed. In order to stir its populace to uprising, cadres of Paonese people are schooled in three languages: Valiant, a language of strong, aggressive verbs and a vocabulary based on conflict and contrast, is used to shape the mindsets of a warrior class; Technicant, complex and logical, shapes the thoughts of people destined for industrial development; and Cogitant, a language rich with scope for hypocrisy and ambiguity, is used to facilitate trade. This, in itself, turns out to be a plot to take over Pao by Palafox, originator of the plan, whose own language (which is actually Cogitant) shapes a society that is striving and aggressive. Ultimately, Beran, son of the assassinated ruler of Pao, saves the day: A native speaker of Paonese, and fluent speaker of Cogitant as a second language, Beran persuades the three, now warring, factions to speak Pastiche, a new language that combines the Valiant, Technicant, and Cogitant tongues in a flexible whole that allows its speakers to see the world more completely.

Vance is careful to stress that Palofax's plan does not expect language to rigidly control the individual behavior of its speakers, but rather that it would compel the speaker in a certain direction, and that the cumulative effect would be to produce a culture of militarism, of industrialism, and of trade. Some of the most impassioned linguistic science fiction concentrates on the effect on the individual. In Barry B. Longyear's 1979 novella 'Enemy Mine' two soldiers, one human and one alien, must put their warring backgrounds aside and cooperate in order to survive on the surface of a hostile planet. Once they start to learn each other's languages their bond grows and they start to see the world as the other does, their initial xenophobia being eroded as this happens. One powerful illustration of this is when the human Davidge learns to recite the 200 generations of alien Jerry's ancestry, immersing himself in his new buddy's language and culture. When the hermaphrodite Jerry dies in childbirth, Davidge is left to rear the alien child, Zammis, and both pass on its culture and language and somehow explain why the two species are at war—something that, with his newfound empathy for the aliens, he struggles to do; at one point, Zammis says, 'I think I would like to be an interpreter and help end the war' (Longyear, 1979/2004, p. 66). Eventually rescued from the planet, Davidge is separated from Zammis, and confronted with his own kind: Even with the war over, humans remain bitterly xenophobic, with hate posters on the walls and people hurling abuse at Davidge the alien lover; traveling to Jerry's home world, Davidge encounters the same hostility from the aliens. Davidge, however, is different, he is more: Immersed in the culture and language of both species, he can see both sides.

In my own 2006 novel *Genetopia* (Brooke, 2006) a devolved human slave race speak an invented Creole called Mutter; the true humans speak their own language, but most speak Mutter too—to be bilingual is not, in itself, an indication of the character or mindset of an individual. There is, however, a distinction between those who use Mutter only as a means of exerting—often brutal—control over the slaves, and those who use it to engage and understand. The novel is all about embracing the *other*, about welcoming change and diversity rather than resisting it at all costs. Those who are open, who communicate and see reality through open windows of language, are ready for the post-human world of Harmony; those who use language to control and close those windows are not. As in *Genetopia*, so in *The Languages of Pao*: 'its message is clear: the characters who suffer are those whose world-view is limited' (Meyers, 1980, p. 169). Douglas Adams' Babel Fish, by removing all barriers to communication, is responsible for more wars and bloodshed than anything else, ever, but Jack Vance, Barry Longyear, Sheila Finch, and other SF authors show a more positive view of the value of opening yourself to language and thus opening your mind to other realities.

Samuel Delany's *Babel-17* asks, 'If there's no word, how do you think about it?' (Delany, 1966, p. 97). Now consider all the things we might not have the language for, but which aliens might. That's what SF writers do all the time. In *Reading the Bones* Sheila Finch's alien Freh says to the Lingster protagonist, 'You understand how words make' (Finch, 2007, p. 227). SF writers are used to describing the indescribable, to hinting and implying so that the reader sees more than the writer . . . or so that they believe they do, so that they sense insight into other mindsets. Just as language does. We understand how words make. Or at least we try to. And one thing that the more linguistically aware science-fiction authors also understand is that multilinguals view reality so much more clearly than their perceptually challenged monolingual peers.

REFERENCES

Adams, D. A. (1979). *The hitchhiker's guide to the galaxy*. London: Pan Macmillan.

Bee, R. (2008). Linguistics, cultural engineering, and world building in the languages of Pao and Babel-17. *Internet Review of Science Fiction*. Online. Available <http://www.irosf.com/q/zine/article/10429> (accessed January 12, 2010).

Brooke, K. (2006). *Genetopia*. Amherst, NY: Pyr.

Delany, S. R. (1966/1987). *Babel-17*. Reprinted 1987. London: Gollancz Classic SF.

Farmer, P. J. (1961). Prometheus. *Fantasy and Science Fiction*, March.

Finch, S. (1998/2007). Reading the bones. Reprinted in Finch, S. (2007). *The guild of the xenolinguists*. Urbana, IL: Golden Gryphon Press.

Heinlein, R. A. (1949). Gulf. *Astounding Science Fiction*, November & December.

Longyear, B. B. (1979/2004). Enemy mine. *Isaac Asimov's SF Magazine*. Reprinted 2004, Lincoln, NE: Authors Guild.

Meyers, W. E. (1980). *Aliens and linguists*. Athens, GA: University of Georgia Press.

Nicholls, P. (Ed.). (1993). *The encyclopedia of science fiction*. St Albans, UK: Granada.

Orwell, G. (1949). *1984*. London: Secker & Warburg.

Vance, J. (1958/1974). *The languages of Pao*. Reprinted 1974. London: Mayflower.

Watson, I. (1973). *The embedding*. London: Gollancz.

Watson, I. (1975). Towards an alien linguistics. *Vector, 71*.

Whorf, B. (1924). *The ruler of the universe*. Unpublished manuscript. Cited in Meyers (1980).

Author index

Subject index